The Formation
of National States in
Western Europe

STUDIES IN
POLITICAL DEVELOPMENT

1. *Communications and Political Development*
Edited by Lucian W. Pye

2. *Bureaucracy and Political Development*
Edited by Joseph LaPalombara

3. *Political Modernization in Japan and Turkey*
Edited by Robert E. Ward and Dankwart A. Rustow

4. *Education and Political Development*
Edited by James S. Coleman

5. *Political Culture and Political Development*
Edited by Lucian W. Pye and Sidney Verba

6. *Political Parties and Political Development*
Edited by Joseph LaPalombara and Myron Weiner

7. *Crises and Sequences in Political Development*
by Leonard Binder, James S. Coleman, Joseph LaPalombara,
Lucian W. Pye, Sidney Verba, Myron Weiner

8. *The Formation of National States in Western Europe*
Edited by Charles Tilly

❖

Sponsored by the Committee on
Comparative Politics of the Social
Science Research Council

Lucian W. Pye, *Chairman*

Gabriel A. Almond
Leonard Binder
Philip E. Converse
Samuel P. Huntington
Joseph LaPalombara
Sidney Verba
Robert E. Ward
Myron Weiner
Aristide R. Zolberg
Bryce Wood, *staff*

The Formation
of National States in
Western Europe

Edited by Charles Tilly

CONTRIBUTORS

GABRIEL ARDANT	WOLFRAM FISCHER
DAVID H. BAYLEY	PETER LUNDGREEN
RUDOLF BRAUN	STEIN ROKKAN
SAMUEL E. FINER	CHARLES TILLY

PRINCETON, NEW JERSEY

PRINCETON UNIVERSITY PRESS

1975

Library of Congress Cataloging in Publication
Data will be found on the last printed
page of this book

This book has been composed in Linotype Caslon Old Face

Printed in the United States of America
by Princeton University Press, Princeton, New Jersey

CONTENTS

LIST OF ILLUSTRATIONS AND TABLES   vii

FOREWORD by Lucian W. Pye   ix

ACKNOWLEDGMENTS   xiii

1. Reflections on the History of European State-Making
by Charles Tilly   3

2. State- and Nation-Building in Europe: The Role
of the Military by Samuel E. Finer   84

3. Financial Policy and Economic Infrastructure of Modern
States and Nations by Gabriel Ardant   164

4. Taxation, Sociopolitical Structure, and State-Building:
Great Britain and Brandenburg-Prussia
by Rudolf Braun   243

5. The Police and Political Development in Europe
by David H. Bayley   328

6. Food Supply and Public Order in Modern Europe
by Charles Tilly   380

7. The Recruitment and Training of Administrative and
Technical Personnel by Wolfram Fischer and
Peter Lundgreen   456

8. Dimensions of State Formation and Nation-Building:
A Possible Paradigm for Research on Variations within
Europe by Stein Rokkan   562

9. Western State-Making and Theories of Political Transformation by Charles Tilly   601

BIBLIOGRAPHY   639

CONTRIBUTORS   687

INDEX   691

LIST OF ILLUSTRATIONS AND TABLES

ILLUSTRATIONS

Figure 1– 1 Ardant's Model of a State   53

2– 1 Development of the Contemporary State   87

2– 2 The Economy-Technology-Format Cycle   91

2– 3 The Beliefs-Format Cycle   93

2– 4 The Format-Options Cycle   95

2– 5 The Extraction-Coercion Cycle   96

2– 6 The State-Building Cycle   97

2– 7 The Interconnection of the Major Cycles   98

5– 1 Structure of National Police Systems   341

5– 2 Political Involvement of Police   364

5– 3 Centralization and Military Involvement   367

5– 4 Accountability   371

5– 5 Variables Used in the Analysis of Police Systems   375

5– 6 Police Organization and Political Life   379

8– 1 Basic Processes of Territorial Differentiation   564

8– 2 The Basic Grid of Dimensions   566

8– 3 Hirschman and Parsons Combined   567

8– 4 A Grid of Primary Variables and Linkage Variables for Europe   569

8– 5 The Location of the Four Time Phases within the Three Dimensional Grid   571

8– 6 The Four Time Phases within Sweden, Norway, and Finland   573

8– 7 A Schematic Geopolitical Map of Europe   579

8– 8 Conceptual Reformulation of the Schematic Geopolitical Map of Europe   586

8– 9 Elite Options in European States   590

8–10 Four Corresponding Sets of "Master Variables"   592

[vii]

TABLES

3–1 Worldwide Production of Gold and Silver, 1701–1800   199

3–2 Gross Agricultural and Industrial Product and State Expenditures   221

6–1 Estimates of European Population in Cities of 100,000 or More, 1500–1950   399

6–2 Estimated Average Yields of Wheat, Rye, and Barley, 1225–1785 (per unit of seed)   416

7–1 Top Level Administrative Personnel in France and Prussia   504

7–2 Output of Top Level Technical Personnel in France and Prussia, 1820–1850   557

FOREWORD

THIS EIGHTH volume in the series of Studies in Political Development represents two new departures in the intellectual history of the Committee on Comparative Politics of the Social Science Research Council: a "return to Europe," and an attempt to collaborate with historians.

From its establishment in 1954 the Committee's focus has been on understanding the processes of political change in the developing countries of Asia, Africa, and Latin America, and in dealing with contemporary problems it has sought collaboration with specialists in the newer areas of sociology, anthropology, economics, psychology, and journalism. In time, however, the Committee felt an increasing need for greater perspective for understanding the current problems of political development in the new states. The idea of examining again the history of state and nation-building in Europe in the light of present developments held great attraction especially since it presented the added prospect of stimulating collaboration between historians and political scientists. Consequently, the Committee was inspired to seek funds from the Ford Foundation to sponsor specifically "the collaboration of American and European historians" in the study of "the formation of nation states in Western Europe."

The ensuing grant made it possible to organize a planning group under the imaginative leadership of Gabriel A. Almond, to invite Charles Tilly to direct the study, to hold a summer workshop of European and American scholars at the Center for Advanced Study in the Behavioral Sciences, and to arrange subsequent meetings, including one at the Villa Serbelloni in Bellagio. The fact that this project has been the most generously endowed enterprise in the history of the Committee on Comparative Politics makes it no more, or less, important than any other Committee product.

During the years of its existence 245 people have participated in Committee activities. The Committee has helped to produce over 300 written reports, including books, chapters, articles in journals, and research memoranda. In addition to providing competition for research support, the Committee has sponsored 23 conferences, co-sponsored 6 others, conducted 5 summer workshops, and produced the series of Studies in Political Development of which this is the latest volume but not the last planned. Throughout its history the Committee has encouraged a wide variety of approaches and viewpoints.

One of the purposes of the study reported in this volume was to discover the extent to which a review of state-building in Europe could usefully inform contemporary efforts at advancing both the practice and the theories of political development. It is, therefore, noteworthy that in many ways the authors highlight the fact that the circumstances of state-building in Europe were quite different from the situation which pertains today in the new states and thus great care must be exercised in generalizing from the past to the present. In Europe the establishment of authoritarian structures occurred well before either the beginning of economic growth or the spread of popular participation. Furthermore, the procurement of specialized skills and talents was not inhibited by citizenship requirements and the sensitivities of nationalism.

Possibly most striking and disturbing is the finding of the authors of this volume that wars and the threats of war played such a critical part in building the strong states of Europe. The ominous phenomenon of war gave telling reality and unquestionable legitimacy to the reasons of state. What was established and learned in the mobilizing of resources for national security persisted to provide funds for peacetime allocations, largely because of the extraordinary ratchet effect universally inherent in the processes of taxation. Specifically, European elites learned early what still escapes the rulers of many new states, and that is the art of taxing the wealthy and also the peasantry. The current scene in the developing world provides no comparable imperatives as war did for Europe, and hence it is not surprising that the new states cannot tap as high a proportion of national income as the early European states did. Yet no one would want an increase in the pervasiveness of war.

Yet in spite of such significant differences in the circumstances of the past and the present, this endeavor by historians succeeds in realizing the prime purpose of the Committee which was to broaden the perspective of those concerned with political development. Although Tilly and his European and American colleagues have chosen to focus on the development of the more authoritative and repressive institutions associated with state-building, and ignored such matters as the dispensing of justice, they have impressively demonstrated the complexity of their select subjects. Scholars will no doubt differ in their interpretations of the matters dealt with in this book, as indeed have the members of the Committee, but it is hoped the ensuing dialogue will advance knowledge, which has been the sole purpose of the Committee.

Cambridge, Mass.   Lucian W. Pye
January, 1974

ACKNOWLEDGMENTS

THIS BOOK is a collective enterprise, as the Contents makes clear. Yet it neglects some important contributors. First, there were the organizations. The Center for Advanced Study in the Behavioral Sciences gracefully accommodated our seminar during the summer of 1970; we owe particular thanks to O. Meredith Wilson and Preston Cutler at the Center. The Rockefeller Foundation gave us a delightful few days of discussion at the Villa Serbelloni, Bellagio, in 1971. The National Science Foundation, via its research grant GS–2674, indirectly supported the preparation of some parts of the book. The Institute for Advanced Study helped in the preparation of some parts of the manuscript, and gave Tilly the leisure to work on it. Thanks to Carl Kaysen for making the Institute a place where social scientists and historians—whether they consider themselves social scientists or not—can work together. The Social Science Research Council (where Bryce Wood did the worrying and scurrying for us during three or four difficult years) not only got our inquiry started, but provided the bulk of its financial support.

Others helped us work out the plan of inquiry and hammer out our arguments. Leonard Binder, Samuel Huntington, Herbert Kisch, Rajni Kothari, Lucian Pye, Robert Ward, Myron Weiner, and Aristide Zolberg all took part in valuable discussions before or during the seminar. While we were in California, Val Lorwin, Peter Paret, and G. W. Skinner lavished their wisdom on the members of the seminar. Lorwin even traveled with us to Italy, and provided salient critiques of our sayings and writings over several years. Gabriel Almond worked with us from the beginning. Nay, more: the seminar, and thus this book, came into being largely because of Almond's zeal to make connections between studies of contemporary political change and analyses of the western past.

Someone also had to help shape a mass of much-corrected manuscripts into the form of a book. The anonymous critics engaged by the Committee on Comparative Politics and by Princeton University Press (who are condemned to receive our thanks anonymously, through the publication of this note) pained our prides somewhat, but contributed significantly to the tightening of our arguments. At the Press, Sanford Thatcher gave us encouragement and cooperation. Mary Weller de Grandpré Sa'id and Louise Tilly prepared translations at some stages in the preparation of the papers. Karen Fonde and Leila Al-Imad did a notable part of the preliminary editing, while Elizabeth Edmonston and Judith Davidson gave intelligent oversight to the manuscript's final preparation. As for its physical production, Margaret Grillot, Anna Marie Holt, Pamela Hume and Debbie Polzin all took part. To this great corps of collaborators, the collective thanks of the authors.

The Formation
of National States in
Western Europe

CHAPTER 1

REFLECTIONS ON THE HISTORY OF EUROPEAN STATE-MAKING

CHARLES TILLY

Political Development and History

THE ANALYSIS OF political development has had about the same relationship to historical experience as a dog on a long leash to the tree at the other end of the leash. The dog can roam in almost any direction. He can even get the illusion of rushing off on his own. But let him rush too far, too fast and his collar will jerk him back; it may even knock the wind out of him. Some political scientists want to break the leash or at least move the tree. The authors of this book want, instead, a leash which is very long but very sure. Our minimum position is this: major political transformations which occurred in the past may not repeat themselves in the present and future, and are very unlikely to repeat themselves in exactly the same way, but any theories which claim to encompass general processes of political transformation must be consistent with past experience, and ought to be checked carefully against that experience before gaining wide acceptance. We often move beyond that minimum position; we consider the historical experience to be more important than contemporary observation in the formulation or verification of some kinds of generalizations about large-scale political changes.

Political analysis as a whole has never strayed far from the tree. The French Revolution, the Athenian city-state, the Chinese bureaucracy have always stood as cases to be conjured with, examples to illustrate an argument, realities against which to dash an opponent's theory. Since World War II, nevertheless, a number of students of large-scale political process have sought to escape the tyranny of the past through the employment of techniques developed in fields oriented mainly to the present: survey research, international quantitative analyses of data from censuses or bureaucratic reporting, and

Warm thanks to Val Lorwin, who threshed several versions of different parts of this chapter, and found plenty of chaff; one of those parts circulated earlier as Tilly 1970 (citations in this form refer to the bibliography at the end of the book).

so on. The creation of scores of independent states made the swing toward the present possible, and even pressing. It had a psychedelic effect; it widened the vision of those whose textbooks had told them that "comparative government" consisted mainly in the systematic scrutiny of republican, fascist, communist, and monarchical constitutions. "Political development" called attention to change, process, emergence in the present and the future.

The move toward the dynamic analysis of the present entailed serious costs, some of which were unavoidable. Two especially concern us here. If the span of time observed is very short—either because the states under study are new or because data are only available for one or two points in time—it will be impossible to detect trends and to verify theories about what the trends should be. The attempt to extrapolate the experience of Ghana, Jordan, or Jamaica from a span of five or ten years is risk itself. And the alternative use of international comparisons at a single point in time (assuming that Ghana, Jordan, Jamaica, Belgium, and Israel, let us say, stand at different points on some continuum of political development all of them will eventually traverse) begs the very question which theorists of political development are struggling to answer.

The second real cost (this one avoidable in principle but nevertheless widespread) is the implicit introduction of misconceived models of Western experience as the criteria of political development. Misconceived, in three senses: (1) they often caricatured the Western experience by assuming a fairly continuous rationalization of government, broadening of political participation, pacification of the masses, and so on; (2) even where reasonably accurate, they skirted the possibility that the Western experience was a lucky shot, an aberration, a dead end, or simply one among many paths open to "modern" government, whatever that may be; (3) the criteria of modernity tended to twist the question of paths of development into another one: under what conditions and through what transformations might we expect the governments of today's new worlds to end up looking like old-world governments?

The most profound historical analysis in the world will not turn us into clairvoyants. Yet careful examination of the longer run of historical experience will at least defend those who ardently desire to make sense of the contemporary world and the world of the future from the two kinds of error I have described. Indeed, we find many political analysts who began with contemporary affairs moving back

[4]

to grapple with the long run: a Barrington Moore transferring his attention from recent Soviet politics to the origins of the world's great political alternatives, a G. W. Skinner gliding from the Chinese in modern Thailand to China over its vast imperial history, a Samuel Huntington bounding from contemporary soldiers to the political development of the major western powers, and numerous others in their company.

This volume, then, may be a leap into a bandwagon already in motion. We hope, at least, that the leap will be graceful and distinctive.

Origins of this Book

The Committee on Comparative Politics gave us a springboard and a starting shove. That committee of the Social Science Research Council had already helped shape the character of American studies of large-scale political change through its patronage of inquiries eventually published under such titles as *Bureaucracy and Political Development, Communications and Political Development,* and *The Civic Culture.* Early in 1969, the committee asked a group composed of five of its members plus two interested outsiders—Samuel Huntington, Robert Ward, Myron Weiner, Aristide Zolberg, Gabriel Almond, Rajni Kothari, and Charles Tilly—to formulate a plan of research on state- and nation-building in Western Europe which the committee might be able to support. The planning group recommended a "workshop" for the summer of 1970. The plan was accepted; Almond and Tilly took on the chief responsibility for organizing the 1970 meeting.

The general plan was straightforward: choose a diverse but interlocking set of activities in which all European states engaged to some degree and whose changes and variations were crucial to the subsequent development of the state as a whole; persuade one or two specialists in the study of each of those activities to prepare synthetic essays comparing the historical experience of several European states; bring together the authors of those essays plus a few other general analysts of political development for two months of discussion of the papers, mutual criticism, further research and rewriting; arrange a regular (but not overwhelming) flow of visiting experts and critics. And that is what we did. The authors of this volume were the core group. At the end of a summer's work at the Center for Advanced Study in the Behavioral Sciences, we were sufficiently convinced that the work we had done was interesting (if not neces-

[5]

sarily valid or definitive) that we decided to bring together the final versions of the papers we had been discussing, plus some general reflections on the papers, in a collective volume. Here it is.

We began our work intending to analyze state-making and the formation of nations interdependently. As our inquiry proceeded, we concentrated our attention increasingly on the development of states rather than the building of nations. There were several reasons for this drift. One was the greater ease with which we could arrive at some working agreement on the meaning of the word "state." "Nation" remains one of the most puzzling and tendentious items in the political lexicon. Another was our early fixation on the periods in which the primacy states was still open to serious challenge; they were not generally periods of nationalism, of mass political identity or even of great cultural homogeneity within the boundaries of a state. The third was the bias in our original set of topics toward the extractive and repressive activities of states.

The bias was deliberate. The singling out of the organization of armed forces, taxation, policing, the control of food supply, and the formation of technical personnel stresses activities which were difficult, costly, and often unwanted by large parts of the population. All were essential to the creation of strong states; all are therefore likely to tell us something important about the conditions under which strong or weak, centralized or decentralized, stable or unstable, states come into being. Of course, other activities might have found their way onto the same list: control of manufacturing, enforcement of public morality, propaganda, colonization and imperialism, and so on. This particular list emphasizes activities which became important early in the state-making experience and remained so for a long time, and on which there already exists a substantial body of historical work. As our work proceeded, the chief omission which the group came to regret was the judicial system. Because courts, judges, and judicial proceedings antedate national states and appear in so many unstately guises, it is easy to forget how large a part certain kinds of courts played in the day-to-day construction of Western states. The issue comes up, of course, in papers dealing with taxation, food supply or policing, but the volume as a whole treats the judicial system much less adequately than we would have liked.

Another deliberate decision significantly affected the character of our work, and of this book. We might have asked our specialists to write their papers as commentaries on some particular set of theories concerning political change. That would have focused our joint inquiry from the very beginning. It would, however, have risked fixing the inquiry on invalid schemes, on problems of terminology, on issues which missed the substance of the phenomena we were trying to understand. Instead, each participant received the invitation to write about his subject as best he knew how, so long as the treatment was synthetic and comparative. (Regardless of native language, incidentally, each participant prepared his contribution in English; where that produced obscurities, I tried to edit the language into comprehensible—but not always idiomatic—English.)

Even the time span was left open. As it worked out, the greatest part of our collective effort went into the seventeenth and eighteenth centuries. An earlier focus would have produced more discussions of the antecedents of full-fledged states than this book contains; a later one would have weighted the discussion toward the accumulation of functions and powers by established states, and the collaboration among existing states in drawing the rest of the world into a system of states. The seventeenth- and eighteenth-century focus has us dealing with periods in which, for most of Europe, both the primacy and the ultimate form of the state were much in doubt. Perhaps that is the most important historical insight the book has to offer: as seen from 1600 or so, the development of the state was very contingent; many aspiring states crumpled and fell along the way.

Of course, all of the participants were aware of open issues in theories of political change to which our conclusions might be relevant; our summer's discussion reinforced that awareness. But the freedom to set each problem in its own terms surely made the individual contributions more valuable, as well as more variable, than they would have been if they had concentrated on a few available general schemes.

The Nature of the Evidence

The materials with which we work in this book will have a spurious familiarity for many a political analyst. They will remind him of faded lecture notes on old constitutions and older states. Yet very few of our readers will currently be attempting to confront theories of political development with systematically assembled historical data. Even fewer will ever have worked firsthand with the actual documents left behind by state-making, as opposed to the standard accounts of state-making bequeathed to us by political historians. In dealing with the broad topics assigned to them, all of our authors have, as one would expect, relied heavily on syntheses prepared by other scholars. In our own routine work, we vary greatly in our use of primary historical sources. Yet in one way or another all of us—readers and writers alike—are ultimately prisoners of the documents. And the chains are hard to see.

The character of the evidence now available concerning the state-building of two or three centuries ago sets important limits on our ability to frame or validate hypotheses about political development. We must rely mainly on the residues of the paperwork carried on as part of the very construction of the states we are studying. Because of the way such records are produced and preserved, the residues overrepresent the final, official, legal, organization, public sides of the affair; we shall always be hard-pressed to find adequate documentation on the preliminary, unofficial, illegal, informal, immoral, and private aspects of state-making. To the extent that our arguments require reliable evidence on the attitudes and intentions of state-makers or citizens, we are bound to be disappointed. What is more, before the nineteenth century the more or less continuous and comprehensive description of the base population now provided by censuses, surveys, and the like is only available for occasional small fragments of time and space; such simple operations as calculating per capita government revenues by region thereby become difficult or impossible.

As compared with historians of the family or of popular culture, nevertheless, we are in a privileged position. For state-makers are papermongers; their files become our archives. From 1500 onward the documentation becomes ever more abundant. By the nineteenth century it is almost inconceivable that a single person could master in his lifetime the whole range of documentary evidence available for more than ten or twenty years of any important European state's operation.

The documentary residues of state-making fall into several distinct categories. For convenience, we might distinguish among (1) direct inside reporting of the conduct of public affairs, (2) routine by-products of organizational work, and (3) records and reports of interactions between governments and members of the general population. Administrative correspondence bulks largest in the first category, both in volume and in value; few sources can give a more rapid and dramatic sense of the problems and preoccupations of state-makers than the exchanges between a Richelieu and his provincial agents. The memoirs, journals, and personal correspondence of statesmen (which are rarer, less accessible and harder to interpret than administrative correspondence) also belong here.

The routine by-products of organizational work include some direct inside reporting, to be sure, but they also include a variety of materials which must be systematically collated and reinterpreted before they yield reliable information on how the government did its work. In Western Europe, the largest stores of this kind are records of taxation and registration, personnel files, budgets and financial materials, and the residues of policing and judicial proceedings.

The records and reports of interactions between governments and members of the general population overlap with the routine organizational by-products, since a major part of governmental activity consists of such things as collecting taxes from individuals, registering births, drafting young men, arresting them or verifying their claims for public assistance. Yet a wide range of relevant documents come into existence outside the bureaucracy: the routine papers of other organizations (firms, monasteries, municipalities, guilds, political associations) which have to deal with the state; the reports of travelers or other outsiders, like the British consuls whose detailed dispatches to London are prime sources for the study of eighteenth-century Italy; the memoirs, journals, and correspondence of individuals outside the government.

With sources as varied as these, an energetic investigator can find documentation of a great range of state-building activities. Yet the nature of the sources sets some interesting constraints on his work. I have already mentioned the difficulty of verifying arguments emphasizing attitudes and intentions with this sort of documentation. The analyst who wishes to get at organizational structure in any but the most formal sense finds himself in a rather different bind: the residues of routine organizational activity are abundant and informative, but their very interpretation requires us to adopt unverified assumptions about how the documents came into existence, which are in fact assumptions about how the organization operated. (I have repeatedly run across this problem in using nineteenth-century French police records to study collective violence and governmental repression—two phenomena which overlap with each other more than one might think.)

The great bulk of the documentary sources, furthermore, do not comprise descriptive testimony in the sense that an eye-witness report describes a crime; they are residues of organizational work resembling the files of any of us who spends part of his time in bureaucracies. Expenditure records provide an excellent example: properly verified and compiled, they describe a major feature of an organization's behavior, but only rarely do they include anything like a narrative of the way the expenditure came about, and the verification and the compilation themselves require a theory of how the organization behaves, if only in the form of guesses about what was disguised or left out. Willy-nilly the historian constructs the history of his sources and of the organizations producing his sources as he reconstructs the phenomena he was pursuing in the first place.

Of course, something like this happens in many other branches of historical inquiry. The student of state-making faces the problem with particular acuteness because the organization he is tracing has itself been the principal accumulator of the sources available to him. The correctives are obvious but difficult: the cross-checking of sources drawn from different positions inside and outside the state, the deliberate bringing to light and testing of implicit hypotheses about the organization's behavior, the devising of internal consistency checks, and so on.

This heady difficulty concerns us here because it means that even in the best of circumstances the comparisons we make between two different states (or between the same state at different points in time) will never quite permit us to distinguish between variations in recordkeeping and variations in the phenomena the records are supposed to reveal. A reader who looks between the lines will notice the difficulty again and again as he goes through this book: in our attempts to judge the relative extent of market production in different periods and places, in our efforts to compare levels of government income and expenditure, in our encounters with the varying repressiveness of different regimes, in our estimates of the redistributive effects of different systems of taxation. We are inclined to think that similar difficulties beset attempts to compare the current experiences of twentieth-century states; they are not peculiar to historical analysis. We are also inclined to think that the advantage of having long spans of time to study outweighs the disadvantages of uncertain comparability.

In the last analysis, the suitability of large historical comparisons for the verification, falsification, and elaboration of theories of political development depends on the scopes of the theories in question. Very general theories about long-term development (like those of

Marx, Weber, or Schumpeter) are ripe for historical criticism; they are indeed difficult to test in any other way. Theories of short-run process in contemporary states, like the party-and-interest-group analyses of V. O. Key, Maurice Duverger or Alessandro Pizzorno, by contrast, do not lend themselves to the same sort of testing very well.

That much is obvious. The interesting case is the establishment of hypothetical relationships among major variables: public liberties as a function of bourgeois dominance, political instability as a function of autonomous military power, the relative bulk of the government's fiscal apparatus as an inverse function of the commercialization of the economy, and so on. Political scientists have customarily sought to establish such relationships through the study of variation across numerous areas at the same point of time. Yet at the same time the theories are commonly evolutionary, developmental, oriented to change over time. In such cases, the cross-sectional comparisons hardly bear on the hypotheses which are supposedly being tested. Data on long-run change are required.

Bruce Russett's *World Handbook of Political and Social Indicators* contains an excellent set of cases in point. Most of the handbook consists of straightforward presentations of quantitative data. But later sections of the book move from simple description of correlations to discussions of (1) "stages" of economic and political development, (2) changing relationships between variables, and (3) multifactor explanations of social change, all on the basis of cross-sectional comparisons of countries in the 1950s. A graph of the logarithm of "deaths from domestic group violence per 1,000,000, 1950–1962" (compiled from the *New York Times Index*, the *New International Yearbook*, *Facts on File*, and the *Britannica Book of the Year* and scattered other sources) against the logarithm of per capita Gross National Product in 1957 bears the caption "Economic Development is Associated with Political Violence, at Least in the Early Stages." And the commentary runs:

> This would suggest—to the extent that our cross-sectional model provides useful insights for change over time—that underdeveloped nations must expect a fairly high level of civil unrest for some time, and that very poor states should probably expect an increase, not a decrease in domestic violence over the next few decades. The reasons, of course, are not hard to suggest. In a traditional society knowledge is limited, aspirations are limited,

and expectations as to the proper activities of government are limited. All this changes with development (Russett 1964: 307).

This passage would be worth squeezing slowly for its implicit view of the world. For present purposes the qualification "to the extent that our cross-sectional model provides useful insights for change over time" is all we need extract. Insight is the most that could come from such comparisons, for they have no logical bearing on propositions about the consequences of change. The cross-sectional differences in deaths from domestic group violence during the 1950s may represent permanent differences between Western and non-Western countries. They are compatible with a world in which collective violence is rising in every country, or falling in every country. And they could result from the ability of the wealthy twentieth-century states to quell dissidence within their own populations, and promote it in poor countries. If we are to formulate essentially historical hypotheses, we shall have to acquire essentially historical data.

The Historical Questions

In their most general terms, all our historical questions go back to one: what are the crucial problems and events in the emergence of the alternative forms of Western states? That immediately raises two issues: common properties and variations. Our attempt to discern the common properties of state-making experiences in different parts of Western Europe has the advantage of extensive documentation, and the logical difficulty of the missing comparison; to really detect the standard features of the West European development, one would want to compare Western Europe with the state-making experience of Eastern Europe, of Asia, of the contemporary world. That we have not done with any zeal.

Our attempt to account for variations *within* the European experience puts us in a somewhat stronger position, since some important differences among, say, Spain, Prussia and England do appear; the main risk we run is of attaching great general importance to what are in fact minor distinctions within the same family of states, or to divisions which are in fact quite idiosyncratic to West European development. The outcome of the Reformation in different European countries, for example, undoubtedly affected subsequent political forms rather seriously; historical peculiarity or general principle?

The problem of variation itself splits neatly into two parts. Part one: what determined the principal variations in the early forms of West European states? Part two: what difference did the character of early state-building make to the subsequent form and substance of political activity in one country or another?

In the first part, we are asking how it is that a centralized monarchy arose early in France, that the Hapsburg domains remained fragmented into ethnic-religious units weakly subordinated to the imperial center, that the regions from Rhine to Oder sustained such a large number of weak principalities, and so on. In the second part, we are asking instead in what respect the early prominence of great landlords and military institutions in Brandenburg-Prussia affected the chances for parliamentary democracy, what features of seventeenth-century Bavaria might have permitted a seer to foretell her failure to survive the nineteenth century as an independent state, whether the long subordination of most of Italy to outside powers somehow determined the special character of Italian unification. That these are enormous questions, and the standard questions of European political history to boot, we are perfectly aware. Our only hope of contributing to their resolution lies in the possibility that the particular variables we have chosen to scrutinize—the variations in the extractive, repressive, control activities of governments—operate in a regular way, and that we have caught some of the regularity in our formulations.

Let me return to the sorts of conclusions we have reached later. What if we *have* made some sense of the Western European experience; why should anyone who is mainly interested in the twentieth-century world outside of Europe pay any attention? For three simple reasons: (1) a large proportion of the reasoning still employed in the analysis of contemporary political change rests implicitly on a reading of European experience, and could therefore be proved wrong on the basis of European evidence; the continued salience of the English, French, and Russian revolutions in contemporary analyses of revolutionary processes illustrates the point perfectly; (2) the European historical experience, for all its special features, is long enough, well-enough documented, and a large enough influence on the rest of the world that any systematic conclusions which did hold up well in the light of that experience would almost automatically become plausible working hypotheses to be tried out elsewhere; in contemporary countries the growing utility for demographic analysis of conclusions concerning the conditions for rising or falling fertility drawn from the close examination of European populations over long periods of time offers an attractive parallel; and (3) conversely, ostensibly general formulations which can already be proposed to account for the contemporary world deserve checking against the vast, well-documented European experience; the least that could come of it would be a delimitation of the applicability of such formulations.

But how we attack the European record will determine the utility of our conclusions. Three choices appear to be crucial: between prospective and retrospective forms of analysis, between probabilistic and deterministic formulations and among the searches for recurrent sequences and recurrent relationships.

Prospective vs. Retrospective Analysis

A retrospective analysis begins with some particular historical condition (within our territory the emergence of stable parliamentary democracy has been a favorite item) and searches back for its causes. Its ideal conclusion appears in something like the form "Y occurs if and only if A, B, C . . . X obtain." A prospective analysis begins with a particular historical condition and searches forward to the alternative outcomes of that condition, with a specification of the paths leading to each of the outcomes. Thus Aristotle tells us that given the existence of a democratic constitution, democracy is likely to persist if the wealthy and well-born are checked but not attacked; that oligarchy is likely to replace it if the demagogues attempt to dispossess the rich; that tyranny is likely to appear if the demagogues employ military might in overcoming their opponents; that kingship, polity, and aristocracy are unlikely to grow from democracy in any circumstances, and so on. The ideal formulation of a prospective argument runs "if A occurs,

W will develop if B, C, D . . . N;
X will develop if C, D, E . . . O;
Y will develop if D, E, F . . . P."

In the case of an ideally complete theory of a phenomenon, to be sure, the retrospective statement will be nothing but a special case of the prospective one made about all possible starting points; then we will know all possible paths to W, X, and Y as well as all possible paths from A, B, and C. As a practical matter, however, retrospective investigation is unlikely to yield valid prospective conclusions, and vice versa. If, then, we are hoping to specify the conditions under which, say, a predominantly peasant population with weak institutions of central government produces (1) military dictatorship, (2) parliamentary democracy, or (3) agrarian socialism, we shall have to set our thinking into a prospective frame.

In beginning our work, we did not fully sense the tension between retrospective and prospective ways of posing questions. That initial uncertainty caused a good deal of trouble, some of which is still visible in the book. We began with a tendency to phrase our most general questions retrospectively, and our detailed historical questions prospectively.

The tension appears in the very selection of a small number of West European states still existing in the nineteenth and twentieth centuries for comparison. For England, France, and even Spain are *survivors* of a ruthless competition in which most contenders lost. The Europe of 1500 included some five hundred more or less independent political units, the Europe of 1900 about twenty-five. The German state did not exist in 1500, or even 1800. Comparing the histories of France, Germany, Spain, Belgium, and England (or, for that matter, any other set of West European countries) for illumination on the processes of state-making weights the whole inquiry toward a certain kind of outcome which was, in fact, quite rare. Having chosen to deal comparatively with those large historical experiences, we never quite escaped the difficulty. Nevertheless, with many fits, starts, stalls, and backtracks, our net movement went away from retrospective questions about political development in general toward prospective questions about the possibilities open at each stage in the formation of Western states.

Probabilistic vs. Deterministic Explanations

Again, any analyst of state-building must choose between probabilistic and deterministic modes of explanation. Having stated the whole range of outcomes theoretically open to the European political situation of the period before states became dominant, we ought to explain why most of those which were theoretically open did *not* occur. That explanation may be probabilistic, and therefore compatible with the conclusion that an unlikely set of outcomes actually occurred in Europe. Or it may be deterministic: in the circumstances, Spain had to develop the kind of political structure it acquired, Brandenburg had to develop its special type. In practice, the "explanation" is more likely to take the logically unsatisfying form of an argument that the most probable set of outcomes actually occurred—a form of argument which would have much more bite if one could run history over and over as a series of tries at the slot machine. In any of these cases, however, we shall be engaged in formulating or accepting general rules for change in political structure.

Yet we have a choice. The search for a deterministic explanation will require us to isolate the effects of a large number of variables, including such items as the genetic inheritance of royal families, the vagaries of war, and the mineral composition of a country's subsoil. It will be correspondingly difficult to extend our conclusions to new political systems—in principle, because the permutations and interactions of the variables outside the range we have already observed are certain to be complicated; in practice, because the more variables, the greater the difficulty of acquiring comparable evidence. The search for a probabilistic explanation will permit many of these variables to be treated as "random" and make it easier to identify and examine the appropriate cases among the new political systems, but it will produce explanations of the old systems which are less satisfactory from the point of view of conventional historical reconstruction, and will run the risk that one of the "random" variables will some day reveal itself as fundamental. Since we are self-consciously seeking to employ historical analysis for the purpose of editing ostensibly general theories of political transformation, we have little choice but to adopt a probabilistic approach.

Events, Sequences, and Relationships

Finally, we must choose among attempts to generalize about recurrent events, recurrent sequences, and recurrent relationships. At the level of events, others have often tried to frame general statements about the patterns of revolutions, of wars, of national crises, and so on. At the level of sequences, we have a number of trials at the delineation of standard stages of political development or the equivalent. At the level of relationships, political analysis abounds in arguments that parliamentary institutions thrive to the extent that a bourgeoisie acquires power, that states in which the army is a primary channel of social mobility are vulnerable to coups and the like —without any necessary implication that certain classes of events recur in essentially the same pattern or that all governments of a certain general type pass through the same sequence of transformations. The choice among events, sequences, and relationships will rest in part on the kinds of theories we hope to confront, in part on our guesses as to whether true regularities at a world scale are likely to appear at the level of events, sequences, or relationships.

The authors of this volume differ more widely on this issue than on the questions of prospective-retrospective analysis or probabilism vs. determinism. In their usual professional work, for example, Fischer and Ardant tend to adopt economic reasoning which concentrates their attention on relationships (for example, between commercialization and fiscal efficiency, or employment opportunity and population growth) and they tend to be skeptical about standard-stage theories. Rokkan, by contrast, has in the past devoted large efforts to the detection of standard sequences of representation, mobilization or even state-building in general. Finer and Tilly, to take the third case, have at least occasionally tried to delineate recurrent features of coups, revolutions, and other transfers of power—of events.

Yet when it comes to the particular task of this book, we converge on the analysis of relationships rather than of events or sequences. There are several reasons for that. First, we find that the arguments about political development which take a propositional form (e.g., if X and Y, then Z) and therefore are susceptible of proof deal almost exclusively with relationships; hypotheses concerning standard sequences and recurrent events ordinarily turn out, on close examination, to be tautological or purely heuristic. Second, the greater logical strength of our position in identifying patterns of difference among European states than in detecting their common properties disposes us to emphasize possible relationships between geopolitical position and military strength, between homogeneity of population and legitimacy of political institutions, and so on. Third (and most important), none of us thinks the European experience will repeat itself as a set of events or sequences. Yet all of us are willing to entertain the hypothesis that some of the relationships which showed up there are quite general.

What the Europe of 1500 Had in Common

Precisely because our object is to look forward from 1600 or 1650, we should step back a bit in time to see what lies behind our vantage point. The processes we are trying to examine were already well in motion by the seventeenth century. At the beginning of the sixteenth —1500—we can get some sense of the common conditions and raw materials on which the state-making processes were operating. By comparison with other eras and other parts of the world, Europeans of the centuries since then have experienced some common conditions which have given their state-making a measure of uniformity and have distinguished it from that now going on elsewhere. First, the Europe of 1500 had a kind of cultural homogeneity only rivaled, at such a geographic scale, by that of China. The earlier unification of the Roman Empire had produced some convergence of language, law, religion, administrative practice, agriculture, landholding, and perhaps kinship as well. In 1500 Celts and Basques held out in the North and West, Magyars and Mongols in the East, Turks and other Muslims in the South; but the populations settled between them shared a common culture and maintained extensive contacts via an active network of trade, a constant movement of persons, and a tremendous interlocking of ruling families. A single relatively centralized church dominated the continent's religious life, an enfeebled empire sprawled over the continent's central sections, clutching fragments of a common political tradition.

In a large part of the area a single family system predominated; bilateral descent leading to the diffuse kindred (rather than a corporate group like the lineage) as the chief larger kinship unit, tendency toward nuclear family residence, small households, relatively late marriage, frequent celibacy, and, consequently, moderate birth rates. These arrangements probably held back the rate of population growth when, in later centuries, mortality fell. But the major significance of this vital and prosperous cultural homogeneity for the emergence of states was the ease it gave to the diffusion of organizational models, to the expansion of states into new territories, to the transfer of populations from one state to another, and to the movement of administrative personnel from one government to another.

I do not mean that variation in position or previous historical experience made no difference in 1500. The *Reconquista* left the Spanish an abundant, often impoverished, nobility which was prepared to alternate between war and disputatious idleness, unlike the monied aristocrats of the Netherlands. The Austrian Hapsburgs were constantly distracted from the work of internal consolidation by the threat of the Turks, a fact which the "most Christian" king of

France did not scruple to use against the projects of the Hapsburg dynasty. Despite the great international web of trade, the economic and social lives of most Europeans were highly localized, market production was not very extensive, internal communications were slow. Well-defined vernaculars (a number of which would later become the identifying features of major states) already divided Europeans into linguistic groups incapable of mutual communication. Nevertheless, in world perspective the cultural homogeneity of the area in which the first powerful national states arose is a condition of prime importance.

The Peasant Base

A second condition is closely connected to it: the prevalence of peasantry. The great bulk of the population and the great bulk of the resources which eventually came under the command of the European state-makers were, in 1500, committed to a peasant way of life. Settled cultivation in which peasant households and communities exercised substantial claims to the land but, under a variety of incentives and pressures, turned over a significant part of their production to town-based consumers (not to mention the idlers of the countryside) in the form of rents, dues, taxes, and cash sales, absorbed most of the working energy expended in the Europe of that time. Nomads, slash-and-burn agriculturalists, fishermen, hunters, and even herders were rare in most of Europe. (Castile and much of northern and western England were heavily engaged in wool production, however, and after 1500 the demand for wool and for meat would hasten the growth of flocks and the dispossession of ploughmen in several parts of Europe.)

The complement, or parasite, of this enormous class of peasants was a small but widespread class of landlords. They were typically titled, which meant that some special relationship to a sovereign guaranteed another special relationship to the land as well as to political power. Their control over the land ranged from (1) symbolic dues paid by peasants who exercised practical freehold, to (2) ownership in the solid nineteenth-century sense of the word, to (3) discretion not only over the land but also over the labor of the men fixed upon it—serfdom. In 1500, however, serfdom of a medieval type was extremely rare, and the alliance between great nobles and statesmen which was to bring something like it into being in Eastern

[19]

Europe during the seventeenth and eighteenth centuries had not yet formed.

Within this peasant world, cities had been growing up as centers of trade, communication, administration and manufacturing for some five hundred years. The Europe of 1500 was, proportionately speaking, most likely more urban than China and nearly as urban as Japan. To be sure, cities spread themselves very unevenly across the European landscape, with the greatest concentration in a central band from south to north. The central band also contained a disproportionate share of European manufacturing. For a century or so before 1500, manufacturing for urban markets had been spreading into the countryside—most notably in the form of the cottage industries of Flanders, southern England, and northern Italy. So the city-based bourgeoisie already had a variety of holds on the countryside: as merchants handling peasant produce, as masters of cities exerting organized pressure on the countryside to assure their own provisioning, as entrepreneurs in rural industry, as lenders of money, and, increasingly, as landlords in the hinterlands of the larger cities.

Why should this set of social arrangements affect the emergence of states? First, it meant that Europe as a whole already had a great deal of wealth and productive capacity, but a wealth and productive capacity not only heavily tied to the land but strongly committed to a large number of individuals and local groups. Second, it shaped the paths by which the state-makers could gain access to those resources. Eric Wolf (1966: 90–91) has framed some powerful general hypotheses about the correlates of the presence or absence of large, kin-based coalitions linking peasants to powerholders outside their communities:

> Such coalitions occur in India, the Near East, and China. They do not occur in manorial Europe, post-Conquest Middle America and the Andean area, the Mediterranean, and neotechnic Europe. The distinction appears to divide societies based on centralized and despotic power, exercised largely through the delegation of prebendal domains, from those in which power is more decentralized. The decentralized systems, however, show two subpatterns. The first, characteristic of the Mediterranean, is built up largely in dyadic terms through patronage relationships. The second, found in medieval Europe and in Middle America and the Andes after the Spanish conquest, usually sub-

ordinated a corporate peasant community to a dominant domain owner in the vicinity. This figure then operated as a patron towards the community as a whole.

The second major distinction divides all the systems from neotechnic Europe, which in its emphasis on associational forms has been able to construct vertical relationships on a single-stranded rather than a many-stranded basis.

As compared with political entrepreneurs elsewhere in the world, therefore, European state-makers had to contend rather little with solidly organized lineages, tribes, and the like. But the landlord was crucial. An ambitious king could form coalitions with the landlords, could attempt to destroy, subvert, or bypass them or (more likely) could try a combination of all of these tactics. He could not ignore them, especially when the chief among them formed a self-conscious hereditary caste, a nobility.

Decentralized Political Structure

This set of power relations drawing its sustenance from a peasant base virtually implies the third general condition of the European state-making experience: the emergence of states from the midst of an extensive, decentralized but relatively uniform political structure. The debris of several unifying empires remained. According to Joseph Strayer, medieval theorists working with Roman tradition, Catholic doctrine, and the realities of feudal life had already fashioned a workable theory of the sovereign state—which is to say a set of coherent justifications which could be widely used in the consolidation of power. The agents of the relatively uniform political structure—princes, popes, *podeste*, parliamentarians—sometimes allied themselves with kings in the making. Indeed, they were themselves often kings in the making. But by the same token they supplied the most obvious rivals of those who succeeded, and the most threatened opponents of the process as a whole.

Two features of the background to European state-making deserve emphasis because our unilinear notions of "political development" tend to disguise them: (1) the early political importance of deliberative assemblies, which the rise of centralized states generally eclipsed; (2) the tenacious and widespread resistance to the expansion of state power.

Before the period of state preeminence, power-wielding deliberative assemblies were acting at all levels of political life from the village council to the Electors of the Empire. The institutions did not, of course, represent individuals in the radical democratic manner of the nineteenth and twentieth centuries. But the Parliament, the Cortes, and Estates did ordinarily incorporate the principal segments of the population which had acquired or maintained liberties, privileges sanctioned by law, in the face of the sovereign. Such assemblies normally had some control of taxation, which typically took the form of an extraordinary grant for a specific purpose. Building strong royal power meant co-opting, subordinating or destroying these institutions; that program absorbed a large part of the energy of seventeenth-century kings, and its outcome strongly affected the next phase of political history. Local assemblies everywhere lost power to expanding states, within a range from the retention of considerable autonomy by Swiss communes to the French absorption of existing communal assemblies into the state structure to the virtual destruction of such institutions in much of the Germanies.

The fate of provincial and national bodies was more various, and no doubt more important to the states' later political experience. In England the Parliament survived serious threats from the Tudors and the Stuarts, then went on to govern. In France and Prussia the kings were able to undermine the Estates after considerable effort, and at the expense of erecting large administrative structures to supplant them. And in Spain crown and Cortes lumbered to a standstill. In 1500 the governments of Europe bore considerably greater resemblance to one another than two or three centuries later. One of the chief reasons for that increasing divergence is the varying course of the contest between central power and power-wielding assemblies from the sixteenth century onward.

Nor were the existing assemblies the only groups which resisted state-making. Three broad classes of people resisted: (1) the ordinary people pressed to surrender men, crops, labor, goods, money, loyalty, and sometimes land to the emerging states; (2) the established authorities pressed to relinquish or share their power; and (3) the rival claimants to sovereignty.

For all their reputed docility, the ordinary people of Europe fought the claims of central states for centuries. In England, for example, the Tudors put down serious rebellions in 1489 (Yorkshire), 1497 (Cornwall), 1536 (the Pilgrimage of Grace), 1547 (the West),

1549 (Kett's Rebellion), 1553 (Wyatt's Rebellion), all responding in one way or another to the centralizing efforts of the crown. These massive provincial rebellions dwindled after 1600. Yet the revolutions of the seventeenth century—despite the modernizing consequences we are now inclined to identify with them—grew most directly from the Stuarts' effort to concentrate power in the crown. The result was an enormous amount of conflict and resistance. As a recent student of the period after the seventeenth-century English revolutions has written: "By 1688 conspiracy and rebellion, treason and plot, were a part of the history and experience of at least three generations of Englishmen. Indeed, for centuries the country had scarcely been free from turbulence for more than a decade at a time" (Plumb 1967: 15). The political transformations of the next three or four decades, according to Plumb, firmly seated an oligarchical state in England, although even that onset of "political stability" did not, by any means, eliminate violent conflict from English political life. Many of the same sequences of demand, resistance, repression and control were, for instance, yet to be repeated in Ireland.

Nor were things calmer across the channel. France experienced the bloody religious wars of the sixteenth century, which pivoted to some extent on questions of royal prerogative versus regional liberties. The clear, concerted, and violent resistance to the imposition of state control rose to its acme in the seventeenth century, as the crown demanded greater tax revenues from the French population, and acted to neutralize or destroy the authorities which stood in its way. While later on the pressing or conscription of men for military service and the forced delivery of grain to cities and armies incited widespread, if localized, rebellions throughout Europe, the earliest, most dramatic, and most influential forms of popular resistance centered on taxation. After all, taxation was the chief means by which the builders of states in the sixteenth century and later supported their expanding armies, which were in turn their principal instrument in establishing control of their frontiers, pushing them out, defending them against external incursions, and assuring their own priority in the use of force within those frontiers. Conversely, military needs were in those first centuries the main incentive for the imposition of new taxes and the regularization of old ones. The need fed itself, furthermore; the overcoming of resistance to taxation required the maintenance of a military force. So turned the tight circle connecting state-making, military institutions and the extraction of scarce resources from a reluctant population.

The state-makers only imposed their wills on the populace through centuries of ruthless effort. The effort took many forms: creating distinct staffs dependent on the crown and loyal to it; making those staffs (armies and bureaucrats alike) reliable, effective instruments of policy; blending coercion, co-optation and legitimation as means of guaranteeing the acquiescence of different segments of the population; acquiring sound information about the country, its people and its resources; promoting economic activities which would free or create resources for the use of the state. In all these efforts and more, the state-makers frequently found the traditional authorities allied with the people against them. Thus it became a game of shifting coalitions: kings rallying popular support by offering guarantees against cruel and arbitrary local magnates or by challenging their claims to goods, money or services, but not hesitating to crush rebellion when the people were divided or a sufficient military force was at hand; magnates parading as defenders of local liberties against royal oppression, but not hesitating to bargain with the crown when it appeared advantageous. Ultimately, the people paid.

There were also a multitude of unsuccessful rival claimants—the princes, bishops, dukes, and brigands who bid for sovereign power but failed. For the reduction of Europe from some five hundred more or less independent political units in 1500 to twenty-odd states in 1900 produced a large number of losers. Unlike the Chinese and Roman state-builders of earlier times, the Europeans of 1500 and later did not ordinarily expand from a highly organized center into a weakly organized periphery. (Which is not to say there are no analogies like the English conquest of Ireland and the expansion of Brandenburg-Prussia through Central Europe, or that regional variations in this regard made no difference.) Only in European colonial expansion did that become the dominant experience.

Nor did the European state-builders often have the chance to seize and strengthen a single preexisting political structure, as has been the frequent experience of anticolonial rebels since the Americans of 1775. Indeed, building substantial states in much of Europe meant absorbing numerous political units which already exercised significant claims to sovereignty—free cities, principalities, bishoprics, and a variety of other entities. The European state-makers engaged in the work of combining, consolidating, neutralizing, manipulating a tough, complicated, and well-set web of political relations. They sought to fashion something larger and stronger than had existed before. In order to accomplish that, they had to tear or dissolve large parts of the web, and to face furious resistance as they did so.

Yet one feature of the earlier political structure greatly favored the enterprise. The Europeans of 1500 had a tradition of kingship which stretched back in diverse ways to Roman times. Just behind them lay seven hundred years of king-making experience which (for all its chaos) had resulted in almost every European's being at least nominally subject to one crown or another. The state-makers who followed were for the most part kings and agents of kings. They were very much members of the system they were gradually destroying. They commanded a measure of submission on quite traditional grounds. The genuine breaks with the tradition came with the formation of federated republics like the Dutch or the Swiss, and with the extension of European power into overseas colonies.

Conditions Favoring the National State

In order to isolate the conditions which favored the increasing dominance of national states over the people of Western Europe, we have to play an unseemly trick on history. We have to consider what could have happened, instead of what was. Without some such comparison—implicit or explicit—between what occurred and what could have occurred, we have no means of separating the trivial antecedents of state-making from the weighty ones. In order to find a time when the national state does not already seem to have preempted all the alternatives, furthermore, we probably have to go back as far as the thirteenth century.

Even then, according to Joseph Strayer, the form of the European state was already well set, the time of its dominance already begun.

By 1300, it was evident that the dominant political form in Western Europe was going to be the sovereign state. The universal Empire had never been anything but a dream; the universal Church had to admit that defense of the individual state took precedence over the liberties of the Church or the claims of the Christian commonwealth. Loyalty to the state was strong-

[25]

er than any other loyalty, and for a few individuals (largely governmental officials) loyalty to the state was taking on some of the overtones of patriotism (Strayer 1970: 57).

Strayer's test for the emergence of a state, however, is a relatively soft one: ". . . the appearance of political units persisting in time and fixed in space, the development of permanent, impersonal institutions, agreement on the need for an authority which can give final judgments, and acceptance of the idea that this authority should receive the basic loyalty of its subjects" (Strayer 1970: 10). The test excludes government by corporate groups or networks which are either geographically fragmented or constantly on the move, even if they exercise primary claims to the obedience of their members. It also excludes government by the coalition or federation (or, for that matter, competition) of multiple authorities exercising jurisdiction over the same populations. It excludes, finally, the incidental exercise of political control by a structure whose principal activity is trade, control of marriage, manipulation of sacred rites and symbols, or something else of the sort. The test does not, on the other hand, require any particular *scale* of government, any particular *degree* of integration among the "permanent, impersonal institutions," or any great concentration of power in the central authority. When it comes to defining the state-making processes of later centuries, those criteria take on the greatest importance.

As a matter of fact, Strayer explicitly brings empires and city-states under his heading; he presumably would not have great difficulty bringing in rule by bishops and popes as well, just so long as they controlled specialized institutions of government. So the claim for early predominance of the state in Europe does not have quite the sweep it first seems to have. In the thirteenth century, then, five outcomes may still have been open: (1) the form of national state which actually emerged; (2) a political federation or empire controlled, if only loosely, from a single center; (3) a theocratic federation—a commonwealth—held together by the structure of the Catholic Church; (4) an intensive trading network without large-scale, central political organization; (5) the persistence of the "feudal" structure which prevailed in the thirteenth century. The rational appraisal of any such list is a peculiar task, since it is so easy to give reasons why events which did not happen could not happen. (On seeing this list, Joseph Strayer has said to me that the political federation was no more than barely possible; the theocratic federation impossible, since the church had already conceded the temporal priority of the state; the persistence of the "feudal" structure equally impossible, because that structure was already gone by 1300.) Nevertheless, each of the unreal outcomes corresponds to developments which did at least begin in Western Europe.

Not only had the Roman Empire prevailed in Europe, not only had the Holy Roman Empire persisted as its shadow, but the Hapsburgs actually kept their own rickety federation operating into the nineteenth century. At times they even dominated the continent. A church-dominated federation seems implausible because we so regularly oppose church and state. Yet some churchmen held great political power well into the modern period. The papal states survived somehow into the nineteenth century. And there are examples elsewhere in the world (including the nearby Near East) of large-scale, yet decentralized, government by priests. The interlocked trading cities of Germany and northern Italy did, in fact, long resist consolidation into national states. They created commercial federations like the Hanse, but not common armies, common bureaucracies or common fiscal structures. Finally, the "feudal" organization of manors, towns, and overlords—for all the imprecision of the word *feudal*—has a special claim: it predominated in Western Europe for several centuries.

The structure which became dominant in Europe after 1500, the national state, differed from these alternative possibilities in several significant ways: (1) it controlled a well-defined, continuous territory; (2) it was relatively centralized; (3) it was differentiated from other organizations; (4) it reinforced its claims through a tendency to acquire a monopoly over the concentrated means of physical coercion within its territory. So, in a sense, explaining how the national state won out amounts to accounting for territorial consolidation, centralization, differentiation of the instruments of government from other sorts of organization, and monopolization (plus concentration) of the means of coercion.

The common conditions we have already noticed as prevailing around 1500 obviously affected all these processes. It is not so clear, however, that they *caused* the dominance of the state. The conditions prevailed earlier than 1500. In 1300 as well, Europe was relatively homogeneous culturally, drew the great bulk of its resources from a peasant base, and maintained a decentralized political struc-

[27]

ture, or, rather, a congeries of political structures. Homogeneity it-self probably did not predispose Europe toward national states. Elsewhere in the world, large homogeneous populations have lent themselves well to the building of empires; although cultural homo-geneity makes the policy of *divide et impera* less feasible, it decreases the difficulty of extending uniform administrative arrange-ments over large populations, and it makes common allegiance easier to promote. The principal way in which the relative homogeneity of the European population facilitated the emergence of the national state rather than some other political dominant, it seems to me, was in making it easy to divide the continent up into mutually exclusive territories which were at once rather arbitrary and subject to con-siderable change.

Nor does there seem to be any particular affinity between peasants and national states; not only have peasants borne the burden of em-pires and city-states, but also European feudal arrangements de-pended from the beginning on the presence of a subordinate peas-antry. My earlier point was not that peasants are essential, or even favorable, to the creation of national states; it was rather that the predominance of peasants drew state-makers willy-nilly into strug-gles and coalitions with the men who controlled the land. The strongest argument one could make for the peasant base as a cause of the state's victory, I suppose, is that the presence of peasants gave power to major landlords, and the necessity of coalitions with re-gional groups of landlords (who had some choice with which au-thorities, or would-be authorities, to ally themselves) both limited the scale at which princes could operate and pushed them toward territorial agglomeration. Those circumstances, however, resulted more directly from the decentralized political structure than from the predominance of peasants.

It seems odd to consider that political fragmentation as one of the conditions contributing to the final dominance of national states. Did not the state-makers struggle continually against fragmentation? Yes, but the very presence of multiple contenders for power, mutually aware and relatively equal in strength, promoted a process of con-solidation by means of shifting coalitions among geographically concentrated elites, made it likely that more than one such process would be going on at a time, and hampered any effort either to im-pose an authority without contiguous territory or to subordinate a large part of Europe to a single authority. We have the *reductio ad absurdum* of the condition S. N. Eisenstadt analyzes in *Political Systems of Empires* (1963): a large, functioning empire goes through a continuous cycle of building up power in its peripheral units only to see those who have direct access to that power turn it to their own ends and against the central structure; when an empire disintegrates as the Roman Empire did, perhaps it follows that its fragments are that much harder to bring back into a common structure.

The weakness of corporate structures, especially those linked by kinship, in Europe probably abetted this process of growth through the manipulation of shifting coalitions. If lineages controlling land, labor and loyalty had sprawled across the European map, it would have been harder to break up the population into discrete territories, co-opt powerful members of local elites without extending privileges to their clienteles or reinforcing the lineages as such, differentiate government from kinship, and so on. The recurrent confrontations in our own time between corporate kin groups and non-Europeans who have sought to construct states on the European model reinforce this speculation. Perhaps the apparent difficulty of state-making in those portions of Europe which *did* harbor fairly powerful corporate kin groups (I have southeastern Europe especially in mind) points in the same direction.

All the "explanations" of the victory of the national state over its theoretically possible alternatives I have proposed so far fall into the category of preconditions. But some features of state-building processes, and of the circumstances which accompanied them in Europe, also deserve inquiry. First, specialized organization works. If the task at hand is well defined and consists of manipulating the outside world, the ruler who builds a special-purpose organization and keeps it supplied with resources tends to have the advantage over his rivals. Success in war is a notable example: the criteria of success are relatively clear, the main elements of the task (if not the secret of their accomplishment) rather clear, and the superiority of the well-supplied special organization quite likely to tell in the long run. For the purposes of routine regional administration, fiscal control or the acquisition of supplies for the needs of government, a record-keeping bureaucracy has a number of advantages over a kin group, a patron-client chain, a trading network or the other structures built into the theoretical alternatives to the national states.

That assertion is, to be sure, far from self-evident. One can challenge it either by recalling the importance of certain kinds of bureaucracy in imperial China and ancient Babylon or by insisting on the costs and inefficiencies of contemporary bureaucracies. I do not want to argue out that whole problem here. I simply want to suggest that in medieval Europe princes who specialized their instruments of government by forming a separate exchequer, a group of legal advisors, and so on gained the organizational advantage—and that the very transformation of the instruments of government in that direction promoted the formation of the large, autonomous, differentiated, territorially distinct organization we call the national state.

Another circumstance which probably favored the fortunes of the national state over its possible alternatives in Europe was the openness of the European periphery. I have in mind both the lack of important concentrations of power around the immediate areas in which states were forming, and the availability of territories for expansion, conquest and extraction of new resources. The Byzantine Empire and the various Muslim empires which formed around the Mediterranean put the most immediate pressure on European political life. Europeans were relatively free from that sort of pressure around some two-thirds of their perimeter. As a consequence, relatively small political units could grow without being gobbled up (or at least dominated) by adjacent empires. Furthermore, the relatively small powers had room—eventually including land across the Atlantic—to expand, colonize, and establish their own imperial control. Without this combination of circumstances, I want to suggest, a much larger organization than the European national state might well have been the only one that could have survived.

We should not, finally, neglect the contributions of cities, trade, merchants, manufacturers, and early capitalism. No doubt if the merchants and burghers of the thirteenth or fourteenth century had laid out a political master plan for Europe, it would not have included national states. They were much more interested in maintaining the autonomy of cities and the links among them. Yet the intensity of mercantile activity in Europe before the national state probably played a major role in freeing resources, making taxation and related forms of governmental extraction feasible, and motivating old authorities to develop new forms of control over the population.

Later on a powerful reciprocal relationship between the expansion of capitalism and the growth of state power developed, despite the frequent efforts of capitalists themselves to fight off state power; Fernand Braudel has made the conjunction a major theme of his

[30]

analyses of the European sixteenth century (Braudel 1949, 1966). Well before then, however, the presence of a taxable wool trade was helping an English monarchy pay for its operations, and the merchants of Paris were discovering that they had to keep the crown supplied with money. The intermittent but substantial expansion of European trade and industry gave a competitive advantage to the political authorities who could devise means of diverting the resources to their own purposes.

In looking back over these supposed causes of the national state's success, we must again distinguish between the easy version of the argument and the hard one. Obviously, all of these conditions (to the extent that I have portrayed the conditions prevailing at the beginning of European state-making accurately) *affected* the way national states formed and grew. That point is trivial. The hard questions are: (1) what structural alternatives were possible; and (2) why this alternative rather than the others? I have identified the empire, the theocratic federation, the trading network and the feudal system as possible alternatives. I have then gone on to propose that the preexisting political fragmentation, the weakness of corporate structures, the effectiveness of specialized organization, the openness of the European periphery and the growth of cities, trade, merchants, manufacturers, and early capitalism weighted the outcome toward the national state. Such a statement implies that a number of other factors like the particular geography of Europe, its cultural homogeneity, and its largely peasant population did not affect the choices among outcomes so much. The way to check out such assertions is through a detailed comparative examination of the correlates of state-making and the alternative processes both in Europe and elsewhere. But this book can be no more than a preface to that noble enterprise.

Different Exits from the Common Conditions

The common conditions—the relatively standard culture, the peasant base, the preexisting, decentralized political structure—shaped the states which developed in Western Europe sufficiently that they have all remained recognizably of the same species up to our own time. Not that their trajectories have been identical; Greece, Switzerland, and Italy produced rather different kinds of states. Let us save the detailed comparison of individual histories for later. Right now the problem is to identify the largest features and grossest variations in the European state-making experience from 1500 onward.

In its simplest version the problem has only three elements. First, there is the *population* which carries on some collective political life —if only by virtue of being nominally subject to the same central authority. Second, there is a *governmental organization* which exercises control over the principal concentrated means of coercion within the population. Third, there are *routinized relations* between the governmental organization and the population. Historians and political scientists have at one time or another called attention to a huge range of characteristics of such populations, governmental structures, and relations between them. In raising preliminary questions about the alternative patterns of state-making in Europe, I want to call attention to only one broad characteristic of each of the elements. First, the pattern of mobilization within the population subject to each state. I mean the identity, sequence, scale, and success of the various segments of the population which formed, acquired collective control over resources, and participated in national struggles for power. The second is the degree of "stateness" of the governmental structure. Borrowing from J. P. Nettl (1968), I mean the degree to which the instruments of government are differentiated from other organizations, centralized, autonomous, and formally coordinated with each other. Third, the forms of political rights exercised by the population with respect to the governmental structure. I have in mind the enforceable claims that members of the population can make on agents of the government—both compelling them to do something and preventing them from doing something else.

Mobilization

Although the cultural homogeneity of Europe restricted the kinds of groups available for mobilization anywhere and although the generality of urbanization, industrialization, and capitalization eventually guaranteed that every country would experience some degree of mobilization on the part of its urban and its rural working classes, the patterns of mobilization have varied strikingly over time and space. Nevertheless since 1500 Europeans have rarely mobilized on the basis of color, kinship, age, sex, or ecological position. The principal exceptions are, no doubt, the nineteenth-century drive for women's rights and the recurrent movements of youth. Europeans have, on the other hand, frequently mobilized on the basis of religion, language, previous political status, community membership, class, and, more narrowly, occupation.

As mass politics grew up from the French Revolution onward, class, language, and religion became relatively more important as bases of mobilization. Stein Rokkan (1970a: 101) analyzes the shift in this way:

> Territorial oppositions set limits to the process of nation-building; pushed to their extreme they lead to war, secession, possibly even population transfers. Functional oppositions can only develop after some initial consolidation of the national territory. They emerge with increasing interaction and communication across the localities and the regions, and they spread through a process of "social mobilization." The growing nation-state developed a wide range of agencies of unification and standardization and gradually penetrated the bastions of "primordial" local culture. So did the organization of the Church, sometimes in close cooperation with the secular administrators, often in opposition to and competition with the officers of the state. And so did the many autonomous agencies of economic development and growth, the networks of traders and merchants, of bankers and financiers, of artisans and industrial entrepreneurs.
>
> The early growth of the national bureaucracy tended to produce essentially territorial oppositions, but the subsequent widening of the scope of governmental activities and the acceleration of cross-local interactions gradually made for much more complex systems of alignments, some of them *between* localities, and others *across* and *within* localities.

The order and relative weight of the diverse forms of mobilization depended, in Rokkan's view, on three main factors: (1) the state-church relationship established, first, at the Reformation and, second, at the advent of mass participation in national politics; (2) the relative timing of participation and of industrialization; and (3) the cultural—and especially religious—diversity of the population under the jurisdiction of the state in question. (Rokkan in Chapter 8

[33]

reformulates and extends the earlier argument, but on the question of mobilization its essence remains the same.)

The extent of mobilization on the basis of language and belief depended to an important degree on the form and policy of the state. Mobilization on the basis of class position within the industrial system occurred regardless of the character of the state, although twentieth-century states sometimes acted to promote working-class mobilization (as in socialist regimes) or to check it (as in fascist regimes). The state's own policy with regard to cultural homogenization, selection of governmental personnel, control of mobilizing groups and other interactions between government and people itself helped shape the pattern of mobilization.

Both peasants and workers were slow to mobilize at a national scale; before fairly late in the nineteenth century, their mobilization was ordinarily short-term and defensive. Before then there was greater variation in the mobilization of the landowning and mercantile classes; everywhere some kind of accommodation between landlords and the crown played an important part in the extension of state power, even though landlords also supplied the most serious resistance to state-building. That is hardly surprising, given the importance and the diversity of the people who qualify somehow as landlords in an agrarian society.

Stateness

During the last century or so, all West European governments arrived at a relatively high level of stateness, as measured by formal autonomy, differentiation from nongovernmental organizations, centralization, and internal coordination. They have collaborated with each other and with their overseas offshoots in promoting the division of the entire world into state-like units. It has not always been so. Although the drift after 1500 throughout Europe ran toward increasing stateness, different governments moved at very different rates. As a result, international disparities in stateness increased during the sixteenth and seventeenth centuries. By this criterion, the sixteenth century was a time of significantly rising stateness, the later seventeenth century a frenzy of state-making, the eighteenth century (outside) and the East a period of consolidation, the nineteenth century and early twentieth century an age of convergence among governments which were still significantly different from each other in 1800.

[34]

Such a summary exaggerates the regularity of the process, and obscures crucial leads and lags. With respect to autonomy, differentiation, centralization, and internal coordination, France led Europe through almost all the period after 1500, while England accumulated stateness at a slower pace and at a lower level. Yet in 1650 England lay under the control of a centralizing military dictatorship, while France underwent the fragmentation of the Fronde; for that brief moment the English government was very likely the most state-like in Europe. All things considered, however, England (which did so much of its governmental business through justices of the peace, private corporations, merchant fleets and similar groups only indirectly attached to the central structure) survived into the nineteenth century with a rather low level of stateness. Again, Spain produced a sixteenth-century spurt of state-making which, if continued, could easily have brought her to Europe's highest level of centralization, differentiation, autonomy and coordination; the process slowed, and sometimes reversed, in the seventeenth and eighteenth centuries. As a result, Spain entered the age of industry and empire with one of the least stately governmental structures of the continent.

Extreme stateness, of course, neither guarantees political stability nor assures power in the international arena. One might guess that an increase in stateness does ordinarily increase a government's command of the mobile resources within its subject population, does increase its capacity to free resources which embedded in traditional networks of obligation, and thereby augments the government's power to apply resources to objectives at a national or international scale. But if the European experience is a guide, the short-run cost is an increase in the likelihood of resistance and revolt. Hence, a close historical connection among increases in stateness, expansion of armed forces, rises in taxation, and popular rebellion.

Political Rights

Between the development of stateness, on the one hand, and the pattern of mobilization, on the other, comes the acquisition of political rights binding on agents of the government by the members of the mobilized groups within the subject population. Extensions of the suffrage, for example, do not follow from the pace of state-making alone, or from the pattern of mobilization alone, but from an interaction between the two processes. One could, it is true, make a credible case for two subtly complementary propositions: (1) among European governments, those which were higher in stateness by the nineteenth century extended the suffrage farther and faster; (2) but extensions of the suffrage were more durable and supported by surer guarantees in the less state-like governments (cf. Rokkan 1970: 82–88). The propositions would, however, break down entirely if applied to changes over time, since the movement to a wider suffrage and the continued growth of stateness occurred together, yet in nothing like the same rhythm. To understand the early (if temporary) advent of manhood suffrage in France (1793) or Prussia (1849), we shall have to grasp the vast mobilization of peasants and workers which occurred just before those years, and the acute political pressure it placed on the managers of the states in question.

A number of other political rights ought (at least in principle) to yield to the same sort of comparative analysis which has aided theorizing about electoral systems: the state's assurance of the forms of justice, the right of assembly, freedom of the press, the right of petition, protection of religious minorities, defense of life and property, and other claims of individuals or groups on the state which are guaranteed in principle and in general rather than through personal influence or special connections. The development of such rights is much harder to define, detect and compare than the acquisition of voting rights. They fluctuate from regime to regime. They are vulnerable to invisible abridgements. Conversely, they often accrete slowly and inconspicuously before being sanctified in law. They always apply unequally in actual practice. And the managers of states always claim that they are more general than reality shows them to be. In compensation for these difficulties in the systematic study of political rights, they cluster to some degree, and may even form a kind of scale.

For present purposes, the significant thing about such rights is not that they should exist in the abstract, but that the state, rather than some other organization, should become the focus of their enforcement. Indeed, rather than thinking of abstract rights which are enforced (or violated) by states, it would be more illuminating to think of political rights as claims binding the agents of the state to specific groups of people: religious minorities can call on the state to defend them against persecution, adult citizens can insist the state give them their day in court, the indigent can claim sustenance from the state. These are political rights in a large sense—political in that they constitute binding claims on the agents of government, rather than on some other group.

That specification clarifies a large historical transformation. The European national revolutions of the last few centuries did not so much expand political rights as concentrate them in the state and reduce their investment in other sorts of governments. A large part of the process consisted of the state's abridging, destroying or absorbing rights previously lodged in other political units: manors, communities, provinces, estates. In cases like the state's seizure of control over justice from manorial lords, churches and communities, the right itself continued in more or less the same form, but under new management. In other cases, the right disappeared entirely. The right of a household to pasture its flock on the village commons is a notorious example, the right of the household's head to punish its members is a less obvious one.

Nothing could be more detrimental to an understanding of this whole process than the old liberal conception of European history as the gradual creation and extension of political rights. Europeans created and used a wide variety of representative institutions (although not, of course, in the image of the nineteenth-century parliaments) before the heyday of the national state. Far from promoting such institutions, early state-makers struggled against them. Bernard Guénée gives us an idea of the fourteenth-century prelude:

In the middle of the fourteenth century, most likely between 1345 and 1360, the chivalric orders were born, the progress of bureaucratization was checked for a long time to come, the first great revolutionary wave swept across Europe, representative assemblies had their first great successes, and the peoples of Europe seized their most handsome rights from their princes.

Fifty years later, the weight of the English Parliament was so great that Stubbs could speak . . . of Lancastrian parliamentarism; a new revolutionary wave was crossing France and Catalonia, the Estates were achieving their greatest strength in Germany, the Council of Constance weakened the foundations of papal monarchy, the Hussite revolution shook the Empire and challenged the social order. After that came the reflux. Little by little, the Pope and the princes got a grip on themselves, demo-

[37]

cratic convictions faded, the orders of chivalry died, and the bureaucratization began again (Guénée 1971: 405).

For a long time after then, the builders of states worked to stamp out or absorb existing rights, not to extend them.

Rights in the form of claims on the state emerged through an interaction between populations mobilizing at a national scale and governments acquiring greater and greater stateness. The mobilizing groups ordinarily made the claims long and insistently before statesmen, with good grace or bad, honored them. The right of assembly illustrates the point very well. Far from being a right well established in the abstract, it comes into being as a claim of specific segments of the population and specific types of groups—Jews, young people, vagabonds, revolutionaries, sportsmen, patriots—to the protection of the state in their collective occupation of public places. For this reason, changes in the law and in the policing of public assemblies are among our most valuable signs of the acquisition and loss of political power by different segments of the population.

The three sorts of political change I have singled out for examination—changes in stateness, patterns of mobilization, acquisitions and losses of political rights—do not fit together into any single pattern we could confidently call "political development." Each includes some of the transformations which analysts of the contemporary world have put under that heading. For our purposes, rather than patching the battered label, it seems more useful to portray the great political changes involved in the emergence of the European state system as an interaction between two partly independent processes, mobilization and state-making, with the acquisition and loss of rights by different segments of the population being a product of that interaction.

What Distinguishes the Survivors and Victors?

Most of the European efforts to build states failed. The enormous majority of the political units which were around to bid for autonomy and strength in 1500 disappeared in the next few centuries, smashed or absorbed by other states-in-the-making. The substantial majority of the units which got so far as to acquire a recognizable existence as states during those centuries still disappeared. And of the handful which survived or emerged into the nineteenth century as autonomous states, only a few operated effectively—regardless of what criterion of effectiveness we employ. The disproportionate distribution of success and failure puts us in the unpleasant situation of dealing with an experience in which most of the cases are negative, while only the positive cases are well-documented.

Yet we ask what distinguishes the positive cases from the rest. We must at least raise the question; we mean to confront available general ideas about state-making, and those ideas have to do mostly with success and failure. Unfortunately, most of the available ideas straddle the level of generality at which we are attempting to work: either abstracting so greatly that the propositions come close to being matters of definition, or staying so close to one historical model that all other cases become, in their own ways, failures. Nevertheless, it is clear enough to what features of political experience most of the available theories call our attention. By and large we get the image of two rather autonomous clusters of processes: the first cluster variously called social change, modernization or social and economic development, the second cluster labeled political modernization, political development, or even nation-building. Obviously the old division between state and society has gone into motion. The two clusters of processes are supposed to interact, disrupting or facilitating each other. Thus the managers of the political structure face two sorts of "problems": (1) coping with the difficulties produced by social change; and (2) directing social change toward some desired set of outcomes. Performance in these two regards (which emphatically include the survival of the government itself) then provides the criteria of success or failure.

The disagreements within this predominant tradition of theorizing generally concern the direction of causal connections between the "social" and "political" processes (to what extent does change in the government simply reflect change in social structure?), the governmental arrangements most likely to produce the two kinds of success, the degree to which each of the two clusters of processes follows the same path in every country, and, alas, the proper terminology for discussing all these difficult questions. Beneath the surface a debate about the proper and possible roles of government also continues. To my mind, the most interesting thing about this way of setting up the inquiry is its perfect consistency with the world-view of the high administrative official. There it is: an outside world to be coped with or transformed by means of governmental instruments, themselves subject to improvement or decay. No doubt that is the phenomenology most compatible with the aspiration to wring state-making instructions for the present from the experience of the past.

The main questions I am raising here, however, are somewhat less instrumental and somewhat more naturalistic. At each point in time from 1500 onward, what features of a political unit would have permitted us to anticipate whether it would (1) survive into the following period as a distinct unit; (2) undergo territorial consolidation, centralization, differentiation of the instruments of government from other sorts of organization and monopolization of the means of coercion; (3) become the nucleus of a national state? What features of a population would have permitted us to make the same kinds of predictions about the political units claiming jurisdiction over it? In general, it seems to me, the answers have to do with whether the managers of the political units undertook activities which were expensive in goods and manpower, and built an apparatus which effectively drew the necessary resources from the local population and checked the population's efforts to resist that extraction of resources. Such a statement, to be sure, simply shoves many of the more interesting questions back one step. (It sidesteps, for example, the problem of how England grew powerful and survived into the nineteenth century with a relatively puny central structure.) Nevertheless, to the degree that the statement is correct we should only consider the form of representation, the geopolitical position, the culture of the local population or any number of other factors in so far as they affect the propensity of political units to carry on expensive activities and the ability of those units to extract the essential resources from the population.

The individual papers in this volume contain a number of observations on these very questions. I shall itemize the salient arguments which emerge from the papers later in this chapter. Here I only want to mention the most general conditions which appear, in the European experience, to predict survival and state-making: (1) the availability of extractible resources; (2) a relatively protected position in time and space; (3) a continuous supply of political entrepreneurs; (4) success in war; (5) homogeneity (and homogenization) of the subject population; (6) strong coalitions of the central power with major segments of the landed elite. A high standing on one of the factors can make up for a low standing on another. Brandenburg-Prussia, for example, began with an impoverished territory, but its succession of political entrepreneurs squeezed every available resource from the population. France, on the other hand, went through several shortages of entrepreneurial talent at the center, but was able to draw continuously on a rich and populous territory.

The availability of extractible resources is hard to disentangle from the actual fact of their extraction. The value of resources depends on their use, and their use depends on their availability. Nevertheless it is safe to say that the chance to tax goods passing through the Sound gave Danish state-making a great, if temporary, boost; that Spain built a substantial state apparatus with American silver before its seventeenth-century slowdown; and that the levying of customs duties on wool eased the English way to a durable national state.

The "protected position in time and space" generally distinguished the Scandinavian powers from the principalities of Germany—although any such generalization depends on where and when *other* concentrations of power are growing up; in the time of Swedish expansion, the other Scandinavian states had a precarious hold on their existence. For much of the time under consideration here the Poles and the Austrian Hapsburgs found themselves in exposed conditions, while Portugal had only her neighbor (and sometime spouse) Spain to worry about. In any case, the political units which were vulnerable to military attack and/or adjacent to expanding states had great difficulty in maintaining their autonomy and in keeping their dissident populations under control.

Where a single dynasty exercises strong claims on the crown, a continuous supply of political entrepreneurs may depend on fertility and genetic endowment. One can make a case that the mediocrity of the later dukes of Burgundy destroyed the real opportunity for a Burgundian kingdom to the northeast of France, or that Spain simply ran into an ungifted string of kings in the seventeenth century. If so, these are not "accidents," but more or less foreseeable consequences of relying exclusively on inheritance to fill the entrepreneurial positions. Royal inheritance was not, for that matter, an immutable fact of life. We ought to remember that the English contrived to change their ruling family three or four times in the seventeenth century; as late as the accession of George I (1714), there was still a real chance that the magnates would intervene to produce a more acceptable king. In any case, over the whole European experience the ability to recruit talented ministers like a Cromwell, a

Colbert, a Pombal, or a Cavour was probably more important than the gene pool of the royal house. And that was no accident.

Success in war will receive a good deal of attention later in this book. I call attention to it now for more than the trivial reason that most of the political units which disappeared perished in war. The building of an effective military machine imposed a heavy burden on the population involved: taxes, conscription, requisitions, and more. The very act of building it—when it worked—produced arrangements which could deliver resources to the government for other purposes. (Thus almost all the major European taxes began as "extraordinary levies" earmarked for particular wars, and became routine sources of governmental revenue.) It produced the means of enforcing the government's will over stiff resistance: the army. It tended, indeed, to promote territorial consolidation, centralization, differentiation of the instruments of government and monopolization of the means of coercion, all the fundamental state-making processes. War made the state, and the state made war.

The homogeneity of the subject population was, by contrast, no more than a contributing factor. The presence of a culturally homogeneous population no doubt lowered the cost of state-making by making uniform administrative arrangements feasible, by promoting loyalty and solidarity of the subject population (so long as the managers of the state belonged to the same culture), and by putting ready-made communication systems at the disposal of the rulers. Joseph Strayer makes the important distinction between the unitary state and the mosaic state: the first, like England, forming by a process which leaves no significant provincial liberties; the second, like France, reflecting the successive absorption of areas with distinct traditions and political institutions in the persistence of variable law and variable administration. (Great Britain, by drawing Scotland and Ireland under the control of a single crown, became more of a mosaic state, but only after its English core had produced quite a sturdy state apparatus.) Strayer gives even greater emphasis to the distinction between the state formed of a single *regnum* (a population which acknowledged its attachment to some particular royal family in the period after the collapse of the Roman Empire) and the state which was only a fragment of such a *regnum*. He argues:

Both these differences are important in the next stage—changing the state into a nation. Where a whole *regnum* became a

[42]

state, nationalism developed early and naturally, with no great strain or exaggerated emotional appeals. In such a state, people were gradually brought into closer and closer association with each other. The ringwall of the state cut them off, to some extent, from the rest of the world; they were forced to work together and to adapt to each other. They had time to gain a clear sense of identity, to smooth out some of their regional differences, and to become attached to their ruler and the institutions through which he ruled. Where the framework of the state was strong enough and persistent enough, it even created a common nationalism out of very different linguistic and cultural groups. Languedoc was very like Catalonia and very unlike north France, yet it finally became thoroughly French.

It is also clear that the unitary state had an advantage over the "mosaic" state. The central government of a unitary state did not have to worry about provincial privileges, nor did it have to create a huge, and often unpopular, bureaucracy to coordinate and control diverse and quarrelsome local authorities. Local leaders did not have to be looked on with suspicion as men whose primary loyalty was to their province. Instead, they could be used to explain and adapt the government's program to their communities. They gradually began to think in terms of the national interest, because there were no provincial interests to distract their attention. Common laws and common institutions created a greater sense of identity than there was in countries where a man from one province could not understand the governmental procedures of a neighboring province (Strayer 1971: 346–347).

As compared with the accounts you will find later in this book, Strayer's analysis has rather a lot of consensus and rather little coercion in the process by which states formed. Once translated into statements about the costs of securing compliance under varying conditions of homogeneity, however, Strayer's summary fits neatly with the line of argument we pursue.

Over and above the early homogeneity of the population subject to a particular political unit, the unit's success or failure of homogenizing its population also affected the likelihood that it would become and remain an autonomous state. Almost all European governments eventually took steps which homogenized their populations:

the adoption of state religions, expulsion of minorities like the Moors and the Jews, institution of a national language, eventually the organization of mass public instruction. The tolerance of the states of Southeastern Europe for linguistic, cultural, and religious diversity stood in sharp contrast to the intolerance of their Northwestern brethren, and surely stood in the way of effective state-making. The failure to homogenize increased the likelihood that a state existing at a given point in time would fragment into its cultural subdivisions at some time in the future.

Finally, the favorable effects on state-making of strong coalitions between the central power and major segments of the landed elite resulted from a simple reality we discussed earlier: the great predominance of peasants in the European population. The predominance of peasantry meant (1) that the bulk of the resources which might be available for the building of states were committed to the land in one way or another; (2) that control over that land was widely dispersed; and (3) that landlords—especially landlords who wanted reinforcement in their efforts to coerce the local peasantry— became indispensable allies and formidable enemies in the effort to tax, conscript, and requisition.

This summary does not in the least contradict the fact that the Prussian electors, the French kings, and most other European sovereigns had to invest a great deal of their energy in struggles *against* great magnates and corporate bodies of the nobility. The electors, after all, helped create a division of labor between Junkers and bureaucrats (at the expense of peasants and townsmen alike) which carried on into the nineteenth century; according to Hans Rosenberg (1958) and Barrington Moore (1966), that division of labor became the key to the authoritarian Prussian state. Where no strong coalition formed and where the landlords completely outweighed the crown—Spain and Poland are two likely examples—the work of state-making tended to halt, or crumble.

At least one big thing is missing from this preliminary inventory of factors promoting the survival of some states and the disappearance of others. That is the international context of any particular state's emergence and growth. I see two sides to the problem: (1) the changing structure of the European economy as a whole; and (2) the emergence and evolution of an international system of states.

Immanuel Wallerstein has done a superb analysis of the way what he calls the "European world-economy" came into being from the mid-fifteenth to the mid-seventeenth centuries (Wallerstein 1974). He points to the emergence in that period of a large-scale economic division of labor, extending outside of Europe to the Americas and elsewhere. Within that world economy, by his account, a small and changing set of core states dominated the commercial transactions, did the lion's share of the manufacturing, and pushed the peripheral areas toward large-scale monoculture. In the process, the once-thriving manufacturing and commerce of the periphery dwindled, sometimes to nothingness; even splendid Venice declined. Formerly tributary areas like England became central.

Wallerstein points out that the formation of the European world economy was exceptional, perhaps unique, in not leading to a single *imperium* of the sort which had come to govern the great economic spaces of Rome, Byzantium, and China. Instead, multiple states, at least partly independent of each other, sprang up. This fact was in itself very likely crucial for the development of capitalism, since it reduced the capacity of any particular government to capture (or smother) the arrangements of investment, lending, production, or distribution. Moreover, state-making efforts at the center of this emerging world-economy, fed by the flow of resources from the periphery and eased by the monetization of economic life around the center, had a far greater chance of success than those at the periphery. The correspondence is imperfect: Holland stood at the middle of the entire process, and yet did not mount a particularly strong state; the commercialized regions of western Germany resisted incorporation into substantial states; nor is it clear that the sixteenth-century eminence of Spain depended on its being a "core state" in the same sense that England was. Still the position of any population or any political unit within the world economy deeply affected its prospects for state-making.

The second international process which my analysis has so far neglected is the crystallization of a *system* of states acknowledging, and to some extent guaranteeing, each other's existence. Perhaps the Treaty of Westphalia (1648), at the close of the Thirty Years War, first made it clear that all of Europe was to be divided into distinct and sovereign states whose boundaries were defined by international agreement. Over the next three hundred years the Europeans and their descendants managed to impose that state system on the entire world. The recent wave of decolonization has almost completed the mapping of the globe into that system.

[45]

The filling-in of the state system significantly constrained the later participants in European state-making. Whereas the territory eventually to be controlled by the Prussia or the Spain of the fifteenth century was still quite open, the maximum space—at least within Europe—which a united Italy could claim in the nineteenth century was essentially set by the outcome of the Napoleonic Wars. Furthermore, the new states came increasingly to form as consequences of wars among established members of the state system and of the negotiations which ended those wars. The Treaty of Westphalia, the Congress of Vienna, and the Treaty of Versailles provide increasingly dramatic demonstrations of the point. As a consequence, the later the state-making experience under examination, the less likely the sorts of internal processes I emphasized earlier are to provide an adequate explanation of the formation, survival or growth of a state.

The Tasks of Our Papers

Still, we have to get those internal processes right. They absorb most of the attention of the essays in this book. Our authors, true to their commissions, have touched on a great variety of questions, each in his own way. Some, like Bayley, have strongly emphasized the systematic, structural questions in a manner clearly influenced by the style of comparative politics. Others, like Braun, have insisted on the byways, particularities, and continuities in a manner just as clearly instilled by historical training. As a result, any attempt to array the papers as if they were repeated answers to the same insistent question will be presumptuous and unfair. Presumptuous, because of the pretense that one knows better than the authors what they were finding out. Unfair, because of the sacrifice of each paper's separate richness and coherence.

Nevertheless, my attempts at synthesis follow just such an unfair, presumptuous course. Here I attempt to see what sorts of general conclusions concerning the ways national states actually formed in Western Europe emerge from our varied essays. In the final chapter, I try to treat the same material more analytically, asking what general statements about the formation of national states might follow if the European experience were the universal one, and how those statements jibe with existing theories of large-scale political change. Although the two essays overlap, the first proceeds mainly from the perspective of history, the second mainly from the perspective of political science. In either case, the best we can hope for is a set of pro-

[46]

visional conclusions: more solid than working hypotheses, perhaps, but less firm than theses one nails up, to challenge all the world, at the end of a long inquiry.

Our authors claim no more. They often have to take sides on questions which they know to be still undecided—as when Finer commits himself to the view that the Brandenburg Recess of 1653 in itself "was to have the most far-reaching consequences for the future polity and to set a distinctive stamp upon the military format until the defeat at Jena in 1806; and in many respects till well on into the third quarter of the nineteenth century." In so saying, Finer commits himself on an open question. He separates himself to some extent from an argument like Barrington Moore's, where 1653 appears as only one of many incidents in the jostling and balancing of the urban commercial classes, the great landlords and the crown in Brandenburg-Prussia.

None of us claims his arguments or evidence will themselves decide the issue. Each of us concedes that if he has adopted a mistaken position on one of the great questions, his more immediate arguments will be weakened as well. My own analysis of food supply, for example, adopts the standard arguments that influential English landlords of the seventeenth and especially the eighteenth centuries were actively involved in the export of grain and pushing the government toward a policy of favoring exports even to the short-run detriment of English consumers. That could be wrong. To the extent that it *is* wrong, my tracing of variations in national food policy to the major class alliances formed by the crown loses plausibility. So it is with a great many positions the other authors have adopted provisionally, and with trepidation.

If the papers in this book have value, it will not be due to the new general explanations they offer for the rise of capitalism or the decline of Spain. Instead, their originality lies in their emphasis on what Gabriel Ardant calls the "physiology" of state-making: how the builders of states actually performed, or tried to perform, the extractive, coercive, and coordinative side of their work. This emphasis on mechanisms draws attention away from the forms of states and the broadest ends of state-making toward the implications of alternative public policies. At many points, our authors are writing as if the years after 1750 or 1800 had not yet occurred, as if the choices were still open, as if they were calculating the probable consequences of one policy or another on the basis of a more powerful analytic system than was actually available to anyone at the time. They generally opt, that is, for a probabilistic analysis over a deterministic one, for the study of relationships over the study of recurrent events or sequences, and for a prospective rather than a retrospective view of state-making processes.

Some Biases of the Papers

From the prospective point of view, however, the papers have some significant biases. They are heavily weighted toward whole states, and big states like France and Spain at that. They make it easier for us to place ourselves in the seats of power in Versailles or Madrid than to reconstruct the calculations of an Andalusian landlord or of a German princeling. They are heavily weighted toward the states which survived past the eighteenth century: England, Prussia, and Sweden rather than Bohemia, Scotland, Lorraine, or even Naples. And they are somewhat weighted toward *features* of states which were visible within the last century: bureaucracy rather than the sale of offices, mass professional armies rather than militias, specialized police forces rather than posses. If venality, militias, and posses were not simply the fading features of the old regime, but the intermediate institutions which were crucial to the emergence of the states we know, our analyses will tend to misrepresent the developmental processes which created and then destroyed them.

I do not mean these remarks as attacks on our authors. These biases result from the original charges we gave them: to compare the carrying out of some particular state-making activity in several major European countries over a substantial segment of the period since 1500. These biases toward what survived, furthermore, pervade the existing historical literature. To some extent, they even pervade the sources themselves. Whatever their origin, the biases mean that we have only been partly successful in our aim of creating a prospective analysis of state-making processes.

The original agenda also gave little weight to several institutions and processes which our papers disclose as crucial to the phenomena we self-consciously set out to study. Churches and religious organization should have received more direct attention from the start, for two reasons: (1) churches and churchmen were significant political actors at the national and international levels throughout most of the period we are examining; at times they comprised the most formidable rivals, allies, enemies, or instruments of the great state-makers;

[48]

and (2) for several centuries of our era, nationalism and antination-
alism alike customarily wore the mantle of religious faith; great
states like France and the Netherlands were rent by struggles which
inextricably combined religion and politics. For those reasons, control of belief and devotion should probably have been on our initial
agenda.

Likewise, linguistic and cultural policies deserve more direct attention than our general plan allotted them. If Stein Rokkan is right
in asserting that early cultural homogeneity within a territory
strongly facilitated the emergence of a durable state, that its absence
significantly limited the capacity of any state to mobilize its resources, and that the successful European states generally engaged
in a deliberate program of homogenization, we have slighted one of
the major dimensions of our problem, and one of the most interesting points of contact between the early history of Europe and the
current experience of the world's many multicultural states.

I mentioned earlier another omission which we often noticed in
our discussions: the administration of law and justice. In passing, the
papers on armies, taxation, police, and control of food supply inevitably make judgments on law and justice. But none of them deliberately treats in its own terms the use of courts, lawmakers, punitive
power and legal jurisdictions as a means of extending the power of
the state. The result, I fear, is to make less clear than need be the
close relationship between policing and the other processes of control and extraction we analyze. Bayley's argument linking changes
in the organization of policing to the emergence of new challengers
to the existing distribution of power points in that direction. It does
not quite bring out the extent to which European states used their
legal apparatus not merely to hold off threats to public order, but to
define "disorder," create "disorder," and press their right to suppress
the same "disorder."

Finally, an omission which now seems odd indeed. None of our
papers contains a sustained discussion of the general administrative
structure of the various European states, or of their changes over
time. Finer's paper naturally says a great deal about the organization of armies, Braun's plenty about the personnel of fiscal administration, and so on. Fischer and Lundgreen are specifically concerned
with the ways Europeans set, judged and acquired the qualifications
for office. Yet just as we tend to assume knowledge of the judicial
system, we also tend to take the general administrative organization

for granted. This weakness, too, flows from our original setting of the problem; we emphasized function rather than form. Since one of our recurrent discoveries has been the constraint set on emerging functions by existing forms, we pay a substantial price for that emphasis.

All this means that our papers fall far short of presenting a comprehensive or balanced portrayal of the whole European state-building process; that was never our purpose. The countries, periods, institutions and processes under study are slanted toward those which yield the clearest pictures of effective extraction, coercion, and control on the large scale. The advantage of that selection is to reveal subtle relationships between different kinds of extraction, coercion, and control; Finer's neat formulation of "cycles" of extraction, economy-technology, etc. lays out the interdependencies more deliberately than the other arguments do, but every paper identifies relationships of this kind. Taxation, for example, ordinarily shows up in European histories (not to mention theories of political development) as an epiphenomenon—and a rather uninteresting one at that. Guided by Ardant and Braun, we begin to see how crucial the form and effectiveness of taxation were to the military strength of different European states, on the one hand, and to the likelihood of mass rebellion against those states, on the other.

Again, specialized policing often seems to be a more or less automatic response to individual or collective threats against public order—a response whose vigor and effectiveness vary from one setting to another, but whose character is pretty much set by the technical problem of controlling criminals and rioters. Bayley shows the differentiation of police forces in the contemporary sense from the much wider range of activities and personnel implied by the German *Polizei* or the Italian *polizia*. He shows that the degree of differentiation varied considerably from country to country, in response to the domestic political situation. Most importantly, he shows (or rather argues, since the hypothesis is fresh and the evidence far from tabulated) that changes in the format of policing depended closely on the national elite's responses to the perceived threats of new groups making bids for power from outside the political system. The analyses of taxation and of policing illustrate very well what it means to analyze state-making as a series of relationships, rather than as a set of recurrent events or of standard sequences.

[50]

A Review

Before examining the entire set of papers for major relationships, let me review them individually for the main themes the authors themselves have stressed. That will, perhaps, relieve the authors of the blame for later misapplications of the conclusions.

FINER ON MILITARY FORCES

S. E. Finer traces the relationship between the development of major features of the modern state (territorial consolidation, specialized personnel, integrity recognized by other states), its special case the modern nation-state (which adds self-consciousness of common identity, as well as some mutual distribution and sharing of duties and benefits) and the changing character of national armed forces (especially as summed up by "format," which includes basis of service, size composition and stratification). His principal method is to compare the transformations of France, Britain, and Prussia-Germany in both regards, arguing causal connections by comparison. And his chief conceptual device is the identification of clusters of variables, or "cycles": (1) economy-technology-format; (2) stratification-format; (3) beliefs-format; (4) format options; (5) extractin-coercion; and (6) state-building. Having identified the cycles in this way, he then forms his argument as a series of statements about links among the cycles.

Within this complicated chainwork, Finer lays particular emphasis on the first cycle, economy-technology-format. He shows how each major military invention over a thousand years (most of the earlier "inventions" being organizational and tactical rather than technical in any narrow sense) drove those rulers who wished to continue the pursuit of their objectives by force of arms to push their subject populations harder and more continuously for the necessary resources. Those who succeeded used their armed strength to consolidate their control of a territorial base as well as to assure external acceptance of that control; since they characteristically promoted the formation of specialized personnel for the performance of these tasks, the military enterprise played a major part in the creation of all three distinctive signs of the modern state: territorial consolidation, specialized personnel, recognized integrity. Many failed; their states or protostates fell into rebellion, disintegration, or absorption by others. For the survivors, instead of a continuous accretion of central power, we witness an alternation of long pauses with giant steps closely following changes in military technology and the scale of war.

Finer is no narrow technological determinist. He sees the political effects of military reorganization as conditioned by the extent and accessibility of resources within the subject population, on the one hand, the degree of popular commitment to the national cause, on the other. This comes out clearly in his discussion of the mass mobilization called for by Napoleonic warfare, and of increasing demands of war since the time of Napoleon. It is also precisely at this point that Finer brings out most sharply another argument which lies hidden through most of the paper: that the state-makers were actually building an interlocking *system* of states: general wars became the principal means by which the realignments of the participants and their boundaries occurred, the principal moments at which multiple changes of membership and alliance occurred, as well as principal occasions on which the relations between rulers and ruled changed rapidly. The French Revolution, the Napoleonic Wars, and the Congress of Vienna bring out these interdependent effects most fully and dramatically. The virtue of Finer's analysis is to show that 1789–1815 was no odd exception to the long run of European experience. That conclusion brings a tragic tone to his final passages. For it comes close to saying that war is the characteristic condition, and armed force the characteristic instrument, of the state system.

ARDANT ON FINANCIAL POLICY AND ECONOMIC INFRASTRUCTURE

Gabriel Ardant is far from an incurable optimist, but he is more intent than Finer on drawing practical lessons from the past. He asks himself which financial policies will work under what social conditions, with what social costs. In his analysis, financial policy centers on taxation, but includes monetary regulation, public credit, and the whole range of procedures by which governments control their revenues. Obviously these procedures intertwine with those by which governments attempt to intervene in the economies on which they are based—income policies, incentives for investment, and so on. Ardant is interested in them mainly in so far as they contribute to the viability of the state itself, and to its ability to pursue the goals its rulers have set for it. The social conditions to which he attaches greatest importance are the forms of production and marketing. And the social costs he considers most seriously are political ones: the impositions of arbitrary rule, on the one hand, the outbreak of bloody rebellion, on the other.

At its simplest moments, Ardant's model of the state contains only a handful of variables: (1) a set of expensive goals articulated and pursued by the rulers of a state; (2) a bundle of financial policies designed to draw the resources necessary for the pursuit of those goals from the population under the state's control; (3) an economic infrastructure producing and containing such resources as the population has at its disposal; (4) financial consequences of applying a particular set of policies to a particular sort of infrastructure; and (5) social and political consequences of variables 2 (policies) and 4 (financial consequences), including the extent to which the rulers' goals were actually accomplished.

Schematically, the model is seen in Figure 1–1.

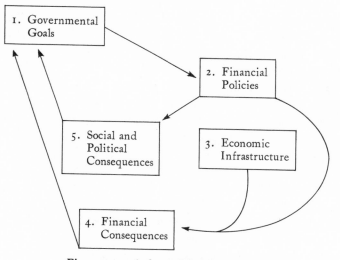

Figure 1–1. Ardant's Model of a State

In his other works, Ardant has paid considerable attention to the impact of financial policy on economic infrastructure, for example, through the tendency of taxation in money to drive self-sufficient peasants into the market. Here, that connection remains almost untouched. Again he is aware of the way that the existing economic infrastructure affects governmental goals; the essay in this volume does not deal systematically with that relationship. The diagram represents the causal sequence he stresses in his argument: from goals to policies to consequences, and then back again to goals.

For purposes of analysis, Ardant generally takes the goals and the economic infrastructure as given. What interests him is the effect of matching or mismatching financial policy with infrastructure. Ordinarily he considers a match to occur when the policy brings the state a high return over the medium and long runs without deterring production. To be sure, he insists that fiscal systems defined and limited by public law work better than capricious force does. With Balzac (in *Cousine Bette*) we hear him saying, "L'arbitraire, c'est la démence du pouvoir" ("arbitrary rule is power gone mad"). He also thinks that in the long run an egalitarian and redistributive policy is not only more just but more effective. However, neither belief appears to be essential to his main argument.

The argument centers on the assertion that a policy apportioning fiscal obligations according to access to wealth tends to produce a high return at low political, social and economic cost to the extent that (1) marketing is extensive and intensive; (2) the fiscal rules are known, binding on the state and widely considered to be equitable; and (3) the economy is productive. Much of Ardant's historical analysis consists of comparing England, Prussia, the Hapsburg possessions and France in these regards: comparing them with the ideal, with themselves at other points in time, and with each other. France is the prime case under discussion, although at many points England provides the standard against which the others are measured. Only at the end does it become clear that the real point of the comparative analysis is to produce lessons for the guidance of contemporary states.

Nevertheless, Ardant makes several fundamental historical observations on his way to the lessons. The first, which only comes *en passant*, echoes Finer: the largest and most persistent stimulus to increases or changes in national fiscal burdens over the great period of European state-making was the effort to build armed forces and wage war. The second observation goes beyond Finer: over that same period, the most serious and persistent precipitant of violent conflicts between European state-makers and the populations they attempted to rule were attempts to collect taxes. Third, in the early period of state-making the most important single spur to the expansion and reorganization of officialdom was very likely the effort to collect taxes from a recalcitrant population; the less extensive the market, the more heterogeneous the population and the greater the demand for revenues relative to total production, in Ardant's analysis, the greater bulk of the governmental apparatus created in the process. Finally, and most controversially, the pressure to extend the suffrage, increase national consciousness, give representation to the working classes, and generally draw the bulk of the national population into political life, which so marked the nineteenth century in Europe, came to an important degree from the fiscal demands of the great military and administrative machines brought into being by the Napoleonic Wars. We shall return to some of these conclusions later on.

BRAUN ON TAXATION AND SOCIO-POLITICAL STRUCTURE

Rudolf Braun adopts a rather different approach to taxation from that of Gabriel Ardant. He devotes himself more assiduously to the construction of a continuous account of fiscal policies in England and Brandenburg-Prussia from the sixteenth century onward. He is much more concerned to pin down the differences between the two countries, and to explain them in historical terms. Whereas Ardant emphasizes the obstacles to the success of different kinds of fiscal policies and the respects in which the economic infrastructure constrained the system of taxation, Braun usually begins with the political situation which led the British or German rulers to adopt a given set of policies at a given time, then takes the existence of that set of policies as a fact whose long-run consequences become the focus of historical investigation.

The trouble with conducting such an analysis through the comparison of two countries is that such a large number of other differences between them are plausible candidates for the explanation of the differences which interest the analyst. In the contrast between the economic histories of England and Brandenburg-Prussia, we have a larger number of interesting candidates than we can possibly handle: the power of the Junkers in Prussia, the greater urbanity of England, the nature of war on the Continent and in England, the variety of agricultural regions within England, the wool trade versus the grain trade, the enclosures versus the "new serfdom," and so on. Given this complexity, one can try to eliminate potentially crucial variables one at a time by intensifying the comparisons and increasing their range in time and space; or one can try to detect differences in the configurations of the variables. Braun chooses the configurations.

He pays particular attention to three classes of long-run consequences of fiscal policy: (1) the kind of national administrative structure it created; (2) its influence on patterns of political power and participation; (3) its impact on economic growth. In this analysis, he deals with the third variable as an outcome of the first two; the direct influence of alternative systems of taxation on investment, saving, factor mobility, etc., hardly figures in his analysis. (Elsewhere, I hasten to add, Braun has shown that he is splendidly capable of dealing with the impact of economic growth on administrative structure, political power and participation.) We get a picture of a Prussian state smothering the economy with its bulk and strangling the economy with its extractiveness. The English state, to oversimplify Braun's subtle account, escaped its evolution in the same direction through a civil war which destroyed the prospering royal bureaucracy.

Here we come upon an historical point which recurs elsewhere in our papers. With the later Tudors and the Stuarts, the English crown was acquiring strength and bulk in ways which resembled the state-building of the continental countries. Although J. P. Cooper complains about the tendency to assimilate English kingship of the early seventeenth century to the absolutism of Spain or Brandenburg-Prussia, he eventually suggests

> that England was well aware of continental political patterns and there were at least the possibilities of similar developments under the early Stuarts; even the parliamentary sphere, if the attempts of Salisbury and Cranfield to solve the crown's problems had been successful, the similarities with other assemblies might have been greater. But in fact the Civil War, though in some ways a reflection of forces generally at work in Europe, finally consolidated a pattern very different from that of most European states (Cooper 1960: 90).

The Civil War consolidated a pattern of government by Parliament in alliance with the notables of city and country. But in the previous century, the ability of the Tudors to draw substantial returns from their own domains had reduced their dependence on Parliament, just as the Hohenzollern monarchs were later to benefit politically from their ability to draw 40 or 50 percent of the government's revenues directly from the royal domain. This partial independence became crucial to royal power; Estates and Parliaments everywhere in Europe used their approval or disapproval of taxes (uncollectable without their collaboration until and unless the crown disposed independently of strong military forces) to secure ratification of their own privileges and to resist the penetration of the royal bureaucracy into their own spheres of influence. As Braun shows, that process went on both in Britain and in Brandenburg-Prussia. Even in autocratic Prussia, the eminent domain of the crown tended to stop at the gates of the Junker estate; the institution of the rural commissioner (*Landrat*) only nominally incorporated the nobility into the vast centralized structure of government.

This way of putting it, however, slightly miscasts Braun's analysis. It suggests a royal authority alone against the world, when in both Britain and Brandenburg-Prussia the class alliances of the crown (and against the crown) were crucial. The tracing of fiscal policy in Brandenburg-Prussia permits us to see the great landlords allying with electors and kings to milk the weakened cities in one way, exploit the helpless peasantry in another way, reinforce their privileged position in a whole variety of ways. For all the wider base of taxation in England, there we find the great English landlords using their influence in the counties to tilt assessments of the land tax away from themselves, and their influence in Parliament to assure such measures as the bounty on exports of grain.

Braun barely mentions another feature of the early modern states that resulted from the search for expedients and alliances which all monarchs had to pursue: what appears (in our virtuous retrospect) to be their extensive corruption and waste. H. R. Trevor-Roper offers a collective sketch:

> So "the Renaissance State" consisted, at bottom, of an ever-expanding bureaucracy which, though at first a working bureaucracy, had by the end of the sixteenth century become a parasitic bureaucracy; and this ever-expanding bureaucracy was sustained on a equally expanding margin of "waste": waste which lay between the taxes imposed on the subject and the revenue collected by the Crown. Since the Crown could not afford an absolute loss of revenue, it is clear that this expansion of the

[57]

waste had to be at the expense of society. It is equally clear that it could be borne only if society itself were expanding in wealth and numbers (Trevor-Roper 1967: 68).

The waste included the open magnificence of the Renaissance court, the conduct of costlier wars, and the ever-present payoffs, bribes, sinecures, or outright thefts which drained away the payments theoretically exacted for public ends.

Trevor-Roper concludes that the Renaissance state destroyed itself in the seventeenth century by pushing its exactions beyond any capacity of the population to support them. That argument dovetails nicely with Ardant's insistence on the centrality of fiscal questions in the frequent rebellions of the seventeenth century. Then Braun and Ardant alike part company with Trevor-Roper. They consider the farming of taxes, the sale of offices, the private handling of royal loans, the enrichment of favorites and financiers to have been almost inescapable consequences of the search for expedients to extend the monarch's power. They attach a relatively small quantitative role to conspicuous consumption as such, and trace the greatest demand for new funds back to the royal efforts to wage war and strengthen their armed forces. The war-making efforts of the Hohenzollerns, the weaker economic base of eastern Germany, the established power of the Junkers combined to produce a far greater extractive apparatus in Brandenburg-Prussia—the coupling of the War State with the Police State.

BAYLEY ON POLICE

That is the point of contact between the studies of taxation and David Bayley's analysis of policing. This historical junction is not overly clear, because Bayley concentrates on the period during which differentiated, professional police forces were forming in European states: the nineteenth and twentieth centuries. Our analysts of taxation have much more to say about the seventeenth and eighteenth centuries. What is more, Bayley takes a deliberatively retrospective view of his problem; he asks himself what accounts for national differences in police forces which are visible in our own times. None of our other authors concentrates so much on present-day outcomes. Finally, Bayley lays out his analysis in a timeless propositional style, relating specific dependent variables—the scope of police tasks, the structure of police forces, the nature of accountability, the

CHARLES TILLY

role-behavior of police—the well-defined general features of the political experience of the state in question. For all of these reasons, a first reading of Bayley's argument gives an impression of detachment from the historical issues which animate most of the other papers. Nevertheless, the paper tells us that the manner and form of policing register with extraordinary clarity the history of the interaction between state-makers and the people they seek to control. Far from being a technical matter subject to its own autonomous exigencies, policing turns out to be an intensely political matter, nicely sensitive to the prevailing pattern of state-making and the prevailing character of resistance to it.

There are, in Bayley's analysis, two dimensions to that influence of the state on the manner of policing. One is temporal, the other international. In the temporal dimension, Bayley argues that there is little regularity in the change of police systems in response to economic transformation, regime changes, external threats, or ideological reorientation. Policing does respond to such changes, he tells us, but irregularly and without major shifts in organization. In the four countries at hand (Italy, Germany, France, and England), he finds more evidence that transformations in the national organization of political power, prolonged violent popular resistance to government, and the "erosion of former bases of community authority" through extended social change induce large shifts toward more differentiated and extensive forms of professional policing.

In the international dimension, Bayley finds a striking correspondence between the organization of police and the general character of administrative organization. To take the most obvious contrast, the high centralization of police forces in Italy and France versus their decentralization in Germany and England conform exactly to the differences in national administrative structure in other regards. Bayley does invoke a number of other factors in accounting for the variations among national police systems: elite reactions to the demand for increased political participation, geopolitical position, and others. He also observes that in our own time the organizational forms of policing are converging to some extent—especially in activities to which uniform standards of efficiency apply. But the central message is the shaping of police structure by political experience.

This message would have come across just as strongly if Bayley had focused on the period before the French Revolution instead of the period since then. He would have had to employ a somewhat

[59]

broader definition of "police" in order to do so, partly because the word itself covered the gamut of domestic regulation, partly because a wide variety of individuals and organizations used to exercise the sorts of coercive powers which subsequently came to be the specialty, profession and near-monopoly of police forces. Those transformations comprise in themselves a significant trend in European state-making. But Bayley's correlations between the organization of coercion and the general character of the state run back to the origins of states.

In France, 1233 brings us the religious police of the Inquisition, complete with armed force and powers of arrest. By 1450 we find a royal provost with his own specialized armed force (including seventy foot patrolmen and thirty-five horsemen) responsible for the tranquillity of Paris and its suburbs. With Francis I we see offices bearing police responsibilities being created and sold to enrich the Crown. And, as Bayley tells us, the great seventeenth-century consolidation of the French state also brought the creation of the distinctive features of the modern French police: centralized structure, plural forces, bureaucratic control, extensive formal tasks, and so on. Colbert himself played a major part in the preparation of Louis XIV's 1667 edict creating the office of Police Lieutenant for Paris, and in the recruitment of a high judicial official, La Reynie, to the post.

From that point on, the extraordinary system of spies and informers which has played an important part in the political work of the French state into our own time took shape. (Sartine, who became *lieutenant général de police* in 1759, is supposed to have said to Louis XV, "Sire, when three people are chatting in the street one of them is surely my man.") Eighteenth-century police manuals like those of Colquhoun in England or Lemaire in France are no less than general treatises on the government's full repertoire of domestic regulation, coercion, and surveillance. Like the routinization of taxation, the regularization of policing imprinted the state's mark on the everyday life of its citizens.

TILLY ON FOOD SUPPLY AND PUBLIC ORDER

My own paper on food supply adds a third kind of control to the list. It is a less obvious kind: citizens of European countries still feel the pinch of the state when they pay their taxes or run afoul of the policeman, but over the last century the day-to-day involvement of government officials in regulation of the food supply has dwindled.

[60]

Everywhere in Europe one kind of government or another was heavily engaged in control of food distribution (if not so heavily on control of food production and consumption) from the medieval period up to 1800. During that time, the most important trends were the supplanting of local authorities by agents of the national state and the increasing commitment of national authorities to the promotion of marketing on a large scale. The interaction between these trends and the resistance they engendered form the main themes of my analysis.

Because it is so workaday, and yet a matter of life and death, food supply provides a valuable field for observation of the state's penetration into the daily routines of its subject population. The history of state intervention in the distribution of food illustrates the tenacity with which large segments of the European population resisted (again, whether consciously or not) the efforts of merchants and officials to drag, shove, or entice them into a world of centralized communications, extensive markets, and large spans of control.

The food riot, it turns out, had a good deal in common with the antitax rebellion, the defense of the commons, the revolt against conscription, and the violent resistance to state control over local churches. More dramatically than other sorts of events, these violent encounters displayed the costs of state-making to ordinary people; they brought into direct confrontation the alternative beliefs about political order and obligation which were at stake in the building of national states. Food riots were not the most important of these events in terms of magnitude or impact on subsequent political developments. They were, however, the most frequent.

The bulk of the paper deals with causes, conditions and consequences of various forms of state intervention in the food supply. We find state-makers directly creating bureaucracies and military forces, and having to assure their subsistence. We find state-makers indirectly promoting the growth of cities (at least of capital cities), adapting the supply apparatus medieval European cities had formed to guarantee their own survival, and eventually fashioning new measures to facilitate the feeding of urban populations as well as to hold off the threat of urban rebellion. We find state-makers promoting or acquiescing in the growth of land-poor and landless labor, and then having to face the problem of nourishing the landless.

The policies different kings and countries adopted to deal with these problems depended largely on the character of agriculture

[61]

within their territories and on the general approaches to state-making they had developed; in both regards, the forms of alliance among state officials, landlords and merchants were crucial. In their turn, the choices of food policies cemented the class coalitions with which the state entered the modern era, affected the success of its fiscal policy by accelerating or impeding the commercialization of agriculture, augmented or diminished the bulk of the national bureaucracy, promoted or hindered economic growth, and governed the form and severity of conflicts over control of the food supply.

The cumulative weight of all these choices produced striking national differences in patterns of regulation. Toward the end of the eighteenth century we can see an England far on the road to a national market and to agrarian capitalism, entrusting such regulation of the domestic market as still went on to the justices of the peace, and giving subsidies to exporters of grain. By contrast, we see a Spain enmeshed in a great web of protective regulation, a France striving energetically but inconsistently to "free the grain trade" and assure deliveries to its great cities, a Brandenburg-Prussia with an enormous regulative machinery geared to the supply of the armed forces. Over the very long run, we can also see what appears to be a general trend in the European state-building experience: a movement away from relatively similar forms of organization in the fourteenth or fifteenth century to a great diversity of solutions in the seventeenth and eighteenth centuries, followed by a certain amount of convergence on the same standard forms of mechanisms during the nineteenth and twentieth centuries.

FISCHER AND LUNDGREEN ON ADMINISTRATIVE
AND TECHNICAL PERSONNEL

That double movement of early divergence and late convergence also appears in the recruitment and training of technical personnel, as portrayed by Fischer and Lundgreen. In comparing the experiences of Britain, France, and Prussia over the entire period since the Middle Ages, they discover an evolution from relatively similar arrangements of personnel among the protostates, to increasing national differences in solutions to broadly similar problems during the epic phases of state-making, to extensive borrowing and standardization of organization in the bureaucratic expansion of the last century or so. Fischer and Lundgreen interpret the term "technical personnel" broadly. So they must, to deal with the changing salience of different sorts of attributes and skills over the centuries they survey. At one time or another, all European state-makers had to create, co-opt or subjugate judges, soldiers, local administrators, tax collectors, engineers, accountants, spies, demographers, scribes, sea captains, bankers, policemen, and propagandists. Which mattered most changed from one decade to the next.

Fischer and Lundgreen insist on the dilemma of loyalty versus effectiveness. Many governments have had servants who were neither effective nor loyal. A few have had servants who were both effective and loyal. Yet the two virtues do not necessarily coincide, especially in the short run. And the government which does not assure itself a minimum of both does not survive.

In the earlier phases of European state-making, loyalty (at least in the sense of some guarantee that officials would not appropriate all the resources entrusted to them, and would not become the ruler's rivals) posed the more pressing problems. That was true for two main reasons: (1) every aspirant builder of a strong and autonomous state in Europe found himself surrounded by serious rivals, both inside and outside the territory currently under his control; his dissatisfied underlings could often find better allies elsewhere; (2) the early rulers had little autonomous coercive power at their disposal; they could not hope to raise armies, collect taxes, or even maintain their dynasties without the assent of powerful organizations which even in principle were largely independent of the ruler. These conditions affect every government to some degree; they constituted the central facts of political life for the early European state-makers.

This situation, as Fischer and Lundgreen say, helps explain the prominence of churchmen as political aides to the early state-makers. It is not just that the church monopolized literacy, legal acumen and formal education. Clerics were useful partners because they brought some of the resources of Europe's largest and wealthiest organization to bear on their work; they found it more difficult than did their brothers the soldiers and landlords to convert the state resources under their control into transmissible private property. They were also less apt to build their own rival dynasties. (These are relative matters; the Borgias did, of course, supply more than their share of bishops and popes; Cardinal Mazarin did, indeed, die wealthy, with his kinsmen well-placed.) However, alliances with churchmen and the church eventually placed serious limits on kingly autonomy. With the obvious exception of the Papal States, all the European states shifted decisively toward lay administrators as their autonomous coercive power increased.

Yet the dilemma of loyalty and effectiveness persisted. Loyalty took a long time to become commonplace. Fischer and Lundgreen suggest that most of the salient features of official recruitment during the great periods of state-making in Britain, France and Prussia resulted from more or less deliberate compromises between the two principles. The sale of offices occurred widely in all three countries, especially with regard to military commissions; the distinction of France was to have used that sale as an important source of government revenue, instead of simply tolerating traffic in offices among private individuals. Although the venality of offices diminished the ability of the state to assign positions according to technical competence, it also expanded the number of people who had a lively interest in the state's survival. Kings followed one of C. Northcote Parkinson's prime principles; they multiplied subordinates, not rivals.

The co-optative procedure operated quite generally. Fischer and Lundgreen point out the extent to which the apparently rationalized and centralized system of Prussian territorial administration grew from the bottom up, with local notables assuming office before the middle levels of administration took shape, and ratified the existing distribution of power, both by putting selection of the Landrat in the hands of a region's landlords and by giving the positions allotted to the landed elite extraordinary precedence within the bureaucratic rank order. Thus they identify some interesting parallels between Britain and Prussia: in both countries the central power carried out a great deal of its work through the partial integration of existing local elites into the state structure. But the manner of integration—for example, through hierarchically arranged offices—had enormous political impact at a later historical stage. Although the French employed similar procedures in the early phases of subordinating the whole country to royal control, once the kings had substantial military forces at their disposal they turned increasingly to the imposition of orders by outsiders directed from the center.

On the other side, Fischer and Lundgreen observe that a number of recruitment systems which appear to reward merit, skill and knowledge actually confirm the hold of a particular class on a set of public offices. The most striking example is Prussia, where the famed eighteenth-century "tightening of standards" strengthened the nobility's claim to high office. Through the expansion of military service and the increasing recruitment of civil servants from the army, the reinforcement of the Junker position within the army may well have increased the aggregate influence of their class. But it did so at the cost of their autonomy as a group.

Likewise, when Fischer and Lundgreen reconsider the famous supplanting of officers (independent representatives of traditional and particularist forces) by commissars (new agents dependent on the king's centralizing will) in France, they have to observe that the commissars came very largely from the same social classes—indeed the same families and career lines—as the officers. Once again what changes is not the class base of a government but the political autonomy of the classes in question. Only with the emergence of the technically trained functionary after 1750 or so, they tell us, do we find government service opening up as a major channel of social mobility. Even there we find the training and the recruitment procedures perpetuating a style and spirit established by the old elite.

Perhaps without intending it, Fischer and Lundgreen raise doubts about the administrative superiority of disciplined, autonomous bureaucracies, as such, over other means of government. But they confirm the significance of the political choices European states made in creating different sorts of staffs to carry on their work. They note, for example, that governmental control over access to technical knowledge was extreme in Prussia, moderately great in France, slight in Britain—a difference which probably influenced the timing and character of industrialization in the three countries, and certainly affected their relative reliance on private corporations, citizen commissions and the like for the solution of public problems. They fill out our picture of an army pervading a population in Prussia, a coalition of landlords and merchants checking royal power in England, and a civilian central authority achieving remarkable autonomy (at the cost of vulnerability to revolution) in France. Despite the convergence in administrative structures due to common problems and mutual modeling since 1800, the choices made in the sixteenth and seventeenth centuries still mark these countries.

ROKKAN ON DIMENSIONS OF STATE FORMATION AND NATION-BUILDING

With Stein Rokkan, we turn to an extraordinary generalization of the variables underlying such international difference. Doubly extraordinary because efforts of this kind are rare, because this effort is rich and stimulating. Rokkan offers a model of the full-fledged nation-state (central control, standard culture, mass political participation, extensive redistributive activity). He converts the model into a set of phases resembling those a number of other scholars have proposed: penetration, standardization, participation, and redistribution. He asks himself what accounts for variations in the loci, timing, and political outcome of these phases within Europe. That leads him to devise several conceptual matrices. The fundamental matrices are schematic maps of Europe; in them large geographic variations in strategic position, culture, and social structure replace strict linear distance.

As Rokkan says himself, the very nature of the exercise fills the paper with contestable generalizations. One can easily argue, for example, with Rokkan's treatment of England and France as broadly similar cases of close interaction between urban and rural economic elites, or with his classification of Savoy with Prussia among the powers making major conquests "inward towards the center of Western Europe." Ultimately such judgments will have to stand up to critical scrutiny. For the scheme to be worth using in the interim, however, it is sufficient that there be an approximate fit among the reality, the specific judgments, and the general scheme. It is rare enough to find a general developmental scheme containing verifiable propositions rather than recurrent tautologies. It is rarer still to find one which simultaneously yields statements about the system as a whole, deals with the full range of variation, and provides unexpected hypotheses concerning the individual instances. Rokkan's scheme does. The present form of the scheme is complicated. The numerate reader, however, will not have much difficulty imagining it as a simple set of simultaneous equations.

Rokkan provides some constants for the equations in the form of common background characteristics which constrained the emergences of states everywhere in Europe: the residual influence of the Roman Empire, the presence of the Catholic Church, the precedent of the autonomous Germanic kingdoms, the continental web of cities, the general growth of the feudal and manorial structure, the early emergence of vernacular literatures. True, internal variation with respect to these features of the European experience made some difference to the development of states in different parts of Eu-

[66]

rope. But within a world perspective these are special properties of European state-making as a whole.

Within the European area, Rokkan brings out several dimensions of variation which generally lie hidden in our other papers: (1) geopolitical position; (2) urbanity, (3) concentration of landholdings; and (4) homogeneity with respect to language and religion. Most of the time he is simply showing that the diverse European experiences do fit without great distortion into the four-dimensional space defined by these variables, and that in combination these four variables yield a plausible account of the geographic pattern of state-making. The implicit argument, however, goes something like this: on functional grounds only a limited number of the large set of possible combinations of these variables could yield viable states; where rulers attempt to build states in the absence of one of these viable combinations, their efforts will fail in characteristic ways; each viable combination will produce a somewhat different but predictable historical sequence and outcome; nevertheless, these controlling conditions do change slowly with time, and are manipulable to some extent, so the geographic pattern shifts in the long run.

This line of reasoning appears in Rokkan's interesting analysis of the slowness of the urbanized region running between Amsterdam, Copenhagen, and Palermo to produce substantial, centralized areas. He considers that the multiplicity of trade-linked cities made it easy for the elites of that region to pool resources in temporary coalitions and federations, and just as easy to band together against the achievement of preponderance by any one of their number. Although a few federations and a few mini-states in the region survived the crystallization of a state system over Europe as a whole, the unifying conquests came from outside. The expansion of Prussia from an eastern base played an important part. The conquests of Napoleon and the Congress of Vienna which settled their outcome gave the last major shoves to the formation of a complete European state system. To an important degree, they cleared the way to a unified Germany and a unified Italy.

The instances of Germany and Italy bring out one of the more intriguing complexities in Rokkan's scheme. For purposes of comparative analysis, how should we set the phases and timing of the state-building? Relatively old states lay at the core of each: Brandenburg-Prussia in Germany, Savoy-Piedmont in Italy. Yet Rokkan's treatment of Germany and Italy as nineteenth-century creations leads him to conclude that they faced a "cumulation of crises" of penetration, standardization, and participation. The plausibility of the argument depends heavily on what we regard as the unit of analysis: Savoy or Italy?

Indeed, the case of Italy identifies the two most embarrassing difficulties in applying a developmental-phase model like Rokkan's to the building of states: (1) If the "phases" can appear simultaneously, repeatedly or in different orders, do they actually constitute more than the elements of a *definition* of the modern state? (2) What is the *unit* which passes through these phases? The difficulties become even more acute when one notices (as does Rokkan) that a number of changes tended to occur at the same time over the whole range of European states, old and new; military innovations are the archetype of these roughly simultaneous changes.

In fact, Rokkan calls attention more directly than any of our other authors to the interaction and interdependence of the changing European states, to the sense in which they formed an operating system. Economically, the industrial North and West fed on the agrarian South and East. Politically, territorial consolidation proceeded at the peripheries of the system rather than at its center. By the end of the eighteenth century the major states were implicitly collaborating in dividing all of Europe into a limited number of sovereign states. What is more, their colonial expansion was spreading the territorial pattern (minus sovereignty) over the rest of the world. By the twentieth century almost the entire world was mapped into well-defined territories which were nominally sovereign, or destined to be so. Struggles over the territory which was to belong to one state or another became rare. (Yes, territorial disputes like those separating India and Pakistan, India and China, Israel and Egypt, or China and the Soviet Union in the 1960s and 1970s still occur, but they have become rare as compared to their prevalence in the nineteenth century.) The main options open to the new state-makers were (1) to occupy the whole territory allotted to them or (2) to break it—or let it break—into smaller states.

Not that this implicit international agreement makes everything easy for contemporary state-makers. It simply changes the nature of their problems. Rokkan's concluding balance sheet offers a bleak outlook for the states acquiring nominal sovereignty after World

War II. It also specifies how the contemporary acquisition of influence over remote parts of the world by Washington, Moscow, or Peking differs from the earlier territorial expansion of a France or a Prussia. Empire there is, but in the form of power relations among formally independent states whose territorial integrity almost all other states collaborate to maintain. The struggle shifts to control over the country's economic resources, its public ideology, its foreign relations, and thence to the personnel of government.

These changes enter Rokkan's argument as a set of models, contacts and pressures from outside the new state. The pressures are more powerful by far than those operating during the great periods of European state-building. The European state-makers constructed, then imposed, strong national governments before mass politics began. In new states, the two processes tend to occur together. That is the "cumulation of crises" already anticipated by the experiences of Germany and Italy.

The reasons that mass politics now arrives so early in a state's life, according to Rokkan's paradigm, almost all have to do with changes in the international system. They are the "high and diversified" pressures from such major centers as London, Paris, Washington, Moscow, and Peking, the "increasing exposure of masses to outside communication," the readily available models of universal suffrage politics, and so on. A skeptic might grumble that the court of Frederick the Great, after all, spoke French, or that the fine hands of the Hapsburgs were to be seen everywhere in sixteenth-century Europe. The fundamental fact—a decided drift toward dependency and interdependence in the twentieth century—would nevertheless remain. Ultimately Rokkan faces us with a paradox: the very international system which eases the creation of new states within the remaining niches in the world map reduces the likelihood that the new state-makers will either retain their personal power or create the sorts of acquiescent, nationalistic populations their European predecessors fashioned for themselves.

Recurrent Themes

Rokkan's survey touches on almost all of the themes which recur throughout the other papers. Their recurrence does not, of course, prove that they are intrinsically important—only that they are important to us. We hardly claim to have arrived at our estimates of importance independently. Nonetheless the common themes deserve mention as pointers toward the general conclusions concerning state-making which one can properly draw from the whole body of papers.

WHAT ARE STATES?

Our seminar did not spend much time discussing definitions. We did not try to legislate a common definition of the state. Sometimes we came to sharp disagreement about the appropriate criteria. (Bayley, in particular, objects to the idea of "stateness" broached earlier in this chapter.) Nevertheless, in their work our authors lean toward a narrow definition of the state. Within the whole historic range of political institutions, they concentrate on a smaller set than Joseph Strayer (1970) sweeps together with his criteria of durability, spatial fixity, permanent and impersonal institutions, final authority, and loyalty. Within the whole range of social relations, they single out what Ralph Miliband (1969) calls the government rather than that entire power structure he calls the "state system."

Finer is more explicit. In his view, a "modern state" is an organization employing specialized personnel which controls a consolidated territory and is recognized as autonomous and integral by the agents of other states. For the most part, Finer and the rest of our authors converge implicitly on the notion of stateness: an organization which controls the population occupying a defined territory is a state *in so far as* (1) it is differentiated from other organizations operating in the same territory; (2) it is autonomous; (3) it is centralized; and (4) its divisions are formally coordinated with one another.

Today's governments differ considerably on each of these dimensions. But over the last five centuries the world as a whole has moved decisively toward "stateness." Thus the processes bringing states into being in Western Europe were: consolidation of territorial control, differentiation of governments from other organizations, acquisition of autonomy (and mutual recognition thereof) by some governments, centralization and coordination. Our authors find the development of national consciousness, participation and commitment—"nation-building"—interesting and important. They exclude it, however, from the definition of the state. They argue that in Europe it generally occurred after the formation of strong states, and by no means as a direct or automatic consequence of state-building alone. In short, they insist on the analytic separation of state-building from

[70]

nation-building, and consider the nation-state only one of several possible outcomes of state-building.

THE HIGH COST OF STATE-BUILDING

Explicitly, our authors agree that the building of states in Western Europe cost tremendously in death, suffering, loss of rights and unwilling surrender of land, goods, or labor. Implicitly, they agree that the process could not have occurred without great costs. (However, we do not agree so completely on the *minimum* costs it would have taken, on how much the actual costs exceeded the minimum, and for what reasons, or on the extent to which the benefits outweighed the costs; all these judgments contain large moral and larger speculative components.) The fundamental reason for the high cost of European state-building was its beginning in the midst of a decentralized, largely peasant social structure. Building differentiated, autonomous, centralized organizations with effective control of territories entailed eliminating or subordinating thousands of semiautonomous authorities. If our analysis of armed forces is correct, most of the enormous cost of military activity—by far the largest single cost of state-making—sprang from the effort to reduce rivals inside and outside the territory. Building states also entailed extracting the resources for their operation from several million rural communities. If our analyses of taxation and food supply are correct, European states could not have acquired much more power than they had at the beginning of the seventeenth century without collaborating in the destruction of the landed peasantry. In any case, they did collaborate.

Most of the European population resisted each phase of the creation of strong states. Our analyses of taxation, of food supply, and (less directly) of policing show that the resistance was often concerted, determined, violent, and threatening to the holders of power. The prevalence of tax rebellions, food riots, movements against conscription, and related forms of protest during the great periods of state-making help gauge the amount of coercion it took to bring people under the state's effective control. Even if we consider that the arrival of effective policing greatly increased the day-to-day security of the average individual, we shall have to weigh that against the coercion the average individual endured along the way, and the long-run increase in his exposure to death and destruction through war.

The incompatibility of the old European peasant social organization with extensive state-building comes out most clearly in the interdependence of financial resources without extensive production for the market. It is true that Postan (1954) has long since warned us against treating "the rise of a money economy" as a general and continuous feature of European experience. It is also true, as Rokkan points out, that the larger European states first grew up outside the most intensely commercialized zone of the continent, the urban band from Flanders and the Baltic ports down into Italy. Intensive marketing did not cause states; it may even have inhibited their formation. If Ardant is right, furthermore, the less commercialized the economy, the more exhaustive the extractive apparatus the state has to mount to get the same return, hence the bulkier the state as such. Yet within such existing states, commercialization facilitated the flow of revenues to the governments. Regions (or periods) of minimal trade blocked governmental efforts to extract resources and carry on expensive tasks. That is one of the main connections Fernand Braudel (1949, 1966) has in mind when he traces the rise and fall of states around the Mediterranean to large swings in the European economy.

In Europe, commercialization and the destruction of the peasantry occurred largely as a consequence of the spread of capitalist property relations and production. Our papers bring out the considerable historical connection between the rise of national states and the expansion of capitalism, especially its agrarian varieties. They do not give us grounds for concluding that the connection was intimate or ineluctable, since early capitalist ventures like the Hanse were quite foreign to state-making, and since early strong states like Spain and France formed outside the principal centers of capitalism. The historical connection had two sides: (1) the expansion of capitalism freed the resources which state-makers captured for national ends; the consolidation of previously fragmented property rights in land, for example, facilitated its taxation; and (2) the growth of cities and of industrial production (often outside the cities) in southern England, Flanders, the Rhineland, northern Italy, and elsewhere in Western Europe produced profitable markets for big agricultural producers elsewhere in Europe, incentives for landlords to hasten the creation of a docile, land-poor labor force, and conditions for political alliance between great landlords and aspirant state-makers. With variations running from the extensive proletarianization of

[72]

Midlands England to the "new serfdom" of Poland and Prussia, that alliance became one of the staples of European state-making.

C. B. Macpherson (1962) has proposed a third relationship between expanding capitalism and the European brand of state-making: the elaboration of a political theory of "possessive individualism" modeled on the property relations of capitalism. Likewise Karl Polanyi (1957) has linked the emergence of the new political and moral doctrines more explicitly to the increasing dominance of the market. Since our papers contain rather little discussion of doctrine, they bear only indirectly on the validity of these arguments. Nevertheless, they suggest that the drift toward governmental adoption of liberal doctrines—which was, in fact, widespread in Europe after 1750—grew not only from the accession of capitalists to political power and the penetration of market relations into everyday life, but also from the experience of statesmen seeking to put larger and larger resources at the disposition of the state.

The relationship was reciprocal and complicated. The growth of governmental staffs, the inflation of armies, the expansion of seats of government, the incessant search for new revenues all contributed in various ways to the drawing (or driving) of peripheral areas into national markets, to urbanization, and to the extension of capitalist property-relations. It remains debatable whether the extent of economic regulation and the sheer weight of government slowed economic growth in countries like Spain and Brandenburg-Prussia. (Among our authors, Ardant and Braun tend to disagree on that point.) The massive expenditure of resources on the military establishment may have drawn capital away from industry. The effect of state-making on the later course of economic change was therefore contingent. But it was powerful.

ARMIES, WARS, AND STATES

The formation of standing armies provided the largest single incentive to extraction and the largest single means of state coercion over the long run of European state-making. Recurrently we find a chain of causation running from (1) change or expansion in land armies to (2) new efforts to extract resources from the subject population to (3) the development of new bureaucracies and administrative innovations to (4) resistance from the subject population to (5) renewed coercion to (6) durable increases in the bulk or extractiveness of the state. The chain stretched more tightly in some states

[73]

than in others; the classic comparison sets military Prussia against civilian England. Even in England, however, the building of a New Model Army entailed the same series of effects.

These connections among state-making, the building of armed forces, and the maintenance of internal control help account for the tendency of revolutions to occur in conjunction with the preparation and the termination of war. As Walter Laqueur says, "War appears to have been the decisive factor in the emergence of revolutionary situations in modern times; most modern revolutions, both successful and abortive, have followed in the wake of war . . ." (Laqueur 1968: 501). Our papers identify two main paths to the revolutionary outcome: (1) the exaction of men, supplies and—especially—taxes for the conduct of war incites resistance from crucial elites or important masses; the European revolutions of the 1640s exemplify this pattern; and (2) the absorption or weakening of a government's repressive capacity by war, coupled with a decline in the government's ability to meet its domestic commitments, encourages its enemies to rebel; the Russian Revolution provides the type case. These are not necessary, or even probable, effects of war-making. They are only likely if the government seriously depletes its coercive reserves. The paradox is that the building up of the government's coercive capacity for war sometimes has that very consequence, because it leads to diversion, dilution, disloyalty or defeat of the forces destined for domestic control.

Where the populations remained docile, wars still weighed heavily. Joseph Strayer (1971: 339) tells us that the first powerful precedent for general taxation by the crown came from the pope's promotion of forced contributions to finance the Third Crusade. Kings were not slow in adapting that newly legitimized procedure to their own secular military needs. Up to our own time dramatic increases in national budgets, national debts, numbers of governmental employees or any other indicator of governmental scale in European countries have occurred almost exclusively as a consequence of preparations for war. The general rule, furthermore, has been for some contraction in governmental scale to occur after a war—but almost never a return to the prewar scale. Preparation for war has been the great state-building activity. The process has been going on more or less continuously for at least five hundred years.

At an international level wars and war settlements have been the great shapers of the European state system as a whole. The Peace of

Westphalia (1648), the Congress of Vienna (1815), the Treaty of Versailles (1919) and the provisional settlements ending World War II produced incomparably greater realignments of the identities, relations, and relative strengths of European states than any long periods of incremental change between them.

To be sure, some of these effects came after substantial delays; to an important degree, Italy and Germany owed their existence as unified, independent states to the course and the settlement of the Napoleonic wars, but those two national states did not actually take shape until decades later. The immediate state-making effects of the Congress of Vienna were nonetheless profound: not only was France shrunken to her nearly definitive borders, but the shrinking process left behind a consolidated Prussia, a consolidated Austro-Hungarian Empire, a Netherlands soon to split definitively into Belgium and Holland, and a two-paneled European map, with the northwestern panel headed for consolidation into a smaller and smaller number of political units without much redrawing of the main national boundaries confirmed in 1815, and the southeastern panel headed for proliferation through the breakup of the Ottoman and Austro-Hungarian Empires. Thus war shaped and reshaped the European state system.

The consolidation of the state system also constricted the opportunities for the building of new states by war. That shift lies behind a paradox which many observers of contemporary state-making have noticed: armies of new states which are unlikely ever to fight an international war adopt the latest armaments, absorb the largest part of the public revenues, employ their might in putting down dissidents and guerrillas, play the parts of arbiters, king-makers and, on occasion, kings, yet fail repeatedly in their efforts to transform the social structure. That they have a "vested interest in the status quo" is of course true . . . but so did the state-making monarchs who nonetheless transformed Europe.

The conventional explanations of militarism in contemporary countries run to the ease with which military models (as opposed to models of industrial production or of family structure) can be imported by new states, the advantage of any army in a power vacuum, and its special significance as the most "modern" institution in a poor country, a major arena for education and communications, a likely instrument for collective tasks running from canal-building to traffic control. Our authors do not deny these effects. Instead, they call attention to their placement within a distinctive twentieth-century international structure: tremendous inequalities of military and economic power, deliberate exportation of military models and assistance by a handful of great powers, likely involvement of several of the same great powers in any war anywhere, consequent irrelevance of the small state's military establishment to its pursuit of international objectives by means of war. As a result of this international situation, military forces become favored links with (and instruments of) the great powers, and become much freer than their predecessors to intervene in domestic politics. The building of substantial armed forces, on the other hand, becomes much less likely to produce the gradual subordination of the subject population, the transformation of the fiscal structure, the freeing and absorption of resources that it did in the European seventeenth and eighteenth centuries. Its state-making impact appears to have diminished and changed.

THE SIGNIFICANCE OF MULTIPLICITY

A state system embracing a relatively small number of participants emerged from centuries of contestation among what had once been quite a large number of virtually independent political units. The thousand state-like units spattering the political map of fourteenth-century Europe dwindled to fewer than thirty by World War I. *E pluribus pauci* might serve as the European motto. Furthermore, throughout the entire reduction process the European system has included not one dominant power but a number of rivals. Unlike much of the Roman or Chinese experience, the multiplicity of medieval and postmedieval Europe almost always made it possible for a coalition to form against the greater power which could overcome that power alone. At an international level, the European political process therefore entailed the constant formation and reformation of coalitions.

Multiplicity marked the European state-making process at a smaller scale as well. In the earlier phases of state-making, every aspiring ruler found himself surrounded by rivals—even within the territories he nominally controlled. Landlords who exercised nearly autonomous control of their own estates (and thereby of most of the resources necessary for the waging of war, the maintenance of courts, and other stately tasks) rivaled and resisted the princes at the local level. Great magnates, royal cousins, and neighboring princes eased or elbowed their way into the prince's own jurisdic-

[76]

CHARLES TILLY

tion. In his essay on armed forces, Finer shows us how mortal a threat the enemies of every prince posed. Successful state-makers had to absorb, check, or destroy most of their immediate rivals.

The variant strategies they employed comprise much of the news of this book. Yet some general features stand out: As a rule the European monarchs of the great state-building period allied themselves with the landlords of their territories, who received a certain license to exploit their own shares of the land and the peasantry. Landowners generally comprised the nerves of the armed forces, the core of the coercion employed in crushing the early forms of resistance to state-making, the bulk of local administration *in nomine principis*. That princes should have formed such coalitions within the matrix of feudal society does not surprise us much in retrospect. That it did happen, nevertheless, hastened the subjugation of the vast mass of peasant population to a state-landlord combine, left power in the Estates even through the so-called age of absolutism, and facilitated the eventual creation of a landless population through such devices as enclosure.

One feature of this coalition process to which several of our papers (notably that of Fischer and Lundgreen) call attention is the co-optation of potential opponents of the state through apparently antistate institutions like the sale of public office. Although France provides the textbook case, most European monarchies at least tolerated the sales of some substantial set of offices during some substantial phase of their histories. In England sales of major offices ended before 1700. Yet even then

in the Exchequer, at least, sinecures abounded. Sir Robert Howard, as bad an administrator as he was poet, could not be removed from his post as Auditor of the Exchequer, which he had bought and so held for life. His security permitted the luxury of political opposition to the King. The Exchequer also provided a notable army of offices that were discharged by deputy, and so provided outdoor relief for the lucky families that held them. Few however, were as fortunate as the family of Walker, who held the office of Usher of the Exchequer. It had been granted this office in perpetuity by Henry II, and members of the family were still drawing their stipends in William III's reign (Plumb 1967: 114).

[77]

For all their dead weight, offices of this kind generally committed their holders to the continued existence of the government. Similarly, the ceding of control over Prussian local government to the regional landlords compromised the power of the state in principle, but helped assure the collaboration of the Junkers in state's exploitation of the peasantry and the urban population.

The form of class alliances thus worked out by the earlier state-makers significantly affected the later political pattern of the state. The coalition of crown, Junkers, and bureaucrats prepared Brandenburg-Prussia for military predominance and revolutions from above, while the opening of the English alliance to the commercial classes cleared the way to liberal democracy. Here the implicit arguments of our papers join the explicit arguments of Barrington Moore's *Social Origins of Dictatorship and Democracy* (1966). The alternatives of autocracy, democracy, federalism, or oligarchy which clearly differentiated European political systems in the nineteenth century were forming in the class alliances made by the state-makers of the previous three centuries.

HOMOGENEITY AND HETEROGENEITY

Largely as a result of the previous unification under the Roman Empire, European state-making began in a setting of considerable cultural homogeneity: in a world perspective, relatively little disparity in language, kinship system, cosmology, religion, aesthetic form, or even political tradition. This relative homogeneity no doubt facilitated the movement of state-making models, ideologies, techniques, and personnel from one area to another. As compared, for example, with the cultural diversity of the Americas or Africa of the time, fourteenth-century Europe provided a favorable setting for the construction of substantial unified states.

Yet European state-making involved a further move toward homogeneity within states, along two criss-crossing paths: (1) via the deliberate attempts of state-makers to homogenize the culture of their subject populations through linguistic, religious, and, eventually, educational standardization; and (2) via the tendency of those states enclosing relatively homogeneous populations to survive and prosper, while those containing wide cultural disparities tended to stagnate or to explode. We need not exaggerate the resultant homogeneity; diversity is the stock in trade of local historians in France, Germany, Italy, or England: historical traditions, dialects, field systems, ethnic

[78]

origins do vary from region to region. In a large perspective, nevertheless, the European state-making process minimized the cultural
variation *within* states and maximized the variation *among* states.
Hence the plausibility of doctrines of national self-determination to
nineteenth-century Europeans—just so long as they were not dealing
with their own ethnic/religious minorities.

Why should homogeneity make any difference? Only the Fischer-
Lundgreen and Rokkan papers take up the issue. They suggest two
complementary reasons. First, a homogeneous population was more
likely to remain loyal to a regime of its own kind, just as it was more
likely to mount a successful rebellion against foreign domination.
Second, centralized policies of extraction and control were more likely to yield a high return to the government (in terms of resources
returned by the subject population per unit of pressure exerted by
the government) where the population's routine life was organized
in relatively uniform ways. There a single successful policy could
easily be generalized to all parts of a state. The more heterogeneous
the population, the more often a policy notably successful in one
place would fail utterly in another, and the more effort and personnel absorbed in the elaboration of alternative plans, and the greater
the relative payoff from policies which put a considerable share of
the available resources into the hands of local magnates and traditional authorities. Hence the incentive of state-makers to homogenize.

Gabriel Ardant's controversial argument about the fiscal incentives for the extension of political participation takes the analysis one
phase further: into what has loosely been called "nation-building."
Gabriel Almond and Bingham Powell distinguish between state-
building and nation-building in the following way:

> We need some way of talking about these challenges which may
> lead to political development, these changes in the magnitude
> and content of the flow of inputs which put the existing culture
> and structure under strain. As a beginning we may suggest four
> types of problems for challenges to a political system. The first
> of these is the problem of penetration and integration; we refer
> to this as the problem of *state-building*. The second type of sys-
> tem-development problem is that of loyalty and commitment,
> which we refer to as *nation-building*. The third problem is that
> of *participation*, the pressure from groups in the society for hav-
> ing a part in the decision making of the system. And the fourth

is the problem of *distribution*, or welfare, the pressure from the domestic society to employ the coercive power of the political system to redistribute income, wealth, opportunity, and honor (Almond and Powell 1966: 35).

Ardant does not go as far into definitions as do Almond and Powell, but he appears to have similar distinctions in mind. In these terms, Ardant is asserting that beyond a certain level of state-building, the builders found that they had to greatly increase the loyalty, commitment, and acquiescence of the subject population (a nation-building task) in order to expand state power and that only substantial increases in participation would accomplish that objective; thus they became willing to accord much wider involvement in governmental affairs to the general population; partly as a result of the expansion of participation, according to Ardant, they found themselves increasingly involved in distribution and redistribution. Of course, Ardant concentrates on the fiscal aspect of these processes. By the very centrality of fiscal activity in the operation of states, however, Ardant's argument has implications for the whole range of state work.

Our papers—on purpose—do not deal with nation-building nearly so fully as with state-building. Therefore, they do not provide the means for testing this portion of Ardant's argument in detail. They provide just enough mixed evidence and contrary argument to make it clear that Ardant's position is a controversial one. He attaches great importance to the needs and plans of state-makers in accounting for the nineteenth-century broadening of participation in national politics. Other papers (notably Bayley's, Rokkan's, and my own) work with a model of strong pressure from below and great resistance from above, leading to a reluctant concession of political rights and guarantees of different mobilized segments of the general population. The controversy is familiar. It is the theme of such distinguished books as Reinhard Bendix's *Nation-Building and Citizenship* (1964), T. H. Marshall's *Citizenship and Social Class* (1950), and E. E. Schattschneider's *The Semi-Sovereign People* (1960). It recalls the very old argument among political historians about the relative weight of popular demands and of statesmen's concessions in the great nineteenth-century transformations of England or Italy. Our papers lead up to that famous old question and connect it with the logic of state-making. They do not resolve it.

[80]

CHARLES TILLY

Why Europe Will Not Occur Again

The European state-building experiences will not repeat themselves in new states. The connections of the new states to the rest of the world have changed too much. The statesmen of the contemporary world find themselves faced with alternative models of state-building, not to mention eager promoters of those models. The manager of a contemporary state may well be ineffective and/or wrong, but he is likely to assume the necessity of promoting an efficient and submissive civil service, a general and uniform system of taxation, a well-trained native military force, and a high level of industrial production. In Europe of the fifteenth or sixteenth century the available models were fewer, different, less well-defined and less obviously appropriate for the objectives of the powerful.

Moreover, the European state-makers and a few non-European collaborators, through war, conquest and alliance, eventually fashioned a worldwide system of states. As the nineteenth and twentieth centuries have worn on, the newcomers to the system have had less choice of the positions they would occupy in it, even down to the exact territories they would control. Among other things, that prior existence of a state system has fundamentally altered the role of the military forces in the smaller states, since their strength or weakness no longer makes the major difference in the territory controlled by the state or in its relations with other states.

Again the resources on which today's state-makers draw and the forces against which they struggle are deeply different from those of the early European experience. All the builders of European states occupied themselves, one way or another, in wresting their wherewithal from largely self-sustaining agrarian populations. They could not borrow military might, technical expertise, or development funds from neighboring states. They could not assume the existence of a world market for any of their products, or the readiness of their producers to respond to a world market if it existed. They could not dispossess foreign capitalists (unless one wants to press the analogy of the Catholic Church with Kennecott Copper). They could not even nationalize the land. On the other hand they could use their personal positions as suzerains and landlords to bring men, food, and rents to the service of the crown; could forge alliances with fellow landlords to assure the acquiescence of the rural population in their grouping; and could drum up public funds

[81]

by such devices as selling offices. Most of these conditions are entirely gone and unlikely to return.

Finally, the managers of contemporary states have undertaken different tasks from their predecessors: building a certain kind of economic system, creating specific facilities like research institutes, steel mills, airports, or holiday resorts; maintaining some minimum of public welfare; promoting one variety of patriotism or another; increasing the supply of scientists; and others. The new tasks flow in part from the available models of state-building, in part from the logic of the international system, in part from pressures within each individual country. In this regard as well, our ability to infer the probable events and sequences in contemporary states from an informed reading of European history is close to nil.

The profundity of all these changes might make worthless any inference whatsoever from European experience to today's world. The authors of this volume take a slightly more sanguine view of the matter. We think there is a reasonable chance that some general relationships among the ways of building state power, the forms of relationship between men and government, and the character of the political institutions which emerge from the process of state-building which held within the European world still hold today. There appears, for example, to be a strong and general connection between the ultimate bulk of national governments and the extent of their reliance on land armies in their formative periods. We propose a number of hypotheses along these lines, and attempt to knit them together: cautiously within our particular areas of competence in the substantive essays on armed forces, police, taxation, and so on, a bit more boldly in the synthetic essays.

The Plan of the Book

At its strongest points, our analysis will present well-founded hypotheses, not conclusions for the ages. The papers which follow are serious; the authors have set themselves demanding questions; they have tried hard to find the answers. Yet everyone of us feels the incompleteness and imprecision of what he has to report. If level of confidence is the measure, in fact, this book takes a step backward from previous statements about "political development," even to the extent of putting the phrase itself into quotation marks. "Not so easy as all that," we frequently conclude. If we have made it clear why it is not so easy and what the possible alternatives to established doctrine are, that will have to do.

The papers themselves appear in a roughly descending order of extractiveness: the most obviously extractive activities first. Samuel Finer, a political scientist-historian, begins with a sweeping comparative analysis of the most expensive governmental activity of all: the building and maintenance of armed forces. Gabriel Ardant, an economist and economic historian, treats financial policy and economic infrastructure, with a strong concentration on the means by which states extracted resources from subject populations. Rudolph Braun, a historian with strong sociological leanings, takes up many of the same themes in a study focused on taxation in Britain and Prussia. David Bayley, a political scientist previously known for his work on new states, carries out a systematic comparison of police systems in West European countries. Charles Tilly, a sociologist who often works with historical materials, follows with a somewhat less systematic survey of problems of food supply and the kinds of conflicts they involved. Wolfram Fischer and Peter Lundgreen, social and economic historians, close the specialized essays with a comparative analysis of state involvement in the recruitment and training of various kinds of officials and technicians. Then we turn to two general essays. Stein Rokkan, a political scientist with fingers in most of the other social sciences, proposes a set of variables with which to analyze the European experience of state-making and nation-building. In the final essay, Tilly considers the implications of the West European experience with states for existing theories of political development and political decay.

CHAPTER 2

STATE- AND NATION-BUILDING IN EUROPE: THE ROLE OF THE MILITARY

SAMUEL E. FINER

~.

Terminology

Just as there are four chief divisions of the mass of the population—farmers, mechanics, shopkeepers and day-labourers—so there are four kinds of military forces—cavalry, heavy infantry, light armed troops, and the navy. Where the territory is suitable for the use of cavalry, there is favourable ground for the construction of a strong form of oligarchy: the inhabitants of such a territory need a cavalry force for security, and it is only men of large means who can afford to breed and keep horses. Where territory is suitable for the use of heavy infantry, the next and less exclusive form of oligarchy is natural: service in the heavy infantry is a matter for the well-to-do rather than for the poor. Light armed troops, and the navy are wholly on the side of democracy; and in our days—with light armed troops and naval forces as large as they are—the oligarchical side is generally worsted in any civil dispute . . . (Barker 1946: 271; cf. also 160, 188).

Here Aristotle is linking three variables: social stratification, style-of-rule, and what I shall be calling the *format* of the military forces. The number of variables involved is, in fact, more numerous than this; for instance, the format of the military is determined by technological advances as well as by terrain, and technology takes us into the sphere of the economy as a whole. Above all, the quotation suggests a static relationship between format and the three styles-of-rule. Now one of my objects is to discover what relationship existed between the development of the modern state and the military format. This posits a relationship between two *processes*—the development of the modern state on the one side, the development of military formats on the other.

I must, therefore, say what I mean by a modern state as contrasted with any other, and presumably, premodern forms; and say something more about this concept of *format*, on the other.

The literature suggests that the term—a "modern" state—can mean rather different things to different authors. Lord Lindsay, for instance, when he writes of *The Modern Democratic State* (Lindsay 1943) appears to be making an implicit distinction between this and the states of classical antiquity. German authors, followed by such scholars as Ernest Barker (Barker 1951: 1–17), evolved however a complex classification of states: the so-called *Ständestaat* of medieval times, then the *Fürstenstaat*, or the Princes' State of the Renaissance, then the *Hausstaat*, or Dynastic State, and so forth. In this view, a "modern" state is that which emerged after the medieval ones. Meanwhile classical concepts of "the state" such as Weber's are of little help for this inquiry which is *genetic*. For instance, in Weber's famous definition, that states are "human associations that successfully claim the monopoly of legitimate use of physical force within a given territory," every single key word begs the historical question of when, at what particular date, the "state" can be said to have emerged. The degree of success achieved by a government in claiming the legitimate use of physical force; the completeness of its monopoly of this, the assurance of its legitimacy, and the extent of its territorial jurisdiction—every one of these fluctuated during the last millennium, and every one admitted and still admits of *degrees*. And so it becomes almost an arbitrary matter to say, "At this date, the area once known as *Regnum Francorum* can be regarded as a state."

I propose to regard the modern European states as those that emerged subsequent to the break up of the Roman polity; hence to regard a medieval kingdom as a form of state and to regard the process of state-building as something that took place between an origin in the early Middle Ages and today. In that case, our contemporary states have, since their amorphous beginnings a thousand years ago, acquired five salient characteristics.

1. Like all states by definition, they are *territorially* defined populations each recognizing a common paramount organ of government.

2. This paramount organ of government is subserved by specialized personnel; one, the *civil* service, to carry out decisions, the other—the *military* service to back these by force where necessary

[85]

and to protect the association from other similarly constituted associations.

3. This state, so defined and characterized, is recognized by other similarly constituted states as independent in its action upon its territorially defined population, i.e., its subjects. This recognition constitutes its international "sovereignty."

4. Ideally at least, but to a large extent in practice also, the population of a state forms a community of feeling—a *Gemeinschaft*—based on self-consciousness of a common *nationality*.

5. Ideally at least and again to a large extent in practice, the population forms a community in the sense that its members mutually distribute and share duties and benefits.

The medieval forerunners of contemporary Britain, France, Germany, and the like, possessed few or none of these characteristics. But somewhere along the line of the second millennium A.D. each acquired them to an extent which would permit us to assign to them a recognizably *contemporary* form. But here it is desirable to distinguish between the first three and the last two of this set of five characteristics. Albeit in England and, somewhat later, in France the last two characteristics were slowly acquired even in the later Middle Ages, for the most part they are markedly later phenomena, developing fast and far only in the late eighteenth and in the nineteenth centuries. These last two characteristics are the ones typically associated with *nation*-building, whereas the first three are characteristic of *state*-building.

As can be inferred from the first and second characteristics, state-building proper involves two major variables: *territoriality* and *function*. (Item 3 is a derivative from these two.) In both these respects the medieval state is anitipodal to the contemporary one. The present territorial entity known as France was in the tenth century a congeries of what at the highest we may style as minor and primitive states, or at the lowest, a welter of competing jurisdictions. Furthermore, whereas today political obedience is a simple function of territorial location in that one owes allegiance to the government of the territory in which one finds oneself, at that time political allegiance was a man-to-man relationship, and obedience might be due, in different circumstances, to several overlords. Nor was there any likelihood that these different claims upon the same individual might not compete. Often, where these lords were in dispute, the

[86]

vassal had to make up his own mind as to where his allegiance lay. By the same arrangement of lordship and vassalage what today we call public and private functions were at that time compounded together. As Mosca puts it (Mosca 1939: 81), "by 'feudal state' we mean that type of political organization in which all the executive functions of society—the economic, the judicial, the administrative, the military—are exercised simultaneously by the same individuals, while at the same time the state is made up of small social aggregates each of which possesses all the organs that are required for self sufficiency." A medieval state as compared with a contemporary one, was fragmented into many hands, and it was crisscrossed with overlapping and sometimes conflicting feudal and subfeudal obligations and pockmarked with "liberties" and "immunities." So *territorially*, the medieval state was *differentiated*. By contrast the public and the private *functions* were *consolidated* in one and the same office or individual.

In contrast the contemporary state consists of formerly differentiated territories which have been brought together and whose populations have become *consolidated* under the same common organ of rule—be it prince, or dictator, or parliament. At the same time a distinction has long been drawn between public and private rights and duties, and by that token, between public officers and private individuals. In brief, public and private services have become differentiated, as shown in Figure 2–1.

	TERRITORIALLY	*FUNCTIONALLY*
MEDIAEVAL	DIFFERENTIATED	CONSOLIDATED
CONTEMPORARY	CONSOLIDATED	DIFFERENTIATED

Figure 2–1. Development of the Contemporary State.

The twin process—from consolidated service to differentiated service and from differentiated territory to consolidated territory—is what constitutes *the development of the modern state*.

Not quite the whole of it, however. For if all contemporary states tend to resemble one another in these two major respects, they may differ from one another in their respective *styles-of-rule*. A contemporary state may be autocratic or representative; it may be centralized or decentralized; its laws may be homonomous or heteronomous, i.e., divaricated according to areas or to functions within the state. Now whereas the twin movement of state-building—from consolidated to differentiated functions, and from differentiation of territory to its consolidation—whereas this twin movement has been on the whole regular, *linear*, and cumulative over the last thousand years, the styles-of-rule have fluctuated.

Nation-building is not the same as state-building. The two have both historical and logical connections. Populations which have been consolidated under a common organ of government may thereby be assisted in attaining the common consciousness (no matter the sentiments or facts on which this is founded), that is the precondition of being a "nation." In return, where such common sentiments or facts of life are self-consciously felt by a population, this may be impelled thereby to seek its own individual political organization, i.e., to make its sense of community and its sense of political allegiance coincide. The literature shows that like the "state" concept, the concept of "nation" has been variously interpreted and two common approaches are often used without distinguishing between them. Yet although they are both historically and logically connected, they are distinct. For some, the sense of nationhood is popular participation in matters affecting the whole population on the one side, and on the other, an identity of benefits received from this association. It is in this sense that the Abbé Sieyes defined the nation as being "A body of associates living under *common* laws and represented by the same legislative assembly." (The emphases are the ones supplied by the Abbé himself—not by me.) This notion contrasts with what some German authors have called the so-called *Ständestaat* or the later "proprietary-territorial state" where the state as such was the "property" not of all, but of its unequal orders (in the former instance) or the prince and his court (in the latter). Here the concept of *nation-state* is the concept of a state of "*all* the state's population, of the whole *nation*, in the name of natural rights and popular sovereignty." On the other hand, a nation can and has been defined as a population conscious of its common *nationality*—Englishness, Germanness, and the like. The two concepts—citizenship with its implication of reciprocal rights and duties among the whole body of the associates, or nationality in the sense of a community of *ethnos* and a sense of shared destiny—are mutually compatible and also self-supportive. Furthermore, insofar as the one embodies the notion of the sovereignty of the people and the other, the notion of the par-

[88]

ticularity of that people among other peoples, the two notions link up both logically and in historical experience with the great principles of the French Revolution. "Equality" of rights in the common association went hand in hand with "fraternity"—brotherhood in the sense that all were equal parts of the same (and distinctive) human family.

In either meaning, the root condition is *community*. Again in either meaning, nation-building began earlier in England than it did in France, and in France earlier than it did among the scattered territories of the Hohenzollern dynasty into whose hand fate and connubial blisses had by 1618 delivered variegated strips of German-speaking territory which later were to be consolidated and to be known as Brandenburg-Prussia and later, just Prussia. For most of the European continent, the phase of nation-building took its great leap forward with the French Revolution and progressed outward from that focus until today when its immense potentialities for nation-building and, by the same token, for state-splitting have reached outward to encompass hitherto little-known peoples of brown, black, and yellow skins, throughout the former imperial territories of the European great powers.

Let me turn now to the other key concept—that of military *format*. It is to the changes in this format that I shall seek to relate changes in the nature of the state.

The role of the military in the state- and nation-building process is not to be taken as identical with the role of coercion. If it were, we should be engaged in an endless and highly subjective enterprise, for we should be trying to establish what role coercion played as against the other factors—commercial, ethnic, linguistic, legal, cultural, and so forth—that have gone into the making of states. Only minds like those of Marx and Engels, obsessively concerned with conflict could so continuously harp upon the role of armed force as the sole force creating and maintaining the state.

Nor is the role of the military in state- and nation-building to be equated with the role of *warfare*. Warfare would at once embrace too much and too little. War embraces elements with which I do not propose to deal—diplomacy, international relations, the effects of foreign occupation, the tolls of pestilence and famine, and the like. Obviously, the format of the armed forces and the resources they require from their host community will significantly alter if they are at war, and this will be an object of my concern. But it will be the in-

[89]

fluence of armed forces in time of war and not war itself with which I shall be concerned. Likewise the equation of the role of the military on state- and nation-building with the role of war would be too narrow; the military format has a domestic role in time of peace.

My purpose is to follow Aristotle and inquire into the relationship between the development of modern states and nations and what I have called the *format* of the armed forces. In its narrow and most explicit definition, format merely signifies the service basis of the forces; i.e., whether they were native or foreign, paid or unpaid, *ad hoc* or permanent. In its more extended definition, I include within the concept, the *size* of the armed forces, the varying composition of its main arms (navy against land forces or artillery components against infantry or cavalry and the like), and I equally include the social stratification of the force. Where necessary, I shall indicate in the text whether I am using the more or the less extended definition of format. On the whole, however, the context will make it clear.

Just as the state has evolved through time, so have the military formats. At any fixed point of time, both have exerted a reciprocal influence on each other. To ascertain the nature of this influence is the object of this essay.

Methodology

This relationship between military format and state-building involves a host of intervening variables as coextensive as the entire field of history itself; which is to say, as coextensive as what Marx very justly defined as "the study of society in motion." At various points of time, we find that we have to explain or understand a development in either of our two key variables by such matters as social stratification, or the condition of the economy, of popular or elite beliefs, or of the role of the ruler (i.e., his ambitions, and his perceptions of risk and opportunity at home as well as abroad).

Some of these variables are more prominent or occur more frequently than others. Additionally some tend to cohere in characteristic clusters, or to speak more precisely, in cycles of mutual interaction. These clusters themselves interact with other characteristic clusters. It will save an infinity of time to identify and then name such clusters, and, in particular, six of the most prominent.

This procedure will not in itself *explain* the data. To put it at its lowest, it will prove a convenient shorthand, where the name of each cluster will resemble a Wagnerian *leit-motiv*, signifying, according to its nature, the entire history of the Volsung family, for instance, or the birth and death of Siegfried. It should prove capable of something more than this though: each "cycle" is, in fact, a *paradigm*, just as the interrelations of these paradigms in Figure 2–2 are a master-paradigm. The paradigm, Etzioni says,

> is more than a perspective but less than a theory. It provides a set of interrelated questions, but no account of validated propositions. It provides a "language," a net of variables, but it does not specify the relationships among those variables. It is less vague than a perspective, providing a systematic, specific, and often logically exhaustive set of foci for research and speculation. A paradigm is often a stage on the way from an old perspective to a new theory. . . . The test of a paradigm is not only that of the validity of the theories constructed through their application, but also its fruitfulness in terms of the spectrum of significant problems whose study is facilitated by it (Etzioni, 1965: 2).

ECONOMY-TECHNOLOGY-FORMAT CYCLE
(BRIEFLY: ECONOMY-TECHNOLOGY CYCLE)

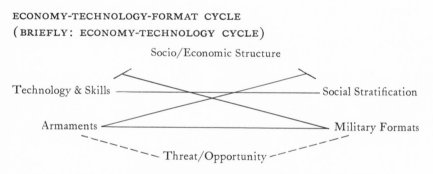

Figure 2–2. The Economy-Technology-Format Cycle

In terms of this "cycle," one can rapidly describe the various factors responsible, for instance, for the introduction of shock-infantry into Europe and the decline of shock-cavalry. The Swiss pike-phalanx outdid the heavy armored shock-cavalry in the course of the fifteenth century. How and why? The French socioeconomic basis was a highly monetized, relatively wealthy, technologically competent society with a large population of at least fifteen million people. Its social stratification was highly unequal as between a warlike and politically and economically privileged class of nobles, and the commoners. These two factors were reflected in the military format

[91]

one of whose main components was still circa 1415 (Agincourt) the heavy armored cavalry first introduced in Frankish times. When one reflects that mail armor alone weighed thirty pounds and cost the equivalent of a small farm, and that plate armor weighed some one hundred thirty pounds and was correspondingly more expensive, that a knight required one or two esquires to equip and support him, and mounts for them as well as a charger and possibly a remount for himself, one can see that only a society similar to that of France could have thrown up and supported such a force. It would be like expecting private individuals nowadays to help form the army by bringing to the battlefield their own Centurion or Patton tank, or their own Phantom plane. Switzerland in all these respects was entirely different. It was a league of, for the most part, poverty-stricken rural mountain cantons, much overpopulated, with a prefeudal social structure of free and egalitarian peasants. The terrain made horses and armor an encumbrance rather than the reverse and in any case few if any individuals would have been wealthy enough to support them. Hence these peasants fought with typically peasant weapons—evolvements from the well-known bill: first the halberd, then, in order to keep the enemy Austrian cavalry still further off, longer pikes with four-feet steel heads. The pikes finally reached the length of eighteen feet. At the same time a special tactic of handling these had to be developed, if they were to be effective: the ranks had to be close so as to admit no charging horses into its gaps. So evolved the typical Swiss phalanx—cheap and plebeian—a square of six thousand men which could form a hedgehog against attacking cavalry and which, faced with enemy infantry, could actually *charge* it with all their impetus and weight of six thousand men. This format proved decisive over the heavy feudal cavalry at Grandison and Muret. Henceforth infantry, armed with pike and bow and then pike and shot, became the linchpin of any military force.

THE STRATIFICATION-FORMAT CYCLE
(BRIEFLY: STRATIFICATION CYCLE)

This cycle and its interrelationships can also be illustrated by Figure 2–2, on which it, too, is located. Moreover, the former example of the Swiss infantry can also serve here. That example makes clear the influence upon the typically Swiss format of the egalitarian structure of its society: an egalitarian social structure, hence an egalitarian military format—even to the point of the Swiss electing their commanders. French social stratification not only perpetuated beyond its useful span the employment of heavy armored shock-cavalry (just as the aristocratic cult of *ye horse* mingled horse cavalry with the tanks in the "Surprise at Cambrai" in 1917); it also made the French cavalry refuse to fraternize with the commoners in their army, whether spearmen or crossbowmen. At Crécy the king of France's reaction to the disorganization of his Genoese crossbowmen was to shout to his knights to "kill me these scoundrels for they block our road."

THE BELIEFS-FORMAT CYCLE (BRIEFLY: BELIEFS CYCLE)

Figure 2–3. The Beliefs-Format Cycle

Once again, the French example cited above can serve to illustrate. Just as society was stratified into noble and commoner, just as the army was similarly stratified, so to the key arm, the shock-cavalry which itself corresponds to a social class, there corresponded a distinct set of beliefs—too inchoate perhaps to be called an ideology. This was the notion of *chivalry*. Knighthood, its duties and also its privileges, incarnated the chivalric ideal. And only knights fought on horseback. Crossbows and the like were *vilain*. Furthermore they threatened the supremacy of the cavalry arm. In this way the chivalric ideals, served to perpetuate an already obsolete mode of fighting.

THE FORMAT-OPTIONS CYCLE (BRIEFLY: FORMAT CYCLE)

It is difficult to reconstruct what prudential considerations went on in the minds of medieval kings in respect to the various options with which their reigns confronted them. It is much clearer after the Renaissance when, even if monarchs did not, albeit obscurely, voice these considerations, publicists and pundits did so on their behalf. So it is that we find Machiavelli, Bodin, Rousseau, Adam Smith, and many others calculatedly balancing up the advantages of using one military format rather than another. Such calculations have continued pretty naturally down to our own era, not to speak of our own day, as I note from a recent publication of the London Institute of Strategic Studies entitled "Military Manpower and Political Purpose."

The considerations are three. The first is the effectiveness of the force for the purpose in hand. Such a "purpose" and such "effectiveness" are the consequences of ultimately *subjective* appraisals; it can be subsumed under two headings: the ambitions of the rulers and the risk-opportunity as they perceive this. Clearly if a force is designed for defense but is likely to run away at the first menacing shouts of its enemy, there is no point in having it at all. If it is predictably useless, then why spend money on it? But if it is not predictably useless, or need not be under certain conditions, then the next consideration is—can such a force, of such a size be afforded? This is the consideration of its *expense*.

But there is also a third consideration and this is the one that Machiavelli dwelt upon. Given such and such a format, would it be loyal to the ruler? This is the consideration of *loyalty*.

Now what was the range of choices from which rulers could choose according to these three considerations? They are basically three, and each can exist in either an *ad hoc* or permanent form. Figure 2–4 shows the basic relationships. Foreign paid volunteers, popularly known as "mercenaries" could be raised *ad hoc* like Swiss pikemen in the fifteenth century, or on a permanent footing like the foreign regiments that had been incorporated into nearly all European standing armies in the eighteenth century. Next reliance could be put on what today we would call "national service," but which admits of many varieties: its basic characteristic is that it is "obligatory." It may be selective. The word "conscription," often used for this kind of service, originally meant merely the common writing down of eligible names for the purposes of a ballot, only the unlucky numbers having to serve. This is, in fact, a kind of "selective service" such as is used in the United States today. In early days, such conscription was highly arbitrary and unfair in its incidence. It was "impressment," in which the weaker, for instance, the unemployed or homeless, were the first to be made to enroll. Alternatively everybody with only relatively insignificant exceptions may be deemed liable; as in Israel today. This is "universal military service." In the feudal period knight service was one component of domestic obligatory service and the *fyrd* or *arrière-ban* its other, and popular, component. But these forces were convened and disbanded *ad hoc*. The permanent or standing version of this format, where a contingent serves in the field and is ready to be supported by a huge reserve of colleagues who have already served, is the most common format in the advanced industrial states of today. Its general introduction dates from the French Revolutionary Wars, and, more generally, from the aftermath of the Franco-Prussian War of 1870; but it had been anteceded in Prussia and the northern states in the seventeenth century, and thence some versions of it were used in France and Savoy. The third format was the domestic paid volunteer troop like the late medieval English "companies" or French *bandes* (in their *ad hoc* form); and of course the regular standing army, typical of the eighteenth century, and still in use in Britain.

In practice few rulers ever used a land or sea force composed of only one of these three major types. Normally they would use a combination. There was a continuous evolution in the preferred formats or combinations of formats during the state- and nation-building period. The main trends will be outlined in the next section "Chronology." Meanwhile let me point out that the choice of the formats was always linked with some of the cycles already discussed: effectiveness with the economy-technology cycle for instance, as well as with the ruler's perceptions of risk-opportunity; loyalty is linked with both the stratification and the belief cycles, and with the state-building cycle itself. And the expense of the armed force is directly related to one of the most visible and (from the state-building point of view) important cycles of all, the *extraction cycle*. Meanwhile Figure 2–4 below indicates in tabular form, the Format-Options Cycle.

	AD HOC	PERMANENT	Consideration
Foreign Paid Volunteers	"Mercenaries"	"Subsidy Troops"	Efficiency
Native Obligatory Service	Feudal Host Popular Militia	Universal Military Service	Expense
Native Paid Volunteers	"Bandes" - Indentured Companies	"Regulars"	Loyalty

Figure 2–4. The Format-Options Cycle

THE EXTRACTION-COERCION CYCLE (BRIEFLY: EXTRACTION CYCLE)

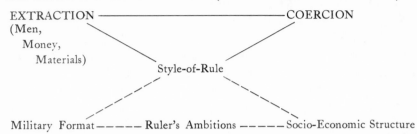

Figure 2–5. The Extraction-Coercion Cycle

Military forces call for men, materials, and, once monetization has set in, for money, too. To extract these has often been very difficult. It has become easier and more generally acceptable as the centuries have rolled on. Where populations proved recalcitrant—and, I may add, they were on the whole and in most countries quite extraordinarily recalcitrant up to the nineteenth century, to a degree that makes popular American recalcitrance to the Vietnam War look like a mere gesture—then rulers had only two alternative courses. They could try to coerce or try to persuade. Now coercion presupposes something very similar to the instrument for which the coercion is itself proposed. Troops extract the taxes or the forage or the carts, and this contribution keeps them in being. More troops—more extraction—more troops: so a cycle of this kind could go on widening and deepening. This is precisely what happened in Brandenburg-Prussia from 1653 onward, and in large measure accounts for the state-building process in that country.

On the other hand, the need for coercion diminishes if, as a result of persuasions, the people—in the language of Deborah—"willingly offer themselves." Religious fervor may provide the incentive sometimes. When the mass hysteria of national sovereignty and national self-determination gripped entire peoples in the nineteenth century, it made possible the provision of armies, navies, matériel, and money on an altogether unprecedented scale—so great a scale indeed that no amount of naked coercion on the part of governments could have extracted a tithe of it. Clearly, it hardly needs saying, this *extraction-persuasion* cycle is linked with the *beliefs* cycle. Beliefs could inspire populations to sacrifices hitherto undreamt of. Hence, it could, and indeed it did become, an object of policy on the part of rulers to substitute beliefs for coercion, and benefits in return for sacrifices, in

[96]

order to extract the vast resources needed. This helped forward the extension of citizenship and welfare services in the nineteenth and twentieth centuries; that is to say that the cycle links up, with not just the state-building, but with the *nation-building* process also.

THE STATE-BUILDING CYCLE

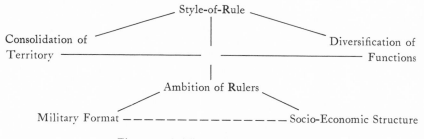

Figure 2–6. The State-Building Cycle

The relationship between style-of-rule, territorial consolidation, and the functional diversification processes has already been explained. But Prussia provides a fairly clear-cut illustration of what these terms look like in concrete events and how they interrelate. The ambition of the Great Elector was to maintain his princely territories and make the resources of each pay for the defense of the others. An ambition to become absolute appears unlikely, at the outset, at any rate; but this was the style-of-rule that resulted. For, to realize his ambitions, he required a larger standing army than his noblemen, who dominated the Estates, were voluntarily prepared to pay for. Here the *extraction-coercion* cycle went into operation, and the Estates were compelled to consent by show of force. The extraction machinery which he established, notably the excise taxation system in the towns and the apparatus for supplying and quartering the troops became more or less standardized throughout the diverse territories. In this process an extractive-cum-military officialdom was set up which went far beyond mere extraction, into expanding the very sources of wealth, and thus interfering in domestic and economic affairs. This led to an expanding and deepening cameralism, a set of territories with more or less uniform institutions (consolidation) and a very numerous specialized bureaucracy, both civil and military (differentiation of functions).

When I began to describe these cycles I pointed out that they themselves interlinked with one another. It is possible to indicate the more obvious linkages by Figure 2–7.

[97]

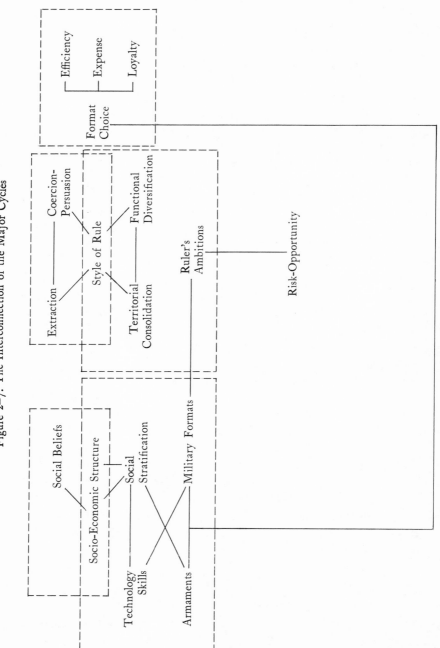

Figure 2-7. The Interconnection of the Major Cycles

Chronology

LAND FORMATS AND WARFARE UP TO THE EIGHTEENTH CENTURY

With one or two notable idiosyncrasies, military formats went through a roughly uniform evolution among the states with which we are concerned. Five major trends stand out. These are related to three parameters: to innovations in armaments (echo of the economy-technology cycle), to the financial and later the industrial development of the state (a similar echo) and to changes in social stratification.

From Ad Hoc to Permanent (Standing) Forces. The first standing force of an exclusively "national" kind, i.e., conceived as owning unique and perpetual allegiance to the nascent state *via* the person of its ruler(s), was the French *Compagnies d'Ordonnance*, set up by Charles VII in 1445. In the Italian Wars (1494 and later), some of France's *ad hoc bandes* were used so frequently as to become, in effect, standing forces and the nucleus of the (later) four *vieux régiments*. By the 1620s supplementary regiments, raised from and paid for by the king, i.e., the *corps entretenus*, would, on disbandment, throw off a small depot force of picked men. Thenceforward, the number and scale of these "skeleton" regiments increased. It may well be that this depot system had been borrowed from the Spanish experiences of the earlier part of the century; there each *tercio* had its own depot force in Spain which supplied it with its replacements. There was no permanent force in England (I except the trainbands of militia), until the New Model Army of 1645. Thereafter there was always some kind of standing force although at the Restoration, 1660, it consisted of less than 6,000 men. As to Prussia, it is not until the War in the North of 1655–1660 that the former *ad hoc* mercenary troops could be said to have been put on a regular footing. Hitherto, though a small body, in fact, had been retained constantly in service, the army was in theory, at any rate, an *ad hoc* one.

From Unpaid Obligatory ("National") Service to Paid Volunteer. Knight service in kind had been generally commuted for cash payments by about 1294 in England, although the last summons of the feudal host—nominal only—occurred in 1385. But militia service for domestic defense or police duty continued unbroken from Saxon times, surviving the passing of the feudal levy. For overseas service, however, the practice became to array militia men and pick a number of them to serve for payment. In the fourteenth century the format altered to a semiprivate cash basis: forces were raised at the king's cost by means of an indenture between the king and the gentlemen he had commissioned. Formats in France followed a similar pattern but with a time lapse; the commutation of knight service lagged by as much as a century behind England, but because of the nobleman's contempt for the *roturier* and the dislike of the townsmen for military campaigning, the popular militia had been abandoned by the close of the fourteenth century. The system of indentured *compagnies*, resembling the English in their format, developed in France, after the early disasters in the Hundred Years War. In the fifteenth century kings put on semipermanent contract foreign paid troops, i.e., the mercenaries proper such as the Swiss and the *Landsknechten*. The *soldatesca* of the Hohenzollerns in the Thirty Years War were of this format, the contracts being known as the *Kapitulationen*.

Here one major exception must be made. After the accession of Henry VII in 1485, England reverted to the popular militia, at least, for home defense, whereas France and Spain and the Hohenzollerns came to depend on paid native volunteers or foreign paid volunteers or both, but *not* on popular militias (exception made, in Spain's case, of the *Hermandad* in the early sixteenth century). By the eighteenth century, however, paid volunteer service had become the rule even in England, though there the militia was retained for domestic service, it is true; but it was more as a political balance to the regular standing army than as a serious fighting force until its reform in 1757. France, though Louis XIV had initiated conscription between 1702 and 1713, relied on a large regular force, many of whose regiments were foreigners. Prussia, too, had a regular standing army of paid troops, but after 1732 this was supplemented by the obligatory service of peasants, each "canton" having to provide the replacements for the regiment assigned to it.

From Semiprivate to Public Control and/or Ownership. Under the system of indentured companies, then that of foreign mercenaries, and then of *corps entretenus*, the common assumption was that the king would commission a gentleman to raise, equip, officer, and lead a given force of men: the king paid him, he for his part did the rest, and if any money stuck to his fingers, this was after all his livelihood. From the late sixteenth through the eighteenth century, rulers increasingly encroached upon the privileges of the "colonel" who raised the regiment. Long before the advent of the revolutionary wars the rulers of France and Prussia had arrogated to themselves the right to appoint the junior officers and the most senior officer of the regiments; to regulate their promotion; to recruit the other ranks; to make the commissariat and logistical provision. True, the sale and purchase of the officer's commission endured until the Revolution in France and, under increasingly stringent regulation, until as late as 1872 in England.

Increasing Size. Accurate figures are notoriously hard to come by. The most significant figures are those for the number of troops called out for a campaign rather than those used in a particular battle or as the regular standing nucleus of the army. The Norman troops at Hastings numbered some 6,000 to 8,000 at the most. For a projected French campaign against England in 1327, an optimistic estimate was that 35,000 troops would be used. In the Italian campaign of 1498, there were 65,000 troops. Against Spain in 1635, the campaign troops numbered 155,000. In 1678 the campaign troops reached 279,000; in the 1691 campaign, as many as 440,000. Napoleon mustered 700,000 men for the Russian campaign in 1812.

For England the figures are always smaller. It must be remembered that throughout this entire period France was far and away the most populous state of the West, in population outnumbering the English by some four or five to one at the various dates in the millennium. At Hastings the numbers roughly equaled the Norman ones— perhaps 6,000 to 8,000 men—but the entire Saxon force available had not been called out. In his campaign of 1513 against France, Henry VIII used 27,000 men; in the 1544 campaign, 42,000; in 1712, at the height of the Spanish Succession War, the number of troops reached 75,000; and at the peak of the Napoleonic campaigns, some 250,000.

In Prussia the figures are roughly congruent with the regular army strength: some 4,000 in 1653; 30,000 in 1688; 80,000 in 1740; 160,000 in the Seven Years War; as many as 300,000 in 1814, when "volunteers" and reservists were added.

It will be seen that the sharp increases come, in every case, after the close of the Thirty Years War, in 1648.

From Multinational to National Armies. Here we need only note that as late as the third quarter of the eighteenth century, from one-half to one-third of the troops of any state would have been foreigners. Over half of Napoleon's *Grande Armée* were not Frenchmen; and over half of Wellington's force at Waterloo (leaving Blücher entirely out of account) were foreigners too. Wholly native armies were a product of the nineteenth century.

THE MILITARY FORMATS AND THE ART OF WAR

From the Age of the Armored Knight to 1300. In "advanced" armies, the principal and necessary arm was the shock-cavalry. Infantry served two different functions. Some were missile infantry, armed with short bows and with the newly resurrected arbalaster, or crossbow. The others, much more numerous, were armed with some type of spear and formed a defensive hedge behind which their cavalry could re-form after an unsuccessful charge.

Three points seem particularly worthy of attention: First, "the fundamental factor in the origin and development of feudal society was the adoption of heavy cavalry by the Franks from the mid-eighth century and the consequent demand for mounted retainers, expensively equipped and elaborately trained to fight on horseback" (Brown 1967: 123). This in turn, as has been demonstrated by Lynn White (White 1962: chap. 1), was due to a simple gadget, equivalent in importance to that later gadget, the bayonet—viz., the iron stirrup. From time immemorial warriors on horseback had ridden up to their enemies and pushed their lance at them with the full strength of their *arm*, i.e., by man power. With a stirrup, the horse and rider were, as it were, glued together. The rider held his long lance under his arm at rest, charged, did not move his arm at all, but, rigidly united to him, it was impelled against the enemy with the full power and momentum of the *horse*. This made the massed charge of heavy mounted cavalry against infantry all but irresistible.

Second, the equipment—a war horse and possibly a remount, two palfreys for esquires to carry the armor to the battlefield and to equip the knight, and the mail armor itself—all these were vastly expensive. A suit of mail cost the price of a small farm at the time of the Third Crusade. Later as plate amor was introduced and the steed had to be the *dextrarius*, a heavier animal altogether, the cost soared still more. In short only very wealthy people could afford to be knights. Alternatively, if a king wanted a particular man or set of men to act as his mounted cavalry, he had to give them the wherewithal. In those nonmonetized days this meant giving a conditional gift of land with peasants to farm it for him. Charles Martel who is credited with introducing the armored cavalry into the West after the battle of Tours in the eighth century appropriated one-third of the lands of the church in order to endow the men whom he wished to serve as his armored cavalry.

Third, as has already been pointed out, this system was like one where a rich man—or a man made rich by government endowment —is expected to contribute to the army his personal tank and its crew, or a Phantom and its crew, and all supporting services. In such circumstances, if the individual renounced his liability, the monarch would have to turn against his tank or his plane, the tanks and planes of those who had decided to honor their pledges. The feudal force was hardly, therefore, a predictably loyal one. Not only that. It was hardly a disciplined force, either. Each tank crew, each Phantom crew, each artillery crew would be an independent entity or, set of entities. Each would have little incentive or inclination to fight under the orders of some common superior. So with the medieval cavalry.

There is a final point. It took a lot of money to equip a knight. Once equipped, however, he had the opportunity for advancement and also for booty. Originally only very rich men could be armed knights. Later, especially on the Continent, where the entire progeny of knights became "noble," the younger sons who were poor strove very hard to acquire the horse and armor, in order to make military careers and so become wealthy. This gave the *noblesse* as whole a vested interest in retaining the existing military system against the nonnoble remainder of the population. It also gave them the military and economic power to do so.

The Decline of the Feudal Cavalry: 1300–1453. The feudal chivalry was eroded by infantry developments of two quite different sorts and in two quite separated geographical areas: in the Atlantic area where the development of the longbow by the English armies felled the French cavalry, and in Central Europe where the Swiss pikemen smashed the Austrian and Burgundian cavalry. But there was never a European "age of the longbowmen" as there was an "age of the pikemen," because, if we are to believe Sir Charles Oman, at any rate, no nation in Europe seemed capable of equaling English skill or achievements with the longbow, and the English never exported themselves as mercenary longbowmen to foreign rulers.

Whereas Swabians, Spaniards, and later many other peoples, did manage to trail pikes as well as the Swiss, the era of the longbow was confined to the Anglo-French struggle. But it so happens that during this period, this struggle was the one that held the attention of Europe. Hence it can be dealt with prior to the infantry phalanx invented by the Swiss.

At Halidon (1332) and Dupplin Moor (1333), the English armies defeated the Scots by utilizing a new tactic—dismounted heavy cavalry (an old trick for the English, first used at the Battle of the Standard in 1138) flanked by the newfangled longbowmen whom Edward I had picked up from South Wales and who were thence forward emulated by the English yeomanry. The longbow could get off some ten or twelve shots a minute compared with the crossbow's one or two. Admittedly the shaft was not as heavy; although it could pierce mail well enough, it was not effective against plate; but, of course, it could also be used against the feudal mounts unless these were protected also. The range was impressive also—some three hundred yards; and the accuracy attainable, quite remarkable. The response of cavalrymen, notably the French, whose entire social status seemed to them to repose on their primacy on the battlefield, was to use plate armor and to try to protect the horses. These cavalry then became incapable of any but direct charges. The bankruptcy of this military format, whether knights were mounted or dismounted, was attested at Crécy, Poitiers, and Agincourt.

But, toward the end of this period a new missile weapon was creeping in. This was the firearm. Cannon proved critical in the French victories of Castillon (1450) and Formigny (1453) which ejected the English from all France excepting only Calais. And the harquebus, firing a two ounce ball farther than the crossbow's quarrel, was slowly ejecting the bow.

Castillon and Formigny—though this was not realized at the time —expelled England from Europe for good. Thenceforward she did indeed equip expeditionary forces for the Continent; but she did not, like Valois and Hapsburg, indulge in continuous warfare lasting some sixty years. The cockpit of Europe ceased to be France and became Italy, and to some extent Flanders. There new methods of warfare were tried out. In their island the English tenaciously clung to their longbows, the success against the Scots at Flodden (1515) contributing much to its continuing favor. Not until 1585 did a British government reluctantly concede that it need no longer be treated as an "official" weapon; yet bows were served out to the northern shire levies for service against the Scots as late as 1638!

On the Continent, however, the art of war developed with great innovations. These ushered in the final downfall of not merely the heavy armored cavalry but cavalry as such, as the prime essential of the military format. The pike and the firearm were responsible for this.

The Age of Pike and Handgun: 1450–1550. Armaments developed rapidly. Heavy artillery for siege, and somewhat lighter though very ponderous guns for battle were fast coming into general use. And so also were handguns. By 1450 the primitive fire tube of 1400 had become the spring-trigger operated harquebus, where a lighted fuse ignited the powder in the pan. Its range was twice that of the crossbow, and its missile very heavy. To counter the new artillery, the tall, thin walls of the medieval castle had to be replaced or girdled by low and thick ones, forerunners of the bastion. In the Italian Wars all manner of combinations of field weapons were tried out with inconclusive results: infantry phalanxes, harquebusiers, the heavy French cavalry—all had their decisive moment, in one or other of the battles. But one fact stood out, one indispensable element. Indeed, the principal and the necessary one was now *infantry.* The Swiss phalanx, perfected from the trial runs of Morgarten (1351) and Sempach (1386), had now become a square of 6,000 men, the front four ranks of which, in elbow close order, wielded eighteen-foot pikes with spearheads four feet long. The rear ranks wielded halberds whose hooks could drag horsemen from the saddle while their blades could lop off the spearheads of enemy infantry. The pike order held off cavalry attacks. The halberd order held off infantry attacks. In revenge, this phalanx, the men holding their pikes over their heads, would trot for a mile and then hurl itself at the enemy infantry shattering it with a shock far greater than that of the feudal cavalry. This formation, after smashingly defeating Charles the Bold at Grandison and Muret, became the favorite of continental Europe. It was copied by the Swabian Germans who called themselves *Landsknechten.* In 1480 *Landsknechten* proved decisive in defeating Louis XI of France at the Battle of Guinegatte. Thereupon he took 6,000 Swiss pikemen into his service on contract; and for the next half century French foot armies were always composed of two elements, either Swiss or *Landsknechten,* and native mercenary *bandes*. But, from his own experiences of the Italian wars against the French, the *Gran Capitan* of Spain, Gonzalvo de Córdoba evolved a more flexible infantry formation. This was the *tercio*. It consisted of three, not six thousand men, divided into three colonelcies (or *coronélias*). At first the armament comprised the indispensable pike, the crossbowman, and sword-and-buckler men. The latter were soon discarded. By about 1540 it had reached its "normal" form—a hollow square, its sides made up of deep formations of harquebusiers, later replaced by the Spanish improvement on this weapon, namely the much heavier musket. As the rate of fire of the handguns increased, so did the proportion of shot to pike. In 1530 it was one shot to two pikes; by the end of the century more like one to one.

The *tercio* became the standard formation of Europe. Its supremacy and prestige did not end until it was shattered by Condé at the Battle of Rocroi in 1643.

The Military Revolution: 1550–1660. Meanwhile the art of fortification, making advances, began to bog down armies into siege and manoeuvre warfare. Field artillery was still too cumbersome to be shifted about a battlefield; it had to be positioned once and for all. As for cavalry, since a use for it had to be found apart from scouting and pursuit—it was adapted to mounted pistoleers who rode to the enemy lines, hastily fired off, and raced back again: the so-called *caracole.*

But the basic element of battle was the infantry square, half shot and half pike. The troublesome problem for the commander was how best to combine these two elements; since the musketeer needed the protection of the pikemen against enemy cavalry or infantry, while the pikemen needed the musketeer's protection too. In this respect quite new tactics were invented by Maurice of Nassau. In the first place, realizing that the Dutch militia were no match for the Spaniards in the open field, he replaced them by a paid volunteer force. These he drilled continually until they could adopt the most diverse formations with great rapidity. The great solid masses of the *tercio* he abandoned for small units, the smallest being only thirty men strong; and these combined with others into larger units, he moved against his enemy in the chequer board formation recommended in the classical *Tactics of Aelius*, the book which served as his constant inspiration.

[106]

The principle of manoeuvrability was carried further by the great Gustavus Adolphus of Sweden. Gustavus, unlike Maurice, was also a very considerable military innovator. He invented a cartridge which much increased the rapidity of fire, he lightened the weight of the musket so that it could be used without a crutch, he invented a leather sheathed copper-tubed artillery—a portable field gun which two men could carry about the battlefield. He abandoned the *caracole* and taught his cavalry to charge home with the saber. And with these improvements, he arranged his troops, with the cavalry on the wings and field guns defended by pike and musket in front of each infantry formation; these formations themselves consisted of pikemen on flank and musketeers in the middle. But, owing to the new rapidity of fire, he could now thin the depth of his musketry formation, since the drill was for the front ranks to fire, and then to file to the rear, to reload, and so forth. With the new speed of fire he had attained, Gustavus could reduce the depth of his formations to eight ranks. Thus from the square he was evolving the infantry into an oblong formation, far longer on its front than in its depth.

From the Battalion Formation to Line, to Manoeuvre, and to Siege. It is now necessary to distinguish even more sharply than ever between grand strategy and tactics. On the battlefield, the movement from square into oblong continued until the oblong became a very long line of some five miles perhaps, but only four or three ranks deep. And this development was consequent upon two prime inventions, gadgets again, in the field of weaponry. The first was the replacement of the matchlock by the flintlock. By 1689 this weapon was standard throughout the French armies and by 1700 throughout Europe. It vastly increased the rate of fire. It could get off a round a minute with an effective range (against a man's body) of some eighty yards. By 1740 the Prussian fusiliers had achieved the rate of three rounds a minute. So the depth of the firing line decreased, and the Prussian fusiliers could safely form in three ranks only. Likewise, since the ranks were thinned, it was possible to extend the troops sideways, and highly desirable too, since this avoided turning of their flanks. So came about the long thin lines of strictly positioned infantry, highly drilled for these complex manoeuvres of getting to and keeping their dressing on the battlefield, and once in position all but impossible to move about quickly.

At almost the same time a second gadget was introduced. This was the simple expedient of fitting a sword blade to the muzzle of the musket. At first (circa 1660) this sword was plugged in, a highly dangerous expedient as was to be shown by the massacre of English soldiers thus equipped, by Highlanders, who swooped out of the mist at Killicrankie in 1689. Instead the socket bayonet which was invented by Vauban in 1680 was widely and rapidly adopted. With this the infantryman became two types of infantry in one person, at once the pikeman, but also the musketeer. He was a missile *and* a shock infantry as desired. This absurdly simple invention was to dominate infantry tactics well past the age of Napoleon up to the eve of the Austro-Prussian War of 1866. The tactic of the eighteenth century was to form the thin line, to advance through the smoke of the field artillery, to pour a curtain of fire in the advance, and then—at about twenty feet from the enemy—to charge home with the bayonet. The cavalry came in to hold, or to overwhelm, or to pursue.

But while this became the set arrangement for the field of *battle*, developments elsewhere were slowing down the pace of *war*. For from the age of Maurice and of Gustavus we have now reached the era of Vauban and Louvois, or Marlborough and Villars. This was the age of sieges, artillery, and above all, of fortification: the perfected asterisk-like bastions of Vauban, and the correspondingly geometrically predictable reduction of similarly constructed fortresses by the lines of circumvallation and approach which Vauban designed. It is the age of "lines" like the lines of the Schellenburg which Marlborough stormed on his way to Blenheim or the *ne plus ultra* lines that Villars threw up and which it took Marlborough an entire campaign season to penetrate. For wars of this kind, evolved to take a strong place here and cut the enemy's communications there, it was necessary to construct magazines, map out forage areas, lay down lines of advance, and see that the extensive transportation was available. In short, the age of logistics had arrived. And it was in logistics, *par excellence*, that Louis's ministers, Le Tellier and Louvois were such remarkable administrators.

By 1713, after the War of the Spanish Succession, the pattern of warfare had been set for the rest of the century until the combination of the notions of Guibert and the extremities of the volunteer soldiers of the French Revolution introduced an entirely different pattern. To that we shall return when we come to "The Napoleonic Watershed."

State and Format in England to 1714

I have suggested that state-building consisted of twin processes: the consolidation together under a common superior of the populations of hitherto disparate territories; and the differentiation between the public and private sectors, and hence between public officials and private individuals. Though the processes are visibly common to England, France, and Brandenburg-Prussia, they occurred in each instance with significant differences in timing, in degree, and above all, in the third aspect of state-building, in style-of-rule. In Brandenburg-Prussia, the outcome was a monarchy even more absolute than that of contemporary France, depending even more than France (where Louis XIV's cannon bore the motto *ultima ratio regum*) upon the support of a docile standing army. But the English outcome was entirely different. There the monarchy had been all but qualified away by an aristocratic-mercantile patriciate, with its central organizational focus in Parliament and effective local ones in the Quarter Sessions. Not only that. The nature of state-building in England smacks far more of a general and relatively rapid reception of common laws and lawcourts than submission to the decisions of specialized executive officers. The administrative and judicial were, for the most part, combined—the most significant illustration being the vast corpus of administrative decision carried out by the Quarter Sessions in judicial form and definitionally by a judicial body. Control of the subject until well into the nineteenth century was on the whole judicial and not administrative. Of course, the laws had, in the last resort, to be enforced. But a verdict was entrusted in the first instance to officers of the court; the police was still an obligatory unspecialized civic force of laymen. Only in the last resort did the public forces in the shape of militia (another civic force) and finally the regular army, intervene to support the verdicts. In short, whereas France and Brandenburg were stuffed with enforcement officers, these were relatively rare in England.

There are further remarkable differences. The processes of state-building are quite visible in the tenth century in England, whereas one must look to the period between the reign of Philippe-Auguste and Philippe le Bel, i.e., the thirteenth and early fourteenth centuries for this to become as prominent in French territory, and the process was incomplete until the second half of the seventeenth. As for Brandenburg-Prussia the processes are entirely a product of the seventeenth and early eighteenth centuries. By that time England, France, Holland, Sweden, Spain, and many other states were in existence to serve, however unconsciously, as a model to the Great Elector and his successors. These had something visible to strive for. By contrast it could be said that the Normans and the Plantagenets, the Capetians, and the Valois were lines of monarchs—each one of whom was setting out on his own individual adventure in self-aggrandizement, a kind of blind progress which only we, with our hindsight recognize as constituting successive milestones in state-building.

Again in each of the three cases, different pockets of territory had to be welded together under a common superior before what we to-day call England, or France, or Prussia began to exist as such. In the English case, this was the heptarchy of Saxon kingdoms. But these were contiguous, the language spoken in them was cognate where it was not the same, and, above all, they were subjugated by common dynasties, whether of Wessex, of Denmark, or of the Wessex line again, at a time when their own native administrative and political institutions were so weak and amorphous as to dissolve into a common form with infinitely less difficulty than was true of the French duchies and counties. There, across the Channel, the territories were too numerous, the distances too great, and the local institutions too well structured by the time they came to have to recognize a common master. As for Brandenburg-Prussia the name speaks volumes. The territories, which were fortuitously brought under the common rule of the Hohenzollern line in 1618 had their own quite separate histories. The economic and social differences between the Rhine areas and the central and eastern ones were very great, and the lands were not even physically contiguous. They did not even speak a common tongue—at least, many districts of the Duchy of Prussia did not (some spoke a Slav dialect up to 1919). All they had in common was the Hohenzollerns.

Next we must bear in mind the demographic and economic differences among the three. In the seventeenth century the English and French economies were completely monetized with rich agricultural and mercantile resources. The population of the one was some five million, that of the other some twenty million. In contrast Brandenburg-Prussia was a thinly populated poverty-stricken sandbox, its capital town having only fifteen thousand people and its total population not exceeding half a million.

Finally social structure was dissimilar. The French *noblesse*, even under the absolute monarchy of the *Ancien Régime* was a highly complex caste admitting of perhaps six subgradations. Also there were thriving commercial, professional, literary, and artistic classes, as well as numerous sections and corporations among the townsfolk, and there were variegations of condition among the peasantry. Not only that. From its inception and markedly as the centuries passed on, the central government of England had been constricted by rival, even if legally subordinate institutions—the courts of law, the magistrates' benches, not to speak of Parliament itself; and each one of these could and did provide an organizational focus for discontents. This was partially true even of France of the *Ancien Régime* where there were the Parlements and (in the *pays d'états*) the Estates, as well as the powerful guilds and corporations. But in Brandenburg-Prussia at the opening of the eighteenth century, there were but two major classes—noble and peasant, lord and serf; the townsfolk, apart from the Königsbergers were of small account; and whereas until the reign of the Great Elector political power had lain with the noble-dominated Estates, at the close of his reign it resided in his hands alone.

Let us then turn to the specific case of England. Here three preliminary points stand out.

The first is to reiterate the early unification. The second has had an important bearing on the military format in the medieval period. On the one hand, we find the use of paid troops and native militiamen side by side with the feudality, on the other a more open-ended, less privileged and caste-like order of nobility. As a consequence of these factors, as well as the early unification, the crown usually had forces on which it could rely apart from the feudality while the state did not suffer as deeply as French territory from a deep-rooted provincial particularism, nor from the strategic and military status inside such provinces which the French *noblesse* enjoyed down to the middle of the seventeenth century. Parenthetically, it may be added that the open-ended character of the English nobility, its descent by primogeniture and not to the entire progeny, the absence of laws of *dérogeance* in cases where the nobleman should pursue some non-noble occupation, and its lack of fiscal immunity—all these, conjoined with the absence of provincial representative bodies which could compete with the central Parliament (as in France), removed from the development of the English Parliament as a tax-granting assembly many of the obstacles which stood in the way of the French Estates-General.

The third factor is that of geographical location. It is not just that by comparison with the area of modern France, England is a small country—half the size in fact. It is that the land frontiers of England marched with neighbors which were very weak. Wales and Scotland are not to be compared with Burgundy or the Hapsburg dominions. Wales was so weak as to be unable to resist English arms by the close of the thirteenth century, and so inchoate as to be absorbed bag and baggage into the English governmental system by the middle of the sixteenth. Scotland was never strong enough to do more than preserve her separate existence as a state. Insofar as there existed menaces to the continuance of the English state, these lay across the Channel, and until the end of the fifteenth century, the lands across this waterway were as much a prize or an opportunity as they were a threat. It was not until the reaggregation of French territories under Charles VII and Louis IX, and effectively not until the accession of Francis I of France and Charles V of Spain and the Hapsburg dominions in Europe that the formerly rich prizes across the sea turned into deadly threats. If at that time the English southern and southeastern frontiers had been land frontiers, it is impossible to visualize an English monarchy that relied only on an ill-trained militia equipped with the longbow for its defense. As it was, providing that the coast lines were fortified in the new traditions, and a navy created, the militia format might be deemed adequate, if a monarch were sufficiently optimistic. This reliance on the militia under the Tudors and early Stuarts was, however, to have the most profound constitutional consequences. And this is, as demonstrated, conditioned by the geographical location of the English state. At an early era, before the concept had been invented, England had on her vulnerable southern and southeastern corners a *natural frontier*.

Five phases may be discerned in the development of the English military (land) format. The first, which for brevity rather than exactness may be styled the feudal, lasted from the Conquest until the early fourteenth century; moved—rather earlier than in France —into a semifeudal phase in the twelfth and thirteenth centuries when service in kind was being commuted for cash payments. The third phase, that of the Hundred Years War—the fourteenth and most of the fifteenth centuries—is best described as semiprivate—

the era of the indentured companies of which we have already spoken. But whereas in continental Europe this phase was generally succeeded by the era of foreign mercenaries and the nuclei of regular native forces, England reverted to her native militia tradition. This did not end until the middle of the seventeenth century. It was then succeeded by the introduction of a regular standing army; but one which, unlike its counterparts on the Continent, was hardly capable, save in its very earliest phases (until the end of the seventeenth century), of posing any threat to the oligarchic parliamentary regime, or presenting any opportunity for the creation of an absolute monarchy.

By the death of Edgar in 975, England, in stark contrast to France, was recognized at that time by its ruling strata, if not by its population, as a single *regnum*. With the exceptions of Cumberland and Northumbria, the frontiers were much as we know them today. Thenceforward aristocratic reaction against the crown was to seek privileges or to command the whole, but *not* to return to the Heptarchy. Then the Conquest set the seal on such sentiment and provided new sinews of unification. For in the words of Helen Cam,

> the strategic advantage given by the fact of conquest is only fully recognized if we compare the nation-wide extension of the machinery controlled by William with the strict localization of that at the disposal of the kings of France. Only a small region round Paris was administered by officials under their orders. The great duchies and counties of France were governed, like Normandy, by the agents of the dukes and counts not the kings' and to build up a national monarchy the French kings had to pursue a century-long policy of piecemeal annexation resulting in the survival to our days of deeply-rooted provincialism (Cam 1961: 74).

Alongside the Anglo-Saxon militiamen, the *fyrd*, the Norman kings established a feudal host of armored cavalry; some eighteen hundred knights bringing with them their own retainers. At this point we discern a glimpse of the relationship between format and state-building. This feudal host was in military terms more than the match for the Saxon militia's infantry format, as was proved at Hastings even against the trained housecarles of Harold. It was infinitely more expensive, hence the expropriation by and reallocation to the Norman adventurers of the forfeited lands of Saxons. But its politi-

cal loyalty was questionable. Once the last embers of the Saxon resistance had been stamped out, William I and his successors were
plagued by the all too common feudal revolts. At the death of Henry
I, the pretext for such revolt was more colorable than ever before—
the rival claims of Stephen and Matilda; and so, as William of Newbury's *History* has it, *regnum Angliae scissum in duo*.

But if the Norman monarchs succeeded in repressing such revolts
and in creating what is called a "strong monarchy," this was due to
the format of the armies. For in practice the feudal cavalrymen were
not called out often (perhaps never, it is now thought) to go overseas; and even at home the kings tended to rely very heavily on paid
mercenary troops and the Saxon militia who proved consistently
loyal to them and hostile to the Norman barons. Rufus, in particular,
used mercenaries to such an extent that the exactions to raise the
monies for their pay caused him to be execrated by the chroniclers.
No doubt these worthy divines thought he did it for his own amuse-
ment rather than to get professional and hence reliable military
service.

Military feudalism as it had been known was a clumsy expedient
invented in the West by Charles Martel who, in order to utilize the
expensive services of a novel shock cavalry without having any currency or indeed other resources with which to do so, stole one third
of the lands of the church and put it and its peasants at the service
of the cavalrymen. For a like reason the Teutonic Knights adapted
the same system when they colonized Prussia in the fourteenth century, and so did Hernán Cortes when he and his *conquistadores* had
conquered Mexico in the sixteenth century. It was a barbarous expedient and very unmilitary. The knight would keep the field only
forty days. The obligation left him with no discretion as to whether
he wanted to serve or not. The individual independence of each
knight and his retainers made for indiscipline in the field.

Cash service was clearly much better for both parties: for the king
because he could pick, choose his troops, and keep them in the field
for as long as his money lasted and get them to serve in the garrisons
or theaters of war that he selected; for the feudatories because it was
up to them whether they served in person or not.

The twelfth and thirteenth centuries saw the transition from unpaid obligatory service to commutation by means of cash. By the end
of the thirteenth century, few knights, if any, were serving in kind.
They served for the cash raised by the scutages and also by the pro-

ceeds of other taxes such as the extraordinary subsidies voted by the nascent Parliament or from the new customs on wool.

This variation in format, slight as it may seem, was not without a profound significance for state-building. For, from the time of Richard and of John, knights had become increasingly reluctant to serve overseas, and indeed to serve in the old feudal way at all. Scutages or fines were levied on them if they defaulted; alternatively, efforts might be made such as Richard made, to induce a proportion of knights to serve, waiving the remainder of the service owed. Two reasons appear to have been responsible for this. The increasing subdivision of the knight's fees owing to the effects of inheritance by females, and the vastly increasing cost of heavier armor and hence the heavier *dextrarius* horses needed to carry the ironclad knight. Furthermore, it was at the time of Richard and John that the kings of France began their long pressure against the English domains on the Continent that were to end, in 1453, in the English expulsion from Europe. The campaigns became more continuous, and permanent garrisons were required for the castles. The traditional forty days service did not provide what was needed—armies and garrisons that were perhaps smaller, but which were semipermanent. So, as service became commuted for cash, quarrels blew up between the king and his feudatories as to a "fair" scutage. The tug of war thus resolved itself by the thirteenth century into a battle over *taxation*. This battle and the origins and development of Parliament are directly associated.

By the beginning of the fourteenth century, all service was paid service; but the system of raising, leading, and equipping the armies that fought in France now becomes something quite different. It was the system of "indentured" companies, bands of fighting men raised by contract between the king as the purchaser, and gentlemen whom he commissioned as the captains and leaders of these companies. The armament and technique of fighting had changed into that combination of dismounted cavalrymen and longbowmen which shattered the feudal horsemen of France at Crécy, Poitiers, and Agincourt. One effect of these victories was the emergence in England of a military-commercial complex, a war party which for a half-century defied the efforts of monarchs like Richard II to make peace when the war was going badly. This party was made up of great magnates with the companies they raised and the lesser gentry—the knights—bannerets who became the folk heroes of contemporary England, both of these two classes avid for glory, for command, and for the rich ransoms to be got; of traders and contractors of all kinds who supplied the armies with their equipment; and of the wool merchants who needed to see Flanders guaranteed to them. But the principal effect of this type of format was above all political. It reflected and also reinforced a recrudescence of a "feudal" relationship between nobles and the crown, but without the loyalty implicit in the notion of feudality and homage to a feudality, in fact, based on the cash nexus. For in the fourteenth and still more in the fifteenth centuries feudal loyalties had sharply declined. Money commutation of feudal obligations had become universal, and oaths of fealty lost what importance they had ever had. A money and trading economy came in with a vengeance, with the rise of the wool industry which encouraged landlords to turn from arable to pasture.

This was reflected in the indenture system and the rise of the bannerets, men who brought at least ten "lances" to the army. By the time of Richard II, the retained troops of the magnates, sometimes called "affinities," existed on a great scale. The Duke of Lancaster, admittedly the richest man in England at that time, brought 600 cavalrymen and 9,000 archers to the Scottish War, under his own banner. By 1403 the marches of Scotland and Wales could be raised in arms by means of these great "liveries." Under Henry VI the process had spread much more widely and the magnates with their private armies were able to exercise extensive political and judicial influence in their own territories, territories which, for their part, had become extended and consolidated by the kings declining to exercise the right to interfere with politically injudicious marriages between their feudatories as they had done under the Normans and the Angevins. At first decisive only in local politics, there came a point where, given the insanity of Henry VI and the struggle to secure control of his person and his policies, these local dynasties became embroiled in the struggle to control the central government itself. It was the indentured liveries, led by local dynasts with their blood ties or blood claims on the throne, that fuelled the Wars of the Roses. (Both sides, alternately and simultaneously, called out the shire-levies, however, throughout the wars.)

But with the Battle of Bosworth Field, gained by Henry Tudor with the aid of numerous foreign mercenaries, a format that became increasingly commonly used in the progress of the civil wars, a dramatic change came over the English military format. On the one 'hand, Henry not only dismissed his mercenaries, but from thenceforth, with an exception in the reign of Edward VI, they were never again used for domestic purposes on British soil—only collected for foreign expeditions. In short, of two possible formats, foreign paid volunteers (i.e., mercenaries) and domestic paid volunteers (i.e., indentured companies), Henry had reverted to the third and very old English alternative: the shire militia. There was one significant difference between the new Commissions of Array which summoned them, and the old ones of Edward I's time, and it reflected the process of functional diversification that had occurred during the intervening centuries. In the olden days, the "Commissioners" of Array would be local magnates. Now though they might indeed include one or two such, the commissions always included the sheriffs, assisted by the Justices of the Peace, the king's own officers, albeit unpaid, in the localities. (After the accession of Edward VI, Lord Lieutenants were instituted in each county to take the musters and reviews, and generally act as the chief of these Commissioners.)

The militia was certainly cheap. In this respect it answered to Henry VII's very acute sense of economizing. The militia was, by the new continental standards, very inefficient. But then it was meant for home defense. For foreign expeditions, troops were hired—both native and foreign. And the sea lay between, as we have seen. Remained the final consideration: Would a militia be more politically reliable to the new dynasty than the indentured companies or foreign mercenaries? Certainly the loyalty of the officers was a question never far removed from the considerations of the Tudors and the Stuarts, as the choice of gentlemen, of Protestant persuasion, and possessing land and status in the counties amply testifies; nor the efforts to store firearms away from the common folk, in special armories (cf. Boynton 1967; Western 1965). In the end, the answer was to be "No." But that was in 1638 where the disaffected northern militia was in no 'heart to meet the Scots army, and in 1642 where the London-trained bands turned out to bar the route to the capital against Charles. Some of the shire-levies turned out to be obstinately royalist; others, just as obdurately parliamentarian. And both of them, with the exception of the London-trained bands, turned out to be so incompetent that the opposing sides rapidly turned to impressment and volunteers for their forces. For nearly a century and a 'half before that time, however, the monarchs had governed a highly turbulent people with no firmer support than the militia. (The exception is the use of 1,000 Italian and German mercenaries to suppress the various rebellions of the year 1549.) During this period, the shire-levies were loyal against antitax rebellions like those of 1489 or 1497; they were less reliable in the religious risings, like the Pilgrimage of Grace in 1536, and it took Henry VIII a good deal of double-dealing before he was in a position to quell this formidable rising; but when it was done, it was militiamen who did it for him. That this reliance on a militia set limits to the powers of the crown is surely attested by the fate of Wolsey's "Amicable Grant" of 1526, a proposal which led to a widespread "tax strike," and which both Wolsey and the king therefore hastily withdrew. The most interesting cases are those where the dynasty was threatened; in all but one, the shire-levies proved loyal. Militiamen defeated Martin Swart's German mercenaries and the Irish kerns at Stoke in 1487; the population rejected Warbeck at Deal in 1489, and the levies defeated him in the West in 1497. As Warwick pursued Queen Mary in 1558, his militiamen deserted him along the route while the queen was able to rally the levies of the shires she passed through. The wretched Northern Earls, in their rising of 1569, after leading their retinues south a little way, retreated in the face of the advancing levies and finally disbanded their followers. Only Wyatt's rebellion against the Spanish Match provides a partial exception to the rule.

On a closer examination, however, this loyalty of the militia seems to owe most to the *stratification* of the force. To begin with, it must be noted that not all the shire-levies were wholly reliable the whole of the time. Not by any means. The Duke of Norfolk forbore to give battle to the Pilgrims in 1536 because "some of my troops thought and think their (the rebels') quarrel to be good and godly." In 1549 the levies in the West and in East Anglia were judged too unreliable to take on the rebels, and the decisive factor in their defeat was the mercenary forces of Germans and Italians who had been brought in, some two years earlier, to fight in the Scots wars.

In the event, the prevailing loyalty of the militia forces turned on three factors: the officering of the levies, the persistence of noble retinues and followings until late in the seventeenth century, and, exceptionally, in 1549, the use of foreign mercenaries. As to the first factor, Boynton shows (Boynton 1967) that Elizabeth took the greatest care to choose the captains of the militia bands from among the substantial, the Protestant, and the well-effected families of the countryside. Efficiency was set lower than these political virtues, so

that the training of the bands was put in the hands of paid and professional muster-masters, standing in the same relationship to the
young captains as a regimental sergeant major might to a green second lieutenant. The Pilgrimage of Grace of 1536 was so dangerous
because so many local gentry permitted themselves to be "pressed"
into leading the rebels. From the beginning of the period in 1485
right through to the civil wars, it should be taken as read that the
arraying or mustering or reviewing or leading the militia was in the
hands of the noblemen and gentry; and as the civil wars were to
show, there was a long and compulsive tradition that the commoners
followed where "the gentlemen" of the shire decided. The loyalty of
the militia turns out to be, for the most part, the loyalty of the noblemen and gentry. This is why the political and religious alienation of
some half of these persons from the court of Charles I destroyed the
only land forces, albeit decrepit ones, in his possession, and made
the outcome of the Great Rebellion a contingent thing instead of a
military walkover.

Nor was the military potential of the magnates and gentry limited
to their officership of the militia. Until the "pacification" of the magnates at the beginning of the seventeenth century (of which more
later), one of the most impressive, and perhaps the only truly effective component of the royal forces continued to be the private retinues and followings of the magnates. Henry VII had acted firmly
against these private armies, and his successors followed his policy
of strictly licensing and controlling them; but they proved indispensable for conducting foreign expeditions and repressing internal disorders. When Henry VII prepared to meet Simnel before the battle
of Stoke (1487), he certainly "ordered musters" of the shire-levies
in the Southeast and Northwest; but, so Francis Bacon informs us,
he was reinforced by "the Earl of Shrewsbury and Lord Strange, of
the nobility, and of knights and gentlemen to the number of at least
threescore and ten persons, with their companies; making in the
whole, at least six thousand fighting men" (Spedding 1963: 57). In
1549, says Bruce Wernham (Wernham 1966: 189), "it was the gentlemen and nobles with their retinues, and foreign mercenaries, who
had to crush the rebellion." In the invasion year of 1588, the army,
especially intended for the defense of the queen's person with a
paper strength of some 45,000 men, drew over one-third of that
number from the private retainers of the nobility, the court officials,
and the prelates (Boynton 1967).

[119]

The third element mentioned was the foreign mercenaries. Henry VII had gathered some three to four thousand Germans and Italians for service in the Scottish campaign at the end of his reign and, in 1549, providentially for the government of Edward VI, some three thousand of them were in camp at Hounslow. It was detachments of this force that proved decisive in defeating the Western Rising, and the rebellion of Kett in East Anglia.

Tudor and early Stuart England was still a hierarchical society where the concept of "degree" commanded widespread acceptance; the commoners looked to the gentlemen and the nobility as their natural leaders (cf. Tillyard 1962: 10–20, on "The Elizabethan World Order," and his references to contemporary sources such as the *Book of Homilies*, and Higden's *Polychronicon*). Furthermore, there continued to persist, through the civil wars and into the eighteenth century a quasi-feudal link between landlord and tenant. The tenant expected to ride with his lord; indeed, up to the middle of the eighteenth century, on the Border, this was often inscribed into the lease as one of the tenant's obligations.

Thus the nobility and gentry with their companies afforced the militia as well as commanded it. That these conditions did not perpetuate the chronic disorders of the Wars of the Roses was due to a consistent and cumulative royal policy of strict license and control, their progressive disarmament of the private stores of weapons, and of an all but total restriction on private fortification. It was due too, to the mutual destruction of the greatest of the magnate families during the Wars of the Roses; to the progressive reduction in the size of individual estates; and to a very rapid decline in the nobles' experience of taste for warfare which set in at the end of Elizabeth's reign and during the first forty years of the seventeenth century. Lawrence Stone has shown that in 1559, out of sixty-two families, eighteen possessed over seventy manors apiece; but that in 1641, out of one hundred twenty-one families, only six did so. Again he states that in the 1540s, three-quarters of the Peers had participated in battle; in 1576 only one-quarter; in the early seventeenth century a mere one-fifth; and by the time of the civil wars, even less (Stone 1967: 96–134). In France the situation during this period was far different as will be seen. The king's command over the contingents of his regular standing forces was, indeed, as in England, in the hands of the local nobility and the gentry; and as in England the magnates could and did call out their tenants to ride with them. But these were a very different kind of nobleman from the English, in two major respects. First, they had been engaged in warfare almost constantly from the first invasion of Italy in 1494. Second, there remained magnates on a medieval scale, for example, Montmorency who in 1559 owned over six hundred manors.

The Tudor monarch then was limited, limited by the disposition of the militiamen to follow their officers (the magnates and the gentry) in an unpopular cause, but limited again, and more strictly, by the disposition of these magnates and gentry to follow or not follow the royal policy. The magnates and gentry were a tax-paying class. Also, they were the unpaid agents of the crown in everything that was going on in the administration of the shires. And they had a focus in Parliament and in the Quarter Sessions. These strategic positions—over the armed forces, over local administration, and over the tax granting authority, i.e., Parliament—all reinforced each other; and they checked the disposition of any monarch to replace their services by paid soldiers and paid administrators, because they were in a position to deny him the finance required to do so.

When this same militia format was carried over to the early Stuarts, the nature of this limiting power became more obvious. If Charles I did not care to believe that his sovereignty was limited, events taught him otherwise. With a standing army the result could have been very different. This is shown by the very opposite experience of the Protectorate. When, with fifteen hundred men at the back, each major general could rule his portion of the Commonwealth, taxation was *five* times greater than it had been under Charles. If a citizen did not care to pay, then a Colonel and a troop of horses could and did make him. The standing army completed the extraction-coercion cycle, and it buttressed the new style-of-rule absolutism. The interlude ended after the death of Cromwell; and the crisis that led to the fall of the experiment was typically enough provoked by a tax strike of the City of London. A situation which in 1638–1642 had led to defection from the king now led to the opposite result: defection from the Protectorate.

With the Restoration occurred another radical transformation in the military format: the germ of the regular standing army of native paid volunteers. The militia was indeed retained but with significant modifications in its officers corps. Under Charles II the regular army was at first a mere 4,500 men. But James II raised it to some 30,000. A force of this size was ample to suppress uprisings as it did Monmouth's Rebellion. It was expensive, but the sharply increased yield from the customs, which had been voted to James for his reign, saw to the expense. It was also far more efficient than a militia. But how politically reliable was it? It is a common assumption that standing armies are not just a necessary, but a sufficient prop for absolute rule. Yet the defection of Charles I's standing *navy* to the Parliament casts doubts on this, so does the defection of General Monck; and so, certainly does James II's experience. It is here that the belief-cycle enters the calculus. Had James II been a loyal Protestant, he might have gone far to realize his pretensions to absolutism, at least to asserting much greater power for the crown. But when his Twelfth Foot openly refused to accept his Declaration of Indulgence, when troops cheered the acquittal of the Seven Bishops, these were indications that a standing army itself may well have limits of loyalty, equally with a civic militia. The principal commanders went over to a Dutchman (and Holland was not popular with Englishmen) and to his mercenary troops. This was far more than the shire-levies had done when they supported Henry VII against Germans and Irishmen at the Battle of Stoke. In 1688 the commanders of the regular force threw its corporate future as well as that of the monarchy itself into the hands of a Parliament dominated by the greater and the lesser landed families.

Therein lies the key to what, with some reversals and vicissitudes, became the Settlement of 1688 and of 1714.

With the wars against Louis XIV the British military effort took on unprecedented dimensions. Extraction occurred on a vast scale. At one point the British army reached 75,000 men, while the navy had some 200 ships. For this, great sums were necessary. Whereas, before 1688, annual revenue had run at some two million pounds, it amounted to seventy-two million pounds between 1689 and 1702, and to ninety-nine million pounds between 1702 and 1711. Of this 40 percent went to the army and 35 percent to the navy. Part of this sum was met by greatly increased taxation. Between 1688 and 1697 revenue doubled, and it doubled again between then and 1714. Even this did not suffice and the deficit was met by public loans. In the Spanish Succession War thirty-five million pounds was borrowed to cover the gap. The technique of the money market had been mastered, and with the assistance of the recently founded Bank of England, government annuities and other interest-bearing stocks were issued on a considerable scale. Furthermore, these public loans were guaranteed by Parliament, a move that at one and the same time, stabilized public credit, attached the lenders to the 1688 Settlement, and thus stabilized the political situation.

This attests a certain reconciliation to the new fact in national development: a standing army. That this was so is explicable only within the framework of the political settlements. First, Parliament had not only achieved supremacy but the initiative. It could, as Blackstone was to attest, "regulate the succession to the Throne," and by doing it made William III and George I dependent on Parliament for their very titles. The monarch did indeed command the armed forces, as is still true to this day, but his ability to use this as an instrument of personal despotism was limited in four major ways.

In the first place, any such attempt on their part could have brought them into collision with the law courts, since the Bill of Rights declared that the maintenance of a standing army in peacetime without the assent of Parliament was illegal, while the Mutiny Acts, which alone permitted military offenses against discipline to be tried by courts martial, was passed for six monthly or annual intervals.

Second, the attempt would have brought them into collision with Parliament. For the vast sums required to maintain the land and sea forces were specifically appropriated for these uses by Parliament.

Third, the attempt could hardly have found any social support: the settlement confirmed the greater landlords in the possession of Parliament and the squires of the administration of the counties. Whig landlords and their associates in the Bank of England and the mercantile classes favored land as well as sea warfare; many squires and "country party" favored the traditional sea policy only. So many Tory gentlemen hated the standing army, feared it, and seized every opportunity to try to disband it and rely on the fleet and the militia. Now commissions were purchased, and the officers came, for the most part from the younger sons of Whiggishly inclined families. These, affiliated by kinship or class ties with Peers and MP's, were hardly likely to assist the crown to overturn the very settlement of which they were the chief beneficiaries, while the "country party" who detested the standing army, had little influence inside it, and was even less likely to wish to use it to reintroduce despotism. In short the *stratification* cycle now played a decisive part in ensuring the political reliability of the standing army. For it was officered and commanded by an extension of the very same families who controlled Parliament. It was this aristocratic complexion of both which provided the social checks and balances which gave reality to the legal enactments governing the status of the armed forces.

Fourth and finally, the militia had been reestablished in 1660. Two conceptions of its role began to emerge: the militia as the "people in arms," as a counterbalance to the small regular forces; and a select and well-trained militia, to serve as an auxiliary to these regular forces. The first conception, the militia as the people at large, prevailed at first. Used for internal repression against the surviving republicans and against the sectaries, the revived militia rapidly degenerated after about 1670, and was all but ineffectual as a fighting force. But, insofar as it was an armed force at all, it was controlled by officers, from the lords lieutenant downward, who were magnates or gentlemen, i.e., the men of property in the shires. The militia was remodeled in 1757, in the face of yet another invasion scare; this time according to the second conception, of a trained and select auxiliary force. Significantly, this act laid down an explicit set of property qualifications for the officers. A colonel had to possess an income from real estate of at least 400 pounds per annum, a lieutenant colonel and major an income from the same source of 300 pounds, a captain 200 pounds, a lieutenant 100 pounds, and an ensign 50 pounds. This reproduced the social hierarchy of the country landowners. The militia was neither a popular force, nor a royalist one. Militarily it was not very efficient. Costwise it was cheap. Its political loyalty went to the parliamentary settlement.

Thus, this complex combination of arms and format—a powerful standing navy, a tiny peacetime regular army only reluctantly expanded for expeditions to Europe and the colonies, and an aristocratically controlled militia—was linked *via* the social stratification cycle to the political arrangements, i.e., to the style-of-rule. This was rule by the "Venetian Oligarchy" with an aristocratized monarchy; and this itself, reflecting as it did the real sources of wealth in society, was linked to the condition of the economy; and this in turn was linked to the extraction cycle, which, in these circumstances was therefore able to pour out the great sums required for eighteenth-century warfare.

State and Format in France to 1715

The way and the sequence in which the territorial entity we now know as France was created was such that there would be deep

durable separatism in its component parts. Second, the early petri-
fication of nobility into a privileged stratum, without counterpart in
England, created a different relationship between the king and his
nobles. Consequent upon these two factors, vast territorial entities
persisted under the control of local grandee families who assumed,
albeit in the king's name, influence or control over his civil and,
above all, his military servants. In France a specialized civil bureaucracy developed to such a degree that by the time of Charles I
in England, who had some two thousand officers, there were four
thousand in the Province of Normandy alone. For 1562 (some half
a century anterior to this), a conservative estimate puts the number
of officials in France as a whole at over 43,000. Since then the creation of new posts had proceeded with increasing rapidity. (Certainly, if one compared senior ranks of *central* bureaucracies there was
not a wide discrepancy: the vast expansion in France took place in
local servants of the king—all but unknown in England.)

Furthermore France had the first corps of a regular standing
army as early as 1445. Its effects were to help expand the territorial
frontier to something like its present dimensions by the first decades
of the eighteenth century, to create an enormous fiscal burden, unequally shared but which, by the expedient of the venality of offices
contributed a vast pseudobureaucratization. These two factors, combined with the privileged status of the nobility, placed obstacles in
the path of turning the Estates-General into a body similar to the
English Parliament. Most importantly, until the reign of Louis XIV,
the military establishment of France, irrespective of its format—
feudal, semifeudal, semiprivate, or the regular standing army—not
only never excluded the disaggregation of the France created in preceding centuries, but at times positively assisted this process.

First, while England in 975 was a unified kingdom, whose permanent frontiers were still unfixed only in the far north, France was a
number of autonomous counties and duchies, of vast size and
strength, like Normandy, Brittany, Burgundy, Gascony, Aqui-
taine, and the like, owing only a nominal subordination to the
suzerain, the king of France, who effectively controlled through his
own royal officers, only a small strip of demesne around Paris. While
the Danish kings, then the English line, and finally the Norman kings
were gradually effacing the political and administrative particularism of the old heptarchy on French territory, as fast as the Capetian
kings extended their personal sway through their own officers in the

county of Francia, equally so did the counts and dukes in the peripheral counties and duchies. There was a race toward centralization. So by the time when the kings were powerful enough, from the end of the twelfth through the early fourteenth centuries, to impose a real suzerainty over their nominal vassals, they could at best *superimpose* their control over a number of political entities whose institutions were well entrenched. In short, they could aggregate a kingdom of the Franks rather than homogenize a "France." By the end of the reign of Philippe le Bel, on the eve of the Hundred Years War, some two thirds of the territory of present-day France had been brought together in this way.

Second, by this date, after the process commencing in the middle of the twelfth century, it was feudal law that unless the King willed otherwise, only those whose father or grandfather in the male line had been knights could themselves become knights; that the privileges of *noblesse* attached to all the progeny of a noble family not just to the eldest son as in England.

If one adds to the particularism of the French kingdom these privileges of the hereditary caste of the nobility, one has the key to the role of the military in state-building. The process that the school history books talk of as "centralizing" resided essentially in the king having his services rendered him in the localities by his own officers, not *via* the intermediation of the local grandees. In practice, up to the personal rule of Louis XIV, the grandees managed after a lapse of time to acquire or at least to control these "royal" offices. The *baillies* and *seneschaux*, appointed by Philippe Auguste as his personal representatives, had suffered such a fate by the middle of the fourteenth century. Thenceforward, they were, from time to time, superseded by extraordinary lieutenants general. It was they who took over the collection of taxes, and the mustering and disposition of the royal forces. But these, we find, were invariably great magnates, very often princes of blood. By the sixteenth century these, now styled governors, were a permanent institution. Francis I tried to curtail their powers and confine the office only to the militarily threatened border provinces, but in vain. In the Wars of Religion both sides appointed their own local governors in the places they occupied. Richelieu, when he took office in 1536, described all the governors as "great lords." He involved himself in local financial activities by sending out his own royal commissioners, the origins of the *intendants* developed by Mazarin and then by Louis XIV. Only then, at the office of *intendant*, does this progressive relapse of royal offices into the maw of the local magnate come to a stop; and only then does the process of centralization become continuous and cumulative.

Thus in the sixteenth and early seventeenth centuries, in each of the historic provinces, a governor, nominally a king's officer, but in practice a great noble, like the Condés and the Guise, these and their lessers, held the governorships and with them a certain control over local finance and the disposition of the troops. Not only that. The great historic controlling officers of the armed forces, the constable, the admirals, the marshals, were nearly always drawn from one of these great families also. And below them, the field officers were all noble, admittedly many from poor country gentry, but noble nonetheless. In the sixteenth century only about one in ten was a commoner.

Now after the Hundred Years War, while the British military effort went into decline, the French effort greatly increased and was to do so continuously until the Battle of Waterloo. One reason was the extraction-coercion cycle in France. For a number of reasons the Estates-General had failed to make good a claim like the English Parliament's, to control taxation; in the closing years of the Hundred Years War money had been raised, for instance by the Constable de Richemont, by military execution, and folk had got used to this; the Estates had in 1439 voted Charles VII the *taille*, and he acted as though this was for his entire reign; the Estates of Charles VIII had in 1484 given him enough to go on his Italian campaign but he too continued to raise it on his own authority; in any case, it was the numerous local assemblies and Estates who were responsible for agreeing to pay taxes and decide the amount and these undercut the power and prestige of the Estates-General; in sum there was no central constitutional organ of opposition to taxation by *fiat* similar to England's and consequently money for the wars could be found more easily in France than across the Channel. If the taxpayer resisted, the troops would make short work of that.

The *stratification cycle* also had its role. The French nobility, owing to the laws of derogation, had usually no other activity, apart from farming, than warfare. They were always at the ready to urge their monarchs on. The kings for their part were vainglorious: hence the Italian wars. Finally, with the sudden rise of Hapsburg power there arose a genuine threat to the French southern, eastern, and northeastern frontiers.

The effects of the royal and noble perception of risk-opportunity was to add a new twist to the extraction-coercion spiral, already severely deepened by Louis XI. And this cycle has an important side effect, on state-building, in that it vastly speeded up functional differentiation, as well as helping to hold or expand the territorial limits.

The fiscal burden has been estimated by Nef, in his *Industry and Government in France and England* (Nef 1940: 126–129) as follows:

Period	France	England
1537–1546	£ 800,000	£ 200,000
1603–1612	3,600,000	275,000
1636–1642	9,000,000	660,000

Since the population of France was four times greater than England's the real burden per capita, after starting equal, had risen to five times the English rate; and if we accept the estimates of Gregory King that the French per capita national income was half that of England, then the extraction of resources in France was *ten times* heavier than that in England.

To raise money kings of France resorted increasingly to the practice of selling offices; then to creating offices in order to sell them; then, by *la Paulette* of 1604, to imposing a tax on the private right to resell or otherwise transmit this office. An office usually brought tax exemption—it proved a source of investment; often too it carried fees or a salary with it; and sometimes it brought ennoblement. So grew up the *noblesse de robe* who staffed the sovereign law courts, among other great organs of the state. The effects of *vénalité* were to expand the bureaucracy far beyond the requirements of French society. Desmarets, Comptroller of Finance to Louis XIV, once brought his master a list of offices which he proposed to create for sale. Louis expressed astonishment at anybody wishing to purchase such absurd offices to which his comptroller replied: "Sire when the King of France creates an office, God immediately creates an idiot to buy it."

The third and very clear effect of the wars was to expand French territory, but for all that and what the legists proclaimed under Francis I, the realm was not homogenized; it was still a patchwork, an aggregate, a mosaic. The latent centrifugal forces broke out after the Peace of Cateau-Cambrésis of 1559, a peace forced on both Valois and Hapsburg by the simultaneous exhaustion of all their ready sources of war finance, and by their bankruptcy. One immediate effect was the restlessness of warlike nobility, Huguenot and Catholic alike, without warlike occupation. The other was the creation of a veritable set of states inside the state as the Calvinist local organizations sprouted upward into provincial federations. France exploded into the Wars of Religion. In these once more are displayed those two historic factors: the rivalry of great houses—in this case, notably, Guise, Bourbon, and Montmorency; and the particularism of the provinces in which they and their *grandes clientèles* held sway—in Lorraine, in Champagne, in Dauphiny, and in Languedoc particularly—of which they were the governors. The royal army—a standing army—split its allegiance just as the English militia was to do, later; thus, the supposed instrument of royal power and centralization, split into factions, each following its local magnates.

But there was, after all, an alternative format available to the king: foreign mercenary troops. Why, it may be asked, did he not opt for this format? The short answer is that the kings or regents did do so; but so did their Huguenot opponents! The war was fought at first by rival sections of the regular army, then by those afforced by volunteer militias; but all the time, each side called in foreign mercenaries to redress a military balance. In brief, up to this point neither the standing army nor the grossly overswollen bureaucracy was an effective instrument of unification.

The events from the death of Henry IV (1610) to the end of *La Fronde* (1653) confirm these hypotheses. In this half century, the interlinkage of the most important of the cycles is prominent and clear. Style-of-rule, together with state-building, is linked, as before, with the persistence of local particularism via the magnates, many of them the Princes of the Blood; this cycle is linked with the beliefs cycle since the legacy of the Wars was the confirmation of the Huguenots in their possession of a hundred towns and strong places, together with their own troops paid for the public Exchequer, and led by the section of Protestant noblemen whose leader was de Rohan. The beliefs cycle thus strengthened already existant particularism. Both it and the state-building cycle continued to link with the stratification cycle—the continuing political and military power of the Houses, of

[129]

Montmorency, Orleans, or Bourbon, or Vendôme, especially. And this was associated with revolt in the name of reduced taxation, i.e., of the extraction cycle, and this again with the military format of the time.

The kernel of the army was the group of *vieux régiments*: permanent troops, dependent on the king. When further troops were raised, this was in the form of the *corps entretenus*: the king commissioning their recruitment by a nobleman and paying their keep (nominally at least), but the magnate appointing the officers, and generally leading "His" regiment.

With the onset of the Thirty Years War, the upkeep of such troops increased steeply. Between 1607 and 1622 the expense of the army increased from four and one half million livres to twenty-two million. Where did the extra taxes come from? Not from direct taxes which hardly rose in this period, nor indirect ones which rose only from five to eight million livres nor from the extraordinary income, mostly *rentes*. The bulk of the new taxes came from forced loans, special taxes on officials' fees, or from the sale of new (and competing) offices. Thus it hit especially hard at the office holders, the people who had bought their offices as an investment. Thus the military format, the extraction, and the stratification cycles all link up. The official classes, led by the Gentlemen of the Robe (who, it will be remembered formed the lawyer class and staffed the great Sovereign Parlements) therefore became very prominent in leading social unrest. This is most obvious in the case of the first, the so-called Parliamentary Fronde. For this was sparked off when Mazarin, anxious to raise money for the Spanish War, demanded the *petit bénéfice du roi*. This was a plan by which officers (the Parlementaires of Paris sagely excepted) were to forego *four years receipt* of their salaries. In fact, the Parlement, took the lead of the officers who were hit by the plan; and their demands on the court are significant. No new offices were to be created (which would have made the bureaucracy a closed hereditary caste); the Parlement must "register" all new taxes; but, also, the new-fangled *intendants*, who were eroding the power of the local finance "officers" were to be abolished.

The people of Paris were induced to throw in their lot with their *Parlement*. Then the princes threw in their lot for or against *Parlement* and for some four years the tragic-comedy of the Fronde convulsed France. A comedy because it was a Feydeau farce version of the parliamentary struggle then taking place in England; and a tragedy in that it signified, in Lavisse's terms *L'inachèvement de la France*. The king, he pointed out, was saved only "by the loyalty of a few unknown officers of the *vieux régiments*." But also, it must be observed, he was saved by the money power of Mazarin who on one occasion succoured the Court at the head of some 6,000 mercenaries from Germany, and on another occasion was able to intercept and buy off the advance of the Duke of Lorraine and his mercenaries while they were on the march to join his enemies.

Lavisse, in the same passage, described how it was that a prince like Condé could enjoy this formidable power; and it provides a fitting commentary and also an epilogue for all that I have said so far, in respect to the marriage between French local particularism and the French *noblesse*.

> The Princes and the magnates were the patrons of clientèles. Condé had his vassals and subjects in his duchies of Enghien, Chateauroux, Montmorency, Albert and Fronsac. He had his own regiments whose loyalty lay solely to him. In September 1651 these regiments lay on the frontier of Picardy, facing the Spaniards but separated from the other forces. On Condé's orders they left their posts and marched up the Loire to fight the king's army. The officers commanding the fortresses of which he was Governor, Dijon, Bellegarde in Burgundy, Clermont, Janetz, and Stenai in Lorraine, Montrond in the Bourbonnais took orders only from him. His authority was great in the Provinces which he governed in the name of the King. Furthermore great personages were linked to him by commitments and Governors of Provinces like the Comte d'Aubernon who was a Marshal of France, or Tavannes who was an army commander. These personages formed the *grande clientèle* of the Prince. The petty clientèle was extremely numerous. Condé then had all the means of making war. His quality as Prince of the Blood gave him almost the right to do so. . . .

If 1653 saw the triumph Mazarin and the crown over the princes and the *Parlements*, together with the reinstatement and reinforcement of the *intendants* and the consolidation of royal control, then 1661—the personal rule of Louis XIV—saw the triumph, not just of the crown but of the king: the king in his own person. Louis decided to govern personally and without a first minister, and the secular alternation between royal control and aristocratic reaction swung, irrevocably until the pre-Revolution, against the aristocracy. Under Louis's personal direction all the conditions which had established the situation in the previous centuries were done away with. The pomp of the ancient nobility was exaggerated, but its political and administrative and military functions whittled away; the functions were taken over by those of middling rank personally selected by Louis. The provinces came under his own *intendants*. The army came under his own war minister and later on, himself. In St.-Simon's bitter words, it was the advent of the reign of the *vile bourgeoisie*.

Here the technology cycle and the extraction cycle interlink and react on each, and both interact with the gradual style-of-rule.

The style-of-rule was a reflection of Louis's personal ambitions. They were to become absolute, and to seek *la gloire*. He immediately excluded the Princes of the Blood from their traditional place on the Council, even shutting out his brother, the Dauphin. Instead he relied on his own middle rankers: men like Colbert, Le Tellier (and later his son Louvois) and de Lionne. The magnates were extruded from their provincial commands. In his *Mémoires* he relates how he downgraded the governorships:

What had hitherto made the Governors (of the frontier fortresses) so absolute in their strongholds, was the freedom which had been given them to handle tax funds during the war, (the pretext having been to maintain the security and the good repair of these strongholds) but which in so far as they amounted to enormous sums in the hands of individuals, made them too powerful and too absolute. In addition, they were free to make up their garrisons from troops who were their dependents. I therefore resolved to take from them by stealth, both the former power and the latter. From one day to another I so arranged things that only troops of soldiers who depended on me alone should garrison all the important towns. . . . In this way, something that no-one would ever have dreamed of proposing a few years before was accomplished without any difficulty or fuss—with everybody simply waiting upon my orders and, indeed receiving more legitimate rewards from me for carrying out his duties (*Mémoires de Louis XIV*, ed. Charles Dreyss, 1860: vol. II, 402).

As the office of governor was eroded in this way, so in each fiscal *généralité* (at the end of the century there would be twenty-four), there was now an *intendant* (who would be a gentleman of the robe), as the king's personal representative in the locality who, with a growing staff of police, administrative and financial *subdélégués*, asserted royal authority. And this office of *intendant* was not purchasable; and, furthermore, it was revocable by the king.

At the same time he excluded the magnates from their military control. But this deliberate act was made not only possible but desirable by the new twist in the technological cycle. Louis's wars were frequent and on a larger scale than ever before: the War of Devolution, 1666–1668, the Dutch War, 1672–1678, the Nine Years War, 1688–1697, and the Spanish Succession War, 1702–1713. In the first of these, Louis deployed 70,000 troops; in the last, some 400,000. War was now a protracted matter, not turning on the outcome of one set battle. In winter troops went into quarters where they trained, while recruiting officers scoured the country for replacements. In spring, when forage was available and the roads passable, the campaign resumed. War had become a thing of siege and fortifications, lines of communication and marches of manoeuvre. It now depended critically on equipment, forage, rolling stock, quarters. In sum, it had become based on *logistics*. At the same time the French fought in a number of theaters simultaneously: in Flanders, on the Rhine, in Spain, for instance. Many armies took the field at once and had to be provisioned and also manoeuvred simultaneously. In short, something like what we today think of as a general staff had become an operational necessity. This direction was in fact provided by Le Tellier, then Louvois, together with the king himself.

Now the necessity for such a remote control in itself would have reduced the former independence of commanders in the field. But this tendency was quite in harmony with the personal intentions of the monarch. The result was the "civilianization" of the army. The office of constable was abolished; so was the office of colonel of infantry. The office of marshal was downgraded by increasing the number of marshals from one or two to twelve. While the purchase of colonelcies and captaincies was not abolished, a number of intermediate ranks like lieutenant, captain, major, were created whose commissioning lay solely with the crown. Thus the number of officers directly dependent on him enormously increased, and it is significant that in 1702 Louis should have created no less than 7,000 commissions as rewards for the aristocracy. Finally, the operations in the field were made directly dependent on the orders of the office at Versailles. In vain did first Condé and then Turenne protest against this control in 1673. They were told to obey. In vain did General Belmost, a lesser light, protest; Louis threatened to dismiss him.

And so the army, hitherto the preserve of the grandees of each province, became, like the provinces themselves, the docile servants of the king at Versailles. For the first time the theory of the style-of-rule came to correspond more or less closely with the actuality: absolute monarchy.

This had its effects on the extraction cycle. The wars bled France white in money and also in men. To make up the gaps in the ranks, the king ordained the militia (by ballot) between 1702 and 1713. Naturally, there were anticonscription riots. Likewise for taxation. The war budget of 1683 was 38 million livres. In 1706 it was 100 million and if we include fortification, artillery, and provisions, it was 145 million. Between 1700 and 1706 the cost was 1,100 million livres. Some of this was brought in by public loans. Some came through debasement of the currency. A good deal was made on the creation and sale of new public offices. For all that taxation increased very sharply indeed. Unequally distributed it had always fallen with undue severity on the poor. In these years, poor harvests increased the popular misery. The last years of the reign were plagued by anti-taxation riots. But the situation no longer resembled the one after the death of Henry IV or the days of the Fronde. The *intendants* called in the troops and the troops came. By 1715 *format*, i.e., the (regular standing army), extraction, and style-of-rule (absolutism) —all mutually supported one another. And so with some vicissitudes they were to continue to do so until the crippling expenses of the American war led to another financial crisis. Then the gentlemen of the robe would see fit to exploit the popular grievances. The last aristocratic *fronde* would begin with different consequences. Not just king, but aristocracy and the entire constitutional fabric would totter and dissolve away.

State and Format in Brandenburg-Prussia to 1740

In 1619 there was no *state* of Prussia. There was a clutch of distinct territories—states if one wishes—which had all come, by the

[134]

accident of hereditary descent, under the dominion of George William of the ruling line of the Hohenzollerns. On the lower Rhine, adjacent to Holland lay diminutive Clèves. Roman Catholic by faith, its nobles paid taxes, its peasants were freemen. It was dominated by its powerful Estates. So too was the very different Duchy of Prussia far to the east on the borders of Poland to whom its Duke, George William, owed fealty. This area was a once Slav land, conquered by the German Teutonic Order of Knights in the fourteenth century. They held down the native Slavs, while introducing German peasants from the west to colonize the land. The order had been dissolved when its last grand master turned Protestant in 1525, becoming, with the king of Poland's collusion, the duke of Prussia. Apart from Königsberg, Prussia was a poor agricultural economy, where monetization had still not made great strides. Power resided in the hands of the Estates, dominated by the nobles, who, for their part, could always play off the demands of the duke by turning for aid to his suzerain, the king of Poland. The central territory was Brandenburg, a mark originally set up to guard Charlemagne's eastern frontier against the Slavs, and which, like Prussia, had been colonized by Germans from further west. This too was poor agricultural territory, dominated by the nobles in the Estates which, like those of Prussia had by now succeeded in exercising control over all extraordinary taxation (i.e., taxation proper, other than the proceeds from the ruler's own domains which were, however, extensive), over foreign policy, and even over the raising and administration of troops.

In the Thirty Years War, Brandenburg was occupied by Swedish troops who levied taxes without the sanction of the Estates, thereby habituating the peasant population to military exaction. Its only troops were some ten thousand ruffian and inefficient mercenaries who seem to have been more a menace to the native populations than to the enemy. But with peace restored and the territories (apart from Pomerania) back in his possession a new Elector, Frederick William, who had succeeded in 1640, having decided that these territories formed an indissoluble patrimony and that the resources of the one ought to be put to the assistance of the others, tried to get the Estates of Brandenburg to grant him money to raise more mercenaries than the mere 1,300 which he had at the time of the peace. From this starting point we see emerge a state—i.e., a consolidated territory, ruled firmly by a common superior, via a specialized bureaucracy.

By 1740 apart from relatively minor peculiarities in the Rhenish provinces, the territories had a common administrative structure, a population of some 3,000,000, and an army of 80,000; the ruler, now a king, was absolute, with a bureaucracy that was the most numerous per head of population in Europe. At the center of this evolution lay the extraction-coercion cycle. A set of officials, to control the logistics of the expanding army on the one side, and to extract revenue for it on the other, commingled to form a dense, hard-working excessively regulated and regulatory bureaucracy; and this formed the spinal column of a *state*. It must be noted too, however, that the stratification cycle also played an important part; it determined the format of the army, and gave a distinctive stamp to the Prussian form of absolutism.

Frederick William, the Great Elector, convened the Estates of Brandenburg in 1650, in the hope that they would provide him with additional taxes, so as to raise the number of his troops which at that time were barely requisite for garrison duty. Now the standard tax was the *contribution*, a land tax. In the towns, however, it was a gross tax fixed at a traditional rate, while in the rural countryside it was apportioned among themselves by the local nobles in each *Kreis*, who appointed one of their number as *Kreisdirektor*. The nobles themselves paid no tax; it was their peasants who paid. The Elector desired to replace this system by a general excise such as the Dutch were using. The nobility refused. Such a tax, they argued, would bear on them equally with the commoners. Finally, they agreed to grant the Elector half a million thalers over the next six years in return for the most far-reaching social concessions. The excise plan was to be abandoned forever. In addition, the noblemen's lands were protected from falling into nonnoble hands except in very special circumstances. Most important of all, the onus of proof as to whether a peasant were free or servile was now shifted to the peasant. In practice this meant the widespread extension and consolidation of the institution of serfdom throughout Brandenburg. This ratification of the division of the population into (apart from the as yet unimportant towns) lord and serf, noble and commoner was to have the most far-reaching consequences for the future polity and to set a distinctive stamp upon the military format until the defeat at Jena in 1806, and in many respects well into the third quarter of the nine-teenth century.

This solution is known as the Recess of 1653. With the new taxes, the Elector raised the number of his soldiers—all mercenaries—to 4,000. But in 1655 war broke out between Brandenburg's powerful neighbors, Sweden and Poland; and in this the Elector decided to play a part. He requested more money. He was refused. Why for ex-ample, should the Estates of Brandenburg or of Clèves pay for the ambitions of their prince in respect of his Duchy of Prussia? The Elector resorted to collecting the taxes willy-nilly by military execu-tion. The peasants tried to resist; the troops enforced payment. Many peasants emigrated. But in two years alone Frederick William already had raised the half million thalers which the Estates had granted him for the period of an entire six years; and the extrac-tion continued in proportion while the number of troops increased throughout the war period to the peace, in 1660, by which time, from a war strength of 22,000, they remained on a permanent stand-ing basis of 10,000.

In 1666 the Elector convened the Estates and once again tried to introduce the general excise. Again the nobles refused. Frederick William now sanctioned the continuation of the land tax in the rural areas while permitting such towns as desired it to use the excise. In order to assist in the adjudication of the disputes in which this tax frequently involved the town councils, the Elector appointed officials known as *Steuerräte*. The "permissive" excise did not prove very sat-isfactory. In 1680 the Elector made it compulsory in the towns, while retaining the land tax in the country; thus permanently sanctioning the division of the tax system into the town and rural system; excise on the one hand and *Kontribution* on the other. The former being administered by the Elector's own paid officials, the *Steuerräte*, the latter by the nobles and their *Kreisdirektor*, who was nominated by his fellows but appointed by the Elector as his local representative and agent.

An excise is an interfering kind of tax: it requires location and control of the flows of merchandise, their prices, weights, and the like. In a very poor country with a ruler determined to husband his most minute resources, the supervision of the *Steuerräte* soon ex-tended into the minutiae of municipal life. Within a few decades the locally appointed mayors and elected councils had disappeared and municipal affairs lay solely in the hands of the *Steuerräte*: important officers, controlling some ten or twelve towns, and with a numerous petty bureaucracy working under them. The Decree of 1689 specified their duties. They included the control of food prices, weights and measures, house-building, fire precautions, the regulation of streets and rivers, the opening of markets, as well as a large number of functions designed to promote and expand the trade on which the yield of the tax was based.

Not only did the introduction of the excise erode and then destroy municipal self-government, it led to the euthanasia of the Estates. For, this tax being indefinitely expansible, the Elector no longer needed to call the Estates together for further increases in taxation. With the new revenue, the bureaucracy, the standing army, the eclipse of the Estates and the extinction of local self-government, the Elector found himself absolute!

But this was merely in the Mark of Brandenburg. The Elector had wanted the same excise system elsewhere. The Estates of Cleves objected to further taxation. The Elector's troops overawed them. Thereafter, in return for a generous recognition of their privileges, these Estates began the practice of making handsome revenue grants. The result was the persistence of their Estates as a working body well into the eighteenth century. Not so in the Duchy of Prussia. There a constitutional quarrel supervened on the Elector's demands for more money and the introduction of the excise. As a result of his alliance with the King of Poland in the 1655–1660 war, the Duke was now recognized by the King of Poland as sovereign. This undercut the position of the pro-Polish faction in Prussia who had hitherto relied on the Polish King to support them against their Duke. They demanded that their assent be purchased at the price of very considerable concessions. Finally, in exasperation, the Elector quartered some 2,000 troops in Prussia in 1663. He got his money, after confirming the privileges of the Estates and promising to reconvene them in six years time. In 1669 the pro-Polish resistance broke out afresh. This time the Elector sought out the heads of the faction. Its leader was hunted down, brought to Brandenburg, and finally, executed. With this the resistance of the Prussian Diet ended. Its strength had been further undermined by the Elector fixing the excise as the local tax for Königsberg, while leaving the rural nobility with their tax exempt status under the traditional land tax arrangement in the countryside. This split the material interests of the

Estates into those of townsfolk and nobility. After 1715 the Prussian Estates met only for ceremonial occasions.

So, by the 1670s, there were three sets of local officers collecting revenue. First, the *Kreisdirektor* for the land tax. Next, the *Steuerräte* for the excise in the towns; third, the *Amtskammers*, working upward to the central *Hofkammer*, and responsible for farming and managing the prince's extensive estates, which alone provided about half the total revenue.

It is necessary to stress yet again: the extensive tax-gathering machinery had been devised and expanded solely in order to expand and maintain a permanent force of troops. But the troops had other military and administrative needs as well. Here *format* interlinks with the extraction-coercion cycle in the following way.

The troops were paid volunteers, some native and some foreign. In the Thirty Years War the Electors had followed the prevalent continental pattern: they commissioned colonels to raise, equip, appoint officers to, and supply a fighting force for their services. The arrangement was governed by a contract, *Kapitulation*. This was supervised by an official, the *Kriegskommissar*, who checked the arrangements and fulfillment of the contract, and administered the oath of allegiance. Between the Recess of 1653 and the end of the Great Elector's reign in 1688, the number of permanently retained troops rose from 4,000 to 30,000. With this degree of permanency, the office of *Kriegskommissar* became permanent also, and similar degrees of permanency began to attach to other parts of the arrangements for the troops. The Elector drew the contracts in vaguer ways allowing him more scope for interference in the colonels' arrangements; he took up the right to veto the appointments of the junior officers; and his *Kriegskommissar*—a local one in the districts supervised by the *Oberkriegskommissar* of each province—took over the logistical functions: forage, billets, transportation, and supplies. In a non-monetized economy, such services bulked large. Thus the office of war commissar began to interfere very widely with the social and economic life of the district. The War of 1655–1660 brought a temporary expansion of such interference; a field marshal was appointed to command the troops in *all* the territories of the Elector; and a supreme council was established to control and coordinate the work of the provincial *Oberkriegskommissars*. This council was the *General War Commissariat*. Its functions and staff were reduced in the peace after 1660, but when war broke out again in 1679, both

[139]

expanded fast and far. Thus had arisen a military-administrative command, with the General War Commissariat at Berlin, working down to the provincial war commissars, and these again to the local ones; and these were very often the local *Kreisdirektors*. Elsewhere, in the towns, they worked down to the *Steuerräte*. In this way the revenue-bureaucracy and the military bureaucracy was fused at the local and the provincial level, and as this occurred, so they were fused at the central level. The General War Commissariat became the administrative organ of *general* administration and control responsible not only for the supply of the army, and the strategic direction of the army, but also for revenue (apart from the Elector's own domains) and for administration *generally*.

In 1640 the total revnue had been one million thalers, half of it from the Elector's own estates. In 1688 it was 3.3 mills, some half coming from his estates. Of this total, it is estimated that between one half and five-sevenths went to service the army. The per capita taxation of this impoverished country was twice that of contemporary France, itself heavily taxed by comparison with England. Observe: in England, 1640 had seen the Parliament assert itself against its king and in 1688, the Glorious Revolution put the seal upon its triumph. In Brandenburg-Prussia in 1640 the noble-dominated Estates had ruled the roost, and the powers of the Elector, had reached their nadir. But in 1688 this same Elector saw his Estates broken, as in Clèves, or extinguished, as in Brandenburg and Prussia; he had a permanent force of 30,000 men; to pay for it and extract services in kind, he had an elaborate paid body of officials, controlled by his General War Commissariat working down to Provincial War Commissariats, which in their own turn worked down to the nobles who provided the service and logistical supports in the countryside, and to the *Steuerräte* who in the towns had by now taken over control of the entire taxation, administration, and economic life. In short, the Elector was absolute and this result had been brought about by the linkage of format, extraction, and state-building culminating in a style-of-rule utterly antipodal to the English monarchy of William III.

Frederick William's successor, Frederick III, had no taste for things military, and there was a pause in this cyclical progression. It is to be noted, however, that from this time the Electors exchanged their title for that of King in Prussia. But under his successor, Frederick William I (1713–1740) and later still, under Frederick II, the Great (1740–1786), the cycles were deepened, and the extraction-coercion cycle in particular given a new twist.

It was typical of the pietistic psalm-singing Frederick William I, who had campaigned under Marlborough, that he should describe himself as "Chief of General Staff and Minister of Finance to the King of Prussia." This was the ruler who so doted on his army that he created the Potsdam Grenadier Regiment, every man of which had to be at least six feet tall, and who were recruited or kidnapped for his service from all over Europe. His first act on accession was to pare to bare essentials the court budget in order to spend more on his army; and he altered the table of precedence so that the former court functionaries were replaced by the Field Marshal.

Frederick William also modified the format. He raised the size of the army from 30,000 to 80,000. This created a most serious extraction problem not only in respect to taxes, but also in respect to manpower. Second, he ended the contract system. The *Kapitulationen* disappeared as such. He—or, if one likes, the state—now became responsible for recruitment and for the appointment of the officers. These two changes reacted upon the administrative arrangement that he had inherited.

First, who were to be the officers? Hitherto the native nobility had been averse to serving. Frederick William I made them send their younger sons to his *Kaddettenhaus* (established 1722). If they resisted he sent police to fetch the young men. But at the same time he offered inducements: the alterations in the table of precedence which so greatly enhanced the prestige of the officer, the royal custom of wearing always the ordinary uniform of the rest of the officer and cadet corps without distinctive insignia of rank, and above all the regular employment, and the not inconsiderable rates of pay which were attached to an officer's commission. By the end of his reign, the nobility had not been merely won over; they had become enthusiasts for the King and nine tenths of the officers were the sons of nobles; which is the same as saying, they were sons of individuals who acted as *Kreisdirektors* (since 1702 known as the *Landräte*), who organized the logistics and services of the troops in the rural area, who exacted the *Kontribution* from the peasants, and who ran their estates and governed their serfs in a most arbitrary and absolute way (appointing their pastors, and later on, their schoolmasters, exacting feudal services from them, and judging criminal and civil cases in which they were involved with the power to inflict penalties that excluded only the power of life or death). This was to have a vital bearing on the other extraction problem: how to supply the recruits for this almost trebled military force.

Only the scum, or most helpless of Europe's population would voluntarily join an army in those days. The King of Prussia had a thousand recruiting officers scouring not only his own lands, but also those of his neighbors to persuade, to con, or even to kidnap "volunteers." It did not suffice. In Prussia the inherent universal obligation to defend with the native territory, such as had endured in England, and with vicissitudes in France, seems to have fallen into oblivion, but Frederick William's Decree of 1713, implied that it existed. In 1732–1733 another decree made it explicit and established a form of military recruitment that would endure down to the defeat at Jena. It was ordained that the territories would be divided into cantons, each capable of supplying the replacements for a regiment of infantry, or of cavalry as the case might be; five thousand families for the former, twelve hundred for the latter. In each, a regimental recruiting officer was to superintend the supply of recruits. Every male birth was notified to him (he was the son of a nobleman, let us remember again) by the local pastors. The recruiting officer would visit and inspect these young male children when they were ten years old. If passed fit, they would wear a red tie to signify that they were destined for the army. The list of exemptions, however, was such that virtually the entire burden fell upon the peasant, which is to say, upon the serf. In short, the noblemen who were the officers of the army, or whose sons were, provided their own serfs and led them into the field for military service; trained them; and controlled them. Yet the needs of the nobleman's farms must not be neglected either. So, after some two years' induction and training under the control of his noble landlord, the serf was returned to the farm to work for that same noble landlord and provide his serf services for some ten months of the year. Then, when spring came, he would don uniform and be led out by his landlord for the spring manoeuvres. Only in wartime, or during these two months of the year, was the Prussian army at full strength. But by the same token the stratification of the army reflected the stratification of the countryside. This was what had been implicit in the Recess of 1653.

But money also was required. This gave another turn to the extraction-coercion cycle. The General War Commissariat consisted of three divisions: for the army, for taxation, and for general administration. But its local officers were always colliding with those other, royal officers, viz. the ones responsible for enhancing the yield of the king's domains. Their constant bickering, especially in the royal courts at the royal expense, led Frederick William I to a final step: merge the two revenue-raising circuits at both the local and the supreme level. Locally, the Domain Chambers were merged with the *Steuerräte* into the War and Domains Chambers; at the top, the General War Commissariat now took the title of the General-Supreme-Finance-War-and-Domains-Directory. This was broken into four geographical sections; the staff of each met the king personally on its own allocated day of the week. In this way the former War Commissariat had absorbed *all* the administrative jurisdictions in the state!

Not only was this bureaucratic apparatus intensive. It was extensive also. The king transferred it to all the territories—to Prussia, to Pomerania, and, with some modification, to the Rhenish territories. In this way a consolidation of the territories under one common superior occurred, albeit they were geographically separated. They now had common institutions. And finally, the king, who personally controlled the precise machinery which provided one official for every four hundred and fifty inhabitants, was absolute; but absolute in a way which went far beyond that of his contemporary, Louis XV of France. The special style-of-rule in Prussia in 1740 has been perceptively captured by Seeley, in his great *Life of Stein*. This is how he saw it:

Let us then compare the army of Frederick William 1st with other continental armies. It was nearly equal to that of Austria which had a population perhaps about six times as great. It was half as large as that of France whose population was about nine times as great. But if we wish to estimate correctly the effect which this incredible military force must have had upon the state which maintained it, we must take several other facts into consideration. We shall find that both as increasing the absolute power of the Government and as a burden upon the people, the army of Frederick William was much more formidable than could be inferred from its greater proportionate numbers. For about one third of it consisted of foreign mercenaries, and of the rest the rank and file consisted not in any degree of the educated classes who might be capable of some regard for liberty and some jealousy of arbitrary power, but of agricultural serfs, who even in their own homes lived under a subjection as complete as in the camp. Moreover, overwhelming as is the force which a vast unintelligent standing army gives to a government even at the present day, there are now in every state counteracting influences, some shadow of a Parliament, some pretence at a free press. In Prussia the local Parliaments had almost everywhere passed into insignificance—there was no Mutiny Bill—and in the time of Frederick William the press had no freedom. Nothing counteracted the brute force of this mass of armed slaves, ruled with iron severity and officered by their hereditary masters, the noblesse, who 'had made themselves in turn, as it were, serfs to their King and Commander-in-Chief, for the Articles of War bound the officer to obedience "even against his own honour." If we reflect on all this we shall still recognize that Frederick William when he organized the army, achieved a work no less important politically than in a military sense. He created not only a new Great Power in Europe but also a new form of government. For in resting it so mainly on 'his army and drawing from it such unlimited power he contrived a new variety of monarchy so that the Prussian State from this time does not resemble the model of the France of Louis XV but anticipates modern military bureaucracies, and furnishes a model to Napoleon (Seeley 1968: 172).

The Napoleonic Watershed

With the French Revolution and its Napoleonic aftermath, state-building received a new emphasis while the concept of the nation and of the nation-state became full blown both in the sense of a shared community of purposes, privileges, and benefits, and in the sense of a "peculiar people" exercising its right of self-determination. Certainly, the relationship between rulers and subjects was never quite the same and often significantly different at the close of this episode, from what it had been at its outset, while the notion of national particularity, already quite consciously 'held by the English for many centuries, and to a degree by the French also, now became a political dogma that was self-consciously grasped and philosophically elaborated and embellished.

The principal difficulty in assessing this period is to decide what was due to military format and its exigencies, and what was due to the Revolutionary ideas of nationality and citizenship. But three truths stand out. First, it is indisputable that these ideas inhered in the French Revolutionary armies and were carried by them among the peoples they conquered, setting up either a hostile but popular reaction, nationalistic in its feeling, as in Spain, or the Kingdom of Naples, or in Russia, or for that matter in Britain; or else producing some simulacrum of these ideas as a kind of inoculation with which the better to resist the French armies—as in Prussia after 1806. Second, the effects of the events of this period were markedly different in the three countries with which we are here concerned—France itself, Britain, and Prussia. Third, the effects on state-building of the strictly military aspects of these events were relatively restricted, but their prefigurements for state-and-nation-building for the century ahead were enormous.

Let me somewhat expand this last point—as to the immediate effects on state-building of the military formats. In France, the principal effect is in style-of-rule: first, in that for the first time in Europe, with the extraordinary exception of England, 1645–1660, the military emerges as a corporate factor playing its own autonomous role in deciding the succession; second, in the creation of a new type of absolutism, i.e., the military dictatorship of our contemporary model; and third, an altogether excessive degree of centralization of authority. The remainder—the fraternity of social classes, the career open to the talents, the experiments in price control, and acquisition of the "natural" frontiers of France—all turned out to be highly ephemeral. As to England, the principal effect was not upon the style-of-rule, which not only continued unaltered for a decade and a half after the peace and in that period was actively reinforced, but in one of the twin aspects of state-building, an impulsion to the differentiation of functions the "economical reform," which, adumbrated by Burke in 1780 (as a result, be it noted, of the misadventures of the American War), achieved great impetus during the wars, especially in the administration of the finances. In Prussia the events wrought havoc and dislocation, and led to a partial revolution, but typically from above. The administration was made less Kafkaesque and somewhat more related to popular feelings, the network of military recruitment was thrown far wider, and socially the fabric was a trifle less oligarchical; but these modifications in the Prussian state were partial, and followed a reaction after 1819.

If, on the other hand, we look at the period as a prefigurement of the future in the light of the immediate past century, i.e., of the *Ancien Régime*, then its significance is profound in the extreme, and it amply merits the title of a "watershed." The 1914–1945 period witnessed strictly national armies; war *à outrance* and the total mobilization of the entire resources of a country, i.e., extraction on its most extensive scale and industrialized logistics. On the social and political fronts, it saw the completion of the developments in citizenship, popular participation, and of the notion of equality as the social and political counterparts of these; and also, if not democratic forms of rule, then ones that were "populist" in the sense of at least appearing to do something to cater for the needs of the masses. Finally, turning strictly to the military, it saw the wide spreading of the divergence between loyalty to the format (i.e., the corporate interest of the military) and the loyalty to the regime—the precondition of military intervention or takeover of government.

In all these respects, the contrast with the *Ancien Régime* is very great indeed. That was an age of multinational armies; of limited dynastic wars fought for colonies and provinces; and with logistics that were primitive and cumbersome. It was an age too of increasingly oligarchic rule coupled with the oligarchies' lack of interest in making social provision for the subjects they administered. And it was an age where, as we have stressed, in each of our three countries, the loyalty to the format had been assimilated to loyalty to the regime—an age where the military forces had been rendered docile instruments of the public authorities whether Britain's Parliament, or the kings of France or of Prussia.

Yet few of these features were seriously modified in the period under review. Armies were still multinational; for the Wagram campaign of 1809, Napoleon raised 300,000 men but half were foreigners. In the 700,000 strong *Grande Armée*, only 300,000 were Frenchmen. War, despite appearances, was not fought *à outrance*. Only 40 percent of the eligible male Frenchmen were called up, in Prussia the total mobilized in 1813–1814 was only 6 percent of the total population; and the proportion was far less in England. As to logistics, Napoleon's were notoriously improvised; and they were inadequate except for lightning campaigns. As to the social and political innovations, it is certainly true that the notion and practice of citizen equality had appeared in France, but it was the precondition of the military formats, not the result; in Prussia and Britain it was not even that. Nor, aside from the Jacobin interlude in France were governments yet populist. The one major respect in which this period innovated is that it saw, in France, the divergence between format-loyalty and regime-loyalty and hence the succession of military interventions in politics that culminated in Napoleon's *coup d'état*.

What then were the chief characteristics of this period? First of all, it is an *irruption*: a period of incessant war, war in twenty-four out of its twenty-six years, which saw the aggression of an army belonging to the most populous state of Western Europe, of France, with its 28 million people, which levied war at once *ideological*, resembling the seventeenth but not the eighteenth century; *popular*, in which it was quite novel; and *predatory*, in which, once again, it resembled not the *Ancien Régime*, but the seventeenth-century wars. But these innovations did not outlast 1815. The wars of the nineteenth century were not ideological, popular, or predatory; though perhaps motivated by nationalism, they were limited wars with confined objectives. Let us look at this characterization then, first with respect to the formats, the belief and the stratification cycles in France and their interaction, and then at the format options posed by the successful French format, in Prussia and Britain with respect to the efficiency, the expense, and the political loyalty of the alternatives between which they could make their choice. Finally, in the light of the whole, let us try to assess the effects on state-building.

The French army adopted a new format and fought a new kind of war. This was a conjuncture both of military doctrine and of necessity. Probably necessity had more to do with it than the theories of Guibert, whose *Essai sur la Tactique* of 1770 Napoleon and many of those who fought under him had studied. But it is necessary to quote from Guibert because he so adeptly prefigures, whether by the power of his doctrine or the then situation of the French armies, the kind of war those armies were indeed to fight:

Another truth which we may draw from the study of the wars of Rome a truth of which the results are in every way in contrast with our present systems of supply, is that armies lived in and at the expense of the country. "War must support war," said Cato in the Senate, and this maxim of Cato was among the Romans a maxim of state. As soon as an army had set foot in an enemy's country, it was for the general who commanded it to enable it to subsist and that general had most usefully served the Republic who, while conducting the most glorious campaign, had best supplied his army and at the close of the campaign brought the most money to the public treasury.

It is astonishing how much a good military administration can extract from the resources of a country. I speak of a populous and fertile country such as Flanders and the greater part of Germany. I am not exclusive nor excessive in my opinions, I will not say to an army "have no supply trains, no magazines, no transport; always live on the country; advance if needs be into the deserts of the Ukraine: Providence will feed you." I want an army to have provision wagons but as few as possible, proportionate to its force, to the nature of the country in which it is to operate, and to the means required in ordinary operations. If it starts from a river or frontier let it have on this base magazines and dépôts well situated with a view to their defence and to the plan of operations. But if it is necessary to undertake a bold operation and forced marches the army must be able to discard the precise methods of routine. The enemy I will assume takes an unexpected position in which I cannot and will not attack him; I am sure to dislodge him or to take him in rear if I march towards his flank. According to our actual routine I shall require for this change of direction to form new dépôts and new rayons of communication. I shall be asked for fifteen days to reform these new magazines. What I want to avoid is that my supplies should command me. It is in this case my movement that is the main thing; all other combinations are accessory and I must try to make them subordinate to the movements. The enemy must see me marching when he supposes me fettered by the calculation of my supplies; this new king of war must astonish him, must nowhere leave him time to breathe . . ." (Wilkinson 1915: 78–79).

In addition to his strategic doctrine Guibert had a tactical doctrine also. He had become somewhat disenchanted with the *ordre mince* introduced by the Prussians and everywhere copied. These five-mile-long thin lines of musketeers armed with flintlock and bayonet were difficult to move once disposed upon the battlefield. Instead Guibert canvassed the possibilities of the *ordre épais*, i.e., the column: not strictly a column since it was some three hundred men across and some twenty-eight ranks in depth. Its advantage was its ability to march right up to the point of action and to attack from there. Its disadvantage was that in so doing only the first two ranks could fire, while they stood to bear the entire volley of the long extended line of the *ordre mince* which faced them.

In practice the necessities of the Republic forced the tactics of the column upon the new French armies, while the ardor but also the material poverty of these armies forced their generals into the strategic doctrine of Guibert. Both these tendencies were incorporated by Napoleon into his own distinctive style of making war.

As to tactics, at the outbreak of the Revolution the officer corps numbered nearly 10,000 of whom some two-thirds were noble, the commoners being for the most part in the technical arms and the artillery. Under the pressure of the Revolutionary extremism, more and more of the noble officers fled the country, until only one-third of them remained. This defection of about half of the trained officers generated confusion in the tactics of the regiments of the line which was not immediately made good by the well-meaning ardor but the all too frequent incompetence of the *sous-officiers* and warrant officers promoted to fill their places. In addition, the aggressiveness of the Brissotins, and their manoeuvres which proved only too successful, to push France into a war, led to a situation which called for far more men than in the standing army. At first the need was met by one-year Volunteers. By the end of the first year many had returned home; while the fact that one could volunteer in the Volunteers for only one year's service drained off recruits to the regular army, which was a long-term engagement. In 1793, when the military situation was desperate and the Jacobins came to power to form the Committee of Public Safety, the *levée en masse* was decreed. This was a piece of Revolutionary rhetoric, but it was accompanied by a hard fact; the introduction of selective service, i.e., the conscription ballot. This immediately produced 300,000 men. Still the difficulties of the armies were not overcome; for the Jacobins feared the royalist proclivities of the regiments of the line and refused at first to permit the volunteers or the conscripts to mingle with them; these latter were regarded as the pure milk of the Revolution, which must not be tainted by the supposedly royalist regiments. In 1794, however, the compromise of the *amalgame* was adopted; to each battalion of former regulars two battalions of the conscripts were attached.

This initial confusion and the enormous dilution of the armies allowed no time for that rigorous training and drill which alone made the thin battle line and set-piece manoeuvring possible. Instead, at first, individual warriors of the Republic, more intrepid than the rest, tended to run forward and fire off against the enemy as had the Americans in the American War of Independence. These were, in fact, skirmishers. Behind them, the other infantrymen tended to come forward in a bunch, and from both of these was rapidly systematized the skirmishing order supported by the column, which Guibert had suggested could in certain situations prove advantageous. Two considerations gave initial victories to this new tactic: the ardor of the troops which surprised the crowned heads of Europe and their generals, and the really vast numbers (proportionate to the time) which the French rulers were prepared to throw against them. Hitherto an infantryman, difficult to recruit and long to train, had been regarded as a precious asset not to be squandered. But the French were willing to take vast casualties: and as Napoleon was to tell Metternich in 1805: "I can afford to expend thirty thousand men a month." The Jourdain conscription law of 1789 set the seal on the extraction of military manpower. It permitted the government to conscript by ballot from all fit males between the ages of 20 to 25 with a number of exemptions, e.g., for married men. So it was that Napoleon, by 1813, had been able to call up some 1,300,000 Frenchmen: a huge number in the perspective of the *Ancien Régime*.

Equally did necessity impose upon the Revolutionary armies the Guibertain tactic of striking rapidly and living off the enemy. Supply for these vast armies far outran the logistical base that even France could provide. The currency and, still more, public credit was in a mess. The *assignats*, issued against the confiscated *biens nationaux* were printed in even larger quantity, so that inflation was rampant. Yet the armies had to be supplied. The bankers, such as Ouvrard, were prepared (for high interest rates and even higher risk) to advance money against the future proceeds of taxes and to discount the *assignats*. It did not suffice and the materials which the *fournisseurs* supplied were supplemented by requisitioned guns and transport, and by the Jacobin establishment of armament factories. Even so, the armies could only be kept going by exacting formal tributes or indemnities from the conquered territories and by seizing supplies from their cities and their farms; forage, remounts, food, treasure— and even men in the shape of allied regiments—were extracted from the conquered territories.

So much for the new format. But this was also linked up, not merely with the exigencies of the military situation itself, but also with the belief cycle and the stratification cycle. The ideology of the Revolution was one of social equality, of the career open to the talents, and of nationalism. The result expressed itself in *sansculottisme* and "missionary zeal." Hence the volunteers, the national guardsmen, and—up to the 1813–1814 campaigns when the country began to see that the Empire meant perpetual war—a not altogether unfavorable acceptance of the conscription. It would be unwise to exaggerate the proportion of defaulters and recalcitrants who, up to that time, did not exceed some 3 percent. At the same time the Revolution had for the first time opened up promotion to officership, and inside the officer corps, to merit. The army therefore became a great avenue of social mobility attracting some of the best of France. All this linked up with and assisted the development of the new format.

But in turn, this ideology and this change in social stratification alone made possible the vast extractions of men, of material, and of money which the format demanded. One million three hundred thousand Frenchmen had been conscripted by 1813; and in the 1813–1814 campaigns Napoleon raised another million. As to taxes, the inflation, the "rescriptions," which the bankers accepted and discounted, all created a situation that bore progressively on the poorer classes who possessed no property whose value would float upward with the inflation. Indirect taxation had been so unpopular under the *Ancien Régime* that the Revolutionary governments had done their best to dispense with it. Even Napoleon, hard put to finance the Marengo campaign of 1800 had not dared increase it. But the extraction-coercion cycle had its own logic: where money was indispensable for the upkeep of the army, as it was for the 1805 campaign, then the army itself must guarantee the supply of the money. By 1805 Napoleon felt well enough entrenched to use his power to make people pay indirect taxation. "Do I not," he inquired, "have my gendarmes, my Prefects, and my priests? If any one should revolt, I will have five or six rebels hanged and *everyone else will pay!*" (Lefebvre 1969: 186–187). Far otherwise was it in 1813, when the general feeling was that Napoleon and with him the agent of extraction, the army, were about to be defeated. The population ignored the requisition notices, and did not pay their taxes; and the Prefects, not sure of who their next master was to be, did little or nothing to compel them. In the interim up to that date, extraction at home had been lightened by extractions from the foreigner. This had begun under the Republic. As Lefebvre writes, the Directory permitted the spoliation of Holland, of Switzerland, of Italy. It was the only mode of financing the armies in the field. "The army, and even the state, lived on war; this was the origin of a war party whose incarnation was Napoleon" (Lefebvre 1969: 36).

Napoleon was the Chaka Zulu of Europe. Like his African contemporary, he adopted a novel and startling tactic, and extreme rapidity of movement; he went for annihilating the enemy army, not taking a few hostages; he recruited his defeated enemies into his own forces and his own empire, so that it grew greater and greater as his enemies grew weaker and weaker; like Chaka he appropriated all the enemy "cattle." And as for the Zulu nation, the crunch came when other peoples awakened to the new Zulu tactic and format, and adapted it against the Zulu themselves.

Interestingly, however, this is not what Britain did. Initially, her rulers stuck to the preferred tradition: a huge fleet, a tiny expeditionary force in Europe with the bulk of the fighting done by her paid allies; and for the rest, *forays* into the colonies. But this tradition had to be abandoned under the threat of invasion after 1804. Thenceforward Britain accumulated larger and larger regular volunteer forces. They were paid, and it was by increasingly sharp pay rates that, given the poverty-stricken conditions of the southern agricultural laborers and the periodic bouts of unemployment in the industries of the north, the ranks were filled. The militia continued with its "Home Guard" role, but in time of emergency (e.g., 1806) Parliament was induced to allow some of its contingents to serve with the regulars overseas, as in Spain. The army was built up, and by 1814 it numbered a quarter of a million. The costs were enormous. In 1780–1789 total expenditure was nearly 22 million pounds of which military expenditure was 53 percent. By the decade of 1810–1819, total expenditure had reached 81.3 million pounds of which military expenditure accounted for 58 percent. The national debt which stood at 244 million pounds in the 1780–1790 decade, had reached 844 million pounds in the decade of 1810–1819. But public credit was good, and the industrialization of Britain, proceeding rapidly, was able to make available the basis for the increased extraction.

Despite—or perhaps one should say because of—this format did not significantly alter. England had a huge regular army, but it was still officered by gentlemen many of whom were MPs. It was regimental in make up, hence anarchic and noncorporative. The officers had all purchased their commissions. Brave men, no doubt of it; but most had had no formal education since they left school at 15. It often proved a serious trial for them to draft or to read dispatches. The British army won because its troops, who were the so-called scum of the earth, were stolid infantry, very well drilled in eighteenth-century thin line tactics, and ably commanded by Wellington who made great play with the tactical possibilities of terrain. The result, in 1815, was perhaps a little unfortunate. England was left with an army which admittedly was no threat to the constitution because it was so much part and parcel of the governing order—its aristocratic element in Parliament and the countryside; but at the same time, it was an obsolete army, and its victory merely confirmed British ruling-class complacency which was to last for another three generations.

Quite different was the Prussian experience. There the defeat at Jena was traumatic. A state that had had to act simply as supply magazine and hinterland to an army quartered on it, saw this *raison d'être* pulverized. The state itself lost half its provinces. It had to pay a huge indemnity and ally itself with the enemy that had defeated it.

Yet the population accepted this situation with fatalism. They had always been kept out of things. They were still out of things. It was in these circumstances that Stein, Hardenburg, and Scharnost perceived that unless some of the sense and the realities of citizen participation were introduced into the Prussian order, then the state would disappear, or alternatively that they would be imposed by revolution from below. Against the vacillation of their king and against the inclinations of a large body of the noblemen, they sketched the outlines of a massive regenerative effort from above. To begin with the serfs were emancipated; municipal government was restored; the Provincial War and Domain Chambers were replaced by Provincial Diets. The army was backed up by a force of conscripts. The first *Landwehr* was backed up by a second *Landwehr*, and in the last resort by the entire remaining male population, the *Landsturm*.

[153]

But let us beware. Each one of the reforms was in practice a shadow of what was intended, and a curiously grim parody of the French Revolutionary ideal. True the serfs were emancipated: which merely meant that they could move if they chose. For the rest the noble could still exact services from them (unless the peasant paid a quit rent), the noble's exemption from the land tax survived until 1861, his police authority in his district until 1872, and even his domestic jurisdiction over his own peasants until 1848. The municipal reform did indeed begin a new era; but it was only a start. As for the reformed army, its hard core was still the regular army of volunteers, but supplemented by men of the first reserve. It was not long before this force, whose political loyalty was suspect to the king, came under the effective control of the regular army officers. These were still, in their great proportion, noblemen. When 1848 came, the army, at Berlin, far from being the welcome and popular defense force that the reforms had worked for, had regained its reputation of being the police agent of the Junkers and the court. But in one respect a vital move had been made. The format, hitherto a standing army of paid volunteers, had been significantly shifted toward a conscript army, based not just on volunteers, but on the obligatory services of all the male population. This format endured after 1815, unlike in France, where despite the formal application of the 1789 conscription law, the purchase of exemptions turned the army into something much more like a regular army of paid volunteers. In Prussia this conscript force and its organization were to be elaborated and to form the force which in the decade of the 1860's was to score three successive victories; and with it become the model format for all the states in Europe and indeed the world, with the exceptions of the Anglo-Saxon powers.

Finally, what was the contribution of this great irruption to state-building in the three states? In England, virtually none except the important advances in fiscal and revenue administration. In Prussia the limited administrative forms that we have noted, but together with an altogether perfervid nationalism that was increasingly to dominate the state in the next decade and that in alliance with the new military format was to unite the minor states of Germany under Prussian hegemony. But in France some effects were enduring and notably the increased homogenization of the polity. The historic provinces were simply scrapped. In addition their control was enormously centralized. Two situations accounted for that: the social unrest, almost civil war, that afflicted the country from the outbreak of the Revolution to as late as the end of the campaign of Marengo in 1800; and the effort required to keep the armies in the field. Throughout the period, from the earliest days when decentralization had been vogue, there was a steady encroachment on the new-found liberties of the departments and communes. It so happened that this tendency, which had been somewhat relaxed under the Directory, fitted in with the personal predilection of Napoleon himself. So came about the consummation of what had been a secular tendency since the days of the Carolingians, the homogenization of the territories under standard and uniform laws, and their control by agents directly dependent on the central power. What Louis XIV had partly achieved through suppressing the *gouverneurs* with his *intendants*, Napoleon now achieved by replacing the *intendants* with his prefects. The result has endured to this very day.

One final point must be made. It prefigures the next century and total war. The notion which the French had generated: sacrifice, hence equality of sacrifice since the fatherland was a common patrimony—this notion was destined to drive on. In the end it brought its obvious counterpart. Equality of sacrifice, equality of benefits. In the Swedish expression, "one soldier, one rifle, one vote."

Nationalism and Industrialism: 1815–1945

Between 1815 and 1914, the economy-technology cycle, in conjunction with the beliefs cycle dictated the all but universal adoption —save for the Anglo-Saxon countries—of one specific format: the one evolved by Prussia after 1814. The format options in so far as they concerned the *efficiency* of the land forces were based on the Prussian success in 1870. In so far as *political loyalty* was concerned however, the choice was not so simple. A collision occurred between the logic of the beliefs cycle in the European states—with which was associated a corresponding ideal type-of-rule—and the stratification cycle, whereby in all three states concerned, the officer corps remained the appurtenance of, for the most part, the nobility. In other words the stratification and beliefs of the officer corps became increasingly incongruent with the stratification and beliefs of society at large. Finally, in so far as the format choice involves the consideration of *expense*, this new format eventuated in the need for an *unlimited* degree of extraction. This occurred, but it was made possible not by the exercise of coercion, but by the exercise of *persuasion*, i.e., by the utilization of popular beliefs and the granting of social benefits. It is here that once again, the beliefs cycle is linked in, and its principal effect was to convert the extraction-coercion cycle into an extraction-persuasion cycle.

The consequences are to be found adumbrated in 1914–1918, and pursued to a logical conclusion after that date to the Second World War. They are respectively: the pitting of format loyalty against regime loyalty; the trends in military format, outlined on page 99, up to the opening of the eighteenth century were extrapolated to their ultimate limit; while as for state-building, the twin processes of consolidation of territory and the expansion of bureaucracy were accompanied by a bureaucratization of social beliefs—the logical extension of nation-building—to produce states which we describe as "totalitarian."

The first linkage to be examined in this period is that between the economy cycle, the stratification cycle, and the military formats. As to the first, the economy-technology cycle, three great trends stand out. The first was the great demographic advance in Europe, from a population of some 188 million to some 600 million in the 1960s. Such vast populations were a precondition of the mass armies that came into being at the close of this period.

The second trend was technological. From about midway through the last century, a host of relatively minor inventions in armament succeeded each other. By 1860 the rifled percussion musket had come into use, its rate of fire being some seven rounds a minute, while its range was some eight hundred yards, about ten times that of the old smooth bore. Rifled breech loading artillery, with longer range, greater rate of fire, and much greater accuracy had also been invented. On the sea, the steam-powered armored warship was coming into common use. In a later wave of inventions between 1880 and 1900, the magazine rifle and smokeless powder had further increased both the rate and the accuracy of fire; so, to a far greater extent, had the *mitrailleuse*, invented in 1870 and subsequently perfected into the machine gun that was to become a commonplace after 1914. Langlois invented his quick-firing field gun in 1891: it outranged the rifles and added a new dimension to the artillery arm.

Third, the extensive industrialization of Western Europe had three military consequences. First, transport and communications were transformed. The telegraph was first used to convey commands from a distant headquarters to the field army during the Crimean

War. From 1859 onward the European states planned extensive railway networks so as to deploy vast numbers of troops toward any threatened frontier in a minimum of time. Second, arms could now be manufactured in great quantities, and as fire power increased and manpower also—both of them tendencies just noticed—so, of course did the needs for material. In the First World War, for instance, it has been calculated that the French and British armies together used in one single month more than twice the ammunition used in the entire four years of the Civil War by the Union Armies. Finally, it brought about a new logistical system, the staged-resupply, or *etappen*, system of Prussia. Magazines were brought to depots behind the armies; thence a shuttle service took them to the troops. As the armies advanced the railhead was advanced behind them. This plan did sacrifice mobility, but it gave great power and great range to the armies.

Fourth, the stratification patterns of the armies were markedly diverging from those of society at large. The latter was marked by the expansion of an industrial working class, and of an industrial middle class. To each corresponded the characteristic ideologies of socialism and liberalism, respectively. These were at loggerheads; but both, in their different ways were antithetical to the patrimonial-dynastic-autocratic ideology, to the classes that continued to uphold it, and to the systems embodied by it. On the other hand, the stratification of the army was still, by and large, one that opposed plebeian rank and file to a largely aristocratic officer corps. Admittedly, in Prussia for instance, one-half of the officers were not now of noble origin; but in being selected for commissioning, accepted by the commanding officer of the regiment to which they were assigned, and in their new officers' mess, they were expected to and joyfully did—accept the aristocratic traditions and outlook of that corps. In any case the senior posts were held in their vast majority, by the nobility. In France, while the latter did not hold true, the younger sons of the rural *noblesse* began to turn to the army in much larger numbers after 1870, and this aristocratization accounts for its increasing alienation from the Republic which was to culminate in the Dreyfus affair and later in the *affaire des fiches*. In England, it would not be correct to talk of an aristocratic officer corps; but prefectly so to talk of an "upper class" one.

One other factor is very important: the increasing professionalization of the officer corps throughout the nineteenth century. In principle, at least, the aristocratic perquisites to officers' commissions were abandoned or relaxed, in favor of educational and training standards: Sandhurst and Woolwich, St. Cyr and the Polytechnique, the *Kadettenschulen* of Germany, began to mold a profession; examinations and career led to officers corps which, by 1914, were universally imbued with highly conservative social values together with very strong corporate loyalties. These were brought into the open by the Curragh in Britain, the Dreyfus affair in France, and the Zabern incident in Germany.

In this way a chasm opened between the beliefs, structures, and expectations of wide sectors of society at large, and those of the officer corps, with the support of other, conservative sectors.

Turning now, from the economic-technological cycle, from the stratification and beliefs cycles to the third and linking element in all these, we come to the *format* which at once stimulated and was a consequence of these cycles.

The first issue was whether the armies were to be regular or conscript. This involved the familiar considerations of cost, efficiency, and political loyalty. In Britain cost proved the governing consideration. Huge amounts were spent on the fleet. This was supposed to act as a shield behind which the small volunteer regular army could expand. Conscription was shunned partly because of its oppressive nature, its interference with liberties, but also because it was held to disrupt economic life. Hence the small trained regular army remained the format until 1916. In Prussia, at the outset, when the *Landwehr* was introduced by Boyen, the king and many noblemen objected on the grounds that it was not possible to train a soldier in a mere two years and then send him to reserve, and that the political loyalties of the popular *Landwehr* were highly suspect. So began the process by which the *Landwehr*'s autonomy as originally conceived by Boyen was eroded, and it became the ancillary of the regular forces and particularly of the officer corps. In France until 1870 the army was effectively a regular force of men serving a seven-year spell. Even after the defeat of 1870, Thiers and many others resisted its replacement by a conscript army on the grounds that it would not be possible to train the men to the required pitch of efficiency. Hence the compromise law of 1872 where the contingent was divided into two groups, one of which served a five-year term and the other half for two years. Pressure from the egalitarian forces in French politics at last brought in the 1889 law of universal military service for two years, after which one served in the reserve. (Later, as the German population outstripped the French, the period of service was lengthened to three years.) It must be noted, however, that though the German and French armies could now be described as conscript ones, based on the universal obligation to serve the state, this conscription signally differed from the early experiments in the late seventeenth, in the eighteenth centuries, and during the Revolution and Empire. Napoleon never gave his new conscripts more than eight days drilling. After that they were expected to pick up their soldiering on the way to the battlefield. These new conscript armies insisted on a long and rigorous training of the conscript and constant retraining all the time they were on reserve.

Their size rapidly increased. The wars, up to and including the Franco-Prussian War of 1870, did not produce armies particularly large by Napoleonic standards. For instance, in 1870 some 250,000 Frenchmen faced some 320,000 Prussians. But as conscript armies were later developed, the numbers increased vastly. In 1874 Germany had 1,300,000 men in the field or in reserve and France had 1,750,000. In 1897 the former had 3,400,000 trained effectives and France 3,500,000.

Meanwhile the great increase in fire power, due to the new weaponry, had made the old Napoleonic tactics obsolete. Close order, with the advance of the line ending up with the bayonet charge became suicidal where a field of fire extended to 800 yards. So also did frontal attacks. Henceforth manoeuvre and flank attacks became essential. Instead of the old line formation, skirmishing and column formations became general. As to cavalry attack, the last successful one made against the new rifles was in 1870, and there was only one such in the entire campaign. Meanwhile, as infantrymen had found in the American Civil War, when faced by enemy rapid-rifle fire the thing to do was to dig a hole and get in it or shelter behind some barricade. The breast-work and trench became a standard feature of the new tactics. Meanwhile the quick-firing field gun was beginning to outrange the rifles; this led to the advent of the artillery barrage which could prevent the enemy from even coming up to their own front line! Later the development of the heavy caliber piece and the howitzer made this tactic even more potent. By 1914 artillery of these types had become the key arm on the battlefield: it dominated the infantry. Altogether the defensive had grown stronger and stronger. The oddest phenomenon is that this lesson, evident from the American Civil War, the Franco-Prussian War, and the Russo-Japanese War, was lost sight of at the beginning of the twentieth century. Instead the infantry manuals began once again to lay down the doctrines of the offensive and of the frontal charge, finished off with the bayonet attack. It was in response to these tactical manuals that the first troops were flung into the mutual massacres of the First World War.

With this review of the linkage between the cycles: between the economy-technology cycle, the stratification and belief cycles, and the military formats, it is possible to proceed to examine three consequences. The first is the collision of format loyalty and regime loyalty. The second is the extraction-coercion cycle in the new setting. And the third and final one, the state-building cycle.

We have already sketched out the conditions through which a gap opened between the stratification and ideology of the officer corps and that of the population as a whole. This led to a series of collisions. In Prussia the friction was continual throughout the century. Between 1819 and 1847 a gap opened between the army and the artisans, and also the peasantry who were repressed in the so called Potato War of 1847; in 1848 the army was regarded by the Berliners as a reactionary police force and was forced initially to withdraw from the capital; there followed between 1858 and 1866 the collisions between the army high command and the Diet, resolved by Bismarck in an overriding of the legislature's claim to vote the budget. In the *Kaiserreich* that followed 1870 there was constant bickering and tension between the Kaiser with his military cabinet and the Reichstag over the war credits; and so one could continue through the war dictatorship of Ludendorff and Hindenburg, to the role of the *Reichswehr* in the Weimar Republic which it hated and in 1932 chose to destroy. In France the military came on the streets for the June Days of Cavaignac in 1848 and then put themselves behind Napoleon's *coup d'état* of 1851; under him they played the role of the *grande muette* and then, under the Republic when the regime moved leftward and the officer corps once again became aristocratized, opened the series of collisions, the Dreyfus crisis and the *affaire des fiches*. Even Britain was not entirely immune, though the Curragh of 1913 was a pale reflection of the tensions on the Continent; but enough to show how severely an upperclass cavalry-bred corps of officers could feel about the orders of civilians of a liberal complection.

[160]

The extraction-coercion cycle now took on a remarkable dimension. The mass army format, based on a universal obligation to serve, required either massive coercion or alternatively some form of mass persuasion. It is here that the belief-cycle played a decisive role. For, through the nineteenth century and never more strongly than from the opening of the twentieth century to 1945, the ideologies of nationalism and popular sovereignty worked rapidly. Nationalism reached the pitch of desiring to commit politicide against one's enemy nation-state and fearing it for one's own. Popular sovereignty made unquestioned and unquestionable the legitimacy of majorities and of representatives. Out of the amalgamation of the two sprang the possibility of unlimited extraction. Let the First World War serve as a paradigm. It originated as a war of movement—the great sweep of Von Kluck's armies down and across Paris. Then it bogged down, and defensive power had time to catch up with the attack. After six weeks what began as movement ended with a race to entrench two hostile lines of armies from the Juras to the Channel; and on each side some two million men lay staring at each other, while the artillery now took over the offensive and counteroffensive role out of their hands. Thus arose its second stage: from the war of movement to the war of manpower. If two million men could not break the enemy trenches, then see what even more men could do. From this it moved rapidly into its third phase; since all this, and particularly the new use of the mass artillery barrage, required expenditures of matériel vaster than had ever been envisaged. So from the balance of manpower, the war moved to the balance of matériel. Hence the shell shortage that hit all the belligerents. At Hooge in 1915 the British used 18,000 shells; at First Somme, 1916, 2 million shells; at Arras, 1917, 2 million shells; at Third Ypres, 4,300,000. And the cost of these shells was 22 million pounds, which was the total cost of the home army for 1913.

Even more matériel failed to break the deadlock, and so the war moved into its final phase. It became a ghastly exaggerated travesty of those sieges of the eighteenth century except that now, not cities, but entire states were besieged. Blockage warfare had begun, in order to deny the enemy the use of the natural resources on which his matériel relied. So was initiated unrestricted submarine warfare, the blockade of food and materials, and as soon as aerial warfare permitted it, the destruction of the enemy's civilians, since they provided the manpower that manufactured the matériel for the armies. Hence the apotheosis of extraction: 10 million soldiers dead, 20 million wounded, and some 20 million civilians dead of famine and disease. The total costs were some $338,000 million of which $186,000 million were direct costs. The staggering increase can be seen in the English figures alone. Military expenditure in 1890–1899 was 36.4 million pounds; in 1900–1909 it was no less than 876.1 million pounds, a tenfold increase. Similarly with the national debt. In 1890–1899 it was 598.7 million pounds; in 1900–1909 7.6 million pounds; while in 1910–1919 it reached 7460.4 million pounds!

As a result of this gigantic extractive effort; as a result of its buttressing by a new set of beliefs which made populations actually *anxious* to go to the battlefield and sacrifice their material wealth, as a result of these, the trends in the development of military format reached their completion by 1945. First, the increase in size: from the 6,000 at Hastings to the 3,000,000 French in the battle line of 1918. Next permanency: not only this had been achieved—now the entire male population underwent peacetime training, and then became a permanent reserve. Third, the trend away from universal military service to volunteer service and then back again to universal service had been sharply reinforced, so that now every person in the country, whether in the armed forces or not, was expected to subserve the war effort. Fourth, the move from semiprivate enterprises to state enterprises was now carried to an extreme point. Up to Napoleonic times, the states had just managed to achieve control over recruitment and the appointment of the officers. Only in Prussia had it acquired the handling of logistics. Napoleon's logistics were left to monopolies handed out to various private *fournisseurs*. Now not only were the standard logistical requirements of armies catered for by the army or the state; the state went further: it nationalized the economy, it took technology into its own service, and it even took in *ideology*—in great lie-factories that turned out war-propaganda. *All* was now swallowed up in the extraction-persuasion cycle: not just the entire economy, but the press and the mass media.

Finally, what of the effects on state- and nation-building? The first was the completion of a transition which had admittedly begun in England and France many centuries before, from a simple state-association, the state as a *Gesellschaft* to the state as a community, a community of a nationality, a *Gemeinschaft*. Next the completion of a trend from oligarchic and at best paternalistic control of subjects, to states which, even if they did not freely dispense citizen participation in political matters, liberally dispensed welfare benefits. And, finally, the completion of that twin movement of the consolidation of the populations under a common superior and the differentiation of state functions. Under the exigencies of the new formats and the new warfare, these reached grotesque excesses in the Soviet Union, in Germany, and in Italy. There, with a state ideology created and propagated to justify (ostensibly) the defense of the territory, we see the culmination of these trends; by the myths of either the proletarian revolution, or of brotherhood in the nation, the "national" consciousness of community was pushed to its last fanatical degree. Homogenization of populations could hardly have gone further; not only were the laws and the institutions now standardized, so also were to be the ways of thought and feeling of each private individual! And, second, the bureaucratization was pushed to its outer limits where every enterprise was, if not directed by the state's special employees, at least controlled by them and ready to fall under direct bureaucratic control the moment the military situation should prove this desirable. The developments of the modern state here reached its term, and the result, coupled with a style-of-rule of an absolute kind, was to produce the totalitarian regime. Against this the liberal and less state-controlled society of France collapsed; the English, given a breathing spell, put themselves and their goods at the disposal of a state economy. So was reached the penultimate, if not the ultimate, in the development of the nation and the state.

It had been interwoven, over a period of over nine hundred years, with perpetual and cumulative escalation of the military instrument and the uses—that is to say the wars—to which it had been put.

CHAPTER 3

FINANCIAL POLICY AND ECONOMIC INFRASTRUCTURE OF MODERN STATES AND NATIONS

GABRIEL ARDANT

Introduction

THE BUILDING of the state and that of the nation cannot really be understood if we do not begin by looking into the practical, concrete and technical conditions in which states function today and have functioned in the past. What is true on the level of analysis is also true as far as putting it into action is concerned. Those who have insisted on disregarding this kind of consideration have never succeeded in constructing viable political entities. This preoccupation is perhaps best explained by different approaches all of which lead back to the different mechanisms by which the economic structure has been able to, and is able to, exert influence on the structure of the state or of the nation.

First Approach: Financial Bases of the State. Starting with those functions generally considered as essential, the first approach consists of defense, security, justice, education, etc. . . . When examined closely, each of these functions can help us to understand the basic features of the state.

However, we are naturally led to become interested in the common denominator of all the services which supplies them with that which permits them to function: finances. As Trivulce said to Louis XII who was preparing to invade Milan and who asked the *condottiere* how he thought to assure the success of the undertaking: " 'Most gracious King, three things are necessary: money, more money and still more money'" (Guicciardini 1583, quoted in Ehrenberg 1955: 3).

We could likewise quote the instructions of Charles V to his son Philip: "One has always seen that when he has to buy troops in Germany, it is necessary to be ready to shell out money, given this condition, you cannot miss . . ." (Le Her reproduced in Granvelle 1841–1852: III, 272).

It is possible that certain states may have existed within the limits of a subsistence economy of any economy which gave preference to the utilization of resources in kind[1]—those states which we call modern do not give us this picture.[2] The Soviet state, for example, began to take shape with the return to hard currency and to the levying of taxes; even now we can conclude that the economic reforms of Eastern Europe are linked to the wise utilization of the fiscal system.

Finance means money, taxes, budget, credit, a system of banking, machinery for the activating of capital, etc. But, during the centuries prior to the nineteenth century, when the handling of money was especially difficult, taxes constituted the basic resource of the states.

Setting up taxes and collecting them may seem to be secondary considerations of interest only to the specialists. Writers of political science often have the impression that fiscal problems are worth paying attention to only to the degree that they can be explained in terms of the distribution of public obligations. They think that once the principle is decided upon, its effecting poses no serious problems.

This is totally wrong. We cannot understand the history of the state if we are not convinced of the idea that taxation is a very difficult operation, even under a good administration, and that this difficulty has always weighed heavily upon the state.

As evidence we could cite the place that fiscal problems have had throughout history. They are to be found in the beginnings of great social changes, such as the liberation of the serfs of Western Europe, the subjugation of the peasants of Eastern Europe, wars for independence (that of Portugal as well as that of the United States), revolutions, the creation of representative governments, etc.

As a matter of fact, the political repercussions of taxation are above all apparent during one particular period of history: the one which witnessed the development of the administrative framework of the modern state. Why was this so? Must one attribute it to the ignorance of the people of the times, or to their technical incompetence? To a certain extent this may be so. Nonetheless, even when

[1] In this regard, a detailed study could lead us to examine what must have been at given times the functioning of certain empires of the Orient, the importance of the cultivation of the demesne in the empire of Charlemagne, in certain Central European states up until a rather late period, and in given features of the Swedish state from the fifteenth to the seventeenth century, etc.

[2] With the reservation made for times of war during which certain financial systems are profoundly disturbed but do not cease to be, we might likewise make the observation that some economic techniques—price control, for example—often appear to be the means of effecting, under the best circumstances, financial policies.

they had capable finance ministers, rulers came up against an economy, the structure of which was poorly adapted to the levying of taxes by the state. Herein lies a basic phenomenon. An analysis of the system of taxation in contemporary times as well as in the past shows that *tax collection and assessment are indissolubly linked to an exchange economy.* The flow of goods and money are necessary for the understanding and especially for the evaluation of taxable materials. It is not enough to be aware of the volume of production because the economic structure sets a much lower limit. Agrarian societies of the past furnished the states with only minimal tax potential.

By means of this analysis we can understand how the economic structure governed the building up of the state, and why, during the centuries up until the eighteenth, if not even later, rulers continually came up against financial difficulty. For the same reason, the nineteenth century offered to those states affected by the Industrial Revolution ever-increasing possibilities of action, not only because greater production affords more extensive levying of taxes, but also because a more highly developed exchange economy allows one to establish taxes with greater accuracy.

What can be said of taxes can also be said of currency. One kind of economy adapts poorly to the use of bank-issued money, and for this very reason, to the most productive methods of inflation. To understand this it is enough for us to concentrate on the reality of the problem and to seek the reasons why in the case of hard money the inflationary machinery was so difficult to put into action, at the same time asking ourselves just what we would do if we had to do it in the conditions of the past. We would probably be more lenient *vis-à-vis* the behavior of the old mint officials (*officiers des monnaies*).

Second Approach: Uprisings and the Building of the State. The political influence of the economic structure on the state and on the nation has manifested itself in other ways. One of them consists of violent reactions on the part of the individual. One tends to think of uprisings as being annoying but chance happenings—as mere accidents—whereas they have played a really major role in the life of states, the formation of which cannot be understood if such events are disregarded. How can one explain Richelieu's system if he overlooks the fact that the cardinal had to cope with several hundred riots and mutinies among the urban classes alone?

[166]

Throughout one entire period of history, taxation was the outstanding instigator of rebellions. One could add the means of sustenances as an incentive to rebellion, but only secondarily. Religious phenomena alone, at least at some periods of time, have had greater emotional value for and appeal to insurrection.[3] It would be inconceivable to think that states confronted by such threats would not have established their administration, their institutions, and their legal concepts in such a way as to withstand these threats. This is not a guess; when we study such a French institution—the intendancies or administrative law—we discover that it has been created to withstand the unfavorable reactions of taxpayers.

If one had any doubts about this, all he would have to do would be to refer to the correspondence of statesmen. The letters of Richelieu, Mazarin, Séguier, Colbert, Charles V, or of Granvelle and of the officials who were their collaborators make clear their daily concerns. In certain cases, one can follow day by day (or almost) how they strove to predict revolts, put them down, and to avoid their recurring. Thus, for an understanding of the state, such correspondence constitutes a much more important instrument than official texts which are so often removed from reality, memoirs which allow the facts to be disguised, or histories which too frequently describe only the most superficial aspects. They are the means of grasping the structure of the state in its deepest meaning.

Third Approach: Class Contrasts and the Power of the State. The correspondence of statesmen allows us to perceive with accuracy another reality and leads to another approach.

When a riot is on the point of springing up, the minister in whose jurisdiction it lies asks himself and his correspondents who are those who are taking part in it. When all classes—peasants, artisans, bourgeois, and even aristocrats—are involved, he comprehends the extreme gravity of the situation. He then strives to isolate at least a

[3] It goes without saying that in some other types of societies the majority of rebellions have had other causes: slave societies gave rise to slave uprisings. In Russia the uprisings of the serfs were relatively numerous. On the other hand, the *corvée* does not seem to have provoked, at least in Western Europe, many violent reactions. In the same way and in spite of the example set by the Catalan rebellion and the war of the Vendée, obligatory military service has not caused as many uprisings as has taxation. One might keep in mind though, the opposition to conscription during the First Empire, which can be explained by the extent of conscription judged indispensable in a time of almost unceasing wars.

part of these classes from the coalition, the nobility in the seventeenth century, if possible the bourgeoisie, in order to have a kind of auxiliary police force to reinforce the operative force of the army. The struggle against the government is generally accompanied by class conflict, which is more or less clear-cut and more or less deliberate, so the monarch's task is made. easier. Here again we find the influence of the economic structure which gives rise to the class or classes without which the state could not be established except in a very different form.[4]

Of course, we can treat the problem in another way and maintain that the state, being no more than the emanation of the privileged classes, is deprived of all operational autonomy. Without underestimating the value of this approach, we must add that the sovereign, from the day of his investiture on, and from the moment in which he calls together a group of collaborators and clientele, has within his power a minimum of operational possibilities and can strive to play the role of arbiter between the various classes. Analyses of bureaucratic phenomena and of what is known today as the technostructure of the state lead to similar conclusions.

Fourth Approach: Economic Structure and the Building of the Nation. The economic structure acts in another way: it more or less inspires individuals with the eagerness to participate in it. In an agrarian society, such as existed in Europe from the fourteenth to the seventeenth century, with its small units of production and with its farms and villages having only a slightly open economy, the greatest aim of the people was to avoid the interference of the state in their affairs, since such interference meant exacting of them not only labor but above all money which was hard to come by. Members of the community in the small towns with their restricted commercial horizon had reactions of a similar kind.

For this reason the assemblies to which sovereigns had to resort in order to introduce taxation—succeeding to a certain degree—were reduced in importance except in mercantile states, particularly England where one segment of the population was sufficiently involved in business to realize the effects politics would have on their day-to-day interests.

---

[4] It is fitting of course to proceed to a series of distinctions between classes and subclasses, distinctions for which Marx has set a good example in his historical works, notably, in *The Eighteenth Brumaire of Louis Bonaparte* (Marx 1900). Cf. especially the work of the Russian historian, Boris Federovich Porshnev (Porshnev 1963).

The situation changed radically in the nineteenth century. The insurrections at the time of the Restoration and the July Monarchy, the unrest of English workers, especially Chartism, the Revolution of 1848, and similar movements in other countries, demonstrate significantly the need for participation that had extended itself throughout increasingly more numerous strata of the population.

Nations could not really take root, though, unless the constitutional systems, the details of which were developed at this time included at least a minimum measure of response to the needs of the masses: the personal income tax appeared to be the mainstay of this motion of solidarity.[5] Now, this type of tax was linked to the economic structure. In those classes which hung on to many features of the old agrarian society, it yielded only incomplete results. In this lies one of the reasons for the different political evolution of northern countries as distinct from Mediterranean countries.

We must not conceal the fact that the awareness of belonging to a nation depends to a great degree upon the satisfaction that individuals derive or hope to derive from community life. In this respect, in contemporary industrial societies, we must attribute a very great importance to economic growth. Here too we find the effects of financial procedures. For more than twenty years, states have had new methods at their disposal, which have helped them avoid serious crises similar to those that precipitated the Second World War.

But these techniques themselves rest upon an infrastructure: industrial society, where the relatively harmonious advances of all the factors of production and trade permit fluctuations as regards the demand be expressed in terms of advances in production and not by bottlenecks which are in turn generating forces of inflation. Again we find the repercussions of the economic structure in political life, repercussions every bit as important as underemployment in constituting the most important cause of insurrection in our times.

Fifth Approach: Interrelations between the Economy and Institutions. An understanding of the mechanics of taxation, of its economic implications, and of its influence on the spirit of revolt allows us to chart accurately the correlations that exist between the institutions of different European countries throughout the different periods of their existence. In France during the reign of Louis XIV, there was a tight link between the centralized administrative regime, the ab-

---

[5] Cf. as an example of this, the ideas and activities of Léon Bourgeois in France at the end of the nineteenth century.

sence of the Estates General, restrictions on local freedom as well as on individual freedom, a standing army composed in part of mercenaries, the existence of privileges accorded the Church, the nobility, and the bourgeoisie, the institution of the *garde bourgeoise*, and the venality of offices, etc. There is not one of these institutions that can be understood without understanding another, and, more often than not, by the need to levy taxes, and to prevent or retard the occurrence of rebellions. Inversely, in the England of Charles II and William of Orange, the existence of Parliament, the habeas corpus, the place of duties in the fiscal system, the existence of a stock market and local self-government were no less bound one to the other.

All of this goes to show clearly the existence of relationships analogous to those in the field of ecology. Disturbances provoked in nature by the disappearance of a given species find their equivalent in society when, for one reason or another, one of the parts of the whole system is eliminated. For instance, when a king obstructs the privileges of one class without making sure of the support of another class or when he diminishes the rigor of centralization, as in the case of Louis XVI in 1787 who caused a most severe kind of upset, that is, the French Revolution.

We might set up analogous ecological tables for other countries or for other periods, such as for Prussia under Frederick II or for France at the time of Napoleon. We might then see how, for example, the institution of the Legion of Honor and the reconstruction of the nobility—both being in reality very important endowments—would fit into the logic of the system. The same might be said for the July Monarchy as regards, to cite one example, the prime role played by the *Garde Nationale*.

Nonetheless, these tables of interrelations, or interdependencies, have a static character. They do not correspond exactly to our subject: the discovery of those conditions in which a structure—that of the state or nation, to be precise—is formed.

We can try to discover this by dedicating ourselves to the task of stressing those changes in economic structure resulting from technical advances, such as the long economic swings, the activities pertinent to the rulers and to the technostructure, as well as demographic phenomena, etc.

We also have to try to find elements of the solution by means of comparing a given kind of state, such as that formed in Western Europe, with other political entities: those of Eastern Europe and the

Orient, as well as those of new nations resulting from decolonization. By asking ourselves why certain empires have not survived, or, at least, did not open up in the nineteenth century to new avenues of action as did the states of Western Europe, we can hope to understand why the latter states have evolved in the way we know. And it is by comparing the structures and the infrastructures of Western Europe with those of Eastern Europe that we can try to separate from each other the sectors of economic conditions and political conditions found in the overall character of these different entities.

Is it necessary to believe that this bond is such that it leaves no freedom of action to the government, to the administration, or to the citizens?

Such a conclusion would be erroneous because it would not take into account the action of the states which, during the times when the resistance of the milieu of the existing social framework was the greatest, endeavored to modify these forces and to introduce industry and trade, particularly foreign trade, and all that could make the economy better qualified to furnish kings and their ministers with the basic ingredients of power. Mercantile policies presupposed, however, at least a minimum economic development: the rulers of Eastern Europe were led to another type of action; that is, demanding more of the state than of individual initiative, which was still largely lacking. Is it really necessary to state that considerations of this kind have not lost all real meaning?

In an analogous sense, even if financial techniques are dominated by the economic context, it would, however, be an exaggeration to say that technicians and politicians have no options. In the same era and in the same type of society, we might find more or less sensible techniques: certain taxes which were particularly unwieldly had particularly devastating consequences.

These remarks are applicable to an even greater extent to the most important and most delicate of all techniques, namely, money. In this area, reactions are so rapid that they are or, at least, should be immediately visible; for example, the German reaction following the decisions of Chancellor Brüning. It is not certain at the present time that the various financial techniques (the tax system, money, or the budget) correspond either to the potential offered by industrialized society or to the more or less conscious aspirations of individuals.

We have often noticed that political institutions do not change as rapidly as the circumstances from which they arise. This is perhaps even more valid in the case of financial techniques. According to the extent that history points out the origin of all these factors, we are naturally led to ask if they correspond to the needs of our times. We might be tempted to say that a knowledge of history interests us most because it allows us to free ourselves from its legacy, or heritage, or from what is out of date in this heritage.

In this work I have endeavored in particular to stress one of the approaches to the problem by bringing into focus those financial structures which have served as a link between the economic infrastructure and the formation of the state or nation.

All these comments are enough to establish why the history of the state seems to me to be inseparable from the history of taxation. For this reason, I have taken in substance and sometimes in form ideas which already appear in *Histoire de l'impôt* (1971–1972). And, for the same reason, one will also come across certain developments found in *Théorie sociologique de l'impôt* (1965).

The Building of States from the Late Middle Ages to the Eighteenth Century

INTRODUCTION

Everyone knows the seriousness of the financial difficulties against which the builders of modern states 'had to struggle continuously. They adjusted their foreign policy, and were actually induced in some circumstances to forego wars, or end a war prematurely. We can also recognize the financial causes in the establishment of some representative regimes, as well as the triggering of the American and French Revolutions.

However, it seems that we have not always given proper weight to the exact nature, and one might say, to the implacable character of such financial exigencies.

Judging from our experience, we are inclined to condemn ignorance, awkwardness, and corruption in the men who, in Western Europe from the fourteenth to the nineteenth centuries had a most thankless task: that of finances. Actually their contemporaries have given us the model for condemnation. It would be easy to draw up a long martyrology from the list of ministers of finance, *surintendants* or *contrôleurs généraux* of France. Some died on the scaffold, like Enguerrand de Marigny and Semblançay, not to mention the Knights Templar who were horribly tortured for their cleverness in the management of private and public funds. Jacques Coeur and later John Law were luckier, being able to go into exile. Fouquet escaped capital punishment only at the price of life imprisonment. Those financiers and ministers who evaded prosecution were the butt of pamphleteers. The *mazarinades* would cause a library to overflow, and there are many other works which could join them from Turcaret to the polemical books of the eighteenth century.

But this should not surprise us, when we consider the monstrousness of the old regime of taxation, the salt tax collectors bursting into homes to seize salt which did not come from the official monopoly, smugglers condemned to death or to the galleys, systems as archaic as the ancient levy on harvests which continued until the eighteenth or even the nineteenth century, men taxed only because they lived, without taking account of their revenues, toll merchants, etc. . . .

However, the men responsible for public finances should not all be condemned. To appreciate objectively the quality of their financial administration, we must examine the situation more closely.

Although it is true that the distinction between public funds and the private fortunes of those who handled state monies was a long time coming, at least we should recognize that the financial administrators were not all ignorant and incapable. Jacques Coeur, Nicolas Fouquet, and later John Law understood the economic foundation of the wealth of the state. Next to a Chamillart we should note the competence and energy of a Desmaretz, who bolstered French finances during the darkest hours of the reign of Louis XIV. In the seventeenth century a Machault d'Arnouville had the merit to try to establish a system of direct taxes which were both relatively productive and relatively equitable. Turgot has always been counted an exception, but more careful historians have recently begun to rehabilitate Terray, not to mention Calonne.

The history of other countries would doubtless give rise to similar observations. Truthfully, we cannot make impartial judgments on these men, which is a secondary point, but above all we cannot measure the obstacles which faced the modern state-builders unless we recognize the necessity for and the difficulty of taxation in the economic milieu before the nineteenth century.

For several centuries European kings tried to avoid these difficulties by systematic payments in kind or in services. In the empire of Charlemagne and his successors, in the France of the first Capetians, in the empire of Otto the Great and of Frederick Barbarossa, an enormous effort was brought to support the state in a setting that was close to a subsistence economy. History shows the weakness of these systems. From the twelfth to the nineteenth century, European sovereigns tried to eliminate the feudal system and replace payments in kind by payments in money. Taxation meant the possibility of eliminating first the tumultuous and anarchic feudal levies, which were also ineffectual, as the French defeats at Crécy, Agincourt and Poitiers show so clearly, and later the *arrière-ban*, which had little military value, and was called up for the last time under Louis XIV. Without taxation it would have been impossible to replace the network of manorial administrations with an administration in the proper sense of the word, recruited by virtue of its competence, in which the king could put his faith. There were some backward steps, such as the creation of a new nobility and the venality of offices; Maupeou tried to free the French monarchy of these policies, which can be explained to a large degree by inadequate fiscal resources.

Each increase in the power of states was linked to an increased possibility of levying taxes.

An examination of the technical problems shows clearly the strict limits of the fiscal possibilities of states from the thirteenth to the seventeenth, and even in the eighteenth century. These limits were such important constraints that they actually shaped in some ways the administrative, juridical, and political structures which we have inherited.

LIMITS TO THE FISCAL POSSIBILITIES OF STATES
BEFORE THE NINETEENTH CENTURY

Until we approach the nineteenth century, a little earlier or later depending upon the country or region, fiscal possibilities were strictly limited by the structure and trend of the economy.

There were three kinds of obstacles which monarchs faced.

First Obstacle: Insufficient Production. When we are surprised at the financial troubles of sovereigns of the fifteenth, sixteenth, or seventeenth centuries, or even of the eighteenth, we forget that they were taxing societies, the major economic activity of which was agriculture, an agriculture giving low returns.

Estimates naturally differ, and we do not have many precise details. All signs point, nevertheless, to the weak productivity of land and labor. In most of Western Europe and the Mediterranean region, yield was only a small multiple of the seeds planted. Production per

[174]

hectare was ridiculously low, compared to present-day figures, and these results were obtained after long hours of work. Not unreasonably, the Physiocrats stressed that taxation, along with the various rents and dues owed to the property owner, lord, and church, could bear only on the *net product*, on that part of the return left to the farmer after he had put aside what was needed for continued production, that is, seed for the next harvest, food for those who plowed and worked the land, a little manure, a small herd of animals, and maintenance of buildings. The remainder (the net product) was relatively small. One can well understand why important state-building efforts succeeded in relatively wealthy zones, the Parisian basin, the London basin, Flanders, the plain of the Po, and, generally speaking, in the large affluvial plains. We must wait for the agricultural revolution of the eighteenth century for the economic base, or as I am tempted to say, the "nutritional" base, for states to be able at last to expand.

The limit imposed by low productivity was combined with a *demographic* phenomenon of which historians are becoming more and more conscious. When the population increased proportionately, reaching a relatively high density for a basic agricultural economy, the product of the land had to be divided among a growing number of claimants, less fertile lands had to be brought under cultivation in the absence of technological progress, which would have made it possible to overcome temporarily the law of diminishing returns. The result was the phenomenon which Malthus later formulated as an economic law: pauperization of the masses, famines or epidemics which struck down underfed bodies.

The growth of the population beyond certain limits not only increased the possibility of death and sickness, it also made the payment of taxes more difficult. It contributed to the unleashing of revolts, which can be considered partly as the result of an unfavorable ratio of production and population. In some cases, it is difficult to say whether a given uprising was provoked by famine or taxes.[6] The direct cause was sometimes hardship, but behind the outbreak of these rebellions were the reactions of taxpayers physically incapable of paying what was demanded of them.

---

[6] It seems possible to make a relatively clear distinction between the food riots studied by Charles and Louise Tilly and tax riots: beyond certain limits famine directly determined rebellion. But I must admit that within those limits the weakness of production could make payment of taxes more difficult and give impetus to a strong movement against the fisc.

Productivity, especially agricultural productivity, and demography were together the first obstacle, a really physical barrier to the power of the state.

Second Obstacle: Insufficient Markets and Difficulties of Collection. The physical limitation was not the only one. Taxes, because they were levied in monetary terms, faced a second limitation. The net product in itself was not adequate to pay the tax; it had to be transformed, by being sold, into money. For the worker, with only his labor to offer, the problem was the same: wherever he was he had to find a buyer for his labor. For the taxpayer the problem of taxation was the problem of markets.

From this came all the difficulties faced by the many regions in which the subsistence economy dominated, all the provinces removed from the important network of exchanges, those far from navigable rivers.

This difficulty was often disguised, and made people almost forget the problems already discussed. Toward the end of the seventeenth century, when the *intendants* drew up, for the instruction of the Duke of Burgundy, memoirs on the situation in their generalities, what these men, primarily responsible for tax collection, emphasized, was not the small return to agricultural or industrial production, but inadequate commercial outlets, trouble finding markets through which to keep wheat flowing, fairs at which to sell animals. When tax collection was difficult in the Limousin, this was not only due to the poor stony soil, but also because the province had no market for their oxen since the Paris market was not only distant, but also more easily supplied from Normandy.

On the other hand, tax collection was relatively easy in the provinces of the Paris basin, the North and the East, not only because the soil was fertile (not all the prosperous areas were especially fertile), but also because they were able to sell their grains and animals at Versailles and Paris, and to the forts and military storehouses along the frontier.[7] One begins to understand why there was a movement

[7] The memoirs of the *intendants* were published by Boulainvilliers in the eighteenth century (Boulainvilliers 1752). More accurate versions of some of those memoirs have been published in the nineteenth and twentieth centuries (for instance, the memoir on the generality of Ile-de-France edited by Boislisle 1881). In the letters of the *intendants*, notably in Boislisle (1874–1897), a lot of concrete notices show how much the problem of outlets was important for the sake of taxation. The correspondence of Colbert and later of Turgot or other men in charge of finances give the same impression. It is possible to find the same kind of observations in other European countries.

to return to taxation in kind in England, France and elsewhere at the end of the seventeenth century.[8]

The inadequate markets were caused by human as well as by physical geography. The regions most distant from the capital carried a larger burden of taxation than did other regions: money sent to the centralized governments did not return to the outlying provinces, or at best only partially and slowly. One can understand why these regions, apart from other reasons, were the forerunners of the resistance to the centralizing tendencies of the modern states—in Spain, France, and Great Britain.[9] The difficulties were even more noticeable insofar as the payment of taxes emphasized the need of money because the movement of funds was relatively slow up to the eighteenth century, as well as in the nineteenth and twentieth; the incomplete banking network and inadequate financial techniques played an important part in making tax collection more difficult.[10] One of the goals of Law's Bank was to improve the movement of specie from the provinces to the capital and vice versa.

As long as bank paper was unknown, or at best only functioned as a very imperfect substitute for specie, tax collection and consequently the life of governments were strictly dependent on the volume of

[8] In France the best known scheme was that of Vauban (*La dîme royale*) (Vauban 1888), but there were in France, in England and in other countries a lot of propositions that took the same direction. They are recalled in Vignes 1961. In that book you can see that one of the first supporters of that idea was Paul Hay du Chastellet, and in England Petty was one of its proponents. The movement continued during the eighteenth century. Some experiments were made in France, notably the *cinquantième* in 1725. Truly speaking, the object was not chiefly the solution of the problem of collection but that the assessment. *Contrôleurs généraux* (Calonne in the late years of the *Ancien Régime*) thought that the sharing of crops could eliminate more easily the inequality of taxes, *de jure* or *de facto*. For that reason their experiments or propositions were so strongly rejected by the privileged classes.

[9] Since the times of Wycliff or Jan Hus the burden of pontifical fiscality was more noticeable because the money was sent to Rome and did not return, to the countries where taxes had been levied. It was one of the causes of the Reformation. If the kings of France or Spain did not take the same direction, it was because they obtained concessions from the Pope: Ferdinand as Grand Master of the great Orders of chivalry, and Francis I because of the Concordat of 1515, which gave him the same advantages that Henry VIII, Gustave Vasa or others obtained by the way of secularization.

[10] At the beginning of the eighteenth century intendants of some generalities (notably that of Bordeaux) made reports in which they said that movements of money from the province to Paris caused great economic disturbances. They asked for a change in the methods of transferring funds; i.e., by buying letters of exchange to businessmen. At the beginning of the nineteenth century, during the first Empire, Mollien, minister of the treasury put into force a system that could make easier the movements of funds, private and public, between Paris and the provinces (cf. Mollien 1898). For the Spanish Empire, cf. the remarks of Braudel (Braudel 1949).

precious metals, the discovery of mines, the output of a given vein, and the importation of metals.

More generally, the imposition of taxes was shaped by economic cycles. Great waves of economic expansion made the government's job easy, while periods of recession threw up unpleasant barriers to their centralizing policies.[11] There is a striking contrast between the seventeenth and eighteenth centuries because of this single fact.

Third Obstacle: The Problem of the Distribution of the Tax Burden and the Assessment of Taxes in Preindustrial Societies. The structure of production and of trade erected another barrier to the possibilities of taxation: limited trade forced states to use imperfect methods of assessment seizing only a fraction of available revenues, only a fraction of Quesnay's net product. Some historians have argued as if it would have been possible to have a fiscal system like that of today—income tax, sales tax or value-added tax—in the economic setting of the seventeenth and eighteenth centuries, or even at the beginning of the nineteenth. This is a profound error, a complete misunderstanding of the technical problems involved in the distribution of the tax burden and the verification of taxes.

What was the nature of the economy at the end of the seventeenth century? *It was chiefly an agricultural economy, often a subsistence economy, and almost always an economy of small farms.* Financial technicians, assuming that they could forget political considerations, saw their possibilities of choice as strictly limited by these characteristics.

The problems of taxing agriculture in our own time are known. They are not only the effect of weak governments. The consumption of his products by the peasant, which still exists in relatively developed economies, goes far to explain why taxation of the agricultural sector is so difficult. This phenomenon was much more important in the primitive economies of the European old regime, in which each farmer tried to produce all his needs, where he baked his bread, ate the meat, spun the wool from his herd, wove his clothes, pressed his grapes, built his furniture, and made his tools. Where could taxation intervene in this tight economic circle, the shortest of all economic cycles? To make matters worse, they were dealing with small farms. To establish the net earnings of this kind of farm, they would have

---

[11] F. Simand was one of the first to draw attention to this effect of economic cycles.

had to face peasants who had not even the basic idea of keeping accounts.

To estimate the volume of the harvest was not enough. How, given the lack of any sale or exchange, could they establish the value? How could they determine the expenses of family farms where no fixed salaries were paid, and where fertilizers were in the form of animal manure? Industry did exist, but it was also dominated by a large number of small enterprises, even in the most active regions.

In the contemporary world, states do not tax the real profit of the artisan or even of small industries; they are satisfied by an approximate estimate (*forfait*). The administration of old regime France faced the same kind of difficulties, but with the difference that the basis for payment was less certain, and large establishments practically did not exist. One approach could have been to establish an identical tax for all artisanal enterprises of a given type, leaving the occupational group itself to assess and collect it.

Storekeepers, with their small stores spread out here and there, were no easier to tax. A tax on sales was theoretically possible, and was tried in various countries and at various periods. The financial administration understood, in advance, the problems of a turnover tax applied to small business; these problems were impossible to overcome except by another system of conventional estimates.

It would seem better to tax the consumption of storekeepers, small businessmen, artisans, their workers, and also the liberal professions. City life assumed the circulation of foodstuffs and (in the simplest sense) manufactured objects, even in a period when many city-dwellers had their own gardens or country homes. Products could be taxed in transit, preferably at the point through which they had to pass to enter the cities, especially when towns were still surrounded by walls.

One can understand the preference of finance ministers for indirect taxes, but even these taxes faced the same obstacle, a backward economic infrastructure. When the manufacture of a whole series of products is concentrated in one setting, as it is today, it is possible to arrange verification of production: breweries, sugar refineries, distilleries, oil refineries can be almost permanently observed as to their machines, production lines, entries of materials and exits of products, accounts, etc. When there are small scattered enterprises, this solution is impossible: even today there are fiscal problems arising in the cases of small distilleries. The fiscal administration in the sixteenth, seventeenth and eighteenth centuries faced problems of this type. But they were not the exception, as they are today. They were the rule. Scattered production meant that taxable wealth could not be taxed at this stage.[12]

All that remained was to control circulation. In France the *Contrôleur général des finances* and the *ferme générale* built an ingenious mechanism based on systematic use of permissions to move products. From the moment at which a taxable item, a barrel of wine, for example, left the place where it was produced, it had to be accompanied by an official document which listed its destination, the length of the journey, and all relevant facts of the trip, in a way that a check of these documents anywhere along the way could reveal an evasion. Furthermore, inventories kept by wholesale and retail merchants made it possible to know constantly what was in stock and what was actually on hand. This "classical" mechanism was so wisely set up that it has continued to exist, in essence, up to now.[13] It made it possible to make cities pay taxes. It was so effective that at various periods and in various countries direct taxation of city dwellers has been replaced by entry duties. It was not effective, however, for taxing the countryside, where consumption on the farm of the product of the farm was too prevalent.[14] In the countryside there was the taxation of salt, which, being physiologically necessary for all men, was the weak link in peasant autarky. From this came the monstrous duty known as the *gabelle*, which was so exaggerated that

[12] There were several exceptions, such as beer production, which could be measured by the amount of malt used or the number of steamers in operation. This explains why taxes on beer were an early and important part of the fiscal system of German states.

Certain other products could also be taxed at the production stage. Early countries to be industrialized like Great Britain could establish their indirect taxes at the point of production (or more often at the stage of the importing of raw materials).

[13] That mechanism was codified in the ordonnance of Colbert "sur le fait des aides." One can find good analyses in books of the eighteenth century, like that of Lefebvre de la Bellande (Lefebvre de la Bellande 1760). The comparison between the ordonnance of Colbert and the present French fiscal code is very striking.

The French system seemed so good that Frederick II, when he wanted bigger revenues from excise, gave the charge of Prussian excise to a group of French technicians. A critique was made by Mirabeau (Mirabeau 1788).

[14] Notably in Prussia since the time of the Great Elector. This distinction between the fiscal system of the country—direct taxation—and that of towns—excise—can be explained by political reasons, that is to say the opposition by the nobility to indirect taxation. The main explanation can be found in the structure of the economy. Long before, in France, Louis XI had the same idea. He did not put it in action, but later a great number of towns were authorized to replace direct taxation by taxes upon entries.

general evasion was practiced, only to be combatted by an army of enforcement agents and a whole series of checks on fraud. The system just described, which depended to a large degree on the taxation of certain products of mass consumption, is a direct expression of a certain type of society. It assumes at the same time some development of cities and markets. It was more suitable in this sense to the Western European countries than to those of Eastern Europe.[15]

In England, as in France, the state set up about the middle of the seventeenth century a widespread system of indirect taxes, or excise taxes, as the basis of the public budget. The English excise tax of 1643, which Holland imitated, taxed drinks (ale, beer, cider, liquor), meat, salt, alum, ammonia, hats, silk, and woolen textiles, etc. The verification of the taxes was set up at the stage of production or at the first sale of the product: the more advanced economy of Great Britain made it possible to eliminate controls during shipment from this period on.

The emperors of Germany were not able to set up a fiscal system in the true sense of the word. They lived on contributions offered by the various orders and geographical divisions of that large, chaotically organized empire. The separate states and the cities of the empire had real tax systems, which were more advanced and precocious in the urban centers.

Indirect taxes, especially on beverages (beer in particular), but also on meat and grains, were important, to the extent that economic conditions made them possible, and in proportion to those economic conditions. There was a tendency from the second half of the seventeenth century on in some of the states, Prussia and Saxony for example, to concentrate taxation in the cities.

However, despite all the advantages that the ruling classes could find in this kind of tax system, it was not sufficient. Today when the agricultural population is only 30 or 40 percent, or even less, of the active population it is possible to accept a very imperfect system of direct taxation on agriculture. When breeding animals and working land were the principal economic activities, this was impossible. States could not bypass direct taxation of the largest part of the taxable population, the peasants themselves.

[15] More details of those countries and notices of other European countries can be found in a book edited during the eighteenth century by a French civil servant (Moreau de Beaumont 1787–1789). It was the result of a general inquiry made probably with the idea of helping the French government to reform its own taxation system.

By the simple logic of fact, monarchs were obliged to ask themselves the following question: could taxation operate without markets? Various solutions—I am tempted to say every kind of solution—were tried.

The Tithe. The first and most simple solution was the payment in kind of percentage of the harvest, *la dîme* (the tithe). Apparently there was no need for elaborate evaluations, since the tax collector had only to collect his share of the fields or of the granary or storerooms of the peasant.

It is surprising that this ancient tax, present in the earliest civilizations, held an important place for so long in history. Political reasons, and the importance of the clergy, go far to explain why France did away with the ecclesiastical tithe only at the time of the Revolution, and Great Britain, in 1836.

But how can we explain that even the most daring proposals of tax reform involved a return to this kind of tax? Vauban's schemes proposed at the end of the reign of Louis XIV were built around a tithe paid in kind. During the eighteenth century, the French monarchy experimented with the ideas and Vauban, and one of the last *contrôleurs généraux*, Calonne, proposed making this kind of tax the base of a reformed system.

This is one of the most characteristic pieces of evidence of the obstacles which the economic structure offered to the fiscal possibilities and life of states; i.e., the stubbornness with which this archaic tax kept being reconsidered. But the collection of tithes was simple only in appearance. The possibility of cheating was great because of scattered holdings. The holders of benefices complained constantly during the entire sixteenth century: at the Estates-General of 1576 and 1588 in France the First Estate devoted entire books of grievances to the evasion of the tithe.

How could collectors assure a minimum of control? There were evident difficulties in any attempt to inventory the wine cellars, granaries, farm buildings, and houses. Forbidding the farmer to complete his harvest until the tithe collector had collected his share, a second solution tried in France and other countries tended to expose the farmer to the risk of bad weather which would ruin his harvest. A third possibility; i.e., the setting up of a fixed payment agreed upon by taxpayer and tax collector alike was frequently used: but

[182]

like all systems of this type it meant giving up any claim on a large part of the taxable product. Besides these obstacles, we should add that if payments in kind were not needed for immediate consumption, the products would have to be moved, sold, or transformed into money.[16]

There were serious inconveniences for the economy in proportion to the attempts to collect this kind of tax. The "economists" in the broadest sense of the term, from Boisguillebert to the liberal economists, including the Physiocrats, were all critical of the tithe. Their criticisms link up with those of contemporary experts estimating the obstacles to agricultural progress in developing countries. The disadvantages which these latter describe in the share-cropping systems are the same that the men of the Enlightenment saw in the tithe.

Their analysis is extremely simple. As is the case of all levies on gross product, the tithe encourages economies in methods of cultivation rather than increased production. Suppose that with an outlay of 91 units, the farmer can produce a harvest of 100 units. The profit would be lost if there were a levy of 10 percent on the gross product although there is a readily taxable net profit. All other things being equal, the tithe tends to bring about the abandonment of types of farming which require large expenditures of capital or other factors. This effect could be reduced by setting different levels for different types of agriculture, higher for those which require little labor, lower for those, such as vineyards, which require large inputs of labor. The tithe nevertheless would have the effect of discouraging intensive cultivation and hindering economic progress.

Capital Taxation and the Cadastre *Solution.* A secondary category of solutions would also permit—at least in appearance—the freeing of the state and its power from the limitations imposed by the eco-

---

[16] We can understand all the difficulties of the tithe if we look at the fiscal history of Moslem states. The place given to that kind of tax is well known. But, in fact, oriental kings were obliged to seek a lot of methods that could afford practical solutions to the problems of the tithe. Instances can be found in the Mughal Empire of India. Emperors or ministers adopted, successively or simultaneously: the solution of measurement, that is to say an evaluation of the crop before the harvest; a fixed charge on each unit of area sown; a contract between the assessor and the peasant, the latter giving a certain sum independent of the area he might sow; the use of standard yields, each unit being classed good, medium or bad, a tax on each plough, etc. . . . In some regions and in certain times, to avoid the incidence of too heavy taxes upon poor units, the tariff was different with the nature of the crops.
The system was much more complicated because the difficulties of assessment and of collection induced the kings to use intermediaries, headmen or farmers for revenue. The system called the "repartition system" was often used as a facility. (Cf. Moreland 1957.) In other Islamic countries difficulties of this kind might also be found.

nomic infrastructure. Although income was fluctuating and difficult to measure, capital was simpler to observe and levy against. From this follows the prominence of taxes of this kind in the fiscal systems of the past.

One must recognize, however, that the content of a fortune is not easy to estimate except insofar as it consists of real property, land, houses, and shops. That is the explanation, already remarked on by Seligman (1914), why the capital taxes of the past always tended, as by a natural law, to be limited to taxation of real estate.

Again there is the problem of determining value. Since this derives from the income of the property, are we led back to the previous problems? Possibly not. In each village, one could choose several pieces of property, or several parcels and concentrate all means of evaluation on them, searching out the usual level of the harvest, the average price of its sale, the expense of cultivation, etc. Then one could group the properties of the commune in several categories according to the types established by the evaluation, such as the most fertile plowlands, the medium, and the least fertile. This process would avoid endless repetitions of evaluations. Naturally, the area of each parcel of land must be known. This is the *cadastre* solution.

The mere summary of its principles shows how complex this solution was. Measuring acreage is a big job, especially in hilly countries or in regions of irregular, cut-up fields. The evaluation is no less delicate, limited as it is to several parcels. How do the evaluators proceed when there is so little commerce that there are no price lists? How can farm consumption be measured, or the expense of cultivation?

There is a way to deflect some of the difficulty: base the distribution of the tax, or at least the cross-checking of it, on the level of rents. The farmer would not agree to a rent more than the net product of the land, nor would the owner rent his property for a smaller income than the land could produce. This case requires that rental of farm land be the ordinary case. Thus this method was not used except in regions where commerce was adequately developed, in France in the zones of large scale farming such as the Parisian basin, the north, and the east; elsewhere, where sharecropping was more important, this system of dividing the crop between owner and renter offered no help to the tax collectors' attempt to evaluate the value of land.

The *cadastres* were researched and established in various regions, with unequal results due to uneven economic structure. The difficulties involved in drawing up *cadastres* meant that they were often allowed to continue in effect for long years, while the value of lands and even their ownership changed. One finally came to the case (as in the southern provinces of France where the "real" *taille* was imposed) where taxes no longer corresponded to the true income from lands, being too low in some cases, too high in others. When the tax was actually larger than the income from land one saw the phenomenon of abandoned farms, as reported by the *intendants* of the generalities in the south of France during the reign of Louis XIV.[17]

Approximate Estimates. Approximate estimates of wealth were accepted in the rest of France, and in other countries, until the end of the old regime. This was known as the *taille personnelle*: each community was assigned a collective sum due in taxes and then elected men who would work out the assessment of the tax based on their own knowledge of the resources of their neighbors. It was a typical arbitrary tax with all the disadvantages of such taxes: the wealthier potential taxpayers could be undertaxed, the distribution being falsified by the interest, favor, or hostility of the assessors; taxpayers were encouraged to hide their wealth, or to forego investments or technological improvements because of fear of giving too favorable an impression of their capacity to pay. Boisguillebert and Vauban, the Physiocrats and later economists continuously criticized this unfavorable distribution of the tax burden.

The Poll Tax. In the seventeenth century the need to find a satisfactory fiscal system was so strong that various European countries resorted to another tax which had nothing to do with the ability to pay—the *poll tax (capitation)*. Gone were the delicate problems of evaluating wealth, one merely had to count the human beings in a nation and place the same tax on each head or on each group of men in large, ranked categories according to their titles, their status, or their occupations if there was a graduated head tax. The French *capitation* of 1695 included twenty-two classes, from the heir-apparent to the throne down to the simple laborer. To the extent that the system remained simple, it required men of quite different incomes

[17] Examples can be found in letters sent by *intendants* to the *contrôleur général des finances* (cf. Boislisle 1874–1897: passim).

[185]

to pay the same tax. It was inconceivable except at very moderate levels, or there would have been an exodus of the potential taxpayers.

All this comes back to the fact that it is impossible to lay hands on taxable wealth, to recognize, or to estimate it without a minimum of economic exchange. The present-day income tax is relatively easy to operate in a country in which most men live on salaries paid by enterprises and through that link are easy to keep track of. Other taxes are levied against the interest or dividends paid by corporations; interest and dividends are both easy to find out and levy excise duties against, the payment of which could be guaranteed by the corporation itself, as in the above case. Taxes against various kinds of rents are also simple to carry out. Production is sufficiently concentrated so that taxes can be levied at that stage which will eventually be passed on to the consumer. Indeed, there are still difficulties. They are due to the burden of the taxes, which lead businesses or individuals to try to protect profits by fraud, but the larger the corporations, the more sophisticated their organization, and the more difficult it is for them to indulge in systematic tax evasion; the complexity of these corporate bodies assumes many links and involvements and consequent risks in cheating.

In agriculture, governments do not try to tax true profits except when the farms are important or adequately involved in commerce so that the possibilities of taxation are broader. There are still technical problems regarding the taxation of industry or commerce, quite acute in some countries, but these are due to the mediocre size of firms, artisanal businesses, and small stores.

Finally, the tax authorities come closest to full exploitation of taxable wealth in industrial societies. The more industrial the society, the more this is true. Up until the time of such societies, finance ministers had to be satisfied with approximations far removed from reality.

ATTEMPTS TO USE MONETARY AND FINANCIAL EXPEDIENTS
AND THEIR WEAKNESS

States were unable to do without taxes except in relatively limited ways; this fact, like the difficulties of taxation, grew out of the structure and the trend of the economy. Kings did hope to avoid the difficulties involved in creating new taxes;[18] they attempted various ex-

---

[18] They often tried to avoid taxes for political motives, in England during the period of the Stuarts for instance. But the main reason was the difficulty of taxation in

pedients and also more serious solutions. But these soon found limits stricter than those of today. It was impossible to go beyond these limits, and this was in turn one of the explanations of the tyrannical effect of fiscal problems on political management in this period. The monarchs tried both "archaic" methods, a return to past methods, as well as modern ones, analogous to some which are used today.

Archaic Solutions. The first reaction of financially pressed governments was always to confiscate the property of certain social groups, or institutions, especially the Church. The "secularizations" of the Reformation encouraged the "take-off" of the Protestant states. Catholic monarchies had their equivalent confiscations: in Spain the king became grand master of the orders of chivalry and seized control of their assets; in France, the Concordat of 1516 gave the king the authority to dispense benefices and prebends with consequent financial return and influence. Even poorly exploited, the sale of the church properties helped Revolutionary France over its first financial difficulties. This kind of resource, nonrenewable and to a large degree frittered away, would be totally unable to support modern states, even temporarily.

Among the rulers of Western Europe at least, there was no serious thought to go back to feudal mechanisms; that would have been a renunciation of their central goal. Under a different form, however, there was a kind of fractionation of the state. De Tocqueville wrote:

> When we come across any ancient medieval custom which was maintained, with its worst elements willfully exploited in defiance of the spirit of the age, or any new and equally pernicious measure, we always find, if we go to the root of the matter, some financial expedient that has crystallized into an institution. Thus, to meet emergencies of a temporary order, new powers were frequently erected which were to last for centuries (de Tocqueville 1856 in Gilbert 1955: 102).

As examples, he cites the right of *franc-fief* which emphasized the gap between the classes, the guilds, the overturning of municipal institutions, and the venality of offices. He concludes, "For the sake of raising some paltry sums of money the central power deprived itself

---

countries where the economic structure did not offer the easy fiscal method of assessment.

of the right to supervise efficiently the work of its own agents and to keep them under control" (de Tocqueville 1955: 105).

Venality of offices is a typical example of a constraint on the powers of the state arising from measures taken by the king to evade the difficulties which insufficient fiscal resources had imposed on his needs or ambitions. Venality was the resource of countries whose political ambitions went beyond the limits which their own inadequate administration, the power of privileged groups and insufficient trade imposed on resources of the state.

Some historians have emphasized that the venality of offices was not established merely to fill the treasury. They've shown that it was a means also for co-opting the bourgeoisie, buying its support for the monarchy, using it as a backstop at the time of popular uprisings, and strengthening the social system.[19] I would be tempted to limit myself to explanations of this sort if I were not forced to emphasize the importance of all financial prospects, even minimal, for governments, the tax systems of which were more tightly limited than we can even imagine. It is significant that all European states, from the Papacy to the Ottoman Empire, resorted at times to the venality of offices. France simply offers the most striking example of the consequences of such a policy.

The history of the sale of offices began with Louis XII; venality was extended under Francis I, continued under his successors, and greatly developed and systematized in the reign of Henry IV. At that time, the institution was in a sense completed by the creation of the "Paulette," an annual payment by the holders of offices which assured them of the right to pass on the offices to their heirs.

The important place of the venality of offices was particularly characteristic at the end of the reign of Louis XIV, a period in which insufficient commerce, due to war and a lingering economic crisis, offered great handicaps to the needs of a policy of grandeur. Unless he could collect more taxes, the French monarch of the eighteenth century could not do away with venality. It would be superfluous to recite all the limitations which, as a result, weighed on the power of the monarchy.[20]

[19] Although the points they make are not identical, arguments of this sort are found in the article of Pagès (Pagès 1932), in the work of Roland Mousnier, and in that of the Russian historian Porshnev (Porshnev 1963).

[20] In his various works, Marcel Marion (Marion 1910; 1914–1928; 1926) showed that in the fiscal field especially, the opposition of the Parlements was one of the causes making it impossible to carry out necessary reforms.

Borrowing. Governments have found financiers useful since the Middle Ages to ease the movements of funds, anticipate the payment of tax receipts, and even to take charge of running taxation. These bankers helped states profit by banking techniques which transferred payments from one end of Europe to the other. The Empire of Charles V or of Philip II would have been impossible to run without the assistance given by the bankers of Genoa and of southern Germany.[21] Businessmen advanced their own capital to their sovereigns, the capital of their associates, and even the capital that they could borrow due to their credit rating, generally better than that of the most powerful kings. Some statesmen got the idea of borrowing from a broader group. Many formulas were dreamed up, from the *Grand parti* of the Cardinal de Tournon to the *tontines* of the eighteenth century. These resources were limited not only by their disregard of the conditions for public credit but also by the structure of society.

Extensive use of government borrowing assumes a money economy developed to the extent that the holders of money are accustomed to lending it, and intermediate financiers are able to guide large amounts of money toward the state treasury. Just as taxation assumes a market for production, borrowing assumes a market for capital. These conditions were present in some states—the Low Countries and England. Elsewhere, at least until the eighteenth century, they were missing.

Recognizing this gap, the French finance ministers tried to create an artificial financial market by making those who handled public funds at the same time lenders to the state. This policy weighed heavily on both the structure and functioning of the state. It led to assigning both the assessment and collection of taxes to private corporations. It led the *contrôleurs généraux* not to press for rigorous accounting and this resulted in considerable private profits, to the detriment of the state treasury. It was reasoned that these profits increased the private credit of the men who had dealings with the minister of finances. And this in turn made it possible for them to borrow more easily the sums that they would in turn lend to the state.

[21] Fernand Braudel (1949) has emphasized the importance, and the difficulty, of the movement of funds between Spain, where ships unloaded gold and silver from the New World, and Flanders, and banking center, to which, if the actual *pistoles* and *écus* were not shipped, at least some means of assuring payment had to be sent.

The courts would periodically try to recover a part of the exaggerated profits of these *traitants*. But in many cases the solemn machinery of repression was stopped by compromises or promoted by interested powerful persons. One of the risks of this trade was the possibility of being convicted, but this only increased the interest or commissions collected from the treasury. Necker believed the state could free itself from the stranglehold of the *financiers*, which then meant those persons responsible for the collection of public revenues, by borrowing from banks and from the private capital market. He was only able to borrow, however, under very onerous conditions, because of his eagerness to place the loans under conditions which were too favorable to the subscribers, and also because the French financial market was insufficiently organized. Mollien, who built up the treasury of the empire, realized for the same reasons that he needed agents who were half bureaucrats, half bankers, and who would put their personal credit at the service of the state; these were the *receveurs généraux*. There is still a trace of the age when the state felt it necessary to provide a sort of supplementary system for an inadequate banking network in the present setup of the *comptables du Trésor* in France.

Quite the opposite, Holland, at the time of the wars against Louis XIV, and Great Britain in the same period (during the eighteenth century and during the Napoleonic wars), both borrowed a part of the resources which helped them hold off France and beat her to a more developed money economy and capital market. This same reason (that is, the economic structure of the country) allowed England to establish an income tax, float long-term loans, and to find complementary resources for the emission of currency.

Inflation. Past governments, right back to the ancient world, also tried to make use of their coinage. But as long as metallic money was the unique system, inflationary attempts, such as the monetary changes which were so frequent in France from the Middle Ages on, could tap only relatively limited resources, came up against numerous evasions and caused serious disadvantages.

What exactly were the techniques of "metallic" inflation? One could issue coins of the same nominal value as pieces already in circulation but of less weight or of a lower standard of precious metal. This tended to encourage persons to export their higher valued coins or to restrike them themselves in order to get the benefit of the debased coinage. One could issue a *monnaie de billion* (copper coin or other coin not specie), a procedure often used, especially by Spain at various periods, which soon reaches its limits.

One could also avoid making the monetary stock diverse by using a money of account different from the money used for payments, and this was the most common technique used since the Middle Ages. The king decided that the *livre* or the *denier*, which were the money of account in which debts and assets were calculated and prices fixed, were worth so many *louis* or *écus*. He could later change the number of *livres* or *deniers* which equaled them without changing the weight or the standard of specie. Variations of this type could be profitable. By increasing the number of *livres* equal to a *louis* or an *écu* the minister of finances could pay his debts with a smaller amount of money or buy a larger amount of goods, so long as prices had not gone up. He could do the opposite, also, forcing his debtors to pay him with a larger proportion of gold or silver.

These alternating mechanisms of *augmentations* or *diminutions*, or as we would say, devaluations or reevaluations, would bring in relatively limited receipts. The state could turn monetary policy to its account by increasing the number of coinages because of the fee, the *seigneuriage*, which was the difference between the weight of metal brought by individuals to be coined and the weight of the coins returned to them. The various monetary manipulations had for their object an increase in the amount of *seigneuriage* collected.[22] By increasing the number of account money units equal to a given coin, the holders of specie were encouraged to bring their coin to be reminted: the state kept part of the profit of this "augmentation" and granted the remainder to the clients of the mints.

This relative profit was not enough. To force individuals to turn in their precious coins, the state sometimes demonetized them: they were "discredited."[23] Individuals still resisted this levy, they waited for a new depreciation, sent their coin out of the country or reminted them themselves. In short, this technique also had the disadvantage of encouraging hoarding and flight of specie with a consequent reduction of the quantity of money in circulation and all the problems that that caused for the economy.

[22] This is the thesis proposed by Adolphe Landry (Landry 1910).
[23] Not always. Here I am schematizing a group of methods which were very varied, very complex and which furthermore made it possible for the *officiers de monnaie* to make more or less regular personal profits.

Since the invention of paper, monarchs have been able to resort to another type of money, another type of inflation. But again a developed economy was the prerequisite. It was necessary that bank bills be common in all circles and that the state could pay its soldiers, its functionaries, even its peasants in paper money. The suppliers of the state, in turn, had to pay their vendors and their workers with money that was not 'hard cash (*n'était ni sonnante, ni trébuchante*). All this assumes not only usages coming from an already advanced commercial and monetary economy, but also a financial market with skilled technicians. Certain states—England most notably—were able to use bank money early on. The France of Louis XIV resorted to *billets de monnaie* in a very clumsy way. Law's system, although originally well thought out, ended by throwing bank money into disrepute by the excessive use of it. France in the seventeenth century did not have the conditions for a successful state manipulation of the money supply.

In short, the nonfiscal methods of financing were either a partial abdication of the state, or required an advanced economic infrastructure, an infrastructure which was missing in most of the European states until at least the eighteenth, if not the nineteenth century. In all cases these methods could only be used without major disadvantages if they were accompanied by a fiscal system which was substantially productive. The structure of production and of commerce limited the power of states in every way.

EFFECTS OF THE TECHNICAL CONDITIONS OF TAXATION ON THE
BUILDING OF THE MODERN STATE

This part of the analysis explains why and how the structure of the economy had many and varied influences on the life, the possibility of life, and on the building of states, all by way of taxes. The building of modern states, in our sense of the term, with a judicial system and an administration paid for by the state and not by those administered, with an army paid, lodged, and maintained by the state, with storehouses filled with purchases made on the open market and not by requisitions, with public works built by specialized corps and not by forced labor—all this was accomplished only gradually, so far and only so far as the exchange economy became rooted, affected more activities, and extended itself over a larger area, spreading out from ports or trade centers.

This evolution occurred in Western Europe over centuries, with interspersed periods of stagnation or regression, and periods of accelerated growth, all due to variations in the economic conjuncture. All the European countries took part in this evolution, but in unequal ways. Sometimes we are surprised by the political importance of certain cities, merchant cities like Venice or the Hanseatic cities; of certain republics, the United Provinces; of certain monarchies, Great Britain—importance out of proportion with the size of their populations or their level of production. One should look for an explanation in the ability of these political units to levy taxes, thanks to the high level of their commercial activity, to the place of tariffs in their fiscal systems, and to the direct taxes on internal commerce which were based on an agricultural system farther removed from a subsistence economy.

But the states—and by this I mean the ruling class, that is the kings, their chief collaborators, and the entire clientele of these collaborators, in other words all those interested in the strength and wealth of public power, or, what we would call today the "techno-structure" of the state—did not always have, in fact usually did not have, the patience to wait for the level of economic evolution which would give them the means to govern, to make war, or to turn the state as they pleased. The ambitions of kings for several centuries ran ahead of the economic structure of their states and of the evolution of the economic conjuncture. This being-out-of-phase, this distorted relationship, caused the states to resort to overly burdensome taxes and simplistic kinds of assessment which made the tax system very difficult to endure. *This poor adaptation of the fiscal system to economic realities had many consequences.*

The first series of consequences was that economy was crushed by the inevitable blunders of awkward tax policies. The multiplication of tolls and duties paralyzed commerce, actually reducing the resources which it could take advantage of. The tithe hindered technological advances in agriculture. The cadastral type of property tax, poorly assessed, based on an almost nonexistent estimate of values, seldom revised, led to the abandonment of farms. The official papers of the fiscal administrations of the period illustrate that they were aware of all these effects; from the papers of Colbert, those of Turgot and the first economists came vehement denunciations of these distasteful effects of taxation. But such effects were difficult to avoid as long as the economy was underdeveloped and strictly limited the possibilities of taxation. On close examination, proposals of the reformers of these periods appear to be a mixture of a few accurate observations and a large number of illusions.

A second series of consequences of the poor fit between the tax system and economic reality are the violent reactions of taxpayers, reactions which range from verbal complaints to riots, to rebellions. If one leaves aside religious movements, it is striking that most of the rebellions in European states from the fourteenth to the seventeenth, or even the eighteenth century, were tax revolts. This fact has been recognized, but for years the importance of fiscal rebellion has not been understood, and this despite the impressive number of tax revolts, several hundred in France alone under the single ministry of Richelieu. Their violence was spectacular: tax collectors were killed, sometimes with exquisite cruelty, and there were actual fixed battles between rebellious taxpayers and regular troops. Such uprisings were among the causes of the paralysis and decline of the Spanish empire. For an entire decade, the decade of the English Revolution and the Fronde, revolts (of which taxes were the pretext or the cause) checked the process of the construction of the administrative monarchies in Europe.

These reactions against taxation, or the constant possibility of such reactions were so important that the problem of how to handle them was one of the permanent preoccupations of the kings and their ministers. The solutions they adopted affected the constitutions of their states, their systems of administration, their juridical philosophy, and their political economy.

The retort by the taxpayers to taxation, which precipitated rebellion, provoked in turn the so-called reply on the part of the state (or rather, replies, since there were several and of different kinds): (1) they sought to improve fiscal techniques: there were advances, the limits of which we have already seen; (2) they sought to dodge taxation by means of expedients: here again they encountered limitations; (3) they tried economic solutions; and (4) they sought political solutions. There were two kinds of political solution: emphasis on constraint and attempts to obtain assent.

The Emphasis on Constraint. This was the typical political solution of the French monarchy, but we find the same kind of solution in other states, especially Spain. The preoccupation with the collection of taxes and with the putting down of taxpayers' rebellions is expressed by means of a whole group of institutions. In the first place, there is the administrative framework. The mainspring of French administration under the *Ancien Régime*, the *intendant*, owes its creation to fiscal preoccupations. The *intendant* was responsible for the collection of taxes; to do this effectively he had to improve the means of assessment and give all the necessary help to the tax collectors in their activity against the taxpayers. From this derives his role as chief of police. He had to worry about the economic development of his generality, a development upon which depended its tax potential. He had to keep an eye on the finances of municipalities in order that the excesses in spending did not prejudice the collection of royal taxes.

The *intendant* also had a judiciary role. The *contrôleur général des finances* had no confidence in the ordinary courts when clashes broke out between taxpayers and the administration. By means of a whole series of operations, the final word in such conflicts was entrusted to either the *intendant* or to the *Conseil d'Etat*. Thus, two institutions of modern-day France—the prefectoral system and administrative justice—are the result of the tax revolts in the times of Richelieu, Mazarin, and Louis XIV. The preoccupation with avoiding unfavorable reactions among the taxpayers likewise led to restrictions of individual liberties, notably the right of assembly and local freedom—in other words, all that might have provided the taxpayers with the opportunity of banding together to resist the state. The professional army, composed largely of foreign mercenaries, backed up any administrative or judiciary action. Finally, the state had at its disposal a reserve force in the form of the privileged classes. The king and his ministers knew very well that in case revolts took place they had to be able to count on the support of the nobility and, although to a lesser degree, on the urban bourgeoisie.

We find much evidence in the correspondence of statesmen (Richelieu, Mazarin, Colbert) and of the *intendants* of their fears which resulted from any coalition whatsoever of the different social classes of the country directed against the king and the tax system. Whence derived the maintenance of tax privileges, which were, though deliberately, graduated. There was relative coherence in this aggregate of institutions, and when, toward the end of the eighteenth century, the monarchy tried to remove one of the units, the whole structure collapsed.

The System of Consent. What we might call the system of consent, or appeal for the adhesion of the taxpayers, was likewise coherent. The machinery for this operation first appeared in the various European states in the thirteenth or fourteenth centuries, and the Parliaments, the Estates-General, and the Cortes all helped the sovereigns to effect the acceptance of the earliest forms of taxation. But beginning in the sixteenth or seventeenth century, the sovereigns of the major countries turned toward the form of government known as the absolute monarchy, of which we get a rather accurate picture of the state under Philip II and Louis XIV.

In Great Britain, on the contrary, through several serious clashes the parliamentary institution persisted, and as time went on revealed all its distinctive features. We might attribute its relative permanence (there were long eclipses) to the fact that taxes were often less heavy in England than on the Continent and to the fact that its trade-based economy made tax collection easier, at the same time providing a greater incentive for participating in the life of the state. Even though the advancement of the parliamentary institution might have been due, from a given stage onward, to preoccupations that were no longer exclusively fiscal, this institution nonetheless still manifests the stamp of its origin through many traits. In this lies one of the explanations of its imperfections and weaknesses.

Economic Solutions. The governing classes surely realized the inadequacy of political solutions, such as repression or seeking the consent of the governed, and therefore sought economic solutions. We have much evidence that they reasoned quite simply as follows: seeing that taxation requires a certain economic structure, developed economic exchange, active commerce, and the division of labor, it behooves the state, and is in fact vital to its existence as a state, to bring its powers to bear upon that structure and to shape it into a structure better able to support taxation.

Fiscal concerns were at the root of mercantilist policy. They explain the importance assigned to the accumulation of a growing stock of money, to an active system of exchange; they explain the opposition to the family-based economy, grinding grain on the farm, for example, before selling it to mills; they explain the establishment of markets and fairs, places at which seignorial taxation had formerly been and where now royal taxes could be collected; they explain the efforts at urbanization and the policy of industrialization which often tended to sacrifice the agricultural sector. This is not conjecture; the French, English, and statesmen of other countries explained their policies and their goals clearly.

If we admit that mercantilist policy was important in the building of a modern economy, we are forced to recognize that by way of this new direction fiscal concerns shaped our societies. But it was necessary that the structure of the society contribute to the evolution of the economy. The countries of Eastern Europe, especially Russia, realized that they lacked an economy of exchange strong enough on which to base a policy of modern state-building. Cities were too rare, merchants too few, and the subsistence economy too widespread; they could not imitate the fiscal policies of the western monarchies and impose indirect taxes. As to direct taxes, the burden and the inevitably simplistic character of assessment led to a flight of taxpayers. In order to build the infrastructure for both taxation and the state, they had to freeze potential taxpayers in the places of production and reduce the mobility of the peasantry. In order to insure the inflow of taxes the czars reimposed serfdom starting in the fifteenth century and continuing to the nineteenth; this was the same process that had occurred, and for similar reasons, in the Late Roman Empire. All of Eastern Europe and a part of Central Europe underwent this kind of political and social change.[24]

The Building of the State and the Problem of the Nation in the Eighteenth Century

INTRODUCTION

From the point of view of the history of taxation, just as in the case of economic history or general history, the eighteenth century is rather ambiguous[25] since, in one sense, it did nothing more than prolong the preceding period. In France, as in Central Europe and the Iberian Peninsula, the machinery of power continued to exist with all its external manifestations. Moreover, it gathered strength in certain countries as a result of imitating French institutions. The representative assemblies which had disappeared or been obliterated in the seventeenth century did not reappear, and those that survived

[24] I give the broad lines of what has been explained elsewhere with more detail and with evidence (Ardant 1971: vol. I, part II, titre III).

[25] By the eighteenth century I mean the period which extends from the Treaties of Utrecht (or in France, from the death of Louis XIV) up to the French Revolution; in other words, from 1713 or 1715 to 1789, not without calling to mind the period of the wars of the Revolution and of the Empire.

played a role of ever-diminishing importance. There were still some conspiracies in evidence, but in Western Europe revolts became less frequent up to the end of the century at least. What were the reasons for such an increase of power? This is the first question for which we shall try to find an answer.

Inversely, the very machinery of power and society itself were challenged in a greater degree, or at least, in a more open way than previously. Even the rulers themselves were aware of the flaws in their institutions and hoped to reform them. Their attempts, however, came up against some imposing obstacles, and, if some progress was effected, many setbacks could also be listed. The most striking attempts at reform were those of the French monarchy, but they were not the only ones to make such attempts. If this was so, why did all these efforts fail?

Explanations based on an analysis of the character of the rulers would not be sufficient; though they are valid for some rulers, Louis XVI for example, they are not for others, such as Joseph II who lacked neither the willpower nor the stubbornness. Even in this case, are we to accuse an economic structure which, although certainly more developed than in the seventeenth century, was not perfect even taking into account the ambitions of the governments? Must we not take into account the according of privileges, which constituted an undeniable obstacle for reform-minded kings and ministers? Why were not these monarchs more strongly determined to overcome the difficulties, or was it, rather, that they were unable to do so? Was it perhaps that the sovereigns did not understand that their efforts had to be backed by the consent of the bulk of the inhabitants? Or was it that they were unable to see that the building of the state had to be accompanied by the building of the nation? How should we weigh the different explanations which we are taking into consideration? Even the slightest investigation of enlightened despotism and of its most important avenues of action will allow us to answer, or rather, to draw up the outline of an answer.

THE POWER OF STATES IN THE EIGHTEENTH CENTURY
AND THEIR INFRASTRUCTURE

In the eighteenth century, we witness in the European countries taken as a whole (except for those that ceased to exist, such as Poland) a resurgence of the power of states. Armies increased in size,[26]

---

[26] This increase of the effective forces, which had begun in the second half of

and larger battle-fleets were constructed. Throughout Europe (except for England)—in Russia, Spain, Austria, Naples, Portugal, etc. —there was a tendency to establish a bureaucratic monarchy having a hierarchical nature and patterned on the French model, which thus consisted of both a central government and local governments run by delegates appointed directly by the ruler, who were equivalent to the *intendants* sent by Versailles to each generality.

This development was based on the increase of the government's financial resources due to the progress made as regards public finance and, even more so, to the growth of the states' fiscal capacity. *This greater facility in collecting taxes was linked not only to advances in the areas of agricultural and industrial production, but also to the decidedly important increase of trade.* All this resulted from a group of phenomena: from more intensive trade with the countries of Asia and America to the introduction into Europe of a wider scale of products like tea, coffee, cacao, sugar, and cotton. Improvements in techniques of maritime and overland transport, the creation of navigable waterways, improvements in the network of roads, and somewhat faster service as regards communications had for effect the penetration of an exchange economy even in those regions which were not directly in touch with the maritime trade.

This was all made easier by the return to the worldwide production of gold and silver which evolved according to the pattern in Table 3–1.

TABLE 3–1. WORLDWIDE PRODUCTION OF GOLD AND SILVER, 1701–1800 (in kilograms)

Twenty-year Period	Silver	Gold	Coefficient of Growth
1701–1720	335,000	12,820	1.08%
1721–1740	431,200	10,080	21.26%
1741–1760	533,145		23.64%
1761–1780	652,740		22.34%
1781–1800	879,060		34.67%

Source: Soetbeer 1879.

Technical progress made in capital flows and banking operations contributed its results, so that some of the most important operational measures were put at the disposal of the more active commerce.[27]

the reign of Louis XIV, worried the military experts (of theory and practice) who, like Guibert (Guibert 1773), did their best to point out that, as a result, the character of military operations was too unwieldy and, therefore, was far from efficacious.
[27] Obviously we do not have statistics which permit us to measure the development

To the advances in trade we owe one of the features of the eighteenth-century fiscal system: the tendency to rely more on indirect taxes, or more specifically, on the possibility to levy indirect taxes, since governments had always sought to use this type of taxation. Likewise, these advancements made direct taxation easier, because the development of the market economy allowed the peasants greater ease in paying the taxes whose assessment became less burdensome.

Another distinctive feature of the times lay in the fact that, although the trend was toward the creation of more centralized and more costly forms of government, if there was opposition, it did not on the whole result in tax revolts of the proportions of those which the French and Spanish monarchies had had to face in the seventeenth century.[28] It can be seen therefore that political development no longer held the lead over the economy in the way that it had in the seventeenth century. If we made a detailed study, analyzing the causes of the strength of states as are presented to us through wars, the importance of the financial, and more precisely, the fiscal basis of power would stand out even more clearly; however, I will limit myself to a few very simple ideas.

On the whole we can say that France was more powerful than Austria. At the beginning of the eighteenth century, although the Austrian monarchy had territories as extensive and almost as heavily populated as those of the French king, his revenue from taxes was five times less. Spain in the second half of the eighteenth century was two and one-half times less populated than France, but she still possessed her colonial empire: all of Latin America with the exception of Brazil, and the Philippines. The general revenue of the state came to 440 million *reals*, or 110 million pounds *tournois*, while in France the revenue in the treasury totaled 500 million pounds.[29]

We can also compare two other states: in spite of the proportion

---

of the exchange economy in the principal European countries. This development can be assumed on the basis of a series of partial data. It should be noted that historians emphasize a development of exchange operations which was more significant than the development of industry. "In the eighteenth century even more than in the seventeenth, commercial progress outstripped industrial progress," writes Henri Sée (1948–1951: vol. I, 293), and he adds that this is a European—moreover, a worldwide—phenomenon.

[28] Of course there are exceptions such as the opposition of the Estates of Styria, Carniola, and Hungary to the financial reforms of Joseph II. As for the French Revolution, its characteristics make it a tax revolt of a special kind.

[29] Of this 100 million *reals* came from America.

of two to one in population (six million as opposed to three million), the kingdom of the Two Sicilies had an army of the same total strength (30,000 men) as the kingdom of Sardinia. The revenue of both states was about the same: 30 million pounds *tournois* at Naples and 25 million at Turin, capital of a state, the foundation of which was laid on the active economic life of Savoy and the Piedmont with all the advantages that trade could bring to the "gateway to the Alps."

What caused these incongruities? We can answer this question only by investigating the economic foundation of taxation and power. In this regard, Austria provides us with a typical example: advisers to the Emperor proposed setting up his finances on an economic base by exploiting the commercial potential provided his states by the treaties of Utrecht—whence the creation of the Ostend Company whose charter was approved in 1722 (cf. Pirenne 1902: vol. 5, and especially Huisman 1902). We know how much this desire for commercial development worried Great Britain, ever-ready throughout the century to restrain any other country's trade. After a series of diplomatic ups and downs, Charles VI abandoned the Ostend Company in exchange for the recognition of the Pragmatic Sanction, thus hoping to keep his states intact in the interest of his daughter.[30] The result of this policy was a state without money and, consequently, without an army and, historians tell us, it was the great joke among other rulers. The sergeant-king openly made fun of the emperor saying, "The Emperor has no land—he is as poor as a painter."

The English envoy predicted the imminent ruin of the Empire, and the French foreign minister shared his views. From instructions given the duke de Richelieu, French ambassador to Vienna, in 1725 we have extracted the following:

Whatever may be the extent of power that the Emperor has attained because of the important acquisitions he had made, we are not unaware that, in spite of the help he has had from several princes from outside of and within the Empire, the great expenditures for wars have terribly upset his finances. Moreover, the help that he draws from the Low Countries, Hungary,

[30] This attitude can also be explained by the threat of war. As a matter of fact, in 1724, the English government demanded the suspension of the Ostend Company for seven years, the renunciation of the Austro-Spanish Commercial Treaty and the Austrian consent to the reestablishing of English monopolies in Spain and India—this constituted the Emperor's abandoning of his economic plan.

the Kingdom of Naples, Sicily, and from Milan, is hardly sufficient to maintain his position, so that, independently of the fact
that every part of his new acquisitions is a burden on him in
peace-time, he would not be able to sustain war-time expenditures, especially since he would not have the same resources
that England, Holland, and several princes from within the Empire offered him in the course of the last war (Commission des
Archives 1884: vol. 1, 208).

The victory of Prussia under Frederick II over the much more
extensive and more densely populated Austria was the result of this
situation. It seems unnecessary to emphasize what historians have
so often done; that is, the contrast offered by Prussian power which
was based on the parallel development of the economy, finances, and
the army. The lesson did not go unheeded; thus, Maria Theresa did
her best to form (or reform) simultaneously an administration, a tax
system, and an army, and Joseph II sought to augment the work she
had begun.[31] The inadequacy of the economic infrastructure limited
the results of these efforts.

In spite of having much less territory and a much smaller population than the Austrian and French monarchies,[32] England was undeniably the dominant power, to the extent that one historian dealing with the eighteenth century, or more precisely with the period
from 1715 to 1763, entitled his work, *La prépondérance anglaise*
(Muret 1949). It hardly seems questionable that England derived
her power in a great degree from her financial resources. Great Britain's economic structure provided the foundation for her fiscal capacity by allowing her to give the most important role to the taxation
of commercial activities. Thus, from 1736 to 1738 we have on an
average:

Tax	Revenue in Pounds
Land	1,000,000
Windows, Annuities, and Functions	135,000

In contrast to this, we have the much higher totals which were collected much more easily from taxation on trading operations.

[31] The revenue of the state which hardly reached 30 million florins under Charles
VI, rose to 56 million in 1773, and was over 80 million at the death of Maria Theresa.
[32] In 1789 the population of England did not exceed 9 million while France had
26 million inhabitants.

Tax	Revenue in Pounds
Customs	1,400,000
Excise	3,000,000
Stamp	150,000

To be sure, wartime made it necessary to impose direct taxes: in 1739 the land tax rate was doubled, in 1747 the tax on windows was raised, and in 1756 the land tax, which had been reduced in the meantime, was again doubled. But a large part of fiscal endeavors had to be aimed at indirect taxes: for instance, during the War of the Austrian Succession attention was focused on the taxing of salt, wine, vinegar, and imported textiles, and on the raising of duties, while during the Seven Years War, it was focused on the creating of a general customs duty on a range of merchandise from the colonies and on the raising of the tax on beer.

The other European states did not have this possibility to the same extent. Several factors made it inevitable that England have trade, the channels of which were rather easy to keep an eye on, in spite of smuggling: England was an island, her climate practically precluded the production of wine, and her commercial activity brought about the use of other items which she did not produce either, such as tea and tobacco. Even the difficulties Walpole came up against are very instructive. One part of his financial policy was aimed at replacing import duties by domestic taxes in hopes of reducing the losses incurred by extremely active smuggling operations. Popular reaction to "this monster excise tax" was such that he was forced to abandon his scheme.[33] It was Pitt who discovered the right solution: customs duties could yield more if they were lowered. Thus it was that in 1748 Henry Fox pointed out before the House of Commons the type of tax which was easiest to impose and to collect. It was not always possible to stick to this formula. In fact, in 1763 the government was obliged to recommend the taxing of cider and perry (i.e., a fermented pear drink). Since these were common household beverages produced, notably in the "Cider land," by the peasants for home consumption, the Cider bill provoked such opposition that Bute was forced to resign.

These different reactions are significant, because they show that

[33] Cf. Cobbett 1811: vols. VIII, IX; the letters edited in Coxe 1798, Hervey 1848; and the books devoted to the life of Robert Walpole by Brisco (1907), Morley (1919), Plumb (1956), etc. Cf. also Paul Vaucher (Vaucher 1924).

the awareness of the English regarding taxation was perhaps no keener at this period than that of the French, since when put in identical tax situations, they both reacted in the same way. Once again it was the economic structure that facilitated the assessment, supervision, and collection of taxes. Finally, the victory of Pitt's England over the France of Louis XV was, just as in the case of the victory of the Plantagenets and later that of William of Orange a victory for the more mercantile nation.

Because her trade (especially foreign trade) made considerable advances after the Seven Years War, we can understand how France was able to get even with England in the form of the American Revolution, which was touched off by the lack of fiscal daring on the part of the English who had thought it possible to lighten their financial burden at the expense of men who had not consented to taxation. France was victorious, but the fiscal strain on her was such that her financial problems became insoluble for lack of a radical reform, which meant, given the blindness of the privileged classes, revolution. The various European states were not entirely unaware that their power was built on an economic and fiscal base, and this awareness perhaps formed the bedrock of enlightened despotism.

THE INFRASTRUCTURE OF ENLIGHTENED DESPOSITISM

The conditions in which modern states were formed cannot be understood if we leave out the ideas and activities which constitute the movement generally known as enlightened despotism. The sovereigns to whom we attribute this double epithet—Maria Theresa and Joseph II, Frederick II, Charles, King of the Two Sicilies and later of Spain, Grand Duke Leopold of Tuscany, and a certain number of German princes[34]—had in common the will to create an absolute, centralized, administrative form of government. The powers of the representative assemblies, notably the right of consent to taxation, were reduced more and more, and increasingly more affluent administrations made ever greater inroads. What is more, these authoritarian regimes had the support of writers, philosophers, and

[34] I have not mentioned Catherine II on purpose because she cannot qualify as a reformer. She duped a certain number of great European writers, who were really willing to let themselves be duped, but she cannot fool history. As far as France was concerned Louis XV and Louis XVI did not display, strictly speaking, the features of enlightened despots, although they did carry out, and above all wanted to carry out, a number of reforms. It will be better to come back to them and treat their cases in greater detail.

economists. Even those who had advocated that citizens take part in the administration of public affairs, resigned themselves to postponing the establishment of the constitutional form of government to the distant future, to that time when, as a result of educational progress, the citizens themselves would be enlightened.

In the meantime, they placed their trust in those rulers whose absolutism seemed the only means of overcoming all the obstacles which privilege and ignorance had placed in the way of administrative, social, and tax reform. It became more and more apparent that the main preoccupation consisted of rationalizing (to use a modern term) man's life, his behavior, his institutions, and his government. Public opinion became more and more aware of the absurdity of rules which were devoid of all save tradition, and tolerated with increasing impatience groundless discriminations, legal atrocities, ineffectual regulations, and repressive measures opposed to the putting into operation of new techniques the effects of which, it was felt, would have great significance in everyone's life.

Tradition no longer sufficed. Institutions were summoned before the tribunal of reason to justify their existence in terms of their usefulness. Although rulers held more absolute power than their predecessors, this power was no longer held to be sacred. Philosophers, economists, and public opinion which observed them closely, based the authority of heads of government on their capacity to carry out at least some reforms. In this respect, Frederick II, Charles III, and Joseph II were certainly men of their time, since they had the determination, if not the passion, to remodel society and to make it conform more exactly to what they considered to be demands of the mind.

What constituted the background of the desire for reform? First of all, there were government and especially military expenditures. The eighteenth century was no less harsh toward the weak than were the preceding centuries. The country without a relatively strong army and navy was threatened as regards its freedom of action, its territorial integrity, and even its very independence. Those states having the best troops (Prussia under Frederick II) or the best ships (England) imposed on others national defense measures which were comparable, if not equal to their own. The keenly felt military requirements needed for the preparation and carrying out of wars constituted perhaps the main stimulus of reforms—above all, of tax reforms.

[205]

The states of the eighteenth century had more fiscal devices at their disposal than their predecessors, but they did not suffice; professional soldiers equipped with modern artillery were costly, and even technical progress had not reduced the price of warships outfitted with increasingly numerous pieces of artillery. Investments were necessary so that industry could stock the arsenals and armories and so that an increased production could feel the flow of trade so necessary to the life of the state.

Rulers had been aware of these problems for centuries, and in order to solve such problems, they had worked out a mercantile policy, all the while struggling with faulty structures and catastrophic economic trends. Structures had improved, economic trends had become more advantageous, and men tended more spontaneously to produce and invest. We understand how rulers and administrators might have been more willing to listen to men like Quesnay, Gournay, Adam Smith, and Lemercier de la Rivière, who showed them all the benefits the nations' wealth could derive from a more liberal economy, a less strictly regulated market, and from less heavily subjugated initiatives of reform.

The agricultural revolution of the eighteenth century came up against not only superannuated community laws but also against the fiscal system which too frequently penalized their efforts to invest and to produce. The birth of mechanization presupposed the freedom to innovate and to apply the results of innovation in spite of their incompatibility with standing corporate or administrative statutes, and it also presupposed a moderate tax on profits.

Among the conditions for economic progress, one stood out as being more urgently required than ever, precisely because of the prospects offered to investment; this condition was the reduction of arbitrary, illegal despotism. According to the views even of those who favored it, despotism had to be legal; in other words, general rules had to be determined for the framework within which individuals could act freely without fear of any capricious repercussions on the part of the lord or functionary. For this reason, the setting-up of guide lines in the fields of civil law and penal law and for the tax system was seen as one of the features of the reform necessary for both society and the state.

These aspirations were especially characteristic of the bourgeoisie which intended to take over new markets and to turn the capital amassed through trade into productive industries. Needless to say, this class was most intolerant of the legal and fiscal favoritism found within the governmental structure. Although they were limited, improvements in transport operations—the opening of more canals, the bettering of roads and means of conveyance—as well as increases in production made people more keenly aware of the many obstacles in such form as tolls and domestic tariffs that stood in the way of the flow of goods.

This very sketchy presentation is not equally valid for all countries —for Great Britain, for instance, where trade brought in enough so that governmental leaders did not have the same preoccupation with reforms; as a matter of fact, they were of the opinion that there were no further reforms to be carried out. Such a presentation is not true either in the case of the Eastern European countries, at least not for Russia, which did experience developments in commerce and growth in industry, but not in any measure to warrant imperialist expansion. The reasons still remained which had led the czar to introduce serfdom in the first place, in the hope of easing the collection of direct taxes rudimentary as they were. To this let us add the role played by the furnishing of services, including military service, in an economy of insufficient monetary development. The aristocracy constituted at one and the same time the bulwark of the state, the foundation of which was laid on coercion more than anything else, and on its master. Catherine II could not forget that she owed her power of the regiments of the imperial guard and to a handful of officers from the nobility, and that she could not oppose the basic interests of this class. For this reason, she took but little from the ideas of enlightened despotism.

Similar was the case of Frederick II, who also discovered such a disparity between his country's needs and its resources that he could not afford to run counter to the interests of the aristocracy. Moreover, he saw that he would have to play a relatively big part in the state's economic intervention. However, since there was adequate industrial progress in Prussia, he could afford to rely rather heavily on indirect taxation. Lastly, even though he honored the interests of the large landowners, he tried to encourage their adopting more modern methods of production.

RESULTS OF ENLIGHTENED DESPOTISM

What were the results of the activity of the enlightened despots? They were by no means negative, since we cannot deny the progress made on the level of tolerance. In that sense the countries were heading toward the modern idea of the secular state. Some very important penal reforms were initiated, in some countries serfdom was reduced or suppressed, and order was introduced into fiscal administration.

However, the reforms did not reach the heights of the ambitions of the kings and their advisers; in fact, in some countries—the case of the Austrian monarchy is the most striking—there was marked evidence of reversion to former conditions. In France it was more a question of blocking those measures proposed by reform-minded ministers. Some progress was made, but when administrators endeavored to have their plans put into effect, they encountered insurmountable resistance. The reasons for the relative failures of both enlightened despots and ministers are of two kinds: the reformers ran up against the social structure and the power of the privileged classes. They had not always correctly judged the force of the former, and they did not want to undertake the necessary measures to overcome the latter. In other words, these reformers of the state retreated in the face of the building of the nation.

Economic Obstacles. At least some of the reforms of enlightened despotism were to be carried out in an economic situation which indeed had evolved, but not sufficiently. In this respect the attempts of the Hapsburgs are particularly significant. In this country, as elsewhere, one of the sovereigns' major preoccupations centered on agricultural policy. Thus it was that they set high hopes on newly developed techniques: the use of fodder plants, the discontinuation of fallow, and the more extensive use of fertilizer.

All attempts to put these into practice still needed to be sustained by investments and productivity, but such attempts met instead with opposition in the form of existing institutions, vestiges of the manorial system and the fiscal administration. Economists had denounced for a long time the levying of taxes on raw materials and arbitrary taxation of all kinds; these, however, could be replaced by the *cadastre*. Based on the net gain (thus avoiding arbitrary measures) the *cadastre* might, by virtue of this, prompt farmers to increase their investments; the extent of the effects of this might be stressed by refraining from revising all evaluations over a period of many years, say, twenty years, for example.

Considerations taken as a whole suffice to make it clear that enlightened despots warmly welcomed the *cadastre* solution, that some of them put it into practice, and that others attempted to put it into practice or, at least had some inclination to do so. Thus it was that a *cadastre* was established from the very beginning of the eighteenth century in one of the richest provinces of the Austrian monarchy. Introduced in 1719, the Milanese *cadastre* was terminated in 1760. According to one historian of finance, it served as the model for the *cadastre* operations later carried out in France and in other states.[35] As a matter of fact, when we examine the methods used by Austria, we became aware of the place held (just as later on in the case of the French *cadastre*) by the markets, verifications taken from indications found in leases, etc.

It must be said that because of its geographical features (a plain checkered with canals), its development, and by the trade activated in its main city and secondary towns, the duchy of Milan was the ideal place in which to establish a *cadastre*. Such was not the case in other Hapsburg dominions where the reform of the property tax, although inspired by the same principles, did not have the same success. When she initiated the "rectification of taxes" (1748–1756), Maria Theresa faced the opposition not only of the lords with their privileges, but also that of the economic infrastructure. It was probably for these reasons that she had to be satisfied with incomplete declarations in some provinces and with superficial evaluations in others.

We might take another example: France. When we investigate the reasons for the failure of every minister who stubbornly strove to tax the net income from lands, we can and must (we shall come back to this) blame the opposition raised by the privileged classes. In consideration of this, we must not underestimate the resistance of the milieu.

Reformers like Abbé de Saint-Pierre and others were right in advocating a better accounting of everyone's resources and an evaluation of agricultural produce, in other words, everything that constituted the proportional *taille*, or *taille tarifée*; moreover, they were right in assigning the carrying out of this work to the administration

---

[35] This opinion was expressed by Wagner (Wagner 1909: Vol. IV, 142). In fact, these were the methods that the French tried to put into practice by fixing the *taille tarifée* and by attempting to improve the assessment of the *vingtième*.

(the *intendants* in charge of the *taille* or the inspector of the *vingtième*). But, apart from the opposition of the privileged classes, it was not easy to initiate these estimates.

It is a fact that the *taille tarifée* had success only in large agricultural areas where tenant farming was widespread, such as in the generality of Paris and Champagne. In the Limousin the difficulties were greater—Turgot was not wrong, and in *Un mémoire au Conseil sur la surcharge des impositions*, this *intendant* of Limoges wrote:

> In the rich provinces such as Normandy, Picardy, Flanders, Orleans, and the outskirts of Paris, nothing is more simple than finding out the real value of capital assets and their correlation with the tax schedule. All land is farmed out, and their rental value is common knowledge; they even know the value of those estates that the owners develop and that have practically all been leased, all the farmers of the canton know how much they would pay to lease it. The proportion between the taille and the rental value is also widely known and about which there can be no mistake. It can also be said that in these sections the cadaster is, so to speak, tailor-made as regards the evaluation of capital. The situation is very different in the poor provinces in the interior of the realm, such as the Bourbonnais, the Limousin, and all those provinces turned over to small farmers and *métayers* (Turgot 1914: 446–447).

The Physiocrats were not unaware of these difficulties. They tended though to rid themselves of the problem by saying that taxes would be imposed on the net product when all of France would be dedicated to big farming and tenant farming.[36]

The difficulties were such that many capable minds, like Terray, Turgot, and Necker, although they agreed on this point, thought it only possible to get around them by means of assessment (*répartition*). They calculated that, if they left it up to a given community to apportion a fixed amount among its members, they would be able to manage the effective application of the tax because of the clash between conflicting interests.

When the tax rate is established on a region as a whole (a tax sys-

[36] Cf. the statements in these terms of Quesnay, of the Marquis de Mirabeau (V. Mirabeau 1760), and others.

tem known as the quota [*quotité*]), it is not in the interests of a tax-payer to have a hand in taxing his neighbor. Things are different when the tax burden of a given community is established beforehand and when the members or representatives of the group are responsible for effecting the apportionment. When one person is required to pay less, more has to be required of someone else. Thus, the clash of conflicting interests automatically leads the community to establish a tax in proportion to each member's possibilities.

Such was Turgot's idea, and in his "Plan d'un mémoire sur les impositions," he studied the different procedures for determining the assessment as regards territorial taxation. After having indicated his preference on the theoretical level for a proportional tax on revenue (the quota, or *quotité*), he added: "I have to admit that the whole thing seems impossible to me: in the present system the king or the government is one against everyone else, who is interested only in concealing the value of his assets" (Turgot 1914: 307). Necker also believed in the advantages of assessment (*répartition*). In keeping with these views, provincial assemblies were tried out in 1778 and 1779, and became widespread in 1787. These assemblies added some limited but judicious reform measures to tax assessment. The blow dealt to the power of the *intendants*, in other words, to the French administrative system as a whole, was, according to de Tocqueville,[37] not the least of the causes for the state's weakness in the face of the first rumblings of revolution.

In any case, the creation of the provincial assemblies prefigured the local administrative system of the Constituent Assembly which handed over to the departments, districts, and communes the responsibility of establishing and levying taxes. The results were most disappointing and we can understand how this was one of the basic reasons for the breakdown of taxation and of the state, a breakdown which was, due to the opposition it stirred up, one of the causes for the dictatorship of the Convention and of the Napoleonic government. Of these events let us remember only that the stubbornness with which they clung to the myth of the *répartition* remains moreover a proof of the obstacles resulting from tax assessment in a country that had an economic and social structure like France of that time.

[37] Cf. in de Tocqueville in chapter 7, Book III entitled "How revolutionary changes in the administrative system preceded the political revolution and their consequences" (Gilbert 1955).

Resistance of the Privileged Classes. Preoccupation with correcting certain analyses must not make us overlook that other previously mentioned obstacle which caused so many reforms to fail: the resistance of the privileged classes. Because he was one of the most systematically minded of despots, Joseph II was especially sensitive to this. Agricultural progress in his country implied not only fiscal reform, but also a genuine freeing of the peasants who were, at the beginning of the eighteenth century, still under the yoke of serfdom. Maria Theresa had granted them certain rights: the right to marry, to acquire certain plots of land, and the right of due process before the state. The delays in effecting policies of reform brought about uprising which Joseph II, associated with the empire since 1760, was forced to quell by means of the army.

It was very evident that he had to make strides: when he became sole sovereign in 1780 he carried out a series of legal, economic, and fiscal reforms. After bringing the *cadastre* to completion, he decided that the payments made by the peasants to their lords had to be restricted in order that the total amount of these payments plus taxes did not exceed 30 percent of the net income. The nobility put up such opposition that Joseph had to suspend application of the reform. His successor rescinded it and then reestablished serfdom, which was not definitively abolished until 1848.

The overall outlines of the evolution in France during the eighteenth century are no less instructive, since at that time this country had a particularly brilliant corps of administrators. Because of the extent of their learning, the breadth of the prerogatives, the experience they acquired daily, and because of their participation in intellectual movements, the best of the *intendants*, at least, could not avoid feeling the overwhelming need to change social conditions starting with that aspect which had the greatest developmental potential—the fiscal system. Men from this category were brought to power time and again because of the more or less justified but never totally unwarranted reputation they had made according to the enlightened public opinion of the era. Now, these talented and right-intentioned men never stopped running into obstacles whose reliability never ceases to amaze us.

We can summarize the history of the last *contrôleurs généraux* by saying that they lasted only as long as they accepted the system in effect and that they had to resign when they decided to reform it. Such was the fate of Calonne, who after having exhausted the resources of a policy of convenience, ended up by proposing as a guideline for financial recovery the suppression of abuses, which were none other than privileges! His successor could do nothing else but carry on Calonne's projects; after various ups and downs he too was dismissed. The monarchy finally resigned itself to convoking the Estates-General. One can imagine that the contrast between, on the one hand, a rather widespread critical spirit and the desire for reform that had asserted itself on several occasions, and, on the other, the perpetual obstruction of reforms, created an explosive situation that was more dangerous than the situation in other European countries, where the notions held by the rulers were often more advanced than those of the great majority of the population.

We could take other examples, but those of the Austrian and French monarchies seem sufficient. All that is left is to ask ourselves *why rulers gave up trying to overcome the resistance they encountered.* We might be tempted to say that such difficulties caused them to become aware of the basis of their power. They came to understand that the strength of monarchies was not to be found in the Empyrean, and that the purity of their intentions and the quality of their administration were not sufficient guarantees of their authority. Kings could not do without the support of the privileged classes, or at least, the support of one of these classes. They could, if really necessary, dispense with the church, but certain kings or their heirs realized that they had gone too far in this direction. In all cases, it was difficult to do without the backing of the nobility which provided part of the administration and the greatest part of the military cadres, and which strung throughout every region a network of landlords, all interested in maintaining order.

If the generation of enlightened despots was followed by a generation of reactionary rulers, such as those Goya painted, it was not due only to genetic caprices and to the effects of intermarriage, but also because the successors of the reform-minded kings understood into what difficulties a too rational policy could lead them. The monarchs either did not dare or were not daring enough to rely on other classes (the bourgeoisie, the peasants, and the emerging class of industrial workers). By resurrecting ancient traditions they could have established a constitutional government which would have led the representatives of these classes to create a balance with the privileged classes. Besides, they could have had their support, notably in fiscal matters. But they did not want to take this course of action.

Would they have succeeded? We cannot conceal the fact that reforms still run into many obstacles inherent in the economic structure.

"THE STATE NEEDS THE NATION" LOUIS XVI, SEPT. 1789

The Nation Helps the State. From our point of view, which is that of the building of the state and the nation, one could summarize the events that took place in Europe during the eighteenth century in the following way: Improvements in production, and even more in trade, provided sovereigns with taxable material that was more valuable and more easily seized. Such an evolution in the economic structure permitted them to increase their power considerably without provoking the same reactions as in the preceding century. With continually growing needs (essentially, military requirements) kings thought that the means of procuring supplementary resources lay in the rationalization of the administration, institutions, and society. From such an overall reform they expected a more active economy because it would be rid of the many impediments which checked its growth, a more efficient administration because it would be simplified, and finally, more extensive resources. This constituted the basis of enlightened despotism.

However, rulers found many obstacles in their way: an economic structure still insufficiently developed (as much as they would have wished otherwise) to meet the needs of their attempts at fiscal reform, and to an even greater degree, the opposition of the privileged classes, the clergy, and the nobility.

To overcome these obstacles they would have been forced to turn to the masses not having privileges. This would have indeed transformed the basis of monarchical power such as it existed in Continental Europe, and it would have meant giving up the supplementary means of law enforcement furnished by the church and more especially by the aristocracy. On the whole, kings backed down. Apart from a few lukewarm attempts,[38] they gave up reforms. They did not dare appeal to the nation.

France was an exception. *In one sense we could define the French Revolution,* according to the phrase of Louis XVI, *as an appeal of the state to the nation,* then as an irruption of the nation in the state, or as an endeavor aimed at building in a parallel direction, with one

---

[38] It would be interesting to study these attempts: those of the King of Spain and of his ministers with recourse to the societies for progress, and those attempts of Joseph II, etc.

leaning on the other, both the nation and the state. Because of the repercussions of this event throughout all of Europe, it is worthwhile to stress its importance. What made this action take place in this country and at this time? In reality there are two questions to be answered: (1) Why the appeal to the Estates-General? (2) Why was the convocation of May 1789 followed by a revolution?

Why the Appeal to the Estates-General? In the fifteenth and sixteenth centuries the convocation of the Estates-General was an important but relatively ordinary undertaking. After an interruption of two centuries, from 1614 to 1789, one could not mistake the gravity of a solemn meeting of the elected delegates from the whole country. Why did the king bring himself to do it? The answer is quite simple: Louis XVI saw no other means of restoring life, or resourcefulness, to the state. The French monarchy had probably benefited more than others from the development of commerce, which had provided supplementary income from its very appreciable returns. The monarchy had widely adopted indirect taxation. Some might wonder if they had reached or even exceeded, the limits of this type of levy.

In the economic context of the era, it was not possible, rather they did not think it possible, to levy taxes on products by merely inspecting and seizing goods of trade as was done later on. The tax inspector entered the producer's or consumer's shop, his cellar, and even his private dwelling. The inspection of the wine producer's harvest and the inventory which allowed the determining of the ("too much drunk") or ("a great deal lacking") were very keenly resented, as those who drew up the lists of complaints declared openly. Insofar as the inspections by agents of the salt-tax were concerned, no one dared defend them any longer.

Technical progress was conceivable: theoretically they could have imposed a tax on beverages similar to the one worked out at the time of the Empire, and they could have replaced the *gabelle* by a tax collected at the exit of the salt beds or other production sites, with a relatively light tax on economic transactions. Two conditions were necessary: the undermining of the privileges in given provinces and the reducing of the burden of the indirect tax, which meant increasing the direct tax.

The first condition presupposed a more positively asserted consciousness of national unity, just as did the second condition. Men of the times had not realized fully the limited but real possibilities of taxing trades and dwellings, which developed later on in the forms of the licenses to exercise trades (*patentes*) and of the personal property tax (*contribution mobilière*). In effect, the initiating of a direct, productive tax, which was basically a land tax, presupposed the abolition of privileges from a plain technical point of view. To improve assessment it was necessary to tax each piece of property where it actually was located and not where the landlord lived; in other words, they had to give up this "personalization" of taxation to which the privileged classes and their promoters, the *parlements*, were so fiercely attached. Besides, no one could ask the taxpayers to make more of an effort without giving them the feeling of at least a bit of equality and without, in some way, seeking their voluntary participation. Direct taxes, because they are more apparent, have always constituted a more vital stimulus of political awareness than taxes on commerce which go unseen by many people who have to pay them.

This necessary recourse to direct taxation could be presented differently by following the reasoning of Labrousse: price increases had exceeded increases in salaries so that taxation of consumer goods, which made the cost of living go even higher, was resented more and more. Independently of public opinion, which regarded indirect taxes with a jaundiced eye, the *contrôleur general* could not do anything other than look for taxable material, especially the rich material in the form of the income of property owners.

Now, these supplementary sources of revenue appeared indispensable, since the abuse of loans had exhausted this source, the Abbé Terray's bankruptcy was still too fresh to be repeated, the monarchy either did not know how, or did not dare, to make extensive use of inflation, and since the war in America had made practically impossible the solution of an already thorny problem. The *contrôleurs généraux* had never given up attempting fiscal reforms throughout the course of the seventeenth century (except during Fleury's long ministry), but they had always run up against the privileges, and royal authority had proved inadequate. If we admit that revolution is possible in the case where enduring efforts to think out and even to attempt reform have revealed the possibility of and the necessity for radical change, then such was the case in France, more than anywhere else at the end of the eighteenth century, where all these conditions were present.

Why Was the Convocation of May 1789 followed by a Revolution?
The state's cry for help to the nation was the result of financial necessity as well as the consequence of an economic evolution that had
given more room to the bourgeoisie, a bourgeoisie that insisted on
the abolition of the privileges of the other classes. As important as
it might have been, this was not the only reason for their wanting to
take part in governing the state; besides, this desire was felt not only
by the bourgeoisie, but by the aristocracy and clergy as well.

To understand the situation, we must once more go back over the
evolution of the economic structure. The increased flow of trade
brought about greater interest in political decisions among a certain
number of people—landowners, industrialists, and merchants. When
the state revealed that it was incapable of maintaining its colonial
territory (markets in Asia and America), it seriously jeopardized
merchant interests. When the state was menaced by bankruptcy, the
stockholders were beset by worries. And, when the state concluded
a poorly drawn-up commercial treaty with England, a treaty which
resulted in fierce competition with British goods, the industrialists
were unhappy as were those workers out of work. To the extent that
the French economy was one of the better developed among the continental economies, *it made the desire for a share in the power more
keenly felt by a given segment of the population.*

For a whole variety of reasons, the convocation of the Estates-
General caused great reverberations throughout the country—the
gravity with which the lists of abuses (*Cahiers de doléances*) were
drawn up is one proof of this. Thus, the state needed the nation, and
at least one part of the nation felt dependent upon the state.

It seems of little use to dwell at greater length on what happened
afterward. We could summmarize the whole thing by saying that the
king may have suddenly realized, later than the enlightened despots
and too late to do any good, that he had without knowing it upset
the very foundation of his state—whence the hesitation, the setbacks,
and the fraud that ruined his popularity.

It might be wise to stress one point in particular. In its earliest period, the French Revolution manifested itself by *the disintegration
of the state due in large part to the illusions of the reformers of the
eighteenth century.* These men had thought that taxes could be
levied in a painless way by means of the technique (perhaps a gim-
mick) of assessment. This attempt at solving the problem of the distribution of the tax burden had led the king to give up one part of

[217]

the armor of his state, since before the Revolution the monarchy had succeeded in disarming itself. Dupe of the same pipe dreams, the National Assembly built up an administrative system in which taxes and the state would have been separated had the Committee of Public Safety (*Comité de Salut Publique*) and the people's Commissioners on detached service (*en mission*) not seen to their reorganization as a single unit.

All that there might have been in the way of anarchy and confusion during the French Revolution could not help but induce European rulers to preserve the machinery of power. It was this too that allowed Napoleon to re-establish a state which preserved certain reforms resulting from the national uprising, such as the suppression of provincial and class privileges, and at the same time rejected the basic demand that citizens have a hand in running the government.

We have noticed that the rulers at war with France often were beaten because they were unable to appeal to popular sentiment to fight the new vitality that this very sentiment gave to France. In the last years of the Empire, the French occupation of various European countries was no less responsible for stirring up the spirit of nationalism. This spirit, although checked temporarily by the Holy Alliance, ended up by erupting in the mid-nineteenth century.

For this reason this century witnessed simultaneously the continuing buildup of the state and the beginning of the construction of the nation.

The Industrial Revolution, the Power of States, and the Building of Nations

INTRODUCTION

The Industrial Revolution gave to states a material power much greater than had existed in the past. That economic mutation made easier or, at least, oriented the building of nations. More precisely, industrial societies are the basis of financial techniques, taxation, and money that can give to individuals a part of what they expect from community life. In the past, economic infrastructure was too backward to be the foundation of very ambitious financial techniques: a lot of strikes were the consequence of that distortion. Nowadays it might be the reverse. Financial techniques are not perfectly in accord with the physical potentialities of the world. In that sense our analysis can lead to a more accomplished building of nations.

[218]

THE INDUSTRIAL REVOLUTION AND THE POWER OF STATES

After having summarized how much the Industrial Revolution has modified the power of states, it will not be inappropriate to make some distinctions between political entities that did not participate, to the same extent, in that transformation. When considering some facts, the war economy particularly, one could think that fiscal factors have not the same impact as in the past. But when peace has limited the possibility of compulsory methods, we can see how much fiscal abilities can interfere with the stability of states.

The Evolution of the Economy and the Growth of State Power since the Nineteenth Century. During the nineteenth century, accelerating economic change and increased state power went hand in hand. Expenditures in the public sector increased by a large proportion. The gradual spread of compulsory military service throughout Europe (England excepted) meant that some saving could be made over the cost of mercenaries. It was still necessary, however, to feed, lodge, and equip armies which were larger than ever. It was also necessary to buy more technically perfect arms at more and more burdensome costs. Governments built the large, stratified administrations which their predecessors had dreamed of.[39]

New infrastructure expenses—roads, ports, canals, railroads—and new social expenditures, starting with schools, were added to the military and administrative outlay. As an illustration of one field, the budget for public education in France increased one hundred times between 1830 and 1905.

How could those expenditures be financed? The evolution of the banking structure and the development of a money economy were important. The credit of the state was used to a greater extent, while the issuing of nonmetallic money, i.e., paper money and bank money, allowed governments to indulge in much more effective types of inflation than had been possible in preceding centuries. Governments gained flexibility in their activity through the development of public credit and the perfection of inflationary techniques, both tied to the

[39] The failure of certain Mediterranean and Near Eastern countries, the Ottoman Empire, Tunisia, and Egypt to solve their financial difficulties sometimes encouraged the establishment of protectorates or intervention by the industrial nations: those backward states were in a situation not unlike that of the western states one or two centuries before. The desire to imitate the technological progress of Western Europe led to expenditures out of proportion to their economic structure.

progress of the monetary economy. This flexibility had not been possible in earlier times except in Great Britain and other commercial states. In this period, just as in the past, the capability to borrow and the capability promote inflation were based on a considerably increased fiscal capability. From the middle, if not the beginning, of the nineteenth century, taxation no longer raised insoluble problems for the states of Western Europe and North America.

Political changes, both the doing away with legal privilege at the beginning or during the nineteenth century and also the use of parliamentary mechanisms, that is, participation of citizens in the process of taxation, were closely connected to this transformation of the conditions for financial power. Yet it was primarily because of structural economic change that states could assess and collect taxes more easily, that the tax revolts disappeared, except for a few recent skirmishes, and that states found the opportunity to increase their military strength, their administrative activity and even their social intervention. It goes without saying that this economic change had a direct effect: one cannot imagine the armies of the American Civil War, of the Franco-Prussian War, and *a fortiori*, of 1914 in the agrarian societies of the seventeenth century. There is no need to call to mind that industrial potential, particularly steelmaking, then chemicals, forms the basis for armament manufacture, while railroads, in the days before trucks, were necessary for a rapid military mobilization and effective provisioning of armies in the field. The Crimean War is an example of the defeat of a great state because of the lack of an industrial infrastructure and modern means of communication.

The strength of nations was a function (we repeat this often stated fact) of the level of their energy resources. Industrial power also influenced the power of states by way of its incidence on their finances, or more exactly, on their fiscal capability. *The fiscal system was the "transformer" of the economic infrastructure into political structure.*

First we must consider the *increase of production*. All European countries could give us good examples. I will take France, using the figures of scholars who have tried to provide the basis of a quantitative history, from the beginning to the end of the nineteenth century, or more precisely from 1815–1824 to 1905–1913.[40] Table 3–2 gives

[40] The exact figures are in the study of M. Marczewski (Marczewski 1965), figures that take into account the works of MM. Toutain (1961) (agriculture) and Markovitch (1965) (industry).

TABLE 3-2. GROSS AGRICULTURAL AND INDUSTRIAL PRODUCT
AND STATE EXPENDITURES

Ten-year Period	Gross Physical Product (millions of francs)	State Expenditures (millions of francs)	State Expenditures as a Percent of Gross Product
1803–1812	7.012	960	13.6
1825–1834	9.301	1067	11.5
1845–1854	12.586	1609	12.8
1865–1874	18.446	2493	13.5
1885–1894	17.767	3335	18.8
1905–1913	25.814	3832	14.7

the gross product of agriculture and industry in current francs, state expenditures, and their percentage of that product. Although very great, production increased a little less than state expenditures: from the beginning of the nineteenth century to the beginning of the twentieth century what was taken in by state from the gross production of the country rose from 12.6 percent to 14.7 percent. But, and this is essential, production per man had much increased:

$$252^F \qquad 1815-1824$$
$$651^F \qquad 1905-1913$$

The difference between the national product and the minimum needed to sustain population was distinctly larger than during previous centuries. This margin, the net product in physiocratic terms, allowed the state to set aside more for taxation as well as more for investment.

That was not all. The job of fiscal administrations became simpler —we could say it was transformed—by the change in the economic structure. The peasant class, always difficult to tax, diminished compared to the working class. Increased numbers of wage-earners and city dwellers meant more trade in food, drink, and manufactured products between city and country. Various kinds of entry taxes, duties on internal trade, and tariffs were important in the fiscal systems of the nineteenth century: *the ease in levying this kind of relatively painless tax was one of the bases for the growing power of states.*

One should particularly emphasize the debilitating effect vis-à-vis family autarchy of increased consumption of the "colonial products," tea, coffee, cocoa, tobacco—all products which Europe did not produce, or produced only in limited amounts, and which became more and more commonly used by peasants as well as workers.[41] For these products, tariffs at the point of import were relatively simple to collect. Other products of mass consumption, such as sugar and beer, could be produced in Europe or North America. But the manufacturing process was concentrated enough to allow relatively easy supervision. To find the chink in peasant autarchy it was no longer necessary to push the salt tax to its extreme limit. It became less important, or even disappeared. It was highly advantageous to be able to tax what were considered, for the time, semiluxury products such as tea, coffee, tobacco, or even sugar.

The growth of customs income had a particularly striking effect on the financial strength of federalist nations which tended to reserve indirect taxes and tariffs for the national level. Thus the fiscal receipts of the German Empire went from 263 million marks in 1873 to 1,203 million in 1909; 122 million marks in 1873 and 629 million in 1909 came from customs. In the United States, at the beginning of the twentieth century, the returns from tariffs covered a large part of ordinary expenses of the federal government, at least in peacetime. The conveniences of these indirect taxes meant that governments could be satisfied as far as direct taxes went with external evidence, often quite approximate, of people's real wealth. These taxes were paid without major difficulties, from the mid-nineteenth century anyway, because of this reduced impact and also because of the development of the economy of exchanges.

Differences in the Economic, Fiscal, and Political Development of Various States. The overall impact of this evolution was unequal in the various countries. Great Britain was still in a better position, given equal production, than other states. She preserved, during the nineteenth century, the long-term advantages of an economy of exchanges which was already more developed. France, on the other hand, was less strong and only slightly favored considering her population and wealth. The weakness of Austria-Hungary was not only the result of the ethnic and national heterogeneity of the country and the resulting centrifugal effects. It was also the result of her weak finances. Between 1830 and 1848 the economic backwardness of Austria could be seen in the financial sector, as evidenced by her

[41] From 1831 to 1900, consumption of tea per capita in France increased from 0.3 kg. to 2.8 kg.; that of coffee from 25.3 kg. to 211.8 kg.; that of cocoa from 2 kg. to 45 kg.

endemic deficit combatted by loans, as well as in the political field. The projects of Baron de Kubeck, president of the Aulic Council, were designed to face these problems: he promoted the introduction of railroads and reorganized an industrial commission. He failed, however. The Hapsburgs' centralization policy was too heavy for the resources of the country. Russia also was weakened not only because of her social condition, but also because of a backward economy which made her financial situation precarious.

As to the Mediterranean countries, they tried to mitigate their low level of economic evolution by maintaining excise taxes on primary consumption products—Italy thus taxed, at the end of the nineteenth and in the early twentieth century, milk, cheese, eggs, fruits, and vegetables. They also reserved an important place in their budgets for direct taxes. This was the reason why the income tax appeared relatively early in Italy, but the economic infrastructure took its revenge: the return was very low while the whole system was so heavily invested by fraud that Italy was the textbook case, at the beginning of the twentieth century, of the example not to follow. In Spain and Portugal likewise, direct taxes were relatively heavy.

With time, changes occurred. During the nineteenth century, the nations of Western Europe and elsewhere felt the impact of their economic infrastructures on their political power; but they did not always recognize its significance, and some of them believed themselves more powerful than they were in reality. The result was some disconcerting shocks for nations who treasured memories of past power and apparent military strength when they were defeated by nations more advanced economically: the victory of France and England, far from their military bases, over Russia in the Crimean War; the victories of France and Savoy, and then Prussia, over Austria-Hungary; the victory of Germany over France in 1870; the victory of the United States over Spain in 1898; and the victory of Japan over Russia in 1905. The two World Wars were no exceptions, with the early defeats for France and England, then the final victory of these nations most linked to exchanges with their empires, and the victory of North America and USSR over the Central Powers.

But from the nineteenth century onward we can see that states no longer passively accepted the repercussions of their economies on their political and military strength. The phenomenon of government intervention appeared in countries where private initiative was less marked, where there was no strong bourgeois class having the spirit of thrift and enterprise, and ready to industrialize the country and establish conditions for a better financial situation and a stronger military position. These governments themselves tried to create the economic infrastructure which did not emerge spontaneously, or at least not without state intervention. This was the policy of Japan in the Meiji Restoration, and to some extent, that of Austria-Hungary and czarist Russia. This latter-day interventionism was a kind of mercantilism. We should note, however, that the objective of the intervening states of the nineteenth century was less directly fiscal than that of the seventeenth-century mercantilist states. The governments aimed above all at establishing an armament industry and communications networks which their defeats had shown to be necessary.

The War Economy of the Twentieth Century. There has also been in the twentieth century a tendency towards reduction of the role of taxation as a "fiscal intermediary" for power. Certain governments have asked individuals and enterprises to supply the state directly with the crucial resources needed for war preparations and conduct, not by way of taxes, but by requisitions or by means of economic controls on industry.[42] The First World War saw the establishment of so-called war economies by the belligerents. Nazi Germany hoped to dominate Europe by mobilizing its resources more thoroughly and more quickly than countries which were financially superior to it. Germany's enemies were forced to use the same methods of directing the economy: rationing, mobilizing the entire active population, including women, etc. These were the same methods which the French Revolution had used to face the rest of Europe allied against it.

Just as in that period, inflation furnished resources, and had to be contained by a double effort of controls—controls over production and distribution, on the one hand, reduced purchasing power obtained by taxation, on the other. Those countries which had a better-developed system of exchanges found it easier to organize rationing. The English succeeded to a larger degree than the French, among other reasons, because much of their food supply was imported, and thus had to pass easily administered checkpoints. Furthermore, the old closed economy had disappeared so long before in England that

[42] The war economies made it possible for the war to last longer than economists, thinking in terms of "classical" financing of its operations, had predicted.

there were not the resources for secret operations and a black market which were found in a country like France. *Under a new form, no longer fiscal, the exchange economy brought some states supplementary strength.* Despite its rigorous war economy, Germany was defeated by the western powers and by a state which had, to an even greater degree, created a strong infrastructure, building by force the equivalent of the exchange economy which had not come to it spontaneously: the USSR.

The Economic Infrastructure, Fiscal Capacity, and Political Disorders in the Twentieth Century. In wartime, draconian regulations of the economy are possible but the end of hostilities makes them more difficult to continue. After the Second World War as after the First, it was hard to maintain various prohibitions, restrictions, and rationing. To avoid the effects of scarcity it was necessary to reduce the purchasing power of individuals and consumer demand by taxation. Those countries which could not or would not pursue this fiscal policy strictly enough suffered political repercussions which tended to weaken them. After the First World War, some of the states of Central Europe were paralyzed by their inability to overcome inflation. We might count, among the effects of financial disorder of this sort, an instability of political regimes, a discrediting of parliamentary approaches, and an open field for *coups d'état*.

This is clearly seen in the interwar period. Czechoslovakia, which was the only Central European state to preserve minimum stability in its monetary system, was completely free of fascist tendencies. It was just the reverse for Poland, in which Marshal Pilsudski's march on Warsaw was aided by monetary difficulties. The coming of Italian Fascism and of Hitlerism show similar facts. In Italy, the popular unrest which preceded Mussolini's taking of power was partly caused by inflation: the price increases had triggered incessant strikes, and workers raided shops in their protests against the high cost of living, etc. In Germany, it was the middle class whose confidence in the state was shaken because of speculation, continual reduction of the purchasing power of wage-earners, and the ruin of those who had savings. All these factors contributed to the hostile environment in which the regime found itself, while the depression, which stirred up an even larger group of discontented persons, struck the final *coup de grâce*. Analogous examples could be drawn from the other central European countries.

[225]

Now *at the root of these sharp devaluations of money we find the weak fiscal efforts of these states,* an inadequacy that we cannot blame on the failure of men and political parties alone. These countries which were unable to use taxation as a tool against inflation were in general the principal agricultural countries of Central Europe. It was not only because of the energetic statesman Rasin that Czechoslovakian financial policy contrasted so strongly with that of the other successor states after 1918; moreover, we should not forget that Bohemia was more industrialized than the other countries.

Germany, with its very advanced industrial structure, was the exception, but this is easily explained. The collapse of German currency after the First World War was, at least in part, deliberately willed, as a sort of exhibition of the heavy financial burden that the Treaty of Versailles had imposed on the defeated country. From the moment that there was a commitment to reestablish the strength of the money, it was done with a rapidity that astonished the experts. After the last war the speed of German monetary recovery was equally sensational. West Germany had all the possibilities for economic equilibrium because of its economic infrastructure, intact despite much destruction, on which its fiscal capacity was based.

One can criticize the financial policies of France and Italy after the two World Wars as less energetic than those of the Anglo-Saxon nations, but one must recognize the handicap of these countries where the exchange economy was less developed. In France in 1945 the most vigorous mechanism for exchanging money, which would have involved a blocking of accounts and allowed serious fiscal action, was rejected for many reasons. Among them was the fear, right or wrong, that the peasantry would not have understood and supported measures of that kind. The financial policy of France would have been different with another economic structure.

Not only agricultural structure has to be considered. A more energetic fiscal policy would have been more difficult in France than in Great Britain because of the importance of small business; the reactions to the controls reestablished in 1953 offer a negative proof.

The Strength of Contemporary States. Since the Second World War the function of taxation and the role and conception of the state proceeding from this have undergone such a change that one ought to speak of a true mutation. Industrial society is a society with high returns, which quickly transforms scientific discoveries into new and

[226]

large-scale manufactured products; it is also a society in which the individual is more and more tied into the economy of exchanges, where the peasantry grows smaller every year, where business executives are the salaried cadres, of not the stockholders, of more numerous and powerful businesses. The state and its tax system can find ever greater opportunities in this situation. It is due to the extent that outmoded economic structures continue to exist that some countries—France for example—continue to have fiscal problems whose nature and location sometimes are singularly evocative of past centuries.

And that is not all. The role and the importance of taxation has been transformed by the growth of monetary analysis and techniques. In this area lies *the most profound change which has affected the possibilities for action and the perspectives of the industrial societies of Western Europe and North America.* This is not to say that the use of money as a source of public revenue is not today such as it was in the past: the use of inflation came rather quickly in the wake of the creation of money. We have shown that hard currency was not well adapted for that kind of financial manipulation, and it was not even sufficient to invent paper money, because the use of inflation required a certain level of economic structure. These conditions were fulfilled in the course of the eighteenth century in some countries, and during the nineteenth, in many more. As far as the twentieth century goes, it has meant not only more abuse of inflation but also a better understanding of the role of money.

Keynesian analysis has shown how the richest and most evolved industrial societies somehow hide the underemployment of an important section of their labor force and their productive capacity, and also how the increased demand rising from action of the state through its power to issue money can promote the mobilization of these latent resources.

These phenomena existed before they were analyzed. It is precisely because the industrial economies had reserves of unexploited production that the belligerents, in the course of the two world wars, could mobilize not only more resources than economists had imagined, but also for a longer period.[43] What is new is the understanding which has been arrived at in the last thirty years of the possibility of using the same methods in peacetime.

---

[43] These same phenomena had played a part, but to a lesser degree, in some wars before the twentieth century.

From this has come a profound change in the very conception of taxation and of its function. It no longer aims at providing money for the state which the state could get by other means. Taxation now plays a part among the tools which the state can use to influence global demand. To slow down too vigorous a demand the state can employ not only taxation but also economic regulation, such as increasing the interest rate, forced savings, intermediate forms between taxes and loans, etc. This kind of state intervention in the business cycle is one of the essential causes of both stronger and more regular economic growth since the last war—stronger because more regular—than was the case at the end of the last century and the beginning of this. The power of the state has been profoundly transformed by this. The state has the possibility of maintaining a relatively high rate of growth. This has been a political factor of great importance in the post war world.

To summarize, one could say that the state, thanks to its economic progress, has the financial means—taxation, credit, money— much superior to those which were available to it in the past, but *these means themselves have increased the state's responsibility*. It would be an error not to try to perfect these financial tools, which will appear peculiarly archaic and singularly inadequate sooner than we think. The continuance of a certain kind of a state is linked to the conditions in which this transformation will be assured. We must now try to see if the study of the economic infrastructure of modern nations will lead us to the same conclusions.

THE INDUSTRIAL REVOLUTION AND THE BUILDING OF NATIONS

Until now we have spoken mainly about the creation of the state in the limited sense of that word, the sense given it by the men of the *Ancien Régime* when a Richelieu could talk of peasants as "Beasts of Burden" who must provide the means of grandeur for political institutions, when a Louis XIV could say, without a general claim, "L'Etat c'est moi." This minister, this king, and others were aware of their task and of their duty vis-à-vis the majority of their subjects. They considered themselves personifications of the state, and some of them declared themselves to be the first servants of that state. Their rule was accepted; they had some support of their people when civil or foreign wars occurred because they tried to maintain order, to administer justice (a justice more impartial than feudal justice) and even, in a very imperfect way, to limit arbitrary actions.

[228]

Speaking in these terms is an oversimplification. National feeling was born and grew in great crises; such was the case of the wars at the end of the reign of Louis XIV. Notwithstanding, the building of states appeared, in the European continental countries, at least, as relatively foreign to the life of the individual. The end of the eighteenth century, the nineteenth and the twentieth give another impression.

During the French Revolution the provinces accepted, not without reticence, their being united into one nation. The wars and conquests of the armies of the Convention as of the Empire made manifest in occupied countries their common origin, fate and interest. The nineteenth century was the century of the "Rise of Nationalism," to take the words of historians. During that century men of Western Europe were more and more closely associated—at least formally— with the management of the state. During the twentieth century that evolution continued, and decolonization was, in the last decades, its most obvious effect. One of the tests of the building of nations is the fact that members of a state accept to pay for the support of other provinces or other members of the same state.

How can we explain so significant an evolution as that of the nineteenth and twentieth centuries? Intellectual, juridical, or political explanations naturally come to our mind. Since the theory of social contract and its application, or what has been considered as its application in the form of the representative system, the broadening of the right of suffrage, as well as local self-government to a certain extent, subjects have become citizens. Is it more than an appearance? For critics of contemporary society, constitutions of the Western type are mere lies. They point out insufficient equality and the fact that citizens are not real participants in the running of the state. Moreover, in some countries the constitutional system of Great Britain or of the United States has been transferred but not actually applied: the number of *coups d'état* is a test, since it means the lack of a national community with a real, even imperfect and limited, meaning.

Following Marxist analysis, political scientists have come to understand the necessity of research which would look, beyond political superstructures, to the infrastructure of national feeling. Obviously, community consciousness is bound to a lot of conditions, such as language, way of life, historical traditions; but none of those elements is sufficient to build a nation; the converging of some of them, however, gives some support to that feeling. Nonetheless, since the nineteenth century, it has been observed that *nation* meant another thing: it was a choice, the desire for a common life, for a common destiny, and that desire must be explained.

Without an excessive research into the economic basis of human behavior and of social institutions it is almost necessary to look at that aspect of the problem. A correlation has been noticed between the standard of living of different countries and the stability of their political superstructure. Such an approach is not sufficient. It is really impossible to conceal the strength of national feeling in relatively poor communities. But it seems possible to perceive *a relation between the sense of nation and the minimum effort toward the abolition of excessive inequalities.* In fact, during the nineteenth century something had begun in that direction. Egalitarian taxation appeared and was considered by some politicians as a great tool for building that society where solidarity should be more than a mere word: the nation. It will be necessary to discover the technical means and the economic infrastructures of that policy.

Nowadays the political impact of fiscal problems seems, right or wrong, less important. Workers are much more interested in progressive augmentation (by the continual increasing of wages, of real wages) that relies upon the growth of national product. Figures of the last decades have been very much influenced by the progress of economic policy; the use of Keynesian analysis has given to industrial societies the possibility of avoiding the great crises that interrupted progress for years and were responsible for catastrophies. But what we call Keynesian techniques, budgetary, fiscal, or monetary are only possible in certain kinds of societies—in industrial societies. Thus, we find *again in a new form the economic infrastructure of financial techniques and of building nations.* We must go further. Full employment is not only the condition of real, wide, and continuous progress in production, it is also necessary for giving to all citizens the feeling that they are in a society that can offer to them the possibility of living not like beggars but like responsible men and women.

If we look at the situation of developing countries or if we look at the history of the nineteenth and twentieth centuries, we very strongly feel the importance of the problem of unemployment, one of the main problems of nation-building. Workers did not fail to understand it. At the beginning of the Industrial Revolution, the right to work was one of their first claims. They stirred up riots, they caused revolutions, and they died for it. Some critics of democracy forget that if nations in the formal sense were built, with more and more numerous assemblies elected by citizens, it was because the Industrial Revolution, with all its problems, gave to industrial workers— as to burgers themselves, the feeling that participation in the state— that is to say the building of a nation—was almost necessary for the betterment of their daily life. So must we begin with this point.

The Industrial Revolution and Political Revolutions of the Nineteenth Century. The fiscal origin of representation is obvious. Taxation, a very sensitive question in past centuries, has awakened political consciousness, led to wars of independence, created Estates-General, Cortes, and other assemblies of that kind. In that sense taxes were not only at the origin of states but also of nations. But taxation was not sufficient to sustain the representative system with a real continuity. Parliament or other Estates had a quasi-permanent life only in Great Britain, or in some commercial republics, where some men strongly advocated participation in the management of public affairs: on that island, linked to the world, some men understood that their daily life depended upon the decisions of kings, upon the foreign policy of the Tudors or of the Stuarts. When the kings were in opposition with the general sentiments of the most active part of the population, the claim for the extension of a representative system was all the more strong.

On the contrary, on the Continent the main preoccupation of members of Continental Estates was the limitation of what they paid for public affairs. They did not really try (that observation has been made by historians of the French Estates-General) to buy the permanence of the representative institution by means of a greater benevolence in the discussion of the amount of taxes.

In the nineteenth century, in France as in other countries, *the bourgeoisie knew how much its profits were dependent on the management of the state.* They wanted their share in investments, canals, railways, and mines. They wanted to be heard when tariffs were to be fixed or treaties of commerce, negotiated. The extension of trade had raised the value of representation and participation. For not having understood that evolution, Louis-Philippe was obliged to ab-

[231]

dicate. The policy of the liberal bourgeoisie was supported by industrial workers. Taxation was not so heavy as a century before, or at least it was not so apparent, and we have seen why. But the industrial working class had the burden of a "liberal" economy which left men without any protection against the abuses of managers, without the simple right of association as prohibited by law. *For the protection of their interests they had to participate in the assemblies where laws were made*—hence, the revolutions of the nineteenth century for the extension of suffrage. By the will of the workers during the nineteenth century and at the beginning of the twentieth, universal male suffrage was put in force; taxation had little to do in that transformation. Poverty and unemployment were the strongest incentives. But fiscality had a new aim after the middle of the nineteenth century, when taxes appeared as a means to bring about greater equality, or, let us say less inequality.

Egalitarian Taxation and National Consciousness. Because of its dependence by and large on consumption taxes, the fiscal system of the nineteenth century weighed most heavily on the popular classes. It was surely one of the most striking manifestations of the triumphant bourgeoisie. One can understand why it was so highly favored by Thiers, and that Bismarck envied his chance to use it.

The very changes in society made it difficult to retain a fiscal mechanism which gave no importance to equitable distribution. Because of this shift the financial system could afford violent political upsets. But new prospects appeared for politicians with the progress of industrial society, the increased numbers of wage-earners, the concentration of enterprises, the relative weakening of agriculture, and the diminution of a subsistence economy. The flow of income and expenditures could be taxed directly, sometimes even at their source. Progressive tariffs and personal deductions could be devised. Great Britain, more advanced economically as usual, offered its example, and tax formulas of the German type were tried here and there in the nineteenth and early twentieth centuries.

Governments had at their disposal a means of income redistribution via inheritance taxes with progressive rates and income taxes. *They could maintain the structure of the liberal economy while at the same time modifying some of its effects by the redistribution of wealth.* This characteristic aspect of financial policy in Western Eu-

[232]

rope and North America at the turn of the nineteenth and twentieth centuries was also a result of a new fiscal tool, or rather of an infrastructure without which such a technique would have been impossible.

In the first analysis, one is tempted to derive from the political evolution the introduction of this new kind of tax. There were attempts to levy egalitarian taxes during the French Revolution. Awkwardly administered, they contributed to the coming to power of Bonaparte. In Austria and various German states income taxes and other progressive taxes had been tried during the revolutions of 1848. On the whole, they disappeared with the restoration of traditional powers. After 1870 and with the increasingly powerful tendency toward universal suffrage, there was a reduction of the strength of the conservative parties in favor of more liberal ones.

Income taxes began to be adopted, governments tried to tax "unearned" income, that is the profit of capital, and progressive rates were first used for inheritance taxes, then for income taxes. The principle of progressive taxation was first accepted in the group of countries which were considered most democratic before 1914: Switzerland, Australia, and New Zealand. The Liberal victory of Great Britain in 1891 led to the introduction of the progressive principle on the inheritance tax and the emphasis on exemptions from the income tax. When the Liberals came to power again in 1906, they came to blows with the House of Lords over a series of projects, especially those of Lloyd George in 1906, inspired by the same preoccupations with, in the end, limitations of the powers of the Lords. In France each victory of the "Left" raised the question of the income tax. One can thus link the history of this tax to political change and to social movement.

But there are other no less significant correlations. With a little exaggeration one can observe that *the income tax was permanently established in a country at about the period when the development of trade made it possible*. England, home of the Industrial Revolution, established the first income tax worthy of the name, if not in 1793, the tax of that year being still quite imperfect, at least in 1803. After an interruption from 1816 to 1841, it was reimposed in 1842. In Germany the income tax first was used in the more commercial and industrial states. Of the four states which had adopted income taxes before 1870, two, Hamburg and Lübeck, were essentially commercial cities. This kind of tax, or a similar one, then appeared in

Prussia in 1871, in Saxony in 1874, in Baden in 1884, in Württemberg and Bavaria only in 1910. The two Mecklenburgs did not have income taxes until 1913. In 1892 and 1893 the Low Countries established a wealth tax and an income tax with progressive rates.

There are apparent exceptions. The United States established a federal income tax only in 1913, but besides the period from 1862 to 1872, when there was a wartime income tax, another income tax law was passed in 1894 which was never put into force because it was declared unconstitutional. Inversely, Italy had a tax on the income from mobile wealth, combined with a real estate tax from 1864, thus, a fiscal system inspired by the income tax concept. But the application of these taxes was very defective; fraud was extremely common, so common that a book was written on that subject alone. Austria had an income tax in 1896, but it was only of secondary importance, and its application depended on external signs of wealth.[44] Indeed one can argue that the economic evolution determined the creation of taxes on income by triggering the social movement and the consequent coming to power of reformist political parties. It is nonetheless true that it was the increased economy of exchanges that allowed the *application* of taxation of this sort.

The social evolution of industrial countries had taken other forms; the progressive improvement in the conditions of work and of pay had been obtained as much through the intervention of the state as through workers' pressure. One should not underestimate the importance of measures which, at the end of the nineteenth century and after, accepted as social charges to the state a series of expenditures for education, medical insurance, retirement insurance, and housing with all these outlays covered by a fiscal regime with egalitarian tendencies.

I would emphasize the influence of that evolution on the very conception of the state and of the nation. *In those countries in which this broader view of taxation had been most widely accepted, it contributed to the relative stability of the political regime*; this was the case of the countries in northwestern Europe, especially Great Britain, and even more so Scandinavia. In these various nations, the governments had used taxation as an essential instrument of social progress. The more agitated political life of nations like France and Italy, in contrast, could be attributed to a series of phenomena among

[44] In certain of the Scandinavian countries it appears that the creation of the income tax did anticipate industrialization.

which was the insufficient strength of tax power.[45] The imperfect tax system meant that the income tax could not be used as an efficient instrument for equality. Raising rates above a certain limit always carried the risk of increasing fraud and causing discontent in large sections of the population. It is significant that, between the two World Wars a simple means of tax verification, the *carnet* or *bordereau de coupons* played a very appreciable political role in France. The imperfection of the fiscal system hindered an increasing egalitarian tendency.

What were the causes of this situation: a relatively effective fiscal mechanism in the northwest of Europe, but a less satisfactory operation of the same mechanism in the countries to the south? To a large degree, this was the result of insufficient commitment on the part of the governments and a certain indifference to public opinion. It was also the effect of an economic structure which still was heavily involved with small peasant holdings and small industrial and commercial firms, all of which were difficult to tax. Whenever the parties of the left tried to remedy this situation, they had to introduce control measures which were particularly opposed by these groups of people. In countries such as England, on the contrary, the dominant place of wage earners, and in rural areas, tenant farmers, made it easier to tax.

Egalitarian fiscal policy has not disappeared since the Second World War. Moreover progressive taxation has been reinforced in certain countries. But those of us who could be the most interested by that policy seem the least concerned. Some reasons can be given for that behavior. People are perhaps more conscious of fiscal evasion. By the incentive of progressive taxation, fraud becomes very important. By a kind of paradox, salaried workers do not pay very great attention to a fact which has a very strong impact upon their daily life.

That is not all. Egalitarian fiscal systems of industrial societies have effects not so different from the past, upon production, productivity, saving, and investment. Some reforms have been effected to correct most obvious distortions and to maintain "fiscal neutrality." For the sake of productivity a new kind of tax has been established: the tax on value added which no longer gives favor to certain forms of activity that are perhaps not the most economically suitable.

[45] France established its first income tax in the war of 1914–1918.

Other reforms could be quoted, the aim of which was to give more incentives to scientific and technical research.

It is not sufficient to correct the incidence of present systems. As did the first economists, we must analyze the economic incidence of taxation more carefully and search for new solutions. We must try to discover if indirect taxes could be more egalitarian. If it is possible we must seek to levy taxes on those activities most important for economic progress and to surtax benefits that come from monopoly situations, and, moreover, from all that jeopardizes the welfare of the community. It must be possible to use more and more fiscal systems for greater equality, for greater economic progress, and for better environment. In that sense the economic infrastructure of nations could be better used by states. If we do not underestimate the importance of taxation—of taxation in the past, of taxation in the present, of taxation in the future—we must also ask, as do some politicians, if the building of nations can rely mainly upon that kind of redistribution of wealth. More or less consciously citizens of industrial societies feel that their way of life depends also upon the functioning of the economy, particularly upon the rate of growth of production and productivity.

Economic Growth and National Consciousness. If the political impact of taxation seems lessened since the Second World War, it is perhaps because the greatest attention has been paid by industrial workers, during the last decades, to the evolution of prices, to the readaptation of nominal wages to the cost of living, and also to the feeling that a continual progression of real wages could be obtained.

Such behavior is a kind of incidence of economic infrastructure upon the national consciousness of workers of industrial societies. Living in a highly technical world, among more and more sophisticated machinery, they cannot understand why they are unable themselves to afford the products of this mechanical monster, this modern Leviathan—cars, freezers, air conditioning, etc. They do not understand how with all this power some daily problems could not have been really solved—housing for instance. Their claim to a rapid increase in wages and in their standard of living is the direct consequence of their environment. If they do not obtain what they think possible, they think themselves to be foreigners in their own country. If fact, real progress has taken place by comparison with what happened between the two World Wars. Studies of the European Organ-

[236]

ization for Cooperation and Development (OCDE) and others have showed that the rate of growth had been higher since 1945 than between 1920 and 1939.

Hence two questions: What is the reason for this evolution? Is it sufficient? At the origin of this deep modification we find the development of economic analysis. The work of Keynes and other studies of this kind were the intellectual foundations of a lot of techniques—budgetary, fiscal, and monetary—that are commonly used in western industrial countries. By means of such tools, governments can more or less stop recessions before they attain a certain level, and they can, much more easily than in the past, determine new advances in production. We must insist upon these possibilities that have been given to modern states, because they are essential for the building of nations.

Full Employment and National Consciousness. It is really not possible to speak of the building of nations without a glance at the full employment policy even if its achievements are yet far from our hopes. Elimination of violent crises and of huge unemployment is not only the means of a relatively high rate of growth, it is also an aim. When we go to the roots of inequality and of the privation of freedoms (elements that are opposed to national consciousness), when we try to understand why so many people do not feel themselves to be participants in a real community where men are really brothers, we are obliged to point out something that is curiously underestimated by political scientists: *the political incidence of economic instability, or more precisely, of unemployment and underemployment.*

When Marx spoke of the "industrial reserve army," that reserve of workers which weighed so heavily upon the level of wages, he put his finger upon an essential characteristic of the proletariat: the instability of his condition, unemployment, or, the permanent possibility of being unemployed. The equivalent for peasantry is *mévente*, or slump. The man who cannot always win money for his life and for the life of his family cannot feel himself really free. When he seeks a job, he does not have a normal bargaining position. He cannot be conscious of national solidarity. It seems to him that the state does not fulfill its essential function.

Since fiscality is no more the great instigator of insurrections, since economy of exchange has deprived men from the weak but effective potentialities of the economy of subsistence, unemployment is one of

[237]

the greatest motives for rebellion. *Days of economic crisis are days of riots.* So it was during the nineteenth century. At the roots of the revo-lution—or better of the revolutions—of 1848 we find lack of subsist-ence and, even more, unemployment. The June Days took the same path.

Without stressing the movements at the end of the century in the urban and rural areas of North America and Western Europe, it is sufficient to look at the period between the two World Wars. Unem-ployment was the cause of great disorders in all industrial countries. In Germany the crisis was most acute. The number of unemployed al-ready large in 1928 rapidly rose to 1,892,000 in 1929, to 3,041,000 in March 1930, when Chancellor Brüning took office. On the basis of 100 percent in 1929, industrial production had fallen to 67.6 percent in 1931. To meet the situation the chancellor used deflationary measures; the result was 6,034,000 unemployed in March 1932. These six million men plus the fear of those who were still at work were among the im-portant causes of Hitler's rise to power.[46] So a policy of unemployment is at the origin of the Second World War. Curiously, scientific and practical conclusions have not been really drawn from such a fact which nobody can seriously contest.

Other examples can be found in the area of developing countries. More than poverty, unemployment is one of the causes of political movements. It was not the cause of decolonization claims or of de-colonization wars, but the incidence of unemployment reinforced these movements. Multiple examples could be shown. In Algeria, a country where, according to official figures, nearly 1,000,000 people were unemployed or underemployed, the rebellion of 1954 began in the *département* where the percentage of unemployment was highest, i.e., the *département* of Constantine. In Latin America great zones of unemployment include the Caribbean Islands, North-East Brazil, Andean regions, etc. In all there have been riots or revolutions. Some of them have succeeded, as the one in Cuba where the percentage of unemployment was peculiarly high, others have not. If political sci-entists looked at this aspect of developing countries they would find the explanation for the political instability of numerous countries of Asia, Africa or Latin America.[47]

[46] For some more details and for other examples of the effects of politics of this kind, cf. the book I have written with Pierre Mendes-France (Ardant and Mendes-France 1955).

[47] I apologize for referring to my book *Le Monde en friche* (Ardant 1959) where I tried to give a summary of the geography of unemployment that is the same as the geography of revolts.

These facts, and many others that could be cited, very clearly show the infrastructure of what we can call Keynesian techniques. We must never forget that Keynes observed industrial societies. He noticed that, because of their wealth, in these countries the desire to put money into savings could be stronger than the desire to invest it. The behavior of individual savers reduced the global demand to a level inferior to the possibilities of production. Hence a part of the means of production were unemployed, but those means, plants, machinery, wagons or trucks, and also industrial workers remained ready to be used, ready to work as soon as an augmentation of demand occurred, whatever the cause of that augmentation might be. In the beginning at least, production was ready to follow an increasing demand without any bottlenecks.

So industrial structure is the infrastructure of Keynesian techniques. The example of developing countries is very illustrative. They cannot use Keynesian techniques without a strong augmentation of prices, because the production apparatus is not ready to respond. In those countries the industrial worker is not unemployed because his plant is closed; he is unemployed because plants do not exist. We will see conclusions to draw from that simple analysis. For the time being let us observe how much Keynesian techniques are bound to the infrastructure of industrial societies.

Keynesian techniques, although they can fend off depressions like that of 1929, are not effective enough to assure full use of all available capacity. Before that point is reached, inflation sets in and the government slows down expansion. Such periodical blockages are one of the main characteristics of a postwar economy. The volume of unemployment that remains is contrary to the national community spirit.

Is it possible to avoid such a situation? It is impossible to examine here in detail the different kinds of solutions. Better analyses of business cycles, quick use of budgetary means (modification of taxation, public works) and of monetary tools, better training of young people and of adult workers, and perhaps what is called a *policy of revenues* must be carefully considered. Some economists think that measures of that kind would not be sufficient and that a complete transformation of monetary structures would be necessary. Others consider that economic structures themselves must be completely transformed. It is a scientific, technical, and naturally, also a political problem, a problem of major importance for the building of nations.

To summarize I could say first that progress of industrial societies has made citizens more anxious to obtain more and more, and better and better results. In the seventeenth century technicians of finance and economy were obliged to follow the ambitions of princes; technicians of the present must follow the ambitions of the people. They cannot assess without a sound revision of their techniques, of their fiscal, monetary, budgetary, and of their economic techniques. They can provide not only to the majority of people, but to those who live marginally, and also to those who even contest the whole of society, reasons for being more and more integrated into the life of the nation.

WESTERN EUROPEAN STATES AND OTHER KINDS OF POLITICAL ENTITIES

It is difficult to speak of state- and nation-building in Western Europe as if it were alone in the world.

Collectivist States. The comparison with *collectivist states* is outside the limits of our subject. Let us observe only that, by their structure, countries of this kind can more easily solve the problem of employment. This is obviously a factor of social and political stability that must not be underestimated. This does not mean that these states have no economic problems. Their leaders themselves say how much progress must be made in the field of productivity. Without trying to stay in that field, it seems possible to make some observations about one particular aspect of what could be called the economic recovery of nations of that kind. A careful study perhaps might show us that their problems of state and nation are, in some respect, of the same kind as those in industrialized countries.

I must emphasize that *the hope to develop productivity leads to giving an important place to fiscal mechanisms.* How, in effect, can the communist state give to its production managers greater initiative and greater responsibility, without assigning costs to the individual firms, or without charging them a part of what the means of production at their disposal would produce if assigned to others? The state cannot give to the individual enterprise, its cadres, and its personnel an important fraction of its profits unless the state makes it its business to keep that part of the profit which does not arise from the actual running of the business by its managers and workers but from its monopoly situation, or from rent or chance profits. One of the key problems of all fiscal policies is to differentiate between earned and unearned profit. The success of economic reforms in Eastern Europe depends on the ways in which these problems can be solved. In this sense, the function and reform of taxation are not so different in Western and in Eastern countries as one might think. All this brings us back to the point that, no matter what the regime, industrial states are at the same time freer to plan their methods of financing and more responsible for their choices.

Developing Countries. The above analysis applies to industrial societies. The young developing countries are in a situation like that of the European nations before their economic transformation. Their infrastructures limit their fiscal capacity in ways analogous to those we have shown in France, Italy, or Germany before the nineteenth century. The same inadequacy of their economic base prevents them from using Keynesian techniques, which were conceived for industrial economies where production is at least able to respond to increased demand. These techniques do not fill the needs of countries where numerous bottlenecks intervene between demand and any response of agriculture or industry. This is not to say that there is no solution; however, *solutions must be sought in different forms.* These countries should not therefore adopt the fiscal systems or financing methods of industrial nations: they should find solutions adapted to the structure of their own economies. Their leaders are in the shoes of a Burleigh, a Laffemas, a Colbert, a Patino. Like the men of mercantile states, they should act directly on the structure of their economy.

Their fiscal systems could well take inspiration from the methods that have been tested. A tax of the cadastral type, although rather delicate to impose, ought to encourage agricultural production, just as the Physiocratic analysis expected of real estate tax, and just as the French First Empire reported with its *Recueil méthodique* which clearly emphasized the economic effect of a tax on the potential value of land. This is just one example of what a judicious fiscal reform could do for the countries of Asia, Africa or Latin America. In a neighboring field, full employment, they could use some simple techniques, such as limiting money payments which cause an overly rapid growth of purchasing power, and instead, they could encourage the peasants to invest, especially in the improvement of their lands (cf. Ardant 1964).

This is not to say that the aid of the industrialized states is of no use. I propose not only economic cooperation, which could expand into a sort of international taxation, but also the organization of markets and monetary reform. It is to the extent that the industrial nations remove monetary obstacles to economic development, that they establish a regulatory system for the prices of raw materials and basic products of the developing countries, that they assure financing of stabilization mechanisms and link them to monetary reform, and to the extent that they encourage throughout the entire world the possibility of expansion which will not be weakened by the instrument of exchanges, that they will give each country, to each man of each country, the chance to change and improve his future by using his capabilities. In this sense, I would state again, the greater possibilities of financing today also mean a more burdensome responsibility for the industrial states.

CHAPTER 4

Taxation, Sociopolitical Structure, and State-Building: Great Britain and Brandenburg-Prussia

RUDOLF BRAUN

~~~~~~

Introduction

"Financial means are the nerves of the state"; this celebrated sentence of Jean Bodin's, written in the formative phase of modern state-building, was cited or paraphrased over and over again in the contemporary literature and later in the mercantilistic-cameralistic writing of the seventeenth and eighteenth centuries. (Bodin 1583: L, VI, chap. II, p. 855).[1] At the end of World War I, Joseph A. Schumpeter reflects on whether or not the modern state, which he labels the "tax state," will have a chance to survive. His essay "The Crisis of the Tax State" combines an historical analysis of the origin and nature of the modern democratic state with a sociology of taxation. According to Schumpeter "fiscal demands are the first sign of life of the modern state. This is why 'tax' has so much to do with 'state' that the expression 'tax state' might almost be considered a pleonasm. And this is why fiscal sociology is so fruitful for the theory of the state" (Schumpeter 1954: 19).[2]

These quotations from Bodin and Schumpeter illuminate right at the beginning the significance of taxation, fiscal policy and public finance in the process of state-building and sociopolitical changes. They might serve as a point of departure to set forth the problems,

---

[1] Cited by F. K. Mann (Mann 1937: 5ff.). Mann cites writers of the seventeenth and eighteenth century who paraphrased Bodin's maxim.

[2] In the last two decades historians have come to emphasize more and more the importance of socioeconomic aspects for the analysis and interpretation of general history; financial history, however, as part of an integrated history remained, at least in the German speaking countries, fallow ground. This is all the more surprising because the research could have resurrected the tradition of the so-called German Younger Historical School of Economics (with Gustav Schmoller as its head), which had been animated by such outstanding and original scholars as Joseph A. Schumpeter, Max Weber, Otto Hintze, Rudolf Goldscheid and Karl Mann (the last two specialized in the field of historical sociology of public finance). I am glad to state right at the beginning that I am much in debt to all of those just mentioned scholars.

outline their ramifications, and sketch the analytical framework of this rather tentative essay.

From a modern point of view, taxes are regularly paid compulsory levies on private units to produce revenues to be spent for public purposes. In regard to the period and the topic under discussion, however, this definition not only helps little, but also forestalls the raising of relevant questions. One of the problems to be dealt with is the extent to which various forms of compulsory levies, at a given time and place, can actually be considered as producing regularly "public" revenues, used wholly for "public" purposes. Up to the eighteenth century, the traditional concept of taxation, in theory if not in fact, evaluated tax collection as an "expedient in times of emergency and even an abuse which as soon as possible should be replaced by income from public property, particularly domains, and by voluntary contributions." But common opinion gradually acquiesced in the permanent character of compulsory levies; it came to accept taxation as a permanent institution and as the "inseparable twin of the modern state" (Mann 1943: 225).

Hence, we have to broaden our scope: we must treat not only taxes in a modern sense, the permanent, compulsory and public character of which is not questioned, but also feudal dues and sources of income accruing to the Crown or the ruling dynasty: revenues in money, kinds of services provided by the royal or seigneurial domains, rights and prerogatives (regalia). Sometimes it is hard to distinguish between taxes in a modern sense and the revenues just mentioned which belonged to the ruling dynasty, inasmuch as the former were in many ways developing out of the latter. The right to impose and collect—that is, to administer—taxes became one of the means by which seigneurial or patrimonial authority over people was transformed into authority over territory, and by which authority and power of a feudal character, with all its mutual rights and obligations, was converted into authority and power of quite a different nature. Taxation was thus important both as weapon and as symbol in the struggle to overcome the feudal order and to build states or nations in a modern sense. The control of wealth by the ruling dynasty was an essential prerequisite for its effective exercise of authority; therefore the amount of property belonging to the ruling dynasty and the efficient administration and utilization of this property were of crucial importance in the struggle for taxation rights and for power in general.

[244]

The struggle for the right to impose and collect new taxes or to convert traditional levies into new forms is closely connected with that for the right to decide what the revenues are to be spent for and the right to control the way they actually are disbursed. This aspect, concerning the allocation of revenues, suggests that we cannot consider problems of taxation without taking into account the side of expenditure; that is, the whole complex of what today is called "public" or "national" expense, budget, credit, debt, and finance. Here again the meaning of the term "public" presents a problem and raises a series of relevant questions. How far have, for example, the expenditures of the royal or seigneurial household to be evaluated as "public?" In what ways and to what degree is the administration of these expenses separated from that of others? Must the debts of the ruling dynasty be considered as "public" debts? Is the collateral for and amortization of these debts provided by property belonging to the dynasty, or is it based upon other securities? As we shall see, these and other questions are closely related to the transformation of seigneurial and patrimonial rights, obligations, services, and functions of a feudal character into new forms. Such a transformation affects the whole range of sociopolitical and socioeconomic affairs: the military organizations; the civil and ecclesiastical administrations; the judicial systems; means of transportation, communication, and education; the maintenance of law and order; the supply and regulation of coins or other currency; and so forth. Since all of these obligations, services and functions provide and/or require revenues, changes in who has the right to impose, collect, and allocate them are likely to lead to changes in the right or obligation to provide these services and functions. It is obvious that the nature and distribution of authority and power over people and territory are involved with these alterations.

Hence, we certainly can agree with Schumpeter's view that the "modern tax state" has grown out of the crisis of its predecessor, the feudal relationship and the desmesne economy at the close of the Middle Ages, but we have to question his statement "that without financial need the immediate cause for the creation of the modern state would have been absent" (Schumpeter 1954: 8, 16). The financial needs are symptoms and effects as well as causes of new political, social and economic needs and of a new quality of life, which is developing. We might therefore add to Schumpeter's statement that of Fritz Karl Mann: "Without political need the cause for the creation of the modern finance and tax system would have been absent" (Mann 1933–1944: 8). This mutual relationship shows the connection of our topic with the other topics of this workshop. Threat of war, plans of expansion, the danger of insurrection at home, e.g., will not only lead to an increase in military expenses, but also may influence the mode of distribution and collection of the required tax load in order to secure the military and/or political support of strategically crucial social groups. Tax privileges and tax exemptions of certain social groups often have this motivation, though it may be concealed. In short, the form, amount, and allocation of revenues are closely related with a variety of internal and external factors: social, political, and economic conditions; foreign relations; and so forth. In the transition from the feudal order to the modern state, a process which stretched over centuries, it is our main task to analyze the financial components. Yet in doing so we cannot ignore the changes in other spheres of life. This leads to a second line of preliminary reflections.

Taxes serve various functions. First, they have fiscal functions; they provide the monetary means for a steadily increasing host of purposes. Second, they have what we might call educational and social functions. Tax policies designed to regulate and influence human behavior have a long history. Direct and/or indirect taxes are used as tools to increase population (tax burden on bachelors; tax reduction for children), to reduce laziness and to force people to work, to check certain human vices, to influence consumption patterns (particularly conspicuous consumption), and so forth. The educational or social goals of such taxes characteristically prevail over the fiscal goals (see Mann 1943: 226ff.).[3] Still more important are social functions of taxes in another area. They regulate, intentionally or not, the distribution of wealth and income. In other words, taxation can be devised either to stabilize or to change the existing social structure by petrifying, leveling out or broadening the existing differences in income and wealth between social groups. From this point of view, both particular taxes and tax systems as a whole can be classified as progressive, proportional, or regressive, the distinction being based upon the ratio of tax liability to net income or net worth. However, we have to be careful, in applying these terms as analytical tools to older times, as they may hinder rather than help us in understanding precisely the social function of

---

[3] Mann writes: "Thus the poor financial result of such taxes may be taken as indicative of their educational success" (Mann 1943: 229).

t'he taxation in question. Certainly any tax privileges, tax exemptions, and regressive taxes granted to groups imply a greater burden upon the rest; and it is likewise obvious that the ruling groups are eager to use taxes as means to strengthen their socioeconomic position. Yet the problem of distribution of the total burden of taxation, on the one hand, and the underlying criteria or standards of distribution, on the other, require that in this period we examine not only people but also institutions; that is estates, social ranks, and certain kinds of property which confer sociopolitical rights. Which social groups, estates, and properties are subject to which, if any, particular taxes? What kind of tax privileges and exemptions exist? In what way are these privileges related to other social as well as political and economic privileges, rights and obligations? What are the prevailing dogmas of social justice and the prevailing social principles upon which tax duties and tax privileges are based? These and other questions are relevant to our inquiry and are part of the general question Max Weber formulated as follows: Will a certain type of social and political power structure (*Herrschaftsverhältnisse*) determine the creation of characteristic forms of revenue and tax systems? (Weber 1964: 49).

This brings up a third function: taxes may have political as well as fiscal and social functions, insofar as they define the character and the degree of political participation of social groups, estates and holders of certain properties. In a variety of ways, for example, the amount of tax liability served as a criterion for enfranchisement. The connections between taxation, enfranchisement, distribution of political rights, and access to political power have to be analyzed. Political participation, for example, may be determined by birth, social rank, and the holding of property; along with these may go a privileged status in terms of tax burdens. Or the case may be quite the reverse: taxation may serve as a barrier to exclude certain social groups from access to political power.[4] According to Montesquieu the 'nature' of a tax system is subject to the specific political system or form of government (Montesquieu 1951: 467-468).[5] Although we disagree with this statement it is evident that a close connection be-

---

[4] In nineteenth-century Prussia we will find both. The amount of tax liability comes to be a criterion for enfranchisement, yet remnants of the old order remain: the so-called *Standesherren*, for example, enjoy political as well as tax privileges by virtue of their birth.

[5] "Que la nature des tributs est relative au gouvernement" (Montesquieu 1911: 467-468).

tween the political system and taxation exists. Constitutional changes often coincide with tax changes, and electoral reforms often become the starting point for tax reforms. It is most likely that the shift of political power between social groups or political institutions and organizations will lead to a new tax policy (see Mann 1961: 646).

Finally, taxes may have economic functions; they have a long history as instruments of economic policy in various ways. "Incentive" and "punitive" taxes, for example, are found not only in the social sphere, but in the economic as well. On the other hand, particular taxes or tax systems as a whole have side-effects which are not intended. They may hamper particular sections of the economy or the economy as a whole, or they may create windfall-profits.

Not only the form and amount of taxes, but also the collection, administration, and allocation of revenue influence the economy. To mention but one example: it is a one-sided point of view that the degree of monetization of the economy will determine the forms of levies. The collection, administration, and disbursement of taxes serve in turn as agents to promote the monetization of an economy. We are in full agreement with the statement of Fritz Karl Mann that the financial and tax administration helped shape the "capitalistic spirit": the "tax state" has to be regarded as educating its people towards a spirit of *Rechenhaftigkeit* even in branches, like agriculture, where rational accounting was still relatively undeveloped (Mann 1933–1934: 9).

The fiscal, social, political, and economic functions of taxation may support or conflict with each other. A certain level of taxation may be desirable, for example, from a fiscal or a social point of view, but may not be compatible with a defined economic policy. Which effects of taxation are intended and which are not? Which goals will come to have priority if a conflict occurs? How is the priority justified? Will the settlement of such a conflict lead to readjustments or reinterpretations of previously defined goals, and if so, how? On the other hand, the same sequence of questions should be applied to the allocation of revenues. Social, political or economic functions, goals and effects of taxation can either be supported or obstructed by the way the revenues are spent.[6]

In regard to the analytical framework of the historical problems of taxation, we should be concerned with the goals or intentions of

---

[6] From this point of view, taxes might be considered as negative subsidies, and subsidies in turn as negative taxes (see Mann 1959: 55).

particular taxes or tax systems as a whole, with the needed amount of revenue and the desired distribution of the burden of taxation. Second, we have to correlate these goals or intentions with the socio-political and socioeconomic conditions, above all with social and political power structure. Third, we should ask which prevailing fiscal, social, political, and economic theories, principles, or dogmas under-lie these purposes and intentions.[7] Finally, the methods of attaining the desired goals as well as the actual successes and failures of these methods have to be investigated.

In order to have more space to discuss the various aspects of our topic, we decided to limit our investigations to Britain and Branden-burg-Prussia, two contrasting cases which illustrate well the inter-relationship between taxation and sociopolitical and socioeconomic modernization. The following section is devoted to what might be called the formative phase of state-building whose end is marked for Britain by the first meeting of the Long Parliament (1640) and the Civil War, for Brandenburg-Prussia by the accession of the Great Elector, Frederick William of Brandenburg (1640), at the end of the Thirty Years War, and the *de jure* transfer of the *ius territoriale* or the *droit de souveraineté* (as the French draft of the Treaty of Westphalia termed it) from the German emperor to the reigning princes (1648).

The Formative Phase of State Building

The Holy Roman Empire remained until its collapse essentially a feudal organism with increasingly anachronistic features. It never succeeded in shaping the sociopolitical structure of its realm towards a centralized modern state or nation. One of the indications, and at the same time one of the causes, of this lack of power to adjust may be found in the fact that unlike the French Crown, the Roman Emperors were unable to develop a system of contributions for the exigencies of the empire, to say nothing of a modern system of taxation covering the peoples and the territories of the empire. All attempts to impose on the Estates of the empire (*Reichsstände*) a regular tax burden and to collect customs duties at the boundaries of the empire failed or had at best a very limited success.[8] At the same time, a continuous ero-

---

[7] As noted above, such theories, principles, or dogmas may become subject to reinterpretation even without changes in the prevailing system of taxation.

[8] The imperial sources of income yielded totally inadequate returns. More and more the Emperors had to rely on their own financial means, that is on revenues accrued from property rights belonging to their dynasty and not to the Imperial Crown. The

sion of the imperial rights and prerogatives which provided revenues or could be used to create new financial means took place. These were grasped by the princes of the empire, including the ecclesiastical ones. Apart from the cities, modern forms of taxation and public finance were developed in the realms of these princes; the changes were part of a sociopolitical and socioeconomic transformation or modernization in general.[9]

The emancipation of the princes from their imperial overlords was well under way in the High Middle Ages. This process was essentially a struggle of the princes to convert a conditional and qualified feudal tenure into a tenure that was unconditional and unqualified, to lessen the feudal vassalage with its defined services and obligations, and to get possession of a host of rights, prerogatives, and privileges hereditarily belonging to the Crown. The dispute about investiture, which saw the Emperor on the losing side, helped both the Church and the princes of the empire to eventually free themselves from the imperial authority and to strengthen their own power over their peoples and territories.[10]

All these changes differed, of course, in path, pace, and degree from region to region. On the whole and in the long run, however, the development had similar features throughout the empire. The

---

free cities and other subjects of the Emperor alone, as well as imperial prerogatives, provided some revenues. An attempt by the Emperor in 1427 to impose taxes failed. The Diet of Worms (1495) granted for a limited time-period the collection of the so-called Ordinary Penny (*Gemeiner Pfennig*), but no regular taxes developed out of this grant. In 1521 agreement was reached that the Estates of the empire had to provide proportionate payments (the so-called *Matrikularbeiträge* or *Römermonate*). The yield of this revenue, however, could not at all meet the financial needs of the empire. In 1522 the Emperor again was turned down in his attempt to impose customs duties. Afterward no further serious efforts were made to put forward schemes of imperial taxation (see Mayer 1926: 210ff.).

[9] Important changes took place in the cities in terms of socioeconomic regulations, new methods of taxation, new forms of public credit and finance, and in administration in general. It was the Golden Age for the cities and towns. Hans Rosenberg writes: The numerous cities "devised the rudiments of a modern system of public administration, public taxation, public finance, public credit, public works, and public utilities" (Rosenberg 1958: 6–7).

[10] In the late fourteenth and the fifteenth century the serious socioeconomic consequences of the Black Death further accelerated this process. In this period of rapid and ruthless political, social, and economic changes the princes could, as a rule, enhance their political positions, no matter how doubtful the legality was. They were able to increase the exercise of power in their territories by virtue of an extended executive system and new governmental administration. Often as an outflow of emergency regulations to check effects caused by the Black Death, intrusion of the government into the socioeconomic affairs of its subjects became common to a degree never known before (see Lütge 1963: 281ff.; and Ziegler 1969: passim).

[250]

reigning princes not only were able to gather political rights, privileges, and power into their hands enlarge the sphere of central government (*protectio, administratio, jurisdictio*) and extend their control over social and economic affairs, but they also strove for sovereignty. This latter aspiration was fortified in the late fifteenth century by the revival of Roman Law with its absolutist principles, which civil lawyers as a new group of servants and councillors at the courts of the princes were eager to stress. Moreover, the princes succeeded in attributing to their authority over people and territory the divine sanctions hitherto reserved for the Imperial Crown, thus adding to their secular authority power over the minds and consciences of the subjects in their realm. For the development of the modern doctrine of sovereignty, this supremacy over the Church was as important as the revival of Roman Law.

Yet this is but one side of the coin; the claim of political supremacy and sovereignty by the princes was resisted and checked by the estates of the various territories: the towns and especially the nobles. Until the beginning of our period, that is, until the end of the Thirty Years War, the nobles and the towns more or less prevented the attempts of the princes to base government on personal absolutism. The result of this struggle was a kind of dual system, of checks and balances between the prince and the estates of the territory (see Hartung 1961a: 62ff.; Rosenberg 1958: 8ff.).[11] The main weapon of the Estates in this struggle was their right to grant or refuse "extraordinary" contributions. The main weakness of the princes was their ever more inadequate financial and fiscal basis in a time of increasing governmental obligations, mounting expenditures and, with the beginning of the sixteenth century, a long price revolution. Hence, a few remarks should be made on the sources of income of the princes in the Late Middle Ages and in early modern times.

Until the seventeenth century, the Estates generally insisted on the principle that their princely rulers should "live of their own." This maxim, which had been regarded as fundamental in the Middle Ages, referred to two sources of revenues: (1) the income from the princes' domains; the relative amount of this source of income to the total income varied appreciably from territory to territory (see Droege 1966: 145ff.);[12] and (2) the sources of income provided by the various seigneurial rights, prerogatives and privileges: mining,

---

[11] In German this sociopolitical setting is called *Ständestaat*.
[12] The domain property of Brandenburg was relatively large.

minting, hunting, forest, milling, brewing and market monopolies; border, road, river and bridge customs; the right to impose duty on the Jews; revenues derived from the judicial functions; fees from the bestowal of privileges, offices, or titles. From both an institutional and a psychological point of view these revenues paved the way for schemes of excise and indirect taxation generally.

The utilization and administration of these sources of income, which might be called "patrimonial," were of utmost importance in the formative stage of modern state-building. On the one hand, the *patrimonium* was crucial as a means to maintain and extend the central power. It was fully at the disposal of the princely ruler, could be sold or farmed out, and determined his borrowing power, inasmuch as it served as collateral for various sorts of loans.[13] On the other hand, the administration and utilization of the *patrimonium* came to be one of the nuclei of modern revenue administration, public finance, public credit, and central governmental bureaucracy, although these institutions were growing out of medieval concepts of authority and government, which lacked the modern distinction between "private" and "public" spheres. We will deal with this aspect later on.

In addition, taxation itself was a source of income for the princes, despite the maxim that they "should live of their own." Unlike the Emperors, the princes succeeded as early as the High Middle Ages in imposing direct taxes (the *Bede*, the Tenths, and the Fifteenths,

---

[13] The pledges were of two different kinds: the older form, the so-called traditional pledge (*Traditionspfand*) in which the property pledged was given to the use of the creditor; and, at a later period, the so-called contract pledge (*Vertragspfand*) in which the income derived from the property pledged remained in the hands of the debtor, but had to be used to pay interests on and for amortization of the debt. The variety of credit sources were at the disposal of the princes for the financing of their ordinary and extraordinary expenditures. The Estates, that is the municipalities of the cities and towns, the aristocracy and Church institutions, were drawn on as creditors. Indeed, this was often done through force. At least as important were the private creditors. It is well known what an important role in this regard the north Italian money-changers (the Lombards), the wealthy merchants, and big commercial houses of southern Germany, and up to the end of the *Ancien Régime*, the court Jews played. Another form for mobilizing capital was the issuing of annuities (annuity for a term or for life), which was innovated in the Italian city-states and widely used by the city municipalities during the Late Middle Ages. But after the princes began to adopt this form of mobilizing capital, the annuities fell in the sixteenth century more and more into discredit, so that the princes often had to levy annuities; they became a kind of forced loan. With the beginning of the seventeenth century the bourses, particularly those of Amsterdam and, later, of London, increasingly gained prominence as institutions for public financing and loans. It was only in the late seventeenth and eighteenth centuries that private, municipal, semistate and state banks gained importance in providing public capital and credit.

for example). These extraordinary contributions were usually property taxes.[14] As a source of revenue they had, by the Late Middle Ages, lost most of their significance, but as symbols of authority and as precedents in the struggle for the right to institute taxes they remained relevant. Up to the beginning of our period, the Estates successfully claimed the right to grant taxes. It was the unwavering principle of the Estates that these contributions should be granted only for "extraordinary" expenditure (e.g., warfare, marriage, coronation) and for a limited duration. They were eager to earmark these revenues for specific purposes and to control their custody, allocation and disbursement. Furthermore they exerted every effort to decide the standards of distribution and assessment themselves. Even the entire administration (assessment, collection, custody, and disbursement) of these taxes came in the hands of the Estates, due to the fact that they found themselves again and again confronted with the need to allow their properties to serve as collateral for the mounting debts of the princes. The so-called credit-purse of the Estates (*Ständisches Kreditwerk*), used for the payment of the interest of the princely debts and for their amortization, served to maintain or restore the borrowing power and credit-worthiness of their ruling houses, and at the same time to encourage the latter to husband its resources and to preserve its property undivided. The prince's solvency was of necessity a matter of concern for the Estates, because their fate was tied to that of their ruling House. The development of such an estate tax system, administered by local institutions of the Estates, reached its peak during the second half of the sixteenth century.

The Estates used their tax grants as bargaining power to demand sociopolitical concessions from their princes. The tax administration became the basis of estate autonomy in other matters. Behind the efforts of the wealthy and powerful to handle the assessment and distribution of taxes themselves stood many selfish interests. True, the fiscal policy and practice of the Estates were marked by many features of a reactionary "feudal" nature. Yet we have to recognize and to emphasize the "modern" progressive features of these activities. In various ways they might be evaluated as genuine elements for the creation of the "tax state": From both an institutional and psychological point of view, they helped to accomplish the undis-

[14] For the *Bede* in Brandenburg see Schmoller 1877: 35ff., and for the Tenths and the Fifteenths see Kennedy 1964: 17ff.

puted acceptance of taxes as regularly paid compulsory levies on private units used for public purposes, and accelerated the process of a clear separation between "public" versus "private" income and expense.

Moreover, the willingness of the Estates to share the expenses and to secure the debts of their princes manifests a concept of the territory as a commonweal with its own—that is, public—interests against the private or "patrimonial" interests of its ruling houses. The Estates thus contributed to the development of a consciousness of "the state" in the modern sense contradicting the traditional concept of authority and government as a hereditary personal "patrimony" of the ruling houses, which could be the object of division, sale, or pledge.

These aspects lead us to the center of a crucial problem: the formative stage in the process of modern state-building and the growth of princely absolutism. The concentration of rights and prerogatives in the hands of the princes not only enlarged their obligations, duties, and services, but changed the very nature of these functions as well as the essence of the relationship to their subjects. Correspondingly the expenditure increased. The protective function (*protectio*) alone became an enormous burden for the princes when the feudal military system, which rested on the principle of clientship, decomposed in the Late Middle Ages and at the same time the costs for war and defense were being drastically raised by firearms and other innovations in warfare. To bear the costs of war out of the ordinary revenues of the *patrimonium* was for most of the princes simply impossible; even minor warfare heaped up debts and usually led to insolvency. But the protective function referred not only to enemies from without, but also to those within the border of the territory. For the maintenance of law and order as well as for the exercise of central power, the princes needed loyal military forces. In order to get and maintain the military and political support of the power elite of the territory, the princes had to pay pensions, annuities and a host of other costly rewards to these groups. The rapid development of the spoils systems, nepotism, and favoritism during the formative stage of modern statebuilding was both a factor and a symptom of sociopolitical changes and a heavy financial burden for the ruling houses. The same can be said in regard to the rising costs of the princely household and court life: the conspicuous consumption of the court was not only a symptom of changing taste and style of life, but a real political factor: the prince was forced to live up to his new dignity (see Dietz 1967: 124). In addition, the diversification of the administrative functions and a set of other new governmental obligations likewise required more financial means.

Even for such as were considered normal peacetime expenditures, the financial basis of the princes became increasingly inadequate; the maxim of the Estates that their ruling House should "live of its own" proved to be more and more unrealistic. Against this background arose the princely demand for the power of disposition over the property of the subjects of the realm. This was the claim for the so-called *dominium eminens*, which had to be evaluated together with the princes' new functions, their claim of sovereignty, and the divine sanction of their authority. At first the *dominium eminens* was restricted to cases of emergency and had to serve public needs. Later, the absolutist doctrine extended the scope of application of the *dominium eminens*; it no longer referred only to the public weal, and it was not connected with the state as an institution but with the princes and their Houses: it became interpreted as part of the *dominium excellenciae*. This interpretation served the princes as a rationale to deduce their right to use the property of their subjects for all their expenses and debts, even the purely private ones. Furthermore, it played a role in the struggle over taxation rights; the princes used the *dominium eminens* in their attempts to dismantle the Estates' right to grant taxes.

Naturally that the *dominium eminens* or at least the interpretation of its range of application was disputed by the representatives of the Estates. Their position was essentially ambivalent. On the one hand, it was to their interest that the ruling prince be able to fulfill his obligations, duties and services to the commonweal. On the other hand, the Estates were concerned with maintaining their own interests against the princes' absolutistic claims. They had to be especially careful that their contributions to the expenditure of their ruling house and their provision of collateral for the princely debts would not lead to a precedent for legalizing an expansion of the *dominium eminens* in the absolutistic sense. This is why they opposed the princes' attempts to institute unlimited compulsory levies and were willing to agree only to taxes of limited duration. For the same reason they sought to grant only earmarked revenues, to control the collection and allocation of the contributions granted, and to develop their own fiscal administration.

[255]

These few general remarks reveal the significance of taxation and fiscal policy, in theory and practice, in determining the dual character of the first phase of modern state-building. The cases of Brandenburg-Prussia and England illustrate these developments.

With the foregoing general outline in mind, and in view of other chapters of this book, we may be allowed to be very sketchy as regards Brandenburg-Prussia. When the House of Hohenzollern succeeded the House of Luxemburg as margraves of Brandenburg (1411), approximately nine-tenths of all "patrimonial" property (including rights and prerogatives as sources of income) were pawned or had been sold. There was no efficient administration for collection, custody and disbursement of tithes, rents, and other revenues. Hence, the Hohenzollerns were faced with the task of recovering sold or pawned sources of income, of establishing efficient methods of utilizing their property, of innovating a revenue administration, and of winning their Estates over—whether voluntarily or by force—to contribute at least to the "extraordinary" expenditures. It was of utmost importance for the formation of the Brandenburg-Prussian state that during the fifteenth century the Hohenzollern margraves proved able to accomplish these tasks: with the help of commercially and legally trained administrators and court officials a new domain and court administration was organized, new accounting methods and audits at fixed dates were introduced, and even a rudimentary budget planning innovated. In addition, the first Hohenzollerns enforced the reintroduction of a direct tax (the *Bede*) and, after bloody conflicts, imposed a new indirect tax (the beer tax). Even though these direct and indirect taxes covered only a small fraction of the total sources of income and were limited in time and therefore continually had to be approved anew, they were the nucleus of a territorial tax system. They manifested the power of the House of Hohenzollern in getting the fiscal cooperation of its subjects and helped to foster the principles of taxation in the consciousness of the Estates and the people (see Schmoller 1877: 44ff.).

To strengthen the central power and government further, judicial reforms were also undertaken: the highest court of justice was reorganized (the so-called *Kammergericht*) and the traditional local law was supplemented by Roman Law. The so-called *Dispositio Achillea* (1473) attempted to secure primogeniture succession of the electorate and to prevent a division of the Hohenzollern property in Brandenburg. Even though the goals of the *Dispositio Achillea*

[256]

could not be realized for a long time to come,[15] they indicated that the private or "patrimonial" conception of authority, government, succession and princely property was giving way to a more public one.

In short, the first Hohenzollerns managed to lay a firm grip on the three most important functions of the government—the *protectio*, *administratio*, and *jurisdictio*—and altered the nature of these functions in principle and practice. The growth of a territorial state and a central power with a host of strikingly "modern" features may clearly be recognized. This development, however, was checked after the death of Joachim I (1535). The financial plight and the mounting debts of his successors, caused by a variety of factors (war and threat of war, costly court life, extension of the territory, less careful management of the "patrimonium," and protracted price rises), enabled the Estates to gain more influence over the central government and administration and to tighten their local authority. Due to the assumption of the debts of the princes, direct and indirect taxes no longer flowed into the princely purse, but into the credit-purses of the Estates. Thus the electors more and more lost control over the administration of finances and budgeting. Instead of a uniform tax system, a multitude of local tax systems and local tax administrations sprang up.[16] The tendency was the same in the towns as in the country: the powerful and the wealthy could virtually shift all the burden of taxes upon the shoulders of the weak and the poor. In the cities there was an increasingly exclusive group of patricians who were eligible to rule. In the country the peasantry lapsed more and more into serfdom. By depressing the status of the peasantry with the exercise of local authority, the landed aristocracy obtained the labor required for the considerably increased arable land under their direct control. Not only did the socioeconomic situation of the subject peasantry worsen in terms of villenage and compulsory labor service, but also the real wages of rural and urban wage earners decreased continuously during this period.[17]

[15] Albrecht Achilles did not succeed with this idea: The contracts of inheritance of his successors again showed divisions. It was not until the House Treaty of Gera (1598, confirmed in 1603) that any division of the electorate was definitely prevented and the rule of primogeniture firmly established for the House of Hohenzollern.

[16] Especially in Cleves and Prussia, territories which had become Hohenzollern possessions at that time, the mode of taxation changed almost from year to year: now it was a livestock, poll, or house tax, now a hidage.

[17] The spirit of the age marked by religious thinking and, particularly in Lutheran territories, by the doctrine of "suffering obedience" (*leidender Gehorsam*) "justified" the suppression of the poor and weak. The traditional concept of society as an organic

The inadequate fiscal basis and the permanent insolvency of the House of Hohenzollern thus reduced the electors' status to a mere *primus inter pares*: "The prince was no more than a landed Junker with the largest estate of the territory."[18] The newly acquired territories could not be integrated into the realm of a central government and administration. The Electorate of Brandenburg-Prussia remained a loosely-knit entity of various parts which had separate governments and administrations, as well as different constitutions, laws and governmental institutions. With this authority, varying in form and degree from territory to territory, the prince had to share his rulership. The representatives of the Estates influenced appointments to governmental offices and determined administrative and governmental affairs. Even military organization and administration came partially under their control. Until the beginning of our period (1640), Brandenburg-Prussia, like so many other territorial states of the German Empire, was marked by a strong, disintegrating localism and all the other weaknesses of the so-called *Ständestaat* or Estates' State. In Britain, the accession of the House of Tudor, often labeled in constitutional history the "New Monarchy," has been regarded as marking the transition from medieval to modern England in terms of radically changing the sphere of government and of shaping the sociopolitical structure toward a modern state or nation. The new dynasty's chances of survival depended heavily upon improvement of the Crown's financial resources so as to overcome the chronic insolvency which had been one of the chief reasons for the decline of the monarchy during the fifteenth century. Though England had a long tradition of direct taxation, these revenues were considered "extraordinary" and were levied only on a grant by Parliament for special purposes such as war. The maxim that the "king should live of his own" still prevailed when the Tudors came to power. However, Henry VII (1485–1509), the first of the Tudor Kings, managed to fulfill this maxim in practice. By improvements in financial administration and a vigilant scrutiny of expenditure in a surprisingly short period of time, the crown began to balance its income and expenditure.

---

unity which is composed of different parts, but interdependent in a mutual privileges-duties relationship, was so transformed under the influence of the doctrine of "suffering obedience" that emphasis was mainly placed on the difference between the parts and little on the reciprocity of privileges and duties.

[18] A sentence of Gustav Schmoller (see Droege 1966: 159).

The innovations with respect to the utilization and administration of the Crown's "own" resources were part of a general transformation of the existing administrative and judicial institutions toward a more centralized government, and here again the reforms of Henry VII were decisive. He instituted the separation of certain governmental functions and administrative institutions from the royal household. A clear distinction between the "public" and the domestic or "private" affairs of the King, however, was not reached for a long time to come.[19] In the course of these changes the government came firmly into the hands of the king: he reached a relatively high degree of independence in appointing and dismissing his ministers and all royal officials; he issued instructions to them; he had the power to allocate revenue, to organize national defense and to intervene in the course of justice. By creating a vastly extended executive system, he strengthened the arm of government immensely. The Privy Council supported by the Star Chamber as a new judicial instrument of the Crown was the chief institution to carry out these governmental functions combining administrative, legislative and judicial power. Their members were more and more drawn from the gentry and the middle class. A type of professional governmental servant and expert administrator replaced the Church dignitaries and members of the ancient aristocratic houses in the Privy Council and the other high civil service offices, forming a new nobility attached to the Crown. The old semi-independent feudal magnates who formerly challenged the Crown were struck down by the Tudors. With the Act of Supremacy (1534), the ecclesiastical authority likewise ceased to be autonomous. The King was now accepted as the "only supreme head in earth of the Church of England"; into his hands fell ecclesiastical property, administration and jurisdiction, as well as the right to define the content of belief and to settle forms of ritual (Keir 1967: 67ff.).[20] In short, Tudor rule —though unsupported by any large professional army—developed toward an absolutistic government: it "undeniably wore a dictatorial, harsh, and remorseless aspect. It put reason of State above the letter

[19] For example, this was indicated by the fact that a substantial amount of revenues, even those derived from parliamentary grants, were withdrawn from the control of the Exchequer and administered in the King's Chamber.

[20] After the death of Henry VIII these rights were, however, challenged by the Parliament. The ecclesiastical supremacy was no longer personal or royal, but was shared by Parliament (see Keir 1967: 87).

of the law and rated the public interest, real or alleged, immeasurably higher than the rights of the subject" (Keir 1967: 99).

The establishment of the Tudors' centralized government and power in place of the essentially feudal monarchy was closely related with the development of a centralized administration and supervision of the Crown's "own" or "ordinary" sources of income. These may be divided into two sections. The first comprised the proprietary revenues from Crown lands and the utilization of the Crown's rights and prerogatives (including revenues provided by the judicial function of the King). The second section of permanent revenue was the customs duties.[21]

For the first category of "ordinary" revenue a centralized system of general surveyors and auditors was introduced in Henry VII's reign designed not only to collect the King's rent but—as Frederick C. Dietz, whom we follow here closely, pointed out—to watch "the minutiae of estate business behind the rents actually paid to the king" (Dietz 1967: 116). The ultimate audit control over the system and its officers was exercised by Henry VII in person and under his successors by committees with delegated royal powers. These committees developed into a series of revenue courts with separate treasuries attached that intentionally neglected the traditional exchequer practice with its built-in localism. In addition, royal commissions were used also to control many of the more important expenditures and disbursements. They were assisted by an office of the auditors of the prests and foreign accounts.[22] In the second half of the sixteenth century, the revenue courts and the office of the prests were amalgamated with the Exchequer, but their forms of procedure were retained within the resulting organization. The introduction of improved methods of bookkeeping and accounting techniques was part of this new scheme of centralized fiscal administration.

Until late in Elizabeth's time the new system of general surveyors and auditors was not applied to the customs. Customs duties remained subject to the Exchequer, a central body but with a built-in

[21] Originally these duties were supposed to provide means for the protection of merchants and the defence of the realm—that is for the expenditures of the Navy. They could therefore not be regarded as the Crown's "own" sources of income. However, under Tudor rule these duties were treated as "ordinary" revenue to be used for ordinary expenditure. Thus, in practice, the customs became "own" or "ordinary" revenues (see Kennedy 1964: 14 and Dietz 1967: 127).

[22] Prests were advances of money to officials entrusted with its expenditure.

localism as far as practice and routines were concerned. However, the trend toward centralization was, for example, indicated by the introduction of seminational, and later on national, valuations as a basis for the collection of rates of duties (Dietz 1967: 114ff.).

The result of these innovations in the field of revenue administration was twofold: an increased yield of the Crown's "own" resources and consequently the enhancement of the Tudors' strength and independence. It was particularly decisive that the first King of the House of Tudor could balance his budget without having to rely on Parliament for financial support; otherwise this dynasty could hardly have seated itself securely on the throne. Second—and in the long run even more important—was the new centralized system of general surveyors and auditors as an instrument to secure royal authority and governmental power. The new fiscal apparatus became a fundamental part of the royal bureaucracy upon which Tudor rule could base its nationwide control.

Although England had a long history of direct taxation (Fifteenths and Tenths) granted by Parliament for "extraordinary" expenditures, Henry VII, after a few cautious attempts with little success, gave up all plans to alter the traditional system of "extraordinary" revenues toward a system of regularly recurring taxes, administered by royal offices and to be used for "ordinary" government expenses. To insist upon innovations in matters of direct taxes, which were customarily disliked and opposed by the people, certainly would have endangered his position. Henry VII felt little need for such a provocation; in peacetime he could manage to "live of his own." Under the reign of his successors, however, the finances of the Crown worsened; even in peacetime the "ordinary" revenue proved ever more inadequate.[23] The Tudors had to rely upon "extraordinary" supplements granted by Parliament, but were unsuccessful in changing the nature of the traditional tax system. Like the Fifteenths and the Tenths, the new supplementary direct tax, the Subsidy (imposed

[23] Henry VIII, though successful in raising extraordinary taxation and in gaining (after the Act of Supremacy was passed) an enormous amount of Church property, nevertheless left his successor a heavy burden of debt and a debased currency. The wars of Edward VI and those of Elizabeth required large sums. But even in peacetime the Crown under Elizabeth was no longer able to live on the "ordinary" revenue and had to rely upon "extraordinary" supplies granted by Parliament. The Church property which the Crown gained was enormous, but a great deal was sold very quickly under Henry VIII and could therefore not provide a permanent source of income. "The gainers were the landed and monied class and not the King" (Keir 1967: 68).

by Henry VIII in 1514), soon became standardized, and its yield was therefore bound to diminish, too. In practice, direct taxation was reduced to a mere land tax, because movable personal property (the standard assessment of merchants and others) could so easily evade taxation. The yield of direct taxes became during the sixteenth-century expansion of commerce and trade more and more incommensurate with the wealth of the nation (see Kennedy 1964: 18ff.).[24] The attempts to create a royal administration for the assessment and collection of these taxes failed. Thus, the traditional disadvantages of the tax system were perpetuated. The crown needed the support and cooperation of the Parliament to obtain these "extraordinary" grants; second, the assessment and collection required the support and cooperation of the local authorities. Consequently, Tudor government was forced to combine royal authority and popular consent on the national and the local levels. This is the other side of fiscal policy and practice which determined the formative stage of modern English rule.

On the national level, the Tudor government had to prevent Parliament from converting its control of "extraordinary" financial supply into a weapon against the royal authority, prerogative and conciliar government.[25] Hence, the Tudors had to be cautious in all attempts to bypass the Parliament as a legislative body or to set royal Prerogative above the Common Law courts. Parliamentary action had to be a function of the monarchy, that is the King had to act both in and out of Parliament in order to maintain parliamentary support without diminishing governmental power. Skillful parliamentary management enabled the Tudors to hold the government firmly in their hands even in times of growing financial strain and insolvency.

On the local level the Tudors likewise established and maintained a balanced combination of royal authority and popular consent. They had to get the support and cooperation of the traditional local authorities in their attempts to extend royal control over social and economic life of the realm. "There was nothing, so far as the Tudor attitude went, which prevented the introduction of a modern type

[24] D. L. Keir writes: "The Subsidy involved taxation of wages, personal property and rents and was assessed by royal collectors. Flexible at first, the subsidy gradually became rigid. . . . Though no standardized collective yield was ever fixed for the subsidy it became difficult to expand" (Keir 1967: 15).

[25] The position and self-esteem of the House of Commons was enhanced by virtue of the decisive role it played in the religious dispute leading to the Act of Supremacy.

of all-controlling paternalistic state during the sixteenth century" (Dietz 1967: 119). Of crucial importance were the Justices of the Peace, usually country gentry and men of property, who had added to their judicial function an increasing number of administrative and other functions.[26] Since they were not professional servants of the government but rather voluntary and unpaid judges and administrators, the practical influence of the Crown and its governmental institutions upon the Justices of the Peace was limited, that is, depended on the cooperation and loyalty of the latter. Hence, apart from the lack of financial means the "paternalistic" ambitions of Tudor government were checked somewhat by the need to rely upon traditional local authorities with their disintegrating localism. The creation of a national tax system, regularly returning an adequate amount of revenues and administered by royal bureaucracy, would have provided both the means and the institutions to live up to these ambitions.

Yet the Tudors failed in attaining such a goal; and this became decisive in terminating the first phase of modern England. When the first Stuart succeeded the Tudors (1603), fiscal matters played a most important part in the power struggle between the Crown and the Parliament.

Unlike the Tudors, the first Stuarts proved unable to establish voluntary support from the Parliament in matters concerning "extraordinary" revenue. Insisting on the unrealistic principle that "the king should live of his own" during peacetime, the Parliament started to use its financial support as a tool for bargaining with the impoverished Crown for political concessions. In the 1620s Parliament even began to withhold (or to give in inadequate measure) "extraordinary" supply in times of threat of war, though it was constitutionally supposed to provide it. It sought to encroach on the Crown's governmental power by forcing the King to dismiss ministers, to deprive him of sole control over the allocation of revenue, to determine his policy (even his foreign and his marriage policy) and to reduce or dismantle the Prerogative. Moreover, Parliament, jointly with the Common Law courts, questioned the Crown's "ordinary" sources of income, particularly the way in which the Stuarts tried to interpret

---

[26] Into their hands fell the maintenance of peace, law and order; they dealt with persons who tried to avoid paying taxes, refused to work, did not attend church services; also as part of their obligation were the maintenance of roads, the granting of ale-house licences, the overseeing of weights and measures, and a host of other duties.

and exploit these sources and their Prerogative (the struggle over Ship Money is a major example).

On the local level the traditional authorities became increasingly reluctant to support the royal government. They frequently refused to execute the Crown's orders in regard to forced loans or the payment of Ship Money. Even the Justices of the Peace began to resist royal orders.

For its part, the Crown, unable to come to terms with the Parliament on financial support, had to utilize its own resources, bypassing the Parliament whenever it could and challenging the Common Law courts with its own jurisdictional power (particularly the Star Chamber). In pursuing this course aimed at the increase of "own" resources the Stuarts approached a kind of personal autocratic absolutism which the Tudor government had been so skillful in avoiding.[27] After 1629 the Crown gradually managed to regain financial strength and could, indeed, hope to govern in an absolutistic fashion without Parliament and its financial supplies. The Scottish rebellion, however, changed this situation: the "Short Parliament" had to be summoned in 1638 but proved unresponsive to the plea for support; the City of London refused loans. The resultant financial weakness rendered the Crown no longer able to cope with the Scottish uprising and the parliamentary opposition. When the "Long Parliament" met in November 1640, the Crown's case was lost. The initial blow was the reduction of the Prerogative; the next steps (1641) aimed at the dismantling of the conciliar government; finally, in June 1642 the Nineteen Propositions were set forth, claiming for Parliament the right to nominate councillors, ministers and judges, along with control of the militia, and also proclaiming the supremacy of the Church. The consequence was civil war.

Let us briefly compare the developments in England (or Great Britain, after the personal union of England and Scotland with the accession of James I) with those in Brandenburg-Prussia. Under

---

[27] In their efforts to increase the revenue and to balance the budget, the Stuarts, on the one hand, reorganized the governmental and financial administration; drastic reforms of household and public expenditures were undertaken. On the other hand, the Stuart government made an all-out effort to increase nonparliamentary sources of revenue: a new kind of import duties, the "Impositions," were levied; monopolistic grants to commercial and manufacturing companies were widely used to collect fees; customs increased several times; attempts to levy an excise and to impose Ship Money generally over the kingdom were made; forced loans were frequently applied to raise money but were often, like the payment of Ship Money, resisted by the Justices of Peace, who refused to execute the Crown's orders (see Keir 1967: 165ff., 184).

Tudor rule the government was firmly in the hands of the King; royal authority and popular consent had been successfully combined. Under the first Stuarts the House of Commons challenged the conciliar government, with the trend toward a parliamentary monarchy. But despite the deprivation by Parliament (with the support of the Common Law courts) of legislative, fiscal, and judicial powers inherent in the Crown's Prerogative, and its encroachments on governmental activity, these inroads are in no way comparable to the dual system in Brandenburg-Prussia. Until the time of the Long Parliament, the Crown had been able to retain a firm grip on government and could during times of peace dispense with Parliament and reduce the influence of the Common Law courts. Britain thus was relatively unified and governed by a powerful royal bureaucracy, whereas the Electorate of Brandenburg-Prussia consisted of various unintegrated parts with separate governments and administrations more or less under the controlling influence of the representative bodies of the estates.

"The destruction of the royal bureaucracy in 1640–1641 can be regarded as the most decisive event in the whole of British history," according to Christopher Hill (Hill 1967: 76). This statement, however, seems somewhat exaggerated; clearly, one of the weaknesses of England's conciliar government was its dependence on the services of the Justices of the Peace, men of property who were inclined to enforce only those statutes, proclamations and laws which suited their interests, as was shown in their refusal to execute the Crown's orders in regard to forced loans. But the Justices of the Peace, though unpaid, were still nominally royal administrators, whereas local authority in Brandenburg-Prussia was solely in the hands of the nobility and the city or town oligarchy, which could widely use their positions for their own socioeconomic interests. The conciliar government under the Tudors and even more under the Stuarts aimed to prevent at least the grosser forms of social injustice and to enforce uniform laws and regulations in regard to wages, prices, poor-relief, enclosure, and other social and economic affairs, though the enforcement was actually inadequate.

To be sure, in England too the laboring poor experienced in this period a steady shrinking of real wages and income; debasement of the coinage and rising prices caused special impoverishment among the lower orders. Sumptuary laws and other statutes helped to maintain social distinctions and a static hierarchical society. The lower

[265]

orders had no political rights; the House of Commons represented property, and "legislators still thought of all people who had no property as semi-servile."[28] The members of the Lower House increasingly used their power and influence, like the representatives of the Estates in Brandenburg-Prussia, for selfish purposes. In the subsidies voted by Parliament, the richer landowners, traders, and merchants were greatly underassessed. The law was heavily weighted against the poor. Certain social groups such as the gentry and the peers enjoyed special privileges; the peers, for example, could not be imprisoned for debts.

Yet, compared with those of Brandenburg-Prussia, the sociopolitical features were markedly benign. The peasantry of England had escaped from villenage and compulsory labor service by the end of the sixteenth century (with the exception of some minor remnants). An economically independent middle order of merchants, better-off artisans, yeomen (independent peasantry) and well-to-do tenant farmers had emerged with their property protected by Common Law, though lacking the privileges of the nobles and gentry. And most important of all, neither the landed nobility and gentry nor the wealthy city merchants were exempted from taxation, and, as in Brandenburg-Prussia, could far less shift the tax burden onto the lower order. On the contrary, both the direct taxes (the Fifteenth and the Tenth, and the Subsidy) and the indirect revenues (Customs, Impositions) had deliberate standards of distribution (forms of assessment and rules of exemptions) which virtually freed the laboring poor from paying revenues.

As for direct taxes, the principle that they should be distributed according to ability or means prevailed.[29] In practice, however, this principle was violated. As we pointed out earlier, the local assessors and commissioners greatly favored the gentry and the wealthier traders and merchants. "This was the price which the government had to pay to its servants and the classes on whom it depended for

---

[28] These are the words of John Clapham, cited by Hill 1967: 41.

[29] As for direct taxes, England had a tradition going back to the High Middle Ages of levying all social groups: the landowner, the merchant, the poor man. The limit of exemption was so low as to cover most of the poor people. When the scheme of direct taxes was reorganized under Henry VIII (the Fifteenth and the Tenth as a land tax; the Subsidy as an innovation for moveables), most of the wage earners were subject to taxation. Only persons earning less than twenty shillings a year escaped. In 1544 the limit of exemption was raised to forty shillings. In the years 1522–1533 wages were explicitly exempted from Subsidy; thereafter, up to the beginning of the period under consideration, the practice was to free the poor from paying Subsidy (see Kennedy 1964: 20ff.).

unsalaried (but not unrewarded) services in local government"
(Hill 1967: 82). Attempts at reassessment in the late sixteenth and
the first half of the seventeenth centuries so as to tap more accurately the real wealth of the nation failed. The so-called Ship Money, a
levy which the Stuarts tried to impose without parliamentary consent mainly contrived to develop naval strength. It was regarded by
the gentry, the merchants, and the City companies as unconstitutional, and met with increasing refusal to pay.

The customs, by far the most lucrative source of "ordinary" revenue under Tudor and Stuart reigns, had a primarily fiscal function.
However, the economic and social effects of this indirect levy were
perceived and discussed in the time of Elizabeth and the first Stuarts.
Though a reorganization (innovation of the Imposition, etc.) and
several increases of the customs duties took place in this period, the
principle set forth (especially under Stuart rule) was that, in order
to relieve the poor, "necessaries of the people" should not be subject
to duty (Kennedy 1964: 13ff.). Hence, the government was well
aware that in practice the burden of customs fell mainly upon the
consumers and less on the merchants. Yet considerations of trade
policy had a certain impact upon the rates of customs duties already
in this period, too, according to William Kennedy, who refers to the
Book of Rates of 1610 (Kennedy 1964: 13ff.). The rising importance
of foreign and inland trade and correspondingly the rising sociopolitical influence of the traders, merchants and financial circles of
the City in the sixteenth century manifested itself in this economic
policy. However, the fiscal needs of the first Stuarts, when they
failed to reach agreement with Parliament and were therefore
forced to exploit fully all "ordinary" sources of revenue, blocked or
hampered this trade policy. The increase of customs duties, the innovation of Impositions and Ship Money, the attempt to levy an excise and the Crown's policy of granting commercial and manufacturing monopolies alienated the trading and manufacturing classes
from the Crown (Keir 1967: 202).

Although a wide gap between proclaimed intention and practice
as to distributing the burden of revenue existed in England, the situation was different from that in Brandenburg-Prussia. Let us recall
that in Brandenburg-Prussia the administration of taxation and at
least partially the financial administration as well were in the hands
of the Estates; a host of regional and frequently changing schemes
of taxation existed; the nobles could virtually escape taxation, and

the city and town oligarchy had ways of shifting the burden of taxation onto the poorer and dependent people. But one common feature marked the situation in Britain and Brandenburg-Prussia at the beginning of our period: in order for "the State" to survive, the entire fiscal and financial organization had to be reformed; both the British and the Brandenburg-Prussian governments were in a state of bankruptcy. As we shall see in the following section, this long overdue fiscal and financial reorganization went hand in hand with drastic changes in the sociopolitical, governmental, and administrative structure of both Britain and Brandenburg-Prussia.

The Crucial Phase of State-Building

The 1640s marked the beginning of the crucial stage of modern state-building for both Brandenburg-Prussia and Britain: In Brandenburg-Prussia a personal or dynastic absolutism emerged and was superseded in the second half of the eighteenth century by bureaucratic absolutism; Britain in turn advanced toward a parliamentary monarchy. What part did fiscal tradition, policies, and practices play in determining these developments?

Three autocratic rulers deserve credit for the formation of modern Prussian absolutism with all its distinct and unique features: the Great Elector (1640–1688), King Frederick William I (1713–1740), and King Frederick the Great (1740–1786). Each of these rulers left his personal imprint, but the reign of the Great Elector was decisive. His innovations and reforms furnished the basis for the centralized and bureaucratized Hohenzollern monarchy.

In attempting to analyze the molding of the modern Prussian state first of all we have to emphasize the syndrome character of these innovations and reforms: the reorganization of the military system, the creation of a central government and administration, the taming of the Estates, the dismantling of the traditional governmental and administrative bodies of the Estates and the provincial territories, the judicial reforms together with supplementing and supplanting the ancient law of the territories by an administrative law of an absolutistic and arbitrary fashion—all these and a set of other changes were closely interwoven with each other. Particularly striking is the interdependence of military, fiscal, and administrative reconstruction. The subjects of the Brandenburg-Prussia Electorate had to get used to both the establishment of a peacetime standing army firmly in the grip of the prince and to regularly recurring direct and indirect taxes, which were designed for and allocated to support the new military system. The military organization in turn enforced the payment of these contributions and eventually collected and administered the revenues with its own apparatus; after the separation of this apparatus from the military organization, it consequently became the prime nucleus of the centralized dynastic bureaucracy. The "militarization," the "fiscalization," and the "bureaucratization," which characterized the nature of Hohenzollern monarchy, particularly after Frederick William I's time, were born inseparable.

These remarks refer to the new system of taxation in order to meet the growing financial and material needs of the army. This is but one side of fiscal matters; as will be seen later on, the Hohenzollerns' "own" resources, the domains and prerogatives, likewise became a focus of Prussian bureaucracy and central power.

Let us first outline the historical development of the new system of taxation, introduced by the Great Elector, and its impact upon the processes of sociopolitical modernization. The genesis of both the new direct tax (the so-called *Contribution*) and the new indirect tax (the so-called *Excise*) reach back into the Thirty Years War. In deciding to keep a standing army for external and even more for internal reasons, the Great Elector relied on a military tradition. During a generation of war the Estates had become accustomed to regularly recurring so-called military contributions (*Kontributionen*) in money, kind, and in services for the support of mercenary troops. The new system of direct and indirect taxes imposed by the Great Elector was in fact little more than an extension of war practice into peacetime.

For direct taxes, during most of his reign, the Great Elector had to depend on old schemes which were in use during the Thirty Years War. Despite several attempts he had but limited success in changing either the overall amount of the Contribution for each district, or the mode of assessment and distribution of the required tax load. The Junkers (i.e., the nobles) still evaded in practice the payment of direct taxes in most of the provincial territories, rationalizing and defending their behavior by referring to ancient tradition which held such revenues to be a symbol of serfdom and therefore unsuited for their social status. Once again the poor and dependent bore the burden of direct taxes, which varied greatly from region to region in the realm.

The new indirect taxation, the Excise, was also an outgrowth of war practice. During the Thirty Years War some districts of the Brandenburg-Prussian electorate applied more indirect methods of taxation in order to raise the required amount of war contributions. The cities and towns used these indirect modes, having a long history of indirect levies and being less suited than the countryside to provide in kind and services for military support. The Great Elector adopted these forms of indirect taxation. Originally he attempted to impose a general Excise throughout his realm, but finally (1667) complied with the request of the Junkers, who vigorously opposed a general excise (seeing their tax privileges endangered), by making only cities and towns but not the countryside and therefore the landed aristocracy subject to the excise. With this decision, Brandenburg-Prussia became divided until the Napoleonic Wars into two different systems of taxation: the countryside with its Contribution, and the cities and towns with their Excise.[30]

To be sure, the introduction of direct and indirect taxes as permanent levies could be achieved only after severe struggles with the Estates, in particular the nobles, varying in duration and intensity from territory to territory according to the status and strength of their power elites. In the long run, however, the Estates entirely lost their rights and influence to grant or withhold revenues. Since these fiscal matters were traditionally the backbone of the Estates' strength, their loss meant the downfall of the Estates as a political counterbalance or challenge to the sovereign's authority and power: the dual system had to give way to a personal or dynastic absolutism. The traditional governmental bodies of the provincial territories were gradually stripped of their rights, functions, and obligations; they saved only part of their judicial functions. Thus to reduce their power, it was essential for the Great Elector to get the collection and administration of taxes in his hands. Again, a military tradition furnished the instrument for this effort. He could rely on an institution which emerged with the rise of mercenary armies and became of prime importance during the Thirty Years War: the system of commissars.

The system of commissars, hierarchically structured, served two functions in dealing with mercenary troops. On the one hand, it

---

[30] Excise regulations were instituted in 1667 in Brandenburg (at first facultatively; revised in 1680), in 1680 in Magdeburg, in 1700 in Pomerania, and in 1713, after the accession of Frederick William I, throughout the rest of the kingdom. Very moderate house-, trade- and poll-taxes, varying from district to district, supplemented the Excise. The duties were collected either at the gates (for goods which were brought into town) or as retail sale and producer taxes. The whole range of consumer goods, including the "necessaries of the People," were subject to the Excise.

served as an instrument of control to protect the princely interests against the mercenary commanders, who operated their corps as a kind of private business enterprise. On the other hand, it provided an apparatus for quartermaster's functions, logistics and in particular for provision of the required war contributions in money, kinds and services. These so-called *War Commissars* (*Kriegskommissarien*) were part of the military organization. In addition, so-called *Country* or *District Commissars* (*Land- oder Krieskommissarien*) served similar functions, but were not part of the military organization. Appointed by the prince from a list proposed by the Estates, they saw themselves as representatives of the Estates and were primarily concerned with the interests of the taxpaying subjects in their realms.

With the establishment of a standing army the Great Elector could prolong the system of commissars, originally used as an extraordinary institution during a state of war, into peacetime. It proved to be the chief vehicle of princely autocracy. Furnished with secret instructions based on an arbitrary administrative law (grown out of martial law), the commissars became "the prime tool for the demolition of the old *Ständestaat* and the creation of a new absolutistic military state" (Hintze 1962: 245). Thus the germ of militarization of Prussian bureaucracy, government, and society, culminating in Frederick William I's time, might be diagnosed as a pathogenic agent of the Thirty Years War.

Making headway, to begin with, only against the strong localism of the estates, the governmental bodies of the provincial territories and traditional law, the system of commissars became the focus of centralized Prussian bureaucracy. With the establishment of the General War Commissariat and the General War Purse, all the affairs of taxation—levying, collection, administration, and disbursement—were gradually taken over by a bureaucratic apparatus firmly in the 'hands of the prince, adding more and more functions, obligations, and rights outside the field of fiscal matters and separating itself from the military organization. It is not our task to outline these developments, but we should say a few words about "the crucial field agents of the central administration and the symbols of its growing power" (Rosenberg 1958: 39)—the Tax Commissar (*Steuerrat*) and the Country Commissioner (*Landrat*).

The predecessor of the Tax Commissar, the so-called *Commissarius loci*, carried out functions of the traditional War Commissar in relation to cities and towns of a taxation district. Still part of the military organization, the *Commissarius loci* was well suited to be used as an instrument for the formation of an all-controlling *Polizei-staat*-pattern of princely rulership. After his separation from the army, the *Commissarius loci* steadily enchanced his influence and competence. Eventually he became the chief administrative and executive power of towns and cities in his district, relegating the traditional self-government of the municipalities to insignificance; "even the ghost of self-government disappeared" (Rosenberg 1958: 39). The Tax Commissar, helped by a staff of subaltern assistants with clerical and/or executive tasks, held the key position for injecting the central bureaucratic machinery into the socioeconomic affairs of its subjects. The cameralistic *Polizeistaat* of the unique Prussian brand, marked by the minute regulation of all affairs of life by an absolutistic government, was personified by the Tax Commissar. Several factors were responsible for his strength and power: On the one hand, the relatively weak position of the cities and towns as Estates and their special tax system (the Excise): on the other, the military origin of the *Commissarius loci* and the close functional connection with the army even after the separation from the latter. The Tax Commissar was not only appointed from outside the provincial territory of his district, deliberately denying the traditional *Indigenats-recht* of the Estates, but was often a former military officer. In the eighteenth century even his staff came more and more to employ former military rank and file. Both in terms of origin and of overlapping and interchange of office holders, the Tax Commissar and his staff were the chief agents for the militarization of Prussian bureaucracy (Hartung 1950: 117; Rosenberg 1958: 64).[31]

During the Great Elector's reign the former District Commissariat was gradually altered into a more absolutistic instrument, but remained essentially a mongrel institution, that is, it still represented the interests both of the sovereign and of the Estates of the rural districts, the landed aristocracy. Early in the eighteenth century it was amalgamated with the traditional County Commissioner (*Landrat*), a semihonorary office reserved for nobles. The County Commissioner served similar functions for his rural district as the Tax Com-

---

[31] Rosenberg writes: "Particularly striking features of the recruitment and promotion policies under Frederick William I were the heavy influx of military bureaucrats and the curb on the career prospects for the old nobility who had no special connections and were not army officers. . . . The employment of professional soldiers and ex-soldiers in the civil branches of the government also became a methodically pursued policy in the eighteenth century" (Rosenberg 1958: 64).

missar for the cities and towns and was likewise assisted by a staff of administrative and/or executive subordinates, but the nature of his position was quite different. The traditional *Indigenatsrecht* continued to be applied for the appointment of the County Commissioner, and the Junkers were invariably privileged to nominate the candidates for this office. These facts mirrored the sociopolitical strength of the Junkers as the main opponents of autocratic rulership. The mongrel character of the County Commissioner was one of the concessions of the prince to obtain the support of the squirearchy. The Junkers were able to ensure their tax exemptions, guarantee their patrimonial rights and local authority (*Gutsherrschaft*), and in general their privileged social status. In short, "the power of the monarch and the bureaucracy and, thus, of the dynastic state ended with the semibureaucratic *Landrat*," and the autocratic *Polizeistaat* was kept away from the realm of *Gutsherrschaft* (Rosenberg 1958: 39).[32]

The General War Commissariat and—at the provincial level—the Head War Commissariats (the predecessors of the War Chambers) were supported by a special judicial institution, the Chamber-court.[33] The Commissars thus belonged to a bureaucratic mechanism with executive and administrative as well as judicial functions. The backbone of its tasks was fiscal affairs of a "public" nature, that is, the new direct and indirect taxes, but the apparatus of the General War Commissariat came to serve more and more as the chief instrument of economic policy and police matters in the broad mercantilistic-cameralistic sense.

The second section of revenue, the sovereign's "own" or "patrimonial" sources of income, was likewise centralized by the Great Elector. Again, this separate bureaucratic body, dealing exclusively with the administration and utilization of the domains and with the regalian prerogatives,[34] was based on a system of commissars, the so-

[32] The so-called Recess of 1653 where the Junkers agreed to grant the Elector an amount of 530,000 Talers over the next six years, considerably enhanced the socioeconomic position of the nobles: Their patrimonial rights and authority were ensured; their landed property was protected from falling into nonnoble hands; connubium-regulations as regards marriage with nonnoble partners were set up; stricter compulsory work regulations for the servile peasantry were approved; last but not least, the onus of proof as to whether a peasant was free or subject to serfdom fell now upon the peasant (see Schmoller 1921: 56ff.).

[33] In the realm of the Chamber-court (*Kammergericht*) fell particularly all fiscal and police matters. The prince's orders to the Chamber-court stated the maxim: *in dubio pro fisco* (Hartung 1950: 114).

[34] With the new fiscal system the formerly innumerable seigneurial prerogatives

called Domain-district Commissars (*Aemterkommissarien*). By virtue of its main property, the domains, the economic policy of this institution was chiefly guided by agrarian interests compared with the more "mercantilistic-cameralistic" interests of the General War Commissariat. Reorganized in 1689 (Secret Court Chamber), the institution lost its importance during the financial mismanagement of Frederick I's reign, but after Frederick William's accession it was reconstructed under the name of the General Financial Directory.[35] Friction and rivalry between the General Financial Directory and the General War Commissariat, caused by their different views of economic policy, soon gave rise to the union of the two separate institutions under the name: *General-ober-Finanz-Kriegs- und Domänendirektorium*, or, abbreviated, the General Directory. The General Directory became the chief governmental administrative organ. Though the purse of the General Financial Directory and that of the General War Commissariat remained separate, the crucial change toward a centralized "state" or "public" fiscal and financial administration, with the corresponding policy change, had taken place.

Likewise important for the structural development of a modern state and for sociopolitical modernization were two other governmental and administrative changes during Frederick William I's

---

(several hundred in number) as sources of revenue were greatly diminished. Some remained and some were added: there were coffee, tobacco, lottery, salt, and other monopolies, a royal post privilege (1712), fees for office appointments or for renewal of guild and other occupational privileges, etc. In comparison with other states, especially France, the practice of utilization of these prerogatives was relatively benign in Brandenburg-Prussia, lacking the grosser forms of exploitation (see Schmoller 1877: 64).

[35] During Frederick I's reign domains were given away in large portions as so-called *Erbpacht* (that is, the grant of a long, hereditary lease) and were no longer administered and utilized by the Crown. Frederick William I changed drastically this mishandling of the Crown's property. By the so-called *Domänenedikt* (1713) he revoked the contracts made under his predecessor and declared the whole of the domains —even the so-called *Schatullengüter* (Privy Estates) which served for the sovereign's purely private expenses—to be inalienable property. Furthermore, he reorganized the administration and utilization of the domains by creating the so-called *Generalpacht* (General Lease-hold): under this, not separate estates but whole districts (*Amt*) of domains were leased for a certain sum of rent-payment to a so-called *Amtmann* (Superintendent of Domains) who was, like a private entrepreneur, in charge of this district, subleasing parts of it to the peasantry. Simultaneously he provided administrative and judicial functions on the local level as a royal official: the *Amtmann* thus had control over the social and economic life of the domain's peasantry. Frederick William I preferred to select men for the function of *Amtmann* who were not of noble stock but were well trained in agricultural matters. The domains became seed-beds for agricultural innovations in regard to methods and techniques of cultivation and to new forms of administration.

reign. The first was a shift from a provincial division of administration toward a division in terms of services and functions.[36] The second had to do with the relationship between sovereign and government: there was a gradual separation of the prince and his staff from the central government and administration after the accession of the Great Elector. The final step toward rule from above or outside the governmental institutions, however, was taken by Frederick William I. He no longer attended governmental meetings, but had to be informed by written reports and gave in turn written orders out of his cabinet to the central government and administration. He and his cabinet were the center of governmental actions and the medium of governmental coordination.

These changes were part of Frederick William I's all-out effort "to support the army of a first-rate power on the resources of a third-rate state" (Dorn 1931: 404). In reaching his goal *Le roi-sergeant* or the "soldiers' King" had to be as fiscal-minded as he was military-minded. Fiscal reforms went hand in hand with the reconstruction of the military system.

Frederick William I made several rather successful attempts to tap the income and property of the nobles more adequately by direct taxes, though the increase was still extremely modest and was accomplished only after hard struggles. The first innovation, the so-called *Generalhufenschoss*, a reform of the assessment of land for tax purposes (with techniques quite modern for the time), was limited to East Prussia, where the Junkers traditionally could less easily escape direct taxation. The reformed assessment of the *Generalhufenschoss* made the property of the nobles more subject to taxation; the Junkers fought against these attempts, and it was on this occasion that the king, not willing to give in, referred to himself as a *rocher de bronze*. The second reform was not limited to specified provinces but covered the entire kingdom. It illuminates the unique features of the contemporary sociopolitical and socioeconomic struc-

---

[36] At first the General Directory had been divided into four provincial departments; each of these departments had, however, to perform certain central functions as well. Hence, the process of change was a gradual one. Frederick the Great (1740–1786) eliminated some functions of the provincial departments and created special departments for those services: the Department for Trade and Manufacture (1740); the Department for Customs and Excise (1766); the Department for Mining and Smelting (1768); the Forest Department (1771). A separate institution had already been founded in 1728 for foreign affairs: the Cabinet Ministry. The Secret Council (but with very limited functions), the Cabinet Ministry, and, the most complex one, the General Directory together formed the central government and administration.

ture of Brandenburg-Prussia: the King had at this time secured 'his personal absolutism; the army and the government were firmly in his hand; the political power of the estates and the governments of the provincial territories were reduced to insignificance. Nevertheless the Crown required both more revenues and the loyal support of the Junkers as officers in meeting his military ambitions. To gain this support and to induce the Junkers to serve in a standing army, Frederick William I had to ensure their material subsistence. He also had to adapt the military organization so as to recruit the Junkers as officers, and their subject peasantry as soldiers, without destroying the traditional subsistence and economy. This he did in a mode which was a strange mixture of feudal and absolutistic traits, combining fiscal and military obligations.

In the first place, Frederick William I imposed the so-called *Lehenspferdegeld* (vassalage-horse money). As the name suggests, this was a commutation of feudal military obligation of the nobles (the knight's services) into money payment. It was actually a revival of a long obsolete obligation attached—as it had been centuries ago —to the vassalage-horses required for each of the nobles' estates (forty thalers annually per horse). This neofeudal levy, however, was counterbalanced by three concessions designed to secure the property of Junkers. First, the Junkers' estate became *allodium* demesne (freehold); the land or estate (including the patrimonial rights) became *de jure* private property. The Crown thus gave up the claim of a broad interpretation of the *dominium eminens* as far as the Junkers' property was concerned. Second, the properties of the nobles could be bought and sold only among members of the nobles themselves; the aim of this special privilege was to prevent a diminishing of the Junkers' property holdings by closing a certain kind of real-estate market (the so-called *Rittergutsgesetz*, i.e., knights' estate law). Closely connected with this was the third institution, introduced in Frederick the Great's reign, the creation of provincial mortgage credit societies (the so-called *Landschaften*), which were at the exclusive disposal of the nobles.

Also Frederick William I reorganized the military system. His so-called Canton system was a combination of a standing army and a militia system that recruited the Junkers for duty as officers and the peasantry as soldiers during a certain time period each year. To secure the peasantry as a recruitment pool the Crown issued several orders to protect the socioeconomic position and the livelihood of

[276]

the peasantry. These orders were a counterpart of the *Ritterguts-gesetz*, though their enforcement proved to be inadequate. In fact, with the new military system, the peasantry fell even more firmly into the hands of the Junkers, who now represented not only a local patrimonial authority, but military authority as well. Even on leave from military duty, the soldier-peasant belonged to the army and was supposed to wear a piece of his military uniform (see Büsch 1962: 27ff.; Rosenberg 1958: passim.). This little detail shows how tightly the fiscal, military, and agrarian systems were interwoven. One system could not be changed without altering the other; each one was strengthened by the other, as we shall see later.

During Frederick William I's reign all spheres of life became subject to police, military, and fiscal controls which formed an interwoven body of absolutistic government, resting upon a new spirit and a new code of values of serving the sovereign and the state. Unlike his predecessor, the "soldiers' King" expected and demanded from his servants not mutual but one-sided and all-out allegiance and obedience similar in nature to that of military officers. And indeed the royal orders to his governmental and administrative officials were as harsh as the command orders in the army. He considered such obedience to be toward himself personally and not toward the state; his rule had all the features of a personal absolutism. Correspondingly, he still considered the property of his dynasty, which became inalienable, that is a feoffment in trust (*Fideikommiss*) by the so-called *Domänenedikt* (1713), primarily as "patrimonial" or "private." This autocrat and his bureaucratic machinery contrived to extract out of a backward economy not only money, kind and services for the support of an oversized military organization, but also could pay off the public debts and liabilities of the Estates, especially those of the cities and towns, and gathered by the time of his death a treasure of eight to nine million thalers, which helped his successor to finance the First Silesian War. He endeavored to control expenditure by innovating uniform methods of accounting and estimations of costs for all governmental and administrative institutions. As far as his "own" sources of income were concerned, he managed not only to redeem all domains, which were pledged during the mishandling of the Crown's property by his predecessor, but to buy for about five million thalers new domain property. Hence, the revenues from his "own" sources of income rose to an amount which nearly matched the yield of all taxes (see Schmoller 1909: 44).

With Frederick the Great a bureaucratic absolutism gradually superseded the personal or dynastic one of the "soldiers' King." This enlightened monarch placed the state above the dynasty. He perceived himself as the first servant of the state and considered the service of his office holders to be tasks for the state, not for the dynasty.[37] In the *General Book of Law*, which was drafted under his reign but published after his death (1791), all domains were declared to be public property of the state; the House of Hohenzollern had only a limited right of usufruct. As a consequence of this new conception of the Crown's function and property, the guidelines of Frederick the Great's fiscal, financial, and economic policy were oriented more toward the purposes of state and less toward enrichment of the dynasty. In fiscal and financial matters, Frederick was as much an economizer as his father was. After the peace of Hubertusburg (1763), he even employed private French enterprisers for the collection of the excise, bypassing the competence of the General Directory (see Dieterici 1875: 7ff.; Grabower 1932: 55ff.). Yet, Frederick the Great approached matters of revenue and expenditure more from an economic and less from a fiscal point of view than his predecessor had, and used fiscal policy as a medium for the development of the state's economy. This brings up the question of prevailing economic and social doctrines as regards taxation during the cameralistic era in Brandenburg-Prussia. Since we must be brief, certain oversimplifications will be unavoidable (see for this part especially Tauscher 1943 and Wilke 1921).

Undoubtedly influenced by Bodin's writing, the mercantilistic-cameralistic literature up to the eighteenth century in theory still considered taxation as an extraordinary levy for special purposes, the primary purpose of which was to provide the necessary means for protecting the life and property of subjects. Therefore, the cameralists of the second half of the seventeenth century dealt extensively with the administration and utilization of domains and prerogatives. They usually prefaced their expositions about taxes with the more or less rhetorical hope that taxes would not be a permanent phenomenon. However, the mercantilists and even more the cameralists actually regarded the various forms of taxation as tools for shaping the structure of the economy and society. The cameralistic version

---

[37] As a demonstration of this, in matters of private law Frederick the Great relinquished all claims of sovereign or absolutistic power and regarded himself and his dynasty as a subject of the state, answerable to the common private law procedure like all the other subjects.

of mercantilism conceived the state as the overall regulative principle. The maxims of every socioeconomic order (*ökonomische Polizei und Cameralverfassung*) can therefore only be derived from the very essence of the state itself.[38] Socioeconomic doctrines have to be oriented toward and formed by the purpose or reason of state. The state must be considered as the main productive force inasmuch as only the state has the know-how and the means to frame the economy and society in the right way, that is, into a proportionate structure: every sector of the economy and correspondingly every stratum of society has to be shaped in such a way that it fits in the right proportion with all the others and in relation to the whole entity, the state, which represents the *droit de bienséance*. The principle of social and economic justice is not guided by equality or uniformity but by the guarantee of the "just" proportion. An organic functional view of a body with different parts and different functions can be recognized as the underlying principle, but all parts and functions are now regulated by and have to serve the same purpose: the reason of state. As the main productive force the governmental institutions have to perform as a heart: they take blood from the organs and distribute it according to need, that is for the well-being and sound development of the body.[39] Taxation serves as an instrument for extracting blood from the organs; the allocation of revenues is the redistribution of this blood. Both tasks have to be accomplished, however, in the "just" or right proportion. The cameralistic government has therefore to develop various schemes of taxation, modes of assessment, and ways of allocation of revenue so as to fulfill the overriding goal, the *droit de bienséance*.

Along with protection of the life and property of the subject, this function of taxation, then, became the main justification of the cameralistic government to impose taxes. Moreover, this function was also used as a justification for an absolutistic interpretation of the *dominium eminens*. Inasmuch as the state is the moving productive force, it is the right of the state and its ruler "to regard all property in the realm as wholly wealth of the state in such a way that it has to be at the disposal of the highest authority of the public and common interests of the state, though this property is chiefly in the possession of private persons."[40]

---

[38] Justi 1755, quoted by Tauscher 1943: 304.
[39] This is a metaphor used by J. Sonnenfels in the preface of his book "*Grundsätze der Polizei, Handlung und Finanz,*" vol. 1 (1776), quoted by Tauscher 1943: 309.
[40] Döhler 1775: 2ff., quoted by Tauscher 1943: 308.

Despite these two widely accepted justifications for taxation, the cameralistic literature was marked by a broad spectrum of opinions regarding forms of taxation, modes of assessment, and schemes of distribution, each reflecting the socioeconomic position and group interests of the writer and his personal predilections. In respect to the motive of protection (the so-called protection theory: *Assekuranz-theorie*), the controversy involved whether life or property needed more protection and had therefore to carry more of the tax burden. The men of property and their spokesmen proclaimed the protection of life to be the more important task, and pleaded for a high poll (or flat rate) tax. The other side held up the principle which was strongly endorsed by Jean Bodin, namely that the levy should be assessed according to the amount of protected wealth and property (see Mann 1937: 60; Wilke 1921: 9).

Beginning around the middle of the seventeenth century, a Europe-wide dispute about excise as a general means of taxation occurred and was to last over generations. The spokesmen of the nobles rejected this form of levy, because it interfered with the nobles' privileged tax position. The majority of the cameralist writers, however, praised the excise as a panacea: it covered all subjects and was therefore a just means of taxation; the levy was so small that it was hardly felt; both assessment and collection were easy and inexpensive (at a time when *cadastres* could not be kept up to date and income and property could easily evade assessment). Last but not least, the excise was credited by the cameralists with being a most suitable tool for the regulation of the economy and society according to the reason of state (see Mann 1937: 50ff.; von Inama-Sternberg 1865: passim). As the example of Brandenburg-Prussia showed, the term excise covered not only levies on consumer goods (collected as retail sales tax) but also a producers' levy and inland customs. A cameralistic government must skillfully apply all these various excises as socioeconomic tools: the flow of goods is controlled by customs; the consumption patterns are determined by differentiated levies on consumer goods; the sphere of production is regulated by producers' taxes of differing amounts (including total exemption in order to stimulate certain branches of production) or by the state's entering the field of production itself with governmental enterprises, using its revenues as investment and working capital.

In this manner taxation was a tool for shaping the economic and social structure into the "just" proportion. If a sector or a branch of the economy were hampered by a too heavy or disproportionate tax load, the government would be acting like "a wild boar tearing out the roots in the field and destroying the future crops," and not like "a good shepherd who shears but does not kill his sheep." On the other hand, the various sectors must be prevented from achieving disproportionate growth, and individuals and groups from becoming lazy and corrupt by too light a tax burden.[41]

In practice, however, these doctrines clashed with group interests and were therefore subject to interest group pressures. In limiting the application of excise primarily to cities and towns, the nobles had maintained their tax privileges. Concerning the laboring poor, the controversy concentrated upon the question of whether and to what extent the "necessities of the people" should be covered by excise duties. This problem was markedly less pronounced in Brandenburg-Prussia (and in the realm of the Roman Empire) than in England; due to a long tradition the former took the levying of "necessities" much more for granted.

In practice taxes were in many ways distorted and perverted because of frequent conflicts among fiscal, economic, and social goals. If interests or goals were incompatible, the fiscal point of view predominated, at least until Frederick the Great. The sociostructural point of view—that is, the preservation of the social structure with all its differences in terms of sociopolitical status and socioeconomic privileges—usually placed second. The purely economic point of view ran third. As for economic principles, cameralistic practice was full of contradictions due to the fact that economic development, though a cherished goal of the government, was not an end in itself, but had to serve the reason of state and was not supposed to disrupt the existing social order. How the tightly interwoven military, agrarian, fiscal, economic, and social structures under the minute regulation of the cameralistic bureaucracy curtailed economic development in Brandenburg-Prussia and retarded sociopolitical modernization needs to be further analyzed. This has to be done through a comparison with the situation in Britain.

The beginning of our period in Britain is marked by one similarity with the situation in Brandenburg-Prussia: the creation of a standing army. The roles, however, were reversed. The Crown had neither sufficient sources of income nor borrowing power to support

[41] The first quotation is a metaphor from W. Schröder 1721, the second from Bornitz 1612; both cited by Tauscher 1943: 314 and 324.

an adequate military force. It was the Parliament which imposed contributions and a variety of taxes, collected customs, and sequestered property of the royalists and the Crown in order to maintain a navy and organize a standing army. This "New Model" army proved decisive for the course of events during the tumultuous and stirring times of the *Interregnum*. By virtue of the Self-Denying Ordinance which disqualified Members of Parliament from holding military commands, the professional army officers soon became a political force of their own, asserting the chief influence over the government and constitutional development until the Restoration.[42]

This was a period of arbitrary rule based not on traditional law but on armed force. The standing army was both the moving and the stabilizing power. After the return to traditional forms of government (1660), the "New Model" army was quickly disbanded; merely a regiment of guards and a few garrison units survived. Whether to increase this small armed force became a matter of dispute between Crown and Parliament for a long time to come. Once again government in Britain was unsupported by any large professional army.

Neither as a focus of bureaucratization nor as a source of financial strain can the army in Britain in any way be compared with the army in Brandenburg-Prussia. Yet the role of the "New Model" army in matters of taxation and public finance might well be viewed in relation to that of the mercenary troops at the beginning of the Great Elector's reign, inasmuch as the financial needs for the maintenance of the navy and upkeep of the "New Model" army made new schemes of revenue and public finance unavoidable, while at the same time this military force was required to enforce new financial exactions along with the payment of the more traditional taxes. Eighteen years of armed force at the disposal of the various *Interregnum* governments were crucial indeed for the imposing of new modes of taxation, as the frequent riots and rebellions connected with revenue matters during these years suggest. Let us outline at first in a very sketchy way the development in terms of taxation and public finance, from the Civil War up to the eighteenth century.

We may distinguish three separate components: the direct taxes, the customs, and the Excise. For all three the *Interregnum* was a

---

[42] The role this body of professional army officers played might be compared with that of the military cadres in many underdeveloped countries today: their constitutional ideas became prevailing; they drafted constitutions, took over the chief functions of government, and even adopted a concept of theocratic rule by a group of the "godly"; finally, out of this officers' junta grew a military dictatorship, the Protectorate.

time of experiments and innovations. The systems of direct taxes under Tudor and Stuart rule fell far short of tapping the wealth of the nation. Under great financial pressure, the Long Parliament attempted to create and impose an equitable scheme of direct taxes with a yield proportionate to the real wealth of the realm. The intention in regard to assessment and distribution was to adopt income as the standard for all who paid direct taxes. In 1641 a graduated poll tax was imposed as one of the emergency measures.[43] However, from the beginning this scheme met with little success in practice. Parliament soon had to rely on fixed sums which each district was required to pay, leaving the distribution of the direct tax burden to the local assessors except for regulation of the limits of exemption. The devices employed were the so-called Weekly Assessment (1643) and, beginning with the year 1645, the Monthly Assessment.

The Monthly Assessment became during the *Interregnum* a regular direct levy; after 1660 (until 1692) it continued at intervals rather than regularly. It was marked by two characteristics. In the first place, the required amount of revenue from each district remained fixed, so that different parts of the country came to pay substantially different rates of tax. In the second place, the Monthly Assessment became chiefly a land tax, levied on a traditional basis and not according to the changing real value of the landed property. Despite all attempts during and after the *Interregnum*, personal and movable property along with income from office were usually exempted or grossly underassessed. After the revolution (1688) and in the reign of William and Mary, the Monthly Assessment was superseded by a new direct tax, the General Aid. This scheme abandoned the system of fixed amounts for each district and imposed a pound rate according to income from land or office holding, and the value of property comprised of goods, merchandise, money, etc.[44]

At first the General Aid seemed relatively successful but the dif-

---

[43] Men were rated at fixed sums according to their rank, office or occupation, and general clauses referring to criteria of income were provided for those not rated specifically. This is a clear indication that the prevailing principle of direct taxation was: men should be levied in consideration of their income and ability to pay.

[44] All persons with property in goods, merchandise, money, etc., were to pay one shilling per pound "according to the true yearly profit thereof." Persons in office, other than naval and military, were to pay one shilling per pound of their salaries or profits. One shilling per pound was to be levied on the true yearly value of all lands. In order to tax the landowner on his real net income, and to bring in the monied man, rent charges and interest on mortgages on land were to be taxed at one shilling per pound by deduction at the source. In 1692 the pound rate rose from one shilling to four shillings per pound of income (see Kennedy 1964: 44).

ficulties of assessing personal property were almost insurmountable. Such property could still easily evade assessment, and landed property was taxed differently from district to district. An attempt to overcome these weaknesses with a so-called Poll Tax as supplemental tax, and later on by combining General Aid and Poll Tax, proved equally unsatisfactory. In 1698 the system of a national pound rate came to an end. Once more a required quota was fixed for each district. This proved to be the surrender of all efforts to achieve an equitable direct tax with a yield proportionate to the real wealth of the nation, a situation that was to prevail for more than a century. The scheme that replaced the pound rate, the so-called Land Tax, became marked with the traditional defects of former direct taxes: an unequal distribution among the districts and the escape of personal movable property. In short, the intended distributive standard of direct taxation, according to income, was not achieved until 1842, when a new property and income tax was introduced (the property and income tax imposed in 1799 was a short-lived war measure).

Furthermore, the Long Parliament broke with the Elizabethan and Stuart tradition of exempting the poor from paying taxes. Though the regular direct taxes exempted the laboring poor, occasional Poll Taxes applied to them.[45] However, with the creation of the Land Tax (1698) the direct taxation of the poor was abandoned. With the exception of the 1740s, the amount of direct taxes (land and assessed taxes) proportionate to the total amount of revenues declined steadily (see Mitchell 1962: 386ff.).

As for the second component, the customs, the Long Parliament paved the way for a new policy toward and a new evaluation and handling of these revenues. Customs were no longer—even in theory —considered as earmarked for "the keeping of the Sea" but were treated like all other revenues as national tax. Correspondingly, these levies gradually lost their justification as a special charge on merchandise for the protection of trade, and could therefore be used more and more as an instrument of mercantilistic trade policy. The tendency during the Long Parliament, which was carried on after the Restoration and the Revolution, was to reduce or abandon totally the export duties on manufactured goods and (from 1656 onward) on certain agricultural products as well. In 1721 Walpole re-

[45] Six pennies in 1641; one shilling in 1660, 1666, 1678, 1689, and 1690; four shillings in 1691, 1697, and 1698. The Poll Taxes exempted paupers and the children of the laboring poor (see Kennedy 1913: 50).

pealed all the remaining duties on exports other than raw materials. Hence, customs became increasingly, and during the eighteenth century almost entirely, a levy on imported commodities. This indicates clearly that Parliament and the government were willing to sacrifice fiscal considerations for the purpose of trade and economic policy. The prohibition of the export of wool (1648) and the trade with France during times of war had the same effect. Moreover, in the case of the so-called corn bounty (introduced in 1673 and remaining in practice with modifications for about a century except in years when home crops were poor) even dumping methods were applied; the corn bounty was a governmental export subvention to ease the burden of direct taxation on the landed gentry. Along with all this, import duties for needed raw materials were reduced or abolished. Parts of this trade and economic policy were the Navigation Acts (the first in 1651, adopted and enlarged in 1660 and 1665) and the treatment of economic affairs of the colonial territories. It is well known that the Long Parliament laid the groundwork in these matters too. It viewed trade policy as the overriding issue of foreign policy. Acts of war and interference on land or at sea were undertaken for trade and economic purposes, and were accomplished with the help of trade and economic weapons.

As far as imported commodities were concerned, fiscal needs, trade policy, and considerations of welfare policy—that is, the protection of the poor—were taken into account in determining the kinds of commodities to be taxed and the relative rates. From the point of view of social welfare, the doctrine that customs should cover only luxuries but not necessaries was widely accepted during the time of the Long Parliament and later on as well. In 1674, Carew Raynall in writing about "The True English Interest" defined the best taxes as those which fell on the vices of the people, including their consumption of needless foreign commodities (see Kennedy 1964: 30). This point of view was followed in practice, certainly to a high degree because it conformed to the prevailing trade and economic policy, which aimed to discourage the consumption of imported manufactured and luxury goods.[46]

[46] In 1690, for example, a heavy import duty was placed on Indian textiles; in 1699 an "Act for the more effectual employing the poor by encouraging the manufactures of this kingdom" was passed, prohibiting entirely the import of Indian textiles for home consumption (Kennedy 1964: 36). It is obvious that merchants would oppose a strict execution of such a policy. Their interests, together with fiscal considerations (among others, the incidence of frauds and smuggling which, of course, increased

Despite the fiscal sacrifices for the purposes of trade and welfare, the absolute amount of customs revenue increased steadily with the exception of years of war (see Mitchell 1962: 386ff.). Customs were regarded by contemporaries as a suitable fiscal means on grounds of distributive justice, ease of collection, and their relatively imperceptible and "voluntary" character (as long as they covered no necessaries). We are familiar with these arguments from the debates about the Excise.

The Excise was an innovation of the Long Parliament. Unlike continental Europe, Britain had no tradition which would prepare the way psychologically for the introduction of Excises, either as regards prerogative revenue (like the beer tax or the so-called *Ungeld*) or Excises introduced by city and town municipalities. Popular opinion in Britain looked upon the Excise as a symbol of serf-like oppression common in continental Europe but incompatible with the tradition of personal and constitutional liberty of England. The imposition of Excise duties by the Long Parliament therefore aroused stubborn opposition and, on several occasions and in several regions, riots. It is hard to imagine that the early Stuart Kings could ever have succeeded in imposing an Excise. It is especially with respect to the innovation of the Excise that eighteen years of armed force at the disposal of *Interregnum* governments were crucial for the adaptation to this new levy, which remained an important mainstay of the revenue system thereafter (see Mitchell 1962: 386ff.). Besides the financial needs which forced the Long Parliament to introduce the Excise, an additional reason was to make the Royalists and neutrals share the costs of the war against the royal forces, and for this, indirect levies, excise and customs as well, were best suited.[47]

It should be noted that the opposition to the Excise was a popular one and not, as in Brandenburg-Prussia, only that of the nobles, who fought for the preservation of their tax privileges. Furthermore, in Britain the discussion of Excise as a mode of taxation centered much more on the question of whether more necessaries of the poor should be covered by this levy than was the case in Brandenburg-Prussia.

---

when customs were extremely high) prevented import duties on such commodities from becoming prohibitory in nature. Nevertheless the increase in rates on certain foreign goods such as wine, tobacco, silks, and other luxuries was enormous.

[47] During the *Interregnum* the term "Foreign Excise" became common; the technical difference between Foreign Excise and Customs Duties was that the former was ordered to be levied on the first buyer from the importer. In practice, however, this was usually ignored (see Kennedy 1913: 27).

The discussion began with the introduction of the Excise and was carried on for generations. The prevailing doctrines were, on the one side, that the poor should share the burden of taxation. This has to be regarded as a break with Elizabethan and Stuart tradition. The political theories of Thomas Hobbes and John Locke among others fortified this principle.[48] On the other side, the doctrine that Excise should fall rather on luxuries than on necessaries was widely accepted. From the period of the *Interregnum* up to the eighteenth century these principles were put forth and contested in parliamentary debates and in contemporary literature, over and over again. The welfare principle clearly influenced what kinds of commodities were to be subject to excise duties, as well as the relative amounts of these duties. Nevertheless, necessaries were subject to Excise from the beginning and remained so, though composition and rates varied greatly from time to time.[49]

Contemporaries were more or less aware of the fact that Excise duties which cover the necessaries are regressive in nature. Nevertheless, Excise was praised as a just means of distributing taxation because it was said to make everybody pay his share, with the richer paying more than the poor. A man's total expenditure or consumption was regarded as a good indication of his socioeconomic standing and therefore Excise duties covering consumption, especially of luxuries, were considered a good method for making everyone share in public expense according to his ability. In a period when the style of living and the pattern of consumption still were to a high degree both status-bound and status-required elements, this assumption was not as erroneous as it may seem from a modern point of view. How-

[48] Kennedy (1964: 66) writes: "But the idea found its most complete expression and justification in Locke's political theory, from which it was a direct deduction, that 'everyone who enjoys his share of the protection should pay out of his estate his proportion for the maintenance of it.' By the end of the seventeenth century this may be said to have become a commonplace."

[49] During the *Interregnum*, for example, beer, ale, cider, perry, salt, meat, soap, and hats, among other things, were levied. During the Restoration excise on necessaries was abolished with the exception of the duty on beer, but a hearth tax introduced in 1662 aroused, as had the meat excise before it, particular opposition, both being regarded as against freedom from governmental interference in private matters. The hearth tax was abandoned by Parliament after the Revolution (1689) as a "badge of slavery" but new excise duties and an increase in rates of the old ones were debated and enacted; among others there were beer, salt, leather, malt, paper, glass, coal, and—for some time—even chimney, window, birth, death, and marriage taxes. The increase of the salt tax by Walpole (1732) and his Excise Bill of 1733, both aimed at keeping the land tax low, stirring, as is well known, such stiff opposition that the powerful leader of the government had to back down.

ever, the contemporary literature also recognized the fact that certain social groups or individuals lived below their means or ability and could therefore evade their fair share of taxation. This was particularly true of nonconformist traders, merchants, money lenders and manufacturers, who had a strong social cohesion and a value code condemning conspicuous consumption. With their personal kind of property and their income escaping much direct taxation, they paid less than their "just" proportion in indirect taxation too.

Up to now we have been concerned only with schemes of taxation. The imposing, collecting, administering, and allocating revenues, and the whole range of what came to be "public finance," have not yet been dealt with. Turning now to this side of our topic, we have to deal again with constitutional, governmental, and administrative aspects.

The so-called Financial Revolution refers to changes in public finance after 1688. However, a sequence of alterations which occurred during the *Interregnum* was of great importance in setting this process in motion. In the first place, direct taxes ceased to be occasional revenue for emergencies; they became regularly paid duties. The same was the case for the traditional and the new indirect levies; they were collected and treated as regular sources of revenue. Correspondingly, the distinction between ordinary and extraordinary revenue vanished during the revolutionary period. Under the Protectorate all the various sources of revenue came to be administered by the Exchequer. "This created the possibility of real Treasury control of revenue and expenditure, a planned budget, and so planned raising of loans" (Hill 1967: 147). These changes, though to some extent repealed during the Restoration, proved to be crucial for new methods of public finance, that is, for new systems of long-term government borrowing.

In the second place, the House of Commons learned during the time of the Long Parliament to handle all the business of the state: taxation, financial matters, war and foreign affairs, trade and colonial (or plantation) policy, the maintenance of the navy and standing army, etc. Even during the Protectorate the Parliament kept its control over taxation and revenue matters. In short, the Long Parliament had given experience, confidence, and power to the House of Commons; after the restoration of the monarchy it could no longer be excluded from the "mystery of state": 1660 marked the beginning of parliamentary monarchy (Keir 1967: 209, 230ff.).

To be sure, Charles II was able to restore and to maintain the conception of the Divine Right of his kingship. The new restoration Parliament, the "Cavalier Parliament," restored in a nostalgic fashion a cult of divine kingship. It was not to be until the Revolution when an informal assembly (the Convention) offered the Crown to William and Mary jointly, presented them with the Bill of Rights, and imposed upon them a new coronation oath with the obligation to govern according to the statutes the Parliament had agreed on, that the idea of kingship by Divine Right would come to be destroyed and royal authority and power become regarded merely as the result of a contract between King and people. True, Charles II and his successor were able once again by virtue of Prerogative to establish royal control over the militia, over the declaration of peace and war, over the summoning and duration of Parliament, as well as to conduct a government headed by a strong Privy Council and administered by committees and departmental ministers.

Yet the authority and power of the Crown and its government was now checked on three levels. First, the Common Law courts triumphed over the judicial power of the King and his government. "English constitutional law was therefore bound, sooner or later, to assume a bias, appropriate to the Common Law tradition, in favor of individual rights and property, and on the whole adverse to the claims of the State to a freedom of action determined by consideration of public policy" (Keir 1967: 233ff.). As regards the socioeconomic development of Britain in the eighteenth century, the importance of its ideological foundation, what Macpherson has called "possessive individualism," can hardly be overrated.

Second, the local authority, represented chiefly in the Justices of the Peace, could emancipate itself further from the control of a central government which was no longer in possession of judicial power: ". . . local officials such as Justices of the Peace relapsed after 1660 into two centuries of virtual irresponsibility. A profound harmony reigned between them and a Parliament drawn from the same classes as themselves" (Keir 1967: 234).

Third, legislation and taxation had become subject to exclusive parliamentary control. In sum: the Crown and its government were forced to seek the consent and cooperation of an upper class of nobles, gentry, men of property and money, who had a controlling influence upon the Common Law courts, local authority, and Parliament, and who came to dominate political life in Britain for two

[289]

centuries. Comparing the nature of the crucial phase of British state-building with that of Brandenburg-Prussia later on, we will have to analyze these aspects further.

With the restoration of the monarchy (1660) the Crown had to be endowed with an annual income by the "Convention Parliament," because the traditional sources of income were either lost or diminished to insignificance. The endowed amount of revenues even in peacetime proved to be inadequate for the expenditure of the Crown and its government, but Parliament attributed the Crown's insolvency to the mishandling of financial affairs and became inclined to encroach anew on the King's sphere of executive power. The once loyal "Cavalier Parliament" became increasingly critical. Two nascent parties began to develop: the Tory party, dominated by the Anglican landed gentry, and the Whig party, led by nobles but drawing its main support from merchants, money-men, and land-owners with a strong dissent bias.

Paradoxically enough, the Crown's financial reputation became severely damaged by the innovation of a credit scheme quite modern in its make-up (patterned after the Bank of Amsterdam); this was the so-called Orders of Payment, introduced in 1665 to mobilize the means for the Dutch War, using the direct taxes authorized by Parliament as security (the Orders were charged against the authorized taxes). Yet the Orders of Payment were soon being charged against the revenues in general and became an instrument of credit, like bank-notes. In other words, the Exchequer (or the Crown) began to exercise a kind of banking function. The debts from the first Dutch War and the financial needs of the second Dutch War led to the collapse of this scheme; in 1672 the result was the so-called Stop of the Exchequer: the Crown had to declare a moratorium on one and three-fourths million of these Orders of Payment (see Dickson 1967: 43ff.).

Nevertheless, in a rudimentary way, these ideas for creating instruments and schemes of long-term public credit led to the revolutionizing of the public finance of Britain after 1688. Two steps were crucial. In the first place, "public" credit and loans became no longer based on the Crown's security but on parliamentary guaranty: the institution which had the sole constitutional power of taxation, the Parliament, now secured the "public" debts; a National Debt came into being (Dickson 1967: 50).[50] This enabled the government (not

---

[50] Dickson writes: "The fact that Parliament guaranteed all these loans made them

immediately but in the long run) to obtain long-term public credit and loans on favorable terms, using direct and indirect revenues as security funds.

In the second place, the establishment of the Bank of England (1694) proved to be of equal importance for the "Financial Revolution."[51] The Bank of England, founded on the basis of the joint-stock principle by approval of the Parliament, became from its beginning the main instrument of governmental credit and loans. Besides its original loan of 1,200,000 pounds (the chief stipulation for its foundation), the Bank of England immediately began to make substantial case advances to the government, became important in mobilizing financial resources from all over the nation, helped the government in floating tontines and annuities, and since 1709 has been associated by statute with the issue of Exchequer bills. Without the Bank of England, the British struggles with France from 1689 until the Peace of Utrecht would have led to a financial disaster. More and more did the financial affairs of government, the national debt, and currency matters become connected with the Bank of England. As a consequence the merchant and banking community of the City (predominantly Whigs) gained increasing political influence: "the Bank (of England) brought government borrowing under direct control of the representatives of the propertied. Henceforth the monied interest played a decisive role in politics; no political group could hope for success without support in the City" (Hill 1967: 147; see also Dickson 1967: 55ff.).

The methods approved by Parliament to mobilize and secure public loans, particularly the scheme of floating annuities with a term of ninety-nine years, influenced taxation in two ways. On the one hand, the indirect taxes (customs and excise) could no longer be limited in time to the life of the King. On the other hand, a large portion of revenue sources became tied up for a long time to come (see Mitchell 1962: 401ff.; Total Debt Charges). This made it necessary that direct taxes become regularly paid levies, and the distinction between "ordinary" and "extraordinary" revenue vanished. The increase of the total debt charges led to the pattern of changing reve-

'debts of the nation' or 'national debts,' and both Englishmen and foreigners were quick to realize that this change from merely royal security was extremely important" (1967: 50).
[51] The foundation of the Bank of Scotland in 1695 and the New East India Company in 1698—as of 1709, the United East India Company—were at the beginning significant for obtaining governmental credit and loans, too.

nue systems (amount of land tax; increase in the rates of the old indirect taxes; the adding of new indirect taxes) so as to make interest payments on the deficit rather than to reduce or amortize it. The reward, however, was long-term governmental borrowing at relatively low rates of interest and, despite a mounting national debt, a permanent solvency of the government. With a grain of sarcasm, Christopher Hill writes: "Payment of interest on the National Debt, guaranteed by Parliament, necessitated heavy taxes, which transferred wealth from the poorer and landed to the monied classes. A national debt is the only collective possession of most modern people: the richer they are, the more deeply they are in debt" (Hill 1967: 148).

It was certainly more than a mere coincidence that the Financial Revolution followed the arrival of the Dutch monarch and his advisers, who were skilled in handling fiscal and financial affairs, particularly long-term government borrowing, and were connected with Dutch banking circles. Concerning "public finance" and banking, Amsterdam, and not the London City still held the lead at this time. Apart from this fact, the "Financial Revolution" has to be analyzed against the background of the "Glorious Revolution" and the war with France. Both incidents helped the effective establishment of parliamentary government and the creation of long-term government borrowing practices guaranteed by Parliament and not merely by royal security. The Bill of Rights altered the essence of the Crown's authority and its relationship to Parliament. The war with France, starting immediately after the coronation of William and Mary, caused heavy financial burdens.[52] The borrowing power of William and Mary, as new rulers, was weak. The Parliament, perennially in session as a wartime consequence, provided the necessary "extraordinary" means. The price the Crown had to pay for this support was the permanent intrusion of Parliament (i.e., the House of Commons) into the sphere of the Treasury by a system of estimate, appropriation and audit. In 1691 a group of members of the Commons were appointed as Commissioners of Public Accounts. Thus,

---

[52] Dickson (1967: 46) writes: "The immediate result of England's entry into the war against France in 1689 was to make public expenditure increase between two and three times. Before 1688 it had been under two million pounds a year. Between 1689 and 1702 it was between five million and six million pounds a year, as the Treasury noted in the books which it now started to keep to record income and expenditure— England being the first major European Power to take this elementary step."

the House of Commons gained the constitutional right to investigate public expenditure (at first only the "extraordinary," but soon all expenses, with the exception of the Civil List), and to approve the raising of money by taxes, loans, lotteries, and other methods. The Treasury had now to inform the House of Commons of its financial needs, suggest methods of meeting them, and give an account of how grants had been spent (Keir 1967: 276ff.).

The financing of the War of the Spanish Succession further accelerated the close cooperation between the Treasury and the House of Commons. It was in those years that the term "ways and means" in connection with what can be regarded as a national financial plan came into use: the treasurer had to discuss with the Commons the "ways and means" of public finance. Consequently, the leading position in the Cabinet came to be associated with the Treasury. The repeal of the clause in the Act of Settlement prohibiting officeholders from sitting in the House of Commons "enabled the ministers and the Lower House to continue in an association which was increasingly to become the essential characteristic of English government" (Keir 1967: 282).

The quarter of a century between the "Glorious Revolution" and the coronation of George I (1714) was marked by party struggles between Tories and Whigs; even with a system of "mixed ministries" (ministers drawn from both parties) the House of Commons was hard to cope with. It was an "ill-defined dualism between a Crown theoretically supreme in matters of administration and policy and a Parliament sovereign in matters of legislation and finance" (Keir 1967: 289). With George I, the stirring times of more than a half century of social unrest and political instability came to an end; the political atmosphere cooled off: Britain entered "an age of almost unbroken internal tranquillity and external progress" (Keir 1967: 289) under the governmental rule of a Whig oligarchy, which had been responsible for the accession of the new dynasty. It was not until the reign of George III (1760–1820), when the Whigs' governmental monopoly was finally challenged by the Crown and the disasters of the American Revolution, that there opened up a new period of constitutional reform.

The harmony between Crown, government, and Parliament during the Whigs' leadership was based on the one hand upon a system of "influence" or "spoils" (from a modern point of view we would call it "corruption"): The Crown and the government employed all the means at their disposal (appointments, titles, sinecures) to get the support of influential circles in and out of Parliament. The Treasury created a host of revenue offices which could be transformed into sinecures by subcontracting the actual tasks. "Spoils" of this kind had a long tradition; even the Long Parliament had been eager to invent offices of a sinecurial nature. But under the Whigs' leadership, "influence" and "spoils" were skillfully applied as a system designed to stabilize and harmonize the upper order of society: the politically, socially and economically dominant groups.

At the same time, a system of checks and balances came into being. It was marked by a separation of powers between the Crown (with its Prerogative), the government and its administration (as the executive power), the Bench, especially the Common Law courts (as the judicial authority interpreting the law), and finally Parliament, which possessed unquestioned legislative sovereignty and held therefore the position of ultimate supremacy.

We have now reached a stage where we may compare the situation in eighteenth-century Britain with that in Brandenburg-Prussia, and approach the central question of our topic: what role did fiscal tradition, policies, and practices take in determining the crucial phase of state-building?

Let us first compare the structure of revenue and expenditure of Britain and Brandenburg-Prussia in the eighteenth century, though the data for the latter are very scanty. In 1740 Brandenburg-Prussia had no debt and therefore no debt charges to pay, but on the contrary had a state treasure of about ten million thalers. Roughly 80 percent of all expenses were for military purposes and 20 percent for the Court and the civil government. In 1786 the state treasury had increased to 54 million thalers and the share of military expense had decreased to a little more than half of the total expenditure (see Meyer 1926: 225ff.). Britain's national debt amounted in 1740 to 47.4 million pounds. Of the total expenditure, 34.1 percent (2.102 million pounds) was for debt charges; 52.1 percent (3.212 million pounds) for army, navy and ordnance; 13.7 percent (0.846 million pounds) for the Court and the civil government (0.792 million for the Civil List). In 1786 the national debt had risen to 246.2 million pounds. At this time 55.8 percent (9.481 million pounds) of the total expense was for debt charges, 32.3 percent (5.483 million pounds) for army, navy and ordnance purposes, 8.9 percent (1.513 million pounds) for the Court and the civil government (1.015 million for the Civil List) (see dia. 2 and 4. See Mitchell 1962: 401ff.).[53]

As far as the sources of income are concerned, in 1740 nearly half of the total net income of Brandenburg-Prussia was provided by the domain economy. This share decreased in the second half of the eighteenth century, but in 1778–1779 the income from all the Crown's properties still amounted to 12 million thalers or 45.7 percent of the total net income. In Britain, after the seventeenth century, the income from the Crown's domain was insignificant in relation to total income.[54]

These differences between Britain and Brandenburg-Prussia regarding sources of revenue, "public" debt, expenditure, and "public" finance are striking indeed. They illustrate not only the structural differences of income and expense, but illuminate two very contrasting stages of modernization. We might paraphrase the assertion of Christopher Hill, quoted earlier, by saying: the more advanced states are, the more deeply they are in debt without being insolvent. Brandenburg-Prussia's structure of "public" finance shows features of a still vital *Hausväter*-tradition; and this corresponds with the image of the prince: despite the enlightened absolutism, the prince was expected to act in matters of finance like a Christian *paterfamilias*, spending no more than his economy could afford and saving by good husbandry for times of special need. This traditional view of financial management was quite compatible with cameralistic doctrines, and determined Brandenburg-Prussian fiscal and financial policy (including currency matters, issue of notes, etc.) up to the early nineteenth century (see R. Tilly 1966: passim.). The impact of this conservative concept upon economic development will be discussed later. But let us note here one aspect, which refers to the evaluation of the Crown's domain. In "Die Epochen der preussischen Finanzpolitik," Gustav Schmoller writes:

> To appreciate the value of such property (the Crown's domains) in correct fashion I would like to confront the one-sided, almost silly statement of Adam Smith, that the income from the domains of every civilized monarchy would cost society more than any

[53] It was not until 1802 that the expenses incurred on behalf of the King and his household and those which, though charged on the Civil List, arose from matters of strictly public concern, were separated (Keir 1967: 383ff.).

[54] For Brandenburg-Prussia, see Meyer 1926: 225ff.; Reidel 1866: Beilage I-XX; Breysig 1895: 291ff.; for Britain, see Mitchell 1962: 386ff.

of the Crown's other sources of income, with the following statement of Stein, which is likewise one-sided but much more true
and ingenious: "The income from the domains is the economic
foundation of the sovereign kingdom and therefore of independent internal and external state-building, because the
Crown's domain is the foundation of the material independence
of kings against the dominion and power of the strong corporations of the estates. Hence, domains exist and will continue to
exist as long as there are kingdoms, inasmuch as the two are not
only historically but also organically linked conceptions"
(Schmoller 1877: 71).[55]

Schmoller's remark highlights a clash between two markedly different conceptions of kingdom, state, society, and economy. On the
one side, there is Adam Smith with his concept that state, society and
economy are distinct from each other and follow separate laws and
rules; the state should interfere as little as possible with economic
matters, which are guided by the self-interests of men. On the other
side, there is Baron Karl vom Stein, from 1804 until 1807 Prussia's
Minister of Excise, Customs, Manufacture, and Commerce, who was
an enlightened, highly sophisticated man and quite familiar with
Adam Smith's writing. Nevertheless his "domains now and domains
forever" clearly indicates that he was still guided by an essentially
absolutistic concept of state, based upon a bureaucratic, utilitarian
and authoritarian monarchy. In order to maintain such a sociopolitical power structure the monarch and his bureaucratic machinery
were forced to rely as much as possible on sources of income which
were at their "own" disposal and not dependent, as far as collection
and allocation were concerned, upon the consent and cooperation
of the people. Thus a parliamentary monarchy after the British fashion, where it was the business of Parliament alone, besides its legis-

---

[55] The original German goes as follows: "Um den Werth eines solchen Besitzes
richtig zu würdigen, möchte ich dem einseitigen, fast albernen Satze von Adam Smith,
dass das Einkommen aus Staatsgütern in der zivilisierten Monarchie die Gesellschaft
mehr als jede andere Einnahme der Krone koste, den ebenfalls einseitigen, aber viel
wahreren und geistreicheren Ausspruch Steins gegenüberstellen, der sagt: 'Die Einnahme aus den Domänen ist die wirtschaftliche Basis des selbständigen Königthums
und mit ihm der selbständigen äussern und innern Staatsbildung; denn sie wird die
Grundlage der materiellen Unabhängigkeit der Könige gegenüber der Herrschaft und
der Gewalt der mächtigen ständischen Körperschaften. Die Domäne dauert daher fort
und wird dauern, so lange es ein Königthum gibt, denn beide sind nicht blos historisch,
sondern organisch mit einander korrespondierende Begriffe.'"

lative sovereignty and other functions, to finance the government and to guarantee the "national debts," seemed to Stein still unthinkable. In short, Stein's laudation of the domains was motivated by a specific conception of the state in its relationship to society and economy, and corresponded not only with Prussia's structural characteristics of revenues (that is the large portion of "own" sources of income) but with the lack of a modern system of public borrowing, the mode of allocation of revenues and the control over expenditure as well. It is not astonishing that Stein is praised by Gustav Schmoller, head of the German Younger Historical School, since that School was a reaction to Adam Smith's (and the classical school of economic theory's) conception of the relationship between state, society, and economy, and was strongly influenced by the post-Kantian political philosophy, especially by Hegel's doctrine of the state as the realization of the moral idea (*die Verwirklichung der sittlichen Idee im Staat*). In line with the views of the Historical Schools, theories of taxation and fiscal policy developed in Germany after the middle of the nineteenth century which were biased toward a historical and organic conception of state, society and economy, and this bias prevailed until the First World War (see Wilke 1921: 65ff.). This leads us to a second aspect, which may be illuminated by an argument between two historians.

Eli Heckscher, the eminent Swedish economic historian, has argued that

> when Cunningham (a British historian of the later nineteenth century) gave the name of "parliamentary Colbertism" to the policy pursued in the period after 1689, he should have added that it was Colbertism not only without Colbert, but also, which is even more important, without the vast administrative machinery created by Colbert—that it was, in fact, a system almost without any administrative machinery at all. . . . How far this explains the fact that what is usually called the Industrial Revolution came to England first, instead of beginning in continental countries—which were probably less backward than England before that time—is of course impossible to decide with certainty. Many other factors made their contribution, and I can only record my personal impression that the absence of administrative control was one of the most important (Heckscher 1936–1937: 47).

The Tudor and Stuart governments (and in a different fashion the Long Parliament as well) at least intended to regulate and control the socioeconomic affairs of their subjects by a centralized machinery furnished by judicial institutions of the Crown's Prerogative (and arbitrary rule of the Long Parliament, respectively), though they lacked the administrative strength at the local level to enforce this policy effectively. The restoration of the monarchy, however, marked the end of such attempts. As D. L. Keir writes,

> the age of paternalistic government closed at the Restoration. Government by the propertied classes in their own interest took the place of government by the Crown in what it held to be the national interest. So far as Parliament bent itself to the task of economic and social regulation, it was not by strengthening administrative control, but by legislative action particularly in the manipulation of tariffs . . . The power of the State in this sphere was effectively limited by the universally accepted principle that all administration was essentially the mere fulfillment of duties imposed by Common or statute law. Such a principle left little or no room for the imposition of direct administrative control by the central government over local authorities. For all practical purposes, moreover, the machinery of control had been demolished when the Privy Council was stripped of its coercive powers in 1641. The eighteenth century was an era of almost complete autonomy for the local institutions of the country. Their duty was to carry out the law, and not to obey the commands of the central executive (Keir 1967: 234, 312).

We might recall the statement of Christopher Hill that "the destruction of the royal bureaucracy in 1640–1641 can be regarded as the most decisive event in the whole British history." To be sure, the Restoration did not leave British government without any centralized administrative apparatus. The fiscal machinery of the Exchequer, which was organized in a complicated set of offices and agencies with collecting, accounting, and auditing functions, and with a judicial tribunal for revenue matters, was a notably large establishment and became increasingly larger and more complicated after the Glorious Revolution. In the eighteenth century the collecting and administrative agencies of customs and excises employed more than 10,000 salaried servants (approximately three-fourths of all the Crown's officials). With few exceptions both sides of fiscal

affairs—receipts and expenditures—were under the central supervision of the Treasury Board (see Binney 1958: 3ff.). Yet functions
and competences of this fiscal machinery as well as the status and
outlook of its officials were in no way comparable with its counterpart in Brandenburg-Prussia.

The centralized administrative apparatus of the British government could not, even if it had attempted to do so, serve as a tool for
the establishment of an arbitrary administrative law and as a
medium for the creation of a *Polizeistaat*-machinery as was the case
in Brandenburg-Prussia. Such attempts would have been checked
by the post-Restoration changes which we have mentioned: the
Common Law courts, which triumphed over the judicial power of
the King and his government; the local authorities, which emancipated themselves further from the control of central government;
and Parliament, which exercised control over the public revenue and
public expenditure, beside its legislative functions. The representatives of these institutions traditionally opposed the encroachment of
government upon the personal sphere of life. In 1689, for example,
Parliament abandoned the recently instituted hearth tax on grounds
of its being a "badge of slavery" contrary to the traditional freedom
from governmental interference.[56] The taxation of movable property
failed in practice over and over again for the same reason. The merchants, traders, manufacturers, and money men rejected vigorously
the intrusion of governmental administration into business matters
for purposes of tax assessment. Adam Smith only stated the popular
opinion among these groups when he called such governmental attempts "an inquisition more intolerable than any tax" (*Wealth of
Nations*), and remarked in a "Lecture on Justice, Police, Revenue
and Arms" (1763): "It is a hardship upon a man in trade to oblige
him to show his books, which is the only way in which we can know
how much he is worth. It is a breach of liberty and may be productive of very bad consequences by ruining his credit . . ." (quoted by
Kennedy 1964: 125). It is needless to go into further detail; obviously
the Whig oligarchy was anxious to avoid encroachment upon the
privacy of the business of those groups from which it drew its political support. Not only the constitutional and institutional framework,
but also the prevailing ideological basis of the sociopolitical power

[56] It was considered "in itself not only a great oppression to the poorer sort, but a
badge of slavery upon the whole people, exposing every man's house to be entered
into and searched at pleasure by persons unknown to him" (parliamentary votum;
quoted by Kennedy 1964: 58).

elite prevented the central administrative apparatus of British government from developing a *Polizeistaat*-pattern.

For the contrasting case of Brandenburg-Prussia, we may well adapt Heckscher's statement and say that here (and in other German territories) the prince and his highest servants not only acted like mini-Colberts, but also created an "administrative machinery" which outdid that of the French in socioeconomic regulations and controls and wholesale bureaucratic encroachment on all affairs of life. The Prussian brand of bureaucracy has found in Otto Hintze and Hans Rosenberg its outstanding historiographers and interpreters. It was a bureaucracy which linked military, police, civil, and economic matters closely with its pivotal function, fiscal affairs and which developed a system of detailed regimentation (based on arbitrary administrative law), secret reporting, and cringing obedience. True, this system attained its prime object: the extraction of the material means and the human efforts "to support the army of a first-rate power on the resources of a third-rate state." Yet it was marked by "obstructiveness and trained mediocrity" (Rosenberg 1958: 194) selfish group interests in the name of the *droit de bienséance*, and last but not least by inefficiency despite—or better—because of an enormous amount of activities. Obedience is not the same as loyalty, and being effective does not necessarily imply being efficient. This may be illustrated by the fact that in a time of great financial stress Frederick the Great employed a French *Régie* for the collection of the Excise.

The Prussian "administrative machinery," armed with the confidence of possessing the know-how and the means to shape the economy and society in the right fashion, hampered economic development in practice, as government not only regulated and minutely controlled the economic sphere from above, but also entered the field of production and commerce by itself, setting up a host of governmental enterprises in various sectors. Quite often these enterprises proved to be unprofitable, despite the fact that they enjoyed many special privileges and advantages (see, for example, Kisch 1968: passim).[57]

[57] Due to the tradition of Prussian historiography, especially the so-called *borussische Geschichtsschreibung*, the function of the Prussian absolutistic bureaucracy as a motor power of modernization was and often still is, in my opinion, much overrated and usually praised without recognizing how strongly this absolutistic policy of modernization was an outflow of socioeconomic backwardness. By the same token, the limitations of this modernization policy was and still is overlooked, namely the fact,

The statement that the Prussian "administrative machinery" and the nature of the system in general hampered economic development is also relevant in regard to the agrarian system, and leads us to a third aspect. Under Prussian absolutism the landed Junkers not only maintained their patrimonial rights and, to a large extent, their tax privileges (among other privileges), but even enhanced their socioeconomic status by adding to their local patrimonial authority military authority over their peasantry. Rosenberg writes:

> In the military establishment the private exploitation of delegated royal authority lived on for another half century in the particularly vicious and brutalizing form of "company management" (*Kompaniewirtschaft*). . . . Thus, until the military reforms after 1806, bureaucratic administration continued to be on a limited scale an object of private ownership and a source of personal gain within the "nationalized" domain of the Prussian state under the central direction of the king, who had staked his political fortune upon the army (Rosenberg 1958: 79).

As we mentioned earlier, the military, fiscal, and agrarian systems were so strongly interwoven that one part could hardly be changed without changing the others; one system reinforced the others. The effect was that the agrarian system of Brandenburg-Prussia had great difficulties in adapting itself to new agricultural techniques and methods of cultivation. The Junkers, led by their King, were well aware of new agricultural techniques and were eager to introduce them. But the petrified socioeconomic structure (land tenure, compulsory labor service, etc.) and the host of military/fiscal obligations in kind and services which rested upon the peasantry proved to be a barrier even after the so-called *Generalseparation*, designed to overcome these obstacles by separating the acres of the Junker's estates from those of his peasantry, was instituted in the second half of the eighteenth century.[58]

---

that in reality the activities of the central bureaucracy often had more retarding than developing effects (see Gerschenkron 1970: 62 ff.); here Gerschenkron tries "to make plausible the proportion that, historically seen, the phenomenon of mercantilism can be usefully regarded as a function of the degree of economic backwardness of the countries concerned" (p. 62).

[58] The highly complex system of logistic provisions in kind and service by the peasantry as part of its fiscal obligations has to be evaluated as a chief barrier. These obligations were either unpaid or low paid; moreover, they confined the freedom of disposition in terms of working arrangements, working time and choice of cultivation. Despite several attempts to curtail these obligations the system remained vital until the

The contrasts with the agrarian conditions of eighteenth-century Britain were striking indeed. The landed gentry in Britain enjoyed no tax privileges; the land bore the bulk of direct taxation. However, the landed gentry and the other groups of larger landholders were compensated for their tax burden in various ways. In the first place, the landed gentry or "Squirearchy" was able to retain a firm grip on the local, administrative, and judicial authority but without using outdated feudal means such as patrimonial rights, villenage, or compulsory labor service. In the second place, the local assessors and acting commissioners of the Land Tax greatly favored the gentry and the larger landholders. This was due to the fact that the administration of the Land Tax differed from that of the other branches of revenues, inasmuch as the personnel that came into contact with the individual taxpayer was directly or indirectly appointed by parliamentary authority and not by the Crown (Binney 1958: 53). In the third place, the corn bounty scheme voted by Parliament was particularly designed to help the gentry and larger landholders, and not the smaller farmers. Most important, the new wave of enclosure, beginning around the middle of the eighteenth century and coming to an end in the early nineteenth, was in the interest of the landed gentry, who used their influence in Parliament, their local authority, and, if necessary, their Common-Law-court connections as well to overcome all opposition against enclosure and to reach settlements in their favor. The enclosure movement was an important precondition for the agrarian reforms of eighteenth-century Britain—a reform which was so successful that the term "Agrarian Revolution" is sometimes used to describe the whole sweep of changes, such as the new land tenure systems, the new crop rotations, the new crops, and the new cultivation methods.

By virtue of these reforms and innovations Britain's agricultural sector was able to meet the food demands of a rapidly increasing population in the eighteenth century. This was of great significance for Britain's balance of payments. As Knut Borchardt pointed out, the Industrial Revolution would have been hampered if the import of needed industrial raw materials had to be curtailed on the

---

end of the *Ancien Régime* and was even enlarged in some instances. The system is much too complex to be outlined here. The main obligations were the provision of oats, hay, straw, pasturage, and *corvée* labor with cart and draught-animal. For a detailed discription of these obligations for the electorate of Brandenburg, see Wöhner 1805: passim.

grounds of balance of payment difficulties caused by food imports. Besides this, the demand for industrial goods by the agricultural sector were crucial as stimuli for the so-called take-off. The agricultural reforms enabled the agrarian sector, up to the middle of the nineteenth century, to provide the bulk of direct taxes, and thus enabled the commercial and monied classes largely to escape direct taxation. The agrarian conditions of eighteenth-century Britain, so markedly different from those of Brandenburg-Prussia in terms of land tenure, labor supply, agricultural techniques, cultivation methods, and taxation, help to explain the fact that the Industrial Revolution came to England first. Let us paraphrase Christopher Hill's remark again: Britain's tax system of the eighteenth century "transferred wealth from the poorer and the landed to the monied classes."

This brings up a fourth aspect, namely the relationship between the monied classes and the laboring poor. The doctrine which arose in Britain in the second half of the seventeenth century that everyone should pay taxes but the richer more than the poor prevailed during the eighteenth century. The disputes over the taxation of necessities went on, too, reaching a climax in the earlier thirties when Walpole attempted to increase the Salt Tax (1732) and presented a new Bill of Excise (1733) in order to keep the Land Tax down. One new point of view was added in opposing taxes on necessaries: this was the theory that taxes on the necessaries of life are not really paid by the poor, who already live close to the margins of subsistence, but by their employers, who consequently have to raise wages. Taking into account the Poor Laws, an innovation of the Tudor government, on the one hand, and the prevailing subsistence theory about wages, on the other, the opposing point of view, stressed by commercial and manufacturing circles, gained ground and remained of importance up to the repeal of the Corn Laws in 1846. Thus behind this opposition stood the selfish interest of the monied classes rather than a welfare policy.

The counterview that the poor ought to be taxed as much as possible in order to oblige them "either to work or starve" was widely discussed too, but was less common as a rationalization for taxing the laboring poor than in Europe.[59] However, in practice the indi-

---

[59] Josiah Tucker (1750), quoted by Kennedy 1964: 117; Kennedy cites other sources in this connection. British colonial policy applied such maxim for the purpose of labor recruitment among natives. See for example, J. C. Mitchell, 1961: 193ff.; see also Mann 1943: 227.

rect and hence highly regressive taxes (Customs and Excise) produced about two-thirds of total revenue in peacetime. Despite the fact that in the last quarter of the eighteenth century various new levies on luxury commodities were introduced, wealth and capital, especially business profits and capital in trade, business, and industry, still remained virtually untapped. The laboring poor and the smaller landholders both were overtaxed. This had the effect of forced saving for the benefit of those groups, which were the motive power of economic development and the Industrial Revolution. The same effects derived from the expenditure side. About half of the expenses went into paying the interest on the national debt. "This was a shift of income from the mass with the higher propensity to spend towards the few with higher propensity to save or to spend on services" (Mathias 1969: 42).

In Brandenburg-Prussia the pattern of tax systems and correspondingly the socioeconomic effects were of a quite different kind. The politically curtailed Junkers, the mainstay of absolutistic monarchy, were supposed to serve their King with loyal devotion as army officers and civil servants. By virtue of their birth they enjoyed social, judicial, economic, and, at the local level, political privileges. Their favorable status as regards taxation was a part of these privileges, that is, a part of the Junkers' special rights by virtue of birth and rank, and has to be considered as a "consolation prize" (Rosenberg 1958: 120) for their integration into the power structure of Prussia's central autocracy.

The peasantry and the laboring poor bore a heavy burden. This was considered justified on the grounds of maintaining the existing social order and for ethical-moral reasons: to prevent the lower order from becoming idle, disobedient and demanding. Unlike in Britain, the potential motive power of economic development, the enterprising middle classes, not only paid their share of taxes, but were also hampered in their efforts by a host of governmental interferences and petrified, outdated regulations. To put it bluntly, Brandenburg-Prussian tax systems were designed for the benefit of an absolutistic state; it was a forced saving in the case for an absolutistic governmental, military, administrative, and police machinery, with the aim of shaping and maintaining the socioeconomic structure in the right and "just" proportion. The design was based on a *geburtsständische* social order (hereditary sociostructural setup). It was not until the Prussian reform period at the beginning of the nineteenth century that this *geburtsständische* social order was seriously challenged by modern liberalism.

Certainly, in Brandenburg-Prussia this was a relatively slow process marked with setbacks and anachronistic survivals. In the long run, however, the peasantry were freed from being hereditary subjects bound to the soil of the estates; landed property became purchasable by all social groups; hereditary barriers to admission to certain professions or certain professional training were removed; nobles were no longer prevented by law (though in some instances by their code of honor) from taking part in certain economic activities; specific social groups were no longer covered by special laws; the manifold socioeconomic distinctions between countryside and city or town (in respect to taxation, economic regulation, etc.) gradually vanished; and so forth. The whole issue ultimately boils down to the relationship between individual, state and society. This leads us to a final aspect: the prevailing concept of society, state and individual in Brandenburg-Prussia and, in particular, in eighteenth-century Britain.

The enlightened absolutism in Brandenburg-Prussia was like a *Hamlet* without a prince of Denmark: an enlightenment without an individual or the concept of autonomous individual freedom. Fritz Hartung writes:

> The defeats (at Jena and Auerstädt in 1806) could only have been so severe because enlightened absolutism generally denied active and free participation to its subjects as regards the affairs of state, claiming rather to command all affairs from above by minutely dictating to every subject his sphere of activity and keeping the subject within this sphere. Moreover, enlightened absolutism regulated the obligations toward the state by the principle of division of labor: only governmental officials and army officers were supposed to take an active part in matters of state, and not the rest of the subjects; the latter were supposed to pay taxes, and even in times of war to live up to the maxim that silent obedience was their primary obligation (*Ruhe ist die erste Bürgerpflicht*) (Hartung 1950: 238).[60]

[60] The original German goes as follows: "So vernichtend konnten diese Niederlagen nur dadurch werden, dass der aufgeklärte Absolutismus grundsätzlich auf die lebendige und freie Anteilnahme seiner Untertanen am Staatsleben verzichtete, dass er vielmehr alles von oben her zu bestimmen unternahm, jedem den Wirkungskreis genau vorschrieb und ihn darin festhielt, dass er auch die Pflicht gegen den Staat nach dem

This characterization of the spirit of Prussia's enlightened absolutism has to be evaluated against the background of what we emphasized earlier about the make-up of the bureaucratic machinery, the outlook of its officials, and the role of the state as the overall regulative principle, representing the *droit de bienséance*. Turning now to the British concept of society and state which came into being, in theory and practice, after the Civil War and prevailed during the eighteenth century, we may apply two catch-phrases for its characterization. The first is provided by William Kennedy; he calls it a "freeholder, non-functional conception of society" (Kennedy 1964: 180ff.).[61] In a sarcastic manner Christopher Hill labels the same phenomenon the "Ritz Hotel view of society"; he writes:

> Locke's philosophy sanctioned a freedom based on property, a freedom with which the state must not interfere: a freedom which, like the doors of the Ritz Hotel, was open to rich and poor alike. "The clash and ferment of economic ideas," said Professor Wilson, "reflected the freedom of a society where trade was allowed to fight its case against the surviving remnants of feudalism: neither the freedom nor the ideas should be underrated as formative influence on economic growth." It was the end of medieval and Tudor conceptions of regulation and control (1967: 128ff.).[62]

The two characterizations are derived from two different interpretations of Locke's political philosophy. Kennedy assumes that Locke's individual rights refer to all men, and therefore sees a great discrepancy between theory and reality:

> In its strict form, such as is found in Locke, every Englishman was supposed to be an individual of the freeholder type; but in

---

Grundsatz der Arbeitsteilung regulierte und eine aktive Betätigung für den Staat nur vom Beamtentum und vom Heere forderte, die breite Masse aber auf das Steuerzahlen beschränkte und selbst in Kriegszeiten für sie die Ruhe als die erste Bürgerpflicht proklamierte."

[61] Kennedy writes: "Men entered into society in order to secure themselves in the rights which individually belonged to them; the state existed to provide this security; the rights to be secured were theoretically 'natural' rights, in practice conceived as the more general and characteristic rights guaranteed by English law; and all men having rights to be protected, which, though different in extent, were essentially similar in kind, every man was a free man and citizen. The basis of political obligation was that the state was necessary to, and in effect did, protect men's rights. Men were born not to functions or service but to rights or enjoyments. They were born freeholders or free merchant adventurers."

[62] Hill is referring to Wilson 1965.

fact, nothing was more untrue. English society was not made up of similar individuals each with similar property and other rights; a large part of it consisted of people whose property rights were very small or non-existent. This inconsistency of theory and fact led to an indefiniteness of feeling which appears in the seventeenth but was more typical of the eighteenth century. The freeholder view of taxation required that everyone should pay taxation; but men often felt that in some way the theory did not satisfy them when applied in practice; whence a sentimental and philanthropic pity for the poor, very different from the more robust attitude of the sixteenth-century moralist. Many other results were also connected with this inconsistency; as an instance take the *laissez-faire* attitude—dominant long before the day of the Philosophic Radicals—which assumed both that cotton operatives were independent individuals in the same essential conditions as mill-owners, and that small yeomen and wage-earning cottagers could be treated, in enclosing village lands, in the same way as lords of manors. It would probably not be incorrect to say that the whole range of social opinion in the eighteenth century was warped by this falsity in the Lockean conception of society (Kennedy 1964: 91).

Accorrding to C. B. Macpherson, author of the famous book *The Political Theory of Possessive Individualism—Hobbes to Locke*, however, it was not a "falsity in the Lockean conception of society," but the very essence of this political philosophy: "Locke was assuming that only those with property were full members of civil society and so of the majority." Locke's constitutionalism therefore was "a defence of the rights of expanding property rather than of the rights of the individual against the state." It was "essentially a defence of the supremacy of property—and not that of the yeomen only, but more especially that of the men of substance to whom the security of unlimited accumulation was of first importance" (Macpherson 1962: 252, 257f.). Christopher Hill's statement indicates that he is in agreement with Macpherson's view. For our topic the interpretation of theories is less important than the question of the reception of theories particularly by the sociopolitical power elite. It is quite obvious that the political ideas of "possessive individualism," especially Locke's philosophy, appealed to those groups which, toward the end of the seventeenth century, came to dominate political life in Britain

[307]

for generations: the upper class of nobles, gentry, men of property and money, "who thought property the central social fact" (Macpherson) and had, as we mentioned earlier, the controlling influence upon Parliament, Common Law courts and local authorities. The "possessive individualism" was designed to serve these groups as an ideological foundation for the rationalization of their sociopolitical status as well as their socioeconomic position.

We cannot enlarge on this theme, but one point might be added: it deals with the somewhat strange symbiosis between the classes of landed and monied property mirrored, for example, in the distribution of the tax load, the funding system of public borrowing, the enclosure acts, and the agricultural reforms generally. How could such a symbiotic relationship emerge and last well into the nineteenth century? How could these divergent interests be linked together by the same ideological fetter? According to Macpherson "Locke was very well aware that there were differences of interest between the landed men, the merchants, and the monied men, and that these differences came out particularly sharply in contests between them about the incidence of taxation." Yet Locke "could assume, as a man of property himself, that the common interest that propertied men 'had in the security of property was more important, and could be seen by any rational self-interested man of property to be more important, than their divergent interests as owners of land, of money, or of mercantile stock" (Macpherson 1962: 253ff.). It is of little surprise that in reality these kinds of thoughts led to a harsher treatment of offenses against personal property. Christopher Hill pointed out that between 1688 and the end of the eighteenth century "the number of offences which carried the death penalty rose from about fifty to nearly five times that number. The vast majority of these were offences against property. . . . A man was hanged for stealing one shilling, a boy of sixteen for stealing 3s.6d. and a penknife, a girl for a handkerchief. . . . By 1740 it was a capital offence to steal property worth one shilling" (Hill 1967: 182, 212). These harsh penalties were in conformity with Locke, who assigned in his *Second Treatise of Government* to the legislative and executive powers the "right of making laws with penalties of Death, and consequently all less penalties, for the regulating and preserving of property. . . ." (II.i.3). In addition, the tendency to regard the nonpropertied men as subordinate and to establish workhouses for the poor could also

[308]

be traced back to the Lockean ideas (about justifying slavery).[63] Thus, whereas the enlightened absolutism in Brandenburg-Prussia was an Enlightenment without individual freedom, Lockean tradition of "possessive individualism" implied that "full individuality was produced by consuming the individuality of others" (Macpherson 1962: 261).

Yet, "the doors of the Ritz Hotel were open": eighteenth-century British society was not a *geburtsständische* society of the continental European fashion but showed strong features of an "achievement" society where property rather than birth and hereditary social rank determined sociopolitical position and access to political power. Against this background arose English liberalism with its concept of society made up of independent individuals motivated by self-interest:

> In the pages of Adam Smith classical expression was given to the already familiar view that the condition of national greatness was the liberation of individual energy, unhampered by anything more than an irreducible minimum of social restraint. The pursuit by every man of his own interest as he conceived it would result, it was assumed, in harmonies which would make regulation of national affairs by government action needless, and, if persisted in, harmful. The main business of government, on this view, was to clear away obstructions which impeded the free play of individual enterprise (Keir 1967: 369).

In looking for the causes and explanations of the fact that Britain became the "workshop of the world" and broke the path toward sociopolitical modernization, this concept of society and state must be considered as crucial. In practice the concept proved to be suited for the introduction of the necessary reforms which were prerequisites of these developments. A bureaucratic machinery of the central government was not the prime mover. Leadership reposed in those, who represented property (Parliament, Common Law courts, local authority). These were political amateurs rather than trained professionals, often even unaided by first-class technical assistants (Binney 1958: 253). Nevertheless, the handling of fiscal and financial affairs after 1688 indicates that the system worked relatively effi-

---

[63] By an Act of 1697 the recipients of poor relief had to wear a payer's badge and thus were stigmatized; an Act of 1723 gave the parish the right to set up workhouses.

ciently. J.E.D. Binney writes in *British Public Finance and Adminis-tration, 1774–1792* as follows: "It may be claimed with a reasonable degree of confidence that the English system (of public finance and administration) for all its acknowledged shortcomings, was superior to that of France or probably any other European State" (Binney 1958:257).

Yet the socioeconomic changes of the Industrial Revolution called for reform. The system had to be reshaped in order to cope with the new problems, tasks and responsibilities: A new fiscal system, an enlargement and professionalization of central government and changes concerning the relationship between Crown, government, and Parliament as well as parliamentary reforms (redistribution of seats, reforms of the franchise) were part of this adaptation process.

Brandenburg-Prussia in turn entered after the defeats of Jena and Auerstädt into a period of reforms. They involved a reorganization of the military system, first attempts to alter the agrarian system, more freedom of trade, changes of the fiscal system, and public finance, as well as the promise of a constitutional monarchy. However, this reform period soon came to an end. The "Decisions of Karlsbad" (1819) marked the turning point. Promises remained unfulfilled, and in many instances the wheel of reforms was turned back. The following decades saw a liberal movement struggling for the creation of a constitutional monarchy and sociopolitical changes. Fiscal affairs and public finance played an important part in this movement, which came to a bitter climax in 1848.

Some Final Remarks

The empirical background of the foregoing two sections may serve for some general conclusions. Let us, first of all, sketch a few interconnections between taxation and the other topics of this book: military force, police, technical personnel, and food supply.

Clearly, the most significant interrelations are those between taxation, warfare, and military forces as many famous writers, among them Tacitus, have emphasized.[64] In 1793 Karl Heinrich Lang published a book about "the historical development of the German tax systems from the Carolingian time up to the present," where he attempted to prove that all changes of tax systems corresponded with foregoing changes of the military systems and techniques of warfare

[64] "Nam neque quies gentium sine armis neque arma sine stipendiis neque stipendia sine tributis haberi queunt"; quoted by Mann 1934:288.

[310]

(see bibliography). Rudolf Goldscheid, a pioneer in the field of fiscal sociology who coined the term "Tax State," evaluated warfare as
the "moving motor of the whole development of public finance."
Hence, "sociology of public finance coincides largely with sociology
of warfare," and public finance has therefore to be treated as "essentially a science of war and not of peace" (1926: 149). Though we
reject these monocausal interpretations, we cannot deny that times
of war played a prime role in the development of taxation and public finance. Even England with its favorable geopolitical position
provides ample illustration. We might recall that the "Financial Revolution" after 1688 had to be evaluated against the background of
the heavy financial burdens of the War of Palatine Inheritance (1688–
1697) and the War of the Spanish Succession. The reforms of the financial and fiscal administration during the last quarter of the
eighteenth century were connected with the War of American
Independence. Pitt's introduction of the first income tax was a wartime emergency measure, because the financial strains of military
expenses were so great that the century-old funding system seemed
in danger of breaking down; at the end of the Napoleonic Wars the
Parliament quickly abandoned this fiscal innovation.[65]

It hardly needs saying that the military costs were by far the largest item of the state budgets. They generally exceeded the sum of all
the other public expenses, because we also have to add under this
heading most of the public debt charges. These debts were mainly
caused by war expenses. The resources needed for the task of securing the territory against interior and exterior threats were determined by a host of factors like: the prevailing military system,
including schemes of recruitment, modes of armament, and traditionally required contributions of equipment by communities and
individuals; techniques of warfare; geopolitical position; potential
threats from outside caused by unensured territorial or dynastic
claims; potential interior threats caused by the sociopolitical power

[65] The Tudors' finances were also severely influenced by war expenditure: In the
fight with France and Scotland Henry VIII and Edward VI spent approximately three
and one half million pounds for military expenses between 1539–1550. Only the
extraordinary chance of selling a good deal of the newly acquired Church property
saved the Crown from bankruptcy. In the last decade of the sixteenth century Elizabeth had to spend more than four million pounds for her forces in Ireland, France,
and the Low Countries; consequently, she left her successor a heavy debt load and a
further loss of the Crown's financial independence. Charles I's campaign of 1640
against the Scots amounted to more than half a million pounds and proved too much
for the Crown's financial capacity (see Dietz 1932: 123ff.).

structure or the constitutional and institutional setting, including the legality of dynastic claims and their popular approval. Yet the actual amount of military expenses is only one side of the coin. For the development of public finance the qualitative aspects of military expenses are likewise important.

To begin with, the maintenance of a loyal and efficient military force caused a variety of hidden and indirect costs. The mode of extracting the necessary means in money, kind, and service had to be designed with a view to the loyalty and efficiency of the armed forces. Hence, the less the rulers had undisputed sources of income and the more their authority had to be based upon a loyal and efficient armed force, the more they were motivated to make costly fiscal and economic concessions to those who were the backbone of military strength. Characteristic features of tax systems like regional or social inequality in the distribution of the tax load and forms of levies or the structure of the tax collecting organs were determined by such military considerations. Tax exemptions of the nobles were traditionally justified by their military function; it was an old maxim that whoever pays with his blood does not have to pay with his goods. As mentioned before, the tax privileges of the Prussian Junkers were motivated by their pivotal functions as officers in the Prussian army. The Prussian tax reform of 1820 left the income of military personnel in active duty again untapped. It was not until 1849 that a royal edict declared the exemption of the military null and void (see von Beckerath 1912: 58ff.).

Times of war required not only large amounts of revenue; to be of use, the money had to be at the disposal of the ruler at the right time. This qualitative criterion determined changes in two directions: first, concerning the development of a tax system; second, regarding the raising of public loans and the funding of public debts.

From both the institutional and psychological point of view, times of war paved the way toward the innovation and less disputed acceptance of regularly recurring direct taxes, because direct taxes were better suited for quick returns than indirect ones, which came in much too slowly. Particularly poll taxes, window taxes, hearth taxes, and various forms of income taxes were favored for war purposes on the grounds of their assessment and collection qualities. Disraeli once called the income tax "a third line of defence" (Buxton 1888: vol. II, 170).

Times of war were even more important for the development of techniques of public borrowing and the handling of public debts. For the efficient execution of military actions the financial solvency of the ruler was of crucial importance, because the loyalty, fighting spirit, and alertness of the armed forces depended heavily upon ensured payment and supply. This refers not only to mercenary troops, but to the militia as well. In the period of modern state-building, where the military system no longer rested on the principle of clientship and the formation of a politically loyal militia based on popularly accepted military obligations of the subjects was at best in a nascent state, ready money was the pivotal point for every military success.

But the demand for ready money in a situation of emergency is always a costly affair; all the more, if the purpose is as risky as warfare usually is. For this reason the rulers were eager to hoard a state or war treasure, but with few exceptions (among them Prussia from the reign of the Great Elector until 1806) these efforts were only of limited practical success. In the period of modern state building the statement of Rudolf Goldscheid that "wars create bad finances and bad finances create wars" bears certainly more than a grain of truth (Goldscheid 1926: 157). Theoretically the ruler had a variety of choices to extract the needed means for war emergency: all sorts of loans by private creditors or public institutions (municipalities, estates, the Church) at home, including forced loans, or from outside the territory; the issuing of annuities; debasement of coins; the imposition of new taxes or brutal confiscation. In reality, however, the choices were determined by a host of factors like the motives of war, the chances of winning the war, the popular support behind the war efforts, and the approval of the warfare and the war motives by other rulers. Yet all modes of extraction were more or less expensive in terms of economic, social, and political costs. Forced loans or new taxes, for example, bore heavy sociopolitical risks; debasement of coins had dangerous economic and social effects; loans from private creditors (wealthy merchants, big commercial houses, court Jews) could usually be raised only by granting expensive concessions in terms of trading privileges, especially war supply privileges, mining rights, or the utilization of other economically valuable royal prerogatives like tax, customs and minting rights, or salt monopoly for a certain time period. Loans from public institutions could in gen-

[313]

eral only be obtained by paying a price in terms of political concessions. With a view to the actual situation the ruler had to set the economic point against the social and political one in deciding how to
meet the task of war financing, if he had a choice at all. These efforts,
which were indeed one of the crucial problems of modern state-
building, were a moving force for the development of new schemes
of private and public borrowing, new funding systems of public
debts and new techniques for the amortization of public debts as
well as public finance generally. As the changes from the so-called
traditional pledge (*Traditionspfand*) to the so-called contract
pledge (*Vertragspfand*), or, later on, to the development of state or
semistate controlled institutions for the purpose of handling public
debts, raising public loans, guaranteeing the supply of money and
providing other functions in the field of public finance suggest, these
innovations and developments, together with the fiscal ones, were an
integrated part of modern state-building. In mutual interaction they
determined the style-of-rule and the characteristic *habitus* of the
state or nation in question. We have stressed the fact that the creation of the national debt in Britain, which was a function of war finance, and the entry of the government into the loan market by the
development of a new funding system and the foundation of the
Bank of England as an instrument of public finance had not only far
reaching economic effects, but also was important for the whole
sociopolitical setting, which came into being after the Glorious Revolution and prevailed for more than one and a half centuries. In
Prussia such a system of public or national debt was lacking. However, the time of occupation and wars after 1806 brought an enormous financial burden. Hence, against tradition and still prevailing
principles the Prussian government, under the leadership of Hardenberg, was also forced to create a national debt. This new system
of public borrowing on permanent funded debt (together with a tax
reform in 1820) was decisive in the efforts to overcome the financial
strains and to regain a basis of sound public finance. Yet in the long
run this new funding system also proved to be crucial in the constitutional struggle (guaranteeing of the national debt, fight for the
right of budget control and so forth).

Yet the problem of extracting the necessary means for military
and war purposes, of lowering the economic, social, and political
costs in meeting these tasks, and, by the same token, of enhancing

[314]

the loyalty and efficiency of the armed forces involved other important aspects of modern state-building too. We are referring to ideological and sociopsychological aspects, i.e., to the indoctrination of
the subjects with adequate value codes, behavioral pattern, public
spirit and civic virtues. The following pointed statement of Rudolf
Goldscheid gives us a key to approach these complex questions:
"The 'just' tax and the 'just' war have the same social and rational
roots" (Goldscheid 1926: 149).

This sentence draws attention to a twin process: On the one hand,
the development toward a loyal and efficient militia based upon a
system of universal or selective military service, which is obligatory
and, as part of the duties of the subjects, virtually unpaid.[66] Samuel
E. Finer in Chapter 2 deals with the slow and gradual formation of
such a military organization. He emphasizes the fact that it was crucial in terms of loyalty, efficiency, and expenses to create a public
spirit where these military obligations were performed not by the
exercise of coercion but the exercise of persuasion, i.e., by the utilization of national or patriotic value codes, *Leitbilder*, behavioral
patterns and virtues.[67]

On the other hand, the twin process involved the development of
modes of extracting the means for military and war purposes. It was
likewise a slow but crucial process to create the adequate institutional framework and a public spirit where these fiscal obligations
rested upon popular consent, i.e., were considered as part of the
public or civil duties. To regard both the conscription and the sub-
scription of war loans as a patriotic obligation needed persuasion
and indoctrination, which were based on the same ideological foundation. More and more, all subjects were destined to sacrifice their
blood as well as their goods for their state, nation, or "fatherland."
Universal conscription and universal liability to pay taxes as part of
the civil duties increasingly became the prevailing principle during
the nineteenth century. They rested on the notion of "equality of sacrifice" (S. E. Finer). We will see later how this notion corresponded
with its counterpart, i.e., equality of political rights and socioeconomic benefits. At this point we may conclude that the military and
times of war played an important role for the popular acceptance of
universal liability to pay regularly recurring levies. Or to apply the
terminology which S. E. Finer invented in his paper as "shorthand

[66] See Chapter 2 above.   [67] See Chapter 2 above.

notation": the military and times of war were significant in converting the "extraction-coercion cycle" into an "extraction-persuasion
cycle."

The Brandenburg-Prussia case illustrates in an ideal-type fashion the interconnection with the second topic: police. The excessive
growth of the police apparatus during the mercantilistic-cameralistic
era was mainly caused by its fiscal functions. Primarily fiscal purposes motivated the minute regulation of and wholesale encroachment upon all affairs of life by governmental institutions. Thus, the
institutional and functional interrelations between fiscal and police
matters became a mainstay of the all-controlling system of the modern absolutistic state and served as an instrument for shaping the
minds and consciences of the subjects with respect to their obligations toward the state. One of the values which had to be implanted
in the minds and consciences of the subjects was the unquestioned
consent to be liable for taxation. From this point of view the police
apparatus, in the broad mercantilistic-cameralistic sense, became
also a medium for converting the "extraction-coercion cycle" into an
"extraction-persuasion cycle." The system of farming out tax collection could never have had this "educational" effect. On the other
hand, during the crucial phase of state-building, the fiscal system
and the fiscal situation of Brandenburg-Prussia required the linkage
of the extraction apparatus with the police apparatus and the military organization. In Britain such a linked system of all-controlling
state interference was absent. The fiscal system and the fiscal situation of Britain favored not centralism but localism. The assessment
as well as the collection of revenues were traditionally carried out
by local authority and the enforcement of revenue payment also belonged to the realm of local authority. The absence of a centralized
apparatus of enforcement and control officers corresponded with the
prevailing principle as far as state interferences were concerned.
"Possessive individualism" fortified these principles. With a less
favorable geopolitical position, however, Britain could hardly have
managed to meet its fiscal tasks without a tighter enforcement and
control apparatus as the reforms of the fiscal administration after the
War of American Independence, which aimed in this direction, indicated (see Binney 1958: 1ff. and passim).[68]

[68] We might recall the Tudor tradition of handling the "own" resources by a
centralized system of general surveyors and auditors, and using this fiscal apparatus
as an instrument of nationwide royal control. Yet this fiscal apparatus as a fundamen-

The assessment, collection, and administration of revenues and the handling of financial affairs in general required special skills and loyalty. The difficulties of recruiting civil servants with adequate skills and guaranteed loyalty are indicated by the fact that up to the end of the eighteenth century the farming out of taxes and the employment of private persons, particularly court Jews, for the management of the financial affairs of the ruling Houses remained in practice. Even obscure international adventurers and projectors like Giacomo Casanova were engaged by princely rulers or high governmental officials to solve fiscal problems, to handle financial transactions or to raise public loans (see Casanova 1965: chaps. II, VI). Sophistication and skill in fiscal and financial matters, as early as the Late Middle Ages, became a vehicle to run a career as court official or councillor without the traditionally required prerequisites in terms of birth and hereditary social rank. The fiscal branches of government were marked by a high degree of professionalization and, as far as the recruitment was concerned, by the early introduction of merit systems, professional qualification requirements and entrance examinations. The General Directory of Brandenburg-Prussia, in charge of fiscal affairs, employed the bulk of those who studied *"Staats- und Polizeiwissenschaft,"* i.e., a university curriculum which was designed for public service and dealt primarily with subjects related to fiscal matters. In the eighteenth century the orders of the Prussian kings as regards professional qualifications and training of public servants were mostly concerned with fiscal functions of the General Directory. Even the British government, which was marked by a relatively low degree of bureaucratization and professionalization of civil service, increasingly employed skilled professionals for fiscal, financial and trade matters, at least below the top level. The personnel of the Treasury and of the Board of Trade were

---

tal part of the royal bureaucracy could not develop into the nucleus of an all-controlling state machinery. The royal bureaucracy was dismantled in 1640–1641 and the Crown lands shrank to insignificance. Once more it should be emphasized that the geopolitical position of Britain had in direct and, even more, in manifold indirect ways an important influence upon public finance in general, the way the increasing financial needs could be met, the manner the revenue were spent, and, last but not least, upon the socioeconomic effects and side-effects of taxation and fiscal policy. In short, a naval, mercantile society like Britain in the eighteenth century could raise and bear public outlays in quite a different way and with quite different effects from those in Prussia. In Britain especially the public outlay for naval purposes as part of the military expenses had quite a different impact upon the economic development and the socioeconomic changes from the kind and magnitude of military costs that Prussian society had to bear.

being chosen more and more for their professional qualifications. The Treasury took the lead in employing new recruitment methods by examining candidates for entry, and placing them on a year's probation if accepted. It was particularly Gladstone as Chancellor of the Exchequer who urged the merit of open competition, condemned patronage and reformed the administrative machinery with the help of experts. Like the administrative reforms of Pitt the Younger in the last quarter of the eighteenth century, Gladstone's efforts to reform the civil service around the middle of the nineteenth century, which marked the beginning of a new kind of bureaucracy, were mainly motivated by the attempt to economize the public service and rationalize the government's finance (see Keir 1967: 425ff.; Deane 1967: 211ff.). Thus, public finance and the fiscal branches of the government had to be evaluated as one of the crucial means in the process of bureaucratization and the development of a modern civil service performed by skilled professionals. The efficiency and loyalty of these "technocrats" were rewarded by social rise and political power. By virtue of their public functions, their educational background and their advantages in terms of know-how and information about public affairs, they increasingly became a fairly homogeneous power elite, with which the old power elite had to enter coalitions in order to maintain its political influence and sociopolitical position. In short, public service directly or indirectly related to fiscal and financial affairs was a nursery for the emergence of new power groups.

Taxation is in many ways related to the last topic: food supply. The commutation of tithes in goods and services into money payment as well as the audit and accounting techniques, cadastral measuring and other methods of calculation in relation with the assessment and collection of direct taxes in the agrarian sector brought subsistence farming closer to the market, promoted the monetization and commercialization of the agrarian sector and, as a side-effect, induced a spirit of *Rechenhaftigkeit* (accountability). On the other hand, outdated schemes of taxation, particularly tithes in goods and services, could severely hamper the pace of agricultural adjustment and progress by preventing the introduction of new crops and new crop rotations or the innovation of new agricultural techniques. The cases of Britain and Brandenburg-Prussia provide ample illustrations of how the amount and the mode of extracting money, goods, and services from the various social groups which were engaged in

[318]

growing food, preparing food for the market and distributing food stuff, had an impact upon food supply and demand. This refers to direct taxes as well as indirect ones.

As far as the direct taxation is concerned the case of Britain shows that changes toward a growth- and market-oriented agricultural production could be reached despite the fact that the agrarian sector had to contribute a disproportionate share of direct taxes. The British land tax system had no built-in barriers against innovations, reforms and expansions. It was not, like the Prussian fiscal system, interconnected with the military and agrarian system, which reinforced and petrified each other and hindered the development of modern commercialized agricultural production. Moreover, England did not know, as Prussia did, the complex and in its economic effects very far-reaching system of the provision of various goods and services mostly but not exclusively for military purposes by the peasantry, for little or no payment, as part of its fiscal obligations —a system which remained vital until the end of the *Ancien Régime* and was even fortified and enlarged in some instances during the eighteenth century.[69] The British Land Tax, which grossly favored the larger landholders, in combination with the corn bounties and other acts of Parliament, especially the enclosure acts, formed a dynamic promoter for the development of large-scale commercialized farming. We might recall that the growth of agricultural production enabled Britain to meet the food demands of a rapidly growing population in the eighteenth century and to carry up to the middle of the nineteenth century the bulk of direct taxes. The Prussian tax reform of 1820 in turn favored again the agrarian provinces and the large landholders. Thus, the agrarian sector, dominated by the old power elite, the landed nobles, received a kind of forced development aid from those productive sectors and those provinces which struggled for the industrial "take-off." This is one of the indications that the coalition between the old power elite and the new one, the bureaucracy, was strengthened after 1820 (see Koselleck 1967: 529ff.). The main barriers to a modern commercialized agricultural production, however, were removed during and after the so-called Reform Period by changing the military, fiscal and, though in a slow process, the agrarian system.

Indirect taxation has an impact upon food supply from the side of demand: Customs and Excise duties on necessities as well as an in-

[69] See footnote 54 above.

flationary monetary policy of the state and other factors depressing real wages affected the nourishment pattern of the growing mass of people, who depended entirely for food supply upon their earning capacities. It is therefore no wonder that indirect taxation, formerly praised as a just means of distributing the tax load, became in the nineteenth century more and more a vital policy issue and the special target of the early working-class and labor movements in Britain and Prussia. Around the turn of the century Britain shifted from an exporter to an importer of grain. Hence, the corn bounties lost their functions and were abolished in 1814. New Corn Laws were introduced to protect the agricultural interest: "In 1815 the existing sliding scale of duties which permitted the imports of corn to vary with the market price was abandoned in favor of absolute prohibition up to a certain price level and duty-free admission above that price. For the next thirty years the Corn Laws were one of the key issues in British social and economic policy, a symbol of the conflict between rich and poor, between agriculture and manufacturing industry and between free trade and protection" (Deane 1967: 191). The movement for repeal of the Corn Laws (revised again in 1828) developed more and more into a "crusade" (Phyllis Deane), but was not successful until 1846, when a disastrous famine swept Britain and particularly Ireland. The repeal of the Corn Laws was the most dramatic and decisive step toward free trade.

This economic policy emerged in the 1820s after tariff rates had soared during the war and postwar years to reach a peak in 1822. But the lowering of the tariff duties could not go very far without an alternative source of revenue. The choice was the imposition, or rather reintroduction, of the income tax in 1842: "The income tax, originally called into existence as a weapon of war, was now to be used as an engine of peace. The repeal of the income tax in 1816 had delayed for many years commercial and financial reforms, its reimposition in 1842 gave them a great impetus" (Buxton 1888: vol. I, 55). It cleared the path for free trade policy and for redressing the inequal pressure of indirect taxation. In the following years the duties on a host of articles were dropped or lowered, culminating in the dramatic repeal of the Corn Laws in 1846.

Certainly, the lowering of the indirect tax burden gave perceptible relief to the laboring poor. Its yield and its proportion of the total revenues increased steadily; correspondingly, the proportion of indirect taxes fell, but amounted at the end of the nineteenth century still to half of the total revenue receipts. As an engine of fiscal reforms the income tax proved successful. At first temporary in nature it was renewed over and over again despite heavy opposition and eventually became a permanent institution. However, it seems no coincidence that a peacetime Income Tax was imposed at a time when wages at least of the upper strata of the working classes began to rise and the attitudes of the employers to living wages and subsistence theories had changed (see Coats 1958). It could therefore be expected that more and more wage earners would reach an income above the exempted minimum level (at first 150 pounds a year) and thus be available for this direct mode of taxation.

In Prussia the need to jettison a multitude of Customs and Excises was even greater than in Britain. The cost of their collection was high (in some instances they outweighed the extracted revenue), and they affected severely trade and commerce. However, the tax reform of 1820 introduced for the larger towns and cities a new indirect levy, the so-called *Mahl- und Schlachtsteuer* (Milling and Slaughter Tax or Corn and Meat Tax). This highly regressive form of taxation fell upon town and city people who had to buy their food. Consequently, they had to change their nourishment pattern by substituting high quality food, i.e., corn and meat, for lower quality food, particularly potatoes. Despite widespread and heavy criticism the *Mahl- und Schlachtsteuer* survived the tax reform of 1851.

Yet the Prussian tax reform of 1820 not only brought the urbanized laboring poor an immense tax burden, but also wrung out of the lower orders outside the larger towns and cities through a new direct tax, the so-called *Klassensteuer* (Class Tax), a highly disproportionate share of revenues. This *Klassensteuer*, designed as a four class-model (each of these four classes was soon divided into three subgroups) attempted to represent and, by the same token, to stabilize the prevailing social structure of the Prussian society. It was based on an anti-Estate concept inasmuch as it covered with few exceptions all subjects, even the civil servants.[70] The selective criteria were not birth but property, education and occupational functions. The effects of the *Klassensteuer* were manifold: the assessment practice, for example, brought the monied and landed interest as well as wealth and education closer together; manual work fell into the two

[70] Only the military personnel, the schoolmasters, the pastors, the midwives, and the *Standesherren*, as well as those who were covered with the *Mahl- und Schlachtsteuer*, were exempted (see von Beckerath 1912: 58).

lower tax-classes and thus was stigmatized. But the most important was that the *Klassensteuer* grossly favored the upper strata of society and hence widened the gap between rich and poor, and promoted pauperism. The lowest tax-class bore the bulk of the tax load, amounting in the years 1821–1826 to 43.3 percent of the total and rising to 49.4 percent in 1845. The share of the first class, on the other hand, was in the years 1821–1826 only 3.6 percent and rose slightly to 3.8 percent in 1845. An indication of increasing poverty may be seen in the fact that the contribution of the lowest subgroup of the lowest main class rose steadily: from 18.2 percent in the years 1821–1826 to 22.9 percent in 1848. The reports of the fiscal organs in the years preceding the revolution of 1848 were full of complaints about the difficulties of collecting the taxes of the laboring poor, even when the hardest measures were applied (see von Beckerath 1912: 15ff.; Koselleck 1967: 537ff.).

The creator of the new tax system of 1820, J. G. Hoffmann, motivated the immense tax burden of the working classes and the lower order of society with an educational goal. The masses should bear the main tax load in order to take an interest in the affairs of state and to become implanted with a spirit of public responsibility and obligation (Koselleck 1967: 534). This educational function as a rationalization of the grossly regressive direct and indirect mode of taxation sounds rather ironic considering the fact that the lower strata of Prussian society traditionally had to bear the bulk of taxes, were subject to a selective conscription system, and, most important, lacked political compensations for their obligations and duties: they still were underprivileged in terms of political participation.

The longer it was in effect, the more the tax system of 1820 came to be a sociopolitical leavening ferment, which added considerably to the unrests climaxing in the "mad year" of 1848. A revision of this tax system was widely discussed in the years preceding the revolution. The liberal movement used it as a political means in the struggle for still unfulfilled constitutional promises. A certain success could be expected: in 1846 a royal order promised to summon the *Vereinigte Landtag* (Joint Provincial Assemblies) for the central purpose of a tax reform. Governmental officials prepared a new concept of taxation. With a view to the British tax reform of 1842 (imposition of the Income Tax), the governmental plan attempted to supplement the old scheme of direct taxation by an income tax for the wealthier. In 1847 the *Vereinigte Landtag* met, rejected the gov-

ernmental proposal, and begged the king to be presented with a revised version. This decision of the *Vereinigte Landtag* proved decisive in preventing a drastic reform of the Prussian system of direct
taxation for decades. Social upheaval broke out and was suppressed
by military force; a constitution was imposed from above, and soon
afterward, likewise imposed from above, a provisional census-suffrage for both Assemblies was instituted (a high census for the First
Assembly and the so-called *Dreiklassenwahlrecht* for the Second Assembly). With taxation liabilities as criteria for enfranchisement and
graduated political participation, the discussion and struggle about
tax reforms became linked with the discussion and struggle about a
permanent system of suffrage and hence became a central political
issue. At first, only these political functions and not fiscal ones were
the pivotal point. On the basis of the proposal of 1847, the government again worked out plans for introducing an income tax; even a
progressive scale (from 3 percent to 5 percent) was suggested. However, these plans met with heavy opposition. Particularly the reactionary First Assembly proved to be an obstacle. In 1850 financial
distresses added fiscal motives to the political ones; for both political
and fiscal reasons a quick decision was now crucial. The landed nobility, high finance and the wealthier business groups could in
this situation water down the governmental plans, because without
their support, no taxation bill could pass the Assemblies, especially
not the first one (*Herrenhaus*). The result was that the new tax system which was approved in 1851 by the two Assemblies was nothing
more than a shadow of the governmental plans: the *Mahl- und
Schlachtsteuer* was not repealed. As regards the direct taxes a revised *Klassensteuer* covered incomes under 1000 *thalers* a year; for
incomes above this level a so-called *klassifizierte Einkommenssteuer*
(Classified Income Tax, scaled in thirty steps) was introduced (the
amount of tax liability in the highest class of this Classified Income
Tax was 600 *thalers* a year). The new tax system of 1851 brought
some changes toward a more equal distribution of the tax load, but
was still to a high degree regressive in nature and favored particularly the highest income groups, i.e., those which at the same time
gained the most in terms of political participation and influence. The
members of the First Assembly were no longer elected by a census-
suffrage but chosen for lifetime by the King. The members of the
Second Assembly were elected by the *Dreiklassenwahlrecht*, a system
of census-suffrage, which increasingly favored the landed nobility

and the well-to-do generally. Erwin von Beckerath writes: "The stricter the principle was applied to base political rights on tax liabilities, the more the plutocratic character of the *Dreiklassenwahlrecht* became evident. Until the early 1890s a step forward in terms of taxation meant at the same time a step back as regards the political structure of the society" (von Beckerath 1912: 93f.).

We cannot enlarge upon this theme: a whole set of changes in connection with the new constitution of 1848 followed in the realms of the judiciary; the military system; the provincial, communal, and municipal administrations; the educational system; and the redemption of traditional obligations of the peasants, to mention only a few. Nor do we have space to sketch the sociopolitical developments in Britain. Our brief outline of the Prussian tax reforms of 1820 and 1851 was primarily intended to guide us back to the general remarks of the introduction by illuminating once more the multifunctional character of fiscal policy.

Long before the great turmoil and reshuffle of the French Revolution and the Napoleonic era, taxation had ceased, in practice if not in theory, to be a voluntary contribution for times of emergency. With more or less popular acquiescence, and more or less arbitrary in nature, taxes had become a regular and compulsory institution at least for most of the subjects. In the nineteenth century, however, the duty to pay taxes universally became defined as part of the new civil obligations and was established firmly in the new constitutional settings. This constitutional anchorage together with the emergence of a wave of national solidarity on the one hand, and the development of more sophisticated techniques and institutions for assessing and collecting the various levies, for handling public debts and managing public finance on the other, clearly enhanced the "presumption of solvency" of the state and hence eased the extraction problems (Mann 1933–1934: 16).

As we indicated earlier, a divergence existed between the new set of civil obligations and the new set of civil rights and sociopolitical benefits. The postrevolution period up to the twentieth century became marked by contests for redistribution of these two sets. By virtue of its multifunctional character fiscal policy played a decisive role in this struggle. Thus, let us close this essay by travelling along this "functional rope."

The social function of taxation and fiscal policy, so widely discussed in the mercantilistic-cameralistic literature in relation with the goal to shape the social structure into the "just" proportion, was approached in the nineteenth century with quite different aims. More and more it was seen as a means for equalizing social class differences and as a tool of social reforms to mitigate the social costs of industrialization and economic changes. True, this role of taxation and fiscal policy was questioned and opposed by the ruling classes, particularly those who represented the monied interest. As part of their *laissez-faire* doctrine they denied the function of taxes as instruments of social reforms and social control; they advocated the so-called Leave-them-as-you-find-them-rule: taxes should have purely fiscal goals, which was, of course, a purposeful fiction (Mann 1933–1934: 4). In the long run, however, the social role of taxation and fiscal policy gained ground in theory and practice. Especially since the middle of the nineteenth century, a redistribution of the fiscal burdens can be recognized in the direction of a less regressive and later on, as far as direct taxes were concerned, even progressive taxation. By developing the system of direct taxes, the income and wealth of the well-to-do people could more adequately be tapped. Admittedly, this was a slow process marked with setbacks (not to speak of the manifold possibilities of legal and illegal tax evasion by the rich). This trend was fortified by the expenditure side of fiscal policy. Increasingly the state used its receipts for social overhead investments: education, public health, social welfare, and so forth. Public spending of this kind might be called "progressive" in nature, because those who pay less taxes are the main beneficiaries of this outlay. At the same time, however, public spending in the field of infrastructural developments increased: canals, turnpikes, railways, harbors, navy, and so forth. These are investments which certainly can be regarded as being in the interest of the commonweal; yet they usually bring more direct and indirect gains for the monied and landed interest and might therefore be called "regressive" in nature. In short, it is hard to evaluate how far overall public spending actually supported the goal of redistributing income and wealth by taxation and fiscal policy. In any case, the ruling classes had ample possibilities to subsidize their increased share of tax burden by influencing the public outlay.

Since they were usually not a homogeneous group in terms of economic and therefore fiscal interest, the ruling classes used both the receipt and expenditure side of fiscal policy to find balanced settlements of these diverging interests. The compromises were crucial in order to act jointly as a political power elite. This indicates the reciprocal relationships between the social and the two other functions of taxation and fiscal policy: the political and economic.

The political functions of taxation and fiscal policy became particularly evident in the constitutional contests of the nineteenth century. Tax reform, the ceiling of the guaranteed public debt and the question of budget control were crucial in the struggle for increased representation of the people. This refers to the relationship between government and legislative bodies. As regards changes in the system of suffrage and political participation, fiscal affairs were likewise important. In Britain the fiscal reforms of the 1840s had to be seen against the background of the parliamentary reform of 1832 with its extension of the franchise and its redistribution of seats. The parliamentary reforms of 1867 and 1884, which brought further extensions of the franchise left also their marks in the field of fiscal policy. The claims of the newly enfranchised groups of the lower strata of society enhanced the pressure for more distributive justice of both the revenue and the expenditure side of fiscal policy. Yet the Prussian case indicates that fiscal policy has a Janus-face: it can look both ways. The Prussian tax reforms of the nineteenth century serve as examples of how changes of tax systems could be connected with the limitation of the franchise, the graduation of political participation, and the preservation of privileged political positions.

We might recall that the cameralistic government attempted to shape the economy in the "just," i.e., proportionate structure with the help of fiscal policy. The receipt and expenditure side were supposed to serve as tools for extracting and redistributing blood from and to the organs of the body. In practice this meant that the economic life was marked by a whole network of governmental regulations, restrictions, controls and interferences. In addition, the government itself took an active part in the economic life by managing its "own" resources: the domains, mine- or saltworks and even manufacturing enterprises. The classical economic theories rejected this role of the state and its corresponding economic functions of fiscal policy. Economic activities of the state were branded as unproductive. The "Leave-them-as-you-find-them-rule" referred to economic as well as social matters. Of course, this was likewise a purposeful fiction; fiscal policy always affects the economy. The wide reception and the durability of these maxims are well known. They had a great impact upon fiscal policy in the nineteenth century, and their influence can be felt up to the present time. They served not only as a rationalization of the ruling classes to oppose the encroachment of economic life by government (where such governmental interference was unwanted), but also provided the chief motivation in keeping the "public hand" poor. Indeed, one of the characteristic features of public finance of our era (disregarding the socialist countries) is the fact that the "public hand" remains poor and the public debt is mounting despite an immense increase of public revenue.

On the other hand, a trend towards increased state interference into economic life has to be recognized. The economic depressions of the late nineteenth century and the war economy of the First World War set the pace; the worldwide economic crisis of the early 1930s, the reception of new economic theories and the war and postwar economic problems brought the final breakthrough. "Planned Economy" lost a good deal of its stigma. Both the receipt and expenditure side of fiscal policy became chief instruments of the anticyclical steering mechanism of the government.

We have attempted to show some interrelations among taxation, public finance, sociopolitical structure and modern state-building. According to Schumpeter, "the public finances are one of the best starting points for an investigation of society, especially though not exclusively of its political life. . . . The spirit of a people, its cultural level, its social structure, the deeds its policy may prepare—all this and more is written in its fiscal history, stripped of all phrases. He who knows how to listen to the message here discerns the thunder of world history more clearly than anywhere else" (J. Schumpeter 1954: 7). It is the multifunctional character of fiscal policy which gives this approach its central place in the analysis of sociopolitical structure and modern state-building, both in terms of "the causal importance of fiscal policy (in so far as fiscal events are an important element in the causation of all change) and of the symptomatic significance (in so far as everything that happens has its fiscal reflection)" (J. Schumpeter 1954: 7).

CHAPTER 5

THE POLICE AND POLITICAL DEVELOPMENT IN EUROPE

DAVID H. BAYLEY

THE PURPOSE OF this chapter is to explore the relationship between the police and political development during the growth of modern European nation-states. Great Britain, France, Germany, and Italy have been chosen for comparison. Four questions will be answered in the course of the analysis: (1) What is the character of the police system in each country? (2) When did these contemporary police systems emerge? (3) What factors account for the emergence and rate of development of these systems? and (4) What factors account for the characteristic solutions each country found for its modern police problems?

Specification of the nature of police is not as easy as it might seem. Organizations called police perform different functions in different countries; different organizations in the same country carry out police duties; police units handle nonpolice duties just as police duties are handled by nonpolice personnel. In order to cut through this tangle of divergent and imprecise usage, it is necessary to delineate the central preoccupation of this paper, that is, what I shall consider the core of "police" activity. The focus of this chapter will be upon the mandate to regulate interpersonal relations within a community through the applications of coercive sanctions authorized in the name of the community. A police force is an organization authorized by a collectivity to regulate social relations within itself by utilizing, if need be, physical force. Therefore, when the word police is used it should be understood in terms of a particular function and not in terms of a given body of men. The definition is most important for what it excludes. Social regulation, after all, is accomplished by a host of community agencies, from health departments to taxing authorities. By and large only the police have an explicit mandate to use physical force in order to resolve disputes or to enforce community directives. Similarly, individuals are commonly accorded the right to defend themselves by physical means, but they would hardly be considered as policemen when they do so. An army is publicly constituted to use force, just as police are, but its jurisdiction is external to the collectivity. An army uses force to defend a community from threats outside itself; a police force protects against threats from within.

When one studies the performance of a task comparatively among different countries, what should one study? The key analytic problem in this chapter is to pose questions which are both important and meaningful comparatively. For example, one might begin by trying to determine when a police system was created in each nation. This is not, it turns out, a very helpful start. Policing is ubiquitous in human society. One would be hard-pressed to find a society where interpersonal relations were regulated either wholly privately or without recourse to physical force. In modern Europe police agencies antedate most other institutions. What is more, it is difficult, as we shall see later, to characterize informatively police arrangements that were replaced by contemporary police systems; public vs. private or state vs. nonstate does not get at a meaningful difference. Another way of providing a meaningful comparative perspective would be to stipulate a particular kind of police system and determine whether developments in various nations have converged toward the model. Is there perhaps such a thing as a modern police system? When did each nation develop such a system? Can it be compared with a traditional or a premodern one? This too is not a very helpful formulation. National police systems are constituted in importantly different ways; each one exhibits unique features requiring explanation. By fitting diverse situations into a Procrustean mold, loss of empirical richness is assured.

In order to meet this problem of describing change meaningfully among disparate systems performing a similar function, I propose to use as a baseline for comparison in each country the nature of each police system as it exists today. This procedure avoids having to determine whether, and then when, each of these systems underwent a generic shift in character from a traditional to a modern system, an underdeveloped to a developed system, a preindustrial to an industrial system, or an unstructured to a bureaucratic system. It may be true that major characterological changes have occurred. This approach does not preclude finding them. If there are common patterns of development, they will become apparent. If there are not, change can still be described, but in this case with reference to explaining what exists contemporaneously rather than what exists only theoretically. In this way empirical diversity is preserved while a meaningful comparative question is answered, namely, when and how did each nation's police system get to be as it is.

It might be argued against this approach that if the entities to be compared are significantly different today, then analysis is almost bound to find few similarities and only unique national differences. This criticism is overdone. Though it is true that this approach assumes a priori that these national systems have nothing in common except their contemporary existence, it does not preclude determining whether their respective development is on a converging course. Indeed, the converse of this formulation is to assume that they are all similar in some respect, for example, modernity, and then to constrain analysis to find similarity in patterns of development. The question of convergence is logically distinct from the question of how several systems developed. Moreover, analysis can be more responsive to unique patterns of national development by disengaging the question of convergence from that of the nature of historical development.

This procedure would not be useful if any of these countries recently experienced a revolutionary shift in police modality, for the baseline of comparison would be unstable. Longevity is the only warrant for concluding that particular features are characteristic. In fact, none of these systems has undergone a major change in the way policing has been performed in the past generation and indeed —with the exception of Germany—in the past half century. The permanence of institutional police patterns in each of these countries is one of the most important findings of this study.

The Character of Contemporary Police Systems

In the following descriptions of the police systems of Great Britain, France, Germany, and Italy, five points of differentiation will be covered: (1) tasks and responsibilities, (2) structure of the national system, (3) nature of accountability, (4) internal organization, and (5) role behavior and professional image.[1] Since the range of descriptive dimensions is very great, any set is incomplete and its adequacy arguable. One dimension particularly is noteworthy by its absence: there is no measure of the efficiency with which policing is accomplished. Surely the most important characterization to be

[1]To facilitate comparison Figure 5–1 (p. 341) summarizes the characteristics of each nation's system.

made deals with the extent to which a police system performs its central function well. While this is true, adequate measurement of efficiency is difficult methodologically; moreover, the effort would be misleading. The perceived need for police varies over time. Police in Cromwell's time were required to be preoccupied with prevention of blasphemy and the keeping of the sabbath; police in Edward Heath's time are required to be stern with drug-takers and violators of motor-vehicle regulations. Prussian police in the eighteenth century enforced residence requirements on peasants and artisans, while police in the Bonn Republic must defend the right of employees to organize and strike. An efficient police in one age is an irrelevant police in another. Crime is a function of social values, hence so is police efficiency. Even if one could determine an unchangeable human need in successive generations which always fell within the domain of the police function, such as the defense of life against unprovoked attack, data simply do not exist which would allow a test for efficiency. Crime statistics, for example, are notoriously unstable and they are of fairly recent invention. Furthermore, the relation between crime statistics and police efficiency is complex: more efficient police forces may have higher crime rates precisely because they know of and record more crimes; a crime prevented may be attributable to police activity or to social circumstances over which they had no control. Finally, due to differences in legal codes even in the present day, international comparisons are highly questionable.

The police function in Great Britain is carried out by forty-nine separate police forces (Critchley 1967: 311–312).[2] Though the personnel of each force is bound in their professional actions by statutory regulations and the Common Law, there is no single authority in the country that can command them in their day-to-day activities. They are led, deployed, and disciplined by local officers. The commanding officers, known as Chief Constables everywhere except London, are accountable to local political bodies: in towns to the Watch Committees and in counties to the Standing Joint Committees.[3] Membership on each committee is composed of two-thirds of elected members of

[2] These figures include England and Wales, but not Scotland, as of 1966. The forces ranged in size from 700 to 7,000 policemen. In 1960 there were 125 forces in England and Wales (Royal Commission 1962: Cmnd. 1728, p. 6). The amalgamations were a direct result of the recommendations of the Royal Commission.

[3] The designation "Standing Joint Committee" is no longer generally used. These bodies are now called "Police Committees." This change in nomenclature occurred in the last few years.

the Town Council and County Council, respectively, and one-third of appointed magistrates.[4] The central government has police authority only in London, where responsibility is in the hands of the Home Secretary who appoints the Commissioner of the London Metropolitan Police. Within any jurisdiction police agency is singular. There is only one police force in each locality and specialization occurs within that organization.

The British system is decentralized in command but unified in its practices. This has been accomplished by statutory direction and through the power of the Home Secretary to inspect local forces and withhold financial support if the force is not judged up to par. Since the central government's grant amounts to half the cost of the force, its bargaining power is considerable.

The extent of police responsibilities is narrow in Great Britain. They are similar to American conceptions of police work, dealing largely with maintenance of law and order, the protection of persons and property, and the prevention of crime. British police officials do not have the power to issue ordinances having the force of law;[5] nor do they undertake regulatory work unrelated to offenses under the criminal law.[6] Their most demanding noncriminal responsibility is the regulation of motor-vehicle traffic.

Day-to-day regulation of political activities by English policemen has been very slight. By and large they respond reactively; initiative is not, and has not been, theirs. Political intelligence is collected by

[4] Until the Police Act, 1964, all members of Watch Committees were elected members of the Town Council. Membership of Standing Joint Committees had been composed half of elected members of the County Council and half of appointed magistrates.

[5] This power does belong to the Commissioner of the London Metropolitan Police by virtue of his having the powers of a magistrate as well.

[6] Royal Commission 1962: 22, summarizes the responsibilities of the police in eight points: "First, the police have a duty to maintain law and order and to protect persons and property. Secondly, they have a duty to prevent crime. Thirdly, they are responsible for the detection of criminals and, in the course of interrogating suspected persons, they have a part to play in the early stages of the judicial process, acting under judicial restraint. Fourthly, the police in England and Wales (but not in Scotland) have the responsibility of deciding whether or not to prosecute persons suspect of criminal offences. Fifthly, in England and Wales (but not in Scotland) the police themselves conduct many prosecutions for the less serious offences. Sixthly, the police have the duty of controlling road traffic and advising local authorities on traffic questions. Seventhly, the police carry out certain duties on behalf of Government Departments—for example, they conduct enquiries into applications made by persons who wish to be granted British nationality. Eighthly, they have by long tradition a duty to befriend anyone who needs their help, and they may at any time be called upon to cope with minor or major emergencies."

the police, and fairly systematically. This work is performed by the Special Branch of the Criminal Investigation Division (C.I.D.).

The uniformed personnel of the British police are selected according to a single set of recruitment procedures. Except in London, top command officers are uniformed police personnel. Chief Constables, as they are known, have almost all attained their positions by promotion from Constable. The only exceptions are in some rural counties, though the practice of promoting nonpolice officers as Chief Constable even here is declining. In London the highest uniformed rank is that of Superintendent. Superintendents are in charge of major regions within London. Until recently the Commissioner was chosen from outside the police establishment, as by and large were his Deputies and Assistants.

Recruit training, apart from simple military drill, was not established in Britain until 1907 (Stead 1957: 139). It now amounts to an initial course of thirteen weeks plus two two-week refresher courses later on (Critchley 1967: 245–246). Special training for higher ranks was begun in 1948. It is an object of considerable suspicion among British policemen who fear the development of an elite corps within the force (Critchley 1967: 249). The primary functional division within the police is between crime prevention and crime investigation.[7] Detectives are recruited from the ranks of the regular police.

The most difficult dimension of any police system to characterize is the role behavior of its personnel and its professional image. Yet no other attribute is more important to the man-in-the-street. I shall try to present a general characterization for each country. It is important to recognize, however, that the material has often been gleaned from reading between lines, from asides and innuendo. In very few countries have the reputations of police forces been carefully studied employing modern surveying techniques. Britain is one of the few exceptions. The Royal Commission, 1962, not only undertook a large public opinion survey, it devoted considerable space in its final report to police-public relations. Presenting a stereotype of the policeman for any country immediately suggests that opinion about the police is homogeneous. This is rarely the case. Though I believe it is fair to make comparisons among the police of different nations, there are also crucial differences of opinion within nations,

[7] The famed Scotland Yard is the headquarters for the London Metropolitan Police. It is not a national criminal investigation unit, though it often lends assistance to other forces when it is asked.

among classes, ethnic groups, and regions. Often these are as great as differences between nations.

The British police are generally perceived as being honest, approachable, trustworthy, and helpful. They are viewed with respect and an admixture of affection. Generally they work as individuals, not in groups. They carry no firearms, and are commonly nonauthoritative and nonpunitive.

The French police system provides a sharp contrast to the British in almost all respects. The French system is completely centralized. Not only on regulations and procedures identical throughout the country, but the Ministry of the Interior has authority to direct police operations in every corner of the land. Policing is conceived as a responsibility of national government.

For practical reasons operational control of the police cannot be exercised from the Paris officers of the Ministry of the Interior. It is delegated to the Prefects of France's ninety (Ridley and Blondel 1965: 88) Departments and from them to Mayors or *Commissaires* in Communes.[8] The *Commissaire* is the chief of police of the Commune; he is responsible both to the Prefect and to the Mayor, though the Mayor himself can be held accountable by the Prefect for police work. There are three distinct police forces in France, not just one as in England. First, there is the *Police Nationale*, which is the civil police force of the central government. Policing in all Communes with a population of over 10,000 is carried out by the *Police Nationale*. Second, in Communes with less than 10,000 inhabitants the Mayor and the Communal Council may create their own police force.[9] Finally, there is the *Gendarmerie*, which is responsible for policing in rural areas where mobility may be important and where the Communes are unwilling to provide adequate forces of their own. Personnel of the *Gendarmerie* are recruited and paid by the Ministry of War, though they are directed in their police work by the Prefects and the Ministry of the Interior. Units of the *Gendarmerie* are posted to all Departments as a reserve police force. The *Garde Mobile*, which is an armed force for riot operations, and the *Garde Républicaine*, which is wholly ceremonial and stationed in Paris, are both units of the *Gendarmerie*.

Police in France are directed by a larger civilian bureaucracy

[8] There are 38,000 Communes in France. A Commune is roughly equivalent to a township in the United States (Ridley and Blondel 1965).
[9] These are the *Gardes champêtres* of rural areas.

than is the case in Great Britain, but they are much farther removed from supervision by elected legislative bodies. Representative supervision exists only through the national Parliament which can call to account the Minister of the Interior. The actions of individual French policemen must be conformable to law. Determination of illegality, however, is made by administrative courts. The French legal system is bifurcated, as is the case in Germany and Italy; one set of courts determines matters of right and privilege between individuals, the other determines the propriety and legality of matters involving the state and the citizen.

Just as the police of London bear a special relation to the central government, so the policing of Paris is constituted somewhat differently than in the rest of the country. In the Department of the Seine, in which Paris is located, the Prefect has been stripped of his police powers; they have been entrusted to the Prefect of Police, as it were a specialized Prefect for police affairs.[10] The Prefect of Police is directly responsible to the Ministry of the Interior; there is no elected Mayor of Paris, and the Municipal Council can withhold funds from the Prefect, but it cannot direct him to perform specific actions. Because of its size and importance, the police of Paris have often tried to become self-regulating, to minimize their links with the Ministry of the Interior, and to aggrandize their influence outside of Paris. Conflict between the police of Paris and the Sûreté has been common.

Police power in France, as well as elsewhere on the continent, is constitutionally indistinguishable from the authority to govern. *Police Générale* refers to the power of government to make binding regulations in the interests of public order and security. It may involve criminal matters, as they would be defined in the United States or Great Britain, or it may encompass more general directions, such as supervision of newspapers and films, control of epidemics, licensing of building construction, control of foreigners, and inspection of asylums and certain children's institutions (Chapman 1953: 506–507). Authority to govern in France is all inclusive and centralized. Since the Prefect is responsible for law and order, as the agent of the central government, many commentators have come to the conclusion that the work of uniformed police personnel is broader than in Eng-

[10] This post was first created in 1800. Until recently the Prefect of Police was responsible for police in all Communes of the Seine Department. Under the terms of a recent reorganization, the Prefect of Police has authority only within Paris.

land and the United States. In the past they were assigned to more distinct formal tasks than were the police in Great Britain. At the same time, they have never been encouraged to undertake the informal work of mediation, assistance, and advising that has been a stock-in-trade of the British or American policeman. Generally the police today are used in France in much the same formal ways as they are in Anglo-Saxon countries; specialization of function has resulted in giving off tasks not immediately related to criminal work. However, there are some administrative tasks performed by police agents which are uncommon in England, such as granting passports, surveying dangerous buildings, scrutinizing prices and the quality of produce, and inspecting factory premises (Stead 1957: 168). The Prefect and the Mayor do have a larger charter of action than any Commissioner or Chief Constable; they are central administrative officials and may issue regulations (*arrêtés*) on a wide variety of subjects.

The police of France have been heavily engaged in politics since their creation. Though this activity has probably declined in the twentieth century—certainly it is less obvious and more restrained— the police continue to be objects of great suspicion by political parties of both left and right. The police are known to keep a very close watch on political opinion and activity. French policemen admit to being able to penetrate most political organizations, regardless of how clandestine these may be. Political intelligence is handled by the *Renseignements Généraux* and counterespionage by the *Surveillance du Territoire*. The police have been sorely tested in France in recent years with respect to maintaining public order. Mundane police dispositions reflect the challenges they face. Paris police lorries are equipped with steel side-panels so that they may be used in barricading broad avenues. London police have nothing comparable.

Until recently officers of the *Police Nationale*, as well as the *Gendarmerie*, were not promoted from the ranks; rather, they were recruited and trained separately as officers. Officers had to have university degrees. This was also the case in Germany and Italy. Now, however, it is possible for lower ranks to take the officer candidate examination, though they must do so before they are thirty-five years of age. Though historically French officers have had higher academic qualifications than their British counterparts, command responsibilities of French officers have been more limited in scope.

[336]

The highest rank for a French officer is that of *Commissaire*. Such individuals have jurisdiction in Communes, which are fairly small areas. They are subordinate to mayors and prefects. French officers are also more closely supervised by a civilian bureaucracy, while the British officers are more closely involved with representative political bodies.

The primary functional division within the police is between the *Police Administrative* and the *Police Judiciaire*: the former handles crime prevention, i.e., patrolling and routine police work, the latter crime investigation. The Ministry of the Interior since 1945 has had its own paramilitary reserves in the *Compagnies Républicaines de Sécurité* (CRS).

Formal training for police officers and men was established in France in 1883 (Stead 1957: 139).

The French police have a reputation for being efficient, indefatigable, and omniscient. They are considered individually to be brusque and rather unapproachable. They are armed, feared, and disliked, though they are not considered especially corrupt.

In West Germany policing is the responsibility of the state of the Federal Republic.[11] This represents a return to the practice of the Weimar period and the Second Reich and a renunciation of the experiment with national responsibility which was tried during the Hitler era. The Bonn government can legislate in any field except education and cultural affairs; thus it can establish principles for the regulation of police agencies. For field administration, however, it has few cadres of its own and must rely upon the bureaucracies of the ten states (Jacob 1963: 162–163). Thus, German police are overwhelmingly state police, accountable to legislatures in each state. The central government maintains only a border police force and a reserve riot force for use in emergencies; it also operates certain forensic establishments and has a small criminal investigation staff for exclusively federal offenses.[12] Operational control is exercised through the mayor in towns or the *Landrat* in rural areas. The *Landrat* presides over county-size units, much like an Indian district officer or a French Prefect, though the *Landrat*'s powers are not so

[11] The police of East Germany are centralized, as they have been since 1946. I have made no attempt to study police organization and practices in East Germany. Attention will be given in this paper only to Prussia, the Second Reich, Weimar, and the Bonn Republic.

[12] This is the Federal Criminal Police Bureau (Jacob 1963). See also Finer 1962: 531–532.

extensive as the Prefect's. The *Landrat* exercises his police authority as an agent of the Ministry of the Interior of his particular state.

The *Landrat* will have at his disposal a state police force and a *Gendarmerie* for use primarily in rural areas. Most states also maintain a heavily armed reserve that receives military training and lives in barracks. The German police make a sharp distinction between officers and men. Recruitment is by competitive examination at different levels of the rank hierarchy. Uniformed command personnel are closely supervised by a civilian bureaucracy, much like their French counterparts.

German policemen are accountable not only to state legislatures, democratically elected after 1949, but to the law. Adjudication of cases against policemen for actions taken in the line-of-duty is handled by administrative courts.

German police authorities have possessed vast rule-making power in the past. Though it is less great than before World War II, it is still substantial. I am unable to provide a precise measure of its extent in comparison with police of other nations. Though the *Landrat*, like the Prefect, presides over all the executive functions of government, the police are given a more specialized set of tasks. They are undoubtedly more extensive than the British and probably more than the French. The state police are divided functionally between criminal police and ordinary police—the one not uniformed, the other uniformed. Within the criminal police division separate offices specialize in particular kinds of crime, such as homicide, burglary, auto theft, and so forth. This pattern is general now among European police forces.

German police were heavily involved in politics in the nineteenth century. This is much less true today. They seem to have adopted the stance of neutral referee, a tradition begun though interrupted during the Weimar period. They undoubtedly collect political intelligence and have a substantial capacity with respect to counterespionage.

German policemen are trusted and honest. They are also formal, rather rigid, and authoritarian in manner. They are not known for approachability. They are armed and do not have a reputation for effective informal mediation.

The police system of Italy is highly centralized; it is also plural, in the sense that there are several forces. The two primary police forces are the *Guardia de Pubblica Sicurezza* (P.S.) and the *Corps de*

Carabinieri. Towns are permitted to raise their own police, known as *Vigili Urbani,* which enforce municipal laws and regulate traffic. Police operations are directed by the Ministry of the Interior through the Prefects of Italy's eighty-eight provinces (Fried 1963: 275). The Prefect is assisted by the *Questore,* who is in effect the provincial chief of police. The *Questore,* like the Prefect, is appointed by the Ministry of the Interior. There is no local political accountability; popular control is exercised only through the national Parliament.

Though the P.S. and the *Carabinieri* are both under the direction of the Ministry of the Interior, they are quite distinct and can properly be considered rivals in the field of police operations.[13] The *Carabinieri* are part of the army; they are recruited, trained, and paid by the Ministry of War. When assigned to police duties, they come under the control of the Ministry of the Interior. In theory the P.S. are given responsibility for normal police duties, both criminal investigation and prevention, while the *Carabinieri* are held in reserve for dealing with problems of public order and security. In fact, the *Carabinieri* also do criminal investigation work as well as political surveillance. Both forces are jealous of their prerogatives and like to demonstrate superior ability over the other. The *Carabinieri* is heavily armed, military in bearing and training, and stratified between officers and men. The P.S., too, is very martial in training; its officers are taken from the army, though they are required to have law degrees and to undergo special training (Cramer 1964: 327–331).

Italian police officers are subject to the law, though adjudication is performed by administrative courts.

The Prefect and the *Questore* have ordinance-making authority. The P.S. especially carries out a greater range of tasks than English police. I am unable to differentiate Italian from French or German police in this regard. Italian police in the nineteenth century played a shamelessly political role. Though they are somewhat more subtle today, they find it difficult to remain above politics for long. This is especially true in the industrial areas of the north and in the "Red Belt" north of Rome. Violence and agitation are commonplace; involvement by police officials is mandatory (Fried 1963: 250–252).

Italian police are considered corrupt, punitive, and unscrupulous.

---

[13] Luigi Barzini (Barzini 1964: 215–216), for example, says that they have been carrying on "a running feud for more than a century." Many Italians, he says, consider their antagonism the best safeguard of the citizen's liberties.

They are feared and disliked. One would not consider going to them for assistance except in time of great stress. They are armed.

It should be obvious now that the diversity among the police forces of Great Britain, France, Germany, and Italy is substantial. The structure of national systems ranges from marked decentralization and local control to extreme centralization and total absence of local control. In one system political control by elected representatives over uniformed personnel is close and direct; in other systems it is screened through layers of civilian bureaucrats. Three countries stratify police between officers and men; two build the police on military lines; all of them specialize according to function within the police. Uniformed police handle very much the same kind of work in all countries, though on the continent their immediate civilian superiors have considerable ordinance-making authority and may direct police into activities that would be considered exceptional in Britain. Some police forces are heavy-handed and set apart from the people; others are trusted and approachable; others are incorruptible and respected; and some are called upon for informal mediation while others are studiously avoided. Quite clearly vigorous national police systems have developed in importantly different ways; these differences will require explanation (see Figure 5–1).

Emergence of National Police Systems

When did the characteristics of these contemporary police systems emerge in recognizable form and what factors account for the timing as well as the rate of subsequent development? The concern in this section will be exclusively with explaining the timing of development. Analysis of the factors which gave each country its unique police features is a separable matter to be taken up in the following section. The first task now is to pinpoint historically the point at which today's characteristics emerged in each country. The second task is to compare political and social processes in each country at these times in order to determine whether similar factors led to the development of national police systems.

Unfortunately for the facilitation of analysis, each police system did not emerge full-blown at a single moment in time. Some features developed earlier than others. Moreover, single features matured over time, surfacing and submerging, so that it is often difficult to say when exactly a particular feature became confirmed in national life. In France, for example, the structure of today's system may be

	Great Britain	France	Germany	Italy
1. Tasks				
a. Formal	Narrow	Extensive	Extensive	Extensive
b. Informal	Extensive	Some	Few	None
c. Political	Very Modest	Modest, Extensive Intelligence	Modest	Extensive
2. National Structure				
a. Nature of Authority Aggregation	Decentralized	Centralized	Decentralized	Centralized
b. Number of Distinct Forces	Singular	Plural	Singular	Plural
3. Nature of Control				
a. Political	Local, Representative	Central, Bureaucratic	Local, Bureaucratic	Central, Bureaucratic
b. Legal	Subject to Unified Legal Code	Subject to Administrative Court System	Subject to Administrative Court System	Subject to Administrative Court System
4. Internal Organization				
a. Rank Organization	Singular	Bifurcated	Bifurcated	Bifurcated
b. Training	Civilian	Civilian	Military	Military
c. Functional Specialization	Considerable	Considerable	Considerable	Considerable
5. Role Behavior and Image				
a. Perceived Character	Trustworthy, Approachable, Respected	Distrusted, Unapproachable, Efficient	Authoritarian, Unapproachable, Honest	Feared, Corrupt, Quixotic
b. Mode of Intervention	Individual, Informal	Formal	Formal, in Groups	Punitive, in Groups
c. Armament	None	Armed	Armed	Armed

Figure 5–1. Structure of National Police Systems

discerned in the late seventeenth century. Even its essential bureaucratic organization can be found at that time. Yet the civil constabulary was not uniformed until 1829 and its period of greatest expansion was probably the middle of the nineteenth century. The development of the characteristics of today's systems emerged over a period of about two centuries. As a result, though one can discern first appearances, the timing of the development of police systems cannot be considered an exact science.

The problem can be made somewhat more manageable by focusing upon only a few of the features of today's systems. The features which are most central to the concerns of political scientists are (1) the structure of the national system, (2) the nature of primary operational units, and (3) the methods of political control. These are the features I shall focus upon. With respect to some of the features which I will neglect, one or two points might be made briefly. Attributes of contemporary internal organization and specialization tend to emerge later than the more political features. Characteristics dealing with role behavior and professional image are very difficult to chronicle at all. The tasks performed by police forces have undergone a similar pattern of development regardless of country; they have gradually been restricted. During the past century many responsibilities have been assigned to separate agencies, until today the work of policemen in each country is very similar.

When did the structure of the national system, its force units, and institutions of political control emerge in Great Britain, France, Germany, and Italy in recognizable contemporary form?

In Great Britain, establishment of a recognizable contemporary system began with the "New Police" in London in 1829 and became implanted throughout the country in the next half-century. In 1829 the central government placed the weight of its authority against the centuries-old and thoroughly discredited parish-constable system. Parliament, acting through the Home Secretary, assumed the responsibility for policing in London and transferred executive responsibility for the police out of the hands of judicial personnel. Sir Robert Peel's police—the "Bobby"—represented the coalescing of bits and pieces of experimentation from the preceding one hundred years. The London Metropolitan Police constable was a full-time, uniformed officer paid from the public rates. The police were organized into a substantial force with jurisdiction coterminous with an entire municipal area. And the force was provided with full-time executive leadership made responsible to an elected political body.

The London police, against enormous public hostility, soon proved its utility over the moribund parish-constable system. In 1839 all former police agencies—except the police of the City of London—were abolished or merged with the metropolitan force; magistrates were stripped of all police authority; and the boundaries of the force were fixed at a radius of fifteen miles from Charing Cross (Critchley 1967: 56–57; Reith 1948: 92). London, however, was not England, and policing in the rest of the country assumed slowly and begrudgingly the form of the London experiment. In 1835 the Municipal Corporations Act allowed towns with charters to establish municipal councils by popular election, which in turn could set up police forces under the direction of a Watch Committee. The precedent of community police forces greater than parish units was expanded to the counties by the County Police Act, 1839. In this case, control was vested in the magistrates corporately and not in an elected body.

Some towns and counties responded to the enabling legislation of 1835 and 1839; many, however, did not. In order to establish some uniformity in policing standards, the County and Borough Police Act of 1856 required creation of full-time professional police organizations in all towns and counties. The central government was empowered to inspect each force and, if found up to the mark, to support them with a grant amounting to one-fourth their total cost. The structure of today's system was now legally in place throughout the kingdom, though with considerable variation in practical detail and performance.

Local political control exercised through representative bodies was not made universal until 1888. The Local Government Act, the last great landmark in the Age of Reform, established Standing Joint Committees in the Counties to supervise the workings of the police. Even so, popular control was not as complete as in the towns. The Standing Joint Committees were composed half of elected representatives and half of magistrates. As we have already seen, the Police Act of 1964, rather than finally abolishing the participation of magistrates, has turned the clock back, appointing magistrates to town Watch Committees as well, though the proportions are now two-thirds elected membership and one-third magistrates in both towns and counties.

Not only did the structure of the British system and its method of control emerge during the sixty-year period after 1829, so also did the distinctive role behavior of its personnel. The "Bobby" was a new kind of police officer. He was unarmed, depending for his success, indeed for his very life, upon his ability to work cooperatively with the populace. He was given little power and told to build respect (Critchley 1967: xiv). He succeeded mightily, and as a result the implacable hostility shown the police in the eighteenth and early nineteenth centuries was transformed into respect and affection.

In France the essential characteristics of today's police system emerged much earlier, becoming recognizable during the years 1660–1700. The first step was the organization of a unique police command in Paris. In 1667 Louis XIV appointed the first Lieutenant-General of Police, superseding the Provost of Paris as chief police officer. The Lieutenant-General was a royal officer, responsible to the king and not to the *Parlement* of Paris (Stead 1957: chap. 1; Arnold 1969: 14–23). Specialization and centralization of police authority succeeded so well that by late 1699 Lieutenants-General of Police had been established in all major cities. During the same period the post of *Commissaire* was created to assist the Lieutenants-General. In the countryside police authority was drawn into the hands of the provincial *Intendants*.[14] The *Intendants* were the predecessors of today's Prefects.[15] Though the office of *Intendant* went into temporary eclipse during the *Fronde*, it was reinvigorated by the reforming Colbert as the primary instrument of central administrative direction.[16] The last region to receive an *Intendant* in regular attendance was Brittany in 1689 (Gruder 1968: 5–10). By 1700 police authority throughout France was held by the Crown acting through *Intendants* in the provinces and Lieutenants-General of Police in cities.

At the disposal of these central police officers were various forces. In the rural areas there was the *Maréchaussée*, a mounted military constabulary. It was abolished during the Revolution, which put in its place in 1791 the national *Gendarmerie*. Though the name was changed, the function and personnel of the two forces were very similar. Both were military units providing police services in rural areas. The cities had a variety of forces during the seventeenth and eighteenth centuries devoted exclusively to policing. In Paris, for example, there were detectives in each quarter and a force of *exempts* whose duty it was to maintain order in all public places. In support of the *exempts* were special bodies of soldiers drawn from the foot guards and dispersed as sentinels throughout the city. Another body of men known as "archers," numbering about one hundred, patrolled the city during the night and for part of the afternoon. Finally, there was a watch-guard, both foot and horse, that

[14] The *Intendants'* full title was "intendants de justice, police, et finances, et commissaires départies dans les généralités du Royaume pour l'exécution des ordres du Roi" (Chapman 1955: 11).
[15] Their jurisdiction was the *généralité*. Thirty-two of them were appointed originally by Richelieu in the reign of Louis XIII.
[16] Robert Fried (Fried 1963: 19) says that police powers had not originally been given to the *Intendants* but continued to be held by Royal Governors. The Governors used their police powers against the Crown during the *Fronde*. As a result, Louis XIV transferred police powers to the *Intendants*, whom he could better control.

patrolled the city night and day. This force was drawn from disbanded infantry and dragoons. Each of its parties was heavily armed. If a situation exceeded the capacity of these considerable police forces, the military garrison of the city could be called in (Radzinowicz 1957: vol. 3, 540–541). This happened most commonly when rioting broke out. In 1829 a uniformed civil constabulary was introduced for the first time; these were the *Sergents de Ville*, later renamed *Gardiens de la Paix*. The force initially numbered only one hundred men (Stead 1957: 98–99). By 1848 the municipal force had expanded to six hundred men, including *Inspecteurs, Sergents de Ville*, and office staff (Stead 1957: 107–108).

It is clear that by the late seventeenth century there were full-time police functionaries in France under the direction of the central government. Policing was a specialized function and personnel were recruited separately for it, though the police force drew heavily from men with military training and relied for support on formal military units. Civilian detectives were well established, having been appointed as early as 1645 by Mazarin (Stead 1957: 24). Permanent police posts, the beginning of the modern police station, were set up in Paris by the Marquis d'Argenson, the second Lieutenant-General of Police (1679–1718). The practice was then expanded to the rest of France (Stead 1957: chap. 2). The French police system of the late seventeenth century was to grow in authority, and to be challenged many times, but its essential lines were to persist unchanged to the present day. The Revolution affected the nature of political authority at the center, but it did not change the balance of power between center and localities. While developments after the Revolution finally confirmed the manner in which central control was to be exercised, whether through a specialized Ministry of Police or the Ministry of the Interior, they did not undermine the principle of central sovereignty in police affairs—if anything, control became more efficient.

The development of the police in Germany was more attenuated than in France and Great Britain. It began in the eighteenth century but did not become fixed until just after unification in 1871. In seeking for antecedents to contemporary police forms, attention will be given to Prussia, for Prussia not only dominated the German empire in geographical size and population, its administrative and political forms, symbolized in the Hohenzollern crown, were carried over into the Second Reich. The key police development in the eighteenth century was the emergence of the *Landrat* and *Steuerrat* as the authoritative instruments of central police power. The *Landrat*, presiding over territories the size of a township or small county, was a royal officer, responsible to Berlin, though he was chosen from the ranks of the local aristocracy. He was not, at least during most of the eighteenth century, a professional bureaucrat but an aristocratic amateur (Muncy 1944: chap. 5; Rosenberg 1958: 166–167; Jacob 1963: 11–12). The *Steuerrat* was responsible for a town. As the positions developed, these officials became the police superintendent with operational control over the *Gendarmerie*, police magistrates, and mayors. They also issued all prohibitory orders, which took the form of police decrees (Jacob 1963: 55). The police authority of the central government was stoutly disputed by the landed aristocracy until 1872 (Holborn 1969: 401). Titled landed proprietors claimed as a traditional right the power to act as sheriffs within their own properties; this right was not repudiated in Prussia until 1872 (Dawson 1914: chap. 1).[17]

Cities were never a source of competing police authority in Prussia, at least not after the decline of city vitality in the fifteenth and sixteenth centuries (Dawson 1914: chap. 4). Frederick II appointed a royal police officer for Berlin in 1742; the post was renamed Police President in 1809.[18] Though the reforms of Baron vom Stein were designed to reinvigorate municipal life in Prussia after the Peace of Tilsit, 1807, towns were expressly denied the right to regulate their own police. It was stipulated, however, that the state could devolve police powers on local authorities if they wished (Dawson 1914: chap. 1).[19] During the nineteenth century preceding unification several royal police presidents were appointed to large Prussian cities, which indicated the growing need for police in the reviving towns (Holborn 1969: 107).

By the time the German Empire was created, police power was aggregated at two levels, the state and the diffused squirearchy,

[17] In 1812, the "Reform Era," a *Gendarmerie-Edict* was promulgated which vested power in the hands of the *Landrat*, on the model of the French sub-Prefect. The Junkers, fearing for their traditional powers, successfully resisted the edict and it was eventually revoked (Rosenberg 1958: 226).

[18] Frederick II sent his officer-designate to Paris to study with Sartine, a famous Lieutenant-General of Police. It is a mark of the prestige of the French system that Maria Theresa of Austria asked Sartine in 1748 to answer sixteen questions about police work, preparatory to her establishment of a Police Commissioner for Vienna in 1751.

[19] One of Stein's most influential young assistants was a Police Director of Konigsberg, J. G. Frey, and a bureaucrat of the central government (Holborn 1966: 401).

DAVID BAYLEY

though the latter was rapidly losing ground. The federal configuration of the Second Reich assured supremacy in police affairs to each member state.

Little information is available about the nature of the police forces created in Prussia during the eighteenth and nineteenth centuries. It is fairly clear that royal officers in the larger cities had full-time, though nonuniformed, police personnel available to them in the eighteenth century. The police of Berlin were not put in uniform until 1848, and it is doubtful that other states showed greater initiative (Fosdick 1915: 109ff.). Military forces were available if needed in the countryside. They were replaced by a *Gendarmerie* on the French model after the defeat of Napoleon (Jacob 1963: 11–12). Thus by the early nineteenth century full-time police existed in the major cities and a *Gendarmerie* in the rural areas.

The police system of modern Italy became recognizable between 1815 and 1870. The political act of unification was a much more important factor in the development of the Italian police than the German. Piedmont did not dominate the Italian peninsula by size or example nearly as much as Prussia did Germany. Moreover, the strict centralization of government in Italy represented a sharp break with the past, while German unification left internal government of the states very much as it had been before. Between 1860 and 1870 a federal system was considered and rejected by the statesmen of the *Risorgimento* (Mack Smith 1968; Fried 1963: chap. 1). A centralized police system in Italy dates from 1870, when Rome and Venice were wrested from foreign domination.

The structure of internal organization and political control of the police built upon practices already tried in Piedmont. Responsibility for law and order had been contested between the Ministries of War and Interior during the first half of the nineteenth century. Preeminence of the Ministry of Interior was fixed by law in 1852 and the instrumentality of the Prefect for police affairs was confirmed in 1858 (Fried 1963: chap. 2). The post of *Questore* was created in 1852 as assistant to the *Intendant-General* of a Division, who became in 1858 the Prefect (Fried 1963: chap. 2).

Italy's two police forces, the *Carabinieri* and the *Guardia de Pubblica Sicurezza*, were created in 1816 and 1852 respectively. Both were Piedmontese innovations. The *Carabinieri* was modeled after the French *Gendarmerie* as a force of armed police maintained by the Ministry of War. The Public Security Guards were created to re-

[347]

place the *Carabinieri*, as well as the National Guard, in Piedmont's largest cities. The *Carabinieri* were considered too rigid to handle the manifold duties of city policing (Cramer 1964: 327–329).

Summarizing this brief essay in comparative history, one finds that the police systems of Great Britain, France, Germany, and Italy developed recognizable modern features with respect to structure, control, and organizational units during a period bounded by 1660 and 1888. The emergence of these features in each country followed a different plan. In Britain the system developed between 1829 and 1888, spreading out from a dramatic experimemt in the nation's capital. The French system was established much earlier. It was not primarily an urban innovation, though the needs were perceived more clearly there, but involved rural and urban areas equally. The police system of Germany could be discerned in important respects during the middle of the eighteenth century. The sovereignty of Germany's several states in police matters survived the formation of the German Empire, as it did the disaster of the Hitler era. The most persistent threat to this sovereignty came not from a central government or even vigorous organs of local government, but from a diffused class of landowning oligarchs. Italy's police system built upon Piedmontese precedents, and in turn upon French, evolving during the period 1816–1858. These were straws in the wind, however, and were not given national life until the drama of the *Risorgimento*, 1859–1870, determined that the Italian peninsula would have a rigidly centralized system of government and administration.

The arrangements for maintaining internal order that were replaced by these new regimes tended to be decentralized in operation, based upon local communities or traditional ascriptive relationships such as were found on feudal estates. The Parish-Constable had been a feature of English life since the fourteenth century, though the Parish itself did not fully emerge as a unit of government until Tudor times (Critchley 1967: chap. 1). The Justice of the Peace, who had the power to direct the constable and to apply the Common Law, bore prime responsibility since the fourteenth century for maintaining the King's peace (Critchley 1967: 7–9). To some extent this responsibility was shared with the Sheriff and Lord Lieutenant of the county. In France, military officers such as the *Prévôt* had acted in a civil defense capacity for two or three hundred years before the seventeenth century. The *Compagnies d'Ordonnance*, for example, France's first standing army, dating from 1455, were directed to clear the roads of highwaymen. At the same time, local authority exercised through *Parlements* for urban and rural areas, dominated by nobles and clergy, assumed responsibility for the maintenance of order, prevention of crime, and application of sanctions against criminal activities. The tradition of local self-help was also to be seen in the *Garde Bourgeoise* of the seventeenth century.[20] Similar to the English yeomanry of a later period, it was a volunteer body composed largely of men of property who banded together to assist in maintaining order. In Prussia, feudal arrangements persisted longer than in either France or England, continuing indeed through the seventeenth and eighteenth centuries, despite the fact that this was the great period of growth in the administrative capacity of Hohenzollern government. From the late fourteenth century through the mid-sixteenth century towns bore autonomous responsibility for policing; in rural areas landed nobles exercised police functions as a prerogative of ownership. The Prussian political settlement, confirmed in the seventeenth century by the Great Elector, ensured both the loss of urban autonomy and the continuation of landed-proprietary privilege.

The point should be underscored that today's police systems, diverse in character, replaced systems of marked longevity that were equally diverse. It would be convenient to be able to say that contemporary police systems reflect a shift from private to public agency, from decentralized to centralized organization, or from feudal to state authority. Beyond noting that the transition to contemporary systems did mark a decline in decentralization, none of these generalizations aptly describe what happened in each country. The Parish-Constable was a public functionary; he was answerable to the Common Law. The French police system had been a composite of central authority, local accountability, and remnants of seigneurial privilege. The transition in Prussia is most clearly from feudal obligations to state responsibility, though even in this case there had been a tradition of vigorous self-government in major trading towns. The problem is that the way in which police functions were carried out can be described in all periods with fair precision, but it is difficult to categorize the operation of police authority in informative developmental terminology. It is quite clear that though the exercise of police functions evolved steadily over the past millennium in Europe, the transition to contemporary systems from pre-existing ones

---

[20] I am indebted to M. Gabriel Ardant for bringing this point to my attention.

does not coincide with a shift in forms that transcends the straight-forward description of the new organizational patterns.

In pinpointing the emergence of modern police systems, it does not seem adequate to confine attention solely to structural characteristics. A police system may exist in embryo, as it were, for many years before becoming an effective force. Surely one needs to consider the growth in capacities of these systems in order to determine a meaningful date for the emergence of a modern system? The simplest and most precise measure of capacity is numbers of police personnel. This is also an indicator of the resources government is willing to expend on policing. Recognizing the importance of data on police recruitment, I scoured sources in the United States for information on the size of foreign police establishments. The conclusion I have reached is that such data do not exist in the United States. Moreover, I doubt very much whether such data exist in English for any country other than Great Britain. Holdings on European policing affairs are extremely meager in the United States regardless of language. Compilation of tables on the strengths of European police forces for the eighteenth, nineteenth, and twentieth centuries will require bibliographic research on the Continent. It will probably involve archival research. I consider the lack of statistical data on police strength a critical shortcoming of this chapter and a point at which research urgently needs to be directed in the future.

Study of impressionistic evidence, as well as the data at hand, convinces me that there is no serious discrepancy between the dating of the development of existing police systems, as I have done it, and police capabilities. Paris was widely recognized during the *Ancien Régime* as being much better policed than London. The coming of the "new police" in Great Britain is considered to have caused a revolution for the better in the security of life and property. Discipline and order were characteristics of German towns and rural districts in the late eighteenth century; certainly the profligacy and criminality of London were unknown. Size of the police establishment in Italy appears to have grown considerably after 1848 and again after 1860. A strong, effective police force centrally directed was continually justified by reference to the brigandage, unrest, and outright rebellion especially in the south after the *Risorgimento*.

Having found approximately when recognizable contemporary police systems emerged in each country, what factors account for their development at these times? The range of factors that might influence development are very great. I shall examine seven general hypotheses, each hypothesis dealing with a distinctive set of variables. The sets are: (1) growth of population and its distribution between cities and rural areas; (2) extent of criminality and insecurity; (3) occurrence of a social or economic transformation; (4) occurrence of a political transformation; (5) marked change in general governmental capabilities; (6) an external threat, and (7) an ideological *démarche*.

Can the timing as well as the rate of development of these police systems be explained by reference to the growth of population or the growth of cities? I do not believe so. There is certainly no threshold of population size which seems to compel development of a police system. The population of Paris was approximately 540,000 when that post of Lieutenant-General was established (Mulhall 1903: 446); that of London was about 1,500,000 in 1829 (Mulhall 1903: 446); and that of Berlin somewhere between 50,000 and 100,000 in the middle of the eighteenth century (Emerson 1968: 4; Mulhall 1903: 446). Rates of population growth also do not appear to be significant. France inaugurated its police system before the period of most rapid population expansion: the population grew by about 23 percent in the seventeenth century and by 42 percent in the eighteenth century (Mulhall 1903: 445). The population of Paris, however, appears to have remained almost the same between 1675 and 1800 (Mulhall 1903: 445). Berlin's population tripled during the eighteenth century, from about 55,000 to above 150,000 (Mulhall 1903: 446). London's population grew exponentially before a new police system was created: it grew by one-third during the eighteenth century and almost doubled during the first thirty years of the nineteenth century. The rate of increase declined somewhat in the next thirty years, to about 87 percent; it continued to decline in the subsequent thirty, falling to a rate of about 50 percent (Mulhall 1903: 445). Furthermore, within England there was a wide disparity in population-per-police ratios between London and the rest of England. During the period 1836–1856 municipal forces outside London generally had twice as many people per policeman as did London (Critchley 1967: 67, quoting J. M. Hart).

In short, considering that the rate of population growth rose in all of Western Europe during the period under review, it is no more than a truism to remark that population growth and the foundation of police systems coincide. The more informative point is that there is no clear pattern of impingement of population size or change in the rate of increase upon the timing of development of police systems.

There has always been a considerable variation among cities of Western Europe with respect to the number of people per police-man.[21] In 1913 the first year for which comparative statistics on police strength for many European cities have been collected, the number of people per policeman ranged from a low of 207 in Rome and 212 in Lisbon to a high of 660 in Berne and 648 in Stuttgart (Fosdick 1915: 401–402). London had 352, Paris 336, and Berlin 324. Edinburgh and Manchester had ratios respectively of 513 and 528, representing 80 percent more people per policeman than in London. The impact of population growth and aggregation on the size of po-lice establishments is indeterminable, except that the more people there are the more policemen there will be. Police establishments are created by human agency, presumably reacting to certain preceived cues. While population growth may enhance those cues, the reading of them is not straightforward; it varies with individual, country, and time.

Can the emergence of police forces be explained in terms of the incidence of criminality or personal insecurity? Because accurate statistics on crime are unavailable for these historical periods, it is exceedingly difficult to be sure. A comparison of events in London and Paris strongly suggests that insecurity is not sufficient to create a police force. London during the eighteenth century was well known for its criminality, violence, and licentiousness. The writings of Henry Fielding and Patrick Colquhoun bear eloquent testimony to the extent of public insecurity. Serious students of British history, such as Sidney and Beatrice Webb, Max Beloff, Charles Reith, T. A. Critchley, Leon Radzinowicz, and members of the Royal Commis-sion on the Police, 1962, seem amazed at the spectacle of that time.[22] European visitors could not understand why an otherwise civilized people did not follow the example of the French or the Germans whose capital cities were models of order. During the eighteenth century Cabinet Ministers went armed in the streets of London at

---

[21] It would be interesting to determine whether there is a convergence in ratios among European cities. Is the difference among cities with respect to people per policeman getting smaller, remaining the same, or increasing? As I have already in-dicated, this fascinating question cannot be answered at the present time.

[22] See, respectively, Webb 1913; Beloff 1938: 22–23; Reith 1948: chap. 14; Critchley 1967: 18–24; Radzinowicz 1957: vol. III; Royal Commission 1962: 13–15.

high noon protected by gangs of retainers; men of property went to bed with firearms at their sides; on the coasts whole towns turned out to plunder shipwrecks, killing sailors or constables who tried to stop the despoilation; brutality to servants and animals was commonplace; gin-mills flourished; prostitution was rampant; and a vast proportion of the population lived utterly outside the law. According to the Royal Commission, 1962, seventeen Parliamentary Committees investigated the problem of law and order in London during the late eighteenth and early nineteenth centuries.[23] Despite this appalling situation, almost nothing was done: "During this long period of more than three-quarters of a century, from 1750 to 1828, there was no section of public opinion, no group in Parliament or outside, no leading newspaper or periodical which would advocate a reform in the traditional machinery for keeping the peace" (Radzinowicz 1957: vol. 3, 374).

England's attempts at curbing crime in these years relied wholly upon deterrence. In 1819 there were 223 capital offenses in the English criminal law; in France there were 6. Never perhaps has the worth of an ounce of prevention been more apparent. England's criminal law was draconian, prevention of crime through policing nonexistent, and crime flourished. In France the criminal law was comparatively more humane, there was a professional police force that patrolled streets regularly, and its cities were relatively law-abiding.[24]

In short, development of police cannot be understood in terms of crime. The reasons for creation are more complex than that. As two careful students of criminology have argued in the case of criminal punishments, for which we may substitute "police":

Punishment is neither a simple consequence of crime, nor the reverse side of crime, nor a mere means which is determined by the end achieved. Punishment must be understood as a social

[23] Jenifer Hart (Hart 1951: 27) gives a different figure. She says there were six Parliamentary Committees between 1770 and 1828.

[24] The picture of indiscriminate hangings in England is seriously overdrawn in much of the writing on the period. No doubt hangings were more frequent per capita in the late eighteenth century than in the late nineteenth century. J. L. Parker (Parker 1937: 959ff.) says that there were twice as many in the former period as in the latter, though the population was only one-third as great. At the same time, precisely because the law was so severe, juries and judges hesitated to convict. Furthermore, though the severity of the law increased in terms of capital offenses, the practice diminished. Transportation was increasingly substituted for hanging as punishment for serious crimes and habitual criminals.

phenomenon freed from both its juristic concept and its social ends. We do not deny that punishment has specific ends, but we do deny that it can be understood from its ends alone. By way of analogy, it might be noted that no one would dream of developing the history of military institutions or a specific army out of the immutable purpose of such institutions (Rusche and Kirchheimer 1968: 5).

Can the emergence of police systems be explained in terms of a major social or economic transformation through which these countries were passing? During the period under review the so-called Industrial Revolution, encompassing the decline of feudalism and the rise of capitalism, shattered and rebuilt European social systems. Though containing the thrust of industrialization in a neat chronology is exceedingly difficult, the periods of most vigorous industrial change, when the economic transformation became confirmed in practice, do not coincide with the rise of today's police systems.

Great Britain is generally considered to have preceded most European nations in this enormous social travail, yet it lagged behind France and Germany in the establishment of its modern national police system. The take-off into industrial growth in France occurred in the early nineteenth century, but its police system had been in place for at least a century. Italy's industrial development was an uneven affair, stronger in the North than in the South. Unification, which established the police system, preceded the most vigorous period of industrial development.

It is also true, however, that economic and social development does impinge on police functions in several pervasive ways. First, it creates new law and order tasks. The forms that crime takes are a reflection of the needs and opportunities confronting individuals. Second, socioeconomic change effects the social basis of community, thus influencing the way in which norms are enforced, rules sanctioned. A feudal society has different control mechanisms than does an urban community composed of autonomous individuals. In modern Germany there are no manors and ascriptive obligations, apart from those of family; policing must be handled, if at all, impersonally. Third, to the extent that economic change thrusts new social strata into politics, government will become increasingly sensitized to a range of enforcement tasks that it may hitherto have neglected. In the United States today, for example, minority groups are continually asking that police meet *their* problems and not be so pre-occupied with those of the affluent suburbs.

Economic and social change constitute a vector during this entire period: in all these countries social and economic forms in the late nineteenth century are vastly different than in the seventeenth century, and it is possible to characterize this change as being singular. But the striking point, as with population growth, is not that police development and social change coincide, but that they exhibit unique patterns of interrelationship in each country. As Barrington Moore has argued for the relation between economic change and political evolution more generally, industrialization impinges differently upon institutions in different countries depending upon the timing of change, the social interests mediating it, and the distribution of political power (Moore 1966). Just as the results for the political system are diverse, so too are they for police systems.[25]

Can the rise of recognizably contemporary police systems be explained in terms of a political transformation? Let us examine various kinds of political changes that have occurred in Europe and see whether they are associated with the establishment of police systems. It would be reasonable to expect that the consolidation of government in an expanded geographical area—state-building—would be associated with the creation of a police system. Formation of national governments would be a particularly critical time from the point of view of social control. This is unambiguously the case in France and Italy. The *Risorgimento* created a national government where none had existed before, and with a rigidly centralized police system. Monarchical absolutism began in France in the seventeenth century. Coincidentally with the consolidation of national power at the royal court came the rise of a new police system in Paris and throughout the country. In Germany it is more difficult to make a case for this linkage. Policing had been in the hands of the landed nobility before the Great Elector and it continued to be so long afterward. Police power in the narrow sense for the *Landrat* and the *Steuerrat* did not develop until the middle of the eighteenth century, during the latter part of the reign of Frederick the Great.[26] Prussian

[25] This analysis is less precise than I would like. It might have been instructive to compare the expansion of police personnel with changes in levels of educational attainment, per capita gross national product, proportion of work-force in agriculture, and so forth. However, until data have been assembled on police strength over time, this analysis will have to be postponed.

[26] It is important to note that police powers in a general sense—the authority to

bureaucratic absolutism was not built on the back of a state police machine. The preoccupation of Prussian government was with taxation and military affairs; it was content to leave policing to the nobles. The famous Boards of War and Domains were not involved with policing. In Great Britain, finally, there is no relation whatsoever between police development and national consolidation.

Association between dynastic consolidation and a new police system is even weaker. Neither Bourbons, Hohenzollerns, Hanoverians, nor the House of Savoy was threatened by a competing dynasty during the time new police systems emerged. One exception was Cromwell's England, where a novel police system was created to support the Commonwealth. Between 1655 and 1657 Cromwell established a national *Gendarmerie*. England was divided into twelve police districts, each covered by a detachment of mounted military police. The purpose of the system was to repress frivolity in support of the social mores of the Puritan revolution. The army was, as a result, brought into enormous disfavor and the system was abandoned. It could be argued that Napoleon III used the police freely to consolidate his regime in the early 1850s. The police were substantially expanded during this period. Generally, however, though regimes certainly use the police to maintain power, whole systems seem rarely to have been inaugurated or expanded in the process of regime-establishment.

Revolutions too have produced little change in modes of policing. They cannot account for the rise of any of our modern systems, unless the *Risorgimento* is termed a revolution. The English Civil War was the occasion of a police experiment, but it was short-lived and left no lasting mark on the Parish-Constable system that continued in a paralyzed state for another century and a half. The French Revolution, certainly the most dramatic and influential political upheaval of this period, promised to sweep into oblivion the police system of the *Ancien Régime*. It singularly failed to do so. If anything, the system was stronger after the revolution. The prefectoral system of Napoleon I was noticeably more efficient than that of the *Intendants* and it did not differ much in principles of organization and control.

Periods of prolonged political turbulence and social violence are associated to some extent with the rise of modern police systems.

---

regulate—were certainly created by the Elector. But the expansion of general "police" power from commerce and taxation into policing in the narrow sense occurred not until the second half of the eighteenth century.

The *Fronde* convinced Louis XIV and Colbert of the importance of holding central power tightly and of the inadvisability of entrusting police powers to provincial *Parlements* and governors. Tax revolts were a common feature of seventeenth-century French life. Ministers from Mazarin to Colbert were preoccupied with problems of domestic order, as their correspondence with Governors and *Intendants* clearly shows.[27] The fact that the *Intendant* was the primary representative of the central government for taxation and police shows the intimate relationship between resource mobilization and social unrest in France at this time. Napoleon III did expand the police of France considerably during the 1850s when memories of political turbulence in 1848 were still fresh in men's minds. The Prussian Kings, by contrast, were not subject to persistent domestic violence during the eighteenth century and Prussian administration nonetheless gradually developed police functions in the narrow sense. During the nineteenth century the relationship is fairly obvious, for Prussian politics was quite repressive after the interlude with Stein and Hardenberg and this is also the greatest period of police development. The British experience is quite anomalous. Rioting was common throughout the eighteenth century; in fact, it was endemic (Rudé 1964; Beloff 1938; Darvall 1934). The Gordon Riots of 1780 devastated London for five helpless days. The first two decades of the nineteenth century were also a period of great unrest in England. A Prime Minister was killed in the lobby of the House of Commons in 1812; Luddite riots the same year brought more troops to the Midlands than Wellesley had taken to the Peninsula in 1808 (Darvall 1934: 1); and the Peterloo massacre of 1819 showed the bankruptcy of the existing police system. Despite all this, the British hesitated to reform the police. Not until after a period of relative calm was a reformed police force inaugurated. And it was a force that was unarmed and nonpunitive in character. If domestic turmoil did play a role in the formation of the "new police," it did so in a way that must surprise and confound most social historians.

Altogether, there is more evidence of an association between the development of police and political changes than with more subterranean social movements such as population growth, urbanization, industrialization, and criminality. Politics and policing are bound together, though similar political events do not always produce the same police development. What is more, dramatic political changes

[27] I am indebted to M. Gabriel Ardant for this point.

[357]

are sometimes completely unassociated with changes in either mode or efficiency of policing.

Has a change in police systems in the past two or three centuries been associated with an expansion of government capabilities generally? Are police developments part of a general growth in government output-functions? The capabilities of all four governments have expanded dramatically since 1660, so that in a general way there is an association. Once again, analysis is handicapped by the lack of data on police strength. The historical evidence suggests that output capacities of government do not expand across the board at the same time. In France, because so much power was held by *Intendants* and then Prefects, reform of the bureaucracy was automatically reform of police control and supervision. More importantly, one can say that regularized, central police capability in France grew together with improvement in the collection of taxes and major changes in the regulation of the nation's economic life—the policy known as mercantilism. In Germany there is no association of this kind. Frederick, the Great Elector and Frederick the Great both concentrated primarily on building the army and improving collection of taxes. They ignored internal policing. The Boards of War and Domains did not deal with domestic law and order problems. In Britain there was a major expansion of central government administration in the period from Charles II through George I, especially from 1689 to 1715 (Plumb 1934). The Parish-Constable system was unaffected. The second great period of expansion came in the second quarter of the nineteenth century. Here police reform marked the onset of reform. Policing was simply one among several areas in which the policy of private, parish, or borough self-help gave way to a national movement of institutional reform. Demands upon government for a national policy with respect to poor-relief, municipal administration, public health, and economic regulation were growing enormously at the time of the new police experiment. Sometimes, then, police arrangements are expanded as part of a general growth of government capability, but the relation is not constant.

Can the development of new police systems be explained by the presence of an external threat to a country? The "Garrison State" hypothesis of Harold Laswell suggests that when a society is under pressure from outside, social groups tend to draw together in the name of national unity, dissent is less freely tolerated, conformity is insisted upon, and regulative capacities of government are strengthened (Laswell 1962). If this is true, development of police systems or their expansion might be associated with wars. There is little evidence for this. None of the really great wars of the past three centuries seems to have impelled police reform. France and Prussia were often at war during the latter part of the seventeenth century. The strains engendered by almost continual war during this period undoubtedly placed a premium on more efficient state operation. In the French case, the foundation of today's police system was laid; in Prussia's, policing was unaffected. The crucial difference appears to lie with the reaction of the populace to mobilization for war: the French were unruly, the Prussians were docile. Napoleon's reorganization of the administrative system actually preceded his external adventures. So did Hitler's centralization of the German police in 1936. The British, though locked in what they considered to be a life-and-death struggle with Napoleon, did not expand or reform police operations until almost a generation after Waterloo. It is true, however, that secret police activities, involving political surveillance, were common toward the end of the Napoleonic wars in Great Britain. But Britain's new police did not stem from her reactionary period but rather from her liberal one. The expansion of civil police capacities throughout Europe in the nineteenth century are unassociated with wars. The Crimean War was certainly quite incidental to the expansion of the French police undertaken by Napoleon III in the 1850s. The fact is that wars fought by Britain, France, and Prussia after 1815 were short, nonideological, or colonial. They did not occasion social unrest. Until ideology was revived as a part of internal politics in the twentieth century, police had a small role to play in a war effort. National security was seldom threatened by internal subversion.

External intervention was part of the Italian *Risorgimento*. Italy faced the prospect of war with Austria in the northeast during the 1860s and had to be concerned with French pride and commitment, especially as Italy menaced papal Rome. These alarms of war receded rapidly after 1870. No particular value can be placed on external threats in explaining the rise of the centralized police machine; they were one of many exigencies that placed a premium on efficient national administration. One might argue that the military character of the police was confirmed, not created, by these threats during the 1860s. It was undoubtedly simpler to organize, train, and support a single force for both internal and external security, when both were so intimately entwined, than to have an army and a distinct civil constabulary.

Can the development of a police system be explained ideologically, in terms of an intellectual reorientation within a country or across the entire Continent? Considering the wide separation in time of the emergence of these systems, no argument can be sustained that a Continent-wide intellectual movement conditioned formation. Within each nation there is some evidence for this association, especially if absolutism is considered an ideology. Perhaps it was, as much as nationalism became in the nineteenth and twentieth centuries. The practice and philosophy of bureaucratic centralization under an absolute sovereign fertilized police development in France and Prussia, though it seems to have blighted it in Great Britain. Sartine and other Lieutenants-General of Police gave advice freely about municipal policing to foreign powers in the eighteenth century. It can be no accident that the Tsar Peter established an imperial police administration in St. Petersburg in 1718, Frederick II a police director in Berlin in 1742, and Maria Theresa a police commissioner in Vienna in 1751 (Emerson 1968: 4–5). There was a pronounced demonstration effect among absolutist states.

Looking back on the emergence of national police systems in Great Britain, France, Germany, and Italy, one finds a remarkable variety in patterns of development. The essential point is that nations develop characteristic solutions to police problems in response to different factors. Very different things were going on in each country when its police force emerged in recognizably contemporary form. The factors which appear to play the most significant role among all the nations are (1) a transformation in the organization of political power; (2) prolonged violent popular resistance to government; and (3) development of new law and order tasks, as well as the erosion of former bases of community authority, as a result of socioeconomic change. But it must be stressed again that even with respect to these factors, there is not an invariant relation between them and either the reform of an existing system or the marked expansion of a new one.

Evolution of Police Forms

Having discovered that contemporary police systems exhibit considerable variation in form, the next task is to explore the factors which account for the differences. Explanations for characteristic differences will be formulated with respect to the following attributes of police systems: (1) nature of tasks, (2) structure of the national system, (3) nature of accountability, and (4) professional image and role behavior. Variations with respect to internal organization will not be explained because this would involve details of public administration and I should like to keep the focus on matters of direct political relevance.

One important difference among police systems is the extent to which police tasks include an active role in political life as opposed to preoccupation primarily with prevention of crime and the maintenance of public order. Some police forces are almost exclusively concerned with the security concerns of individual citizens, others are involved with the political security of a regime. The French police, for instance, have played an active role in politics since their inception; the British police have from time to time been thrust into political life, largely as a result of widespread public disorder, but the role has been slight. Among the countries of our sample, persistent intrusion of the police into politics can be explained by two factors.

First, police will play a political role if creation of effective state institutions and formation of the nation are accompanied by serious social violence. Conflict that touches the legitimacy and capacity of the state at the moment of its creation is most likely to constrain police development and to shape it according to political ends. It is also true, however, that prolonged social conflict, once again particularly if it touches the legitimacy or capacity of existing political arrangements, will over time encourage the use of police in political ways.

To speak of state-building is really an enormous oversimplification. If the essence of the process is the establishment of coherent authority throughout a given territory, then it is clear that such a process does not occur across the board simultaneously. Authority may be made coherent first in law, then in adjudication, then in some sorts of tax powers, then in conscription, then in economic regulative activities, and so forth. The surmounting of distributional economic problems—the creation of the "welfare state"—may be looked upon as another stage in "state-building." States, it seems to me, are very diverse entities. To say that two states have been built by a particular point in time suggests that they are similar in penetration by governmental institutions. Yet one "state" may have only a coherent legal and adjudicative system, while another has efficient tax and military

[361]

capabilities. The differences in nature of institutional penetration among states is as interesting and important as searching for the moment when a "state" in any territorial region can be considered to exist.

The point is that there are problems with the concept of state-building. When I refer to "state-building," I should be understood to be pointing to a process of penetration of a territory by a coherent set of institutions along any of several dimensions. There is no assumption that penetration proceeds along all dimensions simultaneously. Returning now to the police in politics: the police will be utilized in politics if this process of penetration, regardless of dimension, is resisted by violence.

The converse of this proposition is that the violence of interpersonal crime or among private groups may be tolerated at comparatively high levels without police being forced into a political posture. If violence is not perceived in political terms it is unlikely to lead to an expanded police role. In Britain, for example, in the eighteenth century there was enormous personal insecurity as well as great destruction due to riots, but the police establishment was not reformed nor were existing police directed according to partisan political ends.

In seventeenth-century France serious and persistent threats to public order had to be overcome. The roots of conflict were various: resentment at centralization of bureaucratic power, tax impositions, and religious rivalry. State-penetration and formation of the nation were both threatened. Great Britain experienced violence as part of national amalgamation in the nineteenth and twentieth centuries. The C.I.D.'s famous Special Branch, responsible for political intelligence and surveillance, was created in 1884 as a direct response to the intractability of the Irish. If the activities of the I.R.A. and Sinn Fein had continued longer, it is an open question whether the British police would still have a reputation for studious political neutrality. Religious conflict is a species of a larger genus, namely, ideological conflict. Nations today may be as fractured by secular ideological strife as nations have been by religious disorder. A country like China may have the one, while India the other, but both situations will encourage political use of the police.

The police role of the Prussian police stems from another sort of conflict. The police power of the noble estate-owners was used throughout the seventeenth and eighteenth centuries in a very diffused way to maintain the feudal settlement. In the nineteenth cen-

DAVID BAYLEY

tury, when the state police force was developed and expanded most markedly, police were used to counter the growing political assertiveness of new social strata. New classes sought to obtain political power commensurate with growing economic strength; this was bitterly resented. As a result the police were used throughout the nineteenth century to repress "Liberal" and then "Social Democratic" elements. In Prussia a political role for the state's police was not confirmed until considerably after the Prussian state had established substantial centralized governmental capacities. It might be argued for Germany as a whole, after 1870, that the price Bismarck paid for a German Empire was the right of local politicians to use the power of the police within each of the individual states to maintain the existing social distribution of political power. As the centralized Prussian state was founded on dispersed police power to be used for political purposes, so the centralized German Empire was founded on dispersed police power, no less politically utilized.

Second, police forces are more apt to play a political role if there is a traditional insistence in the country upon the importance of right-belief. Such a tradition justifies scrutiny of very personal aspects of individual lives. Where the Inquisition was strong, there police forces active in politics are to be found from an early time. This is certainly the case in France; my impression is that it is also true of Spain. The French word for spy—"mouchard"—is taken from Antoine di Mouchi who was a theologian of the University of Paris appointed by Francis I to prosecute Protestants. He was extremely efficient, sending many people to the stake, and he flooded Paris wtih spies and informers (Radzinowicz 1957: vol. 3, 544). In Britain, on the other hand, outward conformity was considered sufficient. Elizabeth I said that she wanted to open no windows into men's souls.[28] In Prussia Protestantism won a fairly quick though bloody victory; its security made it unnecessary for the police to censor religious thought.

Religious heritage in European countries thus appears to have been an important factor in police development: it has encouraged police intrusion into political life if religious conflict challenged formation of a nation and if religious tradition sanctioned surveillance for the purpose of achieving right-belief.

In summary, police forces are more likely to play an active role in politics if social violence accompanies state- or nation-building, if

[28] I am indebted for this reference to Professor S. E. Finer.

mobilization demands at the time state-penetration is going on occasions popular resistance, if the political system is unable to accommodate without violence demands for increased political participation, and if there is a cultural insistence upon right-belief (see Figure 5–2).[29]

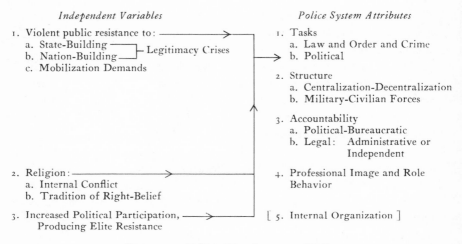

Figure 5–2. Political Involvement of Police

The second aspect of differentiation among national police forces is the structure of the system. Two aspects are important: the extent of centralization and the extent of military participation.

The degree of centralization found in the European examples may be accounted for by four factors.

First, bureaucratic traditions already existing when a new police system is established profoundly influence centralization. Contemporary police systems were not all established at the time state institutions were initially created. In Britain, for instance, state institutions were very much in evidence by the sixteenth and seventeenth centuries; the formation of the contemporary police system was therefore constrained by several centuries of very decentralized bureaucratic tradition. In Prussia, as well, the contemporary system did not begin to grow until almost a century after Frederick the Great Elector. This was a case of an existing centralized bureaucracy becoming involved more and more with a specific new task. It would have been as unthinkable for Prussian administrators to devolve police authority on local government units as it would have been for British

---

[29] A summary of these relationships is presented schematically in Figure 5–2.

statesmen in the nineteenth century to concentrate police authority in the Home Office.

Second, violent public disorder during state- and nation-building encourages police centralization just as it encourages bureaucratic centralization generally. If the legitimacy of new nation-state institutions is jeopardized, resources of the nation-state will be mobilized centrally in their defense.

Third, police systems are more likely to be centralized if mobilization demands are high and stubborn popular resistance is encountered. French kings in the middle and late seventeenth century imposed new taxes and violent resistance was commonplace. The *Intendant* was given power to collect taxes as well as to marshal whatever force was necessary to impose order. These tasks were inextricably mixed. In Prussia, mobilization demands were also great in the late seventeenth century but popular resistance was negligible. As a result, police centralization did not accompany the establishment of the absolutist state. In Great Britain, except for occasional periods such as the Napoleonic wars, mobilization requirements until quite recently have been light and popular violence to state levies has been minimal. In other words, the state could get on financially without coercive instruments in Britain and Prussia but not in France.

Fourth, in all four countries there is a pattern of increased central direction as a result of long-run socioeconomic changes. New law and order tasks have been created in the last hundred years that require national solutions. The boundaries of crime have expanded; crime is increasingly difficult to cope with in small geographical areas. National police agencies, laboratories, training centers, databanks, and communications networks become more and more common.

The argument about centralization can be usefully summarized if the propositions are stated conversely: police systems will be decentralized only if state institutions are created without substantial popular resistance, if mobilization demands are slight or produce little popular resistance, and if bureaucratic traditions derived from state-building are decentralized. The amount of decentralization compatible with efficient policing will decline in the future due to increased intra-national interdependence. This process is already at work.[30]

[30] See Figure 5–3.

Nations differ considerably with respect to the amount of military involvement in domestic policing. In Italy since unification the military has maintained a separate police establishment—the *Carabinieri*. In Britain there has always been a clear distinction between police constables and military personnel. Though the army was often used from the seventeenth to nineteenth centuries to maintain domestic order, such duty was considered exceptional and was the object of deep public suspicion. Three factors account for the extent of military participation among Great Britain, France, Germany, and Italy: (1) the presence of a large standing-army, (2) the earliness of formation of the standing-army in state experience, and (3) the existence of large-scale and persistent civil strife. It should be noted that the creation of a standing army may itself be explained in terms of geopolitical circumstances, thus the first factor could be reformulated in terms of other variables.

The standing army was a feature of continental state-development. Thus, when order had to be maintained at home, the army was ready-to-hand. In Britain a standing-army did not develop until the seventeenth century and it remained small until the Napoleonic wars. The militia, first created in 1660, was prized by the country politicians precisely because it was an irregular force conceived as a counterpoise to the crown's standing army (Western 1965: part 1). As the army grew during the eighteenth century, it was widely used to maintain order. J. L. and Barbara Hammond say, referring to the latter part of the eighteenth century:

> the north and midlands and the manufacturing region of the south-west came to resemble a country under military occupation. The officers commanding the different districts reported on the temper and circumstances of their districts, just as if they were in a hostile or lately conquered country; soldiers were moved about in accordance with the fluctuations in wages and employment, and the daily life of the large towns was watched anxiously and suspiciously by magistrates and generals (Hammond and Hammond 1967; quoted in Radzinowicz 1957: vol. 4, 121).

Though the standing army grew and was used domestically, a tradition of a separate civilian force had been firmly established in political life. The need for army intervention demonstrated to British

[366]

statesmen not that the civil system was expendable but rather that it needed to be made stronger and more efficient. It is not, therefore, simply the presence of a standing army but the timing of its growth in relation to the creation of state political institutions that is important.

If, however, domestic strife persistently exceeds the capacity of civilian forces, the military will play a growing role in internal policing. It also seems reasonable to expect that the more internal disorder is associated with a foreign threat, the more likely civilian and military counterespionage, including political intelligence, will interpenetrate.

The relation between centralization and militarization of police structures is interesting (see Figure 5–3). Militarization will impel

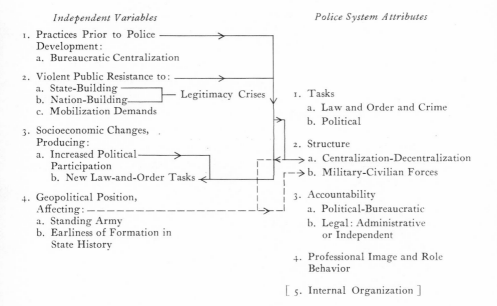

Figure 5–3. Centralization and Military Involvement

centralization, but centralization is irrelevant to militarization. A central police bureaucracy may defend its domain successfully against military influence. It might, in fact, be better able to do so than a decentralized force. A decentralized political elite may welcome military participation in policing. This was the case in Prussia during the eighteenth and nineteenth centuries. Military involvement in policing is more a function of political and bureaucratic disposition than organization circumstances.[31]

The third attribute of police systems to be discussed is the manner in which accountability is achieved. Generally, accountability over the police tends to be exercised at that place in the political system where political power is aggregated. There is remarkable coincidence between the structure and control of the police and the organization of police power in any country. If one had no other information about a country except a description in generic terms of the evolution of its police system, it would be possible to identify the country within a very small margin of error. The police are intimately part of the political system. The significance of this discovery lies in what it indicates about the limits for innovation and change in police establishments. It may also provide clues as to future development. For example, in the United States there appears to be a substantial discrepancy between the places at which political power is aggregated and police authority located. I suggest that the pressure on America's 40,000 police forces to amalgamate as well as to accept more state or national government direction will grow in the near future. Increased jurisdiction will probably be given to national police units relative to local ones. In Great Britain the central government has continually extended its supervisory power over local forces, until today it is only a step away from having a national police for all intents and purposes. From 1856 to 1874 the central government made yearly grants to local forces amounting to one-fourth of costs, contingent upon their passing an inspection (Hart 1951: 36). In 1886 the Home Secretary was given the power to make binding regulations upon county forces. The Police Act of 1964, gave supervisory authority to two authorities, the local committees and the Home Secretary. The Home Secretary may make inspections and he may also demand reports. Because he is subject to the will of Parliament, Parliament may now, for the first time, debate matters of law and order anywhere in Great Britain (Critchley 1967: 293–295 and chap. 5).

Conformity between political institutions and police systems was never more clearly demonstrated than in Germany immediately after World War II. In the British, American, and French zones of occupation three separate police systems were established, each of

[31] Ibid.

them patterned almost exactly on the model of the occupying power.[32] The Americans created small municipal and communal units of government, each with elected bodies, and these units served as the basis for police forces. The Americans gave little attention to police training, believing that radical decentralization and local democracy were sufficient to ensure a freedom-conserving police force (Jacob 1963: 156–158). The British set up district police commands patterned after British counties. Police committees were established in each district composed of elected representatives. The state Ministries of Interior were given power to influence police development through financial grants. The British even tried to create a "highly professional nonpolitical administration" in these units, including making the town clerk the chief administrative officer with the mayor a figurehead. The French, though resisting centralization of police functions across the Allied occupation zones, placed police forces under strict control by the state governments, supervised by French occupation authorities. Police officials were responsible to the *Landrat*, little autonomy was given to local officials (Jacob 1963; Goedhard 1954: especially 109–118 and conclusion). The effect of these experiments upon German policing was negligible; the structure and control of policing in West Germany today is what it was in the Weimar Republic and before that in the Second Reich.

The repressiveness of a police regime is not a function of the place at which political accountability is exercised. Centralized political regimes are not necessarily more repressive in police policy than decentralized ones. The history of Prussia shows that even extreme decentralization of police authority is not incompatible with authoritarian regimentation. Similarly in the United States, it would be difficult to convince Blacks in the South that decentralization of police accountability would augment personal freedom.

Accountability may be obtained through bureaucratic or political agencies. French police officials report to bureaucrats; British ones to representative political bodies. Supervision is more likely to be bureaucratic the greater the scale of police operations and the greater the degree of political centralization. The larger the territorial scale of police operations, itself a function of political aggregation, the more likely that the link between police establishment and political authorities, whether representative or oligarchic, will be bureaucratic.

---

[32] This was also true of the Soviet zone.

Police accountability can also be achieved through legal mechanisms. The British police, both Parish-Constable and Bobby, have always been as responsible under law as any citizen. Italian police, by contrast, as well as German and French, have special status under law as officials of the state. They are responsible to administrative tribunals and to a corpus of law articulating state interests. One should not jump to the conclusion that a fair measure of justice will not be meted out through an administrative law system; any more than one can conclude that a legal system predicated on individuals as actors is always just. The determination of whether accountability is exercised through administrative or nonadministrative courts is a descriptive, not a normative, exercise. What is more important is the extent to which the legal order—meaning both the body of law and the adjudicating mechanisms—is independent of executive perceptions of interest. Three factors have contributed to independent legal accountability in our four national examples. First, if a state-based legal order predates the creation of a central bureaucracy or a police system, accountability is more likely to be independent of executive requirements. This was the case in Great Britain; it was to some extent the case in France; it was not the case in Prussia or Italy. Second, if the creation of state institutions is uncontested the pressures to centralize law and order administration will be weak and the legal tradition is less likely to be state-centered. Third, if the creation of state institutions does not involve mobilization demands and these in turn do not occasion violent popular resistance, police are more apt to be legally responsible to independent judicial bodies. In short, those factors which encourage utilization of the police for political purposes, especially during the creation of viable state institutions, also erode the opportunity to exercise control over the police through an independent legal order. Those states with police active in politics also have administrative legal systems (see Figure 5-4).

From what has been said, it is clear that police systems fit within a context of political practice and experience. There is a wider lesson as well. Police systems exhibit an enormous inertial strength over time; their forms endure even across the divides of war, violent revolution, and shattering economic and social change. The fact is that people seem to become habituated to certain procedures and organizational patterns; they do not know what else to do even when given the chance. Allied occupation policy in West Germany clearly shows

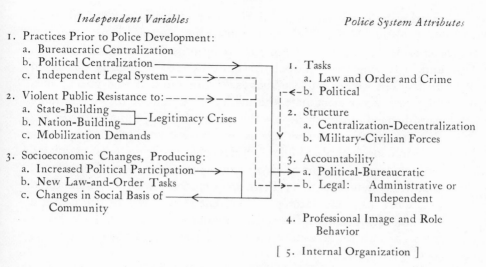

Figure 5–4. Accountability

the enormous power of hallowed ideas and customary behavior over both occupied and occupier.

Among police systems institutional patterns are very unyielding. Consider the reluctance of the British to abandon the thoroughly dilapidated Parish-Constable system. People were put to enormous danger, inconvenience, and expense for a hundred and fifty years without effective remedial action being taken. They refused to accept a paid, professional force even though it would have been responsible to Parliament. Their reluctance cannot be blamed on the absence of alternatives. The French and the Prussian examples were well known. In London itself there had been successful experiments with full-time paid policemen beginning with Henry and John Fielding in the mid-eighteenth century and Patrick Colquhoun's Thames River Police in 1798. One abortive attempt at establishing a metropolitan police force was made by Pitt in 1785, but it foundered on the obstinacy of the merchants of the City of London. So badly burned was the government of the day by this episode that reform was considered untouchable for almost half a century. How does one explain this muddle-headedness, this inability to use known practices to procure elemental security? The answer is that the notion of a paid, professional police force maintained by non-Parish authorities offended the sense of constitutional propriety of England's political elite. It was equated with the destruction of cherished liberties. As Peel put the issue: "I want to teach people that liberty does not consist in having your house robbed by organized gangs of thieves, and in leaving the principal streets of London in nightly possession of drunken women and vagabonds."[33] One can make no greater mistake than to overestimate the ability of circumstances—even quite painful ones—to teach people the value of doing differently. In the British case, the argument against reform was strengthened by international ideological conflict. Professional policing was associated with the tyrannous practices of continental absolutism. Englishmen could not view French or Prussian precedents with an unjaundiced eye. Only after the Jacobin peril receded could the British accept a practice which had continental associations. There may be a lesson in this as well for reform in the United States in our own hardly less ideological age.

The continuity of French administrative practice before and after the revolution is another illustration of the enormous persistence of practice. In the first flush of revolution all the police of the *Ancien Régime* were swept away. But they filtered back, like water rising through sand, both in terms of the forms of administration and the very personnel themselves. As de Tocqueville said, "every time that an attempt is made to do away with absolutism the most that could be done has been to graft the head of liberty onto a servile body" (de Tocqueville 1955: 209). Faced with the requirements of governing, French politicians constructed according to what they knew. Bureaucratic centralism was to persist, constituting a powerful force for stability, continuity, purposeful government, and political socialization.

Even major social dislocations like the Industrial Revolution do not change the course of police history invariably. The structure and control of national police systems continue to display unique features from country to country even though they have felt the effects of what is usually described as a singular economic transformation. Study of the mutations of national police development bears out Dahrendorf's assertion: "Contrary to the beliefs of many, the Industrial Revolution is not the prime mover of the modern world at all. . . . Every country absorbs industrialization into its own traditions; every country assimilates the process in a manner peculiar to it alone;

---

[33] Critchley 1967: 54, quoting a spoken exchange of Peel with the Duke of Wellington, who led the fight for Peel's reform in the House of Lords.

in every country there emerges an amalgamation of cultural traditions and ramifications of industrialization characteristic of it alone" (Dahrendorf 1967: 46–47).

The fourth attribute of contemporary police systems to be explained has to do with professional image and role behavior. Given the general lack of data about this topic and its impressionistic form at best, analysis cannot be as definite as in the preceding discussion. It is possible, however, to link contemporary characteristics with formative historical experiences during the period when these police systems developed.

The London police of 1829 faced enormous public hostility. Peel's system was a revolutionary experiment whose success depended upon persuading people that police did not constitute a threat to cherished liberties. Their behavior was deliberately and dramatically low-key, nonauthoritarian, and informal. They were not allowed to carry weapons. It was not even clear at the time whether it was advisable for them to wear distinctive uniforms. Peel and the first Commissioners, Rowan and Mayne, decided after a great deal of consideration that the police should be uniformed in order to make the constable more visible and hence more responsible. So great was the public dislike of plainclothes policemen that a detective squad was not organized until 1842—and then it numbered only five men—and a formal C.I.D. was not created until 1878. The uniform adopted was dull, completely lacking in military glamor. It consisted of blue tailed coat, blue trousers, and glazed black top hat (Critchley 1967: 51). No suspicion was to be aroused that the police were a state military force in other guise. Police constables were distinguished individually by a number worn prominently on their uniforms. French policemen did not begin to wear numbers until after 1852; German policemen not until after World War II and it may not yet be universal; Italian policemen still do not do so.

British policemen were always imbued with the notion that they were servants, not masters, of the people. Policemen were trained to act individually; rarely did they patrol in groups. They were always accountable to the law. Prevention of crime as well as control of disorder was to be achieved with the least display of force possible. British policemen molded their behavior pragmatically to accomplish very specific ends; being a policeman was not a matter of playing a visible authority-role, though in the end it came to mean that in a peculiarly subtle way.

The French police were created to accomplish state purposes. The ethos was not of service to individual citizens but of responsiveness to state direction. Though public opinion was probably not less antagonistic to the plainclothes police officer in France than in Great Britain, detectives, spies, and informers have been a fixture of the French police establishment since its inception. Uniformed police officers have characteristically worked in small groups, rarely alone. They have always been impressively armed. In the seventeenth and eighteenth centuries considerable reliance was placed on army personnel for preventive patrolling. Recruitment from the military to the police has always been heavy at all rank levels. Separation of executive and judicial functions in the exercise of police powers was not confirmed until the nineteenth century. During the eighteenth century, justice had been swift at the hands of the rural *Gendarmerie*, for its officers possessed full judicial powers.

The relatively more authoritarian character of the Prussian and German police is part of the extensive regimentation that has been a feature of this political heritage. The Prussian police, like citizens generally, were taught to emulate the soldier and to serve the state unquestioningly. That the military model was assiduously adopted can be seen in small things. In the middle of the nineteenth century police campaigned for permission to wear the spiked helmet of the Prussian soldier. Over army protests, the favor was granted (Liang 1970: 28). Until Weimar, police officers were invariably retired army officers. After World War I the requirement of military service for recruits was relaxed, but the physical discipline and training of policemen remained very high and was patterned on the army. As a result, only the most robust youths could join. In Berlin during the Weimar period recruits were drawn heavily from rural East Prussia because they were apt to be stronger and more malleable. While they were probably politically more reliable as well, they could not have had much understanding of the human problems of Berlin during those anxious, violent days (Liang 1970: 58–59). Even today in Germany recruits spend several years living a barracks life before being promoted to municipal or state forces.

The Italian police have been dominated by the military since unification. Today the officers of the P.S., supposedly a counterpoise to the *Carabinieri*, are recruited from the military. Circumstances in Italy over the past hundred years have encouraged army discipline, training, and usage. The south of Italy seethed with uprisings, interpersonal violence, and brigandage during the last years of the nineteenth century. In the burgeoning industrial areas of the north, violence was common. Confrontation continues to be a prime tactic of Italy's labor unions. Italian policemen consider the maintenance of law and order their major responsibility. They are heavily armed and always work in groups.

In sum, the role behavior of policemen in all these countries is a reflection of the purposes for which the force was created and the political culture of the country, especially the way in which authority is manifested by government officials.

The discussion of this section has shown that characteristic solutions to police problems, if one sets aside role behavior and professional image, can be explained in terms of six independent variables. These variables are presented in summary form in Figure 5–5. The

Independent Variables

1. Practices Prior to Police Development:
   a. Bureaucratic Centralization
   b. Political Centralization
   c. Independent Legal System

2. Violent Public Resistance to:
   a. State-Building
   b. Nation-Building } Legitimacy Crises
   c. Mobilization Demands

3. Socioeconomic Changes, Producing:
   ← a. Increased Political Participation →
   b. New Law-and-Order Tasks ←
   c. Changes in Social Basis of Community

4. Geopolitical Position, Affecting:
   a. Standing Army
   b. Earliness of Formation in
      State History

5. Religion:
   a. Internal Conflict
   b. Tradition of Right-Belief

6. Increased Political Participation,
   Producing Elite Resistance

Police System Attributes

1. Tasks
   a. Law and Order and Crime
   b. Political

2. Structure
   a. Centralization-Decentralization
   b. Military-Civilian Forces

3. Accountability
   a. Political-Bureaucratic
   b. Legal: Administrative or
             Independent

4. Professional Image and Role
   Behavior

[5. Internal Organization]

Figure 5–5. Variables Used in the Analysis of Police Systems

reader should note that there are interrelationships among the independent variables. Of special interest is the fact that increased political participation may generate new law and order problems in two ways. Demand for increased participation may be violent. More interestingly, through representation of new strata, existing but hitherto unperceived law and order tasks may at last be noted. The new law and order needs thus find political voice.

One lesson that has emerged from this study is the impermeability of national police systems over time. This, however, is not the whole story. Systems do change. Moreover, they do so to some extent in converging directions. Areas of convergence in police system development are greatest with respect to internal organization and task-definition. Convergence is least noticeable with respect to national structure, control, and role behavior. Training programs have become longer and more elaborate in all these countries in the past half century. There is also much greater specialization of functions within the forces. The detective-patrolman division has been hardened, with the former being the more prestigious, and functional specialties have developed within each branch. Even in Britain, which recently reaffirmed the practice of selecting top command personnel exclusively by promotion, there is growing recognition that command responsibility requires special talent (Royal Commission 1962: 90–95). So far special training for higher ranks has been the only concession to this requirement, but it may not be long before direct recruitment is permitted or much shortened probationary periods as patrolmen are allowed for highly qualified applicants. In general, those elements of police organization change most readily where a standard of efficiency can be brought to bear. Since efficiency is a function of tasks and environment, if both are similar from country to country, different systems will tend to innovate in convergent ways.

There is evidence of convergence at a few points with respect to structure, control, and role behavior as well. Even in decentralized systems, such as Britain's or Germany's, central training and forensic facilities are common. The Germans and British have made great strides in the twentieth century in the direction of ensuring effective cooperation among forces. The Police Act, 1964, in Great Britain makes local forces responsible to Parliament, through the Home Secretary. Britain has not yet grasped the nettle of full nationalization, but it is much closer to it in practice than it was a century ago. Legal accountability, as well, has shown changes. There is strong support in Great Britain for having the government incur the costs of monetary damages assessed against policemen for actions undertaken in the line of duty. Policemen have always been liable individually for their actions as policemen. Since their ability to pay civil damages was slight, scant recompense was to be had by the aggrieved party. Conversely, on the continent my impression is that administrative courts are more anxious than they used to be to provide relief to citizens against individual policemen. Accordingly, more attention is being given to complaint procedures, to making the police officer identifiable individually to citizens, and to specifying those actions government considers improper in a policeman.

The most difficult area to explore is that of role behavior and professional image. The policemen of each nation still display distinctive traits. At the same time, the importance of good public relations has received much more attention in France, Germany, and Italy in the last decade or so. The British, on the other hand, worried about a decline in respect for policemen, are openly wondering whether they need to provide policemen with firearms.

All in all, there are processes of convergence at work: those which are traceable to conditions of task-performance shift more rapidly than those which involve the organization and control of political power.

Conclusion

This chapter has sought to explain why contemporary police systems have assumed the forms they have. Attributes of contemporary systems have been treated as dependent variables. Analysis has been framed in terms of five attributes of police systems, to which have been linked seven independent variables dealing with historical development. In order to pull together the bits and pieces of this comparative analysis, I shall reprise the major propositions about police development that have been generated:

1. The contemporary police systems of Great Britain, France, Germany, and Italy differ substantially with respect to definition of tasks, structure of the national system, manner in which accountability is achieved, internal organization and practice, and role behavior and professional image.

2. Not only are police systems unique nationally, their distinctive features are relatively impermeable in the face of wars, revolutions, and major social and economic transformations. The distinctive characteristics of these police systems have shown remarkable stability over time.

3. The contemporary systems of these nations emerged at different periods of time: Great Britain's between 1829 and 1888; France's in the latter seventeenth century; Germany's (or Prussia's) from the mid-eighteenth century to 1872; and Italy's between 1859 and 1870.

4. The development of today's national police systems cannot be accounted for by population growth, urbanization, incidence of criminality, or industrialization.

5. The development of today's systems can be accounted for in terms of a transformation in the organization of political power, prolonged violent popular resistance to government, and the creation of new law and order tasks as well as the erosion of social bases upon which community authority relations were established.

6. The characteristic forms of police systems can be explained by the interaction among seven variables: practices prior to modern police development having to do with the organization of power, social violence, socioeconomic change, geopolitical position, religion, and elite reactions to demands for increased political participation.

7. Patterns of police system growth are converging very slightly with respect to structure of the national system, nature of force units, and means of exercising accountability. Convergence is most clear in connection with those features involving task-performance where a standard of efficiency may appropriately be applied.

Analysis focusing upon police systems as dependent variables can reveal only half the story about relations between police and their political environment. The other half concerns the effect of police operations and organization upon the encapsulating society. There is a reciprocal relationship between the police and politics. The police are not completely passive; they can play a formative role in determining the character of political life.

The manner and extent to which police have influenced politics in different nations is a complex subject, one that would require extended discussion and considerable further research. Let me only say, at the risk of being provocative without satisfying, that police organizations appear to affect politics in at least five distinguishable ways: (1) by direct impingement of their role activities upon political life; (2) by political socialization of citizens in authoritative contacts; (3) by serving as an avenue for political recruitment and advancement; (4) by socializing policemen to politics; and (5) by being a particular kind of institution, capable of exerting a demonstration effect and creating various kinds of effective demands.

While the characteristics of police systems—tasks, structure, accountability, etc.—can be treated as dependent variables related to conditions of national histories, the political outputs of police systems cannot be treated as dependent variables exclusively related to characteristics of police systems. Another major variable is required to explain political outputs, a variable which is not a function of the police establishment itself. This critical variable is the determination made by a political elite about the use to which it is to be put. Thus, while attributes of police systems do affect their political output, they are not a sufficient cause of the nature of political impingement by the police establishment.

Historical events shape police institutions; police organization and practice affect political life; political life conditions future historical development. This system of interaction feeds back upon itself, though the system is by no means closed. The units of this analysis are presented in Figure 5–6, though the relations among them are too complex for representation in a single chart.

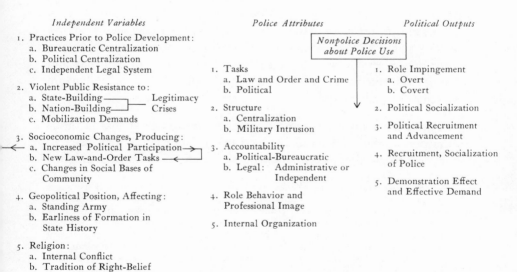

Figure 5–6. Police Organization and Political Life

CHAPTER 6

FOOD SUPPLY AND PUBLIC ORDER
IN MODERN EUROPE

CHARLES TILLY

Men Fight for Food

Era quello il second'anno di raccolta scarsa . . . questa messe
tanto desiderata riusci ancor piu misera della precedente, in
parte per maggior contriaretà delle stagioni . . . in parte per
colpe degli uomini.

This was the second short harvest in a row . . . and this crop was
even more pitiful than the last, partly because the weather was
worse, and partly because of human failings (Manzoni 1966:
310–311).[1]

So begins a chapter of Manzoni's *I promessi sposi*, the famous novel
of seventeenth-century Milan. In such matters, Manzoni (who was
writing in the 1820s) followed the historical record closely. Not long
after that miserable harvest of 1628 came the events of Saturday and
Sunday, November 11 and 12: the *tumulto di San Martino*. Manzoni
sketches the background:

The destruction and turmoil of the war were so great that in the
section of the state most involved many more fields than usual
remained untilled, abandoned by the peasants, who had to go

Freddi Greenberg and Ann O'Shea gave me invaluable bibliographical assistance
in the preparation of this essay. Julian Dent, Val Lorwin, Peter Paret and the other members of our seminar made a number of valuable suggestions and criticisms.
I owe several of the central ideas of the paper to Louise Tilly. Nicolas Sanchez-
Albornoz gave me some important bibliographic leads for Spain. An unpublished
manuscript by Immanuel Wallerstein helped me formulate my ideas concerning the
interaction of Eastern and Western Europe during the sixteenth and seventeenth
centuries. The National Science Foundation supported the research underlying this
paper, and the Institute for Advanced Study gave me the leisure to rewrite it. Perhaps
I should apologize for the breadth of the general title; the paper says little about
Eastern Europe, nothing about the Baukans or Scandinavia and virtually nothing
about the period since 1850.
[1] All translations from sources cited in languages other than English are my own.

begging instead of working for their bread. I said: more than usual, because the insupportable burden of the troops billeted in the country . . . had already been producing that sad effect in the whole Milanese territory for some time. . . . And this particular harvest was not yet in when the provisioning of the army, and the waste that always comes with it, made such a dent in the harvest, that the shortage was felt at once, and with the shortage its unhappy, useful and inevitable effect, a rise in prices. But when the price rise reaches a certain level, people always begin to think that scarcity is not its cause. They forget that they discussed and predicted it; they suppose all of a sudden that there is enough grain, and that the trouble results from the fact that not enough is being sold. . . . The hoarders of grain (real or imagined), the landlords who don't sell everything in one day, the bakers who buy, everyone who has a little, or is said to have a little, take the blame for the shortage and for the rise in prices. . . . People implored the magistrates to take measures, measures which the crowd considers simple, just and certain to bring out the hidden, walled-up, buried grain, and to bring back plenty. The magistrates did do something: fixed the maximum price for various foodstuffs, threatened to punish those who refused to sell, and other edicts of the sort. Since such measures, however vigorous, do not have the virtue of diminishing the need for food, growing crops out of season, or attracting supplies from areas of surplus, the evil lasted, and grew. The crowd attributed that effect to the incompleteness and weakness of the remedies, and shouted for more generous and decisive ones (Manzoni 1966: 311–313).

At that point, much to Manzoni's retrospective disapproval, the grand chancellor of Milan (who was, in that time of Spanish hegemony, an official of the Spanish crown) set the bread price. "He set it," complains Manzoni, "at a price which would have been right if grain had been selling ordinarily at thirty-three lire the moggio,[2] when it was actually selling for up to eighty. He acted like an old woman who makes herself young by changing her birth certificate" (Manzoni 1966: 314–315).

But the people of Milan approved, chanting:

[2] A *moggio* is about 150 liters.

> Viva Spagna e 'l gran cancellier
> ch'ha messo il pane a segno del dover!
> (Nicolini 1934: 179)

The merchants (and, it appears, the nobles, who were deeply involved in the supply of grain to Milan) showed less enthusiasm. The crowd invaded the bakers and grain-merchants, sacked their shops if they resisted selling all they had at the posted price, or if they did not have enough to sell. The troops came out. Four men were hanged. And Milan returned to tranquillity.

About fifteen decades later, a similar chain of events occurred in Paris and its hinterland: the *Guerre des Farines*. For about ten years the royal administration had been contending with the *Parlements* concerning the efforts of the crown to reduce local controls over the distribution of food and remove barriers to the marketing of grain; most of the old apparatus had survived. In 1774 the able and doctrinaire Turgot had become Comptroller General of Finances, the key position in government surveillance of commerce. He soon moved vigorously to free the domestic grain trade. Unfortunately for his plans, the harvest of 1774 was bad, prices rose markedly . . . and Paris still had to eat. The Parisian breadbasket felt the pressure in the spring of 1775. George Rudé tells the tale:

> It began on April 27 at Beaumont-sur-Oise, a market town twenty miles north of Paris. According to the senior magistrate, who was later charged with complicity in the affair, the riots arose from the bakers' refusal to bake more bread and the high prices demanded by the grain merchants. He himself was asked to intervene; but, although entitled as a last resort to adjust the price of bread, having no authority to reduce the market price of wheat, he refused. So the local people, with the porters of Beaumont at their head, and the peasants from neighboring villages took the law into their own hands, invaded the market, and compelled the dealers to sell their wheat at a "just" or reasonable price—in this instance, at 12 francs a *setier* (Rudé 1964: 24; cf. Rudé 1956 and 1961).

The movement spread through a broad band of markets north and south of Paris, reaching the capital itself on the market day of Wednesday, May 3.

At the time, the chief official responsible for *la police* (significantly, *la police* then included surveillance of provisioning as well as control of public spaces) was Jean-Charles-Pierre Lenoir. Lenoir had appealed delicately to Turgot for some authority to act against probable food riots in that season; Turgot had applied an indelicate veto. Lenoir had nevertheless alerted the troops stationed in Paris. Even so, he had the greatest difficulty getting action when the food riots began on May 3, for Turgot had instructed the military not to move without express orders from the king.

As Lenoir confided the story to his memoirs:

The musketeers, who had been warned the day before, hurried to the markets. The fleeing rioters overturned baskets full of bread and blocked the way to the horses. It was 9 A.M.; the watch was supposed to be getting its orders at that hour, and the people had already gone to the bakers and seized the bread they found in the shops. That pillage had a special character. People did it without violence. The shops of the bakers were emptied, but those of the pastry-makers and the dealers in other foods, which were equally exposed, were left untouched (Darnton 1969: 615–616).

For his pains, Lenoir received a request for his resignation. For the pains of the rioters:

In less than a week more than 150 persons were imprisoned by *lettre de cachet* on suspicion of having taken part in various riots. Farmers who had continued to supply the markets of the city and the surrounding area (despite the fact that others had turned them away) were among the prisoners. Two workers were hanged as examples. There was an army camped or billeted in Paris and its surrounding area for six months (Darnton 1969: 617).

And Paris returned to tranquillity.

The two cases we have examined so far, although widely separated in time, were Latin, urban, small in scale and prior to the nineteenth century. Lest we conclude that any of these characteristics is essential to the link between disorder and interruption of the food supply, let us skip to East Anglia in 1816. Here is A. J. Peacock's initial *précis*:

In the early summer of 1816 England was surprised and alarmed by the news that the agricultural labourers of East Anglia had come out in revolt. Conditions had worsened since the ending of the Napoleonic war, and riots and disturbances were everyday occurrences in the towns. The rural population, however, had been regarded as supine, lethargic and, although prone to riot on a small scale, never likely or capable of taking part in a movement serious enough to cause a real threat to society.

The train of events that ended in a specially staged trial of the rioters at Ely and Littleport began in 1815. As conditions worsened, the incidents increased in number. They also altered in character. At first there were attacks on property (usually farm implements) in remote villages. Later, when a really serious rise in the price of bread started, there were attacks on both property and persons in the few large towns in the area—Bury St. Edmonds first, then Brandon, Norwich and Downham Market. Last of all the labourers of Littleport broke out in rebellion on 21st May. The following day they marched to Ely, where they enlisted the aid of the locals and terrorised the millers and magistrates, forcing the latter to capitulate and agree to their demands. Later they took part in an unequal pitched battle with the military in which a life was lost. Five more of their number were eventually executed, dozens of them were transported, and the area was pacified for the next twenty or thirty years (Peacock 1965: 11).

At Littleport, fifty or sixty farm laborers met at a pub. After long discussion, they went to make demands of John Vachell, vicar and magistrate. The demands: work, bread, and his presence at a meeting with the farmers who normally hired them. Despite Vachell's proposal of a minimum wage of two shillings per day and a maximum price for flour of two shillings sixpence per stone, the meeting broke up into attacks on shops and farms, and collections from shopkeepers and farmers who were willing to pay to avoid damage.

That night members of the crowd seized weapons where they could, and prepared for a march to Ely the next day. In the market of Ely, the frightened magistrates set down the following agreement:

The Magistrates agree, and do order that the overseers—shall pay to each family Two Shillings per Head per week, when flour is Half a Crown a Stone; such allowance be raised in proportion when the price of Flour is higher, and that the price of Labour shall be Two Shillings per day, whether married or Single and that the Labourer shall be paid his full wages by the Farmer, who hires him (Peacock 1965: 102).

Which gives a fairly clear idea of what the men were after. They added a last demand: "forgiveness of what had passed." After one more threat ("we will have Blood before Dinner") that demand, too, won out. The crowd then took to exacting cash contributions from the local millers and flour merchants. They spent the contributions in the local inns. Then the rioters of Littleport dispersed.

Troops arrived in Ely, and marched on to Littleport, the next day. The troops met minor resistance, killed one rioter, and made numerous arrests. The trials began almost immediately. On June 28, five of the Littleport men were hanged. And East Anglia returned to tranquillity.

The Physiognomy of the Food Riot

Historians have long known the *tumulto* of 1628, the Flour War of 1775, the riots of 1816. My summaries add nothing to existing accounts. On the contrary, they do injustice to the richness of the record and the complexity of the events. Yet these quick digests have a virtue. They characterize the most frequent form of collective violence setting ordinary people against governmental authorities in most of Europe for at least a century of the modern era. One variety or another of the food riot prevailed in most European countries until well into the nineteenth century. What is more, conflicts over the food supply became more widespread and virulent toward the end, despite the fact that the productivity of agriculture was increasing, the threat of death-dealing famine dwindling.

The first action of the crowd ordinarily struck a presumed hoarder or profiteer. Nevertheless, as our three scenarios make clear, the authorities were in the thick of it from the start, both because of their responsibility for public order, and because of their heavy involvement in surveillance and control of the food supply. Conflicts over the food supply immediately raised a threat to public order. The political authorities of Europe before the twentieth century were

perfectly aware of the connection, but twentieth-century men looking back in time often relegate the food riot and similar conflicts to
the category of impulsive, prepolitical protest.

If we ignore the intimate relation of the food riot to the everyday
administration and politics of the old regime, we shall neglect the
coherent political action the riot represents. Far from being impulsive, hopeless reactions to hunger, bread riots and other struggles
over the food supply took a small number of relatively well-defined
forms. Furthermore, they often worked in the short run; crowd action brought prices down, forced stored grain into the public domain, and impelled the authorities to greater efforts toward assuring
the food supply. Finally, the work of the crowd embodied a critique
of the authorities, was often directed consciously at the authorities,
and commonly consisted of the crowd's taking precisely those measures its members thought the authorities had failed their own responsibility to take—inventorying grain in private hands, setting a
price, and so on. The food riot was a political event, an important
one.

A few distinctions will make the relationship between the food riot
and the politics of subsistence clearer. The term "food riot" actually
identifies three different kinds of action, and suggests a fourth.[3] The
three included under the label are: (1) the *retributive action* in
which the crowd directly attacks the person or property, including
the food supply, of someone accused of withholding or profiteering;
(2) the *price riot*, in which the crowd seizes food, declares a price,
and sells it publicly; (3) the *blockage*, in which the crowd prevents
a shipment of food (whether passing through or originating in the
place in question) from leaving the locality. None of these consumers'
actions should be confused with the fourth, which producers carry
on: (4) the *agrarian demonstration*, in which farmers dump or destroy their produce in protest. The agrarian demonstration, at least
statistically speaking, is quite a new phenomenon; it continues in Europe to this day. The retributive action; on the other hand, is ancient
—probably as old as agricultural marketing systems of any
complexity.

Historically, there were some other occasions in which food became the focus of serious conflicts. Recurrently, artisans and field

[3] Slightly different, but compatible, distinctions appear in L. Tilly 1971 and R. B.
Rose 1959. The discussions of the food riot in this paper (especially in the case of
France) rely heavily on the former, the best general paper on the topic.

laborers who were fed as part of their remuneration mounted complaints against changes in their rations or declines in the quality of their victuals. Along with peace and land, bread often stood for a political program of survival for the little man in movements far broader than any bread riot; the Russian Revolution of 1917 is only the best-known case.

In the nineteenth and twentieth centuries, the high cost of living often became a central theme of strikes and workers protests; the little port riot described earlier came as close to those recent forms as it did to a classic food riot. Struggles over the tithe or over taxation often focused on the seizure of crops by the collector or the imposition of an additional payment for beer, wine, salt, or other foodstuffs. In a more general sense, most attempts to seize common lands or break up estates involved a conflict over the right of some part of the population to a means of raising food. The retributive action, the price riot and the blockage simply reveal in purest form the struggle for control over the existing supply of food.

The blockage and the price riot belong more particularly to the history we are tracing here. Actions to block the shipment of grain characteristically took place in small towns and villages. They acted out the belief that the locals should be fed, at a proper price, before any surplus left town. They rose, therefore, as the effective demand for grain to feed cities and armies extended into agricultural regions previously little involved in production for the market; in those regions the higher prices of the metropolitan market enticed producers and merchants to ship their grain away. But custom, local needs, and, often enough, the village authorities held them back. The blockage gave the village's consumers the means of coercing the sellers and the local authorities. But it could only work (and was, in fact, only likely to be tried) where there were few merchants and where the authorities were sympathetic, weak and/or divided. That means outside the areas of thoroughgoing agrarian capitalism.

Blockages tended to occur in rings around port cities or metropolitan centers, but at some distance from them, because their immediate vicinities were already fully commercialized and because the search for grain in times of shortage led merchants further out in all directions, into villages in which the export of grain produced acute political conflict. At least the pattern seems to hold for France, the only country in which the geography of the food riot has been closely examined.

The blockage sometimes occurred in towns and cities in times of exceptional shortage and extraordinary exports. The city, however, preferred the price riot, and the price riot preferred the city. For the price riot directly and immediately affected the operation of the local market, instead of simply preventing a depletion of the supply. Consumers routinely dependent on the market for their subsistence had the greatest interest in manipulating that market. They concentrated in towns and cities. Furthermore, it was the towns and cities of Europe which developed the most elaborate controls over the marketing of food, precisely because their populations were so vulnerable both to natural disasters and to profiteering. The price riot consisted of the crowd's imposition of some of those elaborate controls in the place of the mayor and his council. So it embodied a criticism of their performance and a usurpation of their functions.

Notice how well the participants in each of these forms of riot knew the script. We are dealing with a neglected but widespread feature of old-regime conflicts: their permeation with ritual and with natural justice. From the Renaissance or earlier, Natalie Davis (1971) has pointed out, European communities periodically carried on festivals in which ordinary people took the part of local elites in caricature and garish disguise. Today's costumed carousing of carnival descends from older celebrations which contained a much more direct and uncompromising critique of the way the authorities were doing their work.

But the festivals of Misrule analyzed by Natalie Davis were sanctioned (however apprehensively) by the authorities. During more serious crises, the ordinary people of Europe sometimes took justice into their own hands, in an almost literal sense of the phrase. They adopted the rituals, formulas and actions of judges as they meted out justice to those whom they condemned. In the Germanic areas, especially Switzerland, the midwinter *Maskenrecht* sometimes turned from its masked mimicry of the privileged classes to direct, organized retribution against them; in the Swiss cantonal wars, masked avengers played an important role (Wackernagel 1956: 222–258).

The taking of the Bastille in 1789 had an even more decided judicial character (Godechot 1970). The crowd condemned de Launey, the governor of the Bastille, as a traitor. They proposed to hang him and drag his body through the streets, tied to a horse's tail; they did decapitate him and display his severed head; all of these belonged to the ritual of executing a traitor in old-regime France.

[388]

Again, the widespread rural rebellions of Great Britain between 1790 and 1830 had recurrent elements of ritual, mystification and natural justice: men costumed as women, as in the Rebecca riots, blackened faces, mythical redressers like Ned Ludd and Captain Swing, the acting out of justice, expansion of the long-established rituals of role reversal. E. J. Hobsbawm and George Rudé (1968) say of the demands made by the participants in the 1830 revolt of agricultural laborers in southern England:

> During the repression these demands came to be defined as "extortion" and used as a pretext for asking the death penalty (which would not have been possible for destroying a threshing machine alone), but in reality they proved the extremely moderate character of the movement, since they were obviously an enlarged form of the periodic rituals in use in English villages in which for a brief moment the social positions were reversed and the poor man had the right to ask a symbolic contribution of the rich before returning to his subordinate role. The rebels adopted that familiar and temporary ritual, and the donors were soon thanked for the gift extorted, precisely because the laborers did not *really* mean to modify the social order or expropriate the rich (Hobsbawm & Rudé 1968: 270).

The food riot, in which ordinary people took the place of authorities in controlling the distribution of the necessities of life, was one of the least dramatic—but most frequent—members of this class of redressing rituals.

The ritual disappeared from most of Europe during the nineteenth century. The efficiency of production and distribution of food increased sufficiently during the nineteenth century to greatly reduce the squeeze on consumers, even in bad years. Furthermore, state-makers and merchants succeeded in dissolving most of the framework of peasant life throughout the continent, in encouraging the emergence of cash-crop producers oriented to national markets, and thus in destroying the bases on which the peasantry resisted and had the capacity to resist. For serious conflicts over the food supply occurred not so much where men were hungry as where they believed others were unjustly depriving them of food to which they had a moral and political right. The dissolution of the peasant community removed the chief defenders of those rights. The food riot vanished as the peasants lost their struggle against the penetration of capitalism into the countryside.

Against the Hydraulic Model

The political ramifications of conflicts over food supply deserve emphasis. A simpler view of the connection between food supply and disorder has generally held sway over historical analyses of the seventeenth to nineteenth centuries. Beloff maintains:

> The afflicted classes themselves varied in temper between a condition of mute resignation, in face of the uncomprehended hardships of their lot, and one of sullen antagonism against those apparently responsible for them. Their resentment, when unemployment and high prices combined to make conditions unendurable, vented itself in attacks upon corn-dealers and millers —attacks which often must have degenerated into mere excuses for crime (Beloff 1938: 75).

The image is hydraulic: hardship increases, pressure builds up, the vessel bursts. The angry individual acts as a reservoir of resentment, a conduit of tension, a boiler of fury. But not as a thinking, political man operating on principle.

Even authors basically sympathetic to the aspirations of ordinary men commonly adopt that sort of theory. Consider the writing of G.D.H. Cole and Raymond Postgate, dealing with the period after the Napoleonic Wars:

> In these circumstances, the post-war collapse of industry was bound to lead to terrible distress. Despite drastic scaling-down of the rates of relief, the sums expended for poor relief, which had been under 2,000,000 before the war, and about £5,000,000 in 1815, rose to nearly £7,000,000 in 1816, and nearly £8,000,000 in the following year; and, in addition, considerable sums were expended out of voluntary funds raised for the relief of distress. Despite this expenditure starvation walked through the land, producing the inevitable reaction in hunger-riots, machine-breaking and other spontaneous outbursts of popular misery (Cole and Postgate 1961: 210–211).

Now, it is true that 1816 was a terrible year through most of Europe, and that years of dearth brought clusters of food riots. It is not true, however, that hunger was enough to bring on rioting, or that the amount of rioting was closely correlated with the amount of hunger. Famished Ireland did not rebel in 1846. For most of the nineteenth century, the better-supplied North produced the bulk of Italy's food riots. What the local authorities, millers, bakers, and merchants did with whatever grain was on hand made the big difference. The so-called rioters responded to the way these worthies did their duty.

The Hammonds caught an important aspect of the phenomenon in their description of the English food riots of 1795:

> These disturbances are particularly interesting from the discipline and good order which characterize the conduct of the rioters. The rioters when they found themselves masters of the situation did not use their strength to plunder the shops: they organized distribution, selling the food they seized at what they considered fair rates, and handing over the proceeds to the owners. They did not rob: they fixed prices, and when the owner of provisions was making for a dearer market they stopped his carts and made him sell on the spot. . . . At Bath the women actually boarded a vessel, laden with wheat and flour, which was lying in the river and refused to let her go. When the Riot Act was read they retorted that they were not rioting, but were resisting the sending of corn abroad, and sang God Save the King. Although the owner took an oath that the corn was destined for Bristol, they were not satisfied, and ultimately soldiers were called in, and the corn was relanded and put into a warehouse. In some places the soldiers helped the populace in their work of fixing prices; at Seaford, for example, they seized and sold meat and flour in the churchyard, and at Guildford they were ringleaders in a movement to lower the price of meat to 4d a pound, and were sent out of town by the magistrates in consequence (Hammond and Hammond 1924: 96–98).

The housewives and soldiers were asserting the right of ordinary people to be fed, and to be fed in a certain way.

The hydraulic view of protest (and not only in the case of the food riot) grows from a series of misconceptions: that both hardship and rapid social change generate undifferentiated tensions which find expression variously as crime, madness, protest or group disintegration; that politics only comes into being when men start acting self-consciously in terms of parties and programs at a national level; that ordinary people are incapable of sustained political thought, but are moved to collective action by impulse. Although such views receive their fullest expression in ideologies of the Right, they do not belong uniquely to any political position; they are, in fact, part of the common-sense sociology of our time.

And they are wrong. There is no solid evidence for the idea that rapid social change as such produces more tension than slow social change, some evidence against the idea that those who suffer most shout the loudest, and a great deal of evidence against the equivalence of different sorts of "disorder." The limitation of politics to programs and parties at a national level ignores the conscious and energetic participation of large numbers of men in local struggles for power long before the nation-state became the principal arena of political contestation. And the condescending view of the ordinary man's political capacities rests on the presumption that theories of how the land should be used, what households owe each other, how much the government can tell a man to do, or who has what right to the local food supply are not really very important in the long run, and are in any case likely to be drawn uncritically from tradition. Knock out these props, and old-fashioned conflicts like the food riot begin to reveal a political structure, prior to the victory of the nation-state over its antagonists, which twentieth-century observers rarely see.

The Political Significance of Food

In the last analysis, the food riot was only an epiphenomenon. Below the surface raged a long struggle by builders of states to secure the survival of the people most dependent on them and most inclined to serve their ends, a struggle to wrest the means of subsistence from a fiercely reluctant peasantry. It paralleled the struggle to extract labor (most notably via *corvées* and conscription) and wealth (most notably via taxation). It complemented those struggles. For a long time, the life of the state depended on the success of the battle for food. "Under the old economic regime," comments Jean Meyer (1966: 1, 477), "the grain problem dominated all the worries of the government, took precedence among all questions of welfare."

That struggle, rather than the food riot, is the real concern of this essay. When did conflicts over the control or distribution of food drive Europeans into collective action, and take on political significance? Under what conditions, and how, did European states intervene actively in the control and distribution of food? What difference did the manner and extent of their intervention make to the subsequent political experiences of the states involved? Answers to such broad questions have to be equally broad. I can best state my tentative answers as a series of straightforward theses; the later discussion will qualify them considerably:

1. Instead of being in any simple sense responses to hunger, serious conflicts over the food supply ordinarily occurred when groups of men felt their established right to a particular source of food was being violated by identifiable groups of others, especially merchants, officials or holders of food.

2. This situation became much more common (and severe conflicts over food therefore prevalent) when states began to assure the subsistence of those populations most dependent upon them and/or threatening to them—notably armed forces, administrative staffs and populations of capital cities—by direct commandeering of food or by promotion of marketing at a national scale. The more extensive and rapid this intervention, the greater the conflict.

3. All states intervened more actively in the control of the distribution (if not the production or consumption) of food as their armed forces, bureaucracies and cities grew, although the extent of their intervention depended on the balance between the growth of these dependent populations and the supply of food already available through the internal and external market. The greater the imbalance, the greater the intervention.

4. In general, the alternate policies for control of food supply adopted by various European states depended on the more general strategies of state-making their leaders had (consciously or unconsciously) adopted, and especially on the relationships to landlords, peasants and merchants which those more general strategies entailed.

5. Nevertheless, the initial choice of methods of extraction, the early form of class coalitions with the crown, and the type of response to conflicts over food supply adopted all independently affected the path and pace of state-making, as well as the structure of power which emerged around the nineteenth- and twentieth-century state.

I am not proposing a Victual Theory of State-making. The ways state-makers raised revenues and waged war surely had more powerful effects on the kinds of states which emerged than did their modes of intervention in the food supply. Subsistence policy deserves separate study for three main reasons: (1) it had some independent influence on the building of the state; (2) it absorbed such a large part of routine governmental work that its study tells us a good deal about the vicissitudes of government in general; and (3) the examination of food supply draws our attention to the critical connections among the expansion of nation-states, the growth of diverse forms of agrarian capitalism, and the creation of industrial nations from a peasant base in Europe.

Now, people have to eat whether they are peasants or not; large governments always find themselves dealing somehow with food. Mesopotamian empires drew much of their tribute in grain, Ch'ing China set up a complex national system of granaries, the Japanese long paid their imperial officials in rice extracted from the countryside, and the establishment of the food market of the *agora* proved important to the development of the Athenian version of democracy. But the problems we are pursuing appear chiefly in populations composed largely of *peasants* and controlled by *states*. In fact, Eric Wolf has built a version of our problem into his very definition of the peasant community as consisting of "rural cultivators whose surpluses serve both to underwrite its own standard of living and to distribute the remainder to groups in society that do not farm but must be fed for their specific goods and services in turn" (Wolf 1966: 4).

Peasants predominated in the population of Europe from the Roman conquest until some time in the twentieth century. Only the Chinese experience with states and peasants is comparable in bulk or continuity. The European experience of the last few centuries stands off from the Chinese and from all others through its combination of a relatively homogeneous culture, numerous and shifting rival states, strongly autonomous local institutions and weak corporate kin groups. The results of these social arrangements have been to disperse and localize control over agricultural production, to multiply the rivals of any particular ruling group both within their own state and outside it, to give landlords great importance as political allies or rivals, to weaken the ability of peasants to act collectively at a scale larger than the village except as landlords themselves served as links among villages, and yet to make possible vigorous local resistance to the expansion of state power.

For our purposes, the most significant implications are that in order to draw food from the point of production merchants or statesmen would have to overcome the resistance of the peasant com-munity and either neutralize or co-opt the landlords. Of course, regional variations mattered: generally speaking, the accretion of power by landlords in Eastern Europe broke the capacity of villages to withhold grain quite early; corporate kin groups showed more vigor around the Mediterranean rim and in the Celtic fringe; large land-lords rarely had great power in the mountain areas; and the pres-ence or absence of cities made a difference even in the Middle Ages. Within a world perspective, nevertheless, the builders of states faced relatively similar conditions through most of Europe.

What is more, multiple states (despite incessant changes in their character and identity) have more or less continuously controlled the European population throughout the two millennia. That fact, too, sets off Europe from most other parts of the world. No need to exaggerate the control: some areas like the Scottish highlands came late to subjection. Parts of such lands as Sicily, Biscay, Brittany, Wales, Montenegro, or Greece periodically eased or wrenched themselves away from the grasp of the state. The states in question fluctuated tremendously in scale, strength, and territorial continuity. Nevertheless, the European experience has for centuries been an ex-perience of living in states populated largely by peasants. In the long run, the resources for both industrialization and state-making came largely from peasant villages. The rulers of European states based themselves in cities. They have in recent centuries recruited large staffs of dependent specialists detached from the land. The inhabit-ants of the cities have not raised nearly enough food on their own to supply their wants. In consequence, the struggle over the food sup-ply has permeated two thousand years of European history.

Here I am only concerned with the last four or five hundred years of that history, the period during which a relatively small number of strong, centralized states came to dominate the whole continent. During that time, one of the principal activities of European politi-cal officials was control of the food supply. Let me recapitulate the main reasons for that involvement of governments in questions of food—again as a series of theses to be qualified as the discussion proceeds:

1. With predominantly peasant populations, the great bulk of the resources of any kind which might be pried loose for governmental use were embedded in agriculture, and therefore most readily

manipulable through some kind of intervention in the production, the consumption or—more likely—the distribution of food.

2. The building of an urban, mercantile and manufacturing population (which was the ordinary, self-conscious objective of European state-makers, regardless of the scales of their states) required the creation of an agricultural surplus and of a reliable means of capturing it for urban consumption.

3. The creation of specialized staffs of government employees— emphatically including standing armies—multiplied the number of hungry mouths for which the government had direct responsibility.

4. Once these processes were underway, rising prices, shortages, and shipments designed to combat the one and the other were likely to mobilize some segment of the general population against the government and, at the extreme, to threaten the overthrow of the government.

State-making, the maintenance of public order and the control of the food supply therefore depended on each other intimately.

The problems we are examining break fairly conveniently into questions of demand, supply, distribution, the impact of state action on each of them, and the further political consequences of variations in that impact. I have already suggested that expanding states notably increased the demand for marketed food; that their intervention in the supply, while often very powerful in the long run, usually took rather indirect forms such as favoring the claims of one class or another to the land, imposing taxation which forced producers into the market, or choosing between the restriction and the encouragement of imports; that the deliberate intervention of European states concentrated on the distribution of food rather than its production or consumption; that the major choices (implicit and explicit) made by European states in these regards corresponded generally to their overall strategies; that the most notable short-run political effects of the choices governed the extent and locus of protests and overt conflicts concerning the right to specific supplies of food; that the most notable long-run effects had to do with the class alliances which emerged as the full-fledged modern state came into its own. In order to see the relations of these matters to each other more clearly, we shall have to consider the demand for food, and then the supply, before moving on to more serious scrutiny of deliberate governmental efforts to influence the food supply.

CHARLES TILLY

Demand and the Expanding State

We have to distinguish between the total demand for food and the demand for *marketed* food. The first is not, in principle, terribly hard to estimate, since it is a function of total population, composition of the population, and slowly changing standards of nutrition. I emphasize "in principle," for the practice is difficult indeed in the present state of knowledge. We have a broad, conventional picture of the rhythms of population growth over Europe as a whole (moderate in the sixteenth century, stagnating in the seventeenth, accelerating in the eighteenth and skyrocketing in the nineteenth) and some fragmentary information on both composition and nutritional standards. Not until another generation of demographic historians has done its work will there be any reliable way of translating these observations into the demand for calories, tons of bread, or something else. Furthermore, the differences within Europe will have to be considered: the frequently greater population growth of areas where landless labor was spreading, the probable loss of population in seventeenth-century Spain, and so on.

Even if we had an accurate moving picture of population change region by region, however, it would not tell us the demand for *marketed* food. For that purpose, we would have to know to what extent European households (and European communities as well) produced all the food they consumed at different points in time. Obviously Europeans already depended on a fairly complicated marketing system to sustain the nonproducing population which existed in 1500, and moved further away from household self-sufficiency as time went on. But, so far as I know, no one has seriously attempted to map those changes over time and space. The scattered and unreliable character of the evidence will make that task very difficult. And there are interesting complications: weighing the demand for salt (which was early in trade and frequently the object of heavy taxation and/or government monopoly) against the demand for meat; considering the effects of seasonal alternations between self-supply and dependency on the market; allowing for the frequency with which people in cities raised their own food inside the walls or drew it directly from properties they controlled outside the walls; figuring what proportion of the time peasant-conscripts of Prussia were away from home and fed through foraging, billeting, central commissaries, or their own purchases.

[397]

In short, all I can do is to enumerate some major sources of demand for marketed food which increased significantly in Europe after 1500, suggest their relationship to the growth of national states, and indicate why it might be worth the enormous effort it would take to actually measure the magnitudes and detect the effects. The sources of demand fall into three overlapping categories: (1) the increase in urban population; (2) the expansion of landless labor; (3) the growth of government staffs.

Cities

A long time ago, Schmoller pointed out the strong demand for marketed food set up by the growth of cities. Starting from the assumption that "Where bread is the principal means of subsistence, one can take some 400 pounds or 200 kilos of grain as the average annual need per capita; a little less when potatoes or other foods play a role, a little more when they are lacking" (1896: 698–699; cf. Braudel 1966: 1, 384–385), and went on to calculate that under the old conditions of production a German town of 5,000 persons would have to draw all the grain from at least eight square miles of agricultural area, while the cost of transport by land was so great that a settlement much larger than 5,000 could not exist without the importation of grain by water. The urbanization of Europe after 1500 therefore entailed both the subordination of an important part of the countryside to the needs of the city and the elaboration of an extensive system of transportation.

From the fragmentary information now available, one can put together Table 6–1. Before 1800 the estimates of city size and of total population in the table are both pocked with uncertainties. As orders of magnitude, they are probably usable. The figures show the urban and the total population maintaining roughly the same moderate pace of growth during the sixteenth and eighteenth centuries, accelerating after 1800, and growing furiously after 1850. Constantinople stood alone in the class of very large cities in 1500. The sixteenth century saw important growth, with Naples and Paris leading the way. Except for the great expansion of London, the seventeenth century brought a slackening of the pace. The table's figures indicate that the total population maintained roughly the same rate of growth —some 0.3 percent per year—from 1600 to 1700 as it did in the centuries immediately before and after. But the population in big cities grew so slowly during the seventeenth century that its share of the

TABLE 6–1. ESTIMATES OF EUROPEAN POPULATION IN CITIES OF 100,000 OR MORE, 1500–1950

Year	Total Population (millions)	Cities of 100,000+ Number	Cities of 100,000+ Population (millions)	Cities of 100,000+ Percent of Total Population
1500	56	6	0.8	1.4
1550	71	7–10	1.1–1.7	1.6–2.3
1600	85	13–14	1.8–2.9	2.2–3.4
1650	100	11–12	2.3–2.5	2.3–2.5
1700	120	14	2.6–3.1	2.2–2.6
1750	140	13–15	3.3–3.7	2.4–2.7
1800	187–190	23	5.4	2.8–2.9
1850	266	43	12.7	4.8
1900	497	143	50.1	10.1
1950	548	384	139.5	24.2

Sources: Carr-Saunders 1936; Durand 1967; Hélin 1963; Mauersberg 1960; Mols 1954–1956; Olbricht 1939; Reinhard, Armengaud and Dupâquier 1968; Ringrose 1969; Russell 1958; Weber 1899: I. From 1850 onward, I have preferred Durand's figures for total population to the many others available. From 1900, the figures are for urban agglomerations rather than cities in the narrow political sense. The latter definition would reduce the statistics for 1950 to 119 million people in 374 places, or 20.7 percent of the total population.

total may well have declined. Perhaps the slowing of urban growth had something to do with the much-mooted "crisis of the seventeenth century." It surely resulted in part from the expansion of industrial activity away from big cities into the surrounding small towns and countryside.

In any case, the growth of both total and urban population, and the urbanization of Europe, resumed in the eighteenth century, and accelerated toward 1800. As Roger Mols (1955: 48) summarizes the earlier period, "we note that the two principal surges occurred during the sixteenth and eighteenth centuries. The first was mainly to the advantage of two Mediterranean peninsulas; the second to the profit of the great modern capitals." That is exactly what a knowledge of the shifting geography of industry and wealth after 1500 would have led us to expect.

The appearance of the factory-based industrial city, from the late eighteenth century onward, dwarfed all previous urban growth. Nevertheless, the earlier growth of large cities significantly affected the demand for marketed food. London, which spurted from 200 thousand people in 1600 to 900 thousand in 1800, is an extreme case, but not an unimportant one. E. A. Wrigley suggests a rise in English agricultural productivity per head of 10 percent between 1650 and

1750, largely as a consequence of the intensification and specialization induced by London's demand. He adds:

> What can be said is that the steady growth in demand for food in London as population there increased, necessarily caused great changes in the methods used on farms over a wider and wider area, in the commercial organization of the food market, and in the transport of food. It must also have tended to increase the proportion of people living outside London who were not engaged directly in agriculture since tertiary employment was sure to increase in these circumstances. Drovers, carters, badgers, brokers, cattle dealers, corn chandlers, innkeepers and the like grew more and more numerous as larger and larger fractions of the year's flocks and crops were consumed at a distance from the areas in which they were produced (Wrigley 1967: 58).

Now we cannot simply extrapolate from the well-documented case of London to all other European urban growth, for the English economy was already exceptionally commercialized in 1650, English landlords were in an unusually strong position vis-à-vis their agricultural laborers and what remained of the peasantry, and the sheer size of London made its situation incomparable with any other cities but Naples and Paris. Smaller cities were still relying, to some extent, on local produce and on individual supply lines during the period of London's great growth. What we can say with the greatest confidence is that food production within cities and reliance on rural properties operated directly by city-dwellers accounted for a decreasing proportion of the total urban supply, especially from the eighteenth century onward, and that the demand for marketed food therefore increased greatly.

Landless and Land-Poor Labor

Before 1800, the growth of landless labor had at least as large an impact on the demand for marketed food as did the development of large cities. The distinction between the two appears a little odd until one realizes that the great proletarianization of the European population which occurred between 1500 and 1800 went on mainly in towns, villages, and open country rather than in big cities. Two related processes accomplished it: (1) the concentration of agricultural land in the control of fewer and fewer landlords, which had as its corollary the creation of a farm workforce consisting of land-poor or landless laborers; and (2) the growth of rural industry, carried on increasingly by full-time workers, although often including men who became agricultural wage-laborers at peak times of planting or harvest.

Again, no one knows the numbers involved. In attempting to estimate changes in the volume of landless labor, historians face formidable obstacles. The first is the ambiguity of both "landless" and "labor." In fact, as Rudolf Braun has shown in great detail for the uplands of Zürich, the early stages of proletarianization produced land-poor families rather than strictly landless ones, but they were nonetheless dependent on the labor market for work and on the commodity market for food. Furthermore, the notion of labor as an entity depends to some extent on the existence of a market for it; both general conceptions and statistical definitions of the labor force tend to become more restrictive (for example, by excluding women who work on farms) as the extent of wage-labor increases. Seasonal alternation between work on one's own plot and work for someone else runs very, very far back in European history; it provides an almost imperceptible entering wedge for the growth of landless labor.

The scrutiny of French experience reveals another ambiguity in the word landless. A large number of French peasants—and, in many regions, the more prosperous segments of the peasantry—owned too little land to survive, but rented or sharecropped enough to keep their households going. They were rather different from the very poor, about whom Pierre Goubert threw up his hands:

> Throughout the Old Regime it is difficult to pin down the most miserable group of peasants. They do not always appear in tax rolls, because they do not usually pay anything; they do not appear in manorial and notarial archives, since they do not usually own anything; one must look for them in the parish registers, or in the gangs of beggars who haunt the highways or the city's back streets, when the police run into them or a charitable institution gives them aid (Labrousse 1970: 598).

If we are attempting to estimate the changing number of European workers who commanded too little land to feed themselves, then both definitions and data stand in our way. All we know for certain is that by the end of the eighteenth century, the numbers were large.

[401]

In areas of concentrated property and cash-crop production, hired laborers often comprised the majority of the agricultural population. According to Gregory King's estimates of 1688, only 350 thousand of the 1.4 million families in England were living from their own land (that is, were landowners, farmers, or freeholders), although up to 1.2 of the 1.4 million drew their principal income from agriculture (Pollard and Crossley 1968: 154). In the Great Britain of 1831, full-fledged farmers (in the substantial English sense of the term) made up only 20 to 25 percent of the 1.8 million persons engaged in agriculture, forestry, and fishing. They were only about 15 percent of the 2.1 million persons in the sector at the 1851 census (Deane and Cole 1967: 143–144). The figures are certainly not comparable, but they point to a large and expanding majority of landless laborers in the agricultural workforce.

Now, England is an extreme case—a sort of Poland without the apparatus of serfdom. The early dissolution of the English peasantry cleared the way for a market-oriented industrial society. Francis M. L. Thompson puts it this way:

> It would have been of fundamental importance if the England of the population explosion and industrial revolution had been a country of peasant owners. Not only would such a structure have responded tardily to increasing demand for food and raw materials, and by its slowness in adapting to new levels of output, and new techniques have damped down the population increase; but also, through its likely spending and saving habits, it would have substantially choked off a large part of the home market support for industrial growth, not simply through the expansion of supplies for a growing non-agricultural sector, but also through its direct demand for industrial products, was an effect of the system of agricultural enterprise fostered by the structure of landownership (1966: 517).

To be sure, the process was mutual: the growth of a national market probably hastened the dissolution of the peasantry, the prevalence of landless labor probably accelerated population growth, the availability of export opportunities for wool, and then for wheat, encouraged the landlords to expand their own production, promoted an alliance between them and the mercantile classes, and helped make the state indulgent to their interests. The growth of landless agricultural labor resulted from the most basic changes in the English economy from 1500 to 1800.

The debatable part is not the fact of expansion but when, where and why it occurred (see e. g., F. M. L. Thompson 1969). The quarrel of Marx with Malthus is still with us, for some scholars would have proletarianization as the direct consequence of dispossession of peasants by capitalists, while others insist on the autonomous rise of rural population as survival became easier.

In their famous *Village Labourer*, the Hammonds laid the blame at the door of enclosures: "The effect on the cottager can best be described by saying that before enclosure the cottager was a labourer with land, after enclosure he was a labourer without land" (Hammond and Hammond 1924: 95–96). Paradoxically, subsequent research has tended to exculpate the enclosures by making them only one of the many means by which large landlords eliminated smallholders and their common rights. A number of modern scholars, such as J. D. Chambers (1957), have attributed far greater importance to an increase in the population on the land. Razzell (1965) and others have discounted "economic" explanations of that increase by stressing the fall in mortality due to improved nutrition and health measures, notably the checking of smallpox.

If we look back to an earlier period, however, we find reasons for suspecting a more intimate connection than that between population shifts and transformations of agrarian structure. Joan Thirsk's generalization for sixteenth-century England carries authority:

The highland zone consisted for the most part of land which was either completely enclosed by the beginning of the sixteenth century or, if the land was worth enclosing at this time, could and often did undergo painless enclosure. In lowland England where common fields were subject to a system of mixed husbandry, where common grazing rights were highly prized because the pasture steadily diminished as the arable enlarged, enclosure constituted, at the beginning at least, a painful and socially disturbing reorganization of land and ways of living (Thirsk 1967: 6).

In the highlands, farmers raised enough grain and garden crops to keep their households going, and acquired their cash through herding. Manorial institutions were weak and settlement was generally dispersed in hamlets and small villages. In the short run, peasants could maintain their established ways well enough under enclosure. In the lowlands, mixed farming prevailed, with extensive communal controls and widespread commercialization of grain production. Settlement was relatively concentrated and manorial controls were more vigorous than in the North and West, with the consequence that the interdependence and mutual awareness of a village's households were greater. In important parts of those regions, enclosure for the purpose of stock-raising meant greatly increased profits for the larger landlords. It also meant forcing many smallholders off the land. Enclosure offered an immediate challenge to the whole structure of the village, and thereby engendered bitter resistance.

Of course (as Thirsk takes great pains to say) the variations were far more subtle than this first approximation indicates. But the simplification has the virtue of identifying three main variables as determining the likelihood of peasant resistance to incorporation in national markets: (1) the profitability of alternative uses of land or dispositions of existing crops; (2) the extent to which those new uses or dispositions could be undertaken within the existing organization of community life; (3) the capacity for collective action on the part of the victims of change afforded by the existing organization of community life. Where alternatives to existing agricultural arrangements are profitable, extensive and spread wide across the community, where they can be absorbed within existing social arrangements and where community structure is weak, the argument implies, shifts toward production in response to national markets are rapid and easy. The three broad conditions constitute, in essence, the obverse of the conditions for peasant rebellions against the penetration of capitalism into the countryside, as outlined by Eric Wolf (1969). They improve on a purely material interpretation (opportunity, hence change) both by denying that misery as such provides a strong incentive to change or rebellion and by laying stress on the structure of power and obligation within the peasant communities.

For our immediate purposes, the more important implication of Thirsk's argument is that in areas like the highlands a gradual expansion of commitment to market production could occur without drastic alteration of the local demographic structure, whereas in the lowlands it produced a direct confrontation between the existing system and the beneficiaries of the market; if the market won, an important segment of the poorer peasantry disappeared and/or changed into landless labor.

To understand the demographic challenge, one must see the systematic side of old-regime demography. To an important extent, the rural population of early modern Europe was self-regulating through arrangements in which opportunities to marry depended on places within the village community and in which age at marriage moved elastically in response to changes in such opportunities. In general, opportunities for work not closely tied to possession of land weakened the self-regulation by making it possible to acquire adult position (and hence the warrant to marry) without waiting for an incumbent to retire or die (see R. Tilly and C. Tilly 1971). Such an implicit system of control operated in England as well as on the Continent (Wrigley 1966). For that reason, it is worthwhile to keep alive the hypothesis that expanding opportunities for landless labor both in agriculture and in rural industry after the seventeenth century themselves played an important part in the rapid population increase of the time.

For present purposes, the fact matters more than its explanation: in England, at least, the demand for marketed food due to the presence of landless labor in agriculture greatly expanded, especially from the eighteenth century onward. In France, the growth of landless labor was slower than in England, as was the overall increase in population. Nineteenth-century French censuses put day-laborers and hired hands at 25 to 50 percent of the agricultural population; the available eighteenth-century estimates run in the same range (Toutain 1963: 108). In the Beauvaisis of Louis XIV's time, Pierre Goubert found that "less than one peasant out of ten in the plain and less than one peasant out of four in the *bocage* was assured of always having enough to feed his family" (Labrousse 1970: 146).

The proof that the proportion of landless and land-poor agricultural workers rose in France over the three centuries before 1800 is fragmentary and inferential. Louis Merle (1958) has shown that the *bocage* ("woodland") landscape of one section of western France came into being through a process parallel to the English enclosures, which continued from the fourteenth into the eighteenth centuries: noble landlords displacing smallholders, consolidating the land into farms of 30 or 40 hectares which they then leased out for cash, and thus creating a surplus landless population. It would not be surprising to find that (1) most French *bocages* took shape in approximately that way; and (2) the availability of that landless labor helps account for the great proliferation of cottage industry in the French *bocages* during the seventeenth and eighteenth centuries. More generally, the underside of the great extension of cultivated land in France during those same centuries was the dispossession of many small-holders who survived through their rights in the commons. As Joseph Kulischer summed it up,

> in France as well the increase of cultivated area led inevitably to a struggle against the remains of agrarian communal property. There, too, the demand for the division of the commons arose. In the sixteenth and seventeenth centuries local lords initiated divisions in which a third of the land went to them (whence the term *triage* for the divisions). In many cases the lord even received two thirds of the communal lands. The wealthier segment of the peasantry had interests in common with the lord. For at this point they acquired the opportunity to lease the allocated land, fenced in and often extended. By contrast the poor peasants (who founded their existence on the possibility of pasturing a few cows on the commons) were hard hit by the divisions (Kulischer 1965: II, 73).

The process did not go as far or as fast as in England; struggles over the commons continued into the Revolution and the nineteenth century. What is more, the French peasantry, as a class, survived into our own time. Barrington Moore (1966) properly emphasizes that point in contrasting the French political experience with that of England. Nevertheless, the rise of agrarian capitalism in France also promoted the multiplication of agricultural workers dependent on the market for their daily bread.

The same is true in different ways for the rest of Europe. The term "agrarian capitalism" overstates the commercialism of the noble landlords in whose hands property was concentrated in Spain after 1500, although it applies well enough to the confederation of sheep-herders which made up the land-hungry Mesta. Among the Italian-speaking areas, the *latifundia* of Sicily and Apulia sent grain actually cultivated by land-poor peasants to a European market, and the Po Valley entered the nineteenth century with a large, swelling labor force of landless agricultural workers. While the changing agrarian structures of the Low Countries and western Germany resembled that of France more than those of England or Italy, in eastern Germany and in much of Eastern Europe the so-called feudalization of the agrarian economy after 1500—the move from *Grundwirtschaft* to *Gutswirtschaft*—consisted of the concentration of property in the control of great grain-exporting landlords pinning down a land-poor labor force through direct repression. Through a number of different paths, the agrarian transformations of early modern Europe led to a greatly increased demand for marketed food on the part of agricultural workers raising too little on their own to keep their families alive.

Beside them stood the millions of workers in rural industry. Again it is Joan Thirsk (1961) who has provided the valuable preliminary statement. She proposes the following general conditions under which cottage industry was likely to expand beyond the usual spinning, weaving, or woodworking for local consumption: (1) accessibility of a potential market for cheap finished goods; (2) prevalence of a form of agriculture (e.g. dairy farming) with relatively little room for intensification of effort; (3) conditions of inheritance and/or demography promoting the appearance of men with insufficient land for survival. Once started, the growth of cottage industry itself often promoted the further extension of these three conditions, and thus fed itself. Fernand Braudel makes a series of suggestions which fall directly into the line of Thirsk's argument. After describing the considerable extension of rural industry in the Mediterranean region during the sixteenth century (he eventually guesses the number of workers at about 1.5 million, about the same as in urban industry), Braudel observes:

> Nevertheless it is probable that rural industries did not have the strength in the Mediterranean region which they already possessed in England . . . or in northern Europe; they never appear in great rural archipelagoes, run at a distance by the merchants of the cities, as will be so often the case in eighteenth-century France. I believe that the constellation of rural industries around sixteenth-century Lyon had no equivalent around the Mediterranean. . . . If correct, that observation would prove two things: that the rural regions of the Mediterranean were better equilibrated within themselves than were many rural regions of the North (and it is possible that the vine and the olive tree were often the equivalent of the rural industries of the northern

[407]

regions—arboriculture puts the peasant budget back in balance);
that the urban industry of the large and medium-size cities was
strong enough to meet the principal demands of a vast market
(Braudel 1966: 1, 392).

Yet even in the Mediterranean, according to Braudel, the seventeenth century brought a shift of industrial activity from the cities
into the countryside.

The great fifteenth-century textile industries of Brabant, Flanders
and Northern Italy, which provided much of the material basis for
the Renaissance, were relatively urban in structure. In England,
however, cottage textile industry was already expanding significantly in the fifteenth century. Herrmann Kellenbenz attributes considerable importance to that early escape of industry from the city:

> The relatively great freedom that the rural situation afforded,
> as contrasted with the gild-ridden urban economy, made it
> easier for members of all social classes to devote themselves to
> the craft of clothier. Some of those who occupied themselves as
> weavers, fullers, dyers and shearers came from established
> crafts; others came from outside: sheep herders, grocers, butch-
> ers, gentry. A little cloth-maker often combined his craft not
> only with agricultural work, but also with other occupations like
> milling or butchering. The large scale manufacturers, often
> enough, were also landlords who acquired some of the wool
> they worked from their own sheep. Here in the world of villages
> (which to some extent grew into townships within the areas of
> manorial control) there was greater freedom to experiment
> (Kellenbenz 1965: 383–384).

And, in Kellenbenz' account, that early freedom helped give England a chance to overtake the industrial power of the Low Countries.
Nevertheless, the cloth industries of Flanders, the Rhineland and
Northern Italy also spread into rural areas to capitalize on their
cheap and elastic labor forces.

The heyday came in the seventeenth and eighteenth centuries.
Then the industrial strength of northern France, the Low Countries,
western Germany and southern England resided mainly in small-
town and rural textile production, and the finished goods of the thriving Atlantic trade came largely from cottage industry. Not that textile
production underwent much *technical* transformation before the

late eighteenth century. "Better than any other sector of the old industry," Pierre Chaunu (1970: 332) tells us, "textiles permit us to grasp the basic structure of seventeenth-century industry, a structure established in the early Middle Ages, including a tremendous fragmentation of economic space." The changes were organizational: increases in the scale of an old system, expanding opportunities for ruthless entrepreneurs, growing coordination of a highly dispersed form of production.

This growth of cottage industry marked modern European economic history profoundly, for it set the basic geographic pattern of nineteenth-century factory-based industrialization. And it produced an expansion of the landless labor force whose magnitude no one has so far dared to estimate, but which certainly ran into millions of workers. By the early eighteenth century, Phyllis Deane (1967: 14) concedes, a tenth of the entire English population may have been "concerned" with woolen production, although some of that involvement was quite subsidiary to agricultural occupations. By the end of the Revolution, a third of the French rural population may have been living from manufacturing, services, and other nonagricultural activities; domestic textile production, smelting, woodworking, tanning, pottery, and basketry were spread wide through the French countryside. During the later eighteenth century, the cottage textile industries of places as far separated as the Rhineland, Silesia, and the hinterland of Moscow went into rapid expansion. It was this very expansion which made the nineteenth-century contraction of rural industry in favor of urban factories so painful. But while it was going on, it probably contributed even more heavily to the proletarianization of agriculture than it did to the demand for marketed food.

The Staffs of Governments

The third large category of growing demand for marketed food is the swelling of the employed staffs of governments, including armed forces. Changes in this source of demand should, in principle, be easier to identify than are increases in urban population or landless labor; the boundaries of government employment became increasingly clear as bureaucratization proceeded, and European governments tended to keep records of such matters. Of course there are complications: the quasi-governmental position of the Justices of the Peace in England, the payment of officials in kind during the earlier years of Brandenburg-Prussia, the uncertainty of the time spent away from home by conscripted peasants in France or Prussia. And again no one has taken the effort to collate the vast, scattered evidence now available. Yet the ballooning of the Prussian standing army from 2,000 in 1640 to 200,000 in 1786 meant a real increase in the demand for food; indeed, it brought into being the art called *Kriegsmagazinverwaltung*: war stores administration. The expansion of the French army from 35,000 in 1610 to 175,000 at the Revolution was less extreme; nevertheless, it too made provisioning a major service of the national government.

The army deserves particular attention because it has been the bulkiest, riskiest, costliest, and perhaps most influential enterprise of Western states throughout their modern history. The army achieved a new importance precisely as the national state rose to preeminence. In the century after 1560, as Sir George Clark (1969: 176) remarks, "Europe underwent a 'military revolution.' Armament, tactics and strategy had changed. They now required new kinds of discipline, a new organization of fleets and standing armies, new and more intensive applications of technical and general knowledge. The financial and administrative machinery of supply, the systems of political control and the social composition of the armed forces were all remodelled. The effects of the military revolution were shown by a salient fact of social history: armies and fleets were much larger than before." Even in England, a country rather late to develop a substantial standing army, military demand made a difference in the food market as early as the Tudor period. In analyzing the increase of private marketing (as opposed to open public sale) of agricultural products from 1540 to 1640, Alan Everitt concludes that the stimulus "originated in the expansion, during the Tudor period, of three special or particular markets: the London market, the export market, and the provisioning of the royal household and armed forces" (Everitt 1967: 507). The royal household itself was no mean consumer:

> The annual supply of 600,000 gallons of beer to Queen Elizabeth's household entailed operations quite beyond the scope of the local market town. It was entrusted to fifty-eight or sixty official brewers, who must have placed very considerable orders for malt and hops with private provincial factors. Even modest transactions like the annual purchase of two hundred sheep and twenty fat oxen in the Parts of Holland might bring regular or-

ders of 350 at a time to men like William Porey of Sutton "a great grazier and a great dealer for cattle in the country of Lincoln." Similarly, the supply of delicacies to the private network of commercial contacts with the specialized farms of different areas demanded a rare professional expertise (Everitt 1967: 507).

Nevertheless, the army and navy were even hungrier. Everitt suggests that the victualling of Henry VIII's armies played a major role in establishing East Anglia as the principal early source of commercial malt, wheat, barley, peas, and beans; Kent was a prime producer of cattle for the market.

The larger armed forces of France pressed even more heavily on the French food supply. In the seventeenth century, mercantile families like the Jacquiers and the Berthelots struck it rich by undertaking provisioning contracts for the army. Although in France, as elsewhere, the practice of placing troops in regular barracks and feeding them from central commissaries did not generalize until late in the seventeenth century, the royal government had to amass the food for campaigns away from home; it set up storehouses along the frontiers for that purpose. One of the major aggravating factors in the devastating French subsistence crises of 1693–1694 and 1709 was the diversion of local food supplies to large concentrations of troops at the frontiers. As Jean Meuvret (1970: 320) describes the background of the earlier crisis, "because of the war, stocks had been moved towards the frontiers. The number of men under arms had grown to a size which, by the standard of the century, was something quite new; their needs led to the channeling of food supplies and the commandeering of transport to the places where they were concentrated."

Even at home and at peace, foraging and billeting did not suffice to feed the army. The payment of subsistence allowances to the soldiers (which was a standard seventeenth-century practice of European armies) itself created a demand for marketed food. The army became a good meal ticket. In a transcript of his Sorbonne lectures, Roland Mousnier offers some intriguing observations on that fact:

You know that seigneurs had the obligation to feed their *censitaires* in times of famine. That was part of the feudal custom: the censitaires owe their dues and corvées and they owe fidelity, but the seigneur owes protection; in times of famine, protection

[411]

implies the obligation to feed their men. I don't know if all the seigneurs fulfilled their obligations in this regard, but it is worth noting that signing men up for the army was a means for captains (and in general for all officers) to offer work, wages and bread to some of the peasants of their villages and their manors, when things went badly, when a series of poor harvests came along and, naturally, when there occurred those periods of epidemics, economic crises and famines, and consequently of deaths which people called The Deaths (which were especially common in the seventeenth century, a time of cold weather and rain which sorely tried the French countryside). In all that period, and naturally in the eighteenth century, even though it was a more prosperous time, enrollment in the army was a way of supplying food and work to men who otherwise would not have found them (Mousnier 1969:97).

Indeed, the growth of the army probably had something to do with the shortage of food and work outside the army.

The needs of the French, English, and Prussian armed forces in these regards are best documented. Nevertheless, there is good reason to think that the demand for marketed food rose proportionately with the growth of armies in Spain, Austria-Hungary, Russia, Scandinavia, and the smaller German states as well. What is less sure is how regularly the expansion of the scale of government outside the army generated new demand. While armies and navies tended to be organized and supplied in broadly similar ways throughout the Continent at any particular point in time, national governments diversified considerably before the great nineteenth-century convergence on centralized, specialized, full-time bureaucracies. In somewhat different ways, the governments of England and Brandenburg did a great deal of their work through the agency of landowners who were powers in their own right, and only indirectly subordinate to the Crown. The Dutch governed themselves through a highly decentralized federation. The French and Spanish governments—for all their differences in effectiveness—pioneered in the creation of distinct, full-time staffs for the conduct of royal business. Yet all these central governments acquired greatly increased power and scope after 1500. And however we define their personnel, the numbers, and thus the mouths to feed, increased importantly.

The Sources of Demand

If we attempt to weigh the three sources of increasing demand for marketed food—urban growth, governmental staffs, and landless labor—against each other, we immediately face the difficulty of their overlap. Landless labor, broadly conceived, includes most of the government employees and almost all the urban population. Furthermore, most government employees based themselves in cities. With these qualifications in mind, it is nevertheless worth reflecting how much each could have contributed to the rising demand from 1500 to 1800. The full-time employees of central governments, including armed forces, might have increased by half a million or a million in Europe as a whole during that time. The population in cities of one hundred thousand or more grew by four to five million people. Landless or land-poor labor (excluding big-city population and government staffs) surely increased by at least twenty-five million, and might have gained up to fifty million persons, not counting dependents outside the labor force.

After 1800, urban growth absorbed a much larger share of the total increase in persons dependent on marketed food. But during the epic period of state-making, the increasing population of wage-workers in towns and villages constituted by far the largest component of increasing demand for marketed food. (The preponderance is so great that I am led to speculate that the greater ease of feeding rural areas, as reflected in lower prices for foodstuffs, promoted the development of cottage industry at the expense of the cities.) The growth of big cities accounted for a much smaller, but still substantial, proportion of the increased demand, and the expansion of central government staffs had a relatively minor quantitative impact.

The immediate involvement of nation-states in the incitement of these changes, however, was inversely proportional to their magnitude. The growth of demand for marketed food through the increase of civilian and military employees of the government obviously resulted from actions of the state. The establishment of national and provincial capitals promoted an urban growth based on the services and supplies required by a courtly or administrative population. St. Petersburg, Berlin, Turin, Naples, Madrid, Paris, and London all illustrate the point. But the expansion of trade and of some forms of

[413]

manufacturing, in which nation-states played a less decisive (but not negligible) part, surely accounted for a larger share of the growth of big cities. The effect of governmental action on the creation of landless and land-poor labor outside the big cities is the most difficult to specify, for it took the form of sanctioning enclosures, favoring exports, backing labor-repressive innovations (like the so-called revival of serfdom in the East) or concentrating taxation on the peasantry. It consists in the class alliances worked out by the builders of states. For all the qualifications which subsequent research has brought to it, I am inclined to agree with the main line of Tawney's declaration:

> The decline of important classes alters the balance of rural society, though the Crown for a long time tries to maintain it, and the way is prepared both for the economic and political omnipotence which the great landed aristocracy will exercise over England as soon as the power of the Crown is broken, and for the triumph of the modern English conception of land-ownership, a conception so repugnant both to our ancestors and to the younger English communities, as in the main a luxury of the richer classes (Tawney 1967: 2).

This is, of course, exactly the note which Barrington Moore's (1966) great comparative analysis of European state-making picks up from Tawney. In one way or another, all the European state-makers allied themselves with the promoters of a commercialized, productive, capitalist economy. But which alliances they formed, how early they did it, and how uncompromising they were in the process deeply affected the subsequent agrarian and industrial histories of their countries.

The Supply of Food

Even on a per-capita basis, the production of food in Europe as a whole rose significantly from 1500 to 1800, and sensationally thereafter. There were many fits, starts, and reversals, of which the various crises of the seventeenth century were the most dramatic. As in the case of demand, however, what we really need to know is how the supply of food to the market fluctuated over that great span of time. We do not know, even within margins of error of 20 or 25 percent.

Slicher van Bath has demonstrated the considerable willingess of farmers in the Low Countries to shift from grain-growing to stock-raising and back depending on prevailing price levels. Bowden (1967) and others have identified the same sort of switching in sixteenth-century England. But these were the highly commercialized agrarian economies of the time. What is less clear is how the landlords and farmers of Spain, of the Germanies, of France outside the Parisian basin responded to changing demand. Technical changes in the strict sense appear to have made little difference to the productivity of European agriculture between 1500 and 1800.

Crop for crop, techniques of sowing, cultivating, fertilizing, and harvesting did not change much; little deliberate improvement of species occurred; and yields did not shift dramatically. Increases in supply had to come mainly from shifts in crops, changes in management, consolidation of holdings or extension of cultivation to unused land. That all these happened widely is simple enough to show. Their timing, extent, regional distribution, and consequences, however, cannot be summarized so easily.

Within the realm of traditional European crops, no significant and durable increases of productivity occurred between 1500 and the later eighteenth century. Indeed, Slicher van Bath (1968) has found some indications of a general decline of productivity (and perhaps of total production as well) during the seventeenth century, from which there was no true recovery until 1750. His estimates of average yields of wheat, rye, and barley per unit of seed for some large blocks of time and space are outlined in Table 6–2.

During the early nineteenth century, comparable figures for Germany and the Netherlands began running from 8 to 15 (Slicher van Bath 1963: 332–333). Such crude figures give us no reliable guide to yields per input of land, labor, or capital. Nevertheless, they are incompatible with very high productivity between the end of the Middle Ages and very recent times. For Europe as a whole, the increased demand had to be met by augmenting the inputs of land and labor.

The individual countries of Europe, however, were far from self-contained producers and consumers of food. Italian wheat sailed great distances in the fourteenth and fifteenth centuries. Poland, Prussia and the Baltic supplied cities all over Europe in the sixteenth and seventeenth centuries (thus allowing Denmark to thrive as a

TABLE 6–2. ESTIMATED AVERAGE YIELDS OF WHEAT, RYE, AND BARLEY, 1225–1785 (per unit of seed)

Period Centering on the Year:	England and Low Countries	France	Germany and Scandinavia	Eastern Europe
1225 ± 25	3.7	3.0		
1275 ± 25	4.7			
1325 ± 25	4.1			
1375 ± 25	5.2			
1400 ± 100		4.3		
1425 ± 25	4.6			
1550 ± 50	7.3			
1575 ± 25			4.4	4.5
1625 ± 25	6.5			
1650 ± 50			4.0	
1660 ± 160		6.3		
1675 ± 25				3.9
1725 ± 25			3.8	
1785 ± 35			8.3	

Source: Slicher van Bath 1968.

customs-grabber, Amsterdam to prosper as the chief *entrepôt*, and Antwerp to grow rich as the principal center for the attendant financial transactions). However, the relative importance of Baltic grain decline after the Thirty Years War. England became a major exporter of grain, with the blessing and subsidy of the crown, until the hunger of her nineteenth-century industrial workers built up pressure against the Corn Laws and shifted the balance toward imports. These shipments of grain by sea take on double importance when we remember that until the expansion of the railroads the movement of grain by land was prohibitively expensive in Europe. No need to exaggerate: around 1600, according to F. C. Spooner (1968: 37), "the shipments by sea probably amounted to one or two percent of the total consumption of grain." That one or two percent was nevertheless exceptionally important, both because of the prosperity it brought to such seafarers as the Dutch and because it represented the margin of survival for capital cities like Lisbon.

The margin of survival for Europe as a whole remained fairly narrow until some time in the eighteenth century. The expansion of the margin shows up dramatically in the French experience: the contrast between the death-dealing famines which periodically shook the country before 1700 and the relatively mild demographic effects of subsistence crises after that time. Exactly why and how the transition occurred in France is still hotly debated, but there is no doubt

[416]

that one component was an increase in the supply of marketed food. On the whole, the rise in productivity occurred first in highly commercialized agricultural regions of Europe, which were themselves mainly adjacent to the chief areas of industrial production.

England led. In accounting for the international increase in agricultural productivity which began in the later eighteenth century, R. M. Hartwell attributes major importance to the stimulus of demand:

> The market force in this change was a sustained upward movement in prices, especially of grain, after 1750, to a high war level after 1790 that was maintained until 1815. The technical changes that enabled increased production were: enclosures, the reduction of fallow with better crop rotations, and the related cultivation of fodder crops; land reclamation and additions to the area of tillage; and improvements to techniques and changes in organisation (in the farm unit and in property and tenurial rights) that increased productivity (Hartwell 1969: 34).

Francis M. L. Thompson (1968) refines this conventional picture of technical transformation into four successive "agricultural revolutions" in the course of the transition from peasant to industrial social organization in Europe. The first, according to Thompson, consisted of the shift from subsistence to cash-crop farming, which involved no necessary change in technique but a great deal of change in the orientation of the farmer. The second consisted mainly of the formation, after 1750, of the classic nineteenth-century commercial farm through the introduction of efficient crop rotation and livestock breeding. The third, later in the nineteenth century, "broke the closed-circuit system and made the operations of the farmer much more like those of the factory owner" through the employment of externally produced seeds, feeds, and fertilizers. The fourth and latest centered on the substitution of machine-power for the labor of men and draft animals, but also included such weird technological innovation as the modern poultry farm, in which nearly immobile chickens fatten on chemical feeds.

Thompson's useful scheme permits us to see one important fact: through most of the great period of European state-making the satisfaction of the rising demand for marketed food occurred mainly through changes in the social organization of production. Technical changes and rising productivity within the same agricultural units had relatively little to do with it until the industrial age had begun. (I do not mean that agricultural change simply reflected the influence of modern industrialization; E. L. Jones [1968] has made a strong case for the stimulation of English industrial development by eighteenth-century agrarian transformations; it seems likely, in fact, that throughout Europe cheap food and surplus agricultural manpower facilitated the growth of factory production.)

Five related varieties of change in agriculture appear to have borne the weight: (1) the introduction of new crops; (2) the intensification of cultivation within producing areas, often accomplished through enclosures and other realignments of propertyholding; (3) the expansion of the cultivated area, likewise often realized by the displacement of one kind of organization by another; (4) an increasing division of labor between exporting areas of large-scale commercial grain production and the market-gardening which grew up in the immediate vicinities of great cities; (5) the diversion of food already produced from local consumption (often quite outside the market) to the consumption of the distant dependent population. The predominance of changes in organization, property, and control is crucial; it meant that those who sought to feed cities, government staffs, and landless labor were engaged, willy-nilly, in the reshaping of rural social structure. In the long run, their work meant the destruction of the peasantry and the subordination of agricultural production to the international market.

This is least true of the introduction of new crops. Within a century after Columbus' voyages to the Americas, a whole series of native American crops were being cultivated regularly in Europe. Maize, green beans, peanuts, potatoes, cocoa, tomatoes, and sweet potatoes were the most important. Within two centuries maize and potatoes had become the dominant sources of calories in some parts of Europe; the cornmeal *polenta* of present-day Piedmont testifies to a seventeenth-century conversion from European grains. Ireland became heavily dependent on the potato in the seventeenth century, and appears to have been responsible for the introduction of this native American crop into New England during the eighteenth century (Masefield 1967: 299). In general, the spread of the new crops increased the production of calories per acre, hence the number of men who could be supported, without substantial changes in the technique or organization of farming.

[418]

However, the population of Europe tripled from 1500 to 1800, and the number of persons producing too little food for their own survival multiplied many more times than that. No one has argued that the introduction of new crops accounts for the major part of the increasing ability to feed the dependent population. No one really knows how it happened. But the conversion of Eastern Europe into a major exporter of grain to the West suggests part of the answer. There a process of colonization (similar in its broadest lines to the transformations of Central America under Spanish domination described by Eric Wolf [1955] and the "agricultural involution" of Java under Dutch domination described by Clifford Geertz [1963]) reversed the growth of an independent peasantry marketing its small surpluses, and brought about the hegemony of great landlords. As S. P. Pach analyzes the process for Hungary, late in the fifteenth century:

> There appeared in Hungary, as well as in a number of other countries of central and eastern Europe, a tendency countering the ordinary movement of the peasantry toward the condition of petit-bourgeois proprietors and countering the trend toward the flourishing of peasant production for the market. That new tendency in Hungarian development sums up economically to the growing participation of the seigneurial class in the trading of goods, and later in the production of those goods.
>
> To achieve that result, the lords moved through three successive stages: 1) by exploiting the seigneurial privilege in the sale of wine; 2) by taking a more and more active part (especially the great landlords and the middle nobility) in the cattle trade; 3) by developing the seigneurial trade in wheat, and even the seigneurial production of wheat (Pach 1966: 1213).

And in a process which is well known in the rest of Eastern Europe despite the confusion which the words "feudal" and "serfdom" have introduced into its discussion, the Hungarian landlord became the predominant figure in the grain trade. He cemented his position by allying with the emerging state, and by coercing his peasantry to stay in place, abandon its independent production for the market, and yield increasing labor services—some of them exacted through the *corvée* and similar devices, others of them remunerated in cash. Thus emerged the *Gutswirtschaft*.

[419]

As Pach suggests, some features of this process paralleled the rise of the great commercial landlord in England. In both countries landlords oriented to distant markets used a variety of means to consolidate property in their own hands, control the local labor supply, and weaken the autonomy of the peasant community. More so than in Spain or France, they involved themselves directly in the production and marketing of crops. As with the formation of the *bocage* in France, the reorganization of landholding in England and Hungary shaped the very landscape. In Hungary, the castles, wheat fields, and peasant hovels of the great estates came to dominate the landscape as the *Gutswirtschaft* took form. In England, the country house, the fenced field and the tenant's cottage began to prevail.

Of course the transformation took time.

The change from peasant husbandry to farming for the market was, it is true, a long-drawn out one. It had begun more than a century earlier under Queen Elizabeth—in some respects much further back,—and it was not completed till the reign of Queen Victoria. Indeed, the two types of agrarian society, of the peasant and of the commercial farmer, co-existed side by side throughout the period 1660–1760. During the eighteenth century, however, the older, more localized, forms of husbandry faced and succumbed to the parliamentary enclosure movement, which more than any other single development destroyed the basis of the peasant world by depriving it of its immemorial rights of common. It was then that the familiar landscape pattern of much of central England took shape, with its small green fields, well-hedged and neatly-tended, in place of the older, larger, more sprawling pattern of open fields and common pastures. By 1760 an economy in which agriculture was chiefly, though still not exclusively, oriented towards the market (Everitt 1968: 60–61).

Everitt's analysis has the virtue not only of stressing the connection between economic transformation and alteration of the landscape, but also of pointing to a significant difference from the east European pattern. In England, the gentry led the drive toward agrarian capitalism, but the commercial classes and the wealthier peasants shared in it. In Hungary and elsewhere in the East, the nobles were almost exclusive beneficiaries.

The process went farther, faster, and more ruthlessly in Hungary. Moreover, the state collaborated there in a more direct and uncompromising manner. The Diet of 1492 required all landlords to impose all the feudal dues to which they had any right; in the next decade the peasants lost their right to hunt. And after the Dózsa rising of 1514 (which began, significantly enough, with a call to a crusade for which 100,000 peasants and other poor folk are supposed to have volunteered) the Diet "condemned all the peasants of Hungary, those of the royal free boroughs alone excepted, to 'real and perpetual servitude,' further imposing on them dues and *corvées* far heavier than anything previously in force" (Macartney 1967: 389).

The largest difference between England and Hungary consisted of the great reliance of the Hungarian landlord on forced labor without monetary compensation. The arrangement did not necessarily make the material condition of the English laborer better than that of his Hungarian counterpart. But it did promote the monetization of economic life in England, and the formation of a "dual economy" in Hungary. In Chapter 29 of *Capital*, Marx, with the English experience very much in mind, treats that thorough monetization as critical for the development of industrial capitalism. In his view, the conversion of peasants to wage-labor not only produced a labor force for industrial production but also formed a home market of sufficient size to make the production of cheap goods profitable. That did not happen in Hungary.

Nor was Hungary peculiar. Marian Malowist (1966) has described the same basic process in Poland, beginning late in the fifteenth century: "The ruin of the peasantry, which was already marked towards the end of the sixteenth century, had a disastrous influence on the economic life of the towns, and in particular of those little towns which were tied to local markets. Industry and small-scale commerce disappeared. The rise in the price of cereals, especially in the second half of the sixteenth century, strengthened the greater and middle nobility as well as the rich merchants of Gdansk, the intermediary between Poland and the western markets" (Malowist 1966: 27).

The transformation was quite general.

The growth of the demand for cereals which was reflected in the rise of prices, especially in the second half of the sixteenth century, and the difficulties caused by the expensiveness of labour had in nearly all the countries of eastern Europe the same influence on the system of agricultural production and through that on the whole economy. There were naturally variations in the time-scale between different regions. The great seigneurial demesnes were established at first mainly on the banks of navigable rivers which facilitated transport towards the Baltic ports. But later the same system spread out towards less well-situated areas (Malowist 1966: 27).

Indeed, the same system and the same transformation extended as far as western Russia. At the same time, Eastern Europe became a major supplier of beef cattle to the West. Because they transported themselves, cattle were the one bulky agricultural product which could profitably move great distances overland. Between 1560 and 1620 about 30,000 steers crossed the Elbe in the average year on their way cross-country to the distant Netherlands for fattening; shortly before the Thirty Years War slowed the trade, the figures ran close to 60,000 (Wiese 1968: 126–127). Both for bread and for meat, the East became an agricultural tributary of the West.

Given no important increase in productivity per input of land or labor, the transfer of greater quantities of agricultural products to the market implies a squeeze on the peasantry. In theory, this could take place through an increase in the work extracted from the peasantry or through a decline in the real incomes of peasants. Both seem to have happened widely at the beginning. The reorganization of the estates centered on capturing the labor of a dependent rural population, and very likely involved an increase in the total work performed by the average man. But during the sixteenth century the real incomes of day-laborers also fell through much of Europe (Abel 1967: 186–189). Nor was the squeeze confined to the great estates east of the Elbe. Emmanuel Le Roy Ladurie (1966: I, 326–328) reports that in Languedoc, where no significant enlargement of farms occurred during the sixteenth or seventeenth centuries, the income of the larger landlords rose, but only through a reduction in the real incomes of the numerous rural workers who depended on wages. The recovery of the wage-laborer's real income in the later seventeenth century accompanied widespread economic contraction and demographic stagnation, a conjunction which again suggests that the poorer segment of the peasantry and the emerging postpeasant class of landless laborers were subsidizing the economic expansion of Europe.

It is possible that the widespread abandonment of villages which occurred through Europe around the end of the fifteenth century (which have sometimes, rather dubiously to my way of thinking, been taken as evidence of a fifteenth-century decline in global population) was a by-product of the same transformation. In England, according to Beresford (1954, 1965) the principal factor was a great wave of enclosures in favor of sheep-grazing. In Spain, the powerful sheep-herding association called the *Mesta* accomplished the same results about the same time (Klein 1920).

But the sheep were raised for wool, not mainly for meat. The wool fed industry. To find major cases of the sacrifice of old villages to the needs of commercial food production, we shall probably have to look eastward. Perhaps that is how we should interpret the explanation that villages near Bremervörde were being abandoned *propter multiplicia servicia quibus quotidie gravantur coloni* (on account of the multiple services with which the farmers are burdened every day) (Abel 1966: 90). The deliberate sweeping away of villages by great landlords did occur in the East; it may also have played an important part in the extraordinary experience of Thuringia, where some two-thirds of all settlements disappeared around the end of the fifteenth century (Lütge 1967: 145). But this is speculation—and speculation which goes against the comfortable situation attributed by Lütge (1967: 188–190) to the region's peasants.

Another speculation comes to mind. It is possible that the extensive population increase which occurred during the sixteenth century grew in part from the same sort of saturation process which Geertz (1963) portrays as a consequence of the destruction of autonomous village communities in Indonesia; in this case the likely demographic mechanism would be a rising birth rate due to a decline in the usual age at marriage, resulting in turn from the weakening of the tie between marriage and access to a farmstead within the village. The creation of a near-proletariat in Eastern Europe through the expansion of noble domains and the coercion of labor on those domains could well have had something like that effect. At present, the demographic evidence is not in.

However these speculations come out, we are touching on the basic processes which, after 1500, resulted in an increasing division

[423]

of labor between the urbanizing, industrializing regions of Western Europe and the series of tributary food-producing areas around Europe's periphery. England was special in that the same island and the same state included full-fledged members of both kinds of economy—a combination which Germany, Italy, and the United States were only to achieve in the nineteenth century, while Spain's effort to keep both kinds going together failed, and France hardly came close. By and large, the states of Europe were firmly tied to one or the other of these economic modes, and their national policies reflected the fact. The determinism ran in both directions, for the early formation of alliances between the Crown and one class or another limited the economic opportunities of subsequent generations.

Again the most telling case is that of Eastern Europe. In Jerome Blum's summary,

> the collapse of the old seigneurial order in the West has been sometimes attributed to the growth of money economy, or to the increase in commerce, or to the development of capitalism. But in the East money economy, trade, and capitalism (as evidenced in the capitalistic farming of the seigneurs) also grew, and yet serfdom was established. It seems to me that the most important reason for this divergence in the evolution of the lord-peasant relation in the two regions lay in their differences in political development. In the struggle for domination of the state, the nobility of the East won out over the princes and the town, or, as in Russia, became the class on which the throne depended. As a result, the Eastern nobility, in pursuit of what it conceived to be its own best interests, was able to establish economic and social control over the peasantry and to dominate over the townsmen (Blum 1957: 836).

In this sense, the formation of different kinds of state in East and West, the creation of a new system of propertyholding, and the creation of a food supply for a growing population producing too little for its own survival turn out to be different aspects of the same fundamental process: the creation of a capitalist world.

Distribution

The growth of western capitalism pivoted on the demand that the market for commodities, land, and labor become the arbiter of value.

CHARLES TILLY

In the classic days of economic liberalism the demand took the form of calls for the freeing of trade from traditional restrictions. The days of liberal historiography produced a parallel view of European economic history as the gradual throwing off of fetters—technical, political, ideological. That is not surprising. Nor is it entirely wrong. In fact, national and international markets did come to play a larger and larger part in determining the flows and prices of commodities, land, and labor as Europe moved toward the nineteenth century. Most of the old controls over these flows and prices did give way. The only surprising thing about the historiography is the widespread, if implicit, assumption that the classic liberals were right: making the market prevail consisted of unfettering a powerful natural process which would, when given free play, produce the greatest good of the greatest number. An excellent presentation of agricultural conditions during the French Revolution like that of Octave Festy, for example, alternates between smiles for the revolutionary attempt to remove "obstacles" and frowns for the reimposition of controls. In the summing up, we discover a Revolution confronted with

> two ways of understanding and dealing with agricultural production in general and that of grain in particular: either continue the method of regulation which, up to then and with rare exceptions, had accompanied an age-old routine which, on that very account, had many partisans in the countryside, or applying to production the principle for which the Revolution had been fought, the principle of liberty, combined with the development of agricultural progress. . . . There remained only one solution, necessarily postponed to an uncertain future: the accomplishment of the agricultural progress in conditions of liberty, thanks to education and the popularization of methods whose favorable results were easy to demonstrate experimentally (Festy 1947: 419–420).

The conflict was real and intense. What is missing in Festy's account is not a sense of the conflict, but a realization of the extent to which the program embodied a deliberate political choice to create a different social order, reject a coherent alternative set of social arrangements, weaken the peasant community, let the market arbitrate, give priority to the bourgeoisie, adopt what C. B. Macpherson (1962)

[425]

calls the "political theory of possessive individualism." And a sense of how many adherents and successes the program had already won by the time of the Revolution.

The economic history which has grown up since the 1930s under the influence of such masters as Labrousse and Braudel has undermined the classic treatment of the West European experience as the unfettering of natural force. The systematic study of long fluctuations in the European economy, of the flow of trade, of the connections among demographic, technical, and economic changes has shattered the static picture of a preindustrial social order. Labrousse himself seems to have moved from a portrayal of the eighteenth-century French economy as fragmented, inefficient and crisis-ridden to a fuller appreciation of its expansion and transformation. In explaining the disappearance of the great sixteenth-century "mortalities" at the moments of food shortage, Labrousse proposes three possible factors: (1) change of the climate, toward milder winters; (2) increased agricultural production; and (3) "still more probably" changes in the distribution of food

> by commercial relations likewise improved, by a wider and more flexible system of supply for the centers of consumption, under the influence of a number of conditions: the long rise in the price of food reduced the proportional cost of transportation; the means of communication, especially roads, showed signs of qualitative and quantitative progress likely to lower the absolute cost of transport in some circumstances. . . . The progress of commerce outstripped by far that of the other sectors of the economy: in its national and international movement it drew with it the products of both industry and agriculture, and helped give the food market, on which the life of the populace depended, a relative, but decisive, equilibrium (Labrousse 1970: 695).

In France, England, and Holland, if not elsewhere in Europe, national markets for food were well on their way.

As the builders of national markets were acutely aware, the social conditions of early modern Europe threw up many barriers to the easy and abundant movement of food in commerce. In the international sphere, customs controls and piracy (which were not quite so distinct from each other as the two words make it sound) threatened long-distance shipments. Within a country, foodstuffs moving in commerce were an obvious target for all sorts of tolls, taxes, and fees. The techniques and facilities for shipment were slow, costly, and cumbersome. How and by what right the available supply of food was to be distributed were frequently questions of the acutest political significance, and therefore risky matters for innovation. Multiple claimants—the lord, the abbot, the vicar, the parish, the miller, the merchant, the municipal agent, the tax collector—often had legal or traditional rights to the same source of food. The available surplus was usually small, often so small that men would fight to resist its seizure. The market-builders had to change the structure of rural life to accomplish their objectives. That is why so innocuous a proposal as "let the grain trade be free" still had a revolutionary meaning in the France of 1789, and why it was so often coupled with a program of enclosing the land, dividing the commons, restricting the right to glean, reducing the number of rural holidays, eliminating the right of the communal herdsman to pasture the flock in unoccupied fields during the off-season, and letting the farmer decide *comme bon lui semblera* what to plant when, and how to harvest it.

The building of a large-scale food distribution system in Europe involved two huge, overlapping phases. The first consisted of the elaboration of multiple, highly various but usually fairly direct links between producers and consumers. The second consisted of the consolidation, standardization, and lengthening of the chains. In the first phase we find a remarkable range of procedures: the drawing of a wealthy urban household's food from its rural estates, the boarding of apprentices in the house of the master, the truck system (in which employers supplied their workers from their own stores in return for wage deductions or scrip), the establishment of regular circuits by street vendors, the maintenance of market gardens within the very walls of big cities, and, most important, the expansion of the local markets in which peasants displayed their own products in a common location at a set time under public control.

Of course, some of these institutions persisted into our own time. Open-air markets still give smaller European towns some of their charm. Disraeli and Dickens left us scorching portraits of the way the managers of nineteenth-century English mills reshaped the truck system to their own advantage. Furthermore, how long and how much food production survived within cities varied considerably from place to place; Jean Sentou's (1969) figures suggest that at the time of the Revolution at least a tenth of the population of Toulouse was engaged in agriculture, although Ingwer Ernst Momsen's study of Husum for the same period gives us fewer than one person in a hundred. According to Hans Mauersberg (1968), the smaller cities of the Rhineland were still able to draw their essential subsistence from the peasants of their own hinterlands well into the nineteenth century. Nevertheless, by that time the nonagricultural population of Europe as a whole depended heavily on standard channels of supply engaging multiple middlemen in the shipment and resale of the food. The proliferation of alternative links between producer and consumer was over, generally speaking, by the eighteenth century.

The phase of consolidation was the one which built relatively coherent regional, national, and international markets for food. Obviously, its timing varied from one part of Europe to another; indeed, it comprises an important part of what most observers have in mind when they speak of England as having commercialized early and Spain late.

Traditional Controls over the Food Supply

The right to be fed had solid political origins. The burghers of medieval Europe had fashioned a clanking, cumbersome but operative system of inspection and control. Municipalities solicitous of their own survival put most of the rules together. They did so in a relatively standard manner throughout Western Europe. Pirenne's description of the rules applying in the Low Countries holds much more generally:

> The legislation, of which some remains still survive to our own days in the police regulation of the municipal markets, was inspired exclusively by the interests of the burghers. Its object was to secure for the townsmen a plentiful supply of necessaries at a low price. It was quickly recognized that each set of middlemen, through whose hands commodities passed on their way from the producer to the consumer, inevitably raised the price. Hence it was needful to bring the countryman, who wished to sell, face to face with the townsman who wished to buy, and to prevent a group of speculators from making a corner in provisions. We have only to look over the communal regulations from this point of view, to realize that this is the spirit that animated them. The *lettre des vénaux* of Liège in 1317 forbade "engrossers" buying, within a radius of two leagues round the city,

poultry, cheese or venison. All these commodities had to be brought to the market, and it was only when the burghers were sufficiently provided for, that traders were allowed to acquire wholesale the unsold surplus. Butchers were prohibited from keeping meat in their cellars; bakers might not procure more corn than they required for their own baking. The most minute precautions were taken to prevent any artificial raising of prices. Not only was a *maximum* established, but also selling outside the market was strictly forbidden. In other words, it was an offense to sell goods otherwise than in public, under the eye of the burghers and the officers of the commune (Pirenne 1963: 80–81; cf. Van Werveke 1955, Klompmaker 1955).

As Pirenne goes on to point out, the system operated almost entirely to protect the urban consumer. It was, in fact, a set of arrangements designed and imposed by burghers for their own protection. It could work quite effectively so long as cities were small enough to supply themselves from their own immediate hinterlands, and so long as they retained political and economic control of the hinterland.

Nevertheless, the system had its counterpart outside the city. Wherever small producers sold grain locally, the same sorts of rules prevailed. The grain available for sale (which ordinarily excluded the grain committed to seed, to household consumption, to rents, taxes, or tithes) belonged first and foremost of the people of the parish. The local authorities had the obligation to make sure the local people had first crack at it, with the price set to exclude excess profit to middlemen. In addition, in times of shortage, the authorities had the obligation, to inventory the grain on hand, to call the salable grain out of storage, to keep shipments from escaping to seek a higher price elsewhere.

Both in city and country, the English justices of the peace had the authority to regulate the public marketing system from the very beginning of their official existence; they very likely acquired some of that authority from even earlier Anglo-Saxon precedent. The *Assisa Panis et Cervisiae*, the best known early codification of the Assize of Bread, is commonly thought to date from 1266 (Webb and Webb 1904: 196). It remained law in the London metropolitan area until 1815, and in the rest of the country until 1836. The law was in a sense a national law, but its administration (like that of so many English laws) relied entirely on the justices of the peace. Its essential features governed the activities of bakers: the relations between the prices they charged and the going price for wheat or rye, the size and quality of loaves, and so on. By extension, it governed the conditions of milling and marketing as well.

Studying the phenomenon in seventeenth-century England, Alan Everitt (1968: 68–69) discovers three important processes going on: (1) this shift of inland trade from the smaller to the larger market towns; (2) an increase in the scale of commercial dealings; (3) the movement of trade from the public market place to corn-chambers, warehouses, and the inns of provincial towns. From one perspective, of course, the third shift constitutes a "privatization" of the distribution system rather unlike the later formation of state-protected commodity exchanges and centralized wholesale markets. But its effect was to consolidate the control of the trade in the hands of a relatively small number of professionals, and to make it less possible for the consumer to buy his food directly from the producer. Those specialists eventually helped make the distribution faster, cheaper, and farther-reaching. Far more than the first phase of expansion, the second phase depended on the wholesale food merchant, and made his fortune.

Here we rejoin the food riot. For it was the age and the agency of the wholesale food merchant which sharpened the conflict between alternative claims to the food supply to the point of violence. The blockage and the price riot were the most common forms of collective violence in Western Europe during the second phase of market-building largely because that was the period in which merchants working to feed the urban population, the dependents of governments and the landless laborers directly confronted groups of people (sometimes drawn, ironically, from that same consuming population) who combined a basis for common action with a conviction that they had a prior right to some particular source of food. The confrontations multiplied, to be sure, when harvests failed and prices rose. Furthermore, they sometimes drew in more participants than consumers and merchants alone, and often involved other grievances than prices and shortage alone. In the Spanish riots of 1856,

"with the pretext of the high price of bread" and for lack of work, the workers of Valladolid and Burgos rose and burned flour stores, mills and inspection offices. The civil governor of

Valladolid, Saldana, intervened to put down the rising, but the rebels overwhelmed him and attacked the chiefs of his forces. The sacking and burning continued. Most likely as a consequence of the spreading of news of the incident, disturbances also spread to the countryside and to other cities. The governor of Palencia tried to hold back the uprising in his city, but had to retreat before a hissing crowd. In Benavente, Rioseco and along the Castile Canal the disorders recurred. They had the characteristics of the old type of rebellion aimed at speculators and hoarders, among whom the masters of workshops were counted. In their hatred, the insurgents set fire to shops and storehouses with the cry of *pan barato* [cheap bread] and attacked the boats which served for the transport of grain as well as putting the torch to grain not yet harvested in the fields (Sanchez-Albornoz 1963b: 94).

The National Militia failed to act (or even fraternized with the rioters), the army intervened, three incendiaries were executed, and, largely because of these conflicts, the government fell.

We begin to see that the nation-state was involved in conflicts over food in a whole series of ways: as the promoter of at least some of the growth in demand which lay beneath the drive to create a national market and wrest food from the peasantry; as the sometime ally of the merchants who sought to satisfy and profit by that demand; as the agency which suppressed or settled the conflict when it offered a threat to public order and the existing structure of power; as the organization which had finally assumed the responsibility of keeping its population from starving. These multiple involvements did not by any means form a harmonious whole. On the contrary, they virtually guaranteed that food policy would be a matter of bitter political debate. In order to grasp the issue of the debate, we must look somewhat more closely at traditional European controls over the food supply, and how the nation-state became involved in them.

The old system was coherent, even elegant. It rested on political and moral assumptions which were widespread in medieval Europe, as curious as their localism and organicism may appear today. It also rested on the assumption of multiple closed economies, each nearly self-sufficient. The conflict between that view of the world and the vision of life at a national or international scale underlay the bitter

[431]

division over the legitimacy of private marketing (as opposed to sale in the public way) in Tudor and Stuart England. Alan Everitt sketches the moral issue:

> In the open market the idea of the "just price" was still a governing consideration. To us that notion may seem antiquated and even chimerical. But it must be remembered that in the eyes of most contemporaries bargains were not simply commercial transactions; they formed part of the network of human intercourse which held society together. Every agricultural transaction both could and should be "equitable." For since every man occupied an appointed place or degree in the body politic, every man had a claim on that body to provide him with the means of livelihood. Transactions or contracts that militated against his right to subsistence, however arrived at, were unjust and invalid. For most people the ultimate appeal in disputed dealings was to social, in contrast with economic, duty (Everitt 1967: 569–570).

Thus traders who insisted that established contracts and debts took precedence over the welfare of the community violated moral sensibilities as well as local interests. Trading privately in warehouses and inns gave them an opportunity to evade surveillance, opprobrium, and, on occasion, retribution. For that reason, among others, merchants tended to favor private marketing, while traditionalists and ordinary people opposed it.

By the eighteenth century, private marketing was winning out in England, and many justices of the peace had given up close regulation of the market. Precisely because both systems were still present, however, conflict over marketing reached new heights. As he encounters the remains of the public marketing system in eighteenth-century England, E. P. Thompson (1963, 1966) assembles them into a vision of a "moral economy" centered on a bread-nexus rather than a cash-nexus. Thompson makes the essential observations:

> 1. The growing commitment of the state, of large farmers and of merchants to the creation of a presumably self-regulating national market (as epitomized in England by the publication of Adam Smith's *The Wealth of Nations* in 1776 and the repeal of laws against forestalling about the same time) undermined the will and the ability of the Justices of the Peace and other local authorities to maintain the old arrangements.

[432]

2. The crowd engaging in what the authorities called a "food riot" ordinarily either a) acted to force the merchants, bakers, J.P.s and others to perform their traditional roles or b) acted in their place by inventorying, seizing, selling, or blocking the shipment of grain.

But by the time England reached the eighteenth century, the rioters and ideologues were looking backward to a world which they had already lost. What they had lost was a system embodying local control and local priority.

The basic system of control had many variants. Four dimensions of variation appear to be most important: (1) the points of intervention in production, distribution, and consumption; (2) the means of intervention employed; (3) the extent and vigor of intervention; (4) the intervening agency. It is not so easy, however, to make refined comparisons in time and space over these dimensions. Prussian local officials long received substantial portions of their income in food, lodging, and other perquisites supplied locally. All the continental armies fluctuated considerably in the extent to which they lived off the land, relied on each man's buying his own meals, or organized their feeding through central commissaries. How shall we weigh the state's demand for resources in such cases, or gauge the choice among extractive policies? If the point is simply to give a comparative historical narrative, one can improvise composite categories. In order to estimate the *effects* of such major policy choices, however, it is necessary to place them all within the same logical framework.

Points of Intervention. Most public controls over food supply in Europe have focused on distribution rather than production or consumption. Controls over consumption itself have been exceedingly rare, except in such special forms as the regulation of alcoholic beverages. Controls over production run far back, in the guise of public regulation of crop rotation, enclosures, harvesting procedure. They belong to the basic structure of the European peasant community. In the eighteenth century, furthermore, quite a few European states took a direct interest in promoting the productivity of their farmers (see Bourde 1967, Ferry and Mulliez 1970).

If the distinction were of great importance here, we might have to debate whether heavy taxes levied on foodstuffs at the point of sale comprised controls over consumption or over distribution. All

[433]

European governments drew some of their income from such taxes. With the exception of the salt monopoly, from which numerous European states once drew considerable revenues, such taxes ordinarily exempted the necessities of life. Publicly consumed luxuries like beer and wine, on the other hand, were prime candidates for taxation. Where the taxes did strike necessities they almost always generated conflicts between consumers and governments; the *macinato*, or milling-tax on grain, incited rebellion after rebellion in Italy. Whether touching necessities or not, such taxes were exceptionally important as points of rebellion, because they so obviously laid the hand of the government on the individual consumer. The great 1647 rebellion of Neapolitan peasants and townsmen against the barons began with the resistance of the people of Naples to a new tax on fruit: "There Masaniello led the people not only against the urban nobles, the financiers and tax collectors, but also against the bandits belonging to the barons' retinues, and sought support from the country" (Cooper 1970: 49). Of course, such taxes symbolized and activated much wider struggles for power, rather than being sufficient in themselves to incite revolutions wherever they occurred. The point is that they symbolized and activated struggles of power rather often.

Means of Intervention. If we include public measures undertaken for other reasons which happen to significantly affect the production, consumption or distribution of food, then the means of intervention vary more than the points at which intervention occurs. The means fall into three big clusters: (1) regulatory, including legislative, judicial and administrative setting of limits to activities affecting the food supply; (2) fiscal, including the imposition of tariffs, duties, tolls, land taxes, excise taxes, licenses, or tithes, as well as the sale or lease of rights directly affecting the food supply; (3) organizational, covering the direct undertaking of production on royal domains, the formation of governmental agencies for the provisioning of the armed forces, and similar measures immediately involving public authorities in production, consumption, and distribution. The traditional European control system was essentially regulatory, but as states grew their fiscal and organizational involvement in the food supply tended to expand for quite a while.

Furthermore, the choice of means for revenues of all kinds affected the ease with which governments called up the necessary food supply. In principle, sovereigns of the sixteenth and seventeenth centuries had quite a range of devices for assuring their income: (1) dispossession of major corporate holders of wealth, such as churches, orders, etc.; (2) rents and other returns from property held directly by the Crown, such as the domain; (3) sale of privileges, honors, offices, etc.; (4) customs duties; (5) taxes on distribution and consumption, such as excise, tolls, licenses, etc.; (6) direct taxes on property and/or production. Furthermore, they had some choice (again, in principle) between exactions in money and exactions in kind.

The dispossession of major corporate holders of wealth often worked well in the short run, but as a long-run strategy it was, to say the least, unreliable. Although the various Estates of Europe lovingly entertained the vision of a king who "lived of his own" from the royal domain, that strategy, too, fell away with the heavy fiscal demands of the sixteenth and seventeenth centuries. The sale of privilege was also self-limiting, although it served the French crown for some time. During the earlier phases of European state-building, choices among the first three means undoubtedly made a considerable difference to the autonomy of the crown; Henry VII's managing to live off his own and Henry VIII's seizure of the monasteries freed those Tudor state-makers from close dependence on Parliament. But as time went on, the choice among customs, excise, and direct taxes became the fundamental ones, at least so far as the impact of national policy on the production, consumption and distribution of food (and vice versa) is concerned. English reliance on customs with a changing policy with regard to the major products of agriculture, Prussian reliance on excise heavily concentrated in the towns and French reliance on direct taxes made unequal by widespread privilege—these are, of course, tendencies, not absolutes—most likely encouraged the capitalization of agriculture in England, slowed all kinds of internal trade in Prussia, and forced peasants (who nevertheless remained peasants) to convert part of their production into cash crops in France. In these broad ways, state-making strategies shaped the development of the European agrarian economies.

The Extent and Vigor of Intervention. How broadly and energetically control agencies intervened in the food supply varied in several different ways: the geographic area affected by any particular regulatory system, the range of products and activities under public control, the energy and effectiveness of surveillance. The staples—bread,

[435]

salt, meat—ordinarily received more careful public attention than did luxury foods. The traditional European system had a relatively narrow geographic and substantive scope, but was quite intense within its defined range. As states entered the scene they tended to broaden the geographic and substantive range of intervention, and to weaken the intensity of control. As we shall see, nevertheless, the closeness of state supervision varied greatly from country to country and time to time; Spain, for example, maintained close national control over the distribution of food for centuries, while England adopted a hands-off policy toward internal flows of grain rather early.

The Intervening Agency. At one time or another, four public or quasi-public organizations involved themselves importantly in control of the European food supply: communities, manors, churches, and states. Households, firms, farms, estates, and groups of merchants, to be sure, also played important parts in food supply, but not as agencies intervening on behalf of some representation of the public interest. As compared with the regulatory role they might have occupied (or have occupied in other times and places), kin groups, craft associations, manufacturing organizations, patronage networks, and ethnic-religious groupings as such appear to have had relatively little to do with control of the European food supply.

Although the manor and the community had overlapped to a considerable degree in many parts of medieval Europe, by the modern period the closest remaining approximation to manorial control of the food supply appeared in the tightening seigneurial control of Eastern Europe. Communities, on the other hand, retained (or perhaps even increased) their share of collective control over food supply well into the modern period. That is especially true of urban communities.

The position of churches was far more variable, for churches were landlords in some places, seigneurs in others, statelike temporal authorities in still others, and collectors of tithes almost everywhere; they once played an important part in the redistribution of food to the poor. Nevertheless, the long-run drift went away from ecclesiastical regulation of the food supply, and toward assimilation of the church's position to that of other producers, consumers, and *rentiers*. Of all these organizations, only states unequivocally acquired greater power to intervene in the food supply over the long run. That is more true of direct intervention than it is of strictly regulatory power, since even before 1500 European kings periodically issued decrees authorizing or forbidding certain marketing practices and putting the authority of their courts behind the decrees. Except for the provisioning of the royal household and the administration of crown domains, most of the apparatus of direct state intervention in food supply—market inspectors, commissariats, corn laws, and so on—did not form or pass under state control until states established their priority over other authorities after 1500.

The Place of Cities in the Control of Food

Cities had a critical, ambivalent, and variable place in the growth of state intervention in food supply. Schmoller pointed out the ambivalence of the "urban interest" long ago:

> Thus two great opposing interests arose in the cities: the old view of provisioning called for cheap and abundant grain; the mass of population wanted, as before, cheap bread and protection against famine as well as against poor wages; and the local authority often identified itself with this interest, or was reminded by riots and uprisings that the general interest did not reside in the commerce of the great merchants, bakers, brewers and grain traders alone, but in cheap bread for the masses. The commercial interests, in opposition to the mass of consumers, had the desire to conduct their business unhindered; price fluctuations and sharp rises in prices promised them great profits (Schmoller 1896: 18–19).

In the long run, the merchants won this contest: early in England, by the early nineteenth century in France and Prussia, rather late in Spain and Italy; but they won. They won via some sort of collaboration with a state concerned to move food to its dependent population and to expand its own revenues from commerce. But in the shorter run the cities undertook a great deal of regulation on their own, and often found themselves at loggerheads with the statesmen and merchants as a result of their activity.

Unsurprisingly, the urban systems of control varied with the commercial position of the city. In sixteenth-century Pavia, the center of a rich agricultural plain, the municipality not only supervised the market, but also registered and taxed the grain as it passed through the gates of the city, and maintained public granaries to meet emergencies. There, too, the arrangements worked to minimize the middleman.

> Every rural proprietor, after having left the part which went to his tenants, hurried to take his grain to the city and, if he did not have enough room in his own place, gave it to a relative, the vicar, a neighbor or, more directly, to the baker who was going to make his bread "for administration" (*in governo*). The rich landlords, who lived in the city, placed the grain in the granges of their palaces and sold the excess beyond their domestic needs on the market, to individuals or to the sellers of bread. The religious communities, the university colleges and everyone else who took in students to board made arrangements to assure a ration of bread for each mouth, if not for the entire year, over a period of at least four or five months. . . . Only the "miserables" —who were still a substantial part of the population—those who lived on slim and irregular income or simply on charity, settled for buying bread from day to day as they could (Zanetti 1963: 51).

In Pavia, the wealthy consumer had rather more latitude in his purchasing arrangements than in Pirenne's Flemish cities, a fact which is probably related to the normally abundant supply of grain in Pavia's hinterland and its role as an *entrepôt* for grain on the way to Milan. Even in Pavia, however, the city fathers kept the whole operation of the grain trade under close surveillance, and took the major responsibility for provisioning the town in times of emergency.

Valencia, like most Spanish cities, ran a closer race with hunger than Pavia. Its organization for food supply was correspondingly more elaborate. From 1555, Valencia had an elected magistrate, the *clavari del avituallement*, whose subordinates (the *administradors de les carns* and *administradors dels forments*) divided the responsibility for meat and grain. In the grain market, "they distinguished sharply between the *forment aventurer*, that is grain which was spontaneously brought to market and the *forment asegurat* which was bought in large quantities by the city and sold at a conventional price, which held down the price of the *forment aventurer*" (Lapeyre 1969: 134–135). In acquiring the "security grains" the city had two major choices to make: (1) where to buy; and (2) by what commercial mechanism. Buying within the Kingdom of Valencia presented no serious difficulties when enough grain was on hand. Buying elsewhere in Spain or in Sicily (the major alternative) required the acquisition, at a price, of a license from the king or viceroy, and the attendant risk of losing either the grain or the money along the way. Although a wide range of commercial techniques came into play at one time than another, the principal choice lay between contracting with a merchant who bought grain on his own with an advance drawn from the city and sending the city's own agent, armed with gold or a letter of exchange, to Sicily, Apulia, Tuscany, Catalonia or somewhere else. Whichever source and whichever commercial mechanism the magistrates chose, the city was committing an important part of its resources to assuring the food supply.

Most of the traditional urban controls affected the *supply* of marketed food locally available. The city fathers, however, had two means of influencing the demand; they employed them only in emergencies. One was to impose rationing. The Pope's capital, Rome, for example, suffered from a precarious relationship to its areas of supply. Joachim du Bellay wrote plaintively of life there in the mid-sixteenth century.

> Quant á l'Estat du Pape, il fallut que j'apprinsse
> A prendre en patience et la soif et la faim.
> C'est pitié, comme là le peuple est inhumain
> Comme tout y est cher, et comme l'on y pinse.

During Rome's terrible hungry winter of 1591, the cardinals had to issue bread tickets, worth 18 ounces per day, to the city's inhabitants; in mid-March they had to reduce the ration to 12 ounces. And when they removed the controls prematurely, Romans began to riot (Delumeau 1957: ii, 622–623).

The other measure was to deliberately reduce the population of the city. Fernand Braudel provides a summary for the sixteenth century:

So there is a threat of famine. Everywhere the steps taken are the same. First act: with sound of trumpet the authorities forbid the departure of grain from the city, double the watch, make a search, inventory the grain on hand. If the threat grows worse, second act: they try to reduce the number of consumers; they

close the city gates; or they expel the foreigners (the usual procedure in Venice), unless the foreigners bring in on their own
account an amount of grain proportioned to their number. In
Marseille, in 1562, they threw out the Protestants, a double victory for a city hostile to Huguenots. In Naples, during the
famine of 1591, the university paid the cost of the disaster; it
was closed, the students sent home to their families (1966: 1,
302).

In Rome, about the same time, the Pope's men threw out the beggars
(Delumeau 1957: II, 562). This was a classic case of fighting an evil
by expanding it, since the control of important parts of Rome's supply area by bandits had helped create the shortage—and the exiled
beggars often joined the bandits. As was so often the case in early
modern urban administration, the interests of the long run and the
exigencies of the moment collided head on.
    The old arrangements for assurance of the urban food supply de-
serve special attention because they provided the models for the
early forms of intervention by the state itself. That is hardly surprising, considering how regularly the first problem which incited active
intervention by the state was the provisioning of its capital. Nevertheless, the intervention of the state did not simply mean more of the
same. Most European states eventually involved themselves somehow in creating a national market and in pursuing the interests of
some of their products, consumers, or distributors at a national scale.
States also brought a kind of muscle to the enforcement of their regulations which individual cities could rarely summon up. National
armies and national police forces acquired some of the form they
brought into modern times in Europe from their considerable involvement during their formative periods in control of the food
supply.

Food and Policing

Words like *Polizei*, police, and policy, etymologists never tire of
telling us, derive from the Greek conception of the *polis*—or more
precisely *politeia*, the governance of a city. The word police did not
lose its general meaning of provision for the public welfare until the
emergence of specialized anticrowd and anticriminal forces during
the nineteenth century. Up to that time, surveillance of public health,
supervision of markets, provision for public order, and a wide range

of other activities directly concerning the safe survival of the population not only hung together in European thinking, but fell into the jurisdiction of the same officials. Nicolas de La Mare's famous *Traité de la Police*, first published in 1705, assembled into a single encyclopedia the lore, law, and doctrine of French policing; perhaps half the four-volume work had to do with food supply. Policing included providing for an adequate food supply, regulating its disposition, and controlling the conflicts which grew up around it.

In this regard, European governments distinguished between their military and nonmilitary forces of order from quite early in their history. So far as I can determine, regular military forces never played a significant part in the routine policing of food supply in Europe. They generated a demand for food, they foraged in the countryside, they organized their own quartermaster corps, they protected threatened shipments, they came in to put down food riots, they ran cities from top to bottom during sieges, but they did not routinely post prices, verify measures, inventory stored grain, send inspectors to markets or any of the other workaday things which made up the *police des blés*. Those were responsibilities of the civil administration.

Some paramilitary forces, it is true, did get involved in the civil tasks. The Bourgeois Militias which provided the night watch for many eighteenth-century French cities sometimes found themselves charged with the inspection of bakeries and mills (Corvisier 1969: 254). Their successors during the Revolution—the directly descended National Guard and the mass-recruited Revolutionary Armies—devoted much of their energy to searching out and securing the urban food supply (Cobb 1963–1964, Cobb 1965). Nevertheless, in France and elsewhere the regular civilian administration bore the real continuing responsibility for policing.

It made sense to link responsibility for public order to responsibility for food supply. Exporting areas with large dependent populations soon learned the risks of playing too freely with the food supply. In Naples,

the immediate cause of the revolt of 1585 was the decision of the Electors to raise the price of bread in the capital. A little while before, the same administration had authorized the exportation of more than four hundred thousand *tomoli* of grain to Spain. Speculative operations of this sort, if less extreme, were not exceptional in the history of the city administration, and thus entered into the normal operation of the grain trade, which was largely controlled by political power. Thus it displayed the nature of the connections between the urban aristocracy and the big grain-growers of the province (Villari 1967: 38).

The rebellion impressed contemporary observers with the extent of mobilization among the ordinary people of the kingdom, and with its call for "death to misgovernment, long live justice." In its repression, thirty-one persons were condemned to death with torture, seventy-one sentenced to the galleys, three hundred banned; another twelve thousand persons are said to have fled the kingdom. Now, of course there was far more to the Neapolitan rebellion than high bread prices. It was precisely that capacity to raise far more general questions of political legitimacy which made conflicts over the food supply a continuing source of threats to public order.

Even conflicts closer to the everyday administration of food supply recurrently produced collective violence. We have already explored the blockage and the price riot, and discovered some very serious conflicts along the way, but it may be useful to reflect on the problem faced by the authorities of Amiens (a market and transit point for an important area of commercial grain production) during the high-price year of 1630.

During the day of July 23, rebels attacked the dwellings of a number of merchants and commissionaires on the rue des Vergeaux and the rue de Beauvais. Those of Jean le Roux and of Grégoire Cordelle, the collector of the abbey of Gard, were sacked completely, the furnishings thrown out the window or stolen; the city councilors, who had rushed to the scene, were stoned and insulted. The bourgeois militia did not gain control of the terrain until after several volleys of musketry, killing five or six insurgents and wounding fourteen. Three looters sent to the Bailliage court were sentenced to whipping and sent to the galleys for nine years. Only the arrival of the Duke of Elbeuf, governor of the province, accompanied with a large group of gentlemen, restored order and fear (Deyon 1967: 437).

This sort of retributive action, which was the most frequent form of violent conflict over the food supply before the eighteenth century, tended to recur whenever prices were rising, supplies were short, and profiteering or hoarding suspected. During the accelerated market-building of the eighteenth and nineteenth centuries, the retributive action tended to give way to the price riot and the blockage. And throughout the modern period—in the first six years of the French Revolution, during the Spanish Revolution of 1868, during the Russian Revolution of 1917—the demand for cheap and abundant bread, for the destruction of the others who profited from the starvation of honest men, compounded the more explicitly political issues of the great revolutionary movements. Great conflicts and small forged a strong connection between public order and food supply.

Yet we must keep the matter in perspective. Food riots alone did not cascade into revolutions. They had greater significance as a symptom than as a stimulus to permanent change. Although the food riot often worked at the local scale by bringing hidden grain into the market, forcing a temporary decline in prices or whipping up the energy of local officials, the scale usually remained quite local. Small in scale, leaderless, and carried on by unarmed men, women, and children, the food riot rarely consolidated into a larger rebellion; even then it was not hard to put down. Although in eighteenth- and nineteenth-century Western Europe the food riot put a steady strain on the apparatus available for policing rural areas, it is not certain that its expansion accounted for any major changes in the practice of repression. It was only when combined with other complaints that conflicts over food proved capable of mobilizing masses of ordinary people for rebellion. Thus control of conflicts over food remained, for the most part, the business of local militias, *gendarmeries* and police forces.

How States Became Involved

Most of those repressive forces remained under the control of local authorities quite far into the modern period. So did most routine supervision of the food supply. As a consequence of their involvement in the expansion of cities, the growth of landless labor and the swelling of governmental staffs, nevertheless, national states intervened in the production and distribution of food with increasing directness and energy from 1500 up to the nineteenth century. I have in mind not just the passing of laws governing transactions among individuals and the organized acquisition of supplies for the royal household (which were, after all, practically as old as king-

[443]

ship) but the erection of a national apparatus engaged in regulatory, fiscal, and organizational intervention in the flow of foodstuffs.

The earliest expansion of state involvement in food supply consisted largely of adapting the traditional community-level controls to a somewhat larger scale. Magnify the controls to the scale of the city-state and to the practice of seizing passing shipments of grain in times of dearth; *voilà*, there is one version of piracy. During the great Spanish famine of 1578, the merchants of Genoa bought grain in Apulia for shipment to the immensely willing buyers of Spain, only to see their ships and cargoes impounded by the Republic of Genoa itself (Braudel 1966: 1, 521). At various times, Venice, Marseille, and many of the other maritime cities of the Mediterranean commissioned corsairs to go out and capture grain ships; the Knights of Malta were in that very business for themselves (Braudel 1966: 1, 303). One more example of the way the fledgling states of the Renaissance employed, or promoted, for their own ends, practices which in retrospect appear to be inimical to the orderly conduct of governmental affairs: brigandage, piracy, venality, corruption. And an important example of the way states as such became involved in the control of the food supply.

In general, the city-based trading states of Italy and Flanders built elaborate procedures for the regulation of the grain trade into their statecraft long before relatively self-sufficient powers like England or France. The maritime states, especially around the Mediterranean, kept a lively international trade in grain going throughout the Renaissance. Jean Meuvret puts it this way:

> From Vidal de la Blache to Fernand Braudel, many writers have spotlighted the role of cities in Mediterranean civilization. But let us stop for a moment to ask where those cities got their means of subsistence, that is their grain, which was the essential part. The answer is clear. . . . Certainly each city had some local production to draw on, sometimes meager, sometimes abundant. Yet none of them would have lived and grown without supplies from outside. At least in times of shortage, shipping took care of the need (Meuvret 1951: 66).

The Mediterranean city-states took full advantage of their "liquid roads," as Fernand Braudel calls them, and were able to meet their needs more successfully than the North European states so long as

[444]

the other foundations of Mediterranean trade stayed in place. This dependence on the outside for the very means of survival, however, made them more vulnerable to piracy, war and routine maritime competition than, say, Sweden, France, or even England. As a result, their governments were extensively engaged in the flow of provisions by the fourteenth or fifteenth century.

Nowhere was the effect clearer than in Sicily, which lay under Spanish domination from around 1400 to 1700. Sicily's main business was the production and shipment of grain. Yet her cities, too, suffered from dearth; they faced riot, or even rebellion, when supplies ran low. The problem was that so many outsiders—the Spaniards, their army and navy, the Pope, and others who had bought *tratte*, export licenses—acquired claims over the harvest which could easily squeeze out Palermo or Messina (Denis Mack Smith 1968: 175–177). From the beginning, Spaniards treated Sicilian wheat as a national (or, more precisely, a royal) resource. The Sicilians themselves often went hungry.

The earlier forms of state intervention in the food supply, then, flowed more or less directly from the efforts of rulers of capital cities to assure the provisioning of their own urban population when demand exceeded the capacity of the politically dependent area. The managers of those states employed expanded versions of the standard urban supply procedures. During the fifteenth century, however, the state-makers of exporting areas like Poland were involving themselves in a rather different manner—by collaborating with the nobles in the creation of the "second serfdom," by favoring exports over the feeding of local cities, and by aiming the tax burden at peasants and merchants rather than landlords. In seventeenth-century Hungary, we even find a shift away from taxation in kind to meet the direct food requirements of the army toward taxation in specie based on the market value of the farm, coupled with the guarantee of preferential access to the market for the great lords (Varkonyi 1968). That combination repeatedly fostered tax rebellions in Europe by blocking the means for peasants to acquire the cash they needed to pay their imposts (Ardant 1965). In this case it was no doubt one of the major precipitants of the "anticolonial" rebellion of Francis II Rokoczi. Rebellion or no, the complex of policies tended to facilitate exports of grain from the big estates, slow the provisioning of the local cities, and increase the dependency of the peasantry. It may also have accelerated the spread of peasant wage-labor as a means of acquiring the money to pay taxes. What was happening, in general terms, was the creation of a colonial system to complement the rise of commercial and industrial centers in Western Europe.

England

The great industrial powers had a different history. In England, one form or another of the standard local controls over the distribution of grain prevailed (with the sanction of the state, but the responsibility of the justices of the peace) everywhere into the eighteenth century. During the sixteenth century, the crown intervened in the international grain trade from time to time, in order to assure the provisioning of the armed forces or to alleviate the impact of bad harvests (Ponko 1968: 8–18). The government only rarely exerted control over the movement of food within the domestic market, and did so chiefly through temporary prohibitions on exports from one county to another. The first extensive national regulation of the grain trade dates from the later seventeenth century; its exponents held up Dutch models for emulation. By that time the domestic grain market—at least the portion centered on London—was already active, extensive, and well-organized.

The chief point of the English national regulation was not to keep Englishmen from starving, but to encourage the profitable export of grain from the country. Unlike the situation in France or Holland, the great landlords of England were still expanding and consolidating their holdings, forcing smallholders off the land, orienting their production to a world market, and using their political influence to ease their way. Domestic consumption appears to have been a less important stimulus to national policy. After their experience with the New Model Army, the English kept their standing armies very small until the nineteenth century, and thus minimized one demand for food which was important on the Continent. The Navy had to be fed (the Pride of Pride's Purge had grown rich as a naval victualer), but its needs for biscuits and beer were relatively small, and could be met in the ports. The influence of London, on the other hand, reshaped the agriculture of southern England. But the state's role, by and large, was to acquiesce in the erosion of the old restrictions on the metropolitan food trade: "London had to be fed, and no practical alternatives were ever suggested. Vested interests could only delay what they could not prevent. City, county and national authorities all learned in time to tolerate what they had previously damned" (Fisher 1954: 151).

Some Englishmen still went hungry. Widespread eighteenth-century food riots signified the continuing conflict between national markets and local needs. But it was not until the manufacturing population grew up in the cities and England became a net importer of grain that the balance of national policy shifted toward the consumer:

> Thus in England the great economic struggle between producer and consumer was fought out over the price of bread and the restrictions on the importation of wheat. The struggle coincided with, and was intensified by, the death struggle with the French Republic and Napoleon. It was the anger spot in the fight for free trade from the rise of Huskisson to the fall of Peel. The act of corn law repeal in 1846 marked the triumph of the consumer and the fulfillment in England of that hard fiscal saying: "Consumption is the sole end and purpose of all production." The country gentlemen and farmers put up a good fight, but they collapsed before the brazen monotone of Cobdenism (Fay 1932: 8).

Fay might have added: and the necessity of feeding an industrial labor force. After that, the supply of bread ceased to be a political issue of durable importance in England.

France

In France as well, truly national policies of food supply only emerged late in the seventeenth century, despite the fact that every commune had its own elaborate regulations. Louis XIV insisted in his memoirs that "the need for food is the first thing a prince should consider," but in fact his officers pursued fluctuating and contradictory food policies. They responded to real differences in interest, and strong differences in doctrine, between center and periphery. As London was the special case and monster market in England, Paris was the exception to most of the rules in France. The great city had long had priority in the purchase of grain within a large, if fluctuating, area to its north and west. The Crown backed that priority. But in the rest of the country, the ritual royal decrees of "freedom of trade" made little difference until Colbert and his successors began directly pressing the creation of a national market apt to keep the grain flowing to an expanding capital and a swelling army.

The pressure to feed the army was surely stronger in France than in England, if only because of the much greater size of the French army. Le Tellier and Louvois, the organizers of the standing army, did much of the work of establishing a regular system of provisioning. During the long wars of Louis XIV, they virtually ended the old practice of having troops live off the land, and organized a military subsistence service with its own storehouses (André 1906: chap. 9). That meant making sure the food was there to buy, especially in years of short supply.

From the end of the seventeenth century onward, high officials of the Crown worked increasingly to promote the free flow of grain out of the provinces, to support the position of the wholesale merchants, and to overrule the frequent resistance of the provincial *Parlements* to the dismantling of the old local regulation of the grain trade. It was precisely in this period (and, I believe, as a direct consequence of the new policies) that the price riot joined the blockage and the retributive action in conflicts over food; food riots of one variety or another became the prevalent form of collective violence in France.

The Revolution of 1789 added a political dimension—or, rather, two political dimensions—to the conflict over food. First, the ordinary complaints about the incompetence and/or immorality of the local authorities and merchants now took on a political cast. "Hoarders and speculators" had always been enemies of the people, but during the early Revolution labels took on a much broader meaning, and carried a much greater threat to their recipients. The improper handling of local problems of subsistence became the occasion not simply of food riots and temporary takeovers of the food supply, but also of demands for the permanent removal of incumbent officials. That leads to the second dimension: the heightened political consequences of conflicts over food. In the multiple local struggles for power which made up the "municipal revolution" of 1789 and 1790, the inability of the old authorities to supply food and check food riots regularly led to their overturn in favor of others allied with the Parisian revolutionaries. In a number of cities, the revolutionary committees and militias (soon to be National Guard units) formed in direct response to the food crisis. Furthermore, the events of 1789 which have entered standard history books as the Peasant Revolt—

the attacks on castles and landlords supposedly carried out by peasants hostile to feudal privilege—often turn out on closer scrutiny to consist of town-based raiding parties scouring the countryside for hoarded grain, and often finding it in the granges of abbeys and castles. Guy Lemarchand sums up the attacks in the region of Rouen:

> Thus these popular uprisings, at first meant to seize grain wherever it could be found, finally challenged the entire social system, even though the rebels themselves never clearly understood that. Their reaction remained negative and shortlived. Because they wanted grain, they were led to attack those who, in eighteenth-century society, were likely to have most. . . . Directed at first against part of the Third Estate, that battle finally touched the feudal segments of the population just as much (Lemarchand 1963: 413).

Eventually this sort of pressure (or rather the version of it which issued from the great conflicts of Paris itself) led to the Jacobin Maximum. The Maximum, which completely reversed the earlier revolutionary attempt to radically free the grain trade, was the first genuine attempt by any French government to fix food prices generally and nationally. The liberal revolution took the most antiliberal measures.

In France, the conflict over food, at least as reflected by the food riot, persisted past the Revolution. It only faded after reaching its maximum intensity during the widespread food riots of 1846 and 1847. (The last round of any significance at all came in 1853–1854.) Although the real explanation for that nineteenth-century rise and fall remains complicated and controversial, I think the main factors were something like these: the number of landless industrial and agricultural workers still located in the countryside grew to its all-time maximum in the early nineteenth century; so long as they were in the countryside, they were vulnerable to the inefficiencies of the rural redistribution of food and yet had the means of local action against merchants and officials; as the century went on, the structure of the peasant community disintegrated in areas of extensive landless labor, the surplus laborers migrated to the city in increasing numbers, the overall productivity of French agriculture rose markedly, and the distribution system, especially through the agency of the railroads, underwent rapid improvement. If this is correct, the explanation of the decline in conflict over food supply is simply the logical extension of the conditions which brought the conflict into being in the first place. Consumers would eventually organize with a vengeance, but only after the long struggle over control of the food supply had been won by the national state and the national market.

Spain

Spain, as usual, presents a more complicated picture. Its long domination of Sicily gave the Spanish crown access to one of the chief granaries of Europe. Its execrable internal transport system made its cities more dependent on external supplies than the peninsula's land mass might lead one to expect. Furthermore, Barcelona and its province of Catalonia frequently operated as a virtually independent city-state. Vilar reports:

> A marked contrast opposes the two capitals: that of the Spanish state set a price on grain and let the bakers free; that of the Catalan region brought grain at the market price and controlled the bankers closely. The explanation is simple. Madrid, as an aristocratic and administrative city, depended less on the variations in the price of bread than Barcelona, a town of artisans, and then of industry. But the unpredictable leaps of the production of Castile could cause quick catastrophes; one had to watch the wheat. In Barcelona, dear bread would make high wages; but the best way to keep down prices in the bakeries was to open the gates to grain coming by sea. So they left the wholesale trade in grain free (it was, in any case, traditionally an important branch of commerce in the city itself); they did not control speculation except in baking (Vilar 1962: II, 390–391).

In Castile and those sections of Spain over which Madrid had effective control, the virtually unchanging policy for centuries was to peg the price of grain and control its distribution carefully. What is more, the policy worked; it kept the poor folks quiet and made the Madrilene population one of the best-fed in Spain (Palacio Atard 1969). A few brief eighteenth-century attempts to free the trade ended in a shambles as Madrid began to starve and its people began to riot.

But control also had its costs. The combination of agricultural decay in Castile and increasingly uncertain access to foreign grains helped strangle the growth of Madrid, make the maintenance of the army more difficult, and promote the decline of Spanish power in the seventeenth century. "The decline of Spain," concludes José Gentil da Silva, "like its expansion, is the history of its agriculture, its villages and, since Castile dominated all else, especially the villages of Castile" (Gentil da Silva 1963: 744). Vicens Vives considers that the decay of Castilian agriculture resulted to an important degree from the food policy of the crown. He argues that the relative cost of Spanish agricultural products rose during the prosperous first half of the sixteenth century:

> Then came the finishing touch, the fixing of wheat prices. Price-fixing was the expression of an agrarian policy based on the principle of favoring the consumer to the detriment of the producer. When prices went up too much, the State simply chose to put a ceiling on them instead of helping production to fight the increase. Thus, price-fixing, which had already been used by the Catholic Monarchs as an occasional measure, was restored as a permanent feature after 1539. This measure, called for by the Cortes (especially after 1535) and supported by the economists of the period, was a result of pressure by the urban proletariat beginning to grow up in the country's large cities. Its effects could not have been more lamentable (Vicens Vives 1969: 346).

Then he enumerates those effects: an economic squeeze on the peasantry, absenteeism among farmers, depreciation in the value of land, reduction of the cultivated area, appearance of a black market, and, finally, famine.

Now, the process was a bit more complicated than Vicens Vives implies. Charles V had asked the Cortes to Castile in 1538 for authority to tax foodstuffs in order to help pay for his Mediterranean warmaking. "The nobles," Carrera Pujal (n. d.: 1, 117) reports, "frankly stated the small sympathy they had with the European enterprises of the Emperor, saying that if he followed the examples of earlier kings, stayed in Spain and freed himself from the problems of other countries, his rents would suffice for his expenses." The fixing of prices was a victory of the Cortes over the crown, and a relatively important step toward the stagnation of state-making which overtook Spain during the following centuries. Nevertheless, the effect was very likely as Vicens Vives (1969) describes it. In the long

[451]

run, this particular choice of controls over distribution probably compromised the effort to build a strong commercial state.

When the Spaniards renewed their efforts to liberalize the economy and create a national market in the nineteenth century, however, they faced the same kinds of conflicts the great industrial powers had encountered earlier. The food riot continued to be a major form of political conflict in Spain through the nineteenth and into the twentieth centuries. It was no more a mechanical response to hunger there than anywhere else. After noting that rural workers had often responded to famine by dying quietly or by emigrating, Diaz del Moral says that in 1905 "the wave of defiance had washed from their souls the Christian resignation with which they had succumbed on similar occasions" (Diaz del Moral 1969: 213–214), and led them and their urban brethren to couple demands for cheap bread with calls for government-promoted work. These conflicts went beyond the usual scale of the classic food riots of 1856 or even of revolutionary 1868 (when one of the origins of conflict was the regime's shift from free importation of grain to protection of the national market for Spanish producers [Sanchez-Albornoz 1968]).

And the food riot appears to have dwindled away over the next few decades. During the Trienio Bolchevista of 1918–1920, high prices sometimes came in for complaint, but the most usual demands of the agrarian strikers had to do with increased wages, expulsion of government officials, rehiring of fired strikers, and abolition of piecework (Levine 1970: 34). By the time of the Civil War, despite the persistence of hunger, the food riot was gone. As in Italy, Spanish rural workers stayed heavily involved in political conflict via land occupations, agrarian strikes and diverse forms of anarcho-syndicalism, but the twentieth-century disappearance of the food riot seems to have followed from the dissolution of the peasant community and its autonomous claims to the food supply.

Brandenburg-Prussia

In Brandenburg-Prussia we have the strongest case of a national food supply shaped by the needs of maintaining a military force. Faced with a ruined countryside at the close of the Thirty Years War, the Elector Frederick William had to negotiate between great noble landlords eager to export the grain squeezed from their estates, and cities just as eager to lay claim to the supplies from their hinterlands in the traditional way. The balance had already, as we know, been shifting toward the landlords for some time. Frederick William leaned toward the landlords, which strengthened their overall position and encouraged them to operate their own lands directly.

Much of the Hohenzollern grain policy went into building up stores and supply systems for a big standing army, and assuring the free movement of grain into those provinces where the army was concentrated. The riveting of agrarian policy to the war machine held into the nineteenth century. Obviously, it served the Junkers of the East, who were simultaneously masters of war and masters of rye. Very likely it also reinforced the unfreedom of the peasantry, inhibited the development of a mercantile class, discouraged the expansion of cottage industry, and thus ultimately slowed the growth of industrialism in Germany. But in the nineteenth century, as Hans Rosenberg (1943) has shown, the Junkers found themselves cooperating in the destruction of their own traditional supports. The legal liberation of the peasantry, the formation of a liberal state, the promotion of industrial growth all broke with their previous experience, although they did not destroy the political power of those old elites. Those same transformations accentuated internal conflicts over the food supply. As in France, food riots reached an all-time peak in the 1840s. Then (rather more slowly than in France) they faded away. So in Germany, too, the pattern of conflict and action with respect to the food supply depended mainly on the changing relations between the state and the major actors in the national economy.

Food Policy and Its National Consequences

The contrasts among national policies we have reviewed have a very familiar air. There are the Mediterranean city-states, bending their governmental policy to the needs of maritime commerce. Here is England, with an influential class of landlords pressing the commercialization of agriculture and acquiring the protection of the state. In France we find the centralizers moving far and fast, assuring a food supply by taxing the peasantry directly, forcing rural producers into the market, and battling the provincial resistance embodied in the *Parlements* all the way. Within Spain the general experience is wide variation from province to province, fluctuation in the degree of central control, acquiescence (at least by Castile) in corruption, stagnation, and the petty influence of the *hidalgo*. And Prussia gives the picture of a bureaucracy devoted with exceptional stubbornness to the creation of military might.

No doubt these are caricatures, familiar masks. If they catch the general direction of differences among the European states, nevertheless, they tell us something important. Food supply absorbed an important part of the energy and organization of every European state for at least some portion of the modern period. The exact nature of the problem in one country or another depended on its geopolitical position, the variety, and organization of its agriculture, the class alliances in which the state-makers themselves were entangled. But how each state's rulers actually dealt with the problem depended on the general state-making policy they adopted. The success or failure of their food policy, moreover, strongly affected their ability to accomplish the other objectives.

To be more precise, the choice of food policies affected the subsequent experience of European states in five fairly direct ways: (1) by forming or cementing the main class coalitions with which the state entered the modern era, the principal choice being the relative strength of the peasantry, the landlords, the mercantile, and the manufacturing classes; (2) by affecting the success of its fiscal policy, the most important relationship being the tendency of commercialized agriculture and high yields from direct taxation to complement each other; (3) by affecting the bulk of the central bureaucracy, with extensive controls at the national level tending to expand the bureaucracy; (4) by promoting or hindering the growth of agricultural and industrial production, both of them being more likely to expand where cash-crop production was encouraged and the capacity of the peasant village to retain its own products destroyed; (5) by governing the timing, extent, and locus of violent conflicts over control of the food supply, with the promotion of a free market tending to generate acute conflict so long as the margin of survival was small, the yearly fluctuations in supply and prices large, and the peasant community still in vigor.

Of course, most of these relationships were reciprocal. Of course, many other factors—geopolitical position, religious and ethnic composition, dynastic accidents, military successes, other fiscal and administrative policies among them—affected the outcomes of the heroic European efforts at building states. Of course, the "choice" of food policy often followed more or less automatically from prior decisions to build armies, favor landlords, or prevent rebellions by whatever means necessary. Perhaps these complications will discourage anyone who hopes to find in bread not only the staff of life but also the key to state-making. To me the moral is more like the homely German tag, *Man ist, was er isst* (you are what you eat). The building of states in the midst of an agrarian economy, where most resources were in one manner or another committed to agriculture and controlled by peasant communities, inevitably involved European state-makers, directly or indirectly, in a struggle for control of food. In watching that struggle we do not necessarily observe all the sources of parliamentary democracy, of fascism, or of military might. We do observe the basic processes of state-making as they touch the everyday lives of ordinary people.

CHAPTER 7

THE RECRUITMENT AND TRAINING OF ADMINISTRATIVE AND TECHNICAL PERSONNEL

WOLFRAM FISCHER AND
PETER LUNDGREEN

~·~

Introduction

STATE-BUILDING can be dealt with by inquiring into the activities in which European states engaged during the early period of their development. The preceding chapters of this book have singled out such activities considered to be of crucial importance. But these activities needed actors who implemented the policies decided upon. The present chapter focuses upon these actors, it deals with the human resources in the process of state-building; it particularly asks for the recruitment and training of both administrative and technical personnel. This means we touch upon fields like administration, taxation, judication, military service, but also military and civil engineering, construction and building, technology and industry.

However, to enumerate these fields does not indicate their relative importance in any specific case of state-building. We have to expect that the countries under consideration will show differences in their patterns of bureaucratic structures, in their ways of recruitment and training of personnel, and in the very degree of bureaucratization itself. These differences may be largely explained by the features of the various countries showed when embarking upon state-building, as has been pointed out in the preceding chapters: differences in preconditions, timing, cumulation of developmental crises, size of tasks either given or deliberately set up, etc. Patterns of personnel formation (mainly studied under the heading of recruitment and training) will therefore serve as an additional indicator, rather than as an independent variable, of Western European state-building. Nevertheless there is good reason not to underestimate the long-term impact of traditions of personnel formation upon the subsequent process of state- and nation-building.

[456]

Administrative Personnel

Comparative analysis tends to stress differences rather than similarities. But we have to keep in mind that in spite of the many varieties of national histories in Western Europe their basic experience, some of their most lasting institutions and cultural traits were common, and that the specific features of each age were shared by all nations. The development of a professional public service was influenced in all European states by the heritage of Roman law and of administrative procedures of the medieval church. They also shared the restrictions of an age without the modern means of communications and therefore of penetration and integration (like roads, railways, and telegraphs).

The few bureaucratic structures available to them at the onset of modern times were that of the church, their own central offices and that of corporations like cities and great enterprises. Fifteenth- and sixteenth-century kings and ministers did not know that they were heading toward the development of a salaried, full-time professional civil service as we are inclined to conclude from the outcome in nineteenth- and twentieth-century Europe. What choices were open to them?

The most obvious choice was to transfer the medieval ecclesiastical hierarchy into the service of the monarch. For centuries kings had used ecclesiastics as their administrative officials at different levels. Since the late fifteenth century even cardinals, like Wolsey in early sixteenth-century England and Richelieu and Mazarin in seventeenth-century France, were leading ministers of the king, and below them bishops and lower clerics served the worldly authority as well as the spiritual. But there had always been the problem of dual loyalty which had led to the tragic fate of such eminent ministers as Thomas Becket or Thomas More. Uncontested loyalty to the supreme authority of the state, the king, had to be assured before an efficient and permanent civil service could develop.

Modern observers tend to look at the civil service mainly from the point of view of efficiency and impartiality. The service has to be able, disinterested, and law oriented. But before it can show such characteristics it had to learn to be loyal. As long as different families strove for kingship, as long as the territory of a state was contested by several princes, as long as the church demanded universal influence, loyalty to a specific house could not be taken for granted. All medieval English kings, and the Tudors as well as the Stuarts, had to face this problem; it was attacked by the Valois in France but solved only by the Bourbons who at least succeeded in uprooting the strong local self-determination. The relatively quick development of efficient government in late-coming Prussia may well be due to the fact that loyalty to the Hohenzollerns was not contested any more after the Great Elector.

Efficiency as a goal of administration for centuries meant mainly the ability to extract resources from the country for the king, his court, and his army. The ever-growing standing armies on the Continent, the similarly growing navy in England, the splendor of the royal household and the administration itself demanded greater means than any of the monarchs could command traditionally from the royal demesne and feudal levies. No early modern king could live "on his own" as the medieval tradition expected him to do. After loyalty the second important virtue of the king's service was, therefore, the ability to raise money. Financial administration was the crucial point of early modern administration. Local administrative offices were set up for this purpose; the penetration of central authorities throughout the king- or princedom meant raising taxes, customs and excises.

The second big task of local administration was to keep law, order, and peace. Administration thus was intermingled with jurisdiction and arbitration. Functions which later became separated and are nowadays regarded as incompatible were united in one office or a single person. If, when, and how they developed into their modern shape characterizes the specific course the state-building process took in the European countries. These differences between the British, French and Prussian experience in their common striving for a "modern" state now have to be studied. This means to outline bureaucratic structures; to estimate the degree of bureaucratization as well as its penetration into the society; to describe the ways and means of recruitment and training; and to reason about possible explanations of the findings and their implications upon state-building. In a second section we will turn to technical personnel.*

* Wolfram Fischer is responsible for the parts on Britain, and Peter Lundgreen for those on France and on Prussia.

BRITAIN

The basic fact from which we have to start is that Britain in her state-building period neither possessed nor developed a civil service as it is defined in the textbooks: a corps of specifically trained, examined, and appointed men, independent from the political conjuncture, impartial in discharging their services, fully salaried and pensioned by the state and fully employed by it, subject to a hierarchical order in which they moved upward according to seniority or merit or a mixture of both.[1] This "ideal-type" civil service is a product of very recent developments and was never fully reached in any country. In Britain a modern civil service was established only in the nineteenth century, when "state-building" in the sense used in this book had already come to a final stage. A number of parliamentary commissions on the reform of public administration, the first appointed in 1780, developed the criteria of a modern civil service one by one: Public officials should work for their money and not hold sinecures; they should discharge their duty in person and not by deputy; they should receive fixed salaries out of public money instead of perquisites, emoluments, and fees; they have the right of superannuation and pension at old age which implied tenure of office; they ought to be servants of the Crown and not of a particular minister; and they have to reach a certain standard of qualification before being appointed or promoted. First limited, then open competition was introduced to substitute merit for patronage, and the service itself was graded (see Cohen 1941).

How can one explain that England could achieve internal peace, authority for the king's orders and parliamentary statutes, an effective judicial system and the exaction of enough means to sustain a court, a government and military forces without employing a modern civil service? As the following pages will show, the answer is partly to be found in definition. If we want to understand early modern European government, we cannot adhere to the stringent notion of civil service used above. England, in particular, though lacking a civil service as a formally trained and regulated body of administrators, possessed experienced servants of the king and of the king's ministers. "Unreformed" as this service was by 1780, governed by haphazardous and obscure rules, full of abuses and discrepancies,

---

[1] For a short definition see Finer 1932: 1163: "The Civil Service is a professional body of officials, permanent, paid and skilled."

it had proved quite efficient by the standards of the sixteenth, seventeenth, and eighteenth centuries. After all England at the end of the eighteenth century was economically the most progressive, politically one of the most powerful countries of Europe. Either "government by amateurs"—as the English governmental system is often called when compared with continental states—was as successful as "government by professionals"[2] or England was not as amateurish as is often supposed, but commanded a group of administrators who, if not professional in the sense of full-time, specially trained and fully salaried, were at least semiprofessional, that is experienced, competent, and reasonably devoted to the service. The thesis offered in this chapter is that a combination of both explains the performance of the English public service before the nineteenth century. Amateur government in early modern times was not *eo ipso* inferior to the crude type of professionalism in France or Prussia, and the English administrators were not as amateurish as we generally believe. A considerable number had some formal training either at the universities or the inns of court (or both), most were thoroughly trained "on the job" either as servants and clerks or higher officials, lawyers or merchants, or as administrators of landed estates and commercial enterprises, and even if they only worked part-time for their government and spent more energy for private business this does not necessarily mean lesser service; there are indications that it induced greater efficiency in discharging public duties in order to gain more time for private aims. Accordingly the lack of adequate salary and dependence on fees, perquisites, and even bribes, or the mixture of public and private affairs so common in the sixteenth to eighteenth centuries, was no decisive drawback against the Continent. Salaries were insufficient everywhere and all public services consequently were deeply corrupt by modern standards. Corruption may have been even less where the pursuit of private enterprise was allowed or expected as where it was suppressed without adequate compensation.

Unfortunately, there are no satisfactory means to measure and to compare the performance of different administrations in earlier modern times. The degree of corruption can only be guessed, the success of administration may be deduced from the degree of penetration a government or the degree of integration a nation achieved —and here England certainly fared no worse than others—but it

[2] This distinction is made *inter alia* by Ernest Barker (Barker 1944: 32).

remains a matter of judgment how far such success can be attributed to efficient administration as compared with other factors. A crude measure is the ratio of administrative personnel to population. However, even these data are deficient. The scarce evidence allows the conclusion that England had a smaller proportion of its population employed in public administration than either Spain, France, or Prussia. At the beginning of the seventeenth century, English central government agencies employed between 1,400 and 2,000 officials. Some hundred customs officials, administrators of Crown lands and local administrators, e.g., Clerks of the Justices of Peace, have to be added. At the same time there were about 650 senior offices in the central French government and 3,000 to 4,000 provincial administrators alone in Normandy. The government of Castile had about 530 *major* posts, and it is said to have employed 60,000 subordinates of its Exchequer and 20,000 in the Inquisition (Aylmer 1961: 440, 452). Even if the Castilian numbers are exaggerated, there remains the basic difference between England's reliance on a relatively small number of local officials and the continental states' employment of a vast number of lesser officials in the provinces. In the central offices, the difference seems not to be very striking. If we assume that between one-quarter and one-third of the English central government employees were senior, they numbered between 350 and 650, which corresponds roughly with the French or Spanish figures. One could also make a case for the necessity of approximately similar central government establishments even if the total population of a country differs. It is in the local administration where the differences in population matter, and in this respect late seventeenth- and eighteenth-century England clearly was less administrated than the Continent.

At the turn of the eighteenth century the number of public servants in Britain was still small. According to E. W. Cohen, in 1797 there were 16,267 officials working in 75 offices; if one excludes the Irish offices the figure is 15,884 in 53 offices. By far the largest establishments were to be found in the Excises and Customs Offices with more than 6,000 servants each, 150 of which at the Customs held sinecures. The Post Office followed with just under 1,000. In contrast the Home Department accounted for only 26, the Foreign Department for 24, the Colonial Department for 12 established officials. But also the military offices were small: 353 at the Ordnance, 160 at the Navy Board, 45 at the Admiralty, 24 at the Commander-in-Chief, and 16 at the Quartermaster-General. Six of the largest ten offices had to deal with revenue collection and administration, two with military services, one with the court, and only one with public service proper (Cohen 1941: 34–35).[3]

Figures for the French and Prussian administration have been collected by Herman Finer (Finer, 1932: 1242, 1167). The 300,-000-odd bureaucrats France is supposed to have employed at the eve of her revolution is hardly comparable to the English figures since it includes every minor city scribe and gate keeper. The Prussian figures for 1800 which in 1930 Dr. Arnold Brecht, then *Ministerialdirektor* at the Prussian Ministry of Finance, furnished to Herman Finer "with reserve," indicate a discernible higher proportion of officials in the population: 23,000 in all central offices including police for a population of 11.6 millions as compared to 15,884 for the 10.7 million in the United Kingdom and 16,267 for the 15.9 million inhabitants of the British Isles at the same time. The ratio would thus be 2 : 1,000 in Prussia, 1.5 : 1,000 in the United Kingdom and 1 : 1,000 in the British Isles.[4] In both cases figures for local government are not included. They would probably widen the difference.

The nineteenth century witnessed a remarkable change, the twentieth century a revolutionary one, in the composition of the public service in all West European countries, but particularly in Britain. Though this development is not our immediate concern in this study, it may be useful to point at some of its most outstanding characteristics to contrast its speed, size and nature with the slow and undramatic developments in the state-building, but preindustrial period. The first feature is the overall growth of public service. Between 1890 and 1950 the total working population in Great Britain grew by

[3] The ten largest offices were:

1. Excise (U.K.)	6.580	6. Taxes	291
2. Customs (U.K)	6.004	7. Navy	160
3. Post	957	8. Treasury	142
4. Stamp	521	9. Victualling	118
5. Ordnance	353	10. Lottery	115

[4] The Prussian figures as given by Brecht and Finer are very doubtful indeed. They seem to include the lesser officials, the number of which is virtually unknown. (For the higher service alone see the table on page 504 of this book compiled by Peter Lundgreen.) Also the population of Prussia in 1800 is not correct. It was closer to 9 million than to 11.6 million; even the greater Prussia of 1816 only counted 10.4 million heads. (See Kirsten, Buchholz, and Köllman, 1955: vol. II, 159.) If the number of officials is correct, Prussia would have had about 2.5 central government employees in 1,000 as compared to 1.5 in 1,000 in the U. K., a more significant difference.

57 percent, government employment (excluding nationalized industries), however, by 450–500 percent. No other single major "industry" which can be traced over the entire period had a similar growth rate. Over 30 percent of the net addition to the working population (between 1931 and 1950 over 60 percent) went into the public service. The share of government employees in the total work force grew from 2.4 to 7.7 percent (Abramovitz and Eliasberg 1957: 26). The second feature is the change in the structure and composition of the public service. At the middle of the nineteenth century, 80 percent of the whole service belonged to the military, not to the civil sector. If we include the civilian staff of the armed forces, their share was about 85 percent in 1851. Over the next century it fell to 55 percent in 1914 and 39 percent in 1950. Among the civil service proper revenue lost its predominant character. Its leading position was first contested by the postal services, then by the agencies regulating the economy and controlling local government, finally by the social services. "On the eve of World War I, the British central government was still mainly a government of soldiers and sailors, postal clerks and tax collectors" (Abramovitz and Eliasberg 1957: 39). By 1950 Britain was a welfare state as far as the size of her civil service was concerned: 40 percent of all civilian government employees served social needs or regulated the economy according to social goals (Abramovitz and Eliasberg 1957: 62–66).

Compared with these fundamental changes the development of the public service in England between the middle of the sixteenth and the nineteenth century seems marginal. We do not have reliable figures for the fifteenth and sixteenth centuries, but from the studies of the different central government offices and their agencies, we can conclude that at the end of Thomas Cromwell's career the number of royal servants cannot have been much less than the 1,400 to 2,000 in Charles I's reign. With the "Tudor Revolution in Government" the main government departments of the English state-building period were established, including those temporary but important offices which aimed at the penetration of government authority into the borderlands, the church and the aristocracy: the Council of the North, the Council in the Marshes of Wales, the Court of Augmentations and the Court of Wards and Liveries.[5]

[5] These conclusions are drawn after consulting the following monographs: Bell 1953; Brooks 1953; Elton 1953; Hurstfield 1958; Reid 1921; W. C. Richardson 1952, 1961; Skeel 1924; Williams 1958.

It would be convenient now if we could prove that the administrative achievements of Thomas Cromwell undoubtedly constituted the definite departure from medieval administrative techniques as G. R. Elton tends to assert. Unfortunately, English history is more complicated. Herman Finer in his comparison of continental and English governmental systems, states that "it is impossible . . . to find a person of the mental calibre and strength of character of Richelieu, Colbert, Louis XIV in France or the Hohenzollerns of the late seventeenth- and eighteenth-century in Prussia devoting themselves with such ardour to the creation of a complete social scheme and administrative system to support it" (Finer 1932: 1281). The beginning of a "state-building period" in England therefore, cannot be dated easily though a case could be made that the Tudor period (1485–1603) does fit this notion better than any other single period of English history. But neither had the Tudor kings to start from scratch (as did the Hohenzollerns), nor was the existence and structure of their realm uncontested when the last Tudor, Elizabeth, died. A century of absolutism, civil war, parliamentary rule, restoration and revolution followed, before the English state was consolidated (see Plumb 1967).

Accordingly, we look in vain for any discernible period in which a premodern civil service was created. The great medieval historian T. F. Tout speaks of the English civil service of the fourteenth century and dates the administrative servants of the English crown back to the "earliest ages of the English state" (Tout 1915), Sir Charles Oman called Henry I (1100–1135) the "father of English bureaucracy" (Oman 1910: 479). G. R. Elton sees the bureaucratic age arise with Cromwell's reform in the 1530s (Elton 1953), others regard Samuel Pepys, the great Treasurer of the Navy Board at the end of the seventeenth century as the first civil servant who introduced rules, procedures and examinations into the service (Bryant 1933–1938), while modern observers might be unwilling to speak of an English civil service at all before the reforms of the mid-nineteenth century. Though it might be possible to exclude all ambiguities by a rigid definition, this would obscure the very problem that we have to solve, namely to find out how the English kings had such a remarkable success as state-builders without creating a service elite.

The answer is sought usually in the nature of the English society, its relative openness, as compared with continental countries, the less privileged situation of its nobility which was not exempt from taxes and left the title only to the eldest son, the gradual merger of nobility, landed gentry, professions, and merchants into a political class large enough to allow merit to be rewarded, open enough to allow office, land management, adventure, and commerce to be linked. Francis Bacon's famous statement has often been repeated—that the institution of the Justices of Peace made England unique because it "knits noblemen and gentlemen together" while "abroad in other countries noblemen meddle not with any parcel of justice, but in martial affairs; matter of justice that belongs to the gownmen; and this is it that makes those noblemen the more ignorant and the more oppressors . . ." (quoted in Hurstfield 1968: 148).

We should, however, not mistake Tudor or Stuart England for a modern society where the middle class ruled, "representative of the rising professional and commercial elements in society rather than the older aristocracy (as in W. C. Richardson 1952: 15–20; similarly Elton 1953). Some of the ministers of the kings still descended from the Norman families who played such a dominant part in most of the middle ages, and a nobleman still had the best chance of holding a great office of state. Lawrence Stone has estimated that the total number of jobs open to a gentleman in the whole of the royal household amounted only to 175 including some sixty pensioners. One of two members of the aristocracy had a chance to get such a job, but only one out of five of the leading five hundred country families and only one out of thirty of the parochial gentry (Stone 1965: 464–467). For a man born in the peerage, personal character was the main factor in determining whether or not he achieved office; no aristocrat was strong enough to impose himself on an unwilling king or queen; but for the lower gentry, the professionals and burgesses ability was not enough—except for the ablest lawyers and exceptional successful merchants like Lionel Cranfield. They needed patronage and favor too. On the other hand, patronage and favor alone—except under James I—were not enough either; among those who enjoyed it, the abler ones had the better chance to rise. The greater mobility and openness of the English society did leave some marks in the sphere of government; however, its proper field of influence was the economy and the social structure. Younger sons of the nobility began to learn professions and participate in enterprise while successful businessmen and officeholders established their families as landed gentry.[6]

[6] For a balanced view see Wilson 1965: chapter 1: "Social Degree and Social Mobility." Also: Hill 1967: 33–35, 185; Notestein 1954; Rowse 1950: chapter VI: "Social Classes."

The sources of Britain's success have to be sought not only in "society," but also in "history," in the "great technical perfection" which the administration of the realm achieved "at a very early date"[7] and the continuity which it enjoyed over more than a thousand years. Few countries can be found which have been built so steadily, gradually and securely. Even the most turbulent periods of English history, the Norman Conquest, the Reformation, or the Civil War and the Revolutions of the seventeenth century, did not interrupt British traditions or suppress ancient institutions in favor of revolutionary new devices. King and Parliament, common law and local self-government prevail in the twentieth-century Britain as well as in medieval England, and "medieval government . . . left as one of its heritages the conception of a professional, organized civil service" (MacCaffrey 1961: 104).

Therefore, the student of the state-building process of Britain cannot help but go back to the earlier medieval times if he wants to identify its beginnings. He also meets considerable difficulties if he wants to single out any period as *the* crucial one in regard to statebuilding. Was it the victory of the Normans over the Anglo-Saxons? Was it the victory of the Tudors over the Roman Church in the sixteenth or that of the Parliament over the king and his court in the seventeenth century? However, as far as the formation of central administrative institutions are concerned most historians agree that the crucial innovations were created during three discernible periods: (1) the Anglo-Norman formation of the centralized feudal state governed by the king and his household (ca. 1080–1230); (2) the Yorkist and early to mid-Tudor period (ca. 1470–1560) in which government departments established themselves definitely as separate institutions run by great officers of the king who recruited a bureaucratic personnel by patronage; and (3) the nineteenth century (more precisely the years 1780–1870), when the modern government-machine based on departments responsible to parliament and staffed by nonpolitical civil servants through open competition was created (Elton 1953: 424–426; Aylmer 1961: 438).

But even if we agree that these three periods were more creative than others in respect to forms of administration and channels of recruitment, we will find that innovations occur in between, that there is no jump from one system into another, and that old institutions

---

[7] This is the judgment of a Russian scholar, Alexander Savine (Savine 1909: 17), quoted by Rowse 1950: 312.

exist long after they have ceased to serve a useful purpose. So it can be argued that the separation of some court offices as government departments occurred long before the "Tudor revolution in government," namely by the end of the twelfth century when the Exchequer was established or during the thirteenth century when the Chancery and the common law courts came into existence.

Difficulties arise particularly if one tries to find the disjunction between medieval and modern times in England. When can separate government departments be clearly distinguished from the king's household? When have "public" servants a status different from that of the king's "private" servants? When is the state-building process in Britain completed? Any time between the fourteenth and the early nineteenth century could be chosen, and this choice could be defended against opposing arguments. Rather than clinging to one specific period of "state-building" in England we will try, therefore, to follow its gradual growth through the centuries up to 1700, pinpointing some of the crucial crossroads.

The Middle Ages. "The public servants of the crown, whose special sphere was administration and finance, and who were professional administrators, not professional soldiers, go back to the earliest age of the English state. They existed, but barely existed, in the later days of the Anglo-Saxon monarchy. They first became numerous, powerful, and conspicuous when the Norman king gave England a centralized administration and a trained body of administrators. Their influence rose to a high level in the reigns of Henry II (1158–1189) and his sons, when England, thanks to their work, was the best governed and most orderly state in all Western Europe." This is the judgment of one of the greatest authorities in English medieval administrative history (Tout 1915: vol. III, 194). Though we may be inclined to cast doubt in the naïve use of terms like "public servants" for such a period, and may cast equal doubt on reported facts like "professional administration" by "a trained body of administrators," we cannot wipe off this evidence by our more cautious use of modern language by insisting on a more precise definition of the criteria of a "trained body of administrators." At about the same time as Tout, C.W.C. Oman in his contribution to the *Encyclopaedia Britannica* of 1910 also speaks of Henry I's autocratic government "through bureaucratic officials" (Oman 1910: 479). More recently (1951) A. L. Poole found that "the descent of English

THE RECRUITMENT OF ADMINISTRATIVE PERSONNEL

bureaucracy from the chamber in which the King slept and the adjacent closet, the wardrobe, where he hung his clothes, is one of the curiosities of history" (Poole 1951: 9), and most recently, Joseph R. Strayer stated that "England by 1200 had permanent institutions run by professional and semi-professional officials," and by the end of the thirteenth century the two pillars of the medieval state—the Treasury and the High Court—"were manned by experienced, professionally minded officials" (Strayer 1970: 33, 42).

Who were these officials and how were they recruited and trained? Beyond doubt the majority of them consisted of clericals, trained in the then rare skills of writing, counting, bookkeeping, Latin and in the use of French. But they must also have known how to survey land, to administer estates and to judicate and some clearly had a business or legal education or both. According to Strayer, the first permanent functionaries of the European kings "were estate-managers, the reeves and shire-reeves (sheriffs) in England, the *prévôts* of France, the ministerials of Germany" (Strayer 1970: 28). It has been often observed that the very existence of the *Domesday Book* points to the fact of a "trained bureaucracy" and of some degree of centralization in government already in the eleventh century.

Perhaps one ought to turn to the early medieval church to fix the beginnings of English state-building since the church gained a spiritual unity for England long before a political unity was attained. Throughout the earlier Middle Ages the church was the only institution which produced men of administrative skills able to administer a country. When Alfred the Great, after his peace with the Danes in 886, restored learning and culture in England—gathering scholars from the Continent, Wales and Ireland, and founding schools—he laid the fundament from which "technical personnel" for the administration of his realm could be drawn. Like Charles the Great in his empire on the Continent, he tried to control and integrate his newly won territory and people with the help of scholars and administrators. Three generations later, a man of the church, Archbishop Dunstan, worked out a body of legislation to establish the rule of law in the English realm. Peaceful state-building was already in progress when internal strife between the magnates, new Danish invasions, and finally the conquest of the Normans put an end to the Anglo-Saxon period of British history.

William the Conqueror's penetration of the country was amazingly thorough. In order to establish the royal rights and to learn how his new land "was peopled, and with what sort of men" (Stenton 1943: 606, 649) he had a group of royal officers, survey the land and evaluate it. It is not entirely clear who the surveying royal officers were, how they were trained and recruited. Though most of the higher ranks may have been Norman and other knights from the Conqueror's entourage, he also seems to have made use of the administrative personnel he found at the English court.

F. M. Stenton considers it possible that the staff of Edward the Confessor's writing office "passed as a whole into King William's service" (Stenton 1943: 633). The following great redistribution of land and power—the combination of several thousand small estates into less than two hundred major lordships—was a remarkable administrative achievement. Since only few details of this process are known, we can only presume that William commanded a considerable staff of military and clerical administrators.

The head of the administrative staff, the chief of the civilian "technical personnel" of the English kings throughout most of the Middle Ages was the chancellor, and the chancery was the first administrative office where clerks were organized (Strayer 1970: 33–35). The second important office which required trained personnel was the Exchequer. Already the Anglo-Saxon kings received a considerable income in money instead of in kind. Collectors and accountants, perhaps auditors too, must have existed and the *Domesday Book* shows that the king's officers already had begun the practice of assaying the money to make sure that the silver content of a payment corresponded to its nominal amount. Probably Alfred the Great possessed a central treasury, William seems to have changed little in the financial system he found, but in the twelfth century the Exchequer, in which the Old English Treasury had been incorporated, can be identified as a separate department in the king's household (Stenton 1943: 636).

Under William a new institution gained a firm footing in England which was to characterize British government perhaps more than any other: the jury. Though, in the first place a device of jurisdiction, it also marked the administrative process. Through centuries governmental decisions were taken through the judiciary. The jury became an essential part of what has become known as amateur government, and it was used already under William in cases which in modern continental Europe would be deferred to an administrative court: to establish facts or rights in disputes between individuals

[469]

and government or between different branches of government. Again the *Domesday Book* proves that at the end of William the Conqueror's reign the entire country had become familiar with the jury system.

A further contribution of William the Conqueror to state-building in England can be found in his relation to the church. Stenton asserts that "he took the position that it was the duty of the secular ruler to supervise the government of the church within his dominions" and that "he never admitted that the Pope was entitled to impose a religious policy on secular princes" (Stenton 1943: 650). Through William's favorite ecclesiastic, Lanfranc, a native of Pavia who had been trained in the Italian tradition of civil law before he turned to theology and finally became Archbishop of Canterbury, the tradition of Roman law achieved a first foothold in Britain. Though weak in judiciary in comparison to common law, the influence of Roman law upon English administration can be traced through centuries.

We cannot follow up in detail here, how the governmental institutions developed during the Middle Ages from the foundations which were laid by the Conqueror. Some remarks must suffice. From Henry I (1100–1135) most English Kings ruled through the *curia regis*, the royal council, in which they assembled their most important officers, the justiciar, the chancellor and the treasurer, together with some knights and clerics. They constituted the supreme court of the realm. The council soon began to delegate special functions to committees. Some members of the council sat as the court of the Exchequer to receive and audit the accounts of the royal revenues and to give legal decisions in all questions connected with finance. Members of the council were sent out to preside over shire courts similar to the commissions the Great Elector used 500 years later in Prussia. Loyal men were appointed sheriffs to do the king's business in the shires according to the rules laid down by the council and subject to its scrutiny. After periods of decay administration was restored from time to time by able administrators like Chancellor Thomas Becket and Justiciar Richard de Lucy. Slowly, the administrative offices of the king began to separate from his household. T. F. Tout dates this development back to Henry II's reign, that is in the second half of the twelfth century. As a main reason he considers the necessity to keep certain officials and the records, registers and rolls, which resulted from the king's administration and jurisdiction, at fixed places while the king and his court were still wandering from one place to another. The Exchequer received a permanent home at Westminster, and by the end of the twelfth century its staff no longer served at the court. The chancery remained longer with the royal household. But the mass of evidence it assembled finally forced it in permanent headquarters in London like the Exchequer, though a part of the staff continued to attend the king on his travels. "By the days of Edward III (1327–1377) the chancery, like the Exchequer since Henry II had become a government office, self-contained, self-sufficing, with its own staff, traditions, methods, and plainly separated from the courts" (Tout 1915: vol. III, 197). For a generation the privy seal took the place of the chancery as the king's immediate writing office. Then, following the demands of the barons, it went out of court too.

Who now were the personnel who conducted these administrative affairs? As in the earlier times, by far the majority of the "civil servants" still were clergymen: they had not necessarily taken the holy orders nor were they learned theologians, often they had not even received the minor orders. The tonsure alone sufficed to enter the status of a cleric and have the benefits of the clergy, e.g. the right of being judged only by clergymen. "Thus the clerical class was very elastic and very large. In fact it comprehended all educated men, most lawyers, most physicians, all scholars, graduates, and students of universities, and most boys in grammar schools" (Tout 1915: vol. III, 200). The only great exception in fourteenth-century England was that of the common lawyers. Study and exercise of common law was open to all laymen. But common lawyers seldom entered the king's service in these times. "It was the civil and canon laws, the law of Rome and the law of the church, not the common law that was most pursued by those who aspired to the public service" (Tout 1915: vol. III, 200). These laws were taught at the universities, and in this respect English public administration seems to have barely differed from the chanceries on the continent.[8] At least the most pretentious posts were filled by university-trained lawyers. Some of the English chancery clerks of the later Middle Ages were doctors of civil and canon law; and for notaries university education was indispensable. Notaries drew up documents in "public form" for diplomatic relations, especially for treaties. "A man had to pass through a long training and a careful examination before he could be admitted to

---

[8] For the overall importance of the legal studies at the medieval universities and for the European culture see Rashdall 1936.

the position of notary, by the pope or the emperor, or by some delegate appointed by the conferring authority (Tout 1920–1933: vol. v, 106). Since nearly all English notaries were empowered by papal authority the "Roman" standards were applied to them. Sometimes the English offices appealed for help to continental chanceries if letters and treaties had to be drafted that were strange to the English officials.

Not all administrative servants of the English kings possessed, however, university degrees. Many in the lower ranks probably were dropouts since the dropout rate of medieval universities was —by modern standards—very high "in spite of the mildness of medieval examiners" (Rashdall 1936: vol. III, 453, also 448). Others came straight from a grammar school with nothing other than a training in Latin and a good handwriting. In the privy seal, as a lesser office, it was unusual for a clerk to be a *magister*; most of them were called *dominus* like any other nonacademic cleric.

The reason why most of the medieval clerks were clerics must not only be sought in education. It was also convenient for the king's control. Most of the medieval offices tended to become heritable. An officer endeavored to make the office his "property" and pass it on to his son, relative or friend. For the king this meant that claims on offices were more easily avoided if a cleric was appointed who usually had no heir. Moreover, a cleric could be more easily rewarded for his services or removed from office by granting him ecclesiastical livings, dignities, prebends, or bishoprics while the laymen usually claimed a grant in land from the royal domain. The most important and confidential office of the Middle Ages, the chancery, was, therefore, up to the fourteenth century exclusively staffed with clerics.

Laymen could more frequently be found in the Exchequer. Here, by the later Middle Ages, many posts had become "hereditary serjeantries"; they were firmly in the hands of certain families who often appointed substitutes to do the real work for them. Accordingly, many of the clerks in the Exchequer were nominated not by the king but by some nobleman. The "patronage" and the "sinecure" system which is so typical a strain in the British public service up to the nineteenth-century reforms can be seen at work already in the twelfth century. T. F. Tout concludes, therefore, that "it was only by employing clerks that the monarch could be master of his own household (Tout 1915: vol. III, 202).

The methods of appointment differed. The Norman kings sold offices "to the highest bidders" (Tout 1915: vol. III, 203). Later the incidents for the sale of higher offices are rare, with exceptions of some reigns, notably that of Richard I, the "Lion Hearted" (1189–1199). He, at the beginning of his reign, sold all offices he could to raise money for the crusade. More often, however, high offices were granted for loyalty or presumed loyalty as a means of strengthening "the king's cause" against rivaling pretenders to the throne or as counterpart against mighty barons. Some of the medieval kings aroused storms by appointing continental vassals or unworthy personal favorites to the highest offices. Frequently high officers had to face charges of corruption which resulted in the loss of office and the confiscation of property; some were impeached for treachery and lost not only office and property but also life. Among the rank-and-file tenure was more secure, but occasionally nearly the whole staff of an office was fired. But such general turnovers were extremely rare. Generally, the rank-and-file servant was as remote from "politics" and its evil consequences as in more modern times. He wrote and counted for the king or his immediate master whoever that was.

It is extremely difficult to establish from which social strata the technical staff of writers and accountants came. The leading officials of course were mostly of high birth. At first they belonged to the Norman nobility, later also to the lesser landed classes. As far as the lower ranks are concerned, we cannot be so sure. Probably they were drawn from quite different classes. Their clerical status often obscures their social origin. Obviously becoming a cleric and receiving a literate education for many was a means of social rise. Medieval barons when criticizing their clerical rivals in the high offices of state sometimes refer to their humble origin. It would probably be wrong to assume that many came from the lowest strata of society, but there are enough instances of men of middle-class origin making their way into the king's service.[9] Best known are of course the famous cases, e.g., Thomas Becket who was born as the son of a Norman merchant family settled in London. After attending a grammar school Becket received a business education at the office of a relative before he entered the household of Archbishop Theobold of Canterbury. Clerics of humbler origin are to be found more often in the less important offices which offered a life-long career rather than a

[9] For some instances see: T. F. Tout 1920–1933: vol. V, 105.

springboard to an ecclesiastical office. Here the son of a vintner—like Geoffrey Chaucer—or a grocer, the bastard of a priest and an unmarried woman, and the poor orphan can be found besides the son from a landed family of Yorkshire or of a king's justice. Middle-class values, the drive for achievement and for accurate work, seems to have been early planted in the offices of the English kings. T. F. Tout judges that the medieval clerks had attained "a respectably high level of general competence." He not only praises the chancery and privy seal clerks for the neat writing and well keeping of their rolls, but also the clerks of the Exchequer for their bookkeeping. "The very addition of Roman numerals was painful enough in itself. It was made more laborious by reckonings by scores and by hundred, by sums, calculated differently in marks and in pounds, shillings and pence, being all mixed up together in the same columns or figures. Yet you will rarely find mistakes in arithmetic even in the most complicated of accounts" (Tout 1915: vol. III, 212).

Where did they acquire these skills? Their basic and formal training seems to have been conducted at schools, universities and inns of court. But the routine the king's servants achieved was by in-service training. Except for those of higher birth or previous ecclesiastical career who entered office at a leading position, the king's clerical officers usually began their services as the clerks of a clerk, as under-officers who were employed by the member of the "establishment" of the office rather than by the king himself or the office as such. With the expansion of the tasks of these offices, the established clerks tended to delegate duties, particularly the routine writing, counting, and bookkeeping work. Many of the medieval clerks claim therefore a much longer service as is shown in the office records. The reason is clearly this tendency to "infeudate" office work. As the medieval tenants-in-chiefs infeudated their land to under-tenants, thus creating a network of feudal obligations, the greater medieval office holder had his tenants and sometimes under-tenants who pledged allegiance rather to him than to the king, or perhaps to the king through him. The poet and civil servant Thomas Hoccleve praised as his "master" the poet and civil servant Chaucer. Though he thought little of his abilities and never received one of the ecclesiastical benefices, Hoccleve was well acquainted with three languages —Latin, French, and English—was familiar with the *belles lettres* of his days; in short, was an educated man. There are many incidents that learned men in science or humanities did make their living during the English Middle Ages not in monasteries or at ecclesiastical prebends but in the king's offices: Walter Map, the twelfth-century satirist, held office in the royal household; Walter Chatillon, a poet of distinction, was employed in Henry II's chancery; and Roger of Hereford, a learned astronomer, served as an itinerant justice of the king (Poole 1951:242).

Earlier Modern Times (Sixteenth to Seventeenth Centuries). Medieval government in England as elsewhere has been checked mainly by two forces which competed with the king for power: the great nobility and the church, the latter commanding a sophisticated administration while also interwoven into the secular government of the king. Competition between the king and the barons had led to a subtle balance of power, a set of "constitutional" rules which secured the prerogative of the king as long as he respected the privileges and rights of the estates and worked through the procedures on which they had agreed. He had to "live on his own" financially and respect the laws; the barons, slowly supplemented by representatives of the greater gentry in the counties and some lawyers and merchants to represent the boroughs, would watch their rights and grant the king taxes whenever they were convinced it was necessary; but they would not interfere in the daily business of administration. By the end of the Middle Ages, this balance was precarious, and the struggle for supremacy was not over, but an arrangement was reached that gave the English king more sovereignty than any continental monarch enjoyed at the same time. If the sixteenth century witnessed a decisive increase in the sovereignty of the king, it was not because of revolutionary developments in this sphere, but because the English king triumphed over the church and destroyed the dualism of spiritual and worldly power. After the Act in Restraint of Appeals of 1533 had declared the realm of England an empire governed by one head and king, and a year later Parliament had granted the king the supremacy over the church, the "king's law in ecclesiastical cases" was substituted for the canon law, and the teaching of canon law forbidden in the universities. The Roman Civil Law with its magnification of princely power took its place. Under Elizabeth I all ecclesiastics, lay officials, and persons in receipt of stipends of the crown were required to take an "oath of su-

[475]

premacy" accepting the queen as "only supreme governor of this realm" promising to her faith and allegiance, and repudiating all foreign jurisdiction and authority (Keir 1966: 80–81). A high commission was appointed which could remove disobedient clergy, coerce dissent among the laity, and exercise censorship over the press.

But supremacy over the church was only the beginning. It was followed by supremacy over society as a whole, an extension of royal action beyond the medieval boundaries. Law laid down by royal proclamation instead of statute in parliament abounded; the council, its offshoots, and the Court of High Commission exercised a mounting control not only over the church and its former property, but over trade and industry, labor, wages, and prices, over local government and its police forces, over the individual and his freedom of belief.

The government apparatus grew and became more efficient in most affairs of public life. The king gained better control over finances, the justice and diplomatic affairs and worked through a more elaborate body of central bureaus. The growing central apparatus of government called for more professional, trained staff. That break with the church at the same time dried up the most important source for recruitment, the literate cleric. This combination was bound to strengthen the other sources of supply for administrative personnel, the universities, particularly its law faculties, the Inns of Court, and the apprentice-like training of clerks in the households of higher royal servants. The university-trained solicitors continued to dominate in diplomacy, which "for the first time" turned into a "regular profession." Permanent embassies, unknown in the medieval world, were established, and "the ablest minds of the age thus enlisted themselves among the king's servants, and magnified the sovereignty of which they were the instruments" (Keir 1966: 99).

The common lawyer prevailed, of course, at the common law courts, the King's Bench, Common Pleas, and the Court of the Exchequer. The judges at these courts, appointed by the king, were required to have reached the degree of sergeant-at-law before they became eligible to the Bench. In marked difference to the Continent where the customary law was overcome and obscured in the state-building process by the principles of Roman Law which the royal bureaucracies implemented, the common law courts in England "remained an imposing fabric of judicial organization and power" (Keir

1966: 28). The new courts were fitted into the old system and amalgamated: they added a new strain in the complicated fabric of English law, but did not set it on a new track. The judges of the common law courts remained close to the crown. They advised the king and his councillors as to the drafting and the effect of legislation, answered questions addressed to them by the executive, and when they traveled through the country and sat as Court of an Assize, they acted "as political as well as judicial representatives of the central authority" (Keir 1966: 29). They were regarded and regarded themselves as kings' servants, not as proponents of a counterpower.

But the Common Law courts remained financially largely independent from the crown; they lived more on the fees they collected than on salary. Though in two of the courts judges held their offices "during the king's good pleasure" and only those on the Exchequer "during their good behaviour," in practice their tenure was secure. The power of the king over them was restricted. He had to rely on their cooperation. Therefore, it is only half of the truth, if one maintains the absolutistic tendencies in Tudor England. Absolute supremacy was gained only over the church, never over Parliament or the common law. The same is true in respect to personnel. The need for an administration staffed by trained experts grew, but the Tudors "never developed a professional and salaried bureaucracy wholly amenable to its own direction and command" because "in the last resort, that service was voluntary and incapable of rigid enforcement" (Keir 1966: 7). This is particularly important for the local administration. There, like in medieval England, the Tudors took their resort to unpaid members of the local gentry. Since the fourteenth century, the justices of the peace had more and more taken over the place of the sheriffs as local representatives of the central government's orders. Originally the duties of the justices of the peace as developed by fourteenth-century statutes, were mainly to keep peace and order; but they also performed a number of administrative duties including the control of wages and prices. In Tudor England more such duties were added: prevention of profiteering on foodstuffs, examination of the by-law of guilds, supervision of weights, and measures, and regulation of apprenticeship and of agricultural labor. In dealing with these matters they employed the methods of jurisdiction in which they had routine. Administration, therefore, was carried out under judicial forms and became impreg-

[477]

nated with judicial characteristics. The execution of the central government's orders depended on the readiness of the justices of the peace to cooperate. Though the council tried to enforce obedience to its orders by citing reluctant justices of the peace before it or removing them from office, its control was limited since the justices also were responsible to the common law courts, and they did not regard themselves—though appointed by the king on the nomination of the lord chancellor—"simply as agents of executive power, but magistrates whose supreme duty was to conform with and carry out the law" (Keir 1966: 31).

One main reason why this should have been so tends often to be overlooked: the dominance of the jurists in the Commissions of Peace. A "quorum" of lawyers was required if the commission sat in quarter sessions. Though only 15 to 20 percent of the justices of the peace were trained in law (as against 55 to 65 percent local gentry), the lawyers attended the sessions more regularly than the other members; a regional study of Somerset has shown that in the early seventeenth century no session took place without at least three lawyers present. About a quarter of the men actually sitting as justices of the peace had been called to the Bar.[10] Moreover, legal education became more and more common for justices of the peace. While in 1562 still 66 percent of the working members of the commission had no training at a university or Inn of Court, in 1636 there were only 16 percent without one, the percentage having steadily declined over the years.[11]

Obedience to the law, moreover, served as protection against royal caprice and despotism. It strengthened independence. These limitations of direct command may have contributed, however, more to the state-building process in England than the imposition of royal commissars (like in France and Prussia) since the cooperation created a sense of common obligation. It was a give-and-take. Thus one can regard the justices of the peace and similar semiofficials in Britain as a factor of social integration, of nation-building by consent. That it was possible to rely on such a type of personnel proves that the state-building process in England was carried much further in late medieval and early modern times than on the Continent.

[10] There are two excellent case studies of local government and its personnel in late Tudor and early Stuart England: Barnes 1961 and Willcox 1940.

[11] The members are from a sample of six counties. See Gleason 1969: 83–95.

It would be misleading, however, to assume that the entire local government was done by unpaid gentlemen or that it went without friction. The justices of the peace had paid clerks at their disposal who performed much of the actual administrative work. The principal officer, the *Custos Rotulorum*, usually had one or two assistant clerks. Officials of the hundreds, the townships and other local subdivisions were the executors of their orders. As a consequence of the supremacy over the church, Tudor England seized upon the ancient parish administration which before the Reformation was ecclesiastic. Now it was made an instrument of poor relief. Overseers were appointed to control the execution of the poor laws, and the parishes developed a civil organization which was also used for other administrative purposes like the upkeep of the highways. Officials of earlier units of local administration filled the lower ranks in this parish administration. Most of the lower officials were paid, and even if they only worked part-time in public affairs they certainly were not honorary officials like the justices of the peace themselves who often *represented* local government rather than *executed* it.

Moreover, the Privy Council in London could, and actually did, concern itself with numerous questions of a local character. For the border regions, special courts were set up—the Council in the Marshes of Wales and the Council in the North which exercised a more tight control, often more reinforced by military means than the local landowners would have done. Direct control could be executed also through the Lords Lieutenant, mainly members of the nobility who were appointed to levy troops in case of war and sedition and to supervise the military organization of their shires. By the end of Elizabeth's reign they also served as "commissars," supervising the local authorities, reporting on their doings, advising the Privy Council on their election or removal (Thomson 1923).

Tudor England, then, was not without some officials who could use coercion. Interestingly enough it did not develop a bureaucracy for recruiting military personnel. Except for some permanent garrisons, a small force of cavalry and a few ships, the yeomen of the guards, and some ordnance officers, the kings had to rely on mercenaries or on shire levies. Modern military technical personnel became important for Britain only after the state-building process was well under way, if not practically completed. It served the maintenance of its supremacy over the waves rather than the accomplishment of internal unity or peace. In the state-building process proper —if one can say so for Britain at all—the English kings relied on pre-modern military personnel.

After this brief survey of the characteristics of the English administration in Tudor England we will take a closer look at the recruitment and training of its personnel.

At the highest and most general level, the King's Council, the Tudors inherited and perpetuated a body of policy makers and advisers emancipated from baronial predominance. Often they became professionals by service.[12] The specialization of functions, e.g., the jurisdiction by committees like the Star Chamber or the Court of Requests, led to a specialization of services. Trained solicitors were appointed to these courts who did not serve at the same time as political councillors or in administrations. The ecclesiastical element lost its predominance. Though one should not assume a sudden break caused by the Reformation, this change is symbolized by the fall of Cardinal Wolsey in 1529, and the rise of Thomas Cromwell as the leading minister of Henry VIII.

The change should, however, not be overemphasized. Cromwell was a trained lawyer as many royal officials before and after him. His career began in the household of a great man close to the king, as a servant's servant, and the service for his immediate master was mixed up with services for the supreme master, the king. Private and public spheres were not yet sharply defined and divided, and not much, if anything, changed in this respect during the sixteenth and early seventeenth century. Double, even manifold loyalties remained common; and the king used part-time service of men who had been successful in business and continued to be so while putting part of their time at the king's disposal (Elton 1953: 307–315; W. C. Richardson 1953; Tawney 1958; Prestwich 1966).

Tudor England needed particularly urgent full-time financial administrators. The wars of the fifteenth century had exhausted the royal finances. One of the first reforms of Tudor England was directed, therefore, toward a more efficient financial administration (see W. C. Richardson 1952; Elton 1953; Hughes 1934). The reform led to a concentration of financial affairs first in the Chamber, a household office, and later to a revival of the Exchequer. After the confiscation of ecclesiastical property huge tasks were added. Though most of the property was soon sold, it first had to be evalu-

[12] See also Strayer 1970: 90–94 on the "professionalization of the inner council."

ated and parts of it remained in royal hands. To deal with the newly acquired rights and estates two judicial and administrative bodies were created, the Court of Augmentation and the Court of First-Fruits and Tenths (W. C. Richardson 1961). Both had to be staffed. At the beginning of the reign of the Tudors, the chancellor of the Exchequer had bitterly complained about the staff he found in the office and as administrators of the crown lands. He described them as inefficient, poorly trained, sometimes illiterate. They lacked the "cunning and discretion to ordre and directe the said lyvelode lawfully." He had proposed, therefore, that only "learned men in the lawe" should be appointed royal stewards (W. C. Richardson 1952: 51). The following reforms aimed not only at better organization, and the establishment of office procedures, but also at a better training and more deliberate recruitment of the administrative staff. In 1485 auditors, surveyors, and receivers were appointed for each unit of the royal estates throughout England. Apparently these men were selected household officers, drawn from different departments according to their knowledge of land surveying and assessing and their training in law.

Some had been in private business before they entered the royal service. This illustrates an important feature of the English way of recruitment and training of administrative personnel: in a higher degree than continental Europe, in contrast especially to Prussia, the English administration relied on the private citizen and his training for his business affairs. England neither established administrative schools (like France), nor drew her personnel from military sources (like Prussia). The lower-upper and the upper-middle classes— whether landowners, businessmen, professional lawyers, or trained administrators, united by a common interest in peace, lawful, profitable, and effective administration, the protection of property and their private affairs—helped the crown to gain control over the country. By virtue of their participation the British government became a civilian, legitimized and respected government; in their own interest they acknowledged the king's sovereignty as long as it was controlled by Parliament which was in turn a "committee" of the same "political society" (Neale 1949).

As long as this educated and well-to-do upper and middle classes were small and well distinct from the large uneducated, propertyless, nondemanding lower classes, the recruitment of the public service from among them could work informally. One knew each other.

[481]

Family and neighborhood, friendship or business associations were reliable sources for judgment of a person's credibility and ability. This was a perfect setting for recruitment by patronage. It did not necessarily mean ineffectiveness. A man who looked for a substitute or an assistant in office was well advised if he chose a capable one. But neither was it foolproof. There were enough sinecure or semi-sinecure posts where one could install an unsuccessful relative. He would not make a career but a living. Those who made a career often were the more capable officers, but not necessarily so. Again favoritism played a considerable role. Personal loyalty was essential as long as the rivalry for the throne and the rivalry for the great offices continued. Men like Wolsey or Cromwell supplanted their personal household with their personal servants into the royal government. Important and lucrative offices went to those whom the leading ministers could count upon. Inheritance of offices was not yet overcome, and reversion for offices generously granted when more aspirants waited than openings occurred (which was usual) or when somebody was to be rewarded for specific services. Often several persons held a reversion for the same office, and lengthy disputes arose when an office finally became vacant. Transfer from one office to another was handled similarly, while the clerks themselves tried to establish a rule of seniority. Those who commanded favor in addition to capacity were much better off than those without a highly placed advocate. No merit system was formally established, but this does not mean that merit remained necessarily unrewarded. As far as departments were subject to formalized procedures, as soon as enough division of labor was established and specific functions were given to specific offices, specific competence could be rewarded, but most of the offices did not yet afford the specialist but the generalist, the literate man who had some knowledge in law and much in office routine. The organizations which Cromwell and others set up were still short-lived and flexible.

Since this unformalized system of recruitment did rely on the co-operation of the upper and middle classes as a whole, it failed to produce a distinct civil service as a career, and consequently as a social caste. Both France and Prussia created a civil service as a professional élite with formalized training, a peculiar value system, an *esprit de corps*, and a characteristic arrogance toward the ordinary citizen. Britain avoided this special feature of forced state-building by the very weakness of her system or informality. The British civil servant remained much more a member of his greater social class.[13] It is true that also in Britain families of public servants developed, but the system itself remained more open, and part-time service, part-of-the-life service, and amateur-service were more frequent than on the Continent. Not only businessmen, but also lawyers kept their private affairs alive while serving the king. In Tudor and early Stuart times there was no incompatibility between government office and a seat in Parliament. On the contrary, the ambitious royal servant secured himself a seat at the Commons as the first step of a public career, and representatives of a borough or a county tried to work more efficiently for their constituency by entering the king's service not with a view of a life-time career but for a specific time. Again professional lawyers or businessmen were particularly prone to divide their time between private and public affairs. Thus the early modern public service in England remained in a much more fluid, adaptable state than on the Continent. Bureaucratization, though growing, remained imperfect.

Thanks to the painstaking study of G. E. Aylmer (1961), we possess some statistical evidence about the king's servants in the first half of the seventeenth century. He explored their social origin, their recruitment, training, promotion, and pay by taking a sample of 194 of the about 900 officers he could identify.[14] The absolute numbers he gives are very small indeed, the ratio of "unknown" factors (e.g., father's status) very high: but since no better figures are available, we have to work with them warning the reader that they are not more than very rough approximations.

The first striking result is the date of entry in public service. Only 1 of his samples was under twenty years of age, 30 in their twenties; the largest group, 42 in their thirties; 23 entered the king's service only in their forties, 16 in their fifties, and 3 were older than sixty when they began their public career (79 unknown). This corresponds well with what we know about the careers of many civil servants in the later Middle Ages and the Tudor time. Many began their

---

[13] The term "civil servant" is used here though it was not yet known at this time. It was first applied to the Indian Civil Service in the first half of the nineteenth century (Tout 1915: vol. III, 193).

[14] Out of a group of over 900 officials Aylmer took 240 whose name began with A, B, or C. About 80 percent of them he could identify. These 194 constituted his sample (see Aylmer 1961: 253–277).

"apprenticeship" not in the king's service but in the household of one of the king's ministers, or they executed business and land administration before entering the royal service.

The father's social status confirms what we know from Tudor times: Most (118) of the officials belong to the upper-middle classes, the landed gentry, the professions, and the businessmen. But a considerable portion (41) belong to the greater landowners, the peers, and especially the knights; the rest (35) are unknown.[15] Twenty-two percent of the fathers of whom rank and occupation are known held office already. The percentage of officeholding fathers is strikingly higher in the nobility: nearly 54 percent of the fathers who were peers of knights also held office in the king's service, while only 11 percent of the fathers who were esquires or below. This shows that for the middle class officeholding was an exception, a means of social rise, while for the nobility it was still usual. It also reinforces the view that the chances to hold office were still much greater for peers and upper gentry than for the middle classes.

Not all known public servants rose in rank. (Some who advanced were imprisoned or were executed.) From the known cases less than one-third remained stationary in rank, 8 percent declined from their father's rank, nearly two-thirds rose, about half of them by one step, the rest by two or more steps.

More than three-quarters of all officials in the sample ended their lives as esquires or better and about 97 percent became at least gentlemen. The picture may be distorted somewhat since the unknown

[15]   The Social Status of the Fathers of 194 Public Servants
1625–1642

Social Status	Known Cases	
	Number	Percent
Peers (New Peers 3 and Bishops 1)	9	5.8
Knights	32	20.1
Esquires and Equivalent		
(Courtesy esquires)	48	30.2
Esquire—Gent—Borderline	9	5.8
Gents	29	18.0
Citizens, Merchants, Sea Captains,		
Yeomen, Plebeians, Other Low-level		
Gents, Foreigners	32	20.1
Total of Known Cases	159	100.0
Unknown	35	
Total	194	

Source: Aylmer 1961: 263.

cases could be those of the lowest in social rank, but they are so few that they cannot alter the pattern of a general rise in rank by public service.[16] This, of course, gives a ready explanation why public service, even part-time, was sought for by many who could do economically without it—merchants, landowners, peers. In this respect England certainly is no exception but fits well into the general European pattern, particularly in the age of baroque when rank and style counted even more than before and thereafter.

As to their formal education, three-quarters of all servants in the sample had a higher education—either university (78 out of 154) or at the Inns of Court (68 out of 154). Practically all descendants of peers and knights entered the king's service with such a higher education: 23 of them had been at Oxford or Cambridge, 1 at a foreign university, 19 at the Inns of Court. In the other ranks the percentage with higher education seems to have been about two-thirds with a slightly but not significantly higher rate for the lower classes as compared to the esquires. The only marked difference is to be found in the choice of the place of education: while sons of esquires and the higher nobility attended somewhat more frequently universities than Inns, the education of the gentlemen's and merchant's sons was nearly equally spread between both institutions (25 Inns of Court, 24 university).[17]

[16]   Final Social Status of 194 Public Servants, 1625–1642

| | Known Cases | |
Social Status	Number	Percent
Peers	24	13.0
Baronets	9	4.8
Knights	64	34.6
Esquires	51	27.6
Esquires or Gents	18	9.7
Gents	14	7.6
Other	5	2.7
Total of Known Cases	185	100.0
Unknown	9	—

Source: Aylmer 1961: 265.

[17] Aylmer's figures on education (Aylmer 1961: Table 21, 273) are somewhat puzzling. He does not indicate whether he could identify the educational background of all the 194 members of his sample. In relating his absolute figures to 194, I assumed he did, otherwise the percentage of servants with higher education would be even higher than 75 percent. Aylmer also fails to indicate whether or not all counted as coming with higher education had reached a degree. Since we know that in the middle ages many did not, it would be an astonishing change, if all had finished their education.

Aylmer has also tried to measure the factors that counted for recruitment into the service and for transfers and promotions. He distinguishes between "patrimony" (family-patronage) and "patronage" (influence or connections other than family). The other modes of entries he found are "purchase of office," "special qualifications" (particular professional abilities), and direct "royal favour," often as a reward for services to the king. Since often a man's career cannot be attributed to only one of these factors, he also counts several (half or part) instances. In three-quarters of all "whole instances" entry in the service was either due to patrimony or patronage (or to patronage in a wider sense). Purchase occurred only 6 times in his sample of 80 "whole instances," or 5 percent, reward for services or royal favor only 5 times (6.5 percent). In 11 cases or 14 percent he assumes that ability was the key which opened the public career. More frequently than the clean cases are those in which more than one factor played a role in the award of a public office. Again patrimony or patronage are the most important advantages for a man. In more than a half of these cases they played some role. Again purchase and special royal favor seem not too frequent (4 and 7 "half instances"). More often, nearly three times as numerous as in the ordinary cases, "special qualifications" appear to have been partly decisive. We can conclude that patronage and the combination of patronage and merit was the most important factor in the recruitment for the king's service. Merit alone was not very strong. Only extraordinary ability seems to have been enough to enter a career in government, but merit helped if patronage was there. Or, to put it differently: among those patronized, the men of ability had a greater chance to succeed than those who possessed only connections.

This statistical evidence seems to be determined by the bulk of less prominent officials. For them the most common way of entrance was the transfer from private to royal service, a mode of entrance which Aylmer counts as a combination of patronage and special abilities. In prominent cases a combination of patronage and purchase happened more often; patronage also could be purchased as Sir Henry Vane, a prominent figure of the 1630s and one of the richest commoners in England around 1640, recalls: "I put myself into Court and bought a Carver's place, by means of friendship of Sir Thomas Overbury which cost me £5,000" (Aylmer 1961:85).

[486]

Open purchase always was disapproved, and several times proposals were made to prevent the sale of offices, particularly since those who had bought theirs were accused of extortion. The servants themselves seem to have not disliked purchase since it helped to secure the office. Purchase meant acquisition of a "property" which could be less easily withdrawn. Sometimes fathers in office bought their office for a son, or more likely, bought a reversion in case of their death. In some cases a legacy was made to a relative *expressis verbis* for buying a place in a government office. Though open and hidden purchases happened, Tudor and Stuart kings never relied on the sale of office to the extent of the French monarchy (Göhring 1938; Mousnier 1945; Swart 1949).

The ways of entrance into the civil service seem to have varied according to the social status. "Those with aristocratic, Court or administrative connexions, were likely to owe most to patrimony or patronage; members of gentry families without these connexions to patronage or purchase, or both, plus, often, some element of ability as well as ambition; businessmen to purchase, plus patronage or ability, or a mixture of the two; lawyers, private secretaries, and confidential servants to patronage with ability, often in the form of linguistic or other special skills" (Aylmer 1961: 96).

The majority of public servants in Aylmer's sample never was transferred or promoted but stayed in the post once awarded to them. This points to the fact that public service was not yet a formalized career. But about 44 percent of the sample made it one. About a quarter of the whole sample was transferred or promoted once, 37 (or 19 percent) were transferred or promoted more than once. These probably were the very same who rose in social status more than one rank. Of the 37 promoted more than once, 30 ended their lives as knights, barons, or peers; 17 of them became privy councillors.

As factors in promotion, patrimony plays practically no part, patronage only about in one-third of all cases. Purchase becomes somewhat more important, but in the sample it occurs only four times as the only reason for promotion or transfer, and four times as half- or part-instance. More important are reward for service or special royal favor and merit. Of 38 plain cases, Aylmer attributes 12 to merit (qualifications, ability, but also seniority=experience), 10 to royal favor, and 11 to patronage. In the split and uncertain cases, patronage still ranks first with 28 of a total of 68, but merit comes close with 23 and favor ranks third with 13 instances. We can conclude that patronage was important also for promotions, but not all-important. Good service and proved ability helped to make a career. This is still far from an objective merit system, but not without it altogether.

Special professional or technical knowledge could be essential. For clerks in the chancery or the common law courts, knowledge of medieval handwriting was required. In seventeenth-century England they had to be specially trained for this purpose. In all offices clerks had to know how to draft legal documents. Letter writing and the keeping of letter books belonged to the general and time-consuming tasks of even senior officials who "must have spent a great deal of time making fair copies of accounts, issuing of receipt books, legal instruments, warrants, orders, and letters" (Aylmer 1961: 154). Some of the foreign experts needed, of course, skill in foreign languages, particularly French; in the Office of Arms the knowledge of heraldry was indispensable, and the noble art of *courteoisie* was required in many of the household offices.

Altogether the "technical knowledge" of the public servant in the early modern England was not yet much specified—and the reformers of the 1780s will complain about it—so that part-time administration and amateur administration still is possible, not only on the local level. G. E. Aylmer claims for the England of Charles I, that "from the Privy Council downwards the country was to a considerable extent governed by part-time officials, by men who were essentially 'amateurs' even if they were paid. . . . If Charles I can be said to have had a bureaucracy at all, about three quarters of it were amateurs" (Aylmer 1961: 282). This holds true, however, only if one accepts his definition of an amateur as everybody who served part-time or was not a "professional." As his own evidence shows best, most of the higher civil servants had a university or legal education; many were trained in the household (office/secretariat) of a higher servant. Others had an in-service training, lawyers often a training and experience at law offices and courts. The businessman had learned how to make business transactions and how to keep books or handle foreign exchange. It can hardly be said that he came as an "amateur" in the customs service or to the provision of army and navy. The noble or gentleman without any preparation is hardly to be found in the public offices of the king, perhaps in some of the household departments. To speak of "amateur-administration" for early modern England is, therefore, misleading. The Prussian sub-altern officer or sergeant who collected taxes when he had finished his military duties would be as much an amateur as the French busi-nessman who bought a customs' office. Defining the amateur status as widely as Aylmer and some other authors do, means to deprive it of any real meaning. Local administration, it is true, had much more of an amateur character than on the continent where the king's central offices sent out their commissars; but even in this respect it is more meaningful to speak of centralized versus decentralized gov-ernment, of government by cooperation and consensus versus gov-ernment by coercion and subjection. The *specificum* of British early modern government is not the amateur-status of its officials but the recruitment of administrators without separating them socially. Gov-ernment officials did not become a social class of its own, a caste of bureaucrats, but through officeholding nobility and greater gentry incorporated lesser gentry, and the commercial and professional bourgeoisie into the "ruling classes." Officeholding, whether full time or part time, whether through being "learned in the law," or possess-ing some other administrative capabilities, meant social rise and adaptation from the lower side, penetration of values and customs from the upper side, meant social integration—not for the nation as a whole, since the lower classes definitely were excluded—but for the old landowners, the newer ones, the businessmen, and profes-sional lawyers.

In this social pattern patronage, sinecure, and service by deputy get a specific meaning. It is not only the way in which the upper classes secure their privileges, place their kinsmen, and augment their income, but also it serves to recruit suitable persons of lower origins as individuals into the "political society." The higher or the senior one is, the more one is able to reduce one's actual work and have it done by a deputy, often a personal servant. The more influen-tial one is, the more one can place persons of one's trust into other offices. Restrictively managed, such a system of recruitment and pro-motion tends to form a service class, a narrow, inbred group of offi-cials separated from the rest of the country. The English upper classes did not manage it in such a way; they allowed people of hum-bler origin to come in.

Why should they do so? We cannot assume that they had a con-ception of the virtues of an "open society"; if they did, it served their own interests. Since service meant income (and status), office property, it was useful to exploit it efficiently. A clever tailor's son like Samuel Pepys or a merchant's son like Thomas Cromwell with a good general education, a bright mind, and personal ambition, promised to be a more useful manager of an admiral's or bishop's affairs than a dull relative. If one could find a kinsman of this sort, all the better. Pepys' first master, Edward Montagu, the joint commander of Oliver Cromwell's fleet, might have taken the young Cambridge graduate as the manager of his affairs because he was distantly related to him, but his next master, the shrewd and calculating Sir George Downing, took him to the Exchequer as his personal servant because of his proved abilities as an administrator (Bryant 1933–1938: vol. 1 passim). A man in the hierarchy of service who wanted to get ahead or stay on at least, was well advised to look for capable assistants. It is true, the higher the birth, the higher one could enter the service. But there were only few absolute limits which prevented others coming from below from competing. And the more incompetent an officeholder of high rank was, the more he needed the services of experienced deputies.

At the end of the eighteenth century a cleavage was found between those "amateurs" who held great offices and the professionals who actually conducted the business. Over the centuries, because of the lack of any systematic approach to governmental organization, more and more posts had become obsolete and served only as sources of income. This was an abuse and offended the minds of people brought up on middle-class values in an age of enlightenment. It was certainly unjust, but not necessarily inefficient. The secret of the English amateur-administrators was that they employed professional deputies. High rank gave name, influence, protection; low rank contributed loyal and efficient service and it was rewarded by social advancement. By keeping the boundaries open, English political society managed to rejuvenate itself without losing its characteristics and remained in control of the government longer than the nobility in most continental countries.

FRANCE

In the course of the history of the major European countries fundamental similarities can be discerned, though chronologically at different time periods. With reference to the development of modern government we may speak of the sequence from medieval constitutionalism to mercantilism, absolutism, bureaucracy; and onward to modern constitutionalism (Friedrich 1950: 25). In terms of the developmental crises theory of state- and nation-building, the first development would be the coming into existence of the modern state (penetration and integration); the second one would indicate the process of restraining and subjecting government to popular influence, i.e., nation-building (identity, legitimacy, participation) (Rokkan 1969: 63ff.). If we center our study on the state-building period of both France and Prussia, we have to outline the evolution and working of absolutism with special regard to the personnel involved as agents. The comparison between France and Prussia seems the more rewarding since the specific course of historical development in Germany, as distinct from the West European one, often has been considered to start only in the beginning of the nineteenth century, its content being the belated nation-building. If this is true, the *Ancien Régime* should provide good conditions for insights by comparative history.

As to state-building and public servants constitutional history knows the evolution of absolutism by superseding the rule of Estates, or, in terms of administrative history, the war to be waged by *commissaires* (i.e., new agents dependent upon the king's centralizing will) as against *officiers* (i.e., fairly independent representatives of traditional and particularist forces). The dichotomy of *officiers* vs. *commissaires* is a useful concept for classification of existing personnel as well as for evaluation of the state-building achievements of France and Prussia respectively. Such an analysis may, however, point out great differences between the two state-building processes.

Differences are to be expected if one considers the sheer length of time France's state-building took, in contrast to Prussia's. For centuries France had gained experience in superimposing royal agents upon an existing structure of administration. The newly installed officials started as a sort of *commissaires* (in control of *officiers*), but developed into *officiers* who were subsequently deprived of some of their responsibilities by the creation of competing new offices until new supervising royal agents (*commissaires*) were installed. Examples are the *baillis*, since the thirteenth century, and the *gouverneurs*, since the sixteenth century. Besides this procedural experience at the disposition of the France of the eve of absolutist government, there were certain preconditions of a modern state because of centuries of existence as a political entity. This leads to the question of dating the modern state of France (a question which hardly arises at all for the case of Prussia).

The territorial unity of France was largely achieved by 1285 and finally completed when, after the end of the Hundred Years War with England, the last great fiefs fell back to the crown. Militarily the fifteenth century witnessed the beginning of a standing army, and fiscally the permanent levy of excise. The war of the Huguenots meant a setback but the great Henri IV stabilized the France of his time in terms of religion. Thus, it has been accepted to speak of the time after 1610 as of French absolutism proper (cf. Lublinskaya 1968). If we concur in this opinion, we have to determine the administrative pattern of 1610 supposedly to be overcome by the forces of absolutism.

Notwithstanding the general unity of France, in 1610, there is hardly any conceivable effective organization to execute a central will. Of course, at the top of the government machinery, the *conseil d'état* in its classic and characteristic threefold composition exists: (1) the *chancelier* being the only one of the old feudal grand officers (like *connétable*, *chambrier*, or *bouteiller*) who was not reduced to a mere holder of title but remained head of the royal chancery and was in charge of judicial administration; (2) the *secrétaires d'état*, usually four in number and being actual ministers of the king, partly without *portefeuille*, partly as heads of certain departments (army, foreign affairs, *maison du roi*, navy); (3) one (or two) *surintendants des finances*. For the time under consideration, Sully filled the latter station and was the most famous officeholder until Colbert reorganized the top level of the financial administration under the name of *contrôleur général*.

Why did these fairly well designed top levels of governmental authority fail to produce an efficient, penetrating, executive administration? It is not the Estates, as the formula "from rule of estates to absolutism" might suggest, which impeded the flow of directives from above. The French Estates did not play any influential role from 1614 to 1789. First and most important, it is the independence of the various corps of *officiers*; second, and perhaps somewhat less important, the provincial particularism which had its stronghold mainly in the power of the provincial governors.

During the upheavals of the sixteenth century these governors, who originally had been in charge of military matters only, had enlarged their powers, thereby becoming a sort of neofeudal lords.

One reason for this was that the governors were recruited from the local nobility. In the 1630s Richelieu destroyed the political weight of this nobility by reducing the governorships to mere decorative offices of title and honor. He transferred their powers to the *intendants*. With respect to the governors (or to the *noblesse d'épée*) French absolutism seemed to have made the game. After all it must have been a manageable task to replace some thirty governors by *intendants*. But what about the corps of *officiers*? Finance and law, the classical branches of inner administration, had their administrators for centuries, neatly organized into a hierarchy of *officiers*, and with the sovereign courts at the top. Especially these *cours souveraines* never acquiesced to consider themselves dependent on the king and his *conseil d'état*. Thus we find, at the top, the competition between the councils (as organization of government) and the courts (as organization of the top of the officers' hierarchy).

It is alleged that Richelieu (and Louis XIV) succeeded in limiting not only the powers of the governors, but also those of the independent corps of *officiers*: by limiting rights and influence of the *parlements*, and by using *intendants* again to direct the execution of the central will. This is precisely the point at which the dichotomy of *officiers* vs. *commissaires* becomes important. Historiography, however, does not agree on the results of the controversy between the two sets of officials. Appraisal of the achievements toward centralization and regularization stands against skepticism in this regard. What are the arguments, and what is the net balance? In order to reach some conclusions we are bound to study separately two layers of the French bureaucracy as a functional and social group: first the *officiers*, second the *commissaires*. The fact that this procedure will not be necessary in the case of Prussia indicates a lack of comparability of the two countries even for the period of the *Ancien Régime*.

The network of judicial and fiscal offices dates back to preabsolutist times. At the top of the judicial branch stood the *parlements* (up to thirteen in number), that of Paris being the most distinguished one and of great political weight. First, the *parlements* considered themselves as courts without further appeal. The institutional stages of appeal ran from the *prévôtées* and seigneurial courts over the *bailliages* (and sometimes still over the *présidiaux*) to the *parlements*. French kings, however, had the means to intervene in this course of instances. At the end of the fifteenth century, they set up the *grand conseil* to counterbalance the *parlements* as last instance. Its special competence referred to conflicts between *parlements* and *présidiaux*. When time went on, however, the *grand conseil* became a sovereign court by itself which made the kings try once again to build up a royal instrument of judicial administration: the *conseil privé*, with the *chancelier* at top of it.

The Paris *parlement*, however, did not only demur about royal interference with the judicial realm but claimed certain political rights which amounted to a judicial control of the government's activities. New laws and ordinances had to show their concordance with traditional and existing law, a procedure which was undertaken by using the rights of *enregistrement* and *remontrance*. Thus it is obvious that French absolutism was bound to clash with these rights.

Before we discuss the conditions and implications of this organization and strong standing of the officership we shall look at the fiscal branch of administration. Fundamentally, the same picture is to be found, modified because of the typical demarcation between ordinary and extraordinary revenues of the state. The ordinary income consisted of the yields of the royal domain and of the fees for fiefs and courts. They were collected, since the early fourteenth century, by the *receveurs* on the *bailliage*-level. *Trésoriers* were the supervisors, and *chambres des comptes* served as sovereign courts, in the same honorable age as the *parlements*. The extraordinary income (*aides*) of the state consisted of the excises levied, mainly the *taille*, collected by *élus* within the *élections* and administered by the *généraux des finances* within the *généralités* (province-level). Again at the top we find, since the late fourteenth century, sovereign courts, the *cours des aides*. A third type of sovereign court within the fiscal realm has been the *cour des monnaies*, established in 1522 and in charge of matters related to the mint. In the course of the sixteenth century the hitherto separated administration of ordinary and extraordinary income was fused into a single one (cf. the War and Domains Chambers in Prussia) with *élections* and *généralités* as fiscal districts/provinces and *élus/receveurs* and *généraux des finances/trésoriers* used synonymously (Holtzmann 1910; Treasure 1966; Bluche 1966b).

We easily can understand the world of *officiers* if we look at its hierarchy cross-sectionally. First, there are some thirty *cours souveraines* which make up the so-called high *magistrature*: the *parlements* and the *grand conseil* (judicial); the *chambres des comptes*, the *cours des aides* and the *cour des monnaies* (fiscal). The distinction between judicial and fiscal competences is yet only a very rough demarcation since there is no clearcut division in practice. On the contrary, the fiscal administration is at the same time judicial instance in cases of conflict (in this realm). Taking this into consideration, we can speak of the middle *magistrature* consisting of the *officiers* at the *bailliages, présidiaux* and *élections*. The *trésoriers* (in the *généralités*) made up a *compagnie souveraine* and were thus part of the high *magistrature* (Mousnier 1958: 330). Below the middle *magistrature* we may speak of the low *magistrature* which comprises the bulk of local officials (like *maires, échevins*) and the subordinate personnel at the courts and administrative district centers.

What about the numbers of the various offices named above, which after all may enable us to visualize the network of offices? It is rather difficult to give exact figures but the order of size may be indicated. For the sixteenth century, we may speak of some 10,000 *officiers* at all levels, with some 4,000 of the high *magistrature* (Göhring 1938: 33f.; von Borch 1954: 108). Since the sixteenth century we find a huge increase of offices especially within the middle and low *magistrature*. The estimates range from 46,000 offices, in 1665, to a total of 300,000 offices in the late eighteenth century, with some 50,000 offices of the upper ranks (probably high and middle *magistrature*) (Finer 1932: 1242; Göhring 1938: 258; Mousnier 1970: 17ff.).

This extraordinary growth in numbers of *officiers*, classified (in 1656) into 629 categories of offices, each class constituting a corps of *officiers* (Göhring 1938: 122), is only partly explained by the common procedure of narrowing competences of existing offices while simultaneously creating new offices for the competences left. This usage of functional differentiation and specialization might have led to greater efficiency though it was mainly undertaken in order to check tendencies of "feudalization" of offices, i.e., taking them as private and unalienable property. Curiously enough, however, the French state of the *Ancien Régime* did its utmost to enforce such tendencies: by tolerating and, afterward, legalizing the peculiar institution of venality of offices. This brings us to the core of the ancient system of French officership.

The custom of an officeholder to resign his office in favor of a benevolent buyer or a relative can be found in the fifteenth century already. This private venality of offices was an attempt to circumvent the state, which, however, soon realized that this could be used as a further source of income. Thus the state started to sell offices (via the *bureau des parties casuelles*) and finally introduced, in 1604, the *Paulette* which meant a kind of tax on offices to be paid yearly, and which consequently made the offices a *de facto* private property. With this state of affairs it was only natural that, when the needs of the state for more money grew heavily (in the seventeenth and eighteenth centuries), the state gave in to the temptation of multiplying the offices again and again, using many devices of attracting the wealthy bourgeoisie to the offices and extracting a maximum of money from them (Göhring 1938; Mousnier 1945).

Several problems arise concerning the venality of offices. The most important question, perhaps, is that of loyalty. On the one hand, the *officiers* were representatives of the monarchy and did not think after all of subverting the ruling house of the king. Perhaps it is even safe to argue that the king as a seller of offices created loyalty by virtue of his patronage. On the other hand, the very institution of venality of offices provided for continuity and irremovability in the French bureaucracy as a corporate organization which eventually made the *officiers* to follow their own interests (of the corps or of the provincial particularism) rather than the king's. This state of affairs could make it nearly impossible to get decisions made at Versailles executed on the provincial and local levels, and it has been said that France has been under-administered in spite of the overabundance of offices (Mandrou 1967: 215). For the late eighteenth century Bosher has recently shown how the royal finances were both collected and spent by various groups of venal accountants (*officiers comptables* such as receivers, payers, and treasurers) who were virtually independent of administrative control and only accountable to the financial sovereign courts. Although they were officials, these venal accountants can be regarded as semiprivate financiers who rendered services to the crown similar to those of the tax farmers and *traitants*. This meant private enterprise in public finance, the state being more a client than the master of the financial agencies (Bosher 1970: 3ff., 67ff., 92ff.).[18]

---

[18] The relationship between the state (as a customer) and an executive agency (as an independent company) holds especially true with regard to the Farmers General who collected the "indirect" taxes (*gabelles, tabac*, customs, etc.) and employed

Second to loyalty ranges the problem of competence or efficiency. If the merit system (like in Prussia) can be regarded as functionally equivalent to the venality of offices insofar as both institutions led to a relative independence of the bureaucracy, there is a major difference in the supply of expertise. To be sure, there were formal prerequisites for officeholding in France, mainly judicial training. As yet this training was only, if at all, a necessary precondition but never a sufficient starting point. Exemptions from the formal prerequisites are always to be found if other factors were favoring the candidate (Göhring 1938: 313ff.; Gruder 1968: 17ff.). Finer summarizes:

> Anybody . . . who desired to acquire an office had to purchase the property from the owner and be installed in the function. The latter gave the Crown the opportunity of demanding guarantees of competence, but in fact the Crown and its officers through whose registers the transaction and the installation passed did not demand such guarantees: they were gallantly content with fees, bribes, and other favors personal or procured . . . Ability . . . , unsupported by money or family, was almost certain of exclusion from public office. The system, in short, was venality tempered by favouritism (Finer 1932: 1242).

Venality of offices, tempered by favoritism, does not necessarily indicate the low competence of officeholders (Eschmann 1943: 161; Van Riper 1958: 8). So far it merely means a strong narrowing of their recruitment. First, it was only the rich and very rich bourgeoisie who could afford to buy those partly very expensive offices (Göhring 1938: passim; Goubert 1959: 63). Second, it was the already established corps of *officiers* who decided upon admission by co-optation rather than by free competition. Considerations of this sort lead us to analyze the *officiers* as a social group. The major catchwords in this context are *noblesse de robe* and *bourgeoisie robine*.

A classical definition of the bourgeoisie, more juridical than social, is: urban citizens who are (1) nonnoble *officiers* (i.e., *roturiers*); (2) merchants; or (3) *rentiers*. In social terms one may draw a line between the many petty *propriétairies* living from their *rentes*; and

---

a huge army of some 35,000 guards, clerks, accountants and inspectors organized into a bureaucracy of hierarchical structure.

the *grande bourgeoisie* serving as wheels which kept the *régime* in motion. It is under the latter heading that Goubert deals with the *bourgeoisie robine* and the *bourgeoisie négociante,* and although the great merchants to a certain degree represent an antipodal type of bourgeois as compared with the many *officiers* in the judicial and financial realm, the sons and grandsons of merchants tended to look for careers of higher social esteem, i.e., within the world of *officiers* (Goubert 1969: 221, 224ff., 229). The logic of this state of affairs was the ever-present goal to get ennobled by officeholding. In order to achieve this goal one had to buy an office which conferred nobility either at once or after twenty years' serving or to one's children or grandchildren. Thus was the *noblesse de robe* developed, no doubt bourgeois in social origin, but juridically part of the second order and even socially merging with the old nobility.

Much has been written about the *noblesse de robe.* One intriguing problem is that this nobility made up the top layer of social stratification, which could be reached via the venality of offices, but at the same time restricted access to it via a co-optative recruitment policy on dynastical grounds. *Grande bourgeoisie* and *noblesse de robe* have hence been seen either as an *élite mixte* of "capitalist-noblemen" or as opposed parties in the so-called feudal reaction (Goubert 1969: 335; Bosher 1970: 317; Ford 1953; Barber 1955). Both interpretations yet agree in that the *noblesse de robe* was a most powerful element in French society which eventually checked the development of a full-fledged absolutist government (cf. Egret 1970). Internally, the *noblesse de robe* exhibits a kind of subculture with its inner traits and slight variations. One of its students, François Bluche, underlines five aspects for characterization and comparison: (1) the nobility of recruitment (i.e., the number of generations of the candidate's family already noble); (2) the dynastical element (i.e., family tradition to serve); (3) the youth of the magistrates (usually younger than prescribed); (4) the mobility and variety of careers within the magistracy; and (5) the quality of outside careers open to magistrates (Bluche 1966a: 22ff.). Taking these indicators into consideration it is possible to rank the *cour des monnaies* at the lower end of the hierarchical high *magistrature* and thereby consider it a "society of transition between the *bourgeoisie robine* of the small courts and that grand *magistrature*" (Bluche 1966a: 28). At the upper end of the hierarchy the *noblesse de robe* did not confine itself to the most prestigious sovereign courts, but kept looking for those outside careers open to magistrates which were mainly to be found in the upper ranks of the royal government and administration, notwithstanding the long-term frictions between councils and sovereign courts.

The intricate nexus of wealth, office, and social mobility, of bourgeoisie and *noblesse de robe* consolidated vested interests which had their stronghold in the largely independent sovereign courts and the corps of *officiers* but which also got a foothold in the very center of royal government and administration. One may wonder, after all, how the *commissaires* fit into this picture. Clearly, if French absolutism meant to build up machinery for the effective execution of a central will, the difficulties to be overcome must have been frightening. Could and did the *commissaires* succeed in cutting the independence and privileges of *officiers?* To answer this question we have to consider their numerical and social weight, their intentions and activities, and their interests as a group.

Commissary functionaries are defined as nonpermanent carriers of an *ad hoc* set and a specially defined commission of inquiry, control, bargain, or arbitration which usually bypasses the existing system of governmental or administrative organization. The historical example of the famous *missi dominici* of Carolingian times serves as prototype for the *commissaires*. In the consciousness of this heritage, France made use again and again of this pattern. This meant that it was necessary to try to control ordinary *officiers* by extraordinary *commissaires*. The one case which is of special interest to us and which is to be considered the crucial inner core of French absolutism and its building of a modern state is that of the *intendants*.

The existing and somewhat narrow controversy on the origins of the *intendants* is due, in a way, to questions of definition. We find single nonpermanent *commissaires* in the late sixteenth century. They are called *intendants de justice, des finances*, or *de police*. It is even safe to speak of military origin of the *intendants* like that of the commissars in Prussia (Finer 1932: 1224f.; cf. Hintze 1962: 248). In contrast, however, to Prussia the military spirit never played any significant role in the French bureaucracy. The *intendants* soon became permanent civil members of the government apparatus. From 1634 onward, the decisive development, is not yet seen either in the permanent officeholding and regional distribution of the *intendants* or in the cumulation of their formerly separated competences for justice, finance, or police. The creation of the *intendants* as a new institution meant the replacement of the old *officiers des finances* in their most important functions. In the words of Roland Mousnier: "From a reforming inspector the *intendant* became an administrator" (Mousnier 1958: 327).

Financial administration was bound to be inefficient and unjust since the traditional *trésoriers de France* claimed the right of *remontrance* and were closely linked to the provincial establishment. The Thirty Years War sharply increased, on the other hand, the needs of the Crown for money. In this situation Richelieu, who had already broken the power of the provincial governors, attempted to use the *intendants* as administrators of finance whereas until then they could only "négocier, obtenir des accords, stimuler" in this realm (Mousnier 1958: 329). In 1634 the first step was to make them presidents of the *bureaux des finances* under the *trésoriers*. This may have led to improved efficiency and pace, but could not touch basic decisions like the *répartition* of the excise. Accordingly, in a second step in 1642, the *intendants* were promoted to chief executives in the field of financial administration, the *trésoriers* being reduced to juridical and technical aspects of the business only (Mousnier 1958: 336). This development found its organizational expression with the *généralités* (and not, as imaginable, the *gouvernements*) which became the administrative units of the approximately thirty provincial *intendants*. Naturally, the regulation of 1642 was heavily opposed by the financial sovereign courts which refused to register it. The death of Louis XIII in 1643 seemed for a moment to give a chance to the *trésoriers*, but the *intendants* became the *de facto* heads of the *généralités* until this kind of financial administration was definitely consolidated under Colbert after 1661.

We now leave the chronological description and analyze the *intendants* as a functional group, their activities and competences: whether (and if so, how) they developed their primarily financial competence into a provincial governship. James E. King gives an appraisal of the *intendants* under the headline "Science and Rationalism in the Government of Louis XIV" (King 1949). He sees a system of inquiry as the rationale of any decision-making process based on rationalism and he consequently outlines the intendancy as a "reportorial bureaucracy" (King 1949: 137): *intendants* were "the legal eyes of the Monarchy," each serving as "a statistical agent of the central government," in order to base administration "on the accumulation of political and social statistics" (King 1949: 128ff.). The sources at hand for the historian confirm this picture. The regular correspondence between Colbert (as comptroller-general, the head of the financial administration) and his *intendants* shows how the decisions were taken: (1) instructions or circular letters of the comptroller-general requested investigation and report on a given issue from the *intendants*; (2) the *intendants* investigated and submitted a report or survey; (3) the reports were studied by the subcommittees and bureaus of the councils; (4) a draft (of an ordinance to be issued or of a policy to be followed) was submitted to the councils of state for decision; (5) the outcome decided upon was communicated to the provincial *intendants* for execution.

Convincing though this procedure may be it had its Achilles' heel: the last link of the chain, the factual execution, the famous question of real vs. legal. Richelieu's achievement, according to Mousnier, had precisely been to have made the *intendants* administrators out of mere inspectors. How far does this hold true with reference to the various fields of reports sent in vis-à-vis the policies decreed?

Generally speaking it is perhaps safe to differentiate between traditional fields of public activity, come down as a legacy and firmly in the grip of the network of *officiers*, and those newly developed, the major case in point being no doubt economics or economic administration. In this respect it was only fortunate that the *intendants* legally and formally were part of the financial administration. When Colbert organized his central department, as a comptroller-general, he set up, besides the intendancies of finance and some other more technically oriented divisions, the bureau of commerce comprising four *intendants* of commerce. Thus he created an instrument to pursue his economic policy (mercantilism, or perhaps Colbertism) of regulation of industry and encouragement of enterprise in which the provincial *intendants* played an important role (King 1949: 192ff.; Parker 1965: 86ff.).

Considering the wide range of tasks to be fulfilled it is yet difficult to present a balanced statement with regard to the success of the *intendants*. Formally, "they administered the unpopular taxes, principally the *taille*, the capitation tax, and the *vingtièmes*; they administered conscription for the militia, undertook the execution of public works, directed the engineers in the construction of roads, maintained public order with the help of the mounted police, administered poor-relief and the workhouses, promoted agriculture, and supervised all the regulations governing industry." In reality, however, according to Mandrou "the *intendant* was not much more than an agent of information, and sometimes of execution in certain economic fields where initiative was possible" (Finer 1932: 1234; Mandrou 1967: 218f.). He was confined to report on the attitude of the *officiers* wherever these were in power, and he had to resort to private subdelegates of his own when he wanted to have a task executed efficiently. If, by contrast, we have a preliminary look into the Prussian administration the picture is much more favorable with regard to the commissars' bureaucracy. The presidents of the provincial War and Domains Chambers (and not the *Landräte*) are clearly to be considered functionally equivalent to the *intendants* of the *généralités*. But what a difference as far as the top level personnel at hand of the provincial chief executives is concerned! The many councillors at the Chambers do not even matter as much as the famous Prussian *Landräte* and especially the *Steuerräte* who do indicate a degree of penetration into the periphery which we cannot perceive in the France of the *Ancien Régime*.

It is true, there is still much controversy about the actual achievements of the *intendants*, about the balance of the daily war against traditional authorities. Surely, during the eighteenth century both the *intendants* and their subdelegates became routinized and firmly established. But the whole question of a throughgoing administration down to the provincial and local levels depends on the relationship between *officiers* and *intendants*. It is a tempting, but probably at least partly misleading picture, to think of both as a functionally coherent body of executives, with the *intendants* enforcing their will via the *officiers*. The latter are simply too well known for their severe observance of rights for which they after all had paid considerably. On the other hand, the *officiers* (and especially the *parlements*) provided for the minimum of assent necessary to make royal warrants more than mere scraps of paper.[19]

[19] Our own inclination to discount the omnipotence of the *intendants* in administrative matters is supported, apart from Mandrou's statement cited above, by Alfred Cobban who compares the French administrative giant with Gulliver being "pinned down by innumerable minuscule claims and customs" serving as the Lilliputians (cf. 1957: 216). Furthermore, G. Durand speaks explicitly of the competition between the parallel hierarchies of *officiers* and *commissaires* (and thirdly, of the *fermiers généraux*) (cf. 1969: 108ff., 139). A more favorable evaluation of the *intendants'* power and effectiveness is given, for instance, by Hubert Méthivier (1966: 88, 114ff.) or on a regional level by Henri Fréville (1953). But even Fréville notes that it is

A second line of argument focuses upon the consideration of the *commissaires* as part of the central government. For it is the positive evaluation of the *intendants* and their actual power which implies that the government deliberately aimed at a sort of bureaucratic absolutism: *commissaires* deciding in the center and executing in the provinces, either against or via the *officiers*. A closer look into the administrative elite is yet necessary if we want to draw the balance between *officiers* and *commissaires* (see Table 7–1).

In theory the central government in France before 1789 had a conciliar structure, the old *conseil d'état* having specialized into several councils: (1) the *conseil d'en haut* or *conseil d'état*, in fact the cabinet deciding on principles of policy, foreign affairs, war and peace, with the king and his ministers present only; (2) the *conseil des finances* under the comptroller-general; (3) the *conseil des dépêches* with competence for most internal affairs besides finances; (4) the *conseil privé* (or *conseil des parties*) under the chancellor in charge of judicial administration. Sometimes it is right to speak of a *conseil d'état privé finances et direction* comprising both the *conseil privé* and a second or subcouncil for financial administration. In addition we may find a *conseil de commerce*. Most of these councils had their own commissions and bureaus where the councillors of state and the *maîtres des requêtes* served who were involved in a host of daily details requiring decision, mainly in terms of legal judgments (Holtzmann 1910: 331ff.; Treasure 1966: 285ff.; Antoine 1970; Bosher 1970: 26ff). In practice this conciliar structure of government was rather confused, due to overlapping, and slow; though adhering to the principle that all decisions be made by the king-in-council, this principle became more and more fictitious and the councils were dominated or bypassed by the secretaries of state and their departments.

The secretaries of state headed the four classic departments (foreign affairs, war, navy, royal household; sometimes a fifth for commerce). In addition each secretary of state was in charge of specific matters (such as the clergy or the lottery) which were more or less

---

mainly the newly-developed fields of activity like promotion of the economy and public welfare where the *intendants* are predominant (Fréville 1953: vol. 3, 337). Unfortunately, Gruder (Gruder 1968) carries her book on the provincial *intendants* precisely to the point only, wherefrom the career of an *intendant* would start after his recruitment and training. We are therefore left in the dark as to what this administrative and social elite did achieve in terms of penetration and integration.

TABLE 7-1. TOP-LEVEL ADMINISTRATIVE PERSONNEL IN FRANCE AND PRUSSIA

	France, 1780 (Population 25,000,000)			Prussia, 1805 (Population 9,000,000)	
	Central Level	*Regional Level*	*Provincial Level*	*Central Level*	*Provincial Level*
Finance	*Cour des monnaies* : 70	*Chambres des comptes* : 830 *Cours des aides* : 280	Treasurers, Receivers, Payers : 1200	Ministers : 12 Presidents, Directors : 15 Councillors : 180 Privy Secretaries : 110	*War and Domains* *Chambers* Presidents : 23 Vice Presidents, Directors : 65 Councillors, Assessors : 480 *Districts* Landräte : 210 Steuerräte : 90
Judiciary	*Councils* Secretaries of State : 40 Councillors of State : 80 Maîtres des Requêtes : 80 *Grand Conseil* : 80	*Departments* Secretaries of State : 6 Intendants of Finance : 10 Premiers Commis : 40 *Parlements* : 1675	*Généralités* Intendants : 30 Subdelegates *Présidiaux* : 1770		*Regierungen* Presidents : 27 Vice Presidents, Directors : 27 Councillors, Assessors : 480

Sources: *Almanach Royal*, 1777; Dahamel, *Etat de la magistrature en France,* 1789; Bosher 1970; *Handbuch über den Königlich Preussischen Hof und Staat für das Jahr 1805.*

related to his main *portefeuille*; second, the provinces and *généralités* were part of the competences of certain departments. This departmental organization on both topical and territorial lines, which is to be found in the Prussian General Directory as well, made it necessary that bureaus were set up within the departments in order to deal with various matters. The largest single department, though not headed by a secretary of state, seems to have been the *contrôle général des finances* under the comptroller-general. In the late eighteenth century, we find some 65 bureaus in this administrative branch. It is these bureaus, headed by *premiers commis* or *chefs*, which eventually outweighed the councils in the decision-making process: many matters had already been dealt with thoroughly when the head of the department put them before the council or directly to the king (Bosher 1970: 47ff.; cf. Cobban 1957: 216ff.).

So far there seems to emerge a picture of the central bureaucracy as powerful machinery for imposing a central will. Two qualifications are yet in order. One relates to the field of actual execution where the departments heavily relied upon the various corps of *officiers*. To take but the prominent example of financial administration: in 1788, of the some sixty-five bureaus of the department thirty-eight had the task "to prepare business for a certain agency or for a certain corps of accountants, and to see that the business was done, much as a customer of a bank or trust company might see to the business he left in their hands" (Bosher 1970: 49). It is only in the fields of public works, trade and industry, health and welfare where the remaining twenty-five bureaus of the department of finances might exercise a more independent will and effective control. This state of affairs corresponds very closely to what has been said about the *intendants* in the *généralités* and their relationship to the network of *officiers*.

The crucial question of *commissaires* vs. *officiers* is yet to be followed not only in the field of executing a decided-upon policy, but also in the very center of the government, and brings up then the qualification of the picture of a powerful central bureaucracy. If we view the whole range of upper-rank personnel as an administrative elite, we may ask about its place in French society and especially within the world of *la robe*. Questions of recruitment and training provide an approach to the social composition of the leading administrators whose hierarchy from top to bottom ran as follows: (1) secretaries of state, regular members of the *conseil d'en haut* and other councils, heads of departments; (2) councillors of state, regular members of the decision boards of the councils other than *conseil d'en haut*; (3) *intendants* of finances; (4) provincial *intendants*, heads of the *généralités*; (5) *maîtres des requêtes*, actual reporters on current issues by inquiring and suggesting, and thereby regular members of the councils via their commissions and bureaus (Gruder 1968: 52ff.). These five categories comprise the administrative elite of the *Ancien Régime*: probably less than two hundred in number and hence a comparatively small group if compared with the thousands of members of the high *magistrature*. The *maîtres des requêtes* who formed the level of entry into the administrative elite clearly deserve our special interest, particularly since nearly all provincial *intendants* formerly practiced this profession. The question of recruitment and training thus has to concentrate on these eighty officers.

After all, it is perhaps not astonishing that the rule of *la robe* dominated this realm. First, it was a legal prerequisite for any *maître des requêtes* to serve several years as a magistrate in a court. This meant the *maîtres des requêtes* (and, consequently, all upper officers including *intendants*) "were judicially trained officers. They were men who had gone through the legal training of the day. This was exceedingly formalistic and could not be said to prepare young men for an administrative career" (Finer 1932: 1233). This disadvantage, however, may have been counterbalanced by the subsequent training-on-the-job which involved the *maîtres des requêtes* with "tax disputes, printing regulations, military supplies, royal domain lands, finances of Paris guilds, religious establishments, or commercial companies, or feudal tolls and proofs of nobility." This "variety of concrete administrative and judicial work" provided a training ground sufficiently related to reality for the prospective *intendants* (Gruder 1968: 79).

The domination of *la robe* in the field of *maîtres des requêtes* was not only a matter of common professional education, but also, and perhaps less understandably, of common recruitment. These two traits are closely connected with each other, and the legal prerequisite of serving some time as magistrate at a court before becoming *maître des requêtes* indicates the background of recruitment. The crucial link, however, between the *officiers de la robe* and the prospective *commissaires* was the simple fact that even the offices of *maîtres des requêtes* were open to venality. The same holds true for the *intendants* of finances in the respective department and the Commissioners for War with the army. In practice this amounted to a highly co-optative recruitment policy including those dynastical elements which we found characteristic of the *noblesse de robe* or the sovereign courts.

In fact the arguments in favor of counting the administrative elite of the *Ancien Régime* as part of the *noblesse de robe* are overwhelming. Thus the crucial question of the relationship between *officiers* and *commissaires* with regard to a loyal and efficient administration comes up again. Are we entitled to conclude that common social origins meant fairly identical interests as a group? Or should we think of differing interests according to distinct functions? Clearly the bulk of the magistrates were of low status compared to the *commissaires*. Consequently, the careers outside the sovereign courts from *maîtres des requêtes* upward must have been of considerable attractiveness to magistrates who might feel it worthwhile to separate from their former colleagues. The extent to which this division of functions, power, and perhaps interests developed is still open to debate. The rather short periods of officeholding of the *intendants* may indicate a certain amount of preventive mistrust on the part of the king, who could not but take the high *magistrature* as the "pépinière des serviteurs de l'Etat" (Bluche 1966a: 11). In fact the *maîtres des requêtes*, *intendants* and secretaries of state formed a governing elite socially embedded within the *noblesse de robe* and constituting a tiny top layer, the *noblesse d'Etat*.[20]

Is there any sense, then, in applying the concept of *officiers* vs. *commissaires* to the history of the French *Ancien Régime*? Perhaps one can argue that French absolutism in the end did not succeed in building up an instrumental bureaucracy either by incorporating the world of *la robe* or by superseding it. The *intendants* and their colleagues of the governing elite "never acquired the social weight necessary" (Mandrou 1967: 220). On the other hand, French absolutism went far enough to give the world of *la robe* ample justification for opposition. Besides the well-known attack against the *parlements* by Maupeou one has to think of contemporary reforms in the finan-

---

[20] Cf. Gruder 1968: especially part II: "The Royal Intendants as a Social Elite: Their Family Origins and Social Evolution," 97ff.; Bluche 1959: 8ff. Mousnier speaks of the *magistrature* and of the *robe du conseil* as of a single social group which was divided into two distinct political groups opposing each other. What this division precisely meant in terms of political power and achievements has not been determined yet. Cf. Mousnier 1970: 331.

cial administration by Necker and others: the number of accountants among the corps of *officiers* became reduced, and, more important, the offices of the *intendants* of finances were abolished. Thus the ministers of finances could not only continue to bypass the councils but initiated a "bureaucratic revolution" which meant "removing the independent, venal magistrates in favor of dependent, salaried administrators," the *premiers commis* of the bureaus (Bosher 1970: 307). However, it was only the French Revolution which, developing to a great extent out of the struggles over administrative reforms, finally paved the way for the establishment of a modern bureaucracy solely relying on the career service of *fonctionnaires*. On the famous night of August 4, 1789, the National Constituent Assembly abolished once and for all the venality of offices, thereby exposing the recruitment and training of officials to the specific problems of parliamentarianism. In Prussia, which saw the victory of the *commissaires*, we have consequently no revolution, but rather bureaucratic autocracy and a slow progression to constitutionalism (Finer 1932: 1241f.).

As our concern is primarily with state-building, it is not possible to give more than a very brief outlook over the recruitment and training of civil servants in France during the post-Revolutionary time of the nineteenth century. The Declaration of Rights of 1791 stated that no "other distinction than that of their virtues and their talents" should decide upon admission of candidates to all public offices (Finer 1932: 1248). The principle seemed to call for application of a merit system and for open competition. The practice, however, showed another picture, The quick succession of republics, consulates, empires, and kingdoms made develop a recruitment policy of high officials based on systematic favoritism or political patronage up to the end of the nineteenth century (Sharp 1935: 102; Finer 1932: 1249). The best case in point is given by Richardson's monograph on the French Prefectoral Corps 1814–1830 (N. Richardson 1966). Political patronage, however, has been no special French experience (like the venality of offices). In general, "the first effect of the development of parliamentarianism was the demoralization of the civil service, and one of the most perplexing and troublesome problems of democratic government has been to secure a public service owing allegiance not to the politicians, nor to any narrow segment of the public, but to the whole" (Mosher, Kingsley and Stahl 1950: 6; cf. F. Mosher 1968).

Taking this general feature into consideration we should add that any merit system does not preclude, as the contrast of Prussia to France might suggest, political patronage on the lines of checks on open competition by co-optative recruitment policy. A merit system is not even necessarily geared to the needs of the state as the example of nineteenth-century China can demonstrate (Van Riper 1958: 8). The concept, however, underlying the application of a merit system as a basic principle of any recruitment of personnel deserves our attention, since it may be designated as that of the (learned and specialized) *fonctionnaire* in contrast to the *officier* as well as the *commissaire*. The *fonctionnaire* undergoes a training and passes examinations before he takes over a rather narrow and often purely technical (as opposite to political) profession. Socially there is no obvious difference between *commissaire* and *fonctionnaire*, and one may say that the Prussian *commissaires* were in fact *fonctionnaires* combining the merit system (introduced remarkably early) of the concept of *fonctionnaire* with the restrictive recruitment policy of elites (whether *commissaires* or *officiers*). The leading officials of France of the nineteenth century show, apart from political patronage, a similar combination, being in fact a meritocracy, i.e., the old administrative elite by virtue of formally tested merit via the *grandes écoles* (Vaughan 1969: 74ff.).[21]

On the other hand, the *fonctionnaire* can be traced back into the eighteenth and even seventeenth centuries. In the fields of science, technology, certain military services, and public works we shall find this kind of technical personnel which will be dealt with separately.

PRUSSIA

The common opinion among scholars is that Prussia's state-building was accomplished under the reign of four successive Hohenzollern kings (1640–1786), three of these being of outstanding caliber and ingenuity. There is also consensus, though perhaps to a lesser degree, that bureaucracy became the means of all means (Schmoller) for this accomplishment and has thoroughly affected the course of Prussian and German history since the seventeenth century, not only in its political, but also in its social and even economic dimensions. Speaking of the emergence of the modern Prussian state, therefore, is almost identical with a study of its bureaucracy, which formed a

---

[21] Reinhard speaks of the *élite de fonction* governing France in the nineteenth century, cf. Reinhard 1956: 5ff.

functional and social body of personnel of the utmost importance. In a general manner, this state of affairs is clearly indicated by the attractiveness of civil service for elites as well as by the content or meaning of the political science of the time. According to Herman Finer;

> in 1688 when the Great Elector died, his legacy was an army and a Civil Service; in 1688 when William of Orange ascended the English throne the English reward of a half-century's efforts was a sovereign Parliament. Thenceforward the cleverest young men in England passed (or did not pass) from the universities to the political parties and the House of Commons, while the clever young German . . . passed through grade after grade of actual and diverse administrative service, to become a states-man . . . Political science in England . . . concerned itself principally with the question of political liberty and obligation. In Germany Cameralism, or the Art and Science of Government by Administrative Departments (Kammer), attracted the best minds of the seventeenth and eighteenth centuries (Finer 1932: 1184).

Constitutional history provides the context for the rising bureaucracy and its importance. Broadly speaking, we follow the sequence of rule of Estates (*Ständestaat*), then the absolutism of the king, in the Prussian case to be superseded by the quasi-absolutism (or autocracy) of the bureaucracy which, in turn, clashes with the forces of liberalism and, later on, socialism (Rosenberg 1958: 18f.). As far as the state-building period (and thereby the birth of bureaucrats as royal servants) is concerned, we may speak of the struggle between the old rule of traditional law, serving the interests of the Estates and the territorial provinces, as against the *Polizeistaat* imposing public law, i.e., administrative law, over and besides the existing units in order to create a centralized monarchy and, above all, to increase the revenue. In this connection it is often stated that the primary factor, in the context of the international military scene, was the decision of the Great Elector to keep a standing army which he could afford only by sharply raising the revenue. At the same time, however, it can be argued that there was no real external need for a Prussian army, but that for internal reasons it made sense to establish a standing army as a relatively cheap instrument for administering an underdeveloped country. Be this as it may be, we are concerned rather with the social implications of the decision for bureaucratization which can be seen right from its beginning. For in the struggle between traditional and public law the emerging *Polizeistaat* had its spearhead, as far as its personnel is concerned, in the commissars (Hintze 1962: 246f.; cf. Rosenberg 1958: 15). Thus the development from the rule of Estates toward absolute monarchy can be described, as in the case of France, by the dichotomy of *officiers* vs. *commissaires*, or, in terms of institutions, by the gradual reduction of the old *Regierungen* to purely judicial matters in favor of the gradual expansion of the War and Domains Chambers (*Kammern* and *Kommissariaten*) in size and tasks. The office of commissar was in existence even before 1640 and was military in origin. The commissar was in charge of affairs of the Quartermaster-General's Department, in fact his first duties being to observe the king's interests with the hired generals of mercenary armies. When the standing army was established, none else was better qualified for purposes of military administration including food supply, logistics, payment, than the commissar. Thus he soon became the main executive in the administration of taxation which by itself was closely connected with the maintenance of a standing army (Isaacsohn 1874–1884: vol. II, 158ff.; Hintze 1962).

The military bureaucrats, the focus of the growing Prussian bureaucracy, easily led to the much discussed militarization of the bureaucracy. Before we come to this point, however, it seems necessary to describe the bureaucracy as a functional (as distinct from a social) group, to ask for numbers, role specification, tasks to be performed, qualifications prescribed, and training facilities. Clearly, there is no distinct line between these questions and the study of bureaucrats as a social group, including recruitment policy, the impact of military personnel both on role behavior and on numerical oversupply, the implications of the merit system, and the like.

At the beginning of any consideration of the bureaucracy as a functional group, there should be a short outline of the history of the institutions. Dorn, who gives a good description of the Prussian bureaucracy from a functional point of view, centers on the reign of Frederick II, but speaks of 1723–1740 as the classic period of the main central administrative institution, the General Directory (Dorn 1931).[22] In order to get an organizational scheme it has always been

---

[22] For the earlier history of the institutions, compare Carsten 1958: 253ff.

convenient to take this period and follow the levels from above to below. The General Directory breaks down into four departments, organized on territorial (and only in addition on topical) grounds and headed by a minister who is assisted by two to five finance councillors (*Finanzräte*). The General Directory, however, could hardly satisfy the king's assumptions of efficient work. It was bypassed by the cabinet, the personal counsellors of the king, and finally saw itself broken down by the establishment of new departments in charge of special subjects without provincial or territorial limitations. This development reached its climax when the administration of taxes, especially the excise, being the nucleus of the commissars' bureaucracy, was cut out of the competence of the General Directory and given to the *Régie* under a completely independent staff which consisted of Frenchmen in the higher ranks at the central and provincial levels (Schultze 1888).

In these circumstances it is perhaps right to consider the provincial and local bodies of the War and Domains Administration, the more important ones. The War and Domains Chambers (*Kriegs- und Domänenkammern*) consisted of one president, two directors, and fifteen to twenty councillors (*Kriegs- und Domänenräte*) as regular members, not to speak of the forty to fifty subordinate officials of the clerical staff (Dorn 1931: no. 47, 86). The two directors indicate the earlier history (before 1723) when there were two separate bodies, the Domains Chamber, in charge of all affairs of the royal domains and forests, and the War Commissariat, in charge of contributions, levying of taxes, military and police matters. Under Frederick II we find seventeen War and Domains Chambers in the Prussian provinces. This organizational pattern lasted, changing names and range of activity notwithstanding, until the end of Prussia in 1945, the Chambers after 1806 being succeeded by the District Governments (*Regierungen*). Thus it is understandable that the Chamber presidents were of high rank in the hierarchy and second only to the ministers. Frederick II even bypassed the General Directory in dealing with the Chambers, the presidents of which, according to Dorn, even "surpassed their ministerial chiefs in actual influence and authority" (Dorn 1931: no. 47, 84).

Finally, we reach the local level of administration which is especially important if one thinks of the difficulties of effectively executing a system still newly imposed and not yet settled. If we do not take the "classic period" for our cross-sectional description of the existing administration but rather follow the course of historical development, we are, therefore, not astonished to find the *Steuerrat* in the towns and the *Landrat* in the country gradually overtaking power long before the whole administrative pyramid was completed and well organized. Indeed, there is much to be said for the view that the Prussian bureaucracy was established from the local level to the national level. This statement is only another way of saying that the commissar was the leading figure in the "new bureaucracy."

Within the preabsolutist state the cities formed an estate as well as the landed aristocracy, but the efficiency of the traditional self-government was of a poor quality, if not really obsolete. Therefore, the levy and administration of the excise which was originally run by city executives was soon taken over by the royal tax commissar who first controlled and then headed the tax collection and administration. Thereby he became the actual governing director of the cities which completely lost their self-government not to be regained until 1808. An ordinance of 1684 describes the function and competence of the *Steuerrat*: he decides upon claims and complaints which were not apt for regular judicial procedure at the courts; he controls food prices, inspects weights and measures, revises the excises rates, intervenes in quarrels between city officials and others, reports on heavy defraudment and irregularity, and executes the decisions taken by the Commissariats (Isaacsohn 1874–1884: vol. II, 187ff.). Besides the controlling and preventive duties he had to look after the welfare of the cities and to safeguard their well being, e.g., building of houses, security against fire, regulation of streets and rivers. He was even in charge of promoting commerce and the trades, e.g., by opening new markets. This wide range of tasks required a fairly large staff of personnel for assistance, partly clerical like cashiers, accountants, writers; partly executives like tax-collectors, controllers at the cities' gates (*Torschreiber*); and the various *Ausreuter*, a police-like personnel to control mills, breweries, mints, and the like.

If we overlook all that is known about the *Steuerrat* activities it seems clearly right to consider him, in accordance with Schmoller, as the perhaps most important official in the new bureaucracy (Isaacsohn 1874–1884: vol. II, 189). This may be indicated by the fact that the *Commissarius loci* (*Steuerrat*) is not a local official in the proper sense of the term. In fact, he headed a taxation district which comprised, on the average, two country districts (each under a *Landrat*) and had therefore to control up to ten or twelve cities. This meant he had to tour those cities twice a year; the actual administration being run by the mayor and the magistrate who anxiously tried to keep the *Steuerrat* in a good frame of mind. The *Steuerrat* reported from his tours of inspection directly to the General Directory and was entitled to consider himself a member of the Provincial War and Domains Chamber, the session of which he attended when he was present. Having his local clerical and executive staff in every city of his district besides himself, the *Steuerrat* had a few assistants for special tasks, i.e., surveyors of construction activities (*Bau-Inspektoren*) and inspectors of trades and industry (*Fabrik-Inspektoren, Kommissarien*), the latter being in charge of keeping up the existing regulations in various trades, the proper distribution of masters and journeymen, and of reporting on the state of affairs for statistical purposes.

As far as the so-called *Polizeistaat* (in the sense of the mercantilistic-cameralistic period) is concerned, it is the cities where we find it best established; here the degree of penetration for the sake of mobilizing resources is higher than in the countryside. The difference in the degree of penetration between cities and countryside can be exemplified by comparing the *Landrat* with the *Steuerrat*. The *Landrat* was the director of the district assemblies of the Estates (*Kreis-Direktor*) in pre-absolutist days; he was chosen as district- or land-commissar in order to protect the rights of the taxpayer against the colonels of the mercenary armies. When the standing army was established he gradually shifted towards a semi-royal servant, being in charge of commissary affairs like military conscription enforcement, Quartermaster General's business, distribution as well as collection of imposed taxes, services, etc., and control of law enforcement.[23] For these functions he was aided by a staff of administrative and executive personnel, similar to that of the *Steuerrat*. But he never gave up his connections with the landed squirearchy of which he remained the first among equals. Thus he remained a mixture between royal servant and Estates' representative, which was already indicated by his coming into office: he is the only official within the Prussian bureaucracy for whom the principle of indigenous origin, otherwise deliberately denied, was constantly applied, even during the nineteenth century (Bleek 1972: 121f.). The King of Prussia did not more than

---

[23] Cf. the Instruction for the *Landräte* in the Electorate of Brandenburg (1766) in Gelpke 1902: 91ff.

approve a list of candidates out of which the *Landrat* was elected by the nobility. This bore consequences for his ranking within the hierarchy. In theory, he was supposed to attend the meetings of the War and Domains Chambers whenever present, like the *Steuerrat*; though this could not be the case very often, he ranked directly behind the Chamber presidents, that is, before the War and Domains councillors including the *Steuerrat* (Isaacsohn 1874–1884: vol. II, 176ff.; vol. III, 169f., 271).

We can extend this reasoning on ranking. Since the Chamber presidents ranked behind the ministers (and before the finance councillors in the General Directory), and since the *Landräte* ranked behind the Chamber presidents (and before the War and Domains councillors in the Chambers), we may speak of the pervasive prestige laid upon the respective top officials on central, provincial, and local levels. As we will see later on, it is just these top officials, mainly of noble birth, who made it nearly impossible either to alter this ranking order or to open it for nonnobles. From the point of view of ranking order, it is interesting to note that the standing of the *Steuerrat* was below the *Landrat*, though the former was functionally of the same level. Perhaps it is permissible to consider the higher grading of the *Landrat* (and the Chamber presidents) as a social consolation prize to the nobility for making peace with the growing *Polizeistaat*. For it is the mercantilistic policy of this state which, considering the rise in productivity and commerce in order to enlarge the taxable national income (or consumption), as well as the amount of customs to be collected from foreign trade, placed the main burden of tasks to be performed on the *Steuerrat* and the War and Domains councillors. This opinion seems to be confirmed when it is learned that work as a *Steuerrat* was regarded as the training ground for the best Prussian officials of the eighteenth century (Finer 1932: 1195, according to Schmoller; cf. Isaacsohn 1874–1884: vol. III, 269). Obviously this kind of work was functionally too important to be performed by personnel recruited otherwise than by merit, regardless of the social prestige or the personal income connected with the office. If this is true, there should have been provisions for recruitment and training of civil servants in order to find the most capable individuals for the many offices to be filled, which we have to reckon in dozens in the 1660s, but in hundreds in the 1740s (Rosenberg 1958: 60).[24]

[24] The figures for 1805 are given in Table 7–1 on page 504 and have been

[515]

This leads to the question of an emerging merit system, and Prussia has been acclaimed as being the first country in modern European history to have elaborated and applied such a system with regard to its civil service. According to Fritz Morstein Marx,

Three outstanding facts have greatly contributed to the success of Prussian personnel policies. First, the rules of recruitment for the public service were laid down in concise terms, and the king himself looked to it that they were strictly applied. When the first president of the United States was born, the system of entrance examinations for administrative positions had already proved its usefulness in Prussia. Second, the higher civil service were never exempt from those principles. In fact, the first regulations dealing with qualifications for public office were primarily written for the leading class of professional administrators . . . And, third the establishment of the merit system as a universal rule, which was not to be broken up by arbitrary exceptions, operated as a means of democratization insofar as the requirement of any specific intellectual or vocational qualification for officeholding always imposes a powerful check on nepotism and class or party patronage (Morstein Marx 1935: 174f.).

The third point mentioned by Fritz Morstein Marx has to be modified when the bureaucracy is viewed as a social group. Before doing so, however, we should point out the functional aspects of the recruitment policy, i.e., the introduction and standardization of the merit system. The main road to administrative skill and upper ranks in the hierarchy was a long period of in-service training. This holds true even for the judiciary where the Berlin *Kammergericht* served as a training center for top level executives in the time of the Great Elector (Rosenberg 1958: 58). But it is the judiciary which, of course, first established the requirement that legal training was to be obtained at a university. The so-called hired doctors were the first academically trained personnel to serve in the emerging *Beamtenstaat*. Successive instructions by the Hohenzollern kings since the late seventeenth century, asked for legal training of the judicial civil servants. By 1775, every candidate had to pass two examinations:

---

drawn from the *Handbuch über den Königlich Preussischen Hof und Staat für das Jahr 1805*. On the basis of the same source figures for the nineteenth century are provided by Koselleck 1967: 689.

one at the university, the other at the State Examination Board (*Ober-Examinationskommission*) (Friedrich 1939: 139f.; Finer 1932: 1198ff.). Between those two examinations there was a period of unpaid in-service training at the courts extending over several years.

The judicial top-level officials, i.e., the academically trained ones, had their main field of activity in the Privy Council and the provincial *Regierungen*.[25] These institutions, which once had been part of the rule of Estates, had gradually lost power to the expanding competences of the General Directory and the War and Domains Chambers. Finally, the old Privy Council and the provincial *Regierungen* saw themselves confined to purely judicial matters, the *Regierungen* being in fact supreme courts of law in the various provinces. Interestingly to note, we find again some kind of social consolation insofar as the judicial councillors (*Regierungsräte*) "retained the flavor of superior social prestige until the remaking of Prussian institutions under the leadership of Stein and Hardenberg" (Rosenberg 1958: 119).

The judiciary could refer to an academic discipline older than the Prussian state. It is more interesting, therefore, to study the functional aspects of recruitment and training of the administrative personnel proper. For one thing, the stress on in-service training is understandable and perhaps quite natural in this realm. If one looks into the great instructions of the Prussian kings for the General Directory (1723 and 1748 respectively) or for the provincial chambers (Isaacsohn 1874–1884: vol. iii, 120ff., 258ff.) it is clear to see that practical skills (or applied science), such as preliminary estimates of costs, drawing up of budgets, preparing reports on current issues, drafting memoranda on measures to be taken, and the like, were most highly regarded. Besides these skills, or perhaps as the necessary underlying psychological make-up of their servants, the kings asked for the severest sense of duty, obedience, vigilance, industry, and similar virtues. In turn, it was the War and Domains Chambers which "became the most vital centers of the entire bureaucratic mechanism. They were the classic workshops of the Prussian mercantilist state through which by the persistent drill of ever watchful officials the sluggish but infinitely malleable and educable inhabitants of the north German plain were galvanized into an active,

---

[25] A recent study of some privy councils in Protestant southern Germany of early absolutist time with special reference to the question of bourgeois vs. noble councillors is given by Gerd Wunder (Wunder 1971).

thrifty, and the most highly disciplined people of modern Europe" (Dorn 1931: no. 47, 83).

Besides the socializing impact of the bureaucracy on society there was, no doubt, a fairly high social mobility within the bureaucracy, owing to the implications of the stress on in-service training. This mobility, however, though unmatched in degree until at least the early twentieth century (Rosenberg 1958: 67), was bound to decline at the very moment when the mercantilistic state established its theory and practices as a distinct academic discipline to be learned at universities. Whatever the sinister preference of nobles for high office may have been, the very academization of service training by itself at the same time democratized, at least in theory, the access to higher ranks and drew insurmountable borders between them and the lower ones. Thus the introduction of academic training for administrative personnel is closely connected with the growing dichotomy between higher and subordinate officials.

The political philosophy of the German mercantilistic state was cameralism, and it was Frederick William I who established, in 1727, the first two chairs in this field at Prussian universities (Halle and Frankfurt/Oder). Gradually, some attendance of classes in cameralism (i.e., economics of the *Polizeistaat* and of private enterprise, especially agriculture, as well as some technology, statistics, and natural science) was required as desirable or prerequisite, until in 1770 a complete course, including the twofold examination pattern similar to the judicial training, was made obligatory (Friedrich 1939: 136ff.; Finer 1932: 1198ff.). The bifurcation, however, between higher and subordinate officials had started much earlier and can be seen in the history of the so-called *Auskultator* (or, later, *Referendar*) institution. Since the councillors in the various branches of the administration were limited in number by the personnel budget, it was usually a matter of waiting, for a long time, before a young candidate could expect to fill a vacancy. In the interim, he could work, as many people of lower social standing did to support themselves, as a subordinate official, and it has already been mentioned that there was "a golden age for select men of common origin," in the time of Frederick William I (Rosenberg 1958: 67; cf. Isaacsohn 1874–1884: vol III, 264, n. 1). But it is the same king who opened a second route of access to the councillor's career by appointing, in 1723, young people of good family standing, belonging to the propertied class, as *Auskultatoren* at the Chambers, i.e., as unpaid aides who would be assisted by the councillors in preparing reports, and taught by them in the specific tasks of their field (Isaacsohn 1874–1884: vol. III, 122; cf. p. 264, n. 2). From a functional point of view, it is clear that it made a difference whether a future councillor got his in-service training by climbing up the hierarchy and thereby perhaps clinging too heavily to the narrow outlook of his former duties familiar to him, or whether he had the advantage, right from the beginning, of a bird's-eye view in looking at the interdependence of the various different tasks due to certain underlying principles. Quite naturally it is precisely this *Auskultator* who was expected, after 1727 and especially after 1770, to have gained his theoretical training at a university, in order to understand the cameralistic concept of state and its politico-practical implications, before he underwent his in-service training, at the end of which he had to pass his second examination. Even then he had eventually to wait for a vacancy before he was appointed as councillor.

The professionalization of government service personnel began in the judicial field and extended to the administrative one, and then led to the growing dichotomy between higher vs. subordinate officials. Though there is, since the eighteenth century, analogous standardization in the formal sense of the prescribed training for judicial and administrative civil servants, i.e., university attendance and in-service training, it is interesting to note that the contents of training were different. However, this status of a special political science to be studied by all applicants to higher posts in the administration did not remain the common feature of Prussian/German recruitment policy and gave way to the jurists' monopoly (*Assessorismus*) dominating the administration in the nineteenth and twentieth centuries (cf. Bleek 1972). Several causes contributed to this development: "Once the task of state-building had been accomplished . . . the struggle for legalizing or constitutionalizing these great administrative mechanisms had begun (Friedrich 1939: 132; cf. Finer 1932: 1252ff.). In the era of economic *laissez faire*, state officials were supposed to be executors of the law rather than managers of the political economy; and a bourgeois-capitalist society was interested to check bureaucratic autocracy by imposing legal restraints upon an arbitrary officialdom. Consequently, cameralism was gradually replaced by legal studies which by 1846 were established as the main and obligatory prerequisite of theoretical training for all higher civil servants. Even with regard to the following in-service training (*Referen-*

dariat), practice in the law courts became the chief preparation for the second examination which opened up for councillorship and the like. Thus we see, in the nineteenth century, the withdrawal of the state from positive economic and social activity and the reduction of the social sciences from an applied science to a literary history of theories (Finer 1932: 1254). It was not until the effects of industrialized economy on society became felt that there arose a debate on the advisability of a purely legal training of the higher officials. From 1879 onward there is to be seen a gradual reintroduction of political science and administrative in-service training into the curriculum of a would-be councillor, but legal studies remained the chief subject (Finer 1932: 1256ff.).

So far we have dealt only with the higher officials. The huge bulk of the civil service, however, belonged to lower ranks and performed subordinate tasks. The main feature in this rank is its use as an institution for maintaining ex-military personnel. The connection between administrative branches and the military via personnel recruitment has always been a close one, even apart from the claim for maintenance laid on the state by disabled soldiers. When the "new" bureaucracy of the Commissariats was established, there were, among others, military bureaucrats like *Regimentsquartiermeister* and *Auditeure* who eventually became *Steuerräte* and the like (Hintze 1964: 90, 103; Rosenberg 1958: 64). But the real impact of the military was felt in the lower ranks of clerical and executive jobs. Here we can speak of a militarization of the Prussian bureaucracy since the days of the Great Elector (Isaacsohn 1874–1884: vol. II, 176; Adam 1939: 886). However, it was Frederick William I and his son who, by extending the standing army to a hitherto unknown per capita ratio and by waging costly wars, greatly enlarged the problem of maintenance of ex-soldiers. Thus, the fundamental instructions for the General Directory, of 1723 and 1748 respectively, laid down the obligation to appoint by preference disabled noncommissioned officers and soldiers to jobs like city gates' comptroller (*Torschreiber*), inspector of mills (*Mühlenbereuter*), and the police-like *Ausreuter*, not to speak of elementary school teachers (Adam 1939: 888ff.). A very high official was in charge of supervising the enforcement of these regulations, i.e., the filling of vacancies, sometimes against the resistance of the affected offices. First, the general aide-de-camp, later on, the ministerial head of the sixth department in the General Directory (Isaacsohn 1874–1884: vol. III, 184, 257).

This militarily overloaded or one-sided recruitment policy of the Prussian bureaucracy, which eventually led even to the preference for military clergymen over civilian ones for appointment to lucrative tenures (Isaacsohn 1874–1884: vol. III, 346), had a profound impact on relationships between bureaucracy and society (cf. Isaacsohn 1874–1884: vol. III, 184f.), and was not to come to an end in the nineteenth century. On the contrary, the introduction of universal conscription (1814) logically raised the claims and problems of "civil maintenance" (*Zivilversorgung*). There was no enthusiasm on the side of the privates to serve longer than the three years requested and eventually to become a noncommissioned officer. To overcome this kind of shortage, king and government introduced an incentive in 1820 for all noncommissioned officers who served at least nine years (in 1874 changed to twelve years) with the army. This incentive was the right to claim preference for appointment to clerical and accounting jobs in the civil service (Adam 1939: 895). From this time onward we find two kinds of ex-soldiers in the first line of the recruitment reservoir, the disabled ones and the noncommissioned officers with a *Zivilversorgungsschein*. And we find even elaborate provisions on how many of the posts of different subordinate rank levels should be filled with these preferred people. No doubt, the noncommissioned officership served as a means of social mobility in the nineteenth century (Hintze 1964: 105), whatever the limiting effect on open competition might have been.

The low requirements of formal education for subordinate officials correspond to those for subordinate military personnel. Noncommissioned officers who applied for admission to civil service were asked only for writing and accounting abilities (Adam 1939: 895). If, on the other side, there was a strong emphasis on professional training for higher civil servants, one can ask how higher military servants, i.e., officers, were recruited and trained. The overwhelming representation of nobles in the officers' corps is too well known to be elaborated on again. From a functional point of view, which interests us at the moment, it can be said perhaps that family tradition served as a kind of substitute training institution providing for homogeneity and *esprit de corps* which, in turn, made up much of the officers' required virtues. An education on rather general lines was offered the future officers at the various *Kadettenanstalten* and, for a minority, at the Berlin military academy (von Poten 1896: 32f, 56ff.). More scholarly or scientific training was only required of officers in the artillery and engineers corps who were more frequently of bourgeois origin and generally regarded of lower standing (Demeter 1962: 71). We shall consider them within the realm of technical personnel and its training.

Thus it was not until 1808 that "knowledge and education" were labeled as the main prerequisites for appointment to an officership in peacetime. What this precisely meant was soon clarified when the simultaneously reorganized general educational system established the *Gymnasium's* upper forms' maturity as equivalent to the privilege of only one year military service, including the appointment to reserve officership. This *Einjährig-Freiwilligen-Privileg* had to be matched in educational level by the regular noble officers' training if they wanted to check or to slow down the access to officership by bourgeois candidates. To be sure, there were special military schools, according to the regulation of 1810, which offered elementary and advanced education, outside the general public system, as a prerequisite for attendance of the purely professional officers' school (*Kriegsschule*) (von Poten 1896: 152f.). But on the one hand, this meant that the noble gentlemen had to attend schools when they were almost too old for it (Demeter 1962: 76); on the other hand, it was precisely the by-passing of general secondary schools which enabled commoners of low social status to obtain ranks of officership. In order to hamper this development the then Prince William tried to introduce, in 1825 and again, in 1844, a common general educational preparation at a *Gymnasium*, with the sons of poor noblemen in the countryside provided with scholarships (Demeter 1962: 76ff.). This policy of protection of the noble class against the implications of an achievement-oriented recruitment policy finally won a partial success when William succeeded as king of Prussia and made it a deliberate practice that officers were not only appointed, according to law, by "knowledge and education," but also by special fulfillment of duties and sound military views (*"Gesinnung"*) (Demeter 1962: 82ff.). However, this ambivalence is already to be found in the famous original regulation of 1808 which spoke of presence of mind, quick perception, punctuality and order, and decent behavior besides knowledge and education (von Poten 1896: 144; Demeter 1962: 76). And it was the commanding officer of the regiment who decided, after all, whether a candidate possessed the necessary qualifications for officership (Hintze 1964: 101; Rosenberg 1958: 217).

The preceding section has tried to delineate, at different levels of higher and subordinate ranks and for the judicial, administrative, and military personnel of the modern Prussian state, the bureaucracy as a functional group; and, with regard to its recruitment and training, the emergence of the merit system. But we could not avoid, here and there, considering the social causes or implications of the outlined features. Clearly, there is a close connection between the functional and social aspect of the Prussian bureaucracy, and we will try to develop a more coherent picture of it as a social group. This is, however, a vast field for scholarly work, and we have to confine ourselves to the questions related either to recruitment and training or, with regard to the emerging merit system, to the checks on open competition.

These checks on open competition within an established merit system can be studied either by pointing to the different forms of exceptions from the rule, such as patronage, nepotism, hereditary claim of offices, purchase of offices, and the like, or by centering on the different positions of certain social groups or classes in the competition process. One big exception to free and open competition has been mentioned already, though it was not confined to a social group proper: the preference of military over civilian personnel for recruitment into subordinate civil service ranks. The impact on socialization and role behavior is easily to be imagined, and may be realized if one thinks of Zuckmayer's *Hauptmann von Köpenick* where the people looking for jobs in a factory are asked for their military service rather than their occupational record.

A narrow study of the question of open competition, however, has to focus, for the sake of precision and sources available, on the high-level personnel. This, at once, brings in the much disputed question of nobles vs. nonnobles in the Prussian recruitment policy. With regard to the military some remarks on this subject have already been made. Indeed, it is true that noblemen were regarded by all royal Prussian state-builders as the material out of which officers were to be made. And even if there are no precise figures on the parental origin of Prussian officers as late as 1806, there can be no doubt that the overwhelming majority of them were of noble birth in the seventeenth and eighteenth centuries (Demeter 1962: 4; Rosenberg 1958: 70). This relationship changed during the Napoleonic wars and slowly worked in favor of a growing percentage of nonnoble officers who in 1860 made up 35 percent (Demeter 1962: 26). The efforts of the old Prussian forces to strengthen the position of the nobility in the age of prescribed educational achievements for officership have been mentioned already. The most effective instrument, however, of controlling the officers' supply was the necessity for a candidate, who had passed all examinations, to get elected by the officers of the regiment he wanted to enter. This, in fact, was a device for a co-optative personnel policy which at the same time made the officers' corps relatively independent of government (i.e., bureaucratic) interference and maintained "the retention of Junker control over the officer class, through the officer over the new, free citizen soldiers, and thus over the bulk of civil society" (Rosenberg 1958: 217). Thus the democratization effect of the merit system, praised by Fritz Morstein Marx (Morstein Marx 1935: 175), turned out to be a tightening up of aristocratic *esprit de corps* (Rosenberg 1958: 217). And it was only the newly enlarged army of the reforms of the 1860s which eventually outstripped the nobility's physical ability to supply sufficient officers.

The top military personnel resisted most strongly the application of the merit system to recruitment and advancement and clung very tenaciously to the connection of birth and profession in its noble officers' corps. Peculiar though this may be for Prussian militarism, we have to ask for the nobility's position in those fields where professionalization began earlier and, perhaps, bore the *stigmata* of bourgeois values of efficiency and industry, namely in the judiciary and administration. As far as the judiciary is concerned, it has to be remembered that it was the stronghold of the Estates against the emerging absolutist dynasty in the seventeenth and early eighteenth centuries, making up the antagonism between traditional and public law, and between old and new bureaucracy (Rosenberg 1958: 53ff.; cf. Isaccsohn 1874–1884: vol. II, 354). The center of the retrieved but still existing power of the squirearchy, apart from the *Landräte*, at this time were the *Regierungen*, in the main supreme courts of law in the provinces. But even in judicial matters they had no monopoly since the very important administrative justice was carried out by the Chambers and Commissariats. The embitterment about losing political influence, the intragroup conflict between "learned bench" and "noble bench," the growing number of deserters to the winning side, and the eagerness of the king and the new bureaucracy to get the support of the highborn finally led, about the 1750s, to an appeasement between old and new bureaucracy, an amalgamation of the two bureaucratic elites (Rosenberg 1958: 116ff.). On the one side this meant the conversion of judicial *officiers* into accountable and removable royal servants, mainly achieved by the judicial reforms of Cocceji (Rosenberg 1958: 129). The introduction of prescribed scholarly qualifications, already mentioned, was highly necessary in the light of the existing circumstances: legal amateurs here and there, nobles being devoted to military service rather than judicial matters, and *roturiers* purchasing their positions in order to make profit rather than find justice. In 1737 Cocceji established the rule that everyone had to pass examinations before appointment, even if he had already paid into the Recruitment Chest (*Rekrutenkasse*) (Rosenberg 1958: 129). Though venality of offices was not very common in Prussia, especially in comparison with France, its very existence in the realm of the judiciary indicates that the latter belonged to the old preabsolutist offices.

This state of affairs was abolished gradually and intentionally by the enforcement of the 1737 and 1755 regulations on training and appointment. But there remained the continuing "flavor of superior social prestige" of the highborn (Rosenberg 1958: 119) to whom, after the noblemen had made their peace with the absolutist state, especially Frederick II paid tribute in his appointments to the top officialdom (Rosenberg 1958: 162). According to Rosenberg, "the 'social' victory of the higher judiciary was more than a consolation prize for political defeat . . . it was also the gratifying symbol of the triumph . . . over the mind of the official parvenu elite" (Rosenberg 1958: 120). This can be demonstrated in the administrative realm where "the rising elite of commissioned officers managed to dilute the emerging 'merit system' " (Rosenberg 1958: 121). The social composition of this new bureaucracy (cf. Rosenberg 1958: 60ff.) varied over time, and it was in fact indigenous nobles who made up a major part of the Great Elector's service class. Thus it was not until Frederick I and Frederick William I that bourgeois jurists, businessmen, bureaucratic subalterns, military bureaucrats and ex-soldiers formed the bulk of the royal servants and eventually reached top positions. This "eventuality" was bound to decline when, on the one hand, the standardization of qualifications took place and led to the bifurcation of higher and subordinate officers and when, on the other hand, the inclination toward recruitment from the nobility grew in the second half of the eighteenth century. The final setup of the 1770 regulations on high level civil service recruitment, in a formal sense the introduction of the merit system, had several counterbalancing social implications. The first was the marked independence of the bureaucracy as a corporation and exclusive group from royal arbitrary intervention in recruitment matters. Second, this newly gained independence led to a recruitment policy by co-optation rather than by competition. For it was not sufficient to pass the prescribed examinations and to undergo the long unpaid in-service training; the candidate who served under the personal observation of a president of a War and Domains Chamber (and, after 1806, of a *Regierung*) was only allowed to enter the training period and the second examination with the president's consent (Hintze 1964: 101). Thereby other than purely intellectual qualifications came into play: "the candidate was required to be 'friendly to the State'—that is to say, conservative, of family standing, a member of students' corps and a reserve officer, and as a rule a Protestant Evangelical" (Finer 1932: 1219; cf. Rosenberg 1958: 180, 212f.). Apart from these ascriptive criteria for the bulk of the higher civil servants, a fairly close connection between the nobility and the very high positions in the administrative hierarchy, such as presidents of the Chambers (Isaacsohn 1874–1884: vol. III, 137; Rosenberg 1958: 69) and, of course, the *Landräte*, existed. This overaverage representation of the nobility in the key positions of Prussian bureaucracy, whether old or new, eased the amalgamation of the two formerly distinct bureaucratic elites and caused the commoners in this distinguished group, once they had arrived, to have their enthusiasm for competition sharply decline (Rosenberg 1958: 121). The main device toward this direction was the ennoblement of the service elite, thus "welding together the old social rank order and the new service hierarchy" (Rosenberg 1958: 139).[26]

To sum up we may say that by sticking to a co-optative recruitment policy and by the "mental corruption" of the successful social climbers there came into being a bureaucratic elite which democratized aristocratic privileges to a certain degree, but which retained its rather exclusive status including the typical features of family connections, patronage, or political commitment. Not even the entrance to the lower level of this group was open to competition.

[26] As far as the excess representation of the nobility within the Prussian bureaucracy of the nineteenth century is concerned, compare Koselleck 1967: 680ff. and Wegmann 1969: 32,110,158.

From the beginning, the high costs of secondary and university education, and especially of the unpaid in-service training, narrowed the social composition of the presumptive candidates to the upper middle class (Finer 1932: 1219). In addition there was the impact of the extramerit prerequisites for appointment and advancement. Thus we have to conclude that the Prussian nobility managed to retain its key position in society as a governing class by using the emerging merit system as a device for modernizing itself. This modernization meant replenishment of the group and the shift toward a likewise exclusive bureaucratic elite, a privileged professional status group similar to the officers' corps (cf. Rosenberg 1958: 211), monopolizing personnel policies as long as there were no mass problems of demand.

The checks on open competition due to social restrictions of an emerging merit system do not necessarily mean a reduction of the functional efficiency of the bureaucracy. However, they belong to the context of the sociopolitical role the bureaucracy could play, and, henceforth, make up a peculiar aspect of Prussian-German state- and nation-building. In the nineteenth century the bureaucracy emancipated itself, becoming the leading political force. As it attracted many an ambitious bourgeois, it contributed to the gradual development of a new upper class. Bismarck, however, made the bureaucracy an instrument at his command, without giving power to the liberal bourgeoisie which, after all, had now been accustomed to acquiesce in obedience, whether to a monarchial or bureaucratic or a chancellor's autocracy (von Borch 1954: 148).[27]

Technical Personnel

The administrative personnel hitherto considered may be labeled as part of the extractive forces of the modern state; indeed its major task has been to secure extractability, the means by which the state could accumulate power. Power was as yet achieved mainly in two ways: (1) building up strong armies or navies; and (2) developing the economy in order to increase the extractable resources. Both ways called for technical, as apart from administrative personnel, as a common general requirement of all countries notwithstanding their greatly differing approaches to solve this problem.

[27] On the impact of nineteenth-century political and social developments on the Prussian bureaucracy cf. Koselleck 1967; Gillis 1971.

To maintain the authority of the king against other contenders, outside and inside the territory, was the task of the army or the navy. Both needed technical personnel; and in the period of state-building in Western Europe, military techniques for the first time called for professionals to discharge this job: gunners and sailors secured not only the European predominance over the rest of the world (see Cipolla 1965), but decided about the rank of the great powers in Europe. To recruit and train men for artillery and the men-of-war was as crucial for the existence of the early modern European state as was the ability of finance power. It was the superiority of British seamanship and gunnery which led to the rise of the British Empire from the defeat of the Armada to Trafalgar, from Drake to Nelson; and it was the superiority of the French, and later the Prussian military techniques which determined control of the Continent.

To support armies and navies meant by necessity a strong and modernizing economy, whether achieved by innovative entrepreneurs or by state intervention or by both. In any case, there arose a great need for technical personnel such as engineers, mechanics, mill- and shipwrights, and the like. At the same time ways and means had to be found for sponsoring and applying science and technology, especially since the scientific revolution of the seventeenth century and the beginning of industrialization in eighteenth-century Britain set the stage of international competition for power. Again it has to be asked how Britain, France, and Prussia responded to this common challenge; and again the differences outlined below seem to fit into the general picture drawn so far.

BRITAIN

If Britain relied for the recruitment of administrative personnel on the society at large, the field for recruitment of technical experts was smaller and wider at the same time: smaller because in certain fields, like shipbuilding or powder making, some families enjoyed a quasi-monopoly, wider because the area of recruitment was not confined to England but extended to the European Continent. Basically, however, the same methods of recruitment and training were employed. Patronage prevailed too; but in this respect it often meant talent hunting and protection of talents. Protection often took the legal form of monopoly which was granted for specific productions or techniques. Since England in the fifteenth and sixteenth centuries was not a technically advanced country, the technical personnel in many fields had to be attracted from the Continent. Fortification and ballistic experts from Italy, navigators from Italy, Spain, and Portugal, astronomers, chemists, and glassmakers from France, horticulturists, mill- and shipwrights, and dyers from Holland, printers and miners from Germany and Hungary, ironmongers from Sweden brought their skills to England between the fifteenth and early seventeenth centuries (for the following see among others Armytage 1965: 24; Nef 1934, Nef 1967). Whether they turned to England on their own initiative, whether they were attracted by good employment opportunities, or whether they were deliberately recruited, is not entirely clear. Peter Mathias asserts that the English state "did not set out energetically to attract foreign capital or foreign skills" (Mathias 1969: 33). It may well be that a little encouragement sufficed in most cases; but certainly in crucial fields deliberate action was taken to secure a particular person or skill. The Italian navigator Sebastian Cabot who had worked many years for Spain "was induced, in 1548, to transfer his allegiance, and the vast store of knowledge and experience he had acquired at the *Casa de Contratación*, to England," where he instructed navigators and produced charts and navigational instruments until his death in 1558 (Marcus 1961: 59). Five years earlier (1543), Henry VIII, pressed by financial difficulties which prevented the purchase of brass for guns from abroad, sent a French cannon-founder from the royal foundry to try the founding of iron cannon which succeeded. The English iron ordnance industry thus was created by deliberate actions of the monarch (Hall 1952: 10). Queen Elizabeth put the saltpeter industry in the hands of Dutchmen and paid one of them 500 pounds to teach two of her subjects to make saltpeter (Nef 1940: 89).

England never relied on foreign skills, however, for very long. The English people quickly absorbed the expertise of the foreign personnel, and within one or two generations often surpassed the country from which they had learned the skills. In the middle of the sixteenth century, England had still to look to Spain or France for pilots; in 1588 the English fleet already outsailed the Armada and fired more powerful guns; ten years later, just before the close of the century, Englishmen were the chief pilots of the Dutch fleets sailing to the East Indies (Marcus 1961: 99; see also Lewis 1959, Lewis 1961).

In metallurgy foreign tutelage lasted longer, and the French artillery remained ahead of the English since it used mathematical methods more strictly, but English cannons soon were sold to the Continent. They were cheap because the English iron industry of the sixteenth and seventeenth centuries was in a few hands, was organized more effectively, and worked with greater units of production. Gunpowder and saltpeter too were produced by royal monopolists, but the government never tried to manage production itself. It relied on the entrepreneurial skill of experienced business families—the Evelyns for gunpowder, the Brownes for cannon—whom it protected legally. When the saltpeter men informed James I that they had difficulties in carrying out their commission because the control of ammunition was not in the hands of a person of high rank, he placed saltpeter commissioners and gunpowder patent under the patronage of the Earl of Worcester whose authority made the landowners more willing to allow the commissioners to search for the valuable earth (Nef 1940: 90–91). James at one occasion also came close to organizing a royal factory for alum making. A group of London merchants had failed to establish efficiently alum manufacturing in spite of a royal monopoly and the hiring of Italian and German skilled laborers; James then appointed three contractors who acted in the name of and with the finances of the king, but they failed too, and in 1615 the alum works were farmed out again to a group of London merchants (Nef 1940: 108–109).

Even in the all-important naval technology, England relied to a great extent on private business. During most of the Middle Ages, English kings hardly ever had possessed a fleet, only a few ships used to be "royal"; in wartime ships were recruited from the "Cinque Ports," which possessed ancient privileges for the duty of providing fifty-seven ships at the service of the king, and from the merchant marine. Though the first-known naval administrator was a cleric, already in 1420 a merchant of Southampton, collector of customs and subsidies of the city and mayor, was appointed to the post of "Keeper of the King's Ships." To make well-to-do merchants administrators of the navy soon became routine. "Besides greater business capacity such a man was useful to the government in that he was expected to advance money, or purchase stores, on his own credit when the crown finance was temporarily strained" (Oppenheim 1896: 3, 16). The Tudors, particularly Henry VIII and Elizabeth, built up the first "Royal Navy" with a greater number of royal vessels. Naval dockyards were developed at Portsmouth, Woolwich,

Deptford, and Erith to build and repair the king's ships. In 1546 the Navy Board was created to administrate under the lord admiral, the navy, and its dockyards. Of the five principal officers of this board,[28] three belonged to the category of administrative personnel (the treasurer, the comptroller, and the clerk of the ships), but two can be regarded as technical experts, the surveyor of ships and the master of the ordnance, though the boundaries were flexible. The first of these technical officers, William Winter, surveyor of ships since 1549 and master of the ordnance from 1557 to 1589, was a trained sea captain and merchant, competent in the technology as well as in the administration of ships (Marcus 1961: 4). In 1577 John Hawkins, son of a sea-faring merchant from Plymouth, a man with experience in many voyages, and son-in-law of his predecessor, was appointed treasurer of the navy. He introduced many improvements in the design of the ships. For seventeen years, in the most crucial period of English naval history, he had the main responsibility for the efficiency of the Royal Navy (Oppenheim 1896: 145).

But the most important technical experts in the long run were the shipwrights who actually built and repaired the ships and designed many themselves. A few families of royal shipwrights oligopolized these posts for more than a century. To this group belonged James Baker, shipwright to Henry VIII, and his son Matthew who laid down the first rules for exact measurement of the tonnage, but above all, the Petts: Peter Pett, chief shipwright of Elizabeth, was succeeded on his death in 1589 by his son Joseph and in 1600 by his younger son, Phineas, who had not only a Cambridge education, but also a solid training as a carpenter. Another son, Peter Pett Jr., built at least three royal ships. In 1631 Phineas became principal officer and commissioner for the navy. While he was still in office, his nephew, another Peter Pett, was appointed to the Navy Board, and in 1649 the fourth Peter Pett, grandson of the first, son of the second, took his place at the Board (Oppenheim 1896: passim). Thus five men of three generations were in active service as technical officers for the navy. This certainly was patronage, but it also meant accumulated experience over generations.

Even more characteristic for the way in which technical expertise was used in modern England is the fact that all these shipwrights remained businessmen in their own right in spite of their paid jobs

[28] Originally six; but the office of Lieutenant of the Admiralty, soon lapsed.

as royal servants. Besides the royal dockyards they conducted private dockyards and undertook all kinds of commissions and under-commissions for the government. Such a system invited abuse, theft, and fraud, e.g., the use of materials and labor from royal dockyards for private purposes. When the early Stuarts put all Navy offices on sale, they were eagerly sought because of the great profit one could make out of them.

Shortly before 1660, however, the office of a royal shipwright and the conduct of private business were declared incompatible. The royal shipwrights were forbidden to indulge in private business. In compensation their salaries were raised. The new rule seems to have been enforced, since we know one instance in which the appointment of a master shipwright was postponed until he had promised to dispose of his private yard (Ehrman 1953: 103–105).

To pay full salaries to royal servants was by no means common at this time. Most of the leading officials had a basic annual salary connected with their office, but their main income was still derived from fees and similar devices, and the clerks fully depended either on fees or on a salary which the master paid out of his own income. Again the navy was among the first government agencies to abolish the system of pay by perquisites and to introduce payment by salary alone. In the summer of 1694, the Admiralty changed the system and made up the first list of officials on its payroll (Ehrman 1953: 562–563). Thus the navy's technical experts were the first royal servants to become full-time, salaried, professional officers. They also received their training inside the dockyards. In the later seventeenth century, a member of this group came closest to the modern notion of a civil servant. Their positions had become permanent much earlier. Already in 1548 three principal designers and master shipwrights were granted pensions of the Exchequer "in consideration of the long and good services, and that they should instruct others in their feats" (Oppenheim 1896: 73). All four principal shipwrights of Elizabeth held patents for lifetime, and one was active at the dockyards still in his eighties.

Other officers of the dockyard followed the shipwrights in securing their jobs for lifetime. In addition they were also the first group of royal servants who could count on a kind of career. Right from the beginning of the Navy Board, lower officials used to be appointed to higher offices on the Board when vacancies occurred.

When the first Treasurer by patent died in 1548, the surveyor of the ships became treasurer and was himself succeeded in his office by the son of the former treasurer; a few years later the master of the ordnance was promoted to lieutenant of the Admiralty. By the seventeenth century technical and clerical service in the Navy was something like a life career with frequent exchange between the dockyards and the Navy Board in London. Even the man who started as purser on a ship or clerk to a naval storekeeper could reasonably hope to make a career in the victualling part of the service rising from smaller to greater vessels and finally to a storekeeper himself. Again the shipwrights took the lead. A young man, apprenticed to a master shipwright at the dockyards could climb many steps on the ladder. When he had distinguished himself enough to become a foreman, his next step was to become a junior officer such as master caulker, master boat-builder, or master mastmaker in one of the yards. From there he might advance to assistant master shipwright and finally master shipwright. Usually along this way he would change his dockyard several times since there existed a hierarchy among the dockyards according to their importance. Even master shipwrights got promotion by transfer from one yard to another. The highest post a shipwright could ordinarily achieve was Resident Commissioner at one of the yards. He then represented the Navy Board at that particular yard; a few shipwrights rose to the position of surveyor of the navy, the top technical officer in royal naval service (Ehrman 1953: 107, 105). Daniel A. Baugh, in a thorough study of naval administration in the age of Walpole, regards the following career as typical for the administrative officers: captain's clerk (usually received through patronage); purser; clerk of the cheque and storekeeper at a port; clerk of the cheque at a naval dockyard; the same at a greater dockyard; commissioner of victualling; extra commissioner at the Navy Board (Baugh 1965: 44–47).

A consequence of the permanence and career possibilities in naval administration was its relative independence from political change and upheaval. To be sure, a strict division between politics and administration was not achieved until the reforms of the nineteenth century. But at the Navy Board, and even more at the dockyards, the personnel changed little throughout the years of revolution, civil war, restoration, and revolution again. The Petts remained the government shipwrights of Tudors, Stuarts, and Commonwealth and so

[533]

did most of the other Navy offices. As for the eighteenth century Baugh states: "The Admiralty could hire, but not fire" (Oppenheim 1896: passim; Ehrman 1953: 288; Baugh 1965: 87).

Permanence, career opportunities, and in-service training given, the entry into the service remains important. How were naval administrators and technicians recruited? The answer is: as in other fields of English administration in the sixteenth to eighteenth centuries, mainly through patronage, family or friendship connections. The Crown only appointed the members of the Navy Board; the Board appointed the main officers of the dockyard; later in the seventeenth century appointment was made by Admiralty warrant. The real selection was usually left, however, to the officer in charge of a particular function: the surveyor chose the dockyards' clerks of the survey, the victualling commissioner the victualling agents. Farther below a wide variety of possibilities existed. The master shipwrights hired their men and, of course, selected their apprentices; so did the storekeepers. The combination of life-long service and family recruitment created a network of connections and relationships. "William Sutherland, who wrote the two best books of the period on shipbuilding, was not an exceptional case, with 32 years' service as a shipwright and junior officer himself, his father and 'several of my relations' master carpenters and one of them a naval surveyor of contract-built ships, his uncle Bagwell master shipwright at Portsmouth, and his grandfather for thirty years a foreman of shipwrights at Deptford yard" (Ehrman 1953: 106).

Not before the eighteenth century the power of appointment was taken from the Navy Board and particular officers and given to the Admiralty. The Duke of Bedford as First Lord of the Admiralty in 1745 expressed his expectation "that my nomination . . . shall be accepted of" (Baugh 1965: 86). This centralized the power of recruitment, allowed to proceed along agreed standards, but led also to political patronage instead of a personal one.

Patronage, however, did not exclude merit and it could not, the more technical the service was. Where generations of shipwrights had accumulated a store of experience and skill in a family, an outsider could not easily match this knowledge. Still in the eighteenth century "there was a tendency to regard shipbuilding skill as a hereditary trait, and the best way to become a master shipwright was to have a father who was one" (Baugh 1965: 303). But sometimes recommendations of an insider were refused by the Board or the Admiralty, and usually the previous career of an applicant was taken into account. Training in the dockyard service meant a definite advantage (Ehrman 1953: 106).

Professional ability was paramount for appointments of Surveyor and Master Attendant in the dockyards. Performance as a seaman could be judged and was critically judged by Navy officers who were consulted before appointments. Baugh states that "no amount of political favor could help a Master Attendant unless his knowledge of seamanship were attested" (Baugh 1965: 303). And while he regards the obvious inadequacies of eighteenth-century naval administration as part of a larger problem—"the problem of governing in a constitutional environment essentially hostile to vigorous administration"—he thinks that the navy administration fared relatively well in the general setting of corruption:

> The Navy Office was not a haven for indolent placemen or political appointees. No one could be appointed a Naval Commissioner unless he was evidently experienced either in sea or clerical affairs; nearly always the clerical experience was gained in the navy service . . . The Surveyor was always selected from the ranks of the Master Shipwrights . . . The Clerk of the Acts was usually a former dockyard officer, so were the three subordinate comptrollers, although occasionally a sea officer might be advanced to one of the Comptrollerships after some seasoning as an extra Commissioner. Extra Commissioners were usually former captains; and experience at sea was an absolute prerequisite for appointment as dockyard Commissioner (Baugh 1965: 5–6, 39–40).

Technical and administrative officers ashore form, of course, only part of the body of naval personnel. Skill and experience at sea counted even more in the struggle for predominance among the major seafaring nations of Europe from the fifteenth to the eighteenth century. How did England recruit and train her sea-officers? The underlying structure is the same as in the field of technology and administration. England relied first on the country at large, mainly its seafaring population, trained in fishery, merchant shipping, voyage, and piracy. With the growth of the Navy in-service training grew more important, but little if any formal naval education was introduced though the leading captains and masters consulted the mathematicians and astronomers in questions of navigation and charting and some secured themselves a sound theoretical training. The Crown took interest in navigation. As in astronomy and exploration, it helped finance (and shared the profit) of the voyages, but it did not set up a national schema or national school for navigators, and only later one for sea-officers.

In the late fifteenth and early sixteenth centuries, the kings of Portugal and Spain had established a scientific and formal approach to explore the sea and train the sea-officers. John II of Portugal in 1484 convened a commission of mathematical experts to work out a method of finding latitude by solar observation. It drew up a greatly simplified version of the tables of Zacuto, a Jewish astronomer at Salamanca, brought them up-to-date and devised a fixed procedure to enable an intelligent and literate seaman to use them. This was one of the first instances in modern Europe where the state deliberately employed a group of scientists to apply theoretical knowledge to the solution of an urgent practical problem. The result was conveniently summarized in a manual which was circulated in manuscript and several printings. To train navigators in celestial navigation and to license them for the East and West Indian voyages, both Portugal and Spain established schools of navigation early in the sixteenth century, one in connection with the *Casa da India* at Lisbon, the other in the *Casa de la Contratación* at Seville where Amerigo Vespucci and Sebastian Cabot taught as pilots major (Parry 1963: 94–96). England succeeded finally in enlisting the aging Cabot for her service, but she did not establish a school or a license system. A plan to introduce a chief pilot also to England with the task to certify the ability of the pilots, master mates, boatswains and quartermasters was not carried out, although a man already had been chosen (Oppenheim 1896: 149, 154). Neither did England employ royal cartographers as did Portugal and Spain in order to verify their explorations (Parry 1963: 104–105).

The English navigation remained backward until the 1570s. The French had acquired the new techniques before the English. Up to the middle of the sixteenth century, England produced no nautical treatises, instruments, or sea charts comparable to the Portuguese, Spanish or French ones. Englishmen did not yet command "the art of the astrolabe." For their Atlantic adventures they had to hire foreign pilots. But by the last decade of the century they sailed often unaided, and soon afterwards English pilots navigated Dutch fleets. Ten years of teaching by Sebastian Cabot and the mathematician

Dr. Dee had sufficed to train some first-class navigators like Richard Chancellor who discovered the Arctic route to Russia, or the brothers Stephen and William Borough (the latter succeeding Chancellor as chief pilot of the Muscovy Company and surveying and charting the White Sea with its coastlines) or John Davis who became the greatest scientific navigator in the latter part of the century.

At the same time the interest in the new sciences and techniques grew in England. Spanish works on navigation were translated into English, sponsored by the Muscovy Company, not the government. In 1574 the first important indigenous treatise in navigation appeared, William Bourne's *Regiment of the Sea*, which was followed by the *Variation of the Compass* by the same author and Captain John Davis' *The Seaman's Secrets* (1594). In 1600 Richard Hakluyt acquainted his countrymen with the *Principal Navigations, Voyages and Discoveries of the English Nation*, mathematicians and astronomers published the result of their research for naval application, and Robert Recorde's textbook *The Whetstone of Witte*, dedicated to the Governors of the Muscovy Company, "brought mathematics out of the scholar's closet into the merchant's counting house and into the sea-captain's cabin" (Waters 1958: 95).

In the second half of the sixteenth century, English instrument makers also acquired their skill for precision work which in the following two centuries proved to be so vital for the economic and technological advance of Britain. In the seventeenth century some of them cooperated with mathematicians and astronomers at Gresham College or the Royal Society and provided them with the precision instruments which were needed for empirical verification of the "new sciences." Theory and practice of hydrography and cartography were taken up successfully in England. But nowhere was the hand of government particularly felt. "Compared with the Spanish system, with its pronounced emphasis on governmental control, regular instruction at an official school of navigation, and careful regimentation, the English approach to the problems of the new age was flexible and individualistic" (Marcus 1961: 66). The Crown encouraged leading seamen like Hawkins, Drake, and Frobisher to apprentice young gentlemen in their craft by taking them to sea and hoped to secure thus a sufficient "store of skylful Pilotes" in the country to advance its commerce and sea power (Waters 1958: 114). Even the certification of masters and pilots competent to undertake oceanic voyages was left to a corporation of seamen, Trinity House, which in 1565, among other privileges, received the right to examine future pilots.

At the beginning of the sixteenth century, the captain of a man-of-war was still an army officer, not a seaman; and the conduct of war at sea was regarded a different matter from the sailing of the ship. The one was done by soldiers, the other by seamen. With the growing importance of naval gunnery, war at sea changed its character; the art of sailing and the technique of gunning became integrated parts of one manoeuvre. The gentlemen captains had to learn seamanship, and the master and his sailors had to learn to fight while sailing. At the end of the century some of the commanders like Drake were professional seamen. As sailors learned to use guns, soldiers became rare on the ships. The "lessons of homogeneous manning and unified command, like the lessons of the great guns," which kept the combatting fleets at distances, "gained acceptance only gradually" everywhere. But it was decisive for England's future that the Spaniards and the Portuguese learned them more slowly than the English and the Dutch (Parry 1963: 123). One lesson the English gentleman officer had to learn when at sea was naval discipline. "I must have," wrote Drake, "the gentleman to haul and to draw with the mariner, and the mariner with the gentleman. If you come on board my ships, you shall obey my officers, whoever you are, and whoever they are" (Lewis 1939: 45).

Under the early Stuarts the nonprofessional officer without much naval experience prevailed again, however, and it was not until the turn of the seventeenth century that the professionalization of the Navy really was carried through. "There were gentlemen and there were seamen," wrote Macaulay about the Navy of Charles II. "But the seamen were not gentlemen and the gentlemen were not seamen" (Macaulay 1913–1915: vol. 1, 294). The seamen, called "tarpaulin officers," had no high social standing. Most were employed by the Royal Navy only in wartime, and even then only for eight to nine months a year, since in winter ships lay in dockyards to be repaired. However, since 1668 the flag officers received half pay during peace time, and gradually this system was extended to the lower ranks. Furthermore, after 1672 pensions were instituted for officers who had served for fifteen years. Junior officers like masters, boatswains, pursers, gunners, carpenters, and cooks received "rigging wages" which amounted to about half of the pay (Ehrman 1953: 139–140). Half pay at first was regarded like pensions mainly as reward for past services; more and more it became, however, a provision for future service in order "to have always a Competent Number of Experienced Sea-Officers, supported on Shore, who be within reach to answer any sudden or immergent Occasion," as an Order in Council put it in 1700 (Baugh 1965: 103). These reserve officers were forbidden to hold any other public employment, to go abroad—hence they could not enter the merchant marine; they had to keep the Admiralty informed of their residences and could be called upon to reside near the dockyards and assist in fitting out ships. They had, in short, to "at all times be ready to obey orders." In 1713 half pay was extended to virtually all commissioned officers. Two years later the Navy Reserve Officers Corps consisted of 4 admirals, 188 captains, and 261 lieutenants (Baugh 1965: 104). The system of half pay secured the Crown enough officers and seamen for emergencies, but it did not in itself create an officer corps. The "tarpaulin-officers" complained that gentleman officers entered above their heads, brought the manners of the court to the Navy and did not know their job. Charles II introduced, therefore, in 1676 the system of "volunteers per-order," designed to encourage "families of better quality to breed up their younger sons to the art and practice of navigation"; if they were sixteen—actually many entered earlier—they were attached to a captain who had to teach them. At the same time a more theoretical preparation was devised for boys of lower social standing. In 1673 a foundation for "forty poor boys" was established, to be taught and instructed in the art of navigation (Lewis 1939: 227). But these "mathematical boys" never were regarded as equally well-trained as the volunteers, the "King's letter boys," and only few future officers chose this way of entry into the navy (Ehrman 1953: 140–143). The "King's letter boys," consequently counted for 48 percent of all officers who passed the entrance examination between 1702 and 1712. Forty-four percent were still merchant mariners, only 16 percent belonged to neither category; they usually entered as servants of sea officers (Baugh 1965: 98, Table 5).

An examination had been introduced in 1677 to get rid of such volunteers, "who having passed some time superficially at sea, and being related to families of interest at court, do obtain lieutenancies before they are fitted for it" (Baugh 1965: 100–101; Lewis 1939: 221). A three-year minimum was required at sea, two of the years as volunteer-per-order and the third as midshipman. This apprenticeship was prolonged to four years in 1703 and to six in 1722. Unlike the requirement of a minimum age (which was raised to twenty years) apprenticeship could hardly be circumvented.

For the instruction of the young gentlemen the navy took schoolmasters aboard around 1700 who before appointment had to pass an examination of the Master and Brethren of Trinity House. The schoolmasters were expected to instruct not only the volunteers, but also "the other youths of the ship" in navigation, mathematics, and writing. But the officers did not appreciate their services and often avoided to take one aboard. At the end of the seventeenth century, the idea of a public school for the navy was developed; but nothing came out of it until the Admiralty decided in 1729 to erect a naval academy for volunteers-per-order. From 1733 onward up to forty sons of noblemen and gentlemen between the ages of thirteen to sixteen could be instructed at Portsmouth. They had to pass an entrance examination in mathematics, and to complete a "Plan of Mathematical Learning" before they received a certificate. The maximum time allowed was three years. Only twenty students attended the Academy on the average and only ten percent of the officers were recruited this way. The rest still went along the old apprenticeship lines, since the volunteer scheme was abolished in 1730. The old distrust of theoretical learning remained; so did the fear that a career was not secure if a young man did not have the patronage of somebody in office. Thus the patronage system remained with the Navy in spite of the built-in features of a merit system (Lewis 1939: 87–90, 272–280; Baugh 1965: 94–100, 123, 299). Compared with other departments of public service, the navy had gone, however, far toward the development of a true professional officer corps. A regulated entrance and training, permanent employment and pay including a superannuation scheme, this all was introduced around 1700, while most other services (with the exception of the colonial service) had to wait until the reforms of the nineteenth century (Lewis 1939: 51).

The question remains how the English naval technology and administration and its personnel compared with that on the continent. After all, Britain ruled the waves. Having done away with Spanish superiority late in the sixteenth century, she successfully fought the Dutch fleet in the seventeenth and the French fleet in the eighteenth century. What made the British Navy superior? Many observers state that Dutch shipbuilding was better than the English for most of the seventeenth century. The English merchant marine found it easier to put Dutch-built merchant ships, bought or captured, into service rather than to improve their own methods of shipbuilding. In this respect, "it was the naval dockyards, building larger ships and disposing larger resources which stood out as leaders in the technology of large-scale shipbuilding" (Wilson 1965: 171). In 1688 the naval dockyards were "the most comprehensive and in some respects the largest industry in the country" (Ehrman 1953: 174; Coleman 1953: 134–135). Nevertheless, French shipbuilding was regarded as more scientific and leading to better results. In the late seventeenth century, conscientious officials in the English Naval Administration had Louis XIV's *Ordonnance du Roi pour les Armées Navales* translated for their private use (Ehrman 1953: 172); in the middle of the eighteenth century they regarded the French vessels as "faster, better-proportioned, and class for class, larger and more powerful than their British opponents" (Marcus 1961: 340).

If not technology—what else counted for British superiority? The experts agree that one reason was that England commanded larger resources, another that the Navy was highly valued in national life which enabled it to attract enough able young men with ample experience at sea. Both led to a superiority of the officer corps. "The average Dutch sailor was a first-class seaman, but an indifferent officer. The Dutch crews were on the whole inferior to the English in training, discipline and morale" (Marcus 1961: 138). The same holds true in comparison with the French. Thus a historian of the English Navy concludes: "The naval superiority of Great Britain depended upon the excellence of the personnel, rather than that of the matériel . . . Perhaps the greatest and most decisive factor of all was the British superiority in the quality of the officers . . . They formed the permanent, effective *cadre* of the service; they were imbued with the strongest sense of professional pride and *esprit de corps*: even in time of peace there were large numbers of them continuously at sea —far more than was the case with the Bourbon navies" (Marcus 1961: 362). Another expert agrees: "British officers generally fought more boldly and more competently. British captains handled their ships, British admirals their squadrons, more aggressively and more expertly" (Baugh 1965: 145).

The technical expertise of the British Army was not as crucial to the country as that of the Navy. The pattern of training of its officers was, however, similar. Again in contrast with the Continent, England developed no formal organization of training, e.g., for the gunners. While Spain had established artillery training schools before the end of the sixteenth century and France had made artillery a mathematically based art, the English Board of Ordnance left design and manufacture of cannon to the experience and ingenuity of the iron founders, "expecting no more than the equality of new guns with those already in existence" (Hall 1952: 17). From time to time, the Crown instructed the officers of the Board of Ordnance to test the value of inventions presented to it. This was the task of the Master Gunner of England and the Firemaster. They experimented, sometimes in the presence of the king or members of the royal family, and with the assistance of mathematicians of the Royal Society. One Master Gunner competed frequently with French and Dutch gunners at Woolwich arsenal where the first ordnance laboratory was set up. The later Stuart period with its active interest of the royal family in naval and military affairs and the close connection between scientists, mechanics and military technicians promoted military technology more than ever before.

The Ordnance Board was responsible for the training of the technical officers who had to learn to construct and to destroy fortifications and to employ guns, mortars, fireworks and mines. The Tudors and earlier Stuarts had employed foreigners in the more technical branches of military service; Sir Charles Moore in the reign of Charles II was the first Englishman to attain the same reputation as the French and Dutch experts. He was a surveyor of the ordnance, a fellow of the Royal Society and an author of books on mathematics, fortification and gunnery. During his service a regular training of artillery officers began. A royal warrant of 1685 provided that "divers of our subjects should be well educated and instructed in the art of an engineer and thereby fitted for our service in our fortifications or elsewhere" (Hall 1952: 20). While in the 1660s complaints about the incompetence of gunners were frequent and the Master Gunner was ordered to train them regularly and dismiss the incompetent ones, by the end of the seventeenth century the technical functions in the army were almost exclusively exercised by officers who had received some training in mathematics and mechanics. Technically qualified officers became more and more the backbone of the middle ranks in the army; by the middle of the eighteenth century the scientific side of gunnery had been so far developed that the bottlenecks were the manufacturing methods which continued on traditional lines. An efficient combination of scientific knowledge, metallurgical skill and military tactics was nowhere achieved, either in France which attracted the best gun founders from many countries and had the best artillery school or in England where the trial-and-error method prevailed.

This failure to implement theory in practice raises the question about the role of science and scientific institutions like the Royal Academy or Gresham College for the technological development. No agreement has been reached on this issue among recent scholars.[29] There is certainly no clear-cut or even one-way causal relationship. For the question of the training of technical personnel the relationship between scientists, government servants and technicians matters. The evidence for such connections is great. England in the sixteenth and seventeenth centuries was a small country with a big capital in which all kinds of men easily could and did meet. Gentlemen and amateur scientists enjoyed the company of "professionals." Navigators and cartographers asked for the help of mathematicians, astronomers, and mechanics. Scientists needed the help of the instrument makers, and the most ingenious of the mechanics showed no contempt for theoretical learning. There were few formal relations before the foundation of the Royal Society in 1660; but interested people attended the lectures of the professors of Gresham College, which was opened in 1597 according to a bequest of Sir Thomas Gresham, the Tudor financier and founder of the Royal Exchange. Here seven professors taught such subjects as astronomy, geometry, and physics. After the lectures and in addition to them, social gatherings and scientific discussions took place out of which the Royal Society was born. Unlike its French counterpart, the Royal Society was not an institution in which salaried scientists worked, but a private gathering of professional and amateur scientists, a platform for exchanging ideas.

Members of both institutions, Gresham College and the Royal Society, and the first Savilian professors of natural science in Oxford and Cambridge had close working contact to many of the government technicians.[30] To take but one example: Henry Briggs, first professor of geometry at Gresham and later first Savilian Professor of Geometry at Oxford, communicated with master shipwrights of the royal dockyards and the mathematician John Wells, Keeper of the Naval Stores at Deptford. Briggs acted as a referee in a dispute

---

[29] English scholars usually deny any great influence for the seventeenth and eighteenth centuries. See, e.g., Hall 1952: 21–22. Also Mathias 1969: 30–33. In favor of this influence argue A. E. Musson and Eric Robinson (Musson and Robinson 1969).

[30] The professorships were founded in 1619 by Sir Henry Savile.

about the design of new ships. He helped in preparing voyages and was a friend of the royal compass- and dial-maker. Many other examples could be added, and there can be no doubt that "the close understanding and co-operation between scholarly scientist and technician was an outstanding characteristic of the scientific movement in England from 1550 onwards" (Johnson 1968:291).[31]

Not less important, however, is the fact that noblemen and great officers promoted the rise of applied sciences, not only as patrons but sometimes also as active researchers. Cuthbert Tunstall, Master of the Rolls under Henry VIII and later Bishop of London and Durham, wrote a textbook on arithmetic (in Latin); in Thomas More's large household mathematics and astronomy were considered to be principal subjects of study, and the noted mathematician Nichols Katzer tutored More's children in astronomy. When John Dee in the third quarter of the sixteenth century assembled a large scientific library in his house near London, it became a center not only for scholars and instrument makers who looked for advice, but also for the great merchants who sought his counsel before voyages, and for members of Elizabeth's court and council who came to study chemistry with him. Lord Burghley, Elizabeth's chief minister, tried to promote both the sciences and scientists. On his request, William Bourne wrote a short treatise on the properties and qualities of glasses for optical purposes. Digges, one of the greatest mathematicians of his time, was called into the service of his country as a military engineer, first to supervise the fortifications at Dover, later as Muster-Master-General of the English forces in The Netherlands. When Spain prepared for the Armada and England feared invasion, the mayor and his aldermen of the city set up mathematical lectures for the officers of the trained bands to help prepare the defense of the city. In 1589–1590 an order of the Privy Council prolonged them for at least two years (Johnson 1968: 199–205). Thus, in effect, the first public lectures in mathematics in England were given for military purposes.

It is true that government as such seldom promoted and never organized science in the sixteenth and seventeenth centuries in England. But where the government as an institution failed, some of the great officers like Philip Sidney, Leicester, Lord Burghley and Sir Walter Raleigh stepped in. Each of Raleigh's voyages was also a scientific expedition, and one of them resulted in an early example of large-

[31] See also Taylor 1930; 1956; 1954; Waters 1958; Wright 1935; Hill 1965.

scale economic and statistical survey: Hariot's "Brief and True Report of the New Found Land of Virginia" (1588) (Hill 1965: 131–224).

The great scheme, however, which was devised in 1572 to provide scientifically trained servants of the Crown, was never realized, because Queen Elizabeth, short of money, "did all by halves" as Raleigh commented (Hill 1965: 159; Johnson 1968: 197). Men like John Dee, Sir Humphrey Gilbert, or Richard Hakluyt had pleaded for the "erection of an Academy in London for education of Her Majestes Wardes and other youths, of nobility and gentlemen" in mathematics and engineering, to apply this knowledge to military fortification, gunnery, geography, and navigation in the queen's service. It took another century before the English government employed scientific methods of rational calculation for its administration, through civil servants like Sir William Petty, the great political economist, and before Oliver Cromwell could advise his son: "Study mathematics and cosmography; . . . these fit for public service for which a man is born" (Hill 1965: 68).

FRANCE AND PRUSSIA

The strong absolutist tradition of both France and Prussia had its concomitant economic theory and economic policy: mercantilism which may be defined as entrepreneurship of the state in a very comprehensive sense. The administration thereby aimed at a sort of general management covering activities in fields like science, technology, education, military services, public works, manufacturing, and trade. To direct, encourage, or develop these fields of action, expert knowledge was required which was clearly beyond that of administrators such as *officiers* or *commissaires*. But these people could define the problem and seek for an institutional solution which, no wonder, laid much more stress on public service than was the case in Britain.

When it was clear that a strong economy meant everything in the international competition for power, one might have concluded that principles of science and technology would have to be applied to practical fields hitherto merely guided by tradition; that the enlightenment necessary for this development might be achieved by education; that education might be the only promising means for a latecoming nation if it wanted to imitate the forerunner. These circumstances gave birth to a third type of public servant, the *fonctionnaire*, the technical expert who never belonged exclusively to the public service but gradually began to play a significant role in private enterprise. This kind of technical personnel is functionally defined by its expert knowledge which it usually gets by education, at least in the cases of France and Prussia. Therefore, it is appropriate to follow an approach of institutional history, i.e., to ask for the formation of technical personnel by educational provisions for diffusion of science and technology. Strong parallels between France and Prussia, as far as the institutional set is concerned, suggest a combined consideration. The common traits seem yet to give way to divergent developments, if the France after 1789 and the Prussia after 1806 are compared.

The traditional institution of higher learning existing since the Middle Ages has been the university (Ornstein 1963: 220ff.; Taton 1964: 13ff.). During the seventeenth, and to a lesser degree, the eighteenth centuries, however, French and German/Prussian universities were kept under the rule of the faculties of theology and clung to classical education within the faculty of arts. Nevertheless universities served the state as much as they offered professional training for law, medicine, and theology. Surprisingly it was Prussia which, in 1727, established the first chairs for cameralism. The Prussian administrators thus had to acquire some knowledge in economics, technology, statistics, and natural science, in addition to law. This state of affairs may perhaps explain why Prussia did not feel the need for technical civil service as early and as urgently as France apparently did. Apart from cameralism or "technology" (in the sense of the cameralists) the representation of mathematics and natural sciences was very poor at the university level. It is justified to state that the scientific revolution of the seventeenth century was largely happening outside the universities and was therefore connected with an organizational revolution: the professionalization of science and its diffusion via learned societies (Hahn 1971: 1ff.).

The French learned society in question is the Academy of Sciences. Only second to the Royal Society, as far as its dating is concerned, it was of profoundly different character. Its mere establishment, in 1666, meant the transformation of a private gathering of scientists into a royal institution of employed and salaried scientists. The concept of professionalized science shared by the members of the Academy coincided with the interests of Colbert's France: to have an advisory council of scientific experts; to draw on their knowledge and research in order to improve navigation, warfare, architecture, engineering; to have the economic policy assisted by systematic application of science to industry and by diffusion of technological knowledge. Under these circumstances, the Academy of Sciences rapidly developed toward the supreme "arbiter of scientific and technological activity" within the French kingdom (Hahn 1969a: chap. 1; cf. Hahn 1969: 231). Its major instruments were the printing privilege for scientific work and the issuance of patent rights for technological work (Hahn 1971: 60ff.).

The close cooperation between administrative and technical personnel can clearly be seen in the history of the Academy of Sciences. We may even speak of the transition or juncture between the worlds of *la robe* and the *fonctionnaires*. If we remember what has been said about the administrative machinery of the established absolutist state, it was the comptroller-general and his *intendants* who tried to enlarge their original field of competence, i.e., fiscal administration, toward the full range of inner politics. The department of the comptroller-general accordingly comprised divisions such as "rivers and forests," "bridges and highways," "powder and saltpeter," and, most important, the "bureau of commerce." This bureau was made up of four *intendants* of commerce each in charge of a certain industrial branch and a number of *généralités*. The decision-making process within the bureau of commerce concerned the following issues: "(1) questions about the access of the factory to fuel, raw material, market, labor, and transportation; (2) principles governing the tests of new processes, the imposition of zoning rules, the regulation of methods of labor and of manufacturing methods, and the granting of such encouragements as to cut wood for fuel, exclusive privileges to manufacture, imposition of tariffs and tolls, and exemption from tariffs and tolls; (3) policies to be pursued for each region and each major industry; and (4) assumptions regarding the nature of the kingdom, the interrelations of agriculture, industry, and commerce, and the necessity of a favorable balance of trade" (Parker 1965: 89).

It is perfectly understandable that French administrators needed informed counsel for their decisions. Once the Academy of Sciences had been established we find a fairly close collaboration between administrators and scientists. Colbert initiated this tradition by instructing, in 1675, the Academy to begin what later became the famous *Descriptions des arts et métiers*. The regulations of 1699 legalized the Academy's position of granting patent rights exclusively. Specific requests for investigations and experiments were laid upon the Academy or individual academicians from 1725 onward. There were academicians serving as permanent consultants to the bureaucracy or to the state's manufactories (Parker 1965; Hahn 1971: 68ff.).

Scientists thus played a key role, via the Academy, in determining the decisions of the administration. This holds especially true for commerce, where the central administration was less hampered by existing competences of *officiers* and therefore could achieve more than merely inspecting and reporting. With regard to state- and nation-building we may join in stating: "France became the first nation to make scientific research a career and to recognize that the possession of highly skilled manpower was a basic factor in national power" (Gilpin 1968: 95). This high evaluation of the scientists of the Old France found its organizational concomitant in the integration of scientists into the social order of the day. The hierarchical structure of the Academy of Sciences (including its co-optative recruitment policy), the privileges ensuing from membership in the Academy, the ennoblement of some *fonctionnaires* show that these people were not socially diverted from the world of *la robe* (Hahn 1971: 72ff.; Taton 1964: 367; Reinhard 1956: 25). At the same time the *Ancien Régime* set the powerful French tradition of employing scientists (and engineers/technicians) as state functionaries, a tradition often imitated but nowhere surpassed.

If we turn to Prussia, we see the Berlin Academy of Sciences established in 1700, after decades of planning and urging by Leibniz. The celebrated founder wanted to combine *theoriam cum praxi* in order to improve not only arts and sciences but country and people, agriculture, manufacture and commerce (Harnack 1900: vol. 1.1, 81). But nothing significant happened in this direction. And when under Frederick II the Berlin Academy had a first peak of activity acknowledged in the world of science, scientists had no influence whatsoever upon the direction of public affairs (Harnack 1900: vol. 1.1, 308). Notwithstanding this general statement the main biographer of the Academy enumerates some activities of the academicians related to practical purposes: lectures on forestry, mining, natural sciences, astronomy; expert judgments on questions of theoretical and applied sciences as well as on inventions and discoveries of all kind; proposing prize subjects and awarding the prizes (Harnack 1900: vol. 1.1, 384ff.). Lack of research into the history of the Berlin Academy may hinder a more favorable or at least substantiated judgment, but Frederick William III argued in 1798, that the Academy failed to take care of improving the mechanical arts (Harnack 1900: vol. 1.2, 528).

Two years before this the so-called Technical Deputation (Matschoss 1911; Straube 1931) was established as part of the Department of Manufactures. After its reorganization, in 1811, the Technical Deputation assumed many of the functions that the Paris Academy had fulfilled before the French Revolution. Though chronologically belonging to another time period we will give attention to the Technical Deputation within the present context for systematical reasons. The mere fact of doing so may indicate the belatedness of Prussia as compared to France. The Deputation consisted mainly of officials in the fields of administration, science, and technology. Their principal occupation was to advise the administration of industry and commerce on all matters demanding special knowledge and to develop practical devices for promoting industry. The larger part of the Deputation's daily work was devoted to matters of patent rights. But there are other close parallels to the Academy: the organization of a library including the international journals on technology; the establishment of laboratories and workshops; the collection of models, machines and products covering the whole range of technology.

The most characteristic name for this kind of collection was chosen for the French prototype. The *Conservatoire des arts et métiers* (Artz 1966: 143ff.) clearly surpassed the collections of the Technical Deputation. It could draw on the collections of the Paris Academy, of Vaucanson's (1775), and others' when it was formally organized in 1794. This industrial museum set the pattern of a fortunate combination of exhibitions, research facilities, and lecturing, but without the rigor of any well-defined college. Such a pattern was perhaps of optimal appeal to people (such as artisans) eager to acquire some technological knowledge but never thinking of becoming a state *fonctionnaire* in the technical service. The state, however, especially if we go back to the *Ancien Régime*, could not be content to have its administration guided by experts on scientific and technological matters; to see the question of granting patent rights handled properly. Administration of an absolutist and mercantilist state needed a technical field service. First, therefore, the diffusion of scientific and technologcial knowledge, which hitherto was given at random as a by-product of the Academy's work, had to be rigorously organized: hence the birth of technical colleges. Second, this technological education aimed primarily at creating state corps of technical personnel (either civil or military): hence the relatively poor provisions for vocational education of the working people.

Military service dates back as long as states exist, and it often involved certain techniques which required some professional education, not to speak of the old relations between warfare and scientific research. The particular military techniques of the West-European state-building period were, roughly speaking, fortifications and artillery. This business brought in two kinds of specialists within the armies, the *génie*-officer (i.e., military engineer) and the artillerist. In both fields France gave the example of training technical personnel via military technical colleges.[32]

Before establishing, however, the later famous *École du génie* (Taton 1964: 559ff.) at Mézières (in 1748), the *corps du génie militaire* was already organized under Vauban, the first great French military engineer who became appointed Inspector General of Fortresses, at the time of Colbert and Louis XIV. The hitherto not regulated recruitment into the corps was bound, in 1697, on passing entrance examinations before Vauban as examiner. Candidates had to look for private opportunities of preparation, until finally the college was established. We may perceive the typical pattern of development in the recruitment practices of the technical corps: (1) admittance into the corps and training-on-the-job afterward; (2) admittance only after passing entrance examinations: hence formal education either privately or through the newly established college. It is not necessary to say that after some time the college again started to limit admission by entrance examinations which accordingly brought preparatory institutions into existence (like the pensions in Paris of the eighteenth century).

The *École du génie* of Mézières achieved high reputation for fine and advanced education, centering on pure and applied mathematics. The college was unrivaled throughout Europe and must be considered as the direct ancestor of the still more famous *École polytechnique* of 1795. As far as artillery is concerned, the second technical service of the military, several schools were established in 1720, and an advanced college in 1756, at LaFère. Of less brilliance than

---

[32] There is no room to touch the general military education. Cf. Taton 1964: 513; Bien 1971.

the sister college of engineering, this *École des élèves* was highly restricted to young nobles who also received preferential treatment at the *École du génie* (Taton 1964: 513ff.; for the officers of the navy cf. 547ff.).

The Prussian corps of military engineers was organized in 1729, but never reached any appreciation on account of high standing during the eighteenth century (von Bonin 1877; von Poten 1896). Regarding the huge Prussian Army, the number of engineer-officers (some sixty at the end of the century) has to be considered small in comparison to the French *corps du génie* of some three hundred officers. A modest attempt to establish an *École de (!) génie* at Berlin, in 1775, under a French professor, did not improve the situation, nor did the opening, in 1788, of an academy for military engineering bring much progress. The same or even a worse picture is to be seen with regard to artillery. Only in 1791 an academy was set up. Thus we have to conclude that Prussia was far behind France as far as the formation of technical personnel within the military realm is concerned. It is only the Prussia after Napoleon's defeat which catches up and gains credit in this respect, similar to what has been said about the respective academies of sciences and the industrial museums.

The major technical service within the civil realm and of crucial importance to the modernizing state comprises civil engineering and architecture (other important branches not being dealt with in this paper are: mining, hydrography, geography, ammunition). Here again France is the pioneer according to the familiar pattern: first creating the corps, then establishing the college. At the time of Colbert the king appointed individual engineers or architects and held them responsible for public works. This state of affairs led, in 1716, to the constitution of the *corps des ponts et chaussées*, like the *corps du génie* of hierarchical structure and distributed into the *généralités* of the kingdom of France. Highways and bridges were, as we remember, part of the comptroller-general's department. Consequently it was an *intendant* of finance, from the *la robe* family of the *Trudaines*, who initiated the beginnings of the *École des ponts et chaussées* (Taton 1964: 343ff.) in 1747.

The founding of this celebrated and unique college is rather interesting since it shows again the precise point, where administrative and technical personnel came together. The practical task to cope with during the 1740s consisted of the general planning and design

[551]

of highways for the kingdom of France. The engineers of the *corps des ponts et chaussées*, appointed to the *généralités*, had to submit their regional designs to the central administration of bridges and highways according to a uniform pattern of information needed. Trudaine as head of the administrative division must not have been satisfied with the result. In 1747 he ordered one of his outstanding engineers, Perronet, who was engineer of the *généralité* of Alençon, to reorganize the bureau of design at Paris, which had been established a few years before. Perronet continued to have the students make cartographical work but included some scientific and technical education. Again reorganized in 1775, by Turgot, the now *École des ponts et chaussées*, still under the direction of Perronet, requested a high standard in theoretical mathematics from its graduates, only comparable to the *École de génie* of the time. It is obvious that the college for civil engineering did not offer technical education to the general public but only to students who filled already the lower ranks of the state corps of engineers. We may summarize that there are close common traits between the history of civil and military technical education in France.

The respective history of civil technical engineering in Prussia follows a similar pattern, though at a later time and of less military-like orientation. The last point is made clear, if one does not find a Prussian state corps of civil engineers. On the other hand, however, Prussian "building officials" form a strong part of the administration and thereby participate in the general pattern of Prussian bureaucracy with its hierarchical structure and rigor of qualifications. The oldest institution which offered some education in the field of civil engineering was the Berlin academy of arts, established in 1696 (Simon 1902: 642ff.; Dobbert 1899: 11ff.). Its fields were painting, sculpture, and architecture. The architectural branch was yet but a stepchild within the academy. When Frederick II tried to establish an *École de génie* for his military engineers (1775) he made a separate class of architecture to be constituted. Since this was very unsatisfactory, the academy of architecture (*Bauakademie*) (Dobbert 1899; Straube 1931) was finally established in 1799. This meant for the first time a comprehensive theoretical education for future building officials, comprising mathematics, mechanics, physics, hydraulics, drawing, a.s.o. Thus we find in the end of Old Prussia a college comparable to the old *École des ponts et chaussées* which at this time had already undergone the changes of the Revolution.

It should be noted that the term "academy" within the Prussian/ German realm corresponds to "college." It is only the Academy of Sciences which refers to a learned society like the numerous French academies. On the other hand we learn that the French *Académie d'architecture* of 1671 may in fact be considered as "the first higher technical school in France" (Artz 1966: 33). Probably it narrowed itself to a learned society while the *École des ponts et chaussées* took its place as a college for civil engineering. Reviewing the eighteenth century as far as technical personnel is concerned France is characterized by (1) organizing civil and military engineers into state corps; (2) establishing colleges for their technical education; (3) setting high standards especially in theoretical knowledge. Prussia's development starts later and attains lower and more modest achievements. In fact it catches up with France only in the nineteenth century, which deserves special interest since it finally led to France's losing its leading position.

At a first glance Prussia seems to achieve, in the early nineteenth century, a pattern and level of technical education for its technical field service (military and civil engineering) which corresponds to the French model before the Revolution. The *Bauakademie* which was established only in 1799 successively raised its standards and continued to educate primarily "building officials." The entrance qualifications comprised knowledge in Latin and French which meant that the students had to attend the *Gymnasium* (grammar school) before entering college. The recruitment possibilities were still further narrowed by awarding special scholarships to sons of Prussian building officials (Dobbert 1899: 43). When Beuth became director of the *Bauakademie* (1831–1845) he redefined the curriculum very closely to the needs of the hierarchy within the civil engineering service. Only in 1849 the college was reorganized with free choice of courses being introduced. This development finally led to the establishment of the *Technische Hochschule* (technical college) in 1879.

The *Bauakademie* of 1799 to 1849 may be compared to the old *École des ponts et chaussées*. The latter college had by now undergone a profound change as part of the overall reorganization of education in general and technical education in particular during the French Revolution. The major achievement in the realm of technical education was the clear division between (1) a general scientific education to be given by the *École polytechnique* (1795) and considered as the common basis for all technical branches; and (2) a specific technical education to be given by the various *Écoles d'application* after attendance of the *École polytechnique*. The concept of the *École polytechnique* was as ingenious as the brilliance of the teachers and students at the college was unmatched. The overwhelming majority of the graduates went into three services: artillery, military and civil engineering (Marièlle 1855: tableau c). Thus the reorganized *École des ponts et chaussées* was one of the major *Écoles d'application* which consequently set higher standards than the Berlin *Bauakademie* of the time prior to 1849 or 1879. Prussian authorities must have realized this since they thought of reorganizing the *Bauakademie*, in 1817, into a sort of polytechnical college (Dobbert 1899: 41).

As a matter of fact military officials joined those of other departments in favoring the establishment of an *École polytechnique* at Berlin, but they did not succeed (Manegold 1966). The military interests in this matter were clearly influenced by the French example. Graduates of the *École polytechnique* who wanted either to join the army or had to do so (more than fifty percent) went to the *École d'artillerie* and *École de génie* which were combined, in 1802, to form the second major *École d'application*. On similar lines the Prussian United Artillery and Engineering College was organized in 1816, but again there was no *École polytechnique* for preparation. This state of affairs leads us to the conclusion, that as far as civil and military engineering is concerned Prussia followed the French model of the time before 1789 during the first half of the nineteenth century. The Prussian colleges for the training of technical public servants never reached the high standing of the respective French institutions of the time up to 1850.

But this is only one half of the story. The powerful and lasting tradition of recruitment for state service, the attraction of high-level education in scientific and technical matters upon intellectually outstanding students—this self-reinforcing combination led to an overloaded accumulation of technical personnel within the realm of public service and was eventually harmful to the needs of industrialization. We cannot go into details with regard to this complicated matter, but the following exposition will present its general outlines.

Where could people who did not intend to enter public service acquire scientific and technological knowledge useful for manufacturing and trades? Universities did not play any remarkable role in these fields either in France or in Prussia, though it has to be stressed that German universities became leading in natural sciences in the latter two thirds of the nineteenth century.[33] Colleges such as the Prussian academies of arts and of architecture were never as exclusively confined to public servants as their French counterparts. In addition there were schools of arts set up in the late eighteenth century to give artisans some basic instruction in mathematics and, above all, in drawing (Simon 1902: 657ff.; Thyssen 1954: 42ff.). This kind of vocational school is to be found in France, too. The leading school of design was established in 1767 and offered courses to 1500 students using a rotary system of attendance (Taton 1964: 441ff.). The beginnings of the French vocational schools proper were laid by the Duc de la Rochefoucauld who founded a trade school in 1788 which became the prototype of the *écoles d'arts et métiers* (Artz 1966: 133ff.; Léon 1968: 77ff., 177ff., 205ff., 241ff.). Up to 1850 only three of these trade schools were founded which gradually raised their standards.

Apparently the pattern of advanced technical education via the *École polytechnique* (with its graduates mostly entering public service); and of the somewhat modest vocational education via the few *écoles d'arts et métiers* could not satisfy the need of the growing French industry for advanced technical personnel. Therefore, the *École centrale des arts et manufactures* (Guillet 1929) was founded in 1829, by cooperation of one distinguished administrative official, two professors and one artillery officer. Only in 1857 the state took over this college which was the first training institution in French history solely aiming at supplying high-level manpower in the fields of mechanics, construction, metallurgy, and chemistry for the purposes of private industry.

Prussia shows a different picture with regard to promoting industry by investment in education. As yet the existing schools of arts of the late eighteenth century did not benefit from the secular reforms of Prussian general and technical education after the breakdown of Prussia. The energetic Beuth preferred to start once more right from the beginning, and in doing so he laid his main emphasis on the central college in preference to the provincial schools. Thus Prussia, while backward compared to France in the realm of technical edu-

[33] On nineteenth-century universities cf. Guerlac 1951: 81ff.; Ben-David and Zloczower 1962: 45ff.; Gilpin 1968; Manegold 1970.

cation for public service, preceded France with regard to technicians for industry, when the *Gewerbeinstitut* (Straube 1931; Lundgreen 1972) was established in 1821. The modest beginnings of this college are perhaps best illustrated by the fact that both the *Bauakademie* and the *Gewerbeinstitut* offered courses in civil engineering. But no graduate of the *Gewerbeinstitut* would have been admitted as a construction official into the civil service. On the other side it is precisely these circumstances which Beuth had in mind. He intentionally aimed at improving the technological knowledge of small artisans without requesting undue entrance qualifications. Gradually, however, his college shifted toward education of technicians who later became employees in the textile and metal-working industries as well as in railway construction. In the rare instances when state authorities wanted to engage a graduate of the *Gewerbeinstitut* Beuth refused them. When time went on and industry became advanced in the size of units and in the degree of technology involved, the *Gewerbeinstitut* was reorganized with its standards raised until it was combined with the *Bauakademie* into the *Technische Hochschule* of 1879.

In the end the two branches of technical education for public service and for industry gave in to a uniform common one. At this time, however, France had lost its leading position compared to Prussia. Science, technology, technical education and industrial progress were considered to be highest in Imperial Germany, even by British observers (cf. Artz 1966: 267f.; Ben-David and Zloczower 1962; Gilpin 1968; Haines 1957–1969). We cannot go into any details about this interesting feature, but we believe that this development had one of its causes in the varying emphasis the two countries put on technical education for public service or for industry before 1850. Variations in this balance may be indicated, on a lower level, if the three *écoles d'arts et métiers* are compared to the some twenty provincial trade schools beneath the *Gewerbeinstitut*. Similar variations are to be seen if we aim at an overall calculation of top level technical personnel thereby summing up what has been said about institutions of higher learning in the technological realm (see Table 7–2).

Up to 1850 the number of engineers trained for military or bureaucratic purposes predominates in both countries, even if we subtract the artillery officers. The grand totals of the output of trained engineers in Prussia and France are in proportion as 1:1.3, the size of the two countries' populations relate as 1:2.3. This means that

TABLE 7-2. OUTPUT OF TOP-LEVEL TECHNICAL PERSONNEL IN
FRANCE AND PRUSSIA, 1820–1850

Sector	France		Prussia	
	Institution	Graduates	Institution	Graduates
Public Service	*École polytechnique*		*Vereinigte Artillerie- und Ingenieurschule*	
	Artillery	1,600	Artillery	1,000
	Génie	850	Military Engineering	500
	Ponts et Chaussées	800	*Bauakademie*	1,000
Industry	*École centrale des arts et manufactures* (1830-1850)	1,400	*Gewerbeinstitut*	1,000
	Total	4,650		3,500
	Total exclusive of artillerists	3,050		2,500

Sources: Dobbert 1899; Guillet 1929; Lundgreen 1972; Marièlle 1855; von Poten 1896.

Prussia trained relatively more technicians. Within the countries' quotas the numerical relation between public and industrial technicians is the same: only 30 percent of all technicians are at the disposition of private enterprise. In quantitative terms Prussia seems to have caught up or even surpassed France. Qualitatively the level of education to be gained at the *École polytechnique* and its *écoles d'application* was certainly higher. This leads back to our main argument. France kept on its highly reputed tradition of technical education for public service. Prussia built up gradually a system of technical education originally geared to the needs of industry and continually adjusted to the state of economic and technological development. Finally, this kind of technical education fused with the civil part of the public service training facilities, the *Bauakademie*. Henceforth the state had to compete with private business when trying to recruit its technical personnel.

So far we have drawn our arguments largely from institutional history. What all this actually meant for the progress of economic modernization during the period of state- and nation-building cannot satisfactorily be answered unless further research scrutinizes the extent to which technicians fluctuated between the public and private sector. No representative statement is possible in this regard. Nevertheless it can be pointed out that public service continued to be of the utmost attractiveness to the French middle class (O'Boyle

1966: 826ff.). The long tradition of *la robe* did find its successor in the *fonctionnaires* who graduated from the *grandes écoles*; the aristocracy of the *noblesse de fonction publique* gave way to the meritocracy of elites having passed the various *concours* (Reinhard 1956: 24ff.; Hahn 1969: 234f.). If, then, there is any example for the alleged affinity (Kocka 1969: 180ff.) between "bureaucrat" and "engineer," France has to be named rather than Prussia.

Summary

The foregoing review of state-building and the recruitment and training of personnel as experienced by three major West-European countries points to a number of similarities as well as differences which shall be briefly summarized. When Britain, France, and Prussia embarked upon state-building, they were confronted with the common problem of creating a loyal and efficient personnel to execute the orders from above. Various differing preconditions, however, determined the respective patterns of state-building and the features, role and impact of the administrative and technical personnel involved. Thus we find different ways and means of securing loyalty and of providing for efficiency which in return lead to divergent social and political implications marking the course of national history.

Notwithstanding the common experience of Roman Law, of medieval church and strong cities of medieval and early modern times, considerable differences between the English and continental ways of recruiting and training personnel can be discerned. In a time when absolutist government was far from reaching its climax in France and when there was no sign yet of its future development in Prussia, it came to an end in Britain. The English nation-state had then been mainly built, but without creating a service elite like that on the continent. It remains even doubtful whether the events of 1640 and 1689 significantly marked the history of administrative personnel in England which shows a long-lasting tradition of strong but cooperative local self-government; of recruiting semi-amateurs from different strata of the society (except the lower classes); and of relatively more restraint in state intervention or activity in economic affairs. Loyalty was basically secured by the alliance of crown and nobility with the gentry and the (rising) bourgeoisie; it was "their" state, and the recruitment to offices via patronage simply meant that there was not much of a separated class of bureaucrats but a relatively open, political society with officeholding as a means of integration.[34] Consequently there is not much to be said in terms of institutional history about the recruitment and training of personnel, in contrast to France and Prussia. Even for the training of technical personnel where more professionalization is required few institutional devices were developed by the state.

Thus we might conclude that the very continuity of state-building (including only a short and early ending period of absolutism) led to a less bureaucratized state which only in the aftermath of industrialization began to increase its administrative personnel on lines similar to all industrialized societies. With regard to technical personnel, both the informal tradition of recruiting administrative personnel and Britain's position as a pioneer of industrialization limited the deliberate attempts of governments to create manpower, in contrast to the continental late-comers and their simultaneously differing bureaucratic traditions. It was only in the late nineteenth century that Britain realized the necessity to embark upon technical education (which also meant enlarging the bureaucracy) in order to keep pace with the now progressive continent.

On the continent we have both the common traits of France and Prussia as against Britain; and the differences between France and Prussia. Both continental states developed a higher degree of bureaucratization than Britain. Considering the strength of provincial particularism and, in the case of Prussia, the outlived remnants of the Holy Roman Empire, state-building was a heavier task for both the continental countries, not to speak of geopolitical disadvantages adding difficulties and costs. As far as Prussia is concerned she represents a contrast to Britain in nearly every respect. Starting extremely late and in a backward economic setting, Prussian kings tried to make up by behaving as technocratic planners in an underdeveloped country: allying with the nobility, the one force existing which could be used as core of a service elite; broadening and in fact creating a service class by institutionalizing professionalism (provision for education and training); recruitment on lines of a merit system tempered by co-optation. A powerful bureaucracy thus came into being which could pretend to represent the commonweal. It is

[34] Cf. Weber's remark that the gentry saved Britain from being bureaucratized. Weber 1956: 1051.

only consequent that we find, in Prussia, enlightened absolutism and bureaucratic autocracy but no successful bourgeois revolution or political victorious bourgeoisie.

With regard to France state-building started earlier and in a more advanced economic environment. There was no vacuum to be filled with public servants but the necessity of coming to terms with competing forces: the complicated play of crown vs. nobility; old vs. new nobility; bourgeoisie vs. nobility. Bureaucracy in this realm meant arrangement which was achieved by making use of the world in *la robe*; venality of offices both as a means of creating loyalty and serving the independence of bureaucracy; high *magistrature* providing for recruitment and training for administrative personnel. On functional as well as on social grounds the praise usually accorded to the French bureaucracy may be discarded. One may only think of the one point that where the Prussian War and Domains Chambers correspond to the *intendants* in France there is no French functional equivalence to the *Steuerräte* and *Landräte* in Prussia.

The French Revolution gave to the bourgeoisie a place within society similar to that in England. The world of *la robe* gave way to a meritocracy of graduates from the *grandes écoles*. Tempered though this merit system has been by patronage (and opportunity costs of education), the principle of recruitment and training on achievement-oriented lines had its outstanding forerunner already in the France of the *Ancien Régime* with regard to technical personnel. This bifurcation of administrators (generalists, trained via the high *magistrature*) vs. technical experts (specialists, trained via technical colleges) calls to mind Weber's distinction between a cultivated person (or leading politician) and a professional (or executive expert) (Weber 1956: 737; cf. 1059–1060). Prussia though adhering to the expert concept for both administrative and technical personnel never reached the performance of French technical education. Being a late-comer, however, Prussia could more easily adjust to the needs of industry (as opposed to public service) whereas France kept on her tradition of breeding excellent talents for civil and military service. Prussia/Germany thus finally caught up and became a model of economic performance to look upon even for the British. French institutions, however, "were resistant to further evolution just at the moment that scientific research entered its greatest period of advancement and just when scientific theory had truly become for the first time the basis of technological innovations" (Gilpin 1968: 84).[35] None of the three "competitors" hence developed an optimal system of training and recruitment of administrative and technical personnel; each had its specific advantages and drawbacks.

[35] Cf. Gilpin 1968: 101: "Secondary and higher education became a prisoner of the examination system."

CHAPTER 8

DIMENSIONS OF STATE FORMATION AND NATION-BUILDING: A POSSIBLE PARADIGM FOR RESEARCH ON VARIATIONS WITHIN EUROPE

STEIN ROKKAN

THE DISCIPLINE of comparative politics faces a double task: the accumulation and evaluation of information about past and present systems of government, the construction and testing of parsimonious models for the explanation of variations in the development, structuring, and performance of such systems. Noticeable progress has been made during the past two or three decades at both levels: we have witnessed remarkable improvements in the organization of information services for political analysts and we have also seen a proliferation of attempts at systematic model-building and hypothesis-testing. But the discipline is still markedly out of balance: for the older, economically advanced polities of the West we have enormous storehouses of solid information, but only sporadic efforts of theory development; for the newer and economically less advanced polities of Latin America, Asia, and Africa we have a plethora of theoretical statements and suggestions, but much less controlled empirical information. It will take very large investments even to begin to right this imbalance on the information front. There may be more immediate payoffs in concerted efforts on the theory front: it *is* a great paradox that so little has been done to develop unifying paradigms for the advanced regions of the world and that so much of what we have in the way of theories of development bears exclusively on the systems with the shortest histories and the poorest documentary records. Clearly to right this imbalance we have to face head-on the challenge posed by the development of the Western systems from the Middle Ages onward: we have to work out meaningful paradigms for comparisons across the best-documented of all our systems. Once we have made some headway with this task, we can move on with greater confidence to the next: the construction of unified models of explanation across all political systems, whether old-

[562]

established and advanced or new and still underdeveloped. Any persistent work in this direction is in turn bound to affect developments on the information front: the effort to bring together in some consistent framework the many strands of theorizing in the literature is not only a challenging intellectual task, it will also help to structure the organizational strategies of the major research centers in deciding on further investments in the gathering and sifting of information about the political systems of the world.

The time is clearly ripe for an attempt at some codification of our knowledge about the sources of similarities and variations in the development of the political systems of Europe. Whether any such effort can help to bridge the great gap in model-building between the West and the other continents still remains to be seen. We are painfully aware of the multitude of dangers and pitfalls in our path, but we think it essential that the attempt be made: without a sustained effort to bridge the gap there is a real danger of stagnation and fragmentation.

We propose to proceed in three steps:

1. We shall first develop an abstract model of what we take to be the *crucial dimensions of variation* across political systems and discuss alternative *time sequences* in the interaction of such dimensions.

2. We shall next show how this model may be used as a basis for a conceptual mapping of *variations within Western Europe*, within the region first to produce viable industrial states and to develop institutions for nation-building through mass participation.

3. We shall then proceed to compare the typical Western European configurations with those of the other regions of the world and try to pin down the *decisive contrasts between the early conditions for state- and nation-building and the conditions for the late-comers of the postcolonial era.*

A Paradigm of Dimensions

Our search for a parsimonious model of explanation starts out from a reinterpretation of the schema underlying Talcott Parsons' discussion in *Societies* (Parsons 1967): see Figure 8–1.

The schema posits four distinct processes of development from the primordial community at a low level of internal role differentiation, with a primitive, locally bounded economy and with a structurally embedded system of religious beliefs and ritual practices: first, the establishment of regular institutions for the settlement of disputes

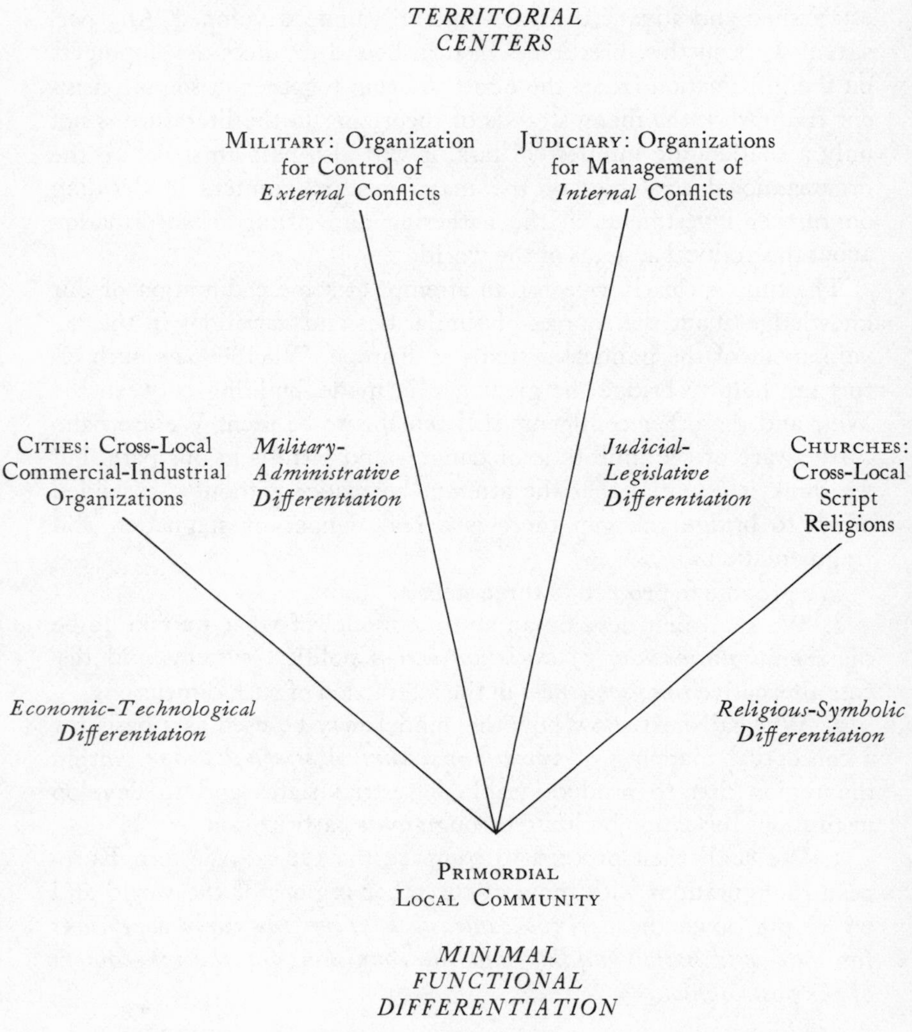

TERRITORIAL
CENTERS

MILITARY: Organization   JUDICIARY: Organizations
for Control of   for Management of
External Conflicts   *Internal* Conflicts

CITIES: Cross-Local   *Military-*   *Judicial-*   CHURCHES:
Commercial-Industrial   *Administrative*   *Legislative*   Cross-Local
Organizations   *Differentiation*   *Differentiation*   Script
                                                                  Religions

Economic-Technological   *Religious-Symbolic*
Differentiation   *Differentiation*

PRIMORDIAL
LOCAL COMMUNITY

*MINIMAL
FUNCTIONAL
DIFFERENTIATION*

Figure 8–1. Basic Processes of Territorial Differentiation

within and across close lineages and the codification of rules of adjudication; second, the growth of militarily powerful conquest center imposing physical control over the surrounding populations through exactions of food, manpower, and other resources; third, the differentiation of a distinct class of priests, the divorce of mythologies and ritual practices from the social structure of the local populations, and the incipient growth of world religions and missionary agencies; and finally, the differentiation of technical skills from the underlying social structure and the growth of independent cross-local networks of craftsmen, merchants, and freighters.

Talcott Parsons used this schema in an effort to establish a typology for the early political systems: the patrimonial kingdoms, the early administrative-religious empires, the city-state confederations, the crucial "seedbed societies" of Israel and Greece. He has also suggested ways of applying it to the nation-states emerging within Western Europe during the Middle Ages and the sixteenth to eighteenth centuries (Parsons 1971). But this effort has so far largely concentrated on the *overall system* of such units and generated only very few propositions about the sources of variations in the *internal structure* of the units. I see a variety of fascinating possibilities in this direction and propose to develop the four-pronged paradigm of differentiation into a *multi-level model for the generation of structural profiles* of political systems.

Figure 8–2 presents the basic model in the form of an octahedron: the primordial communities in the subject periphery are tied in to the differentiated central communities through four channels: the legal, the military, the cultural and the economic.

This three-dimensional model is essentially a device for the ordering of questions and data about similarities and differences among historically given political systems.

First, it allows us to characterize the *subject peripheries* by their level of functional differentiation and their dependence on the center: are they primarily tied in to the total system via the military-extractive apparatus, through communalities in legal traditions, through the city network or through linguistic or religious affinities?

Second, it prompts us to ask questions about the internal and the external resources of the *major components of the central establishment*: what sorts of alliances predominate inside the system and what differences are there among elite sectors in their ability to marshal resources external to the territorial system?

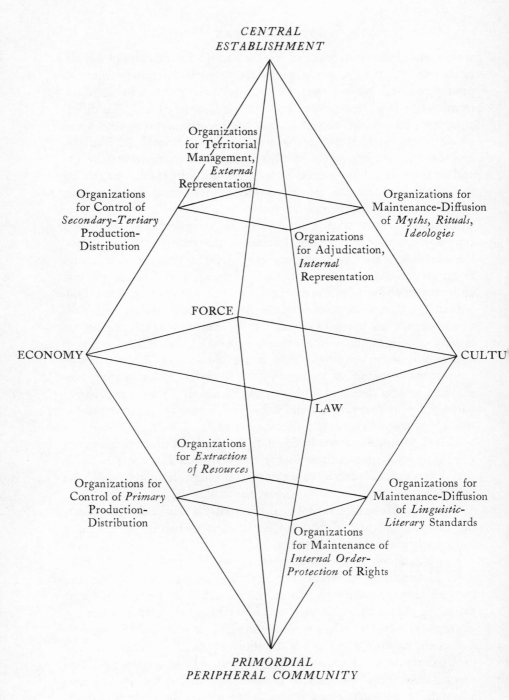

Figure 8–2. The Basic Grid of Dimensions

Finally, the model forces us to inquire into similarities and differences in the *processes of change*: which center-periphery links were established first, which next, which last, and what were the characteristic periphery responses to the successive thrusts from the center?

These three sets of questions reflect concerns very similar to those of Albert O. Hirschman in his brilliant essay on *Exit, Voice and Loyalty* (Hirschman 1970): in fact the model represents an attempt at a fusion of the paradigm of functional differentiation presented by Talcott Parsons and the scheme for the classification of decision systems proposed by Hirschman.

To bring out these isomorphisms, the basic elements of the model can be reorganized and reformulated in a 3 x 4 matrix of Hirschmanian and Parsonian dimensions: see Figure 8–3.

At this abstract level the model obviously leaves a great margin of imprecision: it suggests the general direction of comparative in-

Periphery- Center Balance	Functional Segments			
	Force	*Culture*	*Law*	*Economy*
Degree of Periphery Integration: (at t_1): *Entry* Variables: Potentially *Voice* Variables	Strength of Extractive Agencies, Extent of Opposition to Such Agencies	Strength of Standardizing Agencies, Strength of Counter-Agencies	Strength of Center-Imposed vs. Local/Regional Legal Traditions	Integration/Separation of Primary Economy With/From City Network
Degree of Center Distinctiveness (at t_1): *Exit* Variables	Balance on Internal vs. External Resources of Military Agencies (Alliances, Territorial "Temptations")	Distinctiveness vs. Sharedness of Religious and/or Linguistic Standards	Distinctiveness vs. Sharedness of Territorial Legal System	Openness vs. Closedness of Territorial Economy
Over-Time Processes of System-Building: *Loyalty* Variables	*Penetration*: State-Building *stricto sensu*	*Standardization*: Nation-Building	*Equalization of Rights of Participation*: Establishment of *Political* Citizenship	*Redistribution of Resources/Benefits*: *Establishment of Social* Citizenship

Figure 8–3. Hirschman and Parsons Combined

[567]

quiries but does not generate clear-cut questions for the establishment of multivariate profiles for the comparative analysis of systems.

There is an obvious difficulty about any attempt to concretize the paradigm into a grid of potentially comparable variables: the greater the institutional specificity the narrower the regional range of the comparison. Our strategy in this quandary is to shuttle between an abstract scheme, potentially useful across all regions of the world, and a series of "regional transposes," of regionally specific grids of variables. Let us first look at a possible grid for Western Europe, for the region first to produce differentiated institutions on all the four dimensions of our model: see Figure 8–4.

This grid represents a *flat transpose* of the three-dimensional model: the Force and the Law dimensions have been merged into a center-periphery axis.

This grid may still appear complex and unwieldy, but is in fact generated from the initial model in three simple steps.

The *primary* indicators are estimates of the *comparative strength of the four collectivities-organizations-agencies setting the conditions for center-periphery integration*: the *cities* and the *landholding structures* on the economic front, the *churches* and the *linguistic elites* on the cultural front.

The *secondary* indicators characterize the *two-way linkages* among these four, the center, and each distinctive periphery: the grid gives *one* indication for each of fourteen of the fifteen possible pairs and *two* indicators, one economic and one cultural, for the final pair, the center-periphery axis.

The *tertiary* indicators finally assess the overall strength and distinctiveness of the two poles of the model, the territorial center and the peripheries: one set of these indicators characterizes the *economic resource strength* of each pole, the other set the *cultural distinctiveness*.

The labels given each of the variables in this multiple grid can obviously be questioned: what is important at this stage of the enterprise is not empirical precision but disciplined questioning across all the systems to be compared. The grid is essentially a checklist for the construction of typologies and the testing of regularities across given ranges of historical cases: it is not meant to help single-nation historians in their efforts to account for particular developments, but to guide comparisons across systems, whether pair by pair, region

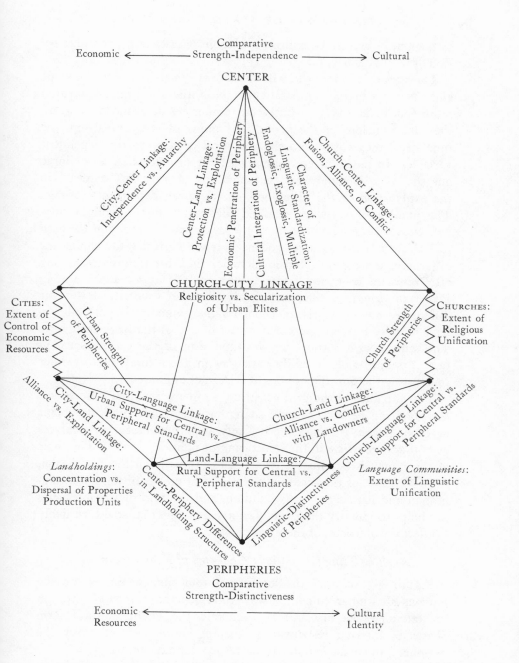

Figure 8-4. A Grid of Primary Variables and Linkage Variables for Europe

by region, or across the entire population of cases at a particular period of world history.

The variables in the grid will clearly vary in weight with the scope
and the focus of the comparative analysis: there are many potential
redundancies in the grid but these cannot be determined a priori,
they are functions of the geocultural range of the comparison, the
time spans they cover, and the analytical distance to the dependent
variables. In any concrete comparison, the primary task is to single
out the most parsimonious configurations of variables required in
the explanation of the differences on the given dependent variable.
The number of variables required for such minimal configurations
will clearly be smaller the more the cases have in common through
joint historical experiences: you need fewer variables to account for
differences among the Nordic countries than for differences among
all Protestant countries, fewer for an analysis of variations among
Protestant countries than among all Christian countries, fewer for
differences among Christian countries than among all political systems initially formed under the impact of one of the world religions.
The same goes a fortiori for the time span of the comparisons: in
fact, it is impossible to study variations in geocultural space without
considering the time dimensions of each source of variation.

The variables in the grid constitute so many potential time series:
the good can be used to map configurations at one particular point
in time, but it is much more likely to prove useful in analyses
of *changes over time* in the structuring of political systems. The logic
of the model is essentially dynamic: the focus is on the description,
stage by stage, of the successes or failures of efforts of territorial unification and national identity-building, and the grid of variables simply helps to identify the major factors in the internal structure likely
to affect the outcomes of these efforts.

The Time Dimension: A Scheme of Four Phases

Figure 8–5 suggests the location of four time phases within the
Parsons-Hirschman model: two center-generated thrusts through
the territory, the first military-economic, the second cultural; two
phases of internal restructuring opening up opportunities for the
periphery, the first symbolic-cultural, the second economic.

Phase I in this model covers the initial *state-building process*: in
Western Europe the period from the High Middle Ages to the
French Revolution. This is typically a period of political, economic,

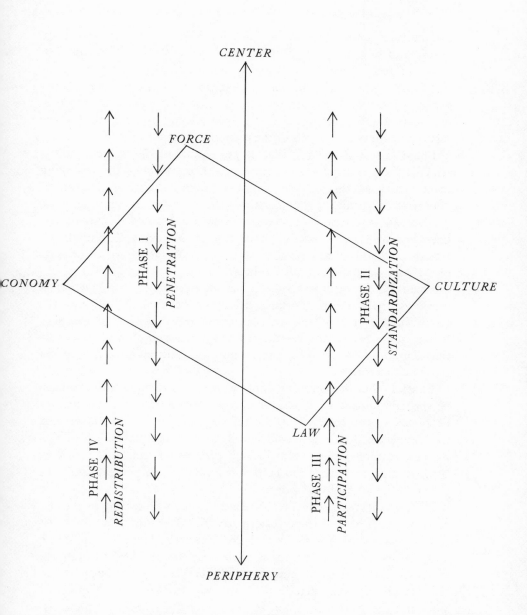

Figure 8–5. The Location of the Four Time Phases within the Three Dimensional Grid

and cultural unification at the elite level: a series of bargains are struck and a variety of cultural bonds are established across networks of local power-holders and a number of institutions are built for the extraction of resources for common defense, for the maintenance of internal order and the adjudication of disputes, for the protection of established rights and privileges and for the elementary infrastructure requirements of the economy and the polity.

Phase II brings in larger and larger sectors of the *masses* into the system: the conscript armies, the compulsory schools, the emerging mass media create channels for direct contact between the central elite and parochial populations of the peripheries and generate widespread feelings of identity with the total political system, frequently, but not necessarily, in protracted conflict with already established identities such as those built up through churches or sects or through peripheral linguistic elites.

Phase III brings these subject masses into *active participation* in the workings of the territorial political system: typically through the establishment of privileges of opposition, the extension of the electorates for organs of representation, the formation of organized parties for the mobilization of support and the articulation and aggregation of demands.

Phase IV finally represents the next series of steps in the expansion of the administrative apparatus of the territorial state: the growth of *agencies of redistribution*, the building of public welfare services, the development of nationwide policies for the equalization of economic conditions, negatively through progressive taxation, positively through transfers from the better-off strata to the poorer, from the richer to the backward regions.

This ideal-typical sequence of phases finds its closest fit in the histories of the older of the Western nations: the political systems recognized as sovereign entities with the Peace of Westphalia in 1648, and the first of the independent settler nations, the United States of America. The fit is not as close for the later Western European states, the secession nations acceding to sovereignty after the Napoleonic wars and the successive waves of revolutionary protest. In these territories Phases II, III and IV often came in a very close succession or even coincided with each other chronologically. Typically, the colonial rulers had left a well-structured administrative machinery for the new masters to take over after independence: there was a distinct Phase I under an alien center, but near-coincidence between

Phases II and III, possibly even Phase IV. The comparison of three neighboring countries in Northern Europe in Figure 8–6 will help to illustrate this point.

	1648	*1815*		*1917*
Sweden	I	II	III	IV
	1536: Vasas' Build-Up of Central Administration	1680s: Systematic Incorporation of Danish-Norwegian Lands	1866–1920: Protracted Participation Crisis	1910s: Distribution Crisis, Build-Up of Welfare State
Norway		I	II	III	IV
	1500s–1700s: Field Administration under Danish Sovereignty	Build-Up of	1814: Independence, Struggle for Separate Identity	1884–1900: Participation Crisis	1930s–1950s: Welfare State
Finland		I	II	II-III	IV
	1500s–1700s: Build-Up of Administration under Swedish Rule	1809: Ceded to Russia with Swedish Administrative Structure	1860s: Identity Crisis, Fennomans vs. Svecomans	1906: Participation-Distribution Crisis	1918: Civil War

Figure 8–6. The Four Time Phases within Sweden, Norway, and Finland

This cumulation of critical challenges during the final struggle for secession from the metropolis and the empire has tended to be even more pronounced outside Europe.[1] The exact chronologies of these sequences are obviously subject to a great deal of questioning: it is difficult to establish equivalent indicators for the "peaking" of the different phases of system development. Quite particularly, it is difficult to state with anything approaching precision the duration of *Phase I*: at what point can the central administrative machineries be said to have penetrated throughout the given territory and what criteria could possibly be used as indicators of the completion of this first phase of system-building? Whatever the difficulties on this score, the crucial message is clear enough: the great majority of the political systems of Latin America, Eastern Europe, Asia, and Africa

[1] For a discussion of the time-phasing of identity struggles, waves of mass mobilization and conflicts over distribution, see Rokkan 1970; this presents a detailed comparison of the liberation-secession histories of Finland and Ireland.

have been faced with a critical cumulation of nation-building challenges over very short spans of time. By contrast to the older, slowly developing nation-states of Western Europe, the great mass of the systems that rose to sovereign status through the break-up of the Iberian, Eastern European, Asian and African empires have had to cope with issues of national-cultural identity, issues of participation, and issues of economic inequality all in one: developments left them with little or no time to reach even temporary institutional solutions to one set of challenges before they were forced to cope with the next set. This is a fundamental contrast between the older Western systems and the newer systems emerging from the break-up of the great empires: the latecomers were not only late in achieving sovereign status, they were left with only a minimum of time to build up their institutions before they were faced with disruptive pressures from outside as well as from inside. The older systems developed in a multicentered international environment without any dominant models of successful development, with very slow transportation networks, and without any technologies for quick mass mobilization. The latecomers are faced with highly visible models of successful development, strong and polarized outside centers of economic and ideological influence, rapid means of communication in and out of each system, advanced technologies of mass mobilization. This cumulation of challenges is a central theme in the comparative study of political development: to get anywhere toward a unifying model of development we shall clearly have to focus attention on the configurations of conditions making for slow and stepwise phase movements in the West and, most significantly, in Japan, and for sudden and often explosive concatenations of critical issues in the great majority of the emerging polities of the twentieth century.

The first step in any such comparison is clearly to map the variations. The contrast between the slow development of the West and the sudden cumulation of challenges in the newer systems is far from absolute: there are important variations within the West, between the older, pre-1648 states and the newer, post-Napoleonic secession states, and between the larger and the smaller nations, and there are even greater differences across the other continents, not only as a function of the character of the overseas settler concentrations, but even more of the character of the inherited style of administrative control and the extent of differentiation between secular and religious institutions. These variations in the time phasing of the four developmental challenges call for a major effort of systematization: this is the primary rationale for the construction of our model and for the establishment of the very elaborate check lists of variables. We cannot go into detail case by case or variable by variable in this one chapter. We shall confine ourselves to a quick mapping of the major sources of variation within Europe and shall then proceed to an even more cursory review of the variations within the other regions of the world. We cannot possibly proceed to any detailed testing of our model in this first round: all we can do is to marshal enough examples of possible applications and enough arguments from concrete comparisons to justify further work along this line.

Dimensions of Variation within Western Europe

Any analytical history of center formation and periphery incorporation in Western Europe must start out from six "givens": first, the heritage of the *Roman Empire*, the supremacy of the Emperor, the systematization of legal rules, the idea of citizenship; second, the supraterritorial, cross-ethnic organizations of the *Catholic Church* and its central role in the channeling of elite communications during the millennium after the fall of the Western Empire; third, the *Germanic kingdoms* and the traditions of legislative-judicial assemblies of free heads of families; fourth, the extraordinary revival of trade between the Orient, the Mediterranean, and the North Sea after the defeat of the Moslems and the consequent growth of a network of *independent cities* across Western Europe from Italy to Flanders and the Baltic; fifth, the development and consolidation of *feudal and manorial agrarian structures* and the consequent concentrations of landholdings in important areas of the West; and sixth and finally the emergence of *literatures in vernacular languages* and the gradual decline of the dominant medium of cross-ethnic communication, Latin, quite particularly after the invention of printing. These "givens" combined to produce a variety of strikingly different configurations during the crucial state-building period from around the eleventh to the eighteenth century.

Four dimensions stood out as crucially important in the generation of these different systems of territorial control: (1) the *geopolitical distance northward, from Rome*, the fountainhead of the old Empire, the focus of Western Christendom after the Schism of 1054 and the symbolic center for the effort of legal unification through the revival of Roman law; (2) the *geopolitical distance westwards or eastwards from the central belt of trade route cities* from Northern Italy to the areas once controlled by the Hanseatic League; (3) the *concentrations of landholdings* and the consequent independence or dependence of the peasantry; and (4) the *ethnic basis* of the early efforts of center-building and the linguistic conditions for early vs. late consolidation.

Let us, to simplify a series of complex territorial histories, first draw a crude conceptual map of Western Europe through the cross-tabulation of the first two dimensions: the North-South "center-culture" axis and the West-East "center-economy" axis. This is done in Figure 8–7 (see pp. 578 and 579). Let us next look at the cells in this tabular map and specify variations in the other two dimensions.

This conceptual map of the territories of Western Christendom tells us a great deal about the sources of diversity with the region first to develop commercial-industrial nation-states.

First of all, it is essential to note the importance of the *city-studded center* for the structuring of efforts of territorial consolidation:

> The decisive thrusts toward the formation of nation-states came at the edges of the Old Empire, first on the seaward fringe, much later on the landward side.

> The cities of the trade-route belt from the Mediterranean to the North Sea and the Baltic were for centuries strong enough to thwart all efforts of military-administration.

Paradoxically the history of Europe is one of center formation at the periphery of a network of strong and independent cities: this explains the great diversity of configurations and the extraordinary tangles of shifting alliances and conflicts.

The trade-route belt produced a variety of short-term confederations of city states. The most famous of these was no doubt the Hanseatic League, at its peak a loose network of hundreds of cities and outposts from London to Bergen, Bruges to Visby. The only lasting systems of territorial control developed at two strategic points of the trade-route belt: in the Alps, and at the estuaries of three of the great northward rivers. The Swiss and the Dutch confederations were essentially defensive in character. There was no strong conquest center in the terminology of our grid of variables, but a network of strategically placed cities willing to pool their resources in defense of their trading privileges.

The only efforts of aggressive state-building took place on the *fringes* of economic Europe. In the smaller of these peripheral nation-states, the typical sequence was one of gradual build-up at the ethnic center, rapid imperial expansion, consolidation within a more homogeneous territory. The Nordic monarchies built up wide-ranging empires before they were forced back to their ethnic heartlands: Denmark and Norway in the Middle Ages only, Sweden again in the seventeenth century. What was important in this sequence was that they could fall back on nationally unified and distinctive systems of law which bounded each territorial system and helped to prevent fragmentation. The English monarchy went through a similar sequence: the retreat from France after the Hundred Years War set the stage for the great period of consolidation under the Tudors. The French monarchy took much longer to consolidate its territory: Breton and "Occitan" ideologists will claim that the conquest of the West and the South built up an empire and not a nation, but these were conquests of a very different nature from the overseas acquisitions of the Norsemen and the English. In fact, the French did not engage in extensive empire-building beyond the consolidated metropolitan base until the seventeenth century, and even then with very little success. What is important in our context is that the French were the first to move successfully across the entire trade-route belt of Europe: after two centuries of absolutist centralization France under Napoleon proved strong enough not only to subject Switzerland and the Low Countries, but also to conquer all of city-state Germany and Italy. This was a short-lived empire, but it paved the way for a major change in the structure of the European system: the integration of the fragmented middle belt within two emerging empires, the Prussian-German and the Italian.

These nineteenth-century developments differed fundamentally from other histories of territorial consolidation in Europe. These were not conquests of peripheral and backward rural lands from a dynastic center, but invasions of economically and culturally advanced urbanized territories from military strongholds at the edges of each system, the German cities and principalities from Prussia, an agricultural-bureaucratic conquest state built up on the Eastern periphery, the Italian cities and possessions from Savoy, a mountain pass state in control of one set of trade routes to the North. The nation-building histories of these latest of the larger states of Western Europe proved very different from those of the earlier ones: they not only had to cope over roughly the same period with issues of administrative unification

WEST-EAST DIMENSION

	"Seaward Peripheries"	"Seaward Empire-Nations"	"City-State Consociations"	"Landsward Empire-Nations"	"Landsward Peripheries"
Strength of Cities:	Weaker	Stronger	Stronger	Weaker	Weaker
Strength of Conquest Centers:	Weaker	Stronger	Weaker	Stronger	Weaker
Geopolitical Type:	*"Seaward Peripheries"*	*"Seaward Empire-Nations"*	*"City-State Consociations"*	*"Landsward Empire-Nations"*	*"Landsward Peripheries"*
Beyond reach of Rome: *Protestant*	ICELAND: Republic 10th Century, later under Norway, Denmark	*Viking Empires* Later Reduced to Ethnically Homogeneous Nation-States: NORWAY: later under Denmark **DENMARK** →		← SWEDEN: State-Building 16th Century, Major Empire 17th Century, Turned Seaward after 1660 through Conquest in West	FINLAND: Province of Sweden, 1809: Grand Duchy of Russia
Territories Once under Roman Empire and/or Influenced by Roman Law: *Protestant*	SCOTLAND: Monarchy 12th Century, United with England 1707 WALES: Subjected 15th Century	ENGLAND: Consolidated 11th Century, Major Overseas Empire 17th-18th Century	*Hanseatic League:* Loose Federation of Cities around Baltic and North Seas 13th to 16th Centuries	PRUSSIA: State-Building 17th Century, Empire 18th Century; Nucleus for Unification of *German Reich*	

SOUTH-NORTH DIMENSION

Figure 8–7. A Schematic Geopolitical Map of Europe

	Religiously Mixed	Catholic	Counter-Reformation Territories
	IRELAND: Subjected 16th-17th Century	BRITTANY: Subjected 16th Century	
	NETHERLANDS: / SWITZERLAND: Confederation 1291, Major City-States added 14th Century; Northern Provinces United in Fight against Hapsburgs, Independence 1648	FRANCE: Consolidated 16th Century, Empire-Building Frustrated except in Indo-China, Africa; BELGIUM: Independent 1830; ARAGON-CATALONIA: United with Castile 1474, Revolt 1640; SAVOY-PIEDMONT: Independent Nucleus for Unification of City-State ITALY	Crusading Empires Built-Up in Fight against Moslems, Major Overseas Empires: PORTUGAL, SPAIN
		BAVARIA	Crusading Empire Built-Up on Dynastic Claims and Wars against Ottomans: AUSTRIA
	BOHEMIA: Subjected by Hapsburgs 1620	Aristocratic Border Empires: POLAND: Divided 18th Century; HUNGARY: Overrun by Ottomans 16th Century, with Hapsburgs 1699	

SOUTH-NORTH DIMENSION

(Phase I in Figure 8–5) and issues of national identity-building (Phase II); the territories they tried to unify were studded with urban centers accustomed for centuries to high levels of autonomy.

Prussia and Savoy made their greatest conquest inward toward the center of Western Europe. Another power at the edge of Roman Europe, the Hapsburgs, had for centuries tried to gain control over the territories of the old Central Empire and for a time was able to assemble a vast patchwork of possessions across the continent. The decisive thrusts of Hapsburg expansion went eastwards, however, against the Ottoman Empire: the great military-administrative strength of the Hapsburgs was built up in continuous wars against the Moslems much in the same way the monarchies of Castile-Aragon and of Portugal built themselves up in the *Reconquista*, in the fight to push the Arabs out of Europe. These power centers at the southeastern and the northwestern corners of the territories of the Roman Church built up *crusading frontier empires* against the threatening infidels, against the rival world religion to the South. This helps to explain the very close symbiosis of Church and State in these empires: the military might of the state was a decisive instrument in the struggle for the expansion of Western Christendom. With the breakdown of Roman Catholic authority in the North, the Hapsburg and the Iberian empires became the leading powers of the Counter-Reformation and developed strong machineries for the repression of heresies. The Iberian empires brought the same fervor of orthodoxy across the ocean to the New World. The conquest of Latin America produced an even stronger fusion of religious, political and economic institutions. These rigid structures proved effective in territories at a low level of mobilization; they proved disastrous in the later phases of development. The Hapsburg Empire could not contain the proliferation of nationalist movements in the Balkans and in Central Europe: the Empire was finally reduced in 1918 to its heartland, the German-speaking provinces of Austria, and for a long period even this entity had to struggle for its sovereign status against the aggressive Pan-German forces centering on Berlin. On the Iberian peninsula only Portugal succeeded in developing a homogeneous national culture: this, however, was achieved at a very low level of political mobilization, and the regime has not yet subjected itself to the full test of mass politics. Spain has to this day remained a state and not a nation: the Catalan and the Basque peripheries have for centuries refused to identify with the power center in Castile and have on several occasions been on the brink of secession. The Latin American empires broke up into a number of fragments from 1810 onward, but the heritage of the fused hierarchical structures weighed heavily on the elites of these new states: they could not get far toward the building of national identities (Phase II) without mobilizing the subject strata into active participation in the system (Phase III), but no effective mobilization could be brought about without changes in the inherited structures of dependence (Phase IV).

The Counter-Reformation brought about a fateful fusion of secular and religious powers in the "crusading empires" of the South. The break with the Roman Church brought about an even greater fusion in the Northern states, particularly in the Lutheran monarchies. The properties of the Church and the Orders were confiscated and the clergy was incorporated into the administrative services of the territorial state. But there was one essential difference. In the North the state churches became major agencies of nation-building, in the South the Catholic Church retained its supraterritorial character and acted as a brake on all efforts to build up strong national identities. In fact the Reformation was as much a revolt against Latin as against the Pope and the Curia; the break with Rome not only nationalized religion, it legitimized the national vernacular standards as languages of worship as well as of statecraft. The Protestant centers of the far North could pass quickly from state-building (Phase I) to nation-building (Phase II) and could develop unified cultures well before the era of mass politics (Phases III and IV).

Much depended, of course, on the initial conditions of ethnic and linguistic unification: how far could the collectivities around each center actually agree on a common standard, how intractable were the linguistic peripheries? Sweden stands out as the most unified of all the Protestant nation-states. The territories acquired from Denmark and Norway at the heyday of her imperial power were quickly integrated into the national culture, and the one linguistically distinctive periphery, Finland, was ceded in 1809. England reached the same level of linguistic unification much earlier, but only within the strict confines of the medieval borders. The Scottish Lowlands and the Celtic fringes proved much more resistant to standardization. Denmark also reached a high level of standardization on the Islands and on Jutland down to Schleswig, but the German possession of the Danish dynasty was to prove an intractable problem for Danish politics during the decisive phase of emerging mass participation from 1848 to 1920.

In two of the Nordic secession states, the early politics of liberation centered on linguistic-cultural divisions. In Norway the conflict over linguistic standards reflected resistance to the centuries-old dependence on Danish culture. In Finland the Fennomans mobilized the peasantry against the linguistic standards imposed on them by the Swedish settler elite. Only Iceland escaped such divisions over linguistic identity. This distant island community had developed such strong literary traditions of its own in the Middle Ages and had reached such a high level of mass literacy at an early stage that there was no serious threat of submersion under an alien culture.

The territories of what we have called "City-State Europe" developed strong linguistic standards without military-administrative centralization: German in the North, Italian in the South. The Empire and the trade-route networks had been strong enough to produce some standardization of the media of communication but too weak to unify the territories administratively. The two great powers on the eastern periphery were both part of this vast language community— Austria and Prussia were rivals for the control of the territories of Middle Europe, but derived much of their strength from their subjection of other language areas to the East. These asymmetries between linguistic unification and military-administrative control go far to explain the intensity of the identity conflicts in the German *Reich*.

Toward the West of this broad Germanic language area only the Dutch could mobilize the cultural resources required for the development of a national standard of their own. The Belgians, the Luxembourgeois, and the Swiss simply accepted standards from outside. The Swiss built up their entire confederation on the principle of linguistic parity and proved able to build up a sense of political identity across two, later three, and even four distinctive language communities. The Luxembourgeois never tried to develop a national standard out of their Germanic vernacular: they simply accepted *Hochdeutsch* and French as their standards. The Belgians were caught between language areas of very different weight in the international system. French was the language of the educated elite, and for a long time Flemish was held in low esteem not only as a peasant vernacular, but also for a period as the language of the hated Calvinist masters to the North. The result was a cumulation of crises: the advent of mass democracy and the economic mobilization of the Flemish peasantry triggered several waves of linguistic demands and in the end forced serious reconsideration of the structure of the Belgian state.

By contrast to Prussia and Austria, France developed a linguistic standard of her own and was able to force its acceptance throughout her territory: not only in Celtic Brittany, in the Languedoc, and in Provence, but even in the Germanic dialect areas of the North, in Alsace and in Lorraine. France and Sweden probably come closest to the ideal type of the "endoglossic" homogeneous nation-state but with one marked difference: in Sweden this great feat of unification was achieved through the integration of the Church, and consequently the schools for mass education, within the apparatus of the State; in France it was brought about essentially through the military and the secular administrative agencies, with only incidental help from the Roman Catholic Church. The French were able to build up a unified nation-state without breaking with Rome. In contrast to the Counter-Reformation empires they were able to set strict limits to the powers of the Church, but they never proceeded to integrate the ecclesiastical agencies into the machinery of the state. The result was a protracted struggle between secular nation-builders and religious authorities throughout the first phase of mass politics: the Church-State issue was to dominate French politics for close to a century and a half after the Great Revolution.

This quick summary of the geopolitical history of Western Europe has limited itself to three variables only: the location of the center-building efforts—to the West or to the East of the trade-route belt from the Mediterranean to the North; the character of the linkage between Church and State in the efforts of territorial consolidation; the character of the efforts of linguistic standardization and the extent of resistances to such efforts.[2]

We have only incidentally touched on the *legal* components of center-building, we have pointed to the importance of the revival of Roman Law for the unification of trade belt Europe, and we have called attention to the distinctive legal developments within the national territories at the Northern and the Western edges of the cen-

[2] This typological-topological scheme owes much to the analyses of conditions of center formation by such political geographers as Friedrich Ratzel, Karl Haushofer, Richard Hartshorne and Derwent Whittlesey. Whittlesey's discussion of the German and the Italian cases in fact contributed directly to my conceptualization of the "middle belt," cf. Whittlesey 1944: chaps. 7, 10. For a detailed classification of the state territories of Europe in the Whittlesey style, see Pounds and Ball 1964.

tral belt. Historians of legal development have repeatedly brought out this contrast in the political geography of Europe: the early development of distinctive national legal systems in the Germanic territories on the periphery, the revival of Roman Law within the territory of the old Central Empire, in Italy, in Catalonia, in Southern France (*pays de droit écrit*), in the Low Countries, and most of city-state Germany (for details see Smith 1928; esp. chaps. 39–44; Koschaker 1953; David and Brierley 1968: 21–118). The Romanization of customary law was an essential characteristic of trade belt Europe. Roman Law cut across the congeries of city-states and principalities, and offered a useful set of principles for the conduct of transactions across open societies. In Hirschman's term it was a law for *exits*. Only the peripheries were able to resist this transnational movement. In their isolation at the edges of Europe they were able to build up strong national or regional systems of law, the Common law of England, the *Jydske Lov* in 1241, the Norwegian code in 1274, the general laws for the cities and the countryside established for Sweden and Finland in 1350. It is no accident of history that the Roman Law countries were the ones to take the lead, centuries later in the struggle for a supranational Europe. The conflict over the extension of the Common Market is very much a conflict between the economically cross-cut city belt at the center and the culturally distinctive territorial systems at the peripheries of this Roman Europe.

This contrast cannot be understood without further analysis of the economic conditions of center-building. We have stressed the difficulties of territorial unification in the urbanized heartland of Europe but we have not discussed the very important variations on the economics of center-building on the edges of this core territory.

Otto Hintze, Otto Brunner, Barrington Moore, and a number of other comparative historians have emphasized the crucial importance of the interaction between urban and rural economic resources for the structuring of the European state. To analyze such interactions within the framework of our geopolitical map we would have to add for each case information about the structure of landholdings during the period of state-building. One regularity stands out with great clarity even after only cursory analysis: *the strongest of the early European nation-states were built up around territories with long histories of concentration in the ownership and control of land.* England was a country of large estates; very similar structures also emerged in Scotland and in Ireland. France was regionally divided in the structure of its landed economy: large estates in the open-field country of the North, smaller holdings in the *bocage* country and the wine-producing areas.[3] On the eastern fringe of trade-route Europe, Austria and Prussia were dominated by large and middle-sized estates of the *Gutsherrschaft* type. To the South, there were vast *latifundia* territories in *Reconquista* Spain, in Sicily and parts of Bourbon Italy. By contrast, the smaller monarchies of the North were less dominated by large estates: Denmark and part of Southern Sweden, it is true, came close to the Prussian structure, but the rest of Sweden and quite particularly Norway had high proportions of small independent peasant holdings. The same was true for large stretches of "consociational Europe": in the Low Countries, in Switzerland and in major parts of what is now Western Germany, the holdings tended to be smaller and the peasantry freer (for details on Germany see Weiss 1970).

These variations in the structure of the primary economy did not in themselves affect the character of the center-forming process. What counted was the balance, the character of the integration between this rural economy and the urban. This is the thrust of Hintze's classic analysis of variations in state-building in Europe (Hintze 1930): it is also the crux of Barrington Moore's discussion of the contrasts between England and France, and England and Prussia (Moore 1966).

The essential elements in these analyses can be brought out in a reformulation of our initial conceptual map of the territories of Western Christendom (see Figure 8–8).

This reformulation helps us sort out a basic difficulty in Barrington Moore's analysis of the economic conditions for the transition to

---

[3] Standard French economic histories emphasize the very high proportion of peasant-owned land even up to the eighteenth century: P. Goubert even thinks that the "conventional" estimate of 30-40 percent is low and suggests ±45 percent peasant-owned as against 25 percent for the nobility, 20 percent for the bourgeoisie and 10 percent for the Church, cf. Goubert 1970: 135. But Eberhard Weiss has recently argued that this still leaves the French rural economy much less in the hands of the peasantry than the economy of the German *Grundherrschaft* territories West of the Elbe. Comparing the French and the West German figures for *domaine utile*, secure tenancies, as well as freehold properties, he concludes that the French peasantry controlled much less of the soil than the West German: possibly some 35 percent against 90 percent or more. The contrast is explained by the difference in *Agrarverfassung*: in petty-state Germany, the nobility and the Church tended to give the peasantry secure long-term leases; in France the rule was short-term *fermage*, various forms of insecure sharecropping. Eberhard Weiss' article (1970) is cited with enthusiastic approval by a leading French eighteenth-century historian, François Furet (1971: 266).

	Distal	Proximal	City-State	Proximal	Distal
	Empire-Nations: Seaward	Empire-Nations: Seaward	Europe	Empire-Nations: Landward	Empire-Nations: Landward
PROTESTANT	Norway	Denmark	Hanse Germany	Prussia	Sweden
MIXED	Britain	France	Low Countries Rhineland Switzerland		
CATHOLIC	Portugal	Aragon-Castile: Spain	Italy	Bavaria Austria	Poland Hungary

Figure 8–8. Conceptual Reformulation of the Schematic Geopolitical Map of Europe

mass democracy: the difficulty of accounting for the contrast between developments in England and developments in France.

Generalized beyond his immediate cases, Moore's thesis might be formulated in two propositions: the closer the ties of interaction and cooperation between the rural and the urban economic elites, the greater the chances for a successful transition to a full-suffrage competitive democracy; the greater the distance between the urban and the landed economies, the greater the likelihood of an unchecked and unbalanced growth of the state, the greater, in fact, the chances for a cumulation of crises in the transition to mass politics.

Barrington Moore has convincingly marshaled the evidence for the importance of this contrast in his analysis of the developments in England vs. Prussia: in the Western case early commercialization of agriculture and a strong alliance between the urban and the rural economies, in Prussia a weakly developed city economy and a highly "labor repressive" rural economy, as a consequence an alliance of the military-administrative power-holders and the land-owning Junkers against the bourgeoisie and the peasantry. Barrington Moore's analysis is much less convincing for France: how could this "seaward empire-nation" with its strong bonds between the rural and the urban economies build up an absolutist regime so very different from the representative rule prevailing in Britain? None of Moore's arguments from the differences in the character of the rural-urban alliances in the two countries carries decisive weight: the contrast between labor-reducing wool production in England and labor-intensive wine production in France, the direct links between the city elite and the estate owners in England, the important role of the

[586]

French monarchy in linking the urban bourgeoisie with the rural nobility through the *vénalité des offices*. Clearly, to account for the differences between England and France, it is necessary to go further in the differentiation of variables: we would have to consider a variety of indicators such as the *openness vs. exclusiveness in the class structure* (England: openness ensured through primogeniture rule; France: large but socially exclusive nobility), the *equalization of tax burdens* (England: no exemptions for peers; France: extensive exemptions), *the ease of resource extraction for the state* (England: customs collection in the harbors; France: greater cost of controls, exemptions a necessary strategy in the reduction of organized resistance against taxation) and, last but not least, the *geopolitical loads and their consequences for the actual fiscal requirements of the state* (England an island, consequently lower defense requirements; France a larger territory with open borders to the North and the Northeast). In our reformulation of the conceptual map we have given pride of place to this geopolitical dimension. France was *closer* to the central trade belt and had to build up a much stronger apparatus to define its national territories; England was *at a safe distance* from the central area and did not have to build up a monolithic apparatus to delimit a distinctive system.

The English-French comparison raises a number of important issues in the study of successive phases of political development. Why did the English Parliament prevail after 1660–1688, while the French *pouvoirs intermédiaires* succumbed to absolute rule for close to two centuries? Why did the Glorious Revolution of 1688 lead England safely through to a gradual solution of its identity and participation crises while the Great Revolution of 1789 left France with a cumulation of crises over these issues throughout the nineteenth century? Why did the English move step by step from one Reform to another to the final phase of mass democracy while the French passed from estate representation to manhood suffrage in two quick jumps in 1792–1793, and as suddenly from *régime censitaire* back to mass democracy in 1848?

Such questions deserve detailed analysis in a broad comparative perspective: great progress can be made through detailed comparisons of pairs of contrasting cases but it is essential to proceed with such comparisons within a broader paradigmatic framework. The contrast between England and France is not unique in all its dimensions: the contrast between slow, stepwise development and sudden, critical restructuring is a universal one, even if the dimensions differ from one configuration to another.

Perhaps the closest parallel to the English-French contrast is the Swedish-Danish: Sweden was able to keep up its estate representation through most of the era of absolutism and moved very gradually, step by step, toward mass democracy; Denmark, by contrast, was an absolute monarchy from 1660 to 1839 and moved quite suddenly to near-manhood suffrage already in 1849. Historians who have compared the developments of the two states during the crucial seventeenth century have been struck by the similarities between Sweden and England on the one hand, Denmark and France on the other. The Danes shared with the French a highly exclusive nobility; the owners of the large estates not only kept the peasantry in a state of near-serfdom, but maintained a posture of aloofness from the urban bourgeoisie. The nobility had for centuries kept the monarchy under control through the institution of the *Haandfaestning*, a contract sworn by the King on the accession to the Throne, guaranteeing the maintenance of privileges. With the increase in commercial activity, notably the greater revenues from the Sound dues, the King was gradually able to strike an alliance with the bourgeoisie and the clergy against the nobility: the result was the coup of 1660 and the introduction of absolute rule. In Sweden there was also a strong nobility, but it was much more open to cooperation both with the Monarchy and with the burgeoning bourgeoisie of the cities. Of major importance in the linking of rural and urban interests were the great iron and copper mines: it is tempting to argue that this trade developed linkages in Sweden similar to those the wool trade did in England. As a result, the Swedish nobility and their bourgeois allies could resist much more efficiently the tendencies to absolute rule which had been strengthened through the successes of the Swedish Kings in building the Baltic Empire.[4] The Estates in fact succumbed for a brief period, from 1680 to 1719, but the decline of the Empire brought back the rule of the Estates: the great Era of Liberty in Sweden is the nearest parallel anywhere in Europe to the era of parliamentary supremacy opened up by Walpole in England.

Again, the factor of geopolitical distance looms large. Denmark was at the tail end of the central trade belt and controlled a crucial

[4] This point has been emphatically stressed by the Norwegian historian Knut Mykland in his analysis of developments up to 1660 (Mykland 1967: 69-62). Cf. Pedersen 1967.

thoroughfare in the European commercial system, the Sound. Sweden had been heavily entangled in the affairs of the trade belt during the Thirty Years War, but later lost out against the Prussians and withdrew to the homeland territories to the north: the Sound and the Baltic isolated it from the central network of continental cities much in the way the Channel did Britain.

We can summarize these comparisons in a 2x2x2 scheme generated from our original model of exit openings for the center-building elites: see Figure 8–9.

This overschematized table posits a dynamic interaction between the structuring of *exit* options and the opening up of channels for *voice*. You cannot build states without controlling borders. In fact, the military-administrative power of any state can best be gauged through an analysis of its success in controlling interaction across its boundaries, in checking the movement of men, commodities and ideas. The absolutist-mercantilist state nearest to the trade belt tried to reduce the *exit* options of its subjects quite drastically. The cities depended for their survival on the freedom of the trade networks and controlled the greatest resources for resistance against the centralizers. But the ability of the cities to resist depended heavily on the structure of alliance options within each territory: who else needed *exit* options? Wherever the cities were weak and isolated, the territorial centralizers succeeded: the result was a reduction in *exit* opportunities and a corresponding increase over time in the pressures for *voice*. But the absolutist-centralist states not only tried to close their borders, they also choked the channels of representation within the territory. In Hirschman's model, you cannot reduce both the *exit* and the *voice* options at the same time without endangering the balance of the system. This is what happened in the absolutist-mercantilist states. They had to go through much more violent transitions to mass democracy (Phases II-IV in our model) than the states which managed to keep a better balance between *exit* controls and *voice* channeling during the crucial phases of state-building. Two types of states in Europe managed to define their borders and to impose a modicum of administrative control without closing the channels of representation: the consociational states in the center (High, High, Low) and the empire nations at one remove from the central trade belt (High, Low, Low). The Netherlands and Switzerland, England, and Sweden, all in their different ways managed to control the processes of mass mobilization with much greater ease

	Western		City-State	Eastern	
	PERIPHERIES	EMPIRE-NATIONS	EUROPE	EMPIRE-NATIONS	PERIPHERIES
Economic Exits: Openness to International City Network	Low	Low	High	High	Low
Legal/Cultural Exits: Openness to Supranational Influences (Shared Legal Systems, Shared Languages)	Low	High	High	High	Low
Territorial/Military Exits:					
Low: Easily Definable Borders, Insulated Geopolitical Position	Iceland	Norway Scotland England	Netherlands Switzerland	Sweden	
High: Borders Uncertain, Unstable Geopolitical Position	Ireland	Denmark France / Castile Portugal	Catalonia Italy	Prussia Bavaria Austria / Bohemia	Finland Poland Hungary

Figure 8–9. Elite Options in European States

than the other states of Europe. France, Denmark, and Spain in the West (High, Low, High and High, High, High), Prussia and Austria in the East (High, High, High) were all caught up in a struggle to define their systems under heavy exit pressures and had to impose stringent controls to check the disruptive forces. On the peripheries of these systems of states all again depended on the permeability of borders: easy transitions to mass politics in such insulated nation-states as Iceland (Low, Low, Low) and Norway (High, Low, Low), much more violent transitions in historically less definite territories such as Ireland (Low, High, High: the Ulster conflict), Finland (Low, Low, High: uncertainties toward Sweden and Russia), Bohemia (High, Low, High: the German-Czech-Slovak tangle), Poland (Low, Low, High: the Prussian-Austrian-Russian border uncertainties), and Hungary (Low, Low, High: uncertainties toward Austria, Croatia and Romania).

The essential message of Figure 8–9 seems to be this: you can expect a smooth transition to the mass politics of Phases III and IV—*either* when the territory is sufficiently remote from the exit promptings of the trade belt to have allowed the early growth of distinctive legal, religious, and linguistic standards (the English, Swedish, Norwegian, and Icelandic cases) *or*, within the central belt, whenever the cities have been able to establish strong enough consociational ties to thwart the development of a centralizing state apparatus (the Dutch and the Swiss cases).

Conversely you should expect difficult, often violent, transitions in all other cases: whenever a strong center had been built up at the edges of the trade belt and had had to develop a national political system through constant struggles to limit the multiple exit options kept up in the trade belt (the Danish, French, Spanish, Prussian, and Austrian cases); whenever center-building, nation-building, and the opening up of the channels of mass politics followed closely on each other (the Italian, Irish, Finnish, Czechoslovak, Polish, and Hungarian cases).

The Uniquenesses of the European Configurations and the Sources of Variation in the Other Regions

We have argued for the use of a simple grid of variables in the explanation of the many variations in the sequences of state-building and national consolidation in Western Europe. We shall conclude our discussion with a brief and necessarily superficial review of the possibilities of constructing a corresponding grid of variables for the differentiation of sequences of development in the other regions of the world.

In our discussion of the variations within Europe we gave pride of place to four variables: on the cultural side the independence-dependence of the Church and the conditions for the development of a distinctive national linguistic standard; on the economic side the level of concentration in the rural economy and the independence-dependence of the city network.

At a higher level of abstraction we can identify four corresponding sets of "master variables," as in Figure 8–10.

	Economy	*Culture*
Exit		
Variables: Conditioning Openness to Cross-System Transactions	Independence of City Network: Openness of Borders	Differentiation of Secular-Religious Institutions: Closeness vs. Openness Towards External Influence
Voice		
Variables: Conditioning Closeness of Ties to Territorial System	Separateness and Concentration of Primary Resources	Distinctiveness and Unification of Territorial Language

Figure 8–10. Four Corresponding Sets of "Master Variables"

Let us review these variables in turn and point out the more striking of the overall differences among geocultural areas:

Master Variables	*Geocultural Area*
1. Secular-Religious Differentiation[5]	
Minimal: Local Religions only	Traditional Tropical Africa
Intermediate: Local Religion Closely Fused with Political System	

[5] This classification relies largely on the distinctions developed by Donald E. Smith (Smith 1972).

Master Variables	*Geocultural Area*
No Corporate Church	Hindu India, Confucian China,
Weakly Incorporated	Moslem Empires
Maximal: Church Differentiated and Strongly Incorporated	
Separate from Society	Buddhist Political Systems
Closely Fused with Political System, but Supraterritorial	Greek Orthodox Church, Counter-Reformation Roman Catholic Church in Latin American Empires
Supraterritorial Organization, Potentially in Opposition to Political Authority	Medieval Catholic Church
Nationally Fused	Protestant State Churches
Separate from National Political System	Protestant Sects

2. Linguistic
Unification/
Distinctiveness[6]

Low-Low

Localized Languages, Little Likelihood of Standardization, Imperial Standard Shared with Several Successor States	Tropical Africa, Latin American Countries with Large Proportions of Indians

[6] This classification draws in part on the work of Heinrich Kloss (Kloss 1968), and on tables assembled by Dankwart Rustow (Rustow 1968).

Master Variables	*Geocultural Area*
Low-Medium	
Highly Diversified, Several Endoglossic, One Exoglossic Standards	India
Medium-Low	
Imperial or Settler Standard Near-Dominant	
One Standard	Arab States, Rest of Latin America English-Speaking Settler States
Several Standards	Europe: Switzerland Belgium Canada S. Africa
Medium-Medium	
One Endoglossic, One Exoglossic Standard	Ireland (Wales) Finland
Medium-High	
Major Dialectal Varieties, One Endoglossic Standard	China
Several Endoglossic Standards	Spain, Norway, Czechoslovakia, Soviet Union
High-Medium	
Shared Endoglossic Standard	Austria, Germany, Thailand/Laos
High-High	Japan Homogeneous European Nation-States

Master Variables	*Geocultural Area*
3. Differentiation- Independence of City Networks[7]	
Low Differentiation from Rural Surroundings, Weak Networks	Tropical Africa, Ibero-American Cities Outside Captaincies, Russian Cities[8]
High Differentiation, Network Dominated by Military-Administrative Centers	Oriental Cities, North African Cities, Ibero-American Capitals, Prussia, Hapsburg Empire
High Differentiation Largely Independent Network	Japan (rise of *Chōnin*, 18th cent.), Cities of "Trade Belt Europe," English-Speaking Settler States
4. Concentration-Dispersal of Landholdings	
No Scarcity of Land Corporate Lineage Ownership	Traditional Tropical Africa[9]
Scarcity, Narrow-Kin Inheritance	
Large Estates	Asia (Must Be Differentiated), North Africa, Parts of Europe, Ibero-America
Smaller Estates Freer Peasantry	Parts of Europe[10] North America

[7] This crude classification is partly inspired by Fernand Braudel (Braudel 1967: chap. 8, 397–404).

[8] On differences between Russian and Western European cities during the decisive period of state-building, see especially Brunner 1956a.

[9] This characterization of traditional tropical Africa is primarily based on Goody 1969a; cf. also Goody 1969b.

[10] For differentiations within Europe see especially Dovring 1960 and Slicher van Bath 1963.

This quick and exceedingly superficial review of major differences among world regions on our four "master variables" obviously will not take us very far toward the construction of differentiating typologies for use in analyses of the preconditions and sequences of political development. The exercise has helped, however, to bring out with greater clarity the *uniquenesses of the European configurations*.

Let us conclude this essay by presenting a series of summary formulations of such uniquenesses: it is too early to present conclusions from any detailed analysis, but it may be worthwhile, even on this meager basis, to set out, however summarily, a few statements for further elaboration and specification once the fuller variable profiles have been established case by case.

The great paradox of Western Europe was that it developed a number of strong centers of territorial control at the edges of an Old Empire: the decisive thrusts of state formation and nation-building took place on the peripheries of the political vacuum left by the disruption of the old Roman Empire.

To this extent there is a tantalizing parallel with the Far East: Japan on the seaward periphery, China in the imperial center, Korea with its centripetal "politics of the vortex," the Asian equivalent to France? But in Asia, Japan was the *only* successful center to rise on the edge of a great empire—the only lasting peripheral center to the landward side of China was an Eastern European power, Russia.

What turned out to be crucial in the European development was that the fragmented center belt was made up of territories at an advanced level of culture, technologically as well as organizationally. First, there was a well-developed *agricultural economy*, innovative in its technology even during the early Middle Ages (see Slicher van Bath 1963: 69–72; White 1940); second, there was a remarkable network of highly autonomous *cities*, institutionally distinct from the surrounding agricultural lands;[11] third, these cities as well as the rural areas were linked together culturally through a common religion as a cross-territorial corporated *church*, through the operation of a major organization for long-distance communication through craft literacy[12] in one dominant standard language, Latin; and fourth, the transactions across these varied autonomous terri-

[11] The distinctiveness of the European city network has been analyzed with great acumen in Brunner 1956b.

[12] This point is developed in Innes 1950, and in Goody 1968: chap. VI, cf. also Cipolla 1969.

tories were controlled under a body of inherited normative precepts, those embodied in long tradition of Roman Law.

At the core of this highly developed region all attempts at military-administrative center-building failed until the nineteenth century. The decisive early developments toward a restructuring of the territory took place at the peripheries of this heartland. These attempts might easily have failed as well, many in fact did. Three circumstances contributed decisively to the success of the center-builders: first of all the development of *literate bureaucracies* and *legal institutions*, largely through the cooperation of the Church with the dynasties of the conquest centers; second, the growth of *trade* and the emergence of *new industries*, developments which allowed the military-administrative machineries to expand without destroying their resource basis; and third, the emergence of *national script* and the consequent attempts to unify the peripheral territories culturally around a standard medium of internal communication: this development was pushed one step further at the Reformation, through the break with the cross-territorial Latin culture, and was accelerated through the invention of printing, through the multiple reproduction of messages without relays.[13]

The extraordinary synchrony of all these developments during the three centuries from 1485 to 1789 goes far to explain the rapid growth of consolidated nation-states on the western and the eastern edges of the Western Europe core territories. What proved decisive for the further growth of these political systems was the *low levels of overall mobilization at the time of state-building*: the new linkages were forged at the level of national and local elites; the masses of the peasantry and the urban workers were only gradually brought in. The decisive thrust toward the consolidation of the machineries of territorial control took place before the full monetization of the economy, before the lower strata could articulate any claims for participation. This gave the national elites time to build up efficient organizations before they had to face the next set of challenges: the strengthening of national identity at the mass level (our Phase II), the opening of channels for mass participation (Phase III), the development of a sense of national economic solidarity and the establishment of a workable consensus on the need for a redistribution of

[13] The decisive impact of printing for the rise of national language cultures has been analyzed by H. A. Innes (1950) and argued with aphoristic exaggeration by Marshall McLuhan (1962).

resources and benefits (Phase IV). There were important differences in the time sequences of these later crises: we have discussed these in some detail above. What is important is that the Western nation-states were given a chance to solve some of the worst problems of state-building before they had to face the ordeals of mass politics.[14]

By contrast to these early state-builders the leaders of the postcolonial polities face a cumulation of challenges in a very different world environment. Let us wind up our analysis by presenting a schematic checklist of such differences in the overall conditions of political action:

	16th-18th Century Europe	*20th Century Postcolonial Systems*
Conditions of Center Formation		
Pressures from Major Centers outside Territory	*Low* Old Empire Disintegrated, Influences from Rome Largely Cultural, Political Only in South	*High and Diversified* London, Paris, Washington, Moscow, Peking
Build-Up through Wars	*Frequent*	*Rare but Exceptions* Vietnam, Israel, Egypt
Center-Periphery Communications	*Slow* Short-Distance Dependencies Favoring Integration; Slowly Expanding Literacy Favoring Integration with National Center	*Rapid* Long-Distance Dependencies Weaken National Center; Increasing Exposure of Masses to outside Communications: Radio, Films
Cultural Unification		
Likelihood of Development of National Linguistic Standard	*High* Outside Standards (Latin, Greek) Politically– Economically Weak	*Low* Outside Standards Politically and/or Economically Strong: Role of Language of Former Imperial Masters

[14] This, of course, is not much more than a reformulation of the argument of Samuel Huntington (Huntington 1968). What we have added is a schema for the analysis of variations *within* Europe and some suggestions for parallel differentiations across and within other regions.

	16th-18th Century Europe	20th Century Postcolonial Systems
Elite Commitment to Unified Culture	*High* Early National Universities Favored Development of Nation-Tied Competences (Careers in Law, Education)	*Low* Dependence on Foreign Universities, Attraction to Outside Alternatives[15]

Participation Challenge

	16th-18th Century Europe	20th Century Postcolonial Systems
Demonstration Effects of Other Regimes	*Low* All Regimes Restrictive until American-French Revolutions	*High* Models of Universal Suffrage Politics in Europe and the West
Institutional Readiness for Mass Participation	*Varying, but Typically High* Historically Given Channels of Representation	*Low*

Distribution Challenge

	16th-18th Century Europe	20th Century Postcolonial Systems
Demonstration Effects	*Low*	*High* Welfare States, Socialist Economies as Alternative Models
Institutional Readiness	*High* Marked Build-Up of Extractive Capabilities, Potential Instruments of Redistribution	*Low* State Machineries Overburdened by Other Tasks
Growth of Cultural-National Economic Solidarity	*Marked* Increase in Willingness to Equalize Economic Conditions within Territory	*Problematic*

[15] This point has been brought out with great force by Ronald Dore in his comparison of endoglossic Japan (in this respect a system very similar to the European nation-states) and Latin America: in Japan the closed national culture encouraged the elites to build up their institutions through internal accommodation; in Latin America the cross-national openness of elite structures sharing the same language always allowed escape options (1964). Cf. the comments by Hirschman 1970: 61.

These are stark contrasts: the actual gradations are finer, the variations have many more strands to them. The lesson of the analysis is nevertheless clear: the European sequence simply cannot be repeated in the newest nations; the new nation-builders have to start out from fundamentally different conditions, they face an entirely different world. But they can learn to develop new combinations of policies from a detailed analysis of the many facets of the European experiences of state-building and national consolidation. They may learn more from the smaller countries than from the large, more from the multiculturally consociational polities than from the homogeneous dynastic states, more from the European latecomers than from the old established nations: what is important is that these experiences be sifted and evaluated, not just case by case, but within an effort of cross-regional systematization. If this paper helps to initiate discussions along these lines it will have served its purpose.

CHAPTER 9

WESTERN STATE-MAKING AND
THEORIES OF POLITICAL TRANSFORMATION

CHARLES TILLY

~~~~~~~~~~~~~~~~~~~~~~~~~~~~~~~~~~~~~

Europe in Theory

WHAT if everything we have said about Western Europe is valid, but irrelevant to the contemporary world? We may have ruled out its validity already, if only by having said contradictory things about European state-making. We certainly have not ruled out the second possibility: irrelevance. In fact, we have called attention to a number of changes in the world situation which make it quite unlikely that the exact sequences of events we have lovingly reconstructed from the European record will ever occur again. Our hope for relevance to the politics of the present and the future rests elsewhere.

Three possible applications of the European experience come to mind. The first is the simple fact that most of the theories which are now available for application to the present and future build, implicitly or explicitly, on ideas of what happened in Europe; at least we can edit those ideas. The second is the (not quite so simple) fact that Europeans and their offspring played the dominant part in creating the international system within which all states of the contemporary world are now operating; most likely getting the previous history of that system right will help us understand its elements and chart the limits on its near future. The third is the chance that the relationships among variables—between the costliness of the armed forces and the extent of the extractive apparatus, for example—which held in European history will continue to hold in our own time, although the specific sequences and forms in which those relationships worked themselves out in Europe will not.

This postscript will not do justice to any of the three alternatives. I will not, for example, scan the literature of "political development"

Once again I am thankful to Val Lorwin for criticism. Gabriel Almond and I wrote early drafts of some sections of this chapter in collaboration. I have lifted a few passages from our joint work, and have built a number of ideas we worked out together into the review of the literature. But (as will no doubt be obvious to a careful reader) Professor Almond bears no responsibility for the way the essay finally came out.

to spot risky analogies and faulty inferences from the European experience. Nor will I make the faintest effort to build a theory of state-making valid for both historical Europe and the contemporary world. This book, I believe, lays some of the groundwork for such a theory. It also identifies some of the ways the new theory must differ from the schemes already on hand. In order to seize these opportunities without returning to the long-windedness of my earlier essays in this book, let me do three things: (1) state a series of positions concerning the usual run of theories about state-making, especially those that have come to be known as "theories of political development," without making a substantial effort to document or defend those positions; (2) indicate what sort of theory seems likely to fit the European and contemporary experiences better than those now available; and (3) enumerate some features of the European experience we have reviewed in this book which are particularly important for the new theories to take into account.

What Theories Are Available?

We are searching for theories which ought, in principle, to give answers to the following questions:

1. Under what conditions do national states (rather than some other sort of political structure) become the dominant organizations in an area?

2. What are the chief forms taken by national states, and what causes one or another of them to appear?

3. What determines how strong, durable, effective, and responsive to its own population a national state is?

We could ask many other questions. I single these out because they define the area of overlap between the historical questions about European experience on which this book has concentrated and the general problems contemporary analysts of large-scale political transformation have been addressing.

What families of theories, then, contain possible answers to the three questions? I see three big sets: developmental, functional, and historical. Each has a number of subdivisions. The *developmental* theories propose some sort of standard process of political transformation to which all social units of some type—societies, regions, nations, or something else—are subject as a consequence of forces which are internal to those social units. The *functional* theories do not specify the process by which national states of a certain kind emerge, but enumerate instead what else must exist if national states of that kind are to operate. The *historical* theories account for the characteristics of any particular government through its individual relationship to some historical transformation affecting the world as a whole.

Developmental, functional, and historical theories are not necessarily incompatible. We might imagine a statement in which the standard developmental process modulates systematically as a world-historical transformation proceeds, because the functional requisites of different kinds of government appear as that transformation unfolds; Marxists have been trying for some time to build such a theory. Nevertheless, the three kinds of argument lead to rather different procedures and evidence. To deal with developmental theories, we shall have to examine the experiences of comparable political units over substantial blocks to time. Functional theories require multiple observations of particular features of national states and of their correlates. Historical theories are at once the most demanding and the least verifiable, for they call for no less than the tracing of a transformation throughout the world.

As a practical matter, then, we shall have to choose among developmental, functional, and historical approaches to our subject matter. Within each category, we may reasonably ask which of the available theories (if any) are consistent with what we know so far about state-making. When it comes to choosing *among* the categories, we must ask not which one is true, but which one leads to the more interesting hypotheses and opens up a feasible program of inquiry. Which one yields the right kinds of propositions? Since the question deals with potentialities, not actualities, any answer we give to it will be risky, tentative, and full of personal judgment. With that understanding, let me lay out opinions on currently available lines of thought.

Developmental Theories

The idea of social development following a standard path and springing from the very nature of societies (as Robert Nisbet has pointed out) pervaded the western social sciences from their nineteenth-century origins, and remained in their tissue into the twentieth century. Marx, Weber, and Durkheim were all developmental-

[603]

ists of sorts. Most of the recent theories to which we turn for accounts of the formation of national states have at least a streak of developmentalism. Nevertheless, some of them emphasize the standard path and the internal logic more strongly than others. Over the last twenty-five years, the phrases "political modernization" and "political development" have come to designate those emphatically developmental theories.

The idea of a partly autonomous process of *political* development came into being in more or less deliberate emulation of the "economic development" which became such a desirable object of public policy after World War II. It entails the same difficulties, and more. Both ideas leave uncertain whether the development in question is a continuous process, an end state or a structural transformation. Both have great difficulty with the problem of determining whether there are one or many paths which qualify as developmental. Both have gone through repeated crises of conceptualization, of definition, of identification of the phenomenon to be explained.

The analysts of economic development have at least two considerable advantages over their political counterparts: (1) relatively wide agreement that whatever else economic development may include, it certainly includes rising material well-being; and (2) the standardized means of description and measurement provided by the different versions of national income analysis. Theorists of political development have not reached consensus on any single criterion: efficiency, strength, representative institutions, or anything else. Nor have political analysts created anything remotely resembling a standard accounting scheme—although many an individual has proposed one general vocabulary or another. We should hardly be surprised, then, at the absence of generally accepted theories or of well-verified empirical generalizations. Instead, the most solid accomplishments of the effort to unravel political development have been a series of interesting case studies and intriguing comparisons; James Scott's analyses of "corruption" in Asia and the essays on Turkey and Japan brought together by Robert Ward and Dankwart Rustow come to mind.

Sequence and Stage Theories

Two main varieties of developmental theory deserve our attention: (1) schemes involving standard stages, sequences, or paths of development; and (2) statements of relationships without well-defined temporal orders. On the whole, theorists have moved away from the attempt to specify stages and toward an effort to specify relationships. Nevertheless, there are still some stage schemes available. We might judge their promise by examining one which is historically well informed. It comes, unsurprisingly, from an historian. Cyril Black speaks of the general phenomenon he is seeking to account for, modernization, as

> the process by which historically evolved institutions are adapted to the rapidly changing functions that reflect the unprecedented increase in man's knowledge, permitting control over his environment, that accompanied the scientific revolution. This process of adaptation had its origins and initial influence in the societies of Western Europe, but in the nineteenth and twentieth centuries these changes have been extended to all other societies and have resulted in a worldwide transformation affecting all human relationships. Political scientists frequently limit the term "modernization" to the political and social changes accompanying industrialization, but a holistic definition is better suited to the complexity and interrelatedness of all aspects of the process (Black 1966: 7).

Within the political realm, Black identifies four "critical problems" which each modernizing country faces; they mark four successive phases of modernization: (1) *the challenge of modernity*: "the initial confrontation of a society, within its traditional framework of knowledge, with modern ideas and institutions, and the emergence of advocates of modernity"; (2) *the consolidation of modernizing leadership*: "the transfer of power from traditional to modernizing leaders in the course of a normally bitter revolutionary struggle often lasting several generations"; (3) *economic and social transformation*: "the development of economic growth and social change to a point where a society is transformed from a predominantly rural and agrarian way of life to one predominantly urban and industrial"; and (4) *the integration of society*: "the phase in which economic and social transformation produces a fundamental reorganization of the social structure throughout the society" (Black 1966: 67–68). Later on Black reminds us that the phases refer mainly to political processes—not, for example, to intellectual transformations—and that they are matters of priority among problems which actually persist over long periods of time. Furthermore, he eventually distinguishes seven different "patterns of modernization"; the distinctions rest mainly on the conditions prevailing in some major part of the world at the time of entry into modernization; since whole subcontinents and even continents have tended to enter the process together, the patterns themselves form a rough temporal sequence. So there are standard phases which differ in their specific features and outcomes depending on which of seven successive patterns they fall into.

What answers does Black's scheme give to our questions about national states? Black considers the second phase of modernization, the consolidation of modernizing leadership, to have three outstanding features: "the assertion on the part of political leaders of the determination to modernize," "an effective and decisive break with the institutions associated with a predominantly agrarian way of life," and "the creation of a national state with an effective government and a reasonable stable consensus on the part of the inhabitants as to ends and means." The answer to our first question (Under what conditions do national states become dominant organizations in an area?) appears to be: when "modernizing leaders" take power, break out of the agrarian mold, and mobilize nationalism for the purpose of modernization. The answer to our second question (What are the chief forms taken by national states, and what causes one or another of them to appear?) seems to be that two things matter most: (a) the character of the modern leaders and (b) the geopolitical position of the territory in question at the beginning of modernization. And the answer to the third question (What determines how strong, durable, effective, and responsive to its own population a national state is?) likewise comes down to the character of modernizing leadership and to initial geopolitical position.

Let me leave aside historical quibbles over the placement of the "phases" and the classification of particular countries, except to note that Black's concentration on survivors leaves out such crucial cases as Brandenburg-Prussia. In his scheme, "Germany" experiences its consolidation of modernizing leadership from 1803 to 1871. The strength of Black's scheme, by the standard of the analyses in this book, is its insistence on a systematic change over time in the limits on state-making set by the international situation. But its weaknesses are multiple: the presentation of the landlords as the fundamental opponents of the modernizing elites, the failure to specify the activities which build up the state apparatus, the neglect of class coalitions as the determinants of different political outcomes, the final appeal to the character of modernizing leadership—which simply drives us back to asking why characteristically different types of leaders appear in the different clusters of modernizing countries. Except for the broad classification by geopolitical position, Black's analysis does not give us the means (even in principle) of taking a set of areas at a particular point in time and assessing the likelihood that strong, durable, effective, responsive national states of one form or another would arise in them by some later point in time.

Of course, one stage model does not represent them all. But Black's stage model is the most sensitive to historical nuances of any I know. By and large, the others present such grossly unhistorical categories or concentrate so heavily on the nineteenth and twentieth centuries as to propose no answers at all to our basic questions concerning the formation of national states. A.F.K. Organski's sequence (politics of primitive unification-politics of industrialization-politics of national welfare-politics of abundance), for example, brushes all our state-making materials into the basket of "unification" (Organski 965). Schemes which smooth out political development into a continuous process without well-defined stages (e.g., Flanigan and Fogelman 1971) invariably begin too late or too vaguely to yield answers to our question concerning the formation of states.

The many efforts to derive a standard sequence empirically from a cross-sectional comparison of a number of states at some recent point in time (e.g., most of the articles on political development in Gillespie and Nesvold 1971) are logically inappropriate for our task, since they do not analyze change over time. Their concentration on existing states elides the problem of how national states emerge where they did not exist before, although a comparison among existing states could conceivably shed light on the sources of the different forms taken by national states, and the reasons for their variable strength, durability, effectiveness, and responsiveness. Finally, the usual results of the cross-sectional analyses—scales at one end of which stand the rich parliamentary democracies—are heavily weighted by the presence or absence of political arrangements which are currently common in the western world. Even in principle, they could not identify the paths to patrimonialism, military dictatorship, or agrarian oligarchy. So far as I can tell, the stage and sequence theories of political development now available do not offer any strong and promising hypotheses concerning the emergence, forms, strength, durability, effectiveness, and responsiveness of national states.

There are, however, some related schemes which look a little more promising. In fact, those schemes had a part in bringing this book into being. They consist of the enumeration of a limited set of transitions, crises, or challenges presumably faced by any unit undergoing political development; in the company of the enumeration we often find a weak hypothesis concerning the order in which the transitions occur, and a weaker hypothesis concerning an historical change in order and pacing of the transitions as political development has moved from the West to the rest of the world. The scheme of "crises of political development" formulated by Lucian Pye, Gabriel Almond and their collaborators looks like this (in Stein Rokkan's concise summary):

Crises, Challenges, Problems	Institutional Solutions: Examples
Penetration	Establishment of a rational field administration for resource mobilization (taxes, manpower), creation of public order, and the coordination of collective efforts (infrastructure development, emergency action, defense)
Integration	Establishment of allocation rules equalizing the shares of offices, benefits, resources among all culturally and/or politically distinct sectors of the national community
Participation	Extension of suffrage to hitherto underprivileged strata of population. Protection of the rights of organized opposition
Identity	Development of media and agencies for the socialization of future citizens into the national community: schools, literary media, institutionalized rituals and symbols (myths, flags, songs)

Crisis, Challenges, Problems	Institutional Solutions: Examples
Legitimacy	Any effort to create loyalty to and confidence in the established structure of political institutions in the given system and to ensure regular conformity to rules and regulations issued by the agencies authorized within the system
Distribution	Establishment of social services and social security measures, income equalization through progressive taxation and transfers between poorer and richer localities (Rokkan 1969: 63–64)

Each of these problems, goes the main hypothesis, tends to concentrate in time, and hence to form a *crisis*. From that point, which is still mainly a matter of definition, the standard formulation proceeds to the idea that the more rapidly and simultaneously these crises appear, the higher the level of strain and the greater the likelihood of intense conflict, breakdown and disintegration. Behind this idea stands an implicit contrast between the long accumulation of political experience by western nations and the recent rush to statehood in the rest of the world. In the European microcosm, we have British gradualism opposed to continental haste. In the world macrocosm, we have European cumulation versus Third World discontinuity.

In these terms, the analyses of taxation, military forces, policing, and so on elsewhere in this book deal primarily with penetration, secondarily with legitimacy, less with integration and identity, hardly at all with participation and distribution. One of the reasons we had the chance to write the papers in this book was the hope of the members of the Committee on Comparative Politics (including Pye and Almond) that a careful look at European history would help edit the scheme—not necessarily confirm it, but at least show whether its categories were historically applicable, determine whether the crises did occur somehow in each country at a distinct point in time, discover whether there were any standard sequences among them, try out the notion of a later cumulation of crises.

Nowhere in this book will you find a self-conscious attempt to match the six crises with historical data. Our analyses only challenge the hypothesis of temporal concentration of each of the problems into a "crisis" indirectly: by treating extraction, control and coalition-formation as the central state-building processes, by portraying the basic "problems" as more or less continuous rather than bunched in time, and by posing great empirical difficulties for any attempt to put the problems or processes into a standard sequence.

They challenge the historical comparisons in the background more directly. Although some of our essays view England's experience as more favorable than that of, say, Prussia, every single one of them calls attention to the immense conflict, uncertainty, and failure that attended the building of national states everywhere in Europe—including England. As a consequence, the idea that latecomers to state-making confront a "cumulation of crises" more concentrated and dangerous than that endured by early state-makers begins to lose plausibility. Perhaps that idea persists because we habitually compare the whole range of contemporary states with the small set that survived from the sixteenth century to our own time. In their days, Poland, the Two Sicilies, Burgundy, Aragon, and Bohemia—all displayed "cumulations of crises" quite worthy of the twentieth-century world. At least the survival of twentieth-century states (if not of their ruling classes or their particular forms of government) is practically assured.

Stripped of their historical references, these criticisms resemble those leveled against the very same sequence scheme by a sympathetic commentator, Sidney Verba. Verba closes a volume concerning the analysis of crises and sequences with a thoughtful critique of the penetration-participation-legitimacy-distribution-identity version of the scheme. ("Integration" has, by this point, disappeared from the set.) There is, he says, "some ambiguity as to what exactly the crises or problems are. In part, the issue is whether they are *crises* (some special kind of event that comes and goes) or persistent problems that political systems face. And, whichever conception of the item is used, they are difficult to place in a sequence because the five items seem to come together" (Verba 1971: 297).

Verba goes on to suggest that the institutions formed by the managers of a state to deal with any particular problem tend to survive beyond the acute phase of the problem and to constrain the response of the state to subsequent problems—a formulation which is surely

CHARLES TILLY

correct, if unsurprising, and which dovetails with this volume's insistence on the durable effects of the expedients adopted for the financing of armies, provisioning of cities, or policing of the countryside. Verba finally supports the hypothesis of cumulation: "What Britain took centuries to do—solve the problems of identity, legitimacy, participation, and distribution—the new nations have to do in the briefest span of time" (Verba 1971: 314). Despite this concession to the conventional argument, Verba's general assessment is that neither the crises, nor the sequences, nor the connections among them, have been reliably identified. I concur.

Developmental Models

Within the category of developmental theories, the chief alternatives to stage and sequence models are those which posit strong relationships among different types of changes without deriving from those relationships any particular developmental paths or priorities. Outside the political realm, sociologists of development have often been content to show that urbanization and industrialization frequently occur together and reinforce each other, without insisting that one of them always comes first, or that their interaction follows a well-defined obstacle course. Similarly, many theories of political development emphasize the interdependence of a specialized governmental staff and a strong executive, without laying out a sequence in which they appear.

Most cross-sectional studies adopt this weaker (but safer) kind of developmental formulation. Phillips Cutright has, for example, conducted a series of comparisons among contemporary states with respect to political development, inequality, and social security systems. In the social security study his most general conclusion is that

national political, economic, and social systems are interdependent. Changes in the complexity of organization in one sphere are followed by changes in organization in other areas. The specific activities that engage the attention of national governments are not independent of the general level of development. Quite the contrary is true. In spite of very great differences among nations in ideological orientation as well as in type of political organization, we found that actual activities of government in the social security field were strongly related to the complexity of social organization in economic, social, and political institutions (Cutright 1965: 548).

[611]

In this particular study, comparing seventy-six governments over the period from 1930 to 1960, Cutright examined the statistical relationships among three measures of the extensiveness of social security programs, a scale of political representativeness (which essentially arrays states by their similarity to those western democracies which have at least two active parties) and several conventional indicators of wealth, urbanity and literacy. Earlier, Cutright had proposed the same scale of representativeness as a general measure of political development (Cutright 1963). There, he displays a high correlation between the index of representativeness (alias political development) and a "communications development index" combining observations on newspaper consumption, newspring consumption, telephones and volume of domestic mail. Having plotted the regression line linking the political index to the communications index, he explicitly adopts a theory of equilibrium at the regression line: a country which has "too much" or "too little" political development for its volume of communications will tend to change in such a way as to bring the two into adjustment.

Whatever one thinks of the general validity of Cutright's analysis, it is obviously a far cry from the specific questions about state-making we are pursuing. His analysis takes the existence of national states for granted, and barely asks what determines their durability, strength or effectiveness. By extrapolation, however, it does offer a *type* of answer to each of our three inquiries:

Q. Under what conditions do national states become the dominant organizations in an area? A. No real answer, but a suggestion that the development of complex social organization in other regards determines the formation of differentiated, centralized, territorially consolidated governments.

Q. What are the chief forms taken by national states, and what causes one or another of them to appear? A. The forms range along a principal continuum from "undeveloped" (characterized by low levels of political participation, by lack of popular representation and little redistributive activity) to "developed" (extensive participation and representation, vigorous redistribution); the various forms succeed each other in an evolutionary progression whose timing depends mainly on nonpolitical transformations: the accumulation of wealth, the formation of complicated communications systems, and so on.

Q. What determines how strong, durable, effective, and responsive to its own population a national state is? A. What position it has reached in the evolutionary progression. All these characteristics rise with political development, although only some of them enter into its definition.

The hypothetical answer to the first question is too general to be verifiable on the basis of European experience since 1500. Its deterministic tone clashes with our general portrayal of the early states as fragile and of their survival as contingent. Answering the second question with an evolutionary continuum running from nonparticipant to participant politics clashes badly with our insistence on the abridgements of political rights which occurred with the formation of national states, on the resistance of ordinary people to the expansion of state power, and on the constant changes in the very units undergoing political transformation. Likewise, our analyses of Europe treat the strength, durability, effectiveness, and responsiveness of a government as (1) only weakly related to each other; (2) only slightly dependent on the wealth or complexity of the population in question with wealth and complexity operating as constraints rather than as determinants; (3) more strongly affected by the class coalitions, past and present, supporting a particular state's government, and by the relationship of that state to the whole system of states, than the evolutionary scheme implies.

Do our analyses therefore *refute* Cutright's? Not really. If they are correct, they limit the field of applicability of his generalizations to the contemporary world and/or the later stages of state-making. If correct, they cast doubt on the functional portions of his argument (e.g., the interdependence of complexity and representation) and offer some support for two alternatives to a functional interpretation: (1) the diffusion of a certain pattern of government among the richer countries of the world; and (2) the imposition of that standard pattern of government on the rest of the world by the richer powers. Finally, if they are correct, they indicate the need for a theory which has more room for expansion, domination, conflict, and destruction than appears in Cutright's.

The same might be said of Talcott Parsons' recent (1971) essay on the emergence of modern western societies. Parsons' treatment differs sharply from Cutright's in dealing extensively with changes in the western world over centuries before our own time, and in argu-

[613]

ing that the unique set of social conditions which emerged in Europe with the decline of feudalism produced a new type of society—the "modern" society—which, after considerable internal transformation, diffused to the rest of the world. What is more, Parsons has a clear conception of a system of states acting on each other and, to some extent, acting collectively. Nevertheless, Parsons and Cutright converge at two crucial points. First, they both consider the formation of governments of the twentieth-century type to be the more or less inevitable accompaniment of complexity in other realms. Second, they both posit an evolutionary path toward democracy and widespread political participation.

Parsons puts forth these points in a passage dealing with England, France and Holland during the seventeenth century:

> These three nations were the "spearhead" of early modernity. The most important developments occurred in their societal communities. The variations among the forms of the three societal communities were immense, but each contributed major innovations relative to national solidarity. In particular, the English conception of national identity provided a basis for a more clearly differentiated societal community. The differentiation proceeded on three fronts—religious, political, and economic —each involving normative considerations. Legal innovations were thus critical, especially those that favored associational rather than bureaucratic potentials of the structure of national community. They were closely related to the emergence of parliamentarism and more developed market economies (Parsons 1971:54).

If we were to apply the three basic questions about state-making to this and related portions of Parsons' analysis, I think we would come out with approximately the same answers that I have already attributed to Cutright: (1) nonpolitical differentiation presupposes or produces political differentiation; (2) political forms belong in a continuum from undeveloped to developed; (3) the quality of a state depends mainly on its position along that continuum. The main difference is that Parsons treats the initial formation of territorial states in France and England as an outcome of renewed cultural creativity in geopolitically favorable niches within the European system. That much of the argument might, if extended, turn out to resemble Stein Rokkan's geopolitical analysis. But the rest raises the same objections I have already stated when dealing with Cutright.

Some General Comments on "Political Development"

Developmental theories have many other variants. It would be tedious and useless to review them one by one. Let me content myself with a few general reflections on the features of available theories which emerge when one grinds away at them with the grit of European history.

The literature concentrates, to a surprising degree, on political processes which only became prominent in the nineteenth century. The recurrent drama is the confrontation between a political structure presumably formed before the development of large-scale manufacturing and the complex of changes surrounding rapid industrialization. Some political structures are supposed to be readier than others to cope with those rapid changes. The readier the structure, the more likely the confrontation is to produce stable democracy. That way of putting it, of course, may simply amount to a definition of "readiness." As a general procedure for the analysis of political development, however, it clashes seriously with a number of the arguments in this book (notably Bayley's) which treat twentieth-century political patterns as outcomes of changes and struggles which occurred well before rapid industrialization.

The literature of political development is also strongly retrospective; it moves from twentieth-century political forms back to their presumed causes. Historical events matter to the extent that they contributed to the creation or survival of conditions actually observable in our own time. One result of this choice is that at its strongest the analysis could lead to a statement of the conditions under which a given political structure would change toward one of the existing models or instructions for producing that change. Such a literature seems unlikely to yield statements about the conditions under which a given political structure will disintegrate, stagnate, combine with others, or transform itself into a variety which has never been seen before. Since a large portion of the European political experience consisted of disintegration, stagnation, combination, and the emergence of political structures of a kind which had never before existed, and since the same will no doubt continue to be true of our world, the existing literature equips us poorly to deal with the analytic problems forced on us by the past and by the present.

[615]

Within the range of processes they do cover, most of these writings remain vague about just what is to be *explained*. The more sweeping and diffuse a conception of "political development" we adopt, the less likely it is that any theory whatsoever could provide an adequate account of its timing, sequences, impact, substance, or anything else. The characteristic uncertainty over the *explicandum* shows up in one of the less confused works in the field, Huntington's *Political Order in Changing Societies*. In general, Huntington is trying to lay out the alternative ways different countries have faced three fundamental political problems—the rationalization of authority, the differentiation of structures, and the expansion of political participation. He distinguishes three different Western patterns: the continental European (which he treats as a single model), the British and the American. The principal point of difference between the British and the continental European patterns is that the processes of centralization on the European Continent were focused in the crown and the state bureaucracy, while in Britain the centralization was focused in Parliament. The American pattern, which, he claims, stems directly from the sixteenth century Tudor distribution of powers, was the least centralized of the three patterns, both in the sense of regional decentralization and separation of powers. Huntington contrasts the long-time period available to the European powers for political problem-solving with the rush to modernity among the new states. His "mobilization-institutionalization" hypothesis asserts that democratic stability depends on a particular symmetry between the processes of mobilization (the breadth and intensity of demands for political participation) and the processes of institutionalization (the development of legitimate roles and political structures). The hypothesis evidently draws on nineteenth-century European history.

Important parts of Huntington's analysis—for instance, his treatment of the "Tudor Constitution" as keeping power away from the royal administration—run afoul of the arguments in this book. Instead of inspecting his historical statements, however, I want to call attention to the uncertainty of exactly what the analysis is supposed to explain. For the most part, Huntington eschews the term "political development"; instead he opposes political modernization to political decay. The basic definition is rather imprecise, but perhaps manageable: "Political modernization involves the rationalization of authority, the differentiation of structures, and the expansion of political participation" (Huntington 1968: 93). Later on, we discover that the Mexican Revolution was "highly successful in political development, that is, the creation of complex, autonomous, coherent, and adaptable political organizations and procedures, and it was reasonably successful in political modernization, that is, the centralization of power necessary for social reform and the expansion of power necessary for assimilation" (p. 324). Elsewhere we receive a warning against confusing "political modernization defined as movement from a traditional to a modern polity and political modernization defined as the political aspects and political effects of social, economic, and cultural modernization" (p. 35). Here and there we also encounter the idea of institutionalization, "Institutionalization is the process by which organizations and procedures acquire value and stability. The level of institutionalization can be defined by the adaptability, complexity, autonomy, and coherence of its organizations and procedures" (p. 12). Eventually, as in the remark on the Mexican Revolution already quoted, we recognize another simple equation:

institutionalization =

formation of adaptable, complex, autonomous,
   coherent political organizations
   and procedures =

political development

By this point, we begin to notice a certain amount of drift—not just in concepts, but in the identification of what is to be explained.

This vagueness of the *explicandum* pervades the field. In fact, the same difficulties beset a whole family of related concepts: modernization, mobilization, not to mention the now-abandoned word progress. With all of them, we attempt to explain so much that we end up explaining nothing.

The complaint about vagueness is as old as the literature itself. There is another problem which is less often noted, yet probably just as serious: the strangeness of the basic unit of analysis. Political scientists lost interest in talking about the state as such twenty or thirty years ago. As they did so, they took to the discussion of societies, political systems and nations. (An interesting example is David Apter's well-known *Politics of Modernization*, which contains absolutely no discussion of the organizational structure of states.) At least two in-

[617]

centives moved them away from the state: (1) the aspiration to "separate out analytically the structures which perform political functions in all societies regardless of scale, degree of differentiations, and culture" (Almond 1960: 5), and thus extend the geographic range of comparative politics outside of the West and into the Third World; and (2) the effort to extend the analytical scope of political analysis to include political culture, political socialization and similar phenomena relevant to government but outside the formal structure of government. This expansion brought a hidden cost: it required political scientists to work with units which were much harder to delineate than states.

One can hardly carry on a systematic analysis—especially a comparative analysis—of nations, political systems or societies without a means of identifying their boundaries. The boundaries need not be geographic; they may separate different groups of people who are scattered or mingled in space. The means may be artibrary, permitting the political scientist to analyze *any* local population as a "political system" in something like the manner that an ecologist designates any localized set of organisms and their environment as an "ecosystem." Or the means may derive from some theory of the social bond, using common language, degree of contact with a particular metropolis, or some such criterion to separate one nation, political system or society from another. In that case, the investigator has a special obligation: he must actually use that criterion to bound his units.

What have political scientists done in practice? For the most part, they have sneaked back to the state. They have treated the people and the territory subject to the control of a particular state as the basic unit to be compared with similar units elsewhere. Colonial territories then cause a certain amount of embarrassment, ordinarily handled by relegating them to a separate analysis. Thus the immense majority of studies in recent political science styling themselves cross-national, cross-polity, comparative and so forth have taken national states (or, more precisely, the territories and populations controlled by national states) as their basic units of analysis. The procedure is convenient and even justifiable. But it has the disadvantage of begging most of the questions which induced comparative political analysts to turn away from the state in the first place.

The choice of contemporary states as units for the long-run comparison of "political development" causes grave difficulties. For everything which is dubious about the coherence of a nation, political system, or society identified by its relationship to a particular state at a single point in time becomes much more dubious when it comes to the study of a very long span of time. Among the areas studied in this volume, England and France seem the least contestable cases; even there we must make hard decisions concerning Scotland, Wales, Ireland, Britanny, and Alsace (not to mention Jersey, Guernsey, Andorra, or Monaco). The difficulties become apparent when we attempt to analyze the development of a unit called "Germany" from, say, 1550 to 1950. What are its boundaries? All the practical solutions of which I am aware divide into two categories: (1) take the population and territory controlled by a particular state at a particular point in time—perhaps the German Reich in 1900—then work forward and backward from that reference point; and (2) choose a particular political organization—the protostate and state of Brandenburg-Prussia would be a likely prospect here—and adjust the populations and territories under consideration to its fortunes. The first choice has the advantage of convenience and the disadvantage of theoretical awkwardness. The second choice provides a better fit to the phenomena about which we are able to theorize coherently, but has two large disadvantages. First, it is hard to do. Second, it leaves aside the continuous histories of the populations and territories which only come under the jurisdiction of the state in question for part of the period being examined. One would want somehow to include the vicissitudes of Bavaria before 1871 among the determinants of German politics after that time. Yet if we are to remain faithful to the analysis of a single coherent political organization, we shall have to drop poor Bavaria and devote our attentions to Brandenburg-Prussia.

Are these difficulties surmountable? If they are, we can retain the hope of generalizing about the process of political development experienced by a nation, political system, or society. If they are not, we shall have to content ourselves with generalizing about either (1) changes in particular kinds of political organizations, including states; in this case, shifts in the sorts of territories and populations with which they are dealing will form a major part of the *explanation* of organizational changes; (2) changes in the political experiences of particular kinds of populations and territories, defined independently of the jurisdictions under which they fall at different points in time, but not (3) both at the same time.

For my part, I do not think the difficulties are surmountable. Even if I am wrong, it should be clear that little more can be done with theories of political development until the actual unit which is "developing" gets more careful specification than it has had in the past.

One more thing about the characteristic unit of analysis deserves a going-over. The extreme concentration on the individual nation, political system, society, *or* state has drawn attention away from the international structures of power within which "development" takes place. The closest most of the literature comes to the kind of analysis we have in mind is in the discussion of influences which disaggregate easily into experiences of individual units: demonstration effects, military support, development funds, external subversion, importation of political technologies. In my review of recent writings, I have encountered impressively little discussion of the way the structure of world markets, the operation of economic imperialism, and the characteristics of the international state system affect the patterns of political change within countries in different parts of the world. Our review of the West European experience, on the other hand, has often brought us face to face with these very phenomena. The interdependent changes in the political structures of Poland, Denmark, Spain, and the Netherlands during the sixteenth and seventeenth centuries provide one of the clearer examples. The profound effects of the Napoleonic Wars, another.

In a few works at the edge of the political development literature —for example, the essays of Amitai Etzioni and of J. P. Nettl and Roland Robertson—one sees a deliberate effort to specify those changes and take them into account. Yet so far I detect few signs that the theory itself is shifting in response to the recognition of its weakness. Something specific about the analysis of political development appears to have blocked the effective introduction of the proper international variables into existing developmental models.

That something could be the implicit policy aims of the models. Taken as a whole, the literature of political development is rather didactic in tone. It runs together description, analysis, prediction, and prescription in a fashion reminiscent of writings on city planning or population problems. Very likely the incentive to offer guidelines for the present and the future has encouraged the analysts to concentrate on the single national states and on the decisions within the reach of its managers. At least that seems a plausible explanation of the neglect of national and international structures of power, of the view from below, of the paths to alternatives the managers do not desire, and so on through most of the weaknesses I have inventoried. Here is one case, it seems, where the effort to produce results relevant to current affairs reduced the strength of the analysis, instead of increasing it.

Functional Theories

Functional theories differ from developmental theories mainly by subtraction: they do not propose any standard stages, sequences or trajectories, but they do state what else must be present if a national state is to exist. By that criterion many of the theories which advertise themselves as developmental are actually functional; indeed, some of the arguments I reviewed under the first heading are more definite about the necessary concomitants of the national states than they are about the processes which produce it. A number of broad evolutionary statements have more to say about function than process.

That is generally the case with anthropological treatments of the state. Anthropologists have worked intermittently on the origins of the state since their discipline crystallized in the nineteenth century. The problem does not have the cachet now that it had in the heyday of cultural evolution. But the students of evolution have never quit; at this point they may well be gaining strength. Recently, for example, Morton Fried has drafted an anthropologist's statement on the evolution of political organization. Characteristically, it links the extent and form of specialized political organization in a society to the system of stratification, which in turn is supposed to depend especially on the organization of production; again characteristically, the scheme divides all societies into a small number of levels: egalitarian, rank, stratified, and state societies. The state

is a collection of specialized institutions and agencies, some formal and others informal, that maintains an order of stratification. Usually its point of concentration is on the basic principles of organization: hierarchy, differential degrees of access to basic resources, obedience to officials, and defense of the area. The state must maintain itself externally as well as internally, and it attempts this by both physical and ideological means, by supporting military forces and by establishing an identity among other similar units (Fried 1967: 235).

This definition and the approach it implies are too broad to serve our immediate purpose of analyzing the alternative patterns of state-making in Western Europe and to draw out their implications for the contemporary world. Yet they draw attention to two features of states which the theories we have been reviewing ordinarily slight: their close ties to existing systems of stratification and their maintenance by means of various forms of coercion. Gerhard Lenski, among others, has taken the same line of argument quite a bit farther in the same direction. His comparisons of the characteristic political structures of agrarian and industrial societies still fall short of the refinement we need to distinguish a Prussia from a Spain or a seventeenth-century Poland from a twentieth-century Indonesia.

Despite the fact that anthropologists are often aware of the diffusion of political forms from one part of the world to another, and of international structures of domination, anthropological theories of the state tend to treat each society as more or less self-contained. To find functional theories of state-making in which relations among states play a major part we have to turn to specialists in international relations. James Rosenau, for example, has titled a monograph *The Adaptation of National Societies: A Theory of Political System Behavior and Transformation*. The name itself announces a whole program of theory and research. In actuality, most of Rosenau's effort goes into the description of four alternative patterns by which "societies" adapt to a changing world environment: acquiescent, intransigent, promotive, and preservative. "For a national society," Rosenau tells us, "adaptation means that the fluctuation in the basic interaction patterns that sustain its social, economic, and political life must be kept within limits minimally acceptable to its members" (Rosenau 1970: 2). His avowed purpose in setting up the problem this way is to examine the interdependence of national and international affairs. What is more, he offers a set of broad, essentially functional, hypotheses which include the idea that "acquiescent" and "preservative" forms of adaptation grow from, depend on, and correspond to stronger influences from the external political system than do the "intransigent" and "promotive" forms. This argument does not quite get us into consideration of the structure of that external system. It does, however, open the way to a formulation of state-making as a function of relations between a particular population and the rest of the world.

[622]

Again, peace researchers are much inclined to connect the structures of power and control among states to their counterparts within states. In a characteristic recent statement, Ekkehart Krippendorff has recalled the close historical connection between the formation of national armies devoted to international warfare and the growth of the state apparatus. Like most of the authors in this book, he regards the building of the armies as a cause of state-making, rather than as a mere symptom of its occurrence. He goes farther; he revives the old idea that the price of domestic tranquillity within the more powerful states was the increase in the intensity of conflict *among* states:

> The Hobbes-Bodin observations about the higher level of international violence being the price paid for domestic pacification can be rephrased, therefore, for our times without losing their basic validity: the increase of violence in new, historically unprecedented forms is the direct function of inter-bloc stability and social pacification within the big industrial powers, which in turn was and still is only possible by means of strengthening state forms of political organization—be it of American, the Soviet or an emerging United European type. There is no doubt that the present pathological international system, better to be called a system of organized disorder, is being maintained only because of the existence of organized states (Krippendorff 1970: 55).

Like most other statements in this field, Krippendorff's analysis obviously leads to a prescription for peace—weaken or dismantle the strong states—and stands as a justification for it. For present purposes, the policy implications of his work matter less than the logical similarity of his basic model of the world to that employed by Rosenau. In both, governments respond to outside pressures and opportunities which are largely set for them by the current international structure of power, and in responding shape the subsequent relations between the government and the people under its jurisdiction. The model assumes a more direct relationship between international and national politics than we find in the literature of political development.

None of the functional theories of which I am aware, however, yields compelling answers to our three basic questions about the

[623]

emergence and transformation of national states. Their main contribution is to call attention to variables—both national and international—which are commonly neglected in developmental theories.

Historical Theories

As things now stand in the analysis of state-making, historical theories offer a more serious alternative to developmental theories than
functional theories do. By "historical" theories I mean those which
account for the characteristics of any particular government through
its individual relationship to some historical transformation affecting
the world as a whole. Perhaps the simplest theory of this type proposes a long-term trend toward wider political participation, equality and responsive government, in which different countries and different social classes join at different points in time. We have already
seen some flickers of those ideas among the developmental theorists.
But to find them fully in view we must turn to writers such as T. H.
Marshall or Reinhard Bendix.

In his *Nation-Building and Citizenship*, Bendix sketches a general
transformation of Western European countries "from the estate societies of the Middle Ages to the absolutist regimes of the eighteenth
century and thence to the class societies of plebiscitarian democracy
in the nation-states of the twentieth century" (Bendix 1964: 2). In
his view, the transformation took place in different parts of Europe
at different tempos, but eventually covered the entire continent. It
entailed several different trends: individualization of authority relationships, equalization of opportunity, the growth of citizenship, bureaucratization. In one important passage, Bendix makes the connection with the formation of the state:

> The simultaneous development of a nationwide authority,
> a corps of public officials formally insulated from "extraneous"
> influences, and the plebiscitarian tendencies in the political
> realm are accompanied by the development of functionally de-
> fined, organized interests. The efforts of public officials to ob-
> tain support, information and guidance from the relevant "pub-
> lics" are matched point for point by the efforts of organized
> interests to influence government actions so as to benefit their
> members or clients. It may be considered a corollary of nation-
> wide authority, on the one hand, and the proliferation of inter-
> ests organized to influence that authority, on the other, that in

Western nation-states consensus is high at this national level. In these political communities no one questions seriously that functions like taxation, conscription, law enforcement, the conduct of foreign affairs, and others belong to (or must be delegated by) the central government, even though the specific implementation of most of these functions is in dispute (Bendix 1964: 136–137).

Bendix does not give an overly explicit account of how, why and when these new political forms developed. (Furthermore, he bypasses the problem of defining the units undergoing the transformation by confining his attention to England, France, Prussia and Russia.) But his basic sequence appears to be: (1) state-makers concentrate authority in the public sphere while authority relations remain relatively unchanged in the private sphere; (2) with the Industrial Revolution and the growth of national markets, demands for political rights and for equality undermine traditional arrangements of authority in the private sphere as well; (3) under these pressures, a more powerful, but participatory, national state comes into being.

Much of Bendix' analysis is compatible with our findings. At two major points, however, we would have to part with the argument of *Nation-Building and Citizenship*. First, if our analyses are correct, Bendix misstates the trajectory and timing of political participation on the part of ordinary people. We see a widespread suppression of political rights and participation by the state-makers, we see recurrent crises of authority (both public and private) from the early days of state-making, frequently as a direct consequence of statemaking. Bendix seems to have relied too heavily on a backward extrapolation of the nineteenth-century nationalization of political action. Second, Bendix' analyses treat developments in one country as more or less independent of developments in the next. The main international connections in his scheme (and the main reasons for changes in the pattern from period to period) consist of different sorts of diffusion of models and beliefs. While our analyses concede the importance of diffusion, they also bring out the influence of the changing international structure of power. The differing relationships of a France, a Russia or an England (and, for that matter, of a seventeenth- and an eighteenth-century France) to the European state system hardly figure in his analysis.

[625]

That neglect is a little surprising, for the German scholarly tradition on which Bendix draws frequently paid attention to the international system. Hintze, for example, pointed out a long time ago that World War I transformed what had been essentially a European state system into a world system, with strong effects on all participants. Writing of the "participation crisis" beloved of later political development theorists, he declared:

> It is worth noticing that the old, well-established democracies showed themselves more resistant to crises than the untested new ones. In addition to these internal sources of shock leading to crises we must not forget the external ones which issued from the transformation which took effect in World War I. With the spread of popular sovereignty, solidarity declined as national rivalries increased. As the situation since the war [Hintze writes around 1930] has shown, these circumstances threaten the survival of the modern state in its historical form (Hintze 1962: 509–510).

In Hintze's analysis, clearly, more than the context in which each individual state "developed" was changing; the world system was changing.

Similarly, analysts of the economic situation of South Asia, the Middle East or (especially) Latin America have frequently attributed some or all of their region's "underdevelopment" to the relations of economic dependency and exploitation between their countries and the major western powers, particularly the United States. André Gunder Frank's *Capitalism and Underdevelopment in Latin America* begins with the contention that

> ... underdevelopment in Chile is the necessary product of four centuries of capitalist development and of the internal contradictions of capitalism itself. These contradictions are the expropriation of economic surplus from the many and its appropriation by the few, the polarization of the capitalist system into metropolitan center and peripheral satellites, and the continuity of the fundamental structure of the capitalist system throughout the history of its expansion and transformation, due to the persistence or re-creation of these contradictions everywhere and at all times. My thesis is that these capitalist contradictions and

[626]

the historical development of the capitalist system have generated underdevelopment in the peripheral satellites whose economic surplus was expropriated, while generating economic development in metropolitan centers which appropriate that surplus— and, further, that this process still continues (Gunder Frank 1967: 3).

This line of argument links neatly to a variety of recent analyses used elsewhere in this book: Immanuel Wallerstein's discussion of the formation of the European world-economy in the sixteenth century, Clifford Geertz' treatment of the "involution" of Indonesian agriculture under the impact of plantation-based production for the European market, Eric Wolf's reconstruction of the ways the expansion of capitalism into the peripheral areas of the world organized around Europe threatened the integrity of peasant communities, and other analyses. In addition to their own intrinsic merits and analyses of particular problems, these recent efforts have the advantage of placing the experience of specific areas squarely within the large international processes which help create that experience. They avoid the characteristic weakness of the "political development" literature: the treatment of each country as a separate, self-contained, more or less autonomous case.

By no means all of the analyses fall into the Leninist tradition on which André Gunder Frank, Paul Baran, and Rodolfo Stavenhagen build their work. The non-Leninist Celso Furtado, for example, speaks of "the international system of division of labor, which enable Latin American countries to initiate their development in the nineteenth century" as creating "asymmetrical relations that were reflected in the close dependence of countries exporting raw materials on the industrialized centers. . . . What was involved was thus a form of dependence consequent upon the very structure of the world economy. By making economic decisions little more than an automatic operation involving the transfer of price mechanisms from the micro-economy to the level of international relations, liberal ideology diverted attention from this problem and hindered perception of its consequences for the national economies and the domestic plane" (Furtado 1970: 151). Furtado's criticism of "liberal ideology" resembles my criticism of conventional theories of political development.

[627]

Not that the contemporary literature concerning economic imperialism contains all the answers to our questions about the formation of national states. For one thing, analysts of contemporary economic change are just as capable of misunderstanding European history as are analysts of political development. The recurrent assumption that the actions of European states had little to do with the growth of their economies is a case in point. Likewise, the recognition of the interdependence of contemporary countries somehow fails to erase the idea that their European predecessors "solved their problems" more or less independently of each other:

> What France, Britain, and America have accomplished through their own revolutions has to be attained in backward countries by a combined effort of popular forces, enlightened government and unselfish foreign help. This combined effort must sweep away the holdover institutions of a defunct age, must change the political and social climate in the underdeveloped countries, and must imbue their nations with a new spirit of enterprise and freedom (Baran 1958: 91).

Furthermore, the analysts of *economic* dependence have not formed a distinct, well-articulated and convincing theory of political dependence. The central conception one finds in the literature on dependency and underdevelopment is of the state as the instrument of a national oligarchy whose position depends on control of local land and capital—a control bolstered by the state's repressive apparatus, but exercised within stringent limits set by the outside powers to which the national economy is subordinate. That Lenin was right in labeling the capitalist state as the "dictatorship of the bourgeoisie" has seemed so self-evident that even Marxist-Leninists have not undertaken a sustained historical analysis of the formation of the state, or of the ways that dominant classes have exercised power over it. (See the complaint of Ralph Miliband at the beginning of his own effort to formulate a Marxist theory of the state; Miliband 1969: 6.)

The clearest statements of the political theory of dependency and underdevelopment have appeared in attacks on the conventional wisdom of political science. Ocampo and Johnson (1972: 399–400), for example, nail up the following theses at the start of a discussion of political development theories:

1. The basic institutional framework of capitalist societies—private property, private initiative, and inequalities in the distribution of wealth and income—generate class structures grounded in inequalities of power and privilege and therefore of antagonistic relations between classes.

2. The fundamental political entity of capitalist society is the state. Any theory of politics and development must take into account the manner in which power vested in control of the economy and power resources of social classes are reflected in the state. The major problem here is identification of the various mechanisms by which the economic power of dominant social classes is translated into institutionalized political power.

3. A crucial problem for the analysis of politics and development is the nature of objective, patterned relations between economy, society, and the state. This involves an identification of the functions, basically of system-maintenance, of the state in and for society. Developmentally, the activities of the state are subject to the structural constraints, which analysis must identify, imposed by the system of capitalism.

4. The different forms of the state—liberal-democratic, authoritarian, fascist, populist, and others—are determined by economic transformations and changes in class relations in historical and cultural contents characteristic of different countries and regions.

5. Development involves the liberation of man from conditions of exploitation and oppression. Politics is the means of human liberation.

The above theses amount to a perspective and a program for inquiry rather than a theory of political change. If we were to extrapolate the statements in the same way that I have tried to squeeze implications for state-making from contemporary analyses of political development, we would arrive at arguments something like these: (1) national states become dominant organizations as the capitalist system expands, and as particular parts of the world become integrated into that system; (2) the chief forms taken by national states depend on the identities of their dominant classes; and (3) the economic strength of those dominant classes (modified by the extent and character of their dependency on the dominant classes of other states) determines the strength, durability, effectiveness and unresponsiveness of the state. These arguments are at least compatible with the main findings of our studies of the European experience.

Nevertheless, such political theory as we now have from the analysts of dependency leave some thorny problems untouched. In order to remain consistent with what we have learned about European state-making, the theory will have to provide an explanation of the large impact of military activity on the form and bulk of the state, an account of fiscal policy which allows for such strange phenomena as the willingness of the English aristocracy to tax itself, a set of categories allowing for class *coalitions* in the formation of different types of state, and a specification of the mechanisms by which dominant classes translate economic into political power.

Marxists and Leninists have been understandably reluctant to attribute separate importance to the political sphere. Contemporary theorists of imperialism (as George Lichtheim argues forcefully in his recent *Imperialism*) have striven so hard to connect the colonial expansion of the eighteenth and nineteenth centuries with the economic penetration of the twentieth that they have blurred the relationship between the political and economic processes. That effort to make the connection has produced some interesting hypotheses, such as the suggestion that the multinational corporation is superseding the national state as a repository of power (e.g., Johnson 1972). But the closest anyone has come to a general restatement of the relationship of political and economic power is in Gustavo Lagos' notions of "international stratification" and "atimia," which allow for the deterioration of status (*atimia*) along the economic and/or the political dimension.

What, then, do we have to learn from the literature of dependency and exploitation? First, the recognition that the nature of the international structure of power, and the relations of particular countries to that structure, account for a major part of the form, change, and variation of the national economic lives of poor countries; there is no obvious reason why that should be less true of political life. Second, the hypotheses of close (but imperfect) interdependence between the international structures of economic and political power, the changes of both being important determinants of the process called state-making. Third, the argument that the class structure of a particular state depends to a large degree on the relations of each major class to the international organization of production of distribution, and strongly affects the form of government within the state. Fourth, the more specific historical hypothesis of the interdependence of a state system forming and growing up in Europe, spreading from there under the promotion and coercion of the European states, eventually encompassing the entire world: according to dependency arguments, the process began with combinations of territory and population open, opportunities for territorial expansion available, multiple political forms feasible, and so on, but it ended with a closed situation: great restraints on the territory, population, governmental form, external relations and development policies of the new member states.

Barrington Moore's synthesis, in *Social Origins of Dictatorship and Democracy*, stands at the edge of this literature, but not completely outside it. Moore deliberately rejects the search for a standard pattern of political development; he resolutely adopts an historicist position: each country's political experience is a specific product of its period. Yet he also tries to bring out the specific features associated with parliamentary democracy of the British type through systematic comparison of the British structural background with that of Germany, France, and Russia. He also assumes that all countries eventually face the challenge of modernization: the formation, that is, of a collective capacity for industrialization.

Where Moore differs most sharply from the theories already reviewed is in his reliance on class structure as an explanation of alternative political paths to modernization. Thus the emergence of representative democracy in Britain (and with variations in France and the United States) is explained by the earlier commercialization of the rural sector, and the dominance of the middle classes in the processes of industrialization and political modernization. In Moore's short formula: no bourgeoisie, no democracy. It is, however, the *coalitions* of classes involved in modernization which eventually turn out to be crucial. Modernization in Germany and in Japan is explained in terms of a process dominated by a monarchic-bureaucratic-aristocratic coalition in which the bourgeoisie is a weaker social formation. The patterns of modernization in Russia and China are explained by societies with extremely weak commercial sectors and dominant, centralized authoritarian regimes. Here modernization is accomplished by means of a violent revolution—led by a revolutionary elite, but supported by an alienated peasantry.

This class analysis of differences in the processes of modernization is surely the dominant theme of Moore's work. Yet his contributions toward more specific explanations of national differences come a bit closer to the "sequence" approach outlined earlier. In the theoretical summary of his point of view (part III of his book), where he is concerned with the prospects of democracy and industrialization in India, Moore refers for the first time to five conditions associated with democratic modernization. The five conditions include other variables than those stressed in the major part of Moore's analysis: (1) the development of a balance somewhere between the extremes of a very strong crown and a very independent landed aristocracy; (2) the commercialization of agriculture; (3) the weakening of the landed aristocracy; (4) the prevention of an aristocratic-bourgeois coalition against the peasantry and the working class; and (5) a revolutionary break with the past. The first and fourth of these conditions take us considerably beyond the massive class variables with which Moore is principally concerned; they take us into the arena of political decision and political structure.

In his effort to differentiate German experience from the British, Moore again relies heavily on other variables than those stressed in his class theory: ". . . at a deeper level of causation, England's whole previous history, her reliance on a navy instead of an army, on unpaid justices of the peace instead of royal officials, had put in the hands of the central government a repressive apparatus weaker than that possessed by the strong continental monarchies. Thus the materials with which to construct a German system were missing or but feebly developed" (Moore 1966: 444). Those are themes which a number of the earlier essays in this book have taken up, sometimes with the direct inspiration of Moore's analysis.

The European Experience as Guide and Corrective

Suppose again that the analyses of European experience in this book have gotten European state-making right. (I apologize for any strain to the reader's imagination.) How would the *substance* of what we say affect existing theories of "political development?" If the world had remained the same kind of place from 1500 to now, some of the inferences would be fairly easy to make. We would return to the general conditions which appear to have favored the survival of particular political units in Europe, and their transformation into national states. To repeat the first chapter, they were: (1) the availability of extractible resources; (2) a relatively protected position in time and space; (3) a continuous supply of political entrepreneurs; (4) success in war; (5) homogeneity (initial or created) of the subject population; (6) strong coalitions of the central power with major segments of the landed elite. We would then add some features of the European state-making process which our analyses have brought out: (7) the high cost of state-building; (8) the intimate connection between the conduct of war, the building of armies, the extension and regularization of taxes and the growth of the state apparatus; (9) the large role of alternating coalitions between the central power and the major social classes within the subject population in determining the broad forms of government; and (10) the further effect of homogenization—or its absence—on the structure and effectiveness of government.

If these were, indeed, the main generalizations one could make about the formation of national states, they would leave untouched many portions the behavior analysts of "political development" have sought to explain; our formulations hardly bear on such questions as how citizens become well-informed, efficacious, concerned, and so on. Nevertheless, they would touch available theories in some vulnerable points. They portray the main processes which bring the national state to a dominant position as coercive and extractive.

Our conclusion in that regard is not the usual observation of hard-nosed government advisers: "some minimum of order" is necessary so the regime can get on with its work of social transformation. Instead, our study of the European experience suggests that most of the transformations European states accomplished until late in their histories were by-products of the consolidation of central control; that the forms of government themselves resulted largely from the way the coercion and extraction were carried on; that most members of the populations over which the managers of states were trying to extend their control resisted the state-making efforts (often with sword and pitchfork); and that the major forms of political participation which westerners now complacently refer to as "modern" are for the most part unintended outcomes of the efforts of European state-makers to build their armies, keep taxes coming in, form effective coalitions against their rivals, hold their nominal subordinates and allies in line, and fend off the threat of rebellion on the part of ordinary people.

If, again, we were dealing today with the same kind of world that fostered the formation of national states in Europe, we would have to challenge the conventional portrait of a "modernizing" elite pitted against "traditional" authorities and a passive, unmobilized and/or traditional mass. I have in the mind the sort of description presented by an M.I.T. study group around 1960:

A society freed from colonial rule or one which has overthrown a traditional government must create a minimally effective national government, a task which confronts such problems as these:

It is almost certain to be the case that much energy and attention must be devoted to overcoming the residues of political authority derived from the traditional society which cannot be harnessed constructively to the purposes of the new modern national government. Examples are the sects in southern Vietnam, the Indian princes, the Chinese war lords, the African tribal leaders.

The new government must also develop a minimum core of technically trained men capable of maintaining order, collecting taxes, and organizing the staff work required for the inevitably substantial role of the government in the economy and in the education process.

Modernization develops aspirations in the minds of various groups of citizens for progress toward many new goals, economic, educational and cultural, which are not regarded by traditional governments as within their responsibilities. The new government must demonstrate effective leadership in establishing programs to promote these new objectives if it is to survive. Means of communication must be developed between the government and its citizens to convey to them a sense that the national goals being pursued are ones which they would sanction.

Political development thus must contend with vested power derived from the traditional society; the lack of trained men; the low literacy rate and the lack of other facilities permitting persuasive mass communication; and the absence of a widespread popular conviction that the new national government is an appropriate vehicle for furthering popular goals.

In the process of contention there are many occasions for frustration and backsliding, many ways in which political life may be diverted to sterile or disruptive goals. The Communist appeal to the underdeveloped areas is designed to exploit precisely these possibilities (M.I.T. Study Group 1967: 32–33).

[634]

No doubt the simplicity and declaratory manner of the statement result from its being addressed to a Senate committee rather than to the scholarly world. Nevertheless, it conveys a familiar image. If the European experience were our only guide, we would have to rule the image quite wrong. For the most part, that experience does not show us modernizing elites articulating the demand and needs of the masses, and fighting off traditional holders of power in order to meet those needs and demands. Far from it. We discover a world in which small groups of power-hungry men fought off numerous rivals and great popular resistance in the pursuit of their own ends, and inadvertently promoted the formation of national states and widespread popular involvement in them. In retrospect, Colbert appears to be a "modernizer." In his time, he sought—quite successfully—to extend and regularize the power of his king. Were the financiers, jurists, burghers, landlords and parliamentarians against whom he struggled "traditional?" Our answer is that the very question obscures the process of aggregation of power that was going on.

What sort of theory would do a better job with the substance of the European experience? The theory we need differs from available theories in several obvious ways:

1. It must refer consistently to a particular kind of unit: a territory, a population, a state, a dynasty or something else, but something specific.

2. Instead of treating the political transformation of that unit as an isolated trial to be accounted for its own terms, it must explicitly relate changes within a unit to shifts in its relationship to the rest of the world.

3. What features of that unit's experience are to be explained must be explicit and limited; "political development" in general is far too broad, much too vague.

4. The theory must proceed in an open-ended and prospective fashion, turning away from the task of specifying the conditions under which stable democracy emerges toward the task of specifying what paths away from, say, traditional kingship are likely and what affects the probabilities that one or another of those paths will actually be followed.

The studies in this book have not, of course, produced the new theory or even followed these principles rigorously. We have maneuvered uneasily between the tracing of particular organizations (the Brandenburg-Prussian state, etc.) and more loosely defined populations ("the English"). We have been more diligent in specifying changes within each unit than in dealing with relations among all the European states. We have dodged and darted from *explicandum* to *explicandum*. And our beginning with the effort to explain how modern France, Germany, or Spain got the way they were hampered the formation of prospective and open-ended arguments. In short, we are preaching about where to go next, not pointing with pride to where we have already been.

Two Paths to the State

There is, however, one feature of the European state-making experience that will help us build a bridge from past to present. That is the existence in Europe itself of two large processes of state formation, and the general shift from one toward the other. The first is the extension of the power and range of a more or less autonomous political unit by conquest, alliance, bargaining, chicanery, argument, and administrative encroachment, until the territory, population, goods, and activities claimed by the particular center extended either to the areas claimed by other strong centers or to a point where the costs of communication and control exceeded the returns from the periphery. Those expansive processes dominated the state-making experience to which we have devoted the greatest attention in this book: Brandenburg-Prussia, France, England, Spain, and so on. Yet we have not been able to ignore a second large process, consisting of the more or less deliberate *creation* of new states by existing states. The carving of Yugoslavia and Czechoslovakia out of the trunk of the Austro-Hungarian Empire is a relatively pure case, Napoleon's formation of the Batavian Republic, the Cisalpine Republic, and other temporary states a more special (but not uncommon) variety of the process, and the final consolidation of Germany and Italy, combinations of the center-to-periphery and external-creation processes. Even in the creation of new states by autonomist rebellions like those of Portugal and The Netherlands in 1640, the acquiescence or collaboration of existing states became increasingly crucial. From 1648 onward, the ends of wars provided the principal occasions on which the creation of new states occurred.

Let me not claim too much. The formation of Zaïre in the 1960s out of what had been for a while the Belgian Congo was not "just like" the creation of a united Italy in the 1860s out of what had been a string of states dominated by Austria. The most important point of contact between the two processes is their involvement in the general movement toward a worldwide state system. We have discussed the movement several times in earlier chapters of this book. Schematically, it goes like this: (1) the formation of a few early national states amid a great variety of other political structures in Europe; (2) the mapping of most of Europe into distinct national states through wars, alliances, and a great variety of other maneuvers; (3) the extension of political and economic domination from that European base to much of the rest of the world, notably through the creation of client states and colonies; (4) the formation—though rebellion and through international agreement—of formally autonomous states corresponding approximately to the clients and colonies; (5) the extension of this state system to the entire world.

If we still dared call these blocks of events "phases" after the difficulties that term has already caused, we would have to place Italy in phase 2, Zaïre in phase 4 of the historical movement. Phases 2 and 3 overlapped considerably in time; indeed, if we consider such cases as the geographic expansion of Russia or the dismemberment of the Ottoman Empire, the distinction between the two begins to dissolve. The extension to the entire world is still going on; Antarctica, for example, remains political limbo. Yet the distinction of that extension from phase 4, the formation of formally autonomous states, is mainly a matter of convenience. The main rhythm, then, has three beats: (1) the formation and consolidation of the first great national states in commercial and military competition with each other, accompanied by their economic penetration of the remainder of Europe and of important parts of the world outside of Europe: roughly 1500 to 1700; (2) the regrouping of the remainder of Europe into a system of states, accompanied by the extension of European political control into most of the non-European world, save those portions already dominated by substantial political organizations (e.g., China and Japan): roughly 1650 to 1850; (3) the extension of the state system to the rest of the world, both through the acquisition of formal independence by colonies and clients, and through the incorporation of existing powers like China and Japan into the system: roughly 1800 to 1950. If this scheme is correct, the study of European state-making has at least one point of relevance to the politics of the contemporary world: Europeans played the major part in creating the contemporary international state-system, and presumably left the imprints of their peculiar political institutions on it. It is probably even true (although not for the reasons usually adduced) that a state which has adopted western forms or organization will have an easier time in the international system; after all, the system grew up in conjunction with those forms.

At the same time as the state system absorbs the entire world, the individual state may be losing part of its significance. I ended this book's introduction with speculations about the devolution of power away from the nation-state both upward and downward: toward the regional grouping and the compact of superstates above, toward the subnational region, ethnic population, or racial group below. Perhaps the two movements are complementary, with the segments of the population which were demobilized as the state became supreme renewing their bids for autonomy as they see the state increasingly constrained by powers outside it. Perhaps the European national state grew up at a scale roughly matched to the markets, capital, communications, and productive organization of the seventeenth or eighteenth centuries, but increasingly irrelevant to the scale and manner of interdependence prevailing in the twentieth century. Perhaps control of a contiguous territory was peculiarly advantageous to the land- and water-bound technologies of the European state-making eras, but an obstacle to full exploitation of technologies of flight, electric power and electronic information-handling.

For all these perhapses, we must wait and see. But remember the definition of a state as an organization, controlling the principal means of coercion within a given territory, which is differentiated from other organizations operating in the same territory, autonomous, centralized and formally coordinated. If there is something to the trends we have described, they threaten almost every single one of these defining features of the state: the monopoly of coercion, the exclusiveness of control within the territory, the autonomy, the centralization, the formal coordination; even the differentiation from other organizations begins to fall away in such compacts as the European Common Market. One last perhaps, then: perhaps, as is so often the case, we only begin to understand this momentous historical process—the formation of national states—when it begins to lose its universal significance. Perhaps, unknowing, we are writing obituaries for the state.

[638]

BIBLIOGRAPHY

Abel, Wilhelm.

1965 "Desertions rurales: bilan de la recherche allemande," in *Villages désertés et histoire économique, XIe-XVIIIe siècle* (Paris: SEVPEN), 515–532.

1966 *Agrarkrisen und Agrarkonjonktur in Mitteleuropa vom 13, bis zum 19. Jahrhundert* (Berlin: Parey; 2d edn.).

1967 *Geschichte der deutschen Landwirtschaft vom früher Mittelalter bis zum 19. Jahrhundert* (Stuttgart: Ulmer; 2d edn.; Gunther Franz, ed., *Deutsche Agrargeschichte*, II).

Abramovitz, Moses, and Eliasberg, Vera F.

1957 *The Growth of Public Employment in Great Britain* (Princeton: Princeton University Press).

Adam, M.

1939 "Deutsche Zivilversorgung," in Ferdinand von Ledebur, ed., *Die Geschichte des deutschen Unteroffiziers* (Berlin: Junker und Dünnhaupt).

Aleati, Giuseppe.

1957 *La popolazione di Pavia durante il dominio Spagnolo* (Milan: Giuffrè).

Almond, Gabriel A.

1960 "Introduction: A Functional Approach to Comparative Politics," in Gabriel A. Almond and James S. Coleman, eds., *The Politics of the Developing Areas* (Princeton: Princeton University Press), 3–64.

———, and Powell, G. Bingham, Jr.

1966 *Comparative Politics: A Developmental Approach* (Boston: Little, Brown).

Añes Alvarez, Gonzalo.

1968 "Production et productivité agricoles dans les deux Castiles de la fin du XVIIe siècle à 1836," *Third International Conference of Economic History, Munich 1965* (Paris: Mouton), II: 85–91.

1970 *Las crisis agrarias en la España moderna* (Madrid: Taurus).

André, Louis.

1906 *Michel Le Tellier et l'organisation de l'armée monarchique* (Paris: Alcan).

Antoine, Michel.

1970 *Le conseil du roi sous le règne de Louis XV* (Geneva: Droz).

Apter, David E.

1965 *The Politics of Modernization* (Chicago: University of Chicago Press).

1970 "Political Systems and Developmental Change," in Robert T. Holt and John E. Turner, eds., *The Methodology of Comparative Research* (New York: Free Press).

Ardant, Gabriel.

1959   *Le monde en friche* (Paris: Presses universitaires de France).

1964   *Plan de lutte contre la faim: rapport présenté au Comité français de la Campagne mondiale contre la faim* (Paris: Presses universitaires de France).

1965   *Théorie sociologique de l'impôt* (Paris: SEVPEN; 2 vols.).

1971   *Histoire de l'impôt* (Paris: Fayard; vol. 1).

Arnold, Eric A.

1969   "Administrative Leadership in a Dictatorship: The Position of Joseph Fouché in the Napoleonic Police, 1800–1810" (unpublished Ph.D. dissertation, Columbia University).

Armstrong, John A.

1973   *The European Administrative Elite* (Princeton: Princeton University Press).

Armengaud, André.

1961   *Les populations de l'Est-Aquitain au début de l'époque contemporaine* (Paris: Mouton).

Armytage, Walter H. G.

1965   *The Rise of the Technocrats: A Social History* (London: Routledge & Kegan Paul).

Artz, Frederick B.

1966   *The Development of Technical Education in France 1500–1850* (Cleveland: Society for the History of Technology).

Aylmer, G. E.

1961   *The King's Servants: The Civil Service of Charles I, 1625–1642* (New York: Columbia University Press).

Bacon, Francis.

1963   "Life of Henry VII," in James Spedding, ed., *The Works of Francis Bacon* (Stuttgart-Bad Cannstaat: G. Holzboog), 6: 3–263.

Baran, Paul.

1958   "On the Political Economy of Backwardness," in A. N. Agarwala and S. P. Singh, eds., *The Economics of Underdevelopment* (New York: Oxford University Press; first published in The Manchester School, 1952).

Barber, Elinor G.

1955   *The Bourgeoisie in 18th Century France* (Princeton: Princeton University Press).

Barker, Sir Ernest.

1944   *The Development of Public Services in Western Europe, 1660–1930* (London: Oxford University Press).

1946   ed., *The Politics of Aristotle* (Oxford: Clarendon Press).

1951   *Principles of Social and Political Theory* (Oxford: Clarendon Press).

Barnes, Thomas Garden.

1961   *Somerset, 1625–1640: A County's Government During the "Personal Rule"* (Cambridge: Harvard University Press).

Barzini, Luigi.
1964 *The Italians* (New York: Atheneum).

Baugh, Daniel A.
1965 *British Naval Administration at the Age of Walpole* (Princeton: Princeton University Press).

von Beckerath, Erwin.
1912 *Die preussische Klassensteuer und die Geschichte ihrer Reform bis 1851* (München, Leipzig; Staats- und socialwissenschaftliche Forschungen, 163).

Bell, H. E.
1953 *An Introduction to the History and Records of the Court of Wards and Liveries* (Cambridge: The University Press).

Beloff, Max.
1938 *Public Order and Popular Disturbances, 1660–1714* (London: Oxford University Press).
1963 *Public Order and Popular Disturbances, 1660–1714* (London: Oxford University Press; 2d edn.).

Ben-David, Joseph and Zloczower, Avraham.
1962 "Universities and Academic Systems in Modern Societies," *Archives Européennes de Sociologie*, III: 45–84.

Bendix, Reinhard.
1964 *Nation-Building and Citizenship* (New York: Wiley).
1968 *State and Society* (Boston: Little, Brown).

Beresford, Maurice.
1954 *The Lost Villages of England* (London: Butterworth).
1965 "Villages désertés: bilan de la recherche anglaise," in *Villages désertés et histoire économique, XIe-XVIIIe siècle* (Paris: SEVPEN), 533–580.

Bergmann, Robert.
1901 *Geschichte der ostpreussischen Stände und Steuern von 1688 bis 1704* (Leipzig: Staats- und socialwissenschaftliche Forschungen, 19, no. 82).

Bernard, R.-J.
1969 "L'Alimentation paysanne en Gévaudan au XVIIIe siècle," *Annales; Economies, Sociétés, Civilisations*, 24: 1449–1467.

Bernier, François.
1699 *Voyages de François Bernier* (Amsterdam: Paul Marret).

Bielfeld, Harald.
1888 *Geschichte des magdeburgischen Steuerwesens von der Reformationszeit bis ins achtzehnte Jahrhundert* (Leipzig: Staats- und socialwissenschaftliche Forschungen, 8: no. 1).

Bien, David.
1969 "Military Education in Eighteenth-Century France: Technical and Non-Technical Determinants," in *Science, Technology, and Warfare. Proceedings of the Third Military History Symposium*, United States Air Force Academy, 8–9 May 1969. Ed. Monte D. Wright and Lawrence J. Paszek (Washington, D.C.: U.S. Government Printing Office), 51 ff.

Binder, Leonard and others.

1971   *Crises and Sequences in Political Development* (Princeton: Princeton University Press).

Binney, John E. D.

1958   *British Public Finance and Administration 1774–92* (Oxford: The University Press).

Black, Cyril.

1966   *The Dynamics of Modernization* (New York: Harper and Row).

Bleedk, Wilhelm.

1972   *Von der Kameralausbildung zum Juristenprivileg. Studium, Prüfung und Ausbildung der höheren Beamten des allgemeinen Verwaltungsdienstes in Deutschland im 18. und 19. Jahrhundert. Historische und Pädagogische Studien* (Berlin: Colloquium Verlag Otto H. Hess).

Bluche, François.

1959   "L'Origine sociale des secrétaires d'Etat de Louis XIV (1661–1715)," *XVIIe Siècle*, 42–43; 8–22.

1966a   *Les Magistrats de la Cour des monnaies de Paris au XVIIIe siècle, 1715–1790* (Paris: Les Belles Lettres; Annales littéraires de l'université de Besançon, 81).

1966b   *Les Magistrats du grand conseil au XVIIIe siècle, 1690–1791* (Paris: Les Belles Lettres; Annales littéraires de l'université de Besançon, 82).

Blum, Jerome.

1957   "The Rise of Serfdom in Eastern Europe," *American Historical Review*, 62: 807–836.

1961   *Lord and Peasant in Russia from the Ninth to the Nineteenth Century* (Princeton: Princeton University Press).

Bodin, Jean.

1583   *Les six livres de la République* (Paris: Chez I. du Puys).

de Boislisle, Arthur André Gabriel Michel.

1874–   ed., *Correspondance des Contrôleurs généraux des finances avec les*
1897   *intendants de province* (Paris: Imprimerie nationale; 3 vols.).

1881   *Mémoire de la Généralité de Paris* (Paris: Imprimerie nationale) Collection de documents interdits sur l'histoire de France.

Boissonade, P.

1897   *La police municipale à Poitiers au XVIIIe siècle* (Poitiers: Blais & Roy).

Bog, Ingomar.

1968   "Das Konsumzentrum London und seine Versorgung 1500–1640," *Third International Conference of Economic History, Munich 1965* (Paris: Mouton), 1: 109–118.

von Bonin, Udo.

1877–   *Geschichte des Ingenieurkorps und der Pioniere in Preussen, Erster*
1878   *Teil* (Berlin: E. S. Mittler; 2 vols.).

von Borch, Herbert.

1954   *Obrigkeit und Widerstand: Zur politischen Soziologie des Beamtentums* (Tübingen: Mohr).

Borchardt, Knut.

1968   "Probleme der ersten Phase der Industriellen Revolution in England," *Vierteljahrschrift für Sozial- und Wirtschaftgeschichte*, 55: 1–62.

Bornitz, Jakob.

1612   *Aerarium sive tractatus politicus de aerario sacro, civili, militari, communi et sacratiori* (Frankfurt: G. Tampachii).

Boserup, Ester.

1965   *The Conditions of Agricultural Growth* (London: George Allen & Unwin).

Bosher, J. F.

1964   "The Premiers Commis des Finances in the Reign of Louis XVI," *French Historical Studies*, 3: 475–494.

1970   *French Finances 1770–1795: From Business to Bureaucracy* (Cambridge: The University Press).

comte de Boulainvilliers, Henri.

1752   *L'Etat de la France* (London: T. Wood & S. Palmer).

Bourde, André.

1967   *Agronomes et agronomie au XVIIIe siècle* (Paris: SEVPEN; 3 vols.).

Bowden, Peter.

1967   "Agricultural Prices, Farm Profits, and Rents," in Joan Thirsk, ed., *The Agrarian History of England and Wales, IV. 1540–1640* (Cambridge: The University Press), 593–695.

Boynton, Lindsay.

1967   *The Elizabethan Militia* (London: Routledge & Kegan Paul; Toronto: Toronto University Press).

Braudel, Fernand.

1949   *La Méditerranée et le monde méditerranéen à l'époque de Philippe II* (Paris: Colin).

1966   *La Méditerranée et le monde méditerranéen à l'époque de Philippe II* (Paris: Colin; 2d edn.).

1967   *Civilisation matérielle et capitalisme* (Paris: Colin).

Braun, Rudolf.

1960   *Industrialisierung und Volksleben, die Veränderung der Lebensformen in einem ländlichen Industriegebiet vor 1800* (Zurich: Rentsch).

1965   *Sozialer und kultureller Wandel in einem industriale Landesgebiet* (Zurich: Rentsch).

Breysig, Kurt.

1895   *Geschichte der brandenburgischen Finanzen in der Zeit von 1640–1697; Darstellung und Akten, I. Die Centralstellen der Kammerverwaltung; Die Amtskammer, das Kassenwesen und die Domänen der Kurmark* (Leipzig; Urkunden und Aktenstucke zur Geschichte der inneren Politick des Kurfürsten Friedrich Wilhelm von Brandenburg, part 1).

Brisco, Norris Arthur.

1907   *The Economic Policy of Robert Walpole* (New York: Columbia University Press).

Broeker, Galen.
1970   *Rural Disorder and Police Reform in Ireland, 1812–36* (London: Routledge & Kegan Paul).

Brooks, Frederick William.
1953   *York and the Council of the North* (London: St. Anthony's Press).

Brown, R. Allen.
1967   "The Norman Conquest," *Transactions of the Royal Historical Society*, 5th series, 17: 109–130.

Brunner, Otto.
1956a   "Europäisches und russisches Bürgertum," in Otto Brunner, *Neue Wege der Sozialgeschichte: Vortrage und Aufsatze* (Göttingen: Vandenhoeck and Ruprecht) 97–115.

1956b   "Stadt und Bürgertum in der europäischen Geschichte," in Otto Brunner, *Neue Wege* (see above, Brunner 1956a) 80–96.

Büsch, Otto.
1962   *Militärsystem und Sozialleben im alten Preussen 1713–1807; die Anfänge der sozialem Militarisierung der preussischdeutschen Gesellschaft* (Berlin: W. de Gruyter).

Burnett, John.
1966   *Plenty and Want* (London: Nelson).

Buxton, Sydney Charles.
1888   *Finance and Politics; an Historical Study 1783–1885* (London: J. Murray; 2 vols.).

Bryant, Arthur.
1933–   *Samuel Pepys* (Cambridge: The University Press; 3 vols.).
1938

Cam, Helen Maud.
1961   *England before Elizabeth* (London: Arrow Books; 2nd edn.).

Carrera Pujal, Jaime.
1943–   *Historia de la economía española* (Barcelona: Bosch; 5 vols.).
1947

Carr-Saunders, A. M.
1936   *World Population* (Oxford: Clarendon Press).

Carsten, Francis Ludwig.
1954   *The Origins of Prussia* (Oxford: Clarendon Press).

Casanova, Giacomo Chevalier de Seingalt.
1965   *Geschichte meines Lebens*, Erich Loos, ed. (Berlin: Propyläen-Verlag).

Castellan, Georges.
1962   "Les céréales dans l'économie rurale de la restauration. L'exemple du département du Rhône," *Revue d'histoire économique*, 40: 175–199.

Chabert, A.
1945   *Essai sur le mouvement des prix en France de 1798 à 1820* (Paris: Medicis).

Chambers, J. D.

1957   *The Vale of Trent, 1670–1800* (London: Cambridge University Press; Economic History Review Supplements, III).

1965   "The Rural Domestic Industries during the Period of Transition to the Factory System with Special Reference to the Midland Counties of England," *Second International Conference of Economic History, Aix-en-Provence,* 1962 (Paris: Mouton), II: 429–455.

1967   "Enclosure and Labour Supply in the Industrial Revolution," in E. L. Jones, ed., *Agriculture and Economic Growth in England 1650–1815* (London: Methuen; University Paperback; first published in *Economic History Review,* 1953), 94–127.

Chambers, J. D., and Mingay, G. E.

1966   *The Agricultural Revolution, 1750–1880* (London: Batsford).

Chapman, Brian.

1953   "The Prefecture of Police," *Journal of Criminal Law, Criminology, and Political Science,* 44: 505–521.

1955   *The Prefects and Provincial France* (London: George Allen & Unwin).

Chaunu, Pierre.

1970   *La civilisation de l'Europe classique* (Paris: Arthaud).

Chayanov, A. V.

1966   *The Theory of Peasant Economy* (Homewood: Irwin).

Cipolla, Carlo M.

1965   *Guns and Sails in the Early Phase of European Expansion, 1400–1700* (London: Collins).

1969   *Literacy and Development in the West* (Harmondsworth: Penguin).

Clark, Sir George.

1969   "The Social Foundations of States" in F. L. Carsten, ed., *The New Cambridge Modern History V. The Ascendancy of France, 1648–88* (Cambridge: The University Press), 176–197.

Coates, W. A.

1958   "Changing Attitudes to Labour in the Mid-eighteenth Century," *Economic History Review,* XI: 35–51.

Cobb, Richard.

1961–   *Les Armées révolutionnaires; instrument de la Terreur dans les dé-*
1963   *partements, avril 1793–floréal an II* (Paris: Mouton; 2 vols.).

1965   *Terreur et subsistances, 1793–1795* (Paris: Clavreuil).

1970   *The Police and the People* (Oxford: The University Press).

Cobban, Alfred.

1957   "The Decline of Divine-Right Monarchy in France," in J. O. Lindsay, ed., *The New Cambridge Modern History VII. The Old Regime* (Cambridge: The University Press), 214–240.

1969   *The Nation State and National Self Determination* (London: Collins; The Fontana Library).

[645]

Cobbett, William.

1811 *Cobbett's Parliamentary History of England from the Norman Conquest, in 1066, to the Year 1803, VIII. A. D. 1722–1733;* and *IX. A. D. 1733–1737* (London: printed by T. C. Hansard).

Cockcroft, James D.

1972 "Last Rites for the Reformist Model in Latin America," in Cockcroft, James D. et al. *Dependence and Underdevelopment* (Garden City: Doubleday; Anchor Books).

Cohen, Emmeline W.

1941 *The Growth of the British Civil Service, 1780–1939* (London: G. Allen & Unwin).

Cole, G. D. H., and Postgate, Raymond.

1961 *The British People, 1746–1946* (New York: Barnes & Noble).

Coleman, D. C.

1953 "Naval Dockyards under the Later Stuarts," *Economic History Review*, 2d series, VI: 134–155.

Colloque de Nice

1969 *Villes de l'Europe méditerranéenne et de l'Europe occidentale du Moyen Age au XIXe siècle* (Nice: Annales de la Faculté des Lettres Humaines de Nice, nos. 9, 10).

La Commission des archives diplomatiques au Ministère des affaires étrangères.

1884 *Recueil des Instructions données aux Ambassadeurs et Ministres de France depuis les traités de Westphalie jusqu'à la révolution française* (Paris: F. Alcan; yearly since 1884), vol. I, *Austria*.

Cooper, J. P.

1960 "Differences between English and Continental Governments in the Early Seventeenth Century," in J. S. Bromley and E. H. Kossmann, eds., *Britain and the Netherlands* (London: Chatto & Windus).

1967 "The Social Distribution of Land and Men in England, 1436–1700," *Economic History Review*, 2d series, 20: 419–440.

1970 "General Introduction" in J. P. Cooper, ed., *The New Cambridge Modern History IV. The Decline of Spain and the Thirty Years War, 1609–58/59* (Cambridge: The University Press), 1–66.

Cornelius, Wayne A., Jr.

1970 "The Political Sociology of Cityward Migration in Latin America: Toward Empirical Theory," in Francine R. Rabinowitz and Felicity M. Trueblood, eds., *Latin American Urban Annual* (Beverly Hills: Sage Publications).

Corvisier, André.

1964 *L'armée française, de la fin du XVII siècle au ministère de Choiseul: Le soldat* (Paris: Presses Universitaires de France; 2 vols.).

1969 "Quelques aspects sociaux des milices bourgeoises au XVIIIe siècle," in *Villes de l'Europe Méditerranéenne et de l'Europe occidentale du Moyen Age au XIXe siècle* (Saint-Brieuc: Les Belles Lettres; Annales de la Faculté des Lettres et Sciences Humaines de Nice, no. 9–10), 241–277.

Coxe, William.

1798   *Memoirs of the Life and Administration of Sir Robert Walpole, Earl of Oxford* (London: T. Cadell, Jun. and W. Davies; 3 vols.).

Cramer, James.

1964   *The World's Police* (London: Cassell and Co.).

Critchley, T. A.

1967   *A History of Police in England and Wales, 900–1066* (London: Constable).

Crouzet, François.

1962   "Les conséquences économiques de la Révolution: à propos d'un inédit de Sir Francis d'Ivernois," *Annales historiques de la Révolution français*, 34: 182–217.

1966   "Angleterre et France au XVIIIe siècle: essai d'analyse comparée de deux croissances économiques," *Annales; Economies, Sociétés, Civilisations*, 21: 254–291.

Cutright, Phillips.

1963   "National political development: measurement and analysis," *American Sociological Review*, 28: 253–264.

1965   "Political Structure, Economic Development, and National Social Security Programs," *American Journal of Sociology*, 70: 537–548.

Dahrendorf, Ralf.

1967   *Society and Democracy in Germany* (New York: Doubleday).

Darnton, Robert.

1969   "Le Lieutenant de Police J.-P. Lenoir, la Guerre des Farines et l'approvisionnement de Paris à la veille de la Révolution," *Revue d'histoire moderne et contemporaine*, 16: 611–624.

Darvall, Frank O.

1934   *Popular Disturbances and Public Order in Regency England* (London: Oxford University Press).

David, R., and Brierley, J. C.

1968   *Major Legal Systems in the World Today*, part 1: "Roman Germanic Family" (London: Stevens) 21–118.

Davies, C.S.L.

1969   "Les révoltes populaires en Angleterre, 1500–1700," *Annales; Economies, Sociétés, Civilisations*, 24: 24–60.

Davis, Natalie Zemon.

1971   "The Reasons of Misrule: Youth Groups and Charivaris in Sixteenth-Century France," *Past and Present*, 50: 41–75.

Davis, Ralph.

1966   "The Rise of Protection in England, 1689–1786," *Economic History Review*, 2d series, 19: 306–317.

Dawson, William H.

1914   *Municipal Life and Government in Germany* (London: Longmans, Green).

Deane, Phyllis.

1967   *The First Industrial Revolution* (Cambridge: The University Press).

————, and Cole, W. A.

1967   *British Economic Growth, 1688–1959* (Cambridge: The University Press; University of Cambridge, Department of Applied Economics, Monographs, 8; 2d edn.).

Delumeau, Jean.

1957   *Vie économique et sociale de Rome dans la seconde moitié du XVIe siècle* (Paris: Boccard; 2 vols.).

Demeter, Karl.

1962   *Das deutsche Offizierskorps in Gesellschaft und Staat, 1650–1945* (Frankfurt, Main: Bernard & Graefe Verlag für Wehrwesen; 2d edn.).

Deprez, Paul.

1965   "The Demographic Development of Flanders in the Eighteenth Century," in D. V. Glass and D.E.C. Eversley, eds. *Population in History* (London: Arnold).

Deyon, Pierre.

1967   *Amiens, capitale provinciale* (Paris: Mouton).

Díaz de Moral, Juan.

1969   *Historia de las agitaciones campesinas andaluzas—Córdoba* (Madrid: Libros del Bolsillo; 2d edn.).

Dickson, Peter George Muir.

1967   *The Financial Revolution in England: A Study in the Development of Public Credit 1688–1756* (London: St. Martin's Press).

Dieterici, Carl.

1875   *Zur Geschichte der Steuerreform in Preussen von 1810 bis 1820* (Berlin: G. Reimer).

Dietz, Frederick C.

1967   "English Public Finance and the National State in the Sixteenth Century," in *Facts and Factors in Economic History: Articles by Former Students of Edwin Francis Gay* (Cambridge: Harvard University Press: 1st edn.; reprint, New York, 1932).

1964   *English Public Finance 1485–1641, I. English Government Finance 1485–1558; II. English Public Finance 1558–1641* (London: F. Cass; 2d edn.).

Dobb, Maurice.

1963   *Studies in the Development of Capitalism* (London: Routledge & Kegan Paul; rev. edn.).

Dobbert, Eduard.

1899   "Bauakademie, Gewerbeakademie und Technische Hoschschule bis 1894. Historische Skizze," in *Chronik der königlichen Technischen Hochschule zu Berlin, 1799–1899* (Berlin: Königliche Technische Hochschule).

Döhler, Jacob Friedrich.

1775   *Abhandlungen von Domainen, Contributionen, Steuern, Schatzungen und Abgaben* (Nürnberg: Stein).

Dore, R. P.

1964 "Latin America and Japan Compared," in John J. Johnson, ed., *Continuity and Change in Latin America* (Stanford: Stanford University Press), 227–249.

Dorn, Walter L.

1931– "The Prussian Bureaucracy in the Eighteenth Century," *Political Science*
1932 *Quarterly*, 46: 403–423; 47: 75–94, 259–273.

Doubleday, Thomas.

1847 *A Financial, Monetary and Statistical History of England: From the Revolution of 1688 to the Present Time* (New York: Greenwood Press, 1968; reprint).

Dovring, Folke.

1960 *Land and Labour in Europe 1900–1950: A Comparative Survey of Recent Agrarian History* (The Hague: Nijhoff; 2d edn.).

Dowell, Stephen.

1965 *A History of Taxation and Taxes in England from the Earliest Times to the Present Day* (London: F. Cass; 6 vols.; 3d edn.).

Droege, Georg.

1966 "Die finanziellen Grundlagen der Territorialstaates in West- und Ostdeutschland an der Wende vom Mittelalter zur Neuzeit," *Vierteljahrschrift für Sozial- und Wirtschaftsgeschichte*, 53: 145–161.

Drummond, J. C., and Wilbraham, Anne.

1939 *The Englishman's Food: A History of Five Centuries of English Diet* (London: Cape).

Dupâquier, Jacques.

1968 "Sur la population française au XVIIe et au XVIIIe siècle," *Revue historique*, 239: 43–79.

Durand, G.

1969 *Etats et institutions, XVIe–XVIIIe siècles* (Paris: A. Colin).

Durand, John D.

1967 "The Modern Expansion of World Population," *Proceedings of the American Philosophical Society*, vol. iii, no. 3: 136–159.

Egret, Jean.

1952 "L'Aristocratie parlementaire française à la fin de l'Ancien Régime," *Revue historique*, 225: 208–216.

1970 *Louis XV et l'opposition parlementaire, 1715–1774* (Paris: A. Colin).

Ehrenberg, Richard.

1955 *Le Siècle des Fugger* (Paris: SEVPEN).

Ehrman, J.

1953 *The Navy in the War of William III, 1689–1697: Its State and Direction* (Cambridge: The University Press).

Eisenstadt, S. N.

1963 *The Political Systems of Empires* (New York: Free Press).

Elliott, John.

1961 "The Decline of Spain," *Past and Present*, 20: 52–75.

1964 *Imperial Spain, 1469–1716* (London: Arnold).

Elton, Geoffrey Rudolph.

1953   *The Tudor Revolution in Government: Administrative Changes in the Reign of Henry VIII* (Cambridge: The University Press).

1962   *The Tudor Revolution in Government: Administrative Changes in the Reign of Henry VIII* (Cambridge: The University Press).

Emerson, Donald E.

1968   *Metternich and the Political Police* (The Hague: Nijhoff).

Emerson, Rupert.

1960   *From Empire to Nation* (Cambridge: Harvard University Press).

Eschmann, Ernst Wilhelm.

1943   *Die Führungeschichten Frankreichs I. Von den Capetingern bis zum Ende des Grand Siècle* (Berlin: Junker und Dünnhaupt).

Etizioni, Amitai.

1965   *Political Unification* (New York: Holt, Rinehart and Winston).

1968   *The Active Society* (New York: Free Press).

Everitt, Alan.

1967   "The Marketing of Agricultural Produce," in Joan Thirsk, ed., *The Agrarian History of England and Wales, IV. 1540–1640* (Cambridge: The University Press), 466–592.

1968   "The Food Market of the English Town, 1660–1760," *Third International Conference of Economic History, Munich 1965* (Paris: Mouton), I: 57–72.

Eversley, D.E.C.

1967   "The Home Market and Economic Growth in England, 1750–1780," in E. L. Jones and G. E. Mingay, eds., *Land, Labour and Population in the Industrial Revolution: Essays Presented to J. D. Chambers* (London: Arnold), 206–259.

Fairlie, Susan.

1969   "The Corn Laws and British Wheat Production, 1829–1876," *Economic History Review*, 2d series, 22: 88–116.

Fay, C. R.

1932   *The Corn Laws and Social England* (Cambridge: The University Press).

Ferry, Guy, and Mulliez, Jacques.

1970   *L'Etat et la rénovation de l'agriculture au XVIIe siècle* (Paris: Presses universitaires de France).

Festy, Octave.

1947   *L'Agriculture pendant la Révolution française; Les conditions de production et de récolte des céréales* (Paris: Gallimard).

Finer, Herman.

1932   *The Theory and Practice of Western Government* (London: Methuen & Co., Ltd.), II.

1962   *The Major Governments of Modern Europe* (New York: Harper and Row).

Fisher, F. J.

1954 "The Development of the London Food Market, 1540–1640," in E. M. Carus-Wilson, ed., *Essays in Economic History* (London: Arnold; first published in *Economic History Review*, 1935), 1: 135–151.

Fischer, Wolfram.

1964 "Das Deutsche Handwerk in den Frühphasen der Industrialisierung," *Zeitschrift für die gesammte Staatswissenschaft*, 120: 686–712.

1966 "Social Tensions at Early Stages of Industrialization," *Comparative Studies in Society and History*, 9: 64–83.

1968 Ed., *Wirtschafts- und sozialgeschichtliche Aspekte der Frühindustrialisierung* (Berlin: Freie Universitat).

Flanigan, William, and Fogelman, Edwin.

1971 "Patterns of Political Development and Democratization: A Quantitative Analysis," in John V. Gillespie and Betty A. Nesvold, eds., *Macro-Quantitative Analysis* (Beverly Hills: Sage Publications).

Ford, Franklin L.

1953 *Robe and Sword: The Regrouping of the French Aristocracy after Louis XIV* (Cambridge: Harvard University Press).

Forman, Shepard, and Riegelhaupt, Joyce.

1970 "Market Place and Marketing System: Toward a Theory of Peasant Economic Integration," *Comparative Studies in Society and History*, 12: 188–212.

Fosdick, Raymond B.

1915 *European Police Systems* (New York: The Century Co.).

Fourastié, Jean, and Grandamy, René.

1968 "Remarques sur les prix salariaux des céréales et la productivité du travail agricole en Europe du XVe au XXe siècles," in *Third International Conference of Economic History, Munich 1965* (Paris: Mouton), 1: 647–658.

Fourquin, Guy.

1964 *Les campagnes de la région parisienne à la fin du moyen âge* (Paris: Presses Universitaires de France; Publications de la Faculté des Lettres et Sciences Humaines de Paris, "Recherches," 10).

Franz, Günther.

1970 *Geschichte des deutschen Bauernstandes vom frühen Mittelalter bis zum 19. Jahrhundert* (Stuttgart: Ulmer; Günther Franz, ed., *Deutsche Agrargeschichte*, IV).

Freudenberger, Herman.

1960 "Industrialization in Bohemia and Moravia in the Eighteenth Century," *Journal of Central European Affairs*, 19: 347–356.

Fréville, Henri.

1953 *L'intendance de Bretagne (1689–1790): Essai sur l'histoire d'une intendance en pays d'états aux XVIIIe siècle* (Rennes: Plihon; 3 vols.).

Friauf, Karl Heinrich.

1968 *Der Staatshaushaltsplan im Spannungsfeld zwischen Parlament und Regierung, I. Verfassungsgeschichtliche Untersuchungen über den Haushaltsplan im deutschen Frühkonstitutionalismus* (Berlin, Zürich: Verlag Gehlen).

Fried, Morton H.

1967 *The Evolution of Political Society* (New York: Random House).

Fried, Robert C.

1963 *The Italian Prefects: A Study in Administrative Politics* (New Haven: Yale University Press).

Friedrich, Carl J.

1939 "The Continental Tradition of Training Administrators in Law and Jurisprudence," *Journal of Modern History*, xi: 129–148.

1950 *Constitutional Government and Democracy: Theory and Practice in Europe and America* (Boston: Ginn; revised edn.).

Furet, François.

1963 "Pour une définition des classes inférieures à l'époque moderne," *Annales; Economies, Sociétés, Civilisations*, 18: 459–474.

1971 "Le catéchisme révolutionnaire," *Annales*, 26: no. 2.

Furtado, Celso.

1970 *Economic Development of Latin America*. Translated by Suzette Macedo (Cambridge: The University Press).

Geertz, Clifford.

1963 *Agricultural Involution: The Process of Ecological Change in Indonesia* (Berkeley: University of California Press).

Gelpke, Franz.

1902 *Die geschichtliche Entwicklung des Landrathsamtes der preussischen Monarchie* (Berlin: C. Heymann).

Georgescu-Roegen, Nicholas.

1969 "The Institutional Aspects of Peasant Communities: An Analytical View," in Clifton R. Wharton, Jr., ed., *Subsistence, Agriculture and Economic Development* (Chicago: Aldine).

Gerschenkron, Alexander.

1970 *Europe in the Russian Mirror: Four lectures on Economic History* (Cambridge: The University Press).

Gerloff, Wilhelm.

1927 "Zur Geschichte der Entwicklung der Personalbesteuerung in Preussen," *Zeitschrift für die gesamte Staatswissenschaft*, 82: 384–393.

Gieysztor, A.

1965 "Villages désertés: bilan de la recherche polonaise," in *Villages désertés et histoire économique, XIe–XVIIIe siècle* (Paris: SEVPEN), 607–612.

Gillespie, John V., and Nesvold, Betty A.

1971 Eds., *Macro-Quantitative Analysis* (Beverly Hills: Sage Publications).

Gillis, John R.

1968 "Aristocracy and Bureaucracy in Nineteenth-Century Prussia," *Past and Present*, 41: 105–115.

1971   *The Prussian Bureaucracy in Crisis 1840–1860* (Stanford: Stanford University Press).

Gilpin, Robert.

1968   *France in the Age of the Scientific State* (Princeton: Princeton University Press).

Gleason, John Howes.

1969   *The Justices of the Peace in England, 1558–1640: A Later Eirenarcha* (Oxford: Clarendon Press).

Godechot, Jacques.

1970   *The Taking of the Bastille* (New York: Scribners).

———, and Moncassin, Suzanne.

1964   "Démographie et subsistances en Languedoc (du XVIIIe au début du XIXe siècle)," *Bulletin d'histoire économique et sociale de la Révolution française*, 1964: 19–60.

Goedhard, Neil.

1954   "Organization and Administration of the Police in Western Germany, 1945–1950" (unpublished M.A. Thesis, School of Public Administration, University of Southern California).

Göhring, Martin.

1938   *Die Amterkauflichkeit im Ancien régime* (Berlin: Verlag dr. Emil Ebering).

Goldscheid, Rudolf.

1926   "Staat, öffentlicher Haushalt und Gesellschaft," in *Handbuch der Finanzwissenschaft* (Tübingen: Mohr), 1: 146–184.

Gonnet, Paul.

1955   "Esquisse de la crise économique en France de 1827 à 1832," *Revue d'histoire économique et sociale*, 33: 249–291.

Goody, John Rankine.

1968   Ed., *Literacy in Transitional Societies* (Cambridge: Harvard University Press).

1969a "Economy and Feudalism in Africa," *Economic History Review*, 2d series, 22: 393–504.

1969b "Succession in Contemporary Africa," *Archives européennes de sociologie*, 10: 27–40.

Gossez, Rémi.

1956   "A propos de la carte des troubles de 1846–1847," in E. Labrousse, ed., *Aspects de la crise et de la dépression de l'économie française au milieu du XIXe siècle, 1846–1851* (La Roche-sur-Yon: Imprimerie Centrale de l'Ouest: Bibliothèque de la Révolution de 1848), 1–3.

Goubert, Pierre.

1959   "Les officiers royaux des présidiaux, bailliages et élections dans la société française au XVIIe siècle," in *XVIIe Siècle*, 42–43: 54–75.

1960   *Beauvais et le Beauvaisis de 1600 à 1730* (Paris: SEVPEN).

1969   *L'Ancien Régime I. La Société* (Paris: A. Colin).

Goubert, Pierre.

1970 "Le paysan et la terre: seigneurie, tenure, exploitation," in Fernand Braudel and E. Labrousse, eds., *Histoire économique et sociale de la France, II. 1660–1789* (Paris: Presses universitaires de France), 119–158.

Gould, J. D.

1962 "Agricultural Fluctuations and the English Economy in the Eighteenth Century," *Journal of Economic History*, 22: 313–333.

Graaf, Bartolome Christian.

1831 *Handbuch des Etats-, Kassen- und Rechnungswesens des Königlich Preussischen Staats* (Berlin: A. Rücker).

Grabower, Rolf.

1932 *Preussens Steuern vor und nach den Befreiungskriegen* (Berlin: C. H. Beck).

Granger, C.W.J., and Elliott, C. M.

1967 "A Fresh Look at Wheat Prices and Markets in the Eighteenth Century," *Economic History Review*, 2d series, 20: 257–265.

de Granvelle, Cardinal Antoine Perrenot.

1841– *Papiers d'Etat du cardinal de Granvelle* (Paris: Imprimerie royale &
1852 Imprimerie nationale; 9 vols.).

Gras, N.S.B.

1915 *The Evolution of the English Corn Market from the Twelfth to the Eighteenth Century* (Cambridge: Harvard University Press).

Gruder, Vivian R.

1968 *The Royal Provincial Intendants: A Governing Elite in Eighteenth-Century France* (Ithaca: Cornell University Press).

Guerlac, Henry.

1951 "Science and French National Strength," in Edward M. Earle, ed., *Modern France: Problems of the Third and Fourth Republics* (Princeton: Princeton University Press), 81–105.

Guénée, Bernard.

1971 "Y a-t-il un Etat des XIVe et XVe siècles?" *Annales; Economies, Sociétés, Civilisations*, 26: 399–406.

Guibert.

1773 *Essai général du tactique* (London).

Guicciardini, Lodovico.

1583 *L'hore di Recreatione* (Anversa: P. Bellero).

Guillet, Léon.

1929 *Cent ans de la vie de l'école centrale des arts et manufactures, 1829–1929* (Paris: M. de Brunoff).

Gunder Frank, André.

1967 *Capitalism and Underdevelopment in Latin America* (New York: Monthly Review Press; rev. edn.).

Habakkuk, H. J.

1965 "La disparition du paysan anglais," *Annales; Economies, Sociétés, Civilisations*, 20: 649–663.

Hahn, Roger.

1969   "Elite scientifique et démocratie politique dans la France révolutionnaire," *Dix-huitième Siècle*, 1: 229–235.

1971   *The Anatomy of a Scientific Institution: The Paris Academy of Sciences, 1666–1803* (Berkeley: University of California Press).

Haines, George, IV.

1957–   *Essays on German Influence upon English Education and Science,*
1959   *1800–1866 and 1850–1919* (New London: Connecticut College;
Monographs 6 and 9).

Hajnal, John.

1965   "European Marriage Patterns in Perspective," in D. V. Glass and
D.E.C. Eversley, eds., *Population in History* (London: Arnold).

Hall, Alfred Rupert.

1952   *Ballistics in the Seventeenth Century: A Study in the Relations of
Science and War with reference principally to England* (Cambridge:
The University Press).

Hamilton, E. V.

1947   *War and Prices in Spain, 1650–1800* (Cambridge: Harvard University Press).

1950   "Origin and Growth of the National Debt in France and England,"
in *Studi in onore di Gino Luzzato* (Milan: Giuffrè), II, 245–258.

Hammond, J. L., and Hammond, Barbara.

1924   *The Village Labourer* (London: Longmans, Green).

1967   *The Town Labourer 1760–1832: The New Civilisation* (New York:
A. M. Kelley).

1794–   *Handbuch über den Könglich Preussischen Hof und Staat auf das
1848   Jahr 1805* (Berlin: n.p.).

Hanke, Gerhard.

1969   "Zur Sozialstruktur de ländlicher Siedlungen Altbayerns im 17. und
18. Jahrhundert," in *Gesellschaft und Herrschaft. Forschungen zur
sozial- und landes- geschichtlichen Problemen vornehmlich in Bayern.
Eine Festgabe für Karl Bösl zum 60. Geburtstag* (Munich: C. H. Beck).

Harnack, Adolf.

1900   *Geschichte der Königlich Preussischen Akademie der Wissenschaften
zu Berlin* (Berlin: Reichsdruckerei; 3 vols.).

Hart, Jenifer M.

1951   *The British Police* (London: George Allen & Unwin).

Hartung, Fritz.

1942–   "Studien zur Geschichte der preussischen Verwaltung (1942–1948),"
1948   in Fritz Hartung, *Staatsbildende Kräfte der Neuzeit; Gesammelte
Aufsätze* (Berlin: Duncker & Humblot, 1961), 178–344.

1950   *Deutsche Verfassungsgeschichte vom 15. Jahrhundert bis zur Gegenwart* (Stuttgart: K. F. Koehler; 8th edn.).

1961a   "Herrschaftsverträge und ständischer Dualismus im ausgehenden Mittelalter (1952)," in Fritz Hartung, *Staatsbildende Kräfte der Neuzeit;
Gesammelte Aufsätze* (Berlin: Duncker & Humblot), 62–77.

Hartung, Fritz.

1961b "Der aufgeklärte Absolutismus (1955)," in Fritz Hartung, *Staatsbildende Kräfte der Neuzeit; Gesammelte Aufsätze* (Berlin: Duncker & Humblot).

Hartwell, R. M.

1969 "Economic Change in England and Europe, 1780–1830," in C. W. Crawley, ed., *The New Cambridge Modern History, IX. War and Peace in an Age of Upheaval, 1793–1830* (Cambridge: The University Press), 31–59.

Haustofen, Heinz.

1963 *Die deutschen Landwirtschaft im technischen Zeitalter* (Stuttgart: Ulmer; Gunther Franz, ed., *Deutsche Agrargeschichte*, vol. 5).

Heckscher, Eli.

1936– "Mercantilism," *Economic History Review*, 7: 99–101 (review by
1937 Jacob Viner).

Heitz, G.

1968 "Produktion und Produktivität in der Landwirtschaft unter Gutsherrschaftlichen Bedingungen im 17. und 18. Jahrhundert," *Third International Conference of Economic History, Munich 1965* (Paris: Mouton), II: 197–204.

Hélin, Etienne.

1963 *La démographie de Liège au XVIIe et XVIIIe siècles* (Brussels: Palais des Académies; Mémoire de l'Académie Royale de Belgique).

Helleiner, Karl F.

1967 "The Population of Europe from the Black Death to the Eve of Vital Revolution," in E. E. Rich and C. H. Wilson, eds., *The Cambridge Economic History of Europe* (Cambridge: The University Press), IV: 1–95.

Herman, Barbara.

1967 "Some Reflections on the Grain Riots in France, 1839–1940" (unpublished paper, Harvard University).

Hervey, John.

1848 *Memoirs of the Reign of George II, from his accession to the Death of Queen Caroline*, Right Hon. John Wilson Croker, ed. (Philadelphia: Lea & Blanchard; 2 vols.).

Hill, John Edward Christopher.

1965 *Intellectual Origins of the English Revolution* (Oxford: Clarendon Press).

1967 *Reformation to Industrial Revolution: A Social and Economic History of Britain, 1530–1780* (London: Weidenfeld & Nicholson).

Hintze, Otto.

1930 "Typologie der ständischen Verfassungen des Abendlandes," *Historische Zeitschrift* 1930, 229–248.

1962 "Der Commissarius und seine Bedeutung in der allgemeinen Verwaltungsgeschichte. Eine vergleichende Studie," in Gerhard Oestreich, ed., *Staat und Verfassung: Gesammelte Abhandlungen zur allgemeinen Verfassungsgeschichte* (Göttingen: Vandenhoeck & Ruprecht; first published in 1910), 242–274.

1962a "Die Entstehung des modernen Staatsleben," in Oestreich, ed., *Staat und Verfassung* (see above, Hintze 1962; first published in 1932), 497–502.

1962b "Der österreichische und der preussische Beamtenstaat im 17. und 18. Jahrhundert," in Gerhard Oestreich, ed. *Staat und Verfassung: Gesammelte Abhandlungen zur allgemeinen Verfassungsgeschichte* (Göttingen: Vandenhoeck & Ruprecht; first published in 1901), 321–358.

1962c "Wesen und Wandlung des modernen Staats," in Oestreich, ed., *Staat und Verfassung* (see above, Hintze 1962; first published in 1931), 470–496.

1964 "Der Beamtenstand," in Gerhard Oestreich, ed., *Soziologie und Geschichte: Gesammelte Abhandlungen zur Soziologie, Politik und Theorie der Geschichte* (Göttingen: Vandenhoeck & Ruprecht; first published in 1911), 66–125.

1967 "Der preussische Militär- und Beamtenstaat im 18. Jahrhundert (1908)," in Gerhard Oestreich, ed., *Regierung und Verwaltung; Gesammelte Abhandlungen zur Staats-, Rechts- und Sozialgeschichte Preussens* (Göttingen: Vandenhoeck & Ruprecht), 419–428.

1967 "Der Ursprung des preussischen Landratsamts in der Mark Brandenburg," in G. Oestreich, ed., *Regierung und Verwaltung* (see above, Hintze 1967; first published in 1915), 164–203.

Hintze, Otto, and Schmoller, Gustav.

1901 *Die Behördenorganisation und die allgemeine Staatsverwaltung Preussens im 18. Jahrhundert, VI, Part 1*: Otto Hintze, *Einleitende Darstellung der Behördenorganisation und allgemeinen Verwaltung in Preussen beim Regierungsantritt Friedrich II, Part 2*: Gustav Schmoller and Otto Hintze, *Akten vom 31. Mai 1740 bis Ende 1745* (Berlin: B. Parey; Acta Borussica. Denkmäler der Preussischen Staatsverwaltung im 18. Jahrhundert).

Hippolyte, Jacques Antoine, comte de Guibert.

1773 *Essai général de tactique; précédé d'un discours sur l'état actuel de la politique et de la science militaire en Europe* (Liège: C. Plomteux, imprimeur).

Hirschman, Albert O.

1970 *Exit, Voice and Loyalty* (Cambridge: Harvard University Press).

Hobsbawm, E. J.

1964 *Laboring Men* (London: Weidenfeld & Nicholson).

1967a "Le agitazioni rurali in Inghilterra nel primo ottocento," *Studi Storici*, 8: 257–281.

1967b "The Crisis of the Seventeenth Century," in Trevor Aston, ed., *Crisis in Europe, 1560–1660* (Garden City: Doubleday; Anchor Books; first published in 1954).

1968 *Industry and Empire: An Economic History of Britain since 1750* (London: Weidenfeld & Nicholson).

Hobsbawm, E. J., and Rudé, George.

1968 *Captain Swing: A Social History of the Great Agrarian Uprising of 1830* (New York: Pantheon).

Holborn, Hajo.

1966 *A History of Modern Germany, 1648–1840* (New York: Alfred Knopf).

1969 *A History of Modern Germany, 1840–1945* (New York: Alfred Knopf).

Holt, Robert T., and Richardson, John M., Jr.

1970 "Competing Paradigms in Comparative Politics," in Robert T. Holt and John E. Turner, eds., *The Methodology of Comparative Research* (New York: Free Press).

Holtzmann, Robert.

1910 *Französische Verfassungsgeschichte von der Mitte des neunten Jahrhunderts bis zur Revolution* (München, Berlin: R. Oldenbourg).

Horowitz, Irving Louis.

1966 *Three Worlds of Development* (New York: Oxford University Press).

Houtte, J. A., and Verhulst, A.

1968 "L'Approvisionnement des villes dans les Pays-Bas (Moyen Age et temps modernes)," *Third International Conference of Economic History, Munich 1965* (Paris: Mouton), 1: 73–78.

Hughes, Edward.

1934 *Studies in Administration and Finance, 1558–1825, with Special Reference to the History of the Salt Tax in England* (Manchester: Manchester University Press).

Huisman, Michel.

1902 *La Belgique commerciale sous l'empereur Charles VI: la compagnie d'Ostende* (Brussels: H. Lamertin).

Huntington, Samuel P.

1968 *Political Order in Changing Societies* (New Haven: Yale University Press).

Hurstfield, Joel.

1958 *The Queen's Wards: Wardship and Marriage under Elisabeth I* (London: Longmans, Green).

1968 "Social Structure, Office-Holding and Politics, Chiefly in Western Europe," in R. B. Wernham, ed., *The New Cambridge Modern History III. The Counter-Reformation and Price Revolution, 1559–1610* (Cambridge: The University Press), 126–148.

Ibarra y Rodriguez, Eduardo.

1926 "El problema de las subsistencias en España al comenzar la Edad moderna. La carne," *Nuestro Tiempo*, 25: 5–29, 26: 206–250.

1941– "El problema cerealista en España durante el reinade de los Reyes
1942 Católicos (1475–1516)," *Anales de Economía*, 1: 163–217, 299–330; 2: 3–30, 119–136.

von Inama-Sternberg, Karl Theodor.

1865 "Der Accisenstreit deutscher Finanztheoretiker im 17. und 18. Jahrhundert," *Zeitschrift für die gesamte Staatswissenschaft*, 21: 515–545.

Innes, Harold Adams.

1950 *Empire and Communications* (Oxford: Clarendon Press).

Irsigler, Franz.

"Getreidepreise, Getreidehandel und städtische Versorgungspolitik in Köln vornehmlich im 15. und 16. Jahrhundert," in Werner Besch et al., eds., *Die Stadt in der europäischen Geschichte. Festschrift Edith Ennen* (Bonn: Röhrscheid, 1972).

Isaacsohn, Siegfried.

1874– *Geschichte des Preussischen Beamtentums vom Anfang des 15.*
1884 *Jahrhunderts bis auf die Gegenwart* (Berlin: Puttkamer & Mühlbrecht; 3 vols.).

Jacob, Herbert.

1963 *German Administration Since Bismarck* (New Haven: Yale University Press).

Jacquart, Jean.

1968 "La productivité agricole dans la France du Nord aux XVIe et XVIIe siècles," *Third International Conference of Economic History, Munich 1965* (Paris: Mouton), ii: 65–74.

Jantke, Carl, and Hilger, Dietrich.

1965 eds., *Die Eigentumslosen. Der Deutsche Pauperismus und die Emanzipationskrise in Darstellung und Deutungen der Zeitgenössischen Literatur* (Alber).

Jecht, Horst.

1959 "Formen der Finanzsoziologie," *Zeitschrift für die gesamte Staatswissenschaft*, 115: 403–414.

John, A. H.

1955 "Wars and the British Economy, 1700–1763," *Economic History Review*, 2d series, 7: 329–344.

1965 "Agricultural Productivity and Economic Growth in England, 1700–1760," *Journal of Economic History*, 25: 19–34.

Johnson, Dale L.

1972 "Dependence and the International System," in James D. Cockcroft et al., *Dependence and Underdevelopment* (Garden City: Doubleday; Anchor Books).

Johnson, Francis R.

1968 *Astronomical Thought in Renaissance England: A Study of the English Scientific Writings from 1500 to 1645* (New York: Octagon Books; first published in 1937).

Jones, E. L.

1965 "Agriculture and Economic Growth in England, 1660–1750: Agricultural Change," *Journal of Economic History*, 25: 1–18.

1967 ed., *Agriculture and Economic Growth in England, 1650–1815* (London: Methuen; University Paperbacks).

1968 "Agricultural Origins of Industry," *Past and Present*, 40: 58–71.

Jones, E. L., and Woolff, S. J.

1969 Eds., *Agrarian Change and Economic Development: The Historical Problems* (London: Methuen).

Justi, Johann Heinrich Gottlob.

1755 *Staatswirtschaft, oder, Systematische Abhandlung aller oekonomischen und Cameral Wissenschaften, die zur Regierung eines Landes effordert werden* (Leipzig: B. C. Breitkopf).

Kaldor, Nicholas.

1965 "The Role of Taxation in Economic Development," in Edward Austin Gossage Robinson, ed., *Problems in Economic Development* (London: Macmillan), 170–195.

Karlbom, Rolf.

1967 *Hungerupplopp och Strejker, 1793–1867* (Lund: Gleerup) (used English summary only).

Keir, Sir David Lindsay.

1967 *The Constitutional History of Modern Britain Since 1485* (New York: Norton; 8th edn.).

Kellenbenz, Hermann.

1965 "Landliches Gewerbe und bäuerliches Unternehmertum in Westeuropa vom Spätmittelalter bis ins XVIII Jahrhundert," *Second International Conference of Economic History, Aix-en-Provence 1962* (Paris: Mouton), ii: 377–428.

Kelter, Ernst.

1941 "Die wirtschaftlichen Ursachen des Bauernkrieges," *Schmollers Jahrbuch*, 65: 641–682.

Kennedy, William.

1964 *English Taxation 1640–1799: An Essay on Policy and Opinion* (New York: A. M. Kelley; Reprints of Economic Classics; first published in 1913).

Kerridge, Eric.

1968 *The Agricultural Revolution* (New York: A. M. Kelley).

Keyfitz, Nathan.

1965 "Political-Economic Aspects of Urbanization in South and Southeast Asia," in Philip M. Hauser and Leo F. Schnore, eds., *The Study of Urbanization* (New York: Wiley).

Kichler, Paul.

1956 "Entwicklung und Wandlung des parlamentarischen Budgetbewilligungsrechts in Deutschland" (Berlin: dissertation, Juristische Fakultät Freie Universität).

Kilian, Fritz.

1882 "Die Pitt'schen Finanzreformen von 1784–92; Ein Bild parlamentarischer Steuerkämpfe," in *Jahrbuch für Gesetzgebung, Verwaltung und Volkswirtschaft im Deutschen Reich* (Leipzig), 6: 1279–1308.

King, James E.

1949 *Science and Rationalism in the Government of Louis XIV, 1661–1683* (Baltimore: Johns Hopkins Press).

Kirsten, Ernst, Buchholz, Ernst Wolfgang, and Köllman, Wolfgang.

1955 *Raum und Bevölkerung in der Weltgeschichte* (Würzburg: Ploetz).

[660]

Kisch, Herbert.

1959   "The Textile Industries in Silesia and the Rhineland: A Comparative Study in Industrialization," *Journal of Economic History*, 19: 541–564.

1964   "Growth Deterrents of a Medieval Heritage: The Aachen-Area Woolen Trades before 1790," *Journal of Economic History*, 24: 517–537.

1968   "Prussian Mercantilism and the Rise of the Krefeld Silk Industry: Variations upon an 18th Century Theme," *Transactions of the American Philosophical Society* (Philadelphia: American Philosophical Society) new series, 58: part 7.

van Klaveren, Jacob.

1960a   *Europäische Wirtschaftsgeschichte Spaniens im 16. und 17. Jahrhundert* (Stuttgart: Fischer).

1960b   "Fiskalismus—Merkantilismus—Korruption. Drei Aspekte der Finanz- und Wirtschaftspolitik während des Ancien Régime," *Vierteljahrschrift für Sozial- und Wirtschaftsgeschichte*, 47: 333–353.

Klein, Julius.

1920   *The Mesta: A Study in Spanish Economic History, 1273–1836* (Cambridge: Harvard University Press).

Klíma, Arnošt.

1965   "The Domestic Industry and the Putting-out System (Verlags-system) in the Period of Transition from Feudalism to Capitalism," *Second International Conference of Economic History, Aix-en-Provence 1962* (Paris: Mouton), II, 477–482.

Klompmaker, Henk.

1955   "Les villes néerlandaises au XVIIe siècle: institutions économiques et sociales," in Société Jean Bodin, *La Ville* (Brussels: Librairie Encyclopedique), Part II, 577–601.

Kloss, Heinrich.

1968   "Notes concerning a Language-Nation Typology," in J. A. Fishman, et al., eds., *Language Problems of Developing Nations* (New York: Wiley), 69–86.

Kocka, Jürgen.

1969   *Unternehmens verwaltung und Angestelltenschaft am Beispiel Siemens 1847–1914. Zum Verhältnis von Kapitalismus und Bürokratie in der deutschen Industrialisierung* (Stuttgart: Klett).

Köllmann, Wolfgang.

1969   "The Process of Urbanization in Germany at the Height of the Industrialization Period," *Journal of Contemporary History*, 4: 59–76.

Koschaker, Paul.

1953   *Europa und das römische Recht* (Munich: C. H. Beck; 2d edn.).

Koselleck, Reinhart.

1967   *Preussen zwischen Reform und Revolution; Allgemeines Landrecht, Verwaltung und soziale Bewegung von 1791 bis 1848*, vol. 7 of Werner Conze, ed., *Industrielle Welt* (Stuttgart: E. Klett).

[661]

Koser, Reinhold.

1903 "Die Preussischen Finanzen von 1763 bis 1786," *Forschungen zur Brandenburgischen und Preussischen Geschichte*, 16: 101–132.

Krader, Lawrence.

1968 *Formation of the State* (Englewood Cliffs: Prentice-Hall).

Krippendorff, Ekkehart.

1970 "The State as a Focus of Peace Research," *Peace Research Society Papers*, The Rome Conference, XVI: 47–60.

Kulischer, Joseph.

1965 *Allgemeine Wirtschaftsgeschichte des Mittelalters und der Neuzeit* (Munich: Oldenbourg; 3d edn.; 2 vols.).

Labrousse, Ernest, et al.

1970 *Histoire économique et sociale de la France, II: Des derniers temps de l'âge seigneurial aux préludes de l'âge industriel (1660–1789)* (Paris: Presses universitaires de France).

Ladero Quesada, Miguel Angel.

1970 "Les finances royales de Castille à la veille des temps modernes," *Annales; Economies, Societes, Civilisations*, 25: 775–788.

Landes, David S.

1969 *The Unbound Prometheus* (Cambridge: The University Press; paperback edn.).

Landry, Adolphe.

1910 *Essai économique sur les mutations des monnaies dans l'ancienne France de Phillipe le Bel à Charles VII* (Paris: H. Champion).

Lang, K. H.

1793 *Historische Entwicklung der Deutschen Steuerverfassungen seit der Karolinger bis auf unsere Zeit* (Berlin and Stettin: F. Nicolai).

Langer, William.

1963 "Europe's Initial Population Explosion," *American Historical Review*, 69: 1–17.

Lapeyre, Henri.

1969 "L'Organisation municipale de la ville de Valence (Espagne) aux XVIe et XVIIe siècles" in *Villes de l'Europe méditerranéenne et de l'Europe occidentale du Moyen Age au XIXe siècle*. (Saint-Brieuc: Les Belles Lettres; Annales de la Faculté des Lettres et Sciences Humaines de Nice, no. 9–10).

Laqueur, Walter.

1968 "Revolution," *International Encyclopedia of the Social Sciences*, XIII, 501–507.

Laswell, Harold.

1962 "The Garrison State Hypothesis Today," in Samuel P. Huntington, ed., *Changing Patterns of Military Politics* (Glencoe: Free Press), 51–70.

Le Clère, Marcel.

1964 *Histoire de la police* (Paris: Presses universitaires de France; "Que sais-je?").

Lefebvre, Georges.

1963   *Etudes Orléanaises. II: Subsistances et Maximum* (Paris: Commission d'Histoire Economique et Sociale de la Révolution).

1969   *Napoleon I. From 18 Brumaire to Tilsit, 1799–1807*, trans. by Henry F. Stockhold (London: Routledge & Kegan Paul; vol. i).

Lefebvre de la Bellande, J. Louis.

1760   *Traité général des droits d'aydes* (Paris: Pour l'auteur chez P. Prault; 2 vols.).

Lemarchand, Guy.

1963   Les troubles de subsistances dans la Généralité de Rouen (seconde moitié du XVIIIe siècle), *Annales historiques de la Révolution française*, 174: 401–427.

Lenski, Gerhard.

1966   *Power and Privilege: A Theory of Social Stratification* (New York: McGraw-Hill).

Léon, Antoine.

1968   *La révolution française et l'éducation technique* (Paris: Société des études robespierristes).

Le Roy Ladurie, Emmanuel.

1966   *Les Paysans de Languedoc* (Paris: SEVPEN; 2 vols.).

Leskiewicz, Janina.

1965   "Les entraves sociales au développement de la 'nouvelle agriculture' en Pologne," *Second International Conference of Economic History, Aix-en-Provence 1962* (Paris: Mouton), ii: 237–247.

Levine, Bruce.

1970   "Economic Development and Social Mobilization: Spain, 1830–1923" (unpublished working paper, Study of Social Change and Collective Violence in Europe, University of Michigan).

Lévy-Leboyer, Maurice.

1964   *Les Banques européennes et l'industrialisation internationale dans le première moitié du XIXe siècle* (Paris: Presses universitaires de France).

Lewis, Michael Arthur.

1939   *England's Sea-Officers: The Story of the Naval Profession* (London: G. Allen & Unwin).

1959   *The Spanish Armada* (New York: Macmillan).

1961   *Armada Guns: A Comparative Study of English and Spanish Armaments* (London: G. Allen & Unwin).

Liang, Hsi-Huey.

1970   *The Berlin Police Force in the Weimar Republic* (Berkeley: University of California Press).

Lichtheim, George.

1971   *Imperialism* (London: Allen Lane; the Penguin Press).

Ligou, Daniel.

1960   "A propos de la révolution municipale," *Revue d'histoire économique et sociale*, 1960: 146–177.

Lindsay, Lord Alexander Dunlop.

1943 *The Modern Democratic State* (London: Oxford University Press).

von Loewe, Karl.

1973 "Commerce and Agriculture in Lithuania. 1400–1600," *Economic History Review*, 2d series, 26: 23–37.

Louis XIV.

1860 *Mémoires de Louis XIV*, ed. Charles Dreyss (Paris: Didier), II.

Lublinskaya, Alexandra Dmitrievna.

1968 *French Absolutism: The Crucial Phase, 1620–1629*, trans. by Brian Pearce (Cambridge: The University Press; first published in 1965).

Lundgreen, Peter.

1972 "Technicians and Labor Market in Prussia, 1820–1850" (To be published in *Annales Cisalpines d'Histoire Sociale*, serie 1, no. 2, Université de Pavie).

Lütge, Friedrich.

1963 "Das 14./15. Jahrhundert in der Sozial- und Wirtschaftsgeschichte," in Friedrich Lütge, *Studien zur Sozial- und Wirtschaftsgeschichte: Gesammelte Abhandlungen* (Stuttgart: G. Fischer), 1: 281–335.

1967 *Geschichte der deutschen Agrarverfassung vom frühen Mittelalter bis zum 19. Jahrhundert* (Stuttgart: Ulmer; 2d edn.; Gunther Franz, ed., *Deutsche Agrargeschichte*, III).

Macartney, C. A.

1967 "Eastern Europe," in G. R. Potter, ed., *The New Cambridge Modern History, I. The Renaissance, 1493–1520* (Cambridge: The University Press), 368–394.

MaCaulay, Lord Thomas Babington.

1913– *History of England From the Accession of James II*, Charles Harding
1915 Firth, ed. (London: Macmillan; 6 vols.).

MacCaffrey, Wallace T.

1961 "Place and Patronage in Elisabethan Politics," in S. T. Bindoff, et al., eds., *Elisabethan Government and Society: Essays Presented to Sir John Neale* (London: University of London, Athlone Press).

MacPherson, C. B.

1962 *The Political Theory of Possessive Individualism: Hobbes to Locke* (Oxford: Clarendon Press).

Makkai, László.

1968 "Production et productivité agricole en Hongrie à l'ère du féodalisme tardif (1550–1850)," in *Third International Conference of Economic History, Munich 1965* (Paris: Mouton), II: 171–180.

Malefakis, Edward E.

1970 *Agrarian Reform and Peasant Revolution in Spain* (New Haven: Yale University Press).

Malowist, Marian.

1950 "Epoque contemporaine," *IXe Congrès International des Sciences Historiques, Paris 1950. I. Rapports* (Paris: Colin), 305–322.

1959 "The Economic and Social Development of the Baltic Countries from the Fifteenth to the Seventeenth Centuries," *Economic History Review*, 2d series, 12: 177–189.

1966 "The Problem of the Inequality of Economic Development in Europe in the Later Middle Ages," *Economic History Review*, 2d series, 19: 15–28.

1972 *Croissance et régression en Europe* (Paris: Armand Colin; Cahiers des Annales, 34).

Mandrou, Robert.

1967 *La France aux XVIIe et XVIIIe siècles* (Paris: Presses universitaires de France; Nouvelle Clio, 33).

Manegold, Karl-Heinz.

1966 "Eine Ecole Polytechnique in Berlin. Uber die im preussischen Kulturministerium in den Jahren 1820 bis 1850 erörterten Pläne zur Gründun einer höheren mathematisch-naturwissenschaftlichen Lehranstalt," *Technikgeschichte*, 33.

1970 *Universität, Technische Hoschschule und Industrie: Ein Beitrag zur Emanzipation der Technik im 19. Jahrhundert unter besonderer Berücksichtigung der Bestrebungen Felix Kleins* (Berlin: Duncker & Humbolt).

Mann, Fritz Karl.

1933– "Finanzsoziologie- Grundsätzliche Bemerkungen," *Kölner Viertel-*
1934 *jahreshefte für Soziologie*, N. F., 12: 1–20.

1934 "Beiträge zur Steuersoziologie," in *Finanzarchiv.*, N. F., 11: no. 2, 281–314.

1937 "Steuerpolitische Ideale: Vergleichende Studien zur Geschichte der ökonomischen und politischen Ideen und ihres Wirkens in der öffentlichen Meinung 1600–1935," *Finanzwissenschaftliche Forschung*, 5: 1–360.

1943 "The Sociology of Taxation," *The Review of Politics*, 5: 225–235.

1959 *Finanztheorie und Finanzsoziologie* (Göttingen: Vandenhoeck & Ruprecht).

1961 "Finanzsoziologie," in *Handwörterbuch der Sozialwissenschaften* (Göttingen: Vandenhoeck & Ruprecht), 3: 642–648.

Manzoni, Alessandro.

1966 *I promessi sposi*, ed. Piero Nardi (Verona: Mondadori; first published in 1825).

Marcus, Geoffrey J.

1961 *A Naval History of England I. The Formative Centuries* (London: Longmans, Green).

Marczewski, Jean.

1965 "Le produit physique de l'économie française de 1789 à 1913—comparaison avec la Grande-Bretagne," *Histoire Quantitative de l'économie française* (Paris: l'Institut de Science Économique Appliquée, Cahiers de l'ISEA serie AF-4, no. 63).

de la Mare, Nicolas.
1729   *Traité de la police* (Paris: Brunet; 3d edn.; 4 vols.).

Marielle, M.C.P.
1855   *Répertoire de l'école impériale polytechnique ou renseignements sur les élèves qui ont fait partie de l'institution, 1794–1853* (Paris: Ecole Centrale des Travaux Publics).

Marion, Marcel.
1910   *Les Impôts directs sous l'Ancien Régime, principalement au XVIIIe siècle* (Paris: E. Cornély).
1914– *Histoire financière de la France depuis 1715* (Paris: A Rousseau; 5
1928   vols.).
1926   *Ce qu'il faut connaître des crises financières de notre histoire* (Paris: Boivin).

Markovitch, T. J.
1965   *L'industrie française de 1789 à 1964* (Paris: Cahiers de l'ISEA), 1–201

Marshall, T. H.
1950   *Citizenship and Social Class, and Other Essays* (Cambridge: The University Press).
1964   *Class, Citizenship and Social Development; Essays* (Garden City: Doubleday; 1st edn.).

Martin, José Louis.
1969   "Organisation municipal de la villa de Gata en el siglo XVI," in *Villes de l'Europe méditerranéenne et de l'Europe occidentale du Moyen Age au XIXe siècle* (Saint-Brieuc: Les Belles Lettres; Annales de la Faculté des Lettres et Sciences Humaines de Nice, no. 9–10), 101–111.

Marx, Fritz Morstein.
1935   "Civil Service in Germany," in Leonard D. White et al., *Civil Service Abroad: Great Britain, Canada, France, Germany* (New York: Mc-Graw-Hill).

Marx, Karl.
1900   *Le 18ème Brumaire de Louis Bonaparte* (Paris: Schleicher).
1970   *Capital* (London: Lawrence and Wishart; 3 vols.).

Masefield, G. B.
1967   "Crops and Livestock," in E. E. Rich and C. H. Wilson, eds., *The Economy of Expanding Europe in the Sixteenth and Seventeenth Centuries* (Cambridge Economic History of Europe) (Cambridge: The University Press), iv: 276–307.

Matejek, François.
1968   "La production agricole dans les pays tschécoslovaques à partir de XVIe siècle jusqu'à la première guerre mondiale," *Third International Conference of Economic History*, Munich 1965 (Paris: Mouton), ii: 205–220.

Mathias, Peter.
1969   *The First Industrial Nation: An Economic History, 1700–1914* (London: Methuen).

Matos, Gustavo Lagos.

1963   *International Stratification and Underdeveloped Countries* (Chapel Hill: University of North Carolina Press).

Matschoss, Conrad.

1911   "Geschichte der Königlich Preussischen Techischen Deputation für Gewerber. Zur Erinnerung an das 100 jährige Bestehen, 1811–1911," *Beiträge zur Geschichte der Technik und Industrie. Jahrbuch des VDI*, 3: 239–275.

Mauersberg, Hans.

1960   *Wirtschafts- und Sozialgeschichte zentraleuropäischer Städte in neurer Zeit* (Göttingen: Vandenhoeck & Ruprecht).

1968   "Die Versorgung der oberdeutschen Städte im spaten Mittelalter und in der Neuzeit," *Third International Conference of Economic History, Munich 1965* (Paris: Mouton), 1: 119–124.

Mayer, Theodor.

1926   "Geschichte der Finanzwirtschaft und Finanzwissenschaft vom Spatmittelalter bis zum Ende des 18. Jahrhunderts," in *Handbuch der Finanzwissenschaften* (Tübingen: Mohr), 1: 210–244.

McLuhan, Marshall.

1962   *The Gutenberg Galaxy* (London: Routledge & Kegan Paul).

Mendels, Franklin.

1969   "Industrialization and Population Pressure in 18th-Century Flanders" (unpublished doctoral dissertation, University of Wisconsin).

1970a   "Industry and Marriages in Flanders before the Industrial Revolution," in *Proceedings of Section V (Historical Demography) of the Fourth Congress of the International Economic History Association* (Winnipeg: University of Manitoba Press), 81–93.

1970b   "Recent Research in European Historical Demography," *American Historical Review*, 75: 1065–1073.

Mendès-France, Pierre, and Ardant, Gabriel.

1955   *Economics and Action* (London: W. Heinemann).

Merkl, Peter.

1970   *Modern Comparative Politics* (New York: Holt, Rinehart and Winston).

Merle, Louis.

1958   *La Métairie et l'évolution agraire de la Gâtine poitevine de la fin du Moyen Age à la Révolution* (Paris: SEVPEN).

Meshalin, I.

1950   *Tekstil'naiá promyshlennost' krest'ian Moskovskoy gubernii v XVIII i pervoy polovinie XIX veka* (Moscow: Izdatel'stvo Akademii Nauk SSSR).

Méthivier, Hubert.

1966   *L'Ancien Régime* (Paris: Presses universitaires de France; 3d edn.).

Meuvret, Jean.

1951   "La géographie des prix des céréales et les anciennes économies européennes: Prix méditerranéens, prix continentaux, prix atlantiques à la fin du XVII siècle," *Revista de Economía*, 4: 63–69.

Meuvret, Jean.

1968   "Production et productivité agricoles," *Third International Confer-ence of Economic History*, Munich 1965 (Paris: Mouton), ii: 11–22.

1970a   "The Condition of France, 1688–1715," in J. S. Bromley, ed., *The New Cambridge Modern History, VI. The Rise of Great Britain and Russia, 1688–1715/25* (Cambridge: The University Press), 316–342.

1970b   "Prices, Population and Economic Activities in Europe, 1688–1715: A Note," in J. S. Bromley, ed., *The New Cambridge Modern History, VI. The Rise of Great Britain and Russia, 1688–1715/25* (Cam-bridge: The University Press), 874–897.

Meyer, Jean.

1966   *La noblesse bretonne au XVIIIe siècle* (Paris: SEVPEN; 2 vols.).

Miliband, Ralph.

1969   *The State in Capitalist Society* (London: Weidenfeld & Nicholson)

comte de Mirabeau, Honoré-Gabriel de Riquetti.

1788   *De la monarchie prussienne, sous Frederic le Grand* (London: N.P.).

marquis de Mirabeau, Victor de Riquetti.

1761   *La théorie de l'impôt* (A la Haye: B. Gilbert).

M.I.T. Study Group.

1967   "The Transitional Process," in Claude E. Welch, ed., *Political Mod-ernization* (Belmont, Calif.: Wadsworth; first published in 1960), pp. 22–48.

Mitchell, Brian R.

1962   *Abstract of British Historical Statistics*, with the collaboration of Phyllis Deane (Cambridge: The University Press).

Mitchell, J. Clyde

1961   "Wage Labour and African Population Movements in Central Africa," in K. M. Barbour and R. M. Prothero, ed. *Essays on African Popula-tion* (London: Routledge & Kegan Paul).

comte de Mollien, Francois Nicolas.

1945   *Memoires d'un ministre du trésor public, 1780–1815* (Paris: Im-primerie de H. Fournier).

Mols, Roger.

1954–   *Introduction à la démographie historique des villes d'Europe du XIVe*
1956   *au XVIe siècle* (Louvain: Université de Louvain; 3 vols.).

Momsen, Ingwer Ernst.

1969   *Die Bevölkerung der Stadt Husum von 1769 bis 1860* (Kiel: Geo-graphische Institut).

Montesquieu.

1949–   *Oeuvres complètes*, texte présenté et annoté par Roger Caillois (Paris:
1951   Gallimard).

Moore, Barrington.

1966   *Social Origins of Dictatorship and Democracy: Lord and Peasant in the Making of the Modern World* (Boston: Beacon Press).

[668]

Moreau de Beaumont, Jean Louis.

1787– *Mémoires concernant les impositions et droits en Europe* (Paris: J. C.
1789   Desaint; 5 vols.).

Moreland, W. H.

1957   "The Revenue System of the Mughul Empire," in Sir Richard Brun,
ed., *The Cambridge History of India, IV. The Mughul Period* (New
Delhi: S. Chand), 449–475.

Morineau, Michel.

1971   *Les faux-semblants d'un démarrage économique: agriculture et démographie en France au XVIIIe siècle* (Paris: Armand Colin), Cahiers
des Annales.

Morley, John.

1919   *Walpole* (London: Macmillan).

Morselli, Emanuele.

1951   "On the Historiography of Thought on Public Finance," *Public
Finance*, VI: 53–80.

Mosca, Gaetano.

1939   *The Ruling Class*, Arthur Livingston, ed. (London: McGraw-Hill).

Mosher, Frederick C.

1968   *Democracy and the Public Service* (New York: Oxford University
Press).

Mosher, William E., Kingsley, J. Donald, and Stahl, O. Glenn.

1950   *Public Personnel Administration* (New York: Harper and Row; 3d
edn.).

Mousnier, Roland.

1945   *La Vénalité des offices sous Henri IX et Louis XIII* (Rouen: Editions
Maugard).

1958   "Etat et commissaire: Recherches sur la création des intendants des
provinces (1634–1648)," in Richard Dietrich and Gerhard Oestreich,
eds., *Forschungen zu Staat und Verfassung: Festgabe für Fritz Hartung*
(Berlin: Duncker & Humblot), 325–344.

1969   *Etat et Société en France aux XVIIe et XVIIIe siècles* (Paris: Centre
de Documentation Universitaire).

1970   et ses collaborateurs, *Le Conseil du roi de Louis XII à la révolution*
(Paris: Presses universitaires de France).

Mulhall, Michael G.

1903   *The Dictionary of Statistics* (London: George Routledge).

Muncy, Lysbeth W.

1944   *The Junker in the Prussian Administration Under William II. 1888–
1914* (Providence: Brown University Press).

Muret, Pierre.

1949   avec Phillipe Sagnac *La prépondérance anglaise, 1715–1763* (Paris:
Presses universitaires de France; *Peuples et Civilisations, histoire général*, vol. II).

Musgrave, Richard A.

1969 *Fiscal Systems* (New Haven: Yale University Press).

Musson, A. E., and Robinson, Eric.

1969 *Science and Technology in the Industrial Revolution* (Manchester: The University Press).

Mykland, Knut.

1967 *Skiftet i forvaltningsordningen i Danmark og Norge* (Oslo: Universitetsforlaget).

Nadal, Jorge.

1966 *La población española* (*siglos XVI a XX*) (Barcelona: Ariel).

Naudé, Wilhelm.

1896 *Die Getreidehandelspolitik der europäischen Staaten vom 13. bis zum 18. Jahrhundert, als Einleitung in die preussiche Getreidehandelspolitik* (Berlin: Parey; Acta Borussica, "Die Getreidehandelspolitik," 1).

1901 *Die Getreidehandelspolitik und Kriegsmagazinverwaltung Brandenburg Preussens bis 1740* (Berlin: Parey; Acta Borussica, "Die Getreidehandelspolitik," ii).

————, Stalweit, August, and Schmoller, Gustav.

1910 *Die Getreidehandelspolitik und Kriegsmagazinverwaltung Preussens 1740–1756* (Berlin: Parey; Acta Borussica, "Die Getreidehandelspolitik," iii).

Neale, John Ernest.

1949 *The Elisabethan House of Commons* (London: Cape).

Nef, John Ulric.

1934 "The Progress of Technology and the Growth of Large-scale Industry in Great Britain, 1540–1640," *Economic History Review*, v. Reprinted in E. M. Carus-Wilson, ed., *Essays in Economic History*, Reprints edited for the Economic History Society (London: E. Arnold, 1954–1962), 1: 88–107 and in *The Conquest of the Material World: Essays in the Coming of Industrialization* (Cleveland: World Publishing Co.; Meridan Books, 1967), 121–143.

1940 *Industry and Government in France and England: 1540–1640* (Ithaca: Cornell University Press; Great Seal Books).

Nelson, Joan.

1969 "Migrants, Urban Poverty and Instability in New Nations" (Cambridge: Harvard Center for International Affairs, Occasional Paper, no. 22).

1970 "The Urban Poor: Disruption or Political Integration in Third World Cities?" *World Politics*, 22: 393–414.

Ness, Gayl D.

1970 "Colonialism, Nationalism and Economic Development," in Gayl D. Ness, ed., *The Sociology of Economic Development* (New York: Harper and Row), 387–401.

Nettl, J. P.

1967 *Political Mobilization* (London: Faber & Faber).

1968 "The State as a Conceptual Variable," *World Politics*, 20: 559–592.

————, and Robertson, Roland.

1968 *International Systems and the Modernization of Societies* (London: Faber & Faber).

Nicolini, Fausto.

1934 *Aspetti della vita italo-spagnuola nel cinque e seicento* (Naples: A. Guida).

Nisbet, Robert.

1969 *Social Change and History* (New York: Oxford University Press).

Nordlinger, Eric.

1970 *Politics and Society* (Englewood Cliffs: Prentice-Hall).

North, Douglass C., and Thomas, Robert P.

1970 "An Economic Theory of the Growth of the Western World," *Economic History Review*, 2d series, 23: 1–17.

Notestein, Wallace.

1954 *The English People at the Eve of Colonisation, 1603–1630* (New York: Harper and Row).

O'Boyle, Lenore.

1966 "The Middle Class in Europe, 1815–1848," *American Historical Review*, 71: 826–845.

O'Brien, P. K.

1959 "British Incomes and Property in the Early 19th Century," *Economic History Review*, 2d series, 12: 255–267.

Ocampo, Jose F., and Johnson, Dale L.

1972 "The Concept of Political Development," in James D. Cockcroft et al. *Dependence and Underdevelopment* (Garden City: Doubleday; Anchor Books).

Olbricht, Konrad.

1939 "Die Vergrossstädterung des Abendlandes zu Beginn des Dreissigjahrigen Krieges," *Petermanns Geographische Mitteilungen*, 85: 349–353.

Oman, C.W.C.

1910 "English History (II)," in *Encyclopaedia Britannica IX* (Cambridge: The University Press; 11th edn.), 474–486.

Oppenheim, Michael.

1896 *A History of the Administration of the Royal Navy and of Merchant Shipping in Relation to the Navy, I. 1509–1660* (London: J. Lane).

Organski, A.F.K.

1965 *The Stages of Political Development* (New York: Alfred Knopf).

Ornstein, Martha.

1963 *The Role of Scientific Societies in the Seventeenth Century* (Hamden, London: Archon Books; 3d edn.; first published in 1938).

Ōtsuka, Hisao.

1965 "The Market Structure of Rural Industry in the Early Stages of the Development of Modern Capitalism," *Second International Conference of Economic History, Aix-en-Provence 1962* (Paris: Mouton), II: 457–472.

[671]

Pach, S. P.

1965 "Über einige Probleme der Gutswirtschaft in Ungarn in der ersten Hälfte des XVIIe Jahrhunderts," *Second International Conference of Economic History, Aix-en-Provence 1962* (Paris: Mouton), II: 217–222.

1966 "En Hongrie au XVIe siècle: l'Activité commerciale des seigneurs et leur production marchande," *Annales; Economies, Sociétés, Civilisations*, 21: 1212–1231.

1968 "Die Getreideversorgung der ungarischen Städte vom XV. bis XVII. Jahrhundert," *Third International Conference of Economic History, Munich 1965* (Paris: Mouton), I: 97–108.

Pagès, G.

1932 "La Vénalité des offices dans l'ancienne France," *Revue historique*, 169: 477–495.

Palacio Atard, Vicente.

1969 "Problems de abastecimento en Madrid a finales del s. XVIII," *Villes de l'Europe méditerranéene et de l'Europe occidentale du Moyen Age au XIXe siècle* (Saint-Brieuc: Les Belles Lettres; Annales de la Faculté des Lettres et Sciences Humaines de Nice, no. 9–10), 279–288.

Palloix, Christian.

1971 *L'Economie mondiale capitaliste* (Paris: Maspero; 2 vols.).

Parker, Geoffrey.

1973 "Mutiny and Discontent in the Spanish Army of Flanders 1572–1607," *Past and Present*, 58: 38–52.

Parker, Harold T.

1965 "French Administrators and French Scientists during the Old Regime and the Early Years of the Revolution," Richard Herr and Harold T. Parker, eds., *Ideas in History: Essays Presented to Louis Gottschalk by his former students* (Durham: Duke University Press), 85–109.

Parker, J. L.

1937 "Law and Police," in Edward Eyre, ed., *European Civilisation: Its origins and development—Economic History of Europe since the Reformation* (London: Oxford University Press), 893–993.

Parker, R.A.C.

1968 "Landlord and Tenant in 18th Century and 19th Century England," *Third International Conference of Economic History, Munich 1965* (Paris: Mouton), II: 127–130.

Parry, John Horace.

1963 *The Age of Reconnaissance* (London: Weidenfeld & Nicholson).

Parsons, Talcott.

1967 *Societies: Comparative and Evolutionary Perspectives* (Englewood Cliffs: Prentice-Hall).

1971 *The System of Modern Societies* (Englewood Cliffs: Prentice-Hall).

Peacock, A. J.

1965 *Bread or Blood. A Study of the Agrarian Riots in East Anglia in 1816* (London: Victor Gollancz).

Pedersen, E. Ladewig.

1967   *The Crisis of the Danish Nobility* (Odense: The University Press).

Pesez, J. M., and Ladurie, E. Le Roy.

1965   "Le cas français: vue d'ensemble," in *Villages désertés et histoire économique, XIe-XVIIIe siècle* (Paris: SEVPEN), 127–252.

Petraň, Josef.

1965   "A propos de la formation des régions de la production spécialisée en Europe centrale," *Second International Conference of Economic History, Aix-en-Provence 1962* (Paris: Mouton), ii: 223–236.

Pirenne, Henri.

1902   *Histoire de Belgique* (Brussels: Lamertin).

1914   "The Stages in the Social History of Capitalism," *American Historical Review*, 19: 494–515.

1963   *Early Democracies in the Low Countries* (New York: Harper and Row; first published in 1915).

Plumb, J. H.

1956   *Sir Robert Walpole: The Making of a Statesman* (London: Cresset Press).

Polanyi, Karl, and Arensberg, Conrad M., editors.

1957   *Trade and Market in the Early Empires; Economies in History and Theory* (Glencoe: Free Press).

1967   *The Growth of Political Stability in England, 1675–1725* (London: Macmillan).

Pollard, Sidney, and Crossley, David W.

1968   *The Wealth of Britain* (London: Batsford).

Ponko, Vincent, Jr.

1968   "The Privy Council and the Spirit of Elizabethan Economic Management, 1558–1603," *Transactions of the American Philosophical Society* (Philadelphia: The American Philosophical Society), new series, 58: part 4.

Poole, Austin Lane.

1951   *From Domesday Book to Magna Carta, 1087–1226* (Oxford: Clarendon Press).

Porshnev, Boris Fedorovich.

1963   *Les soulèvements populaires en France de 1623 à 1648* (Paris: SEVPEN; École pratique des hautes études, 6e section: Centre de recherches historiques: Oeuvres étrangères, 4).

Postan, M. M.

1954   "The Rise of a Money Economy," in E. M. Carus-Wilson, ed., *Essays in Economic History* (London: Arnold).

von Poten, Bernhard.

1896   *Geschichte des Militär-Erziehungs-und Bildungswesens in den Länder deutscher Zunge, IV. Preussen* (Berlin: A. Hofmann).

Pounds, N.J.G., and Ball, S. S.

1964 "Core Areas and the Development of the European States System," *Annals of the Association of American Geographers*, 54: 24–40.

Prestwich, Menna.

1966 *Cranfield: Politics and Profits under the Early Stuarts. The Career of Lionel Cranfield, Earl of Middlesex* (Oxford: Clarendon Press).

Price, Jacob M.

1970 "The Map of Commerce, 1683–1721," in J. S. Bromley, ed., *The New Cambridge Modern History IV, The Rise of Great Britain and Russia, 1688–1725* (Cambridge: The University Press), 834–874.

Pûrs, Jaroslav.

1965 "Die Aufhebung der Hörigkeit und die Grundentlastung in den böhmischen Landern," *Second International Conference of Economic History, Aix-en-Provence 1962* (Paris: Mouton), II: 247–257.

Pye, Lucian W.

1967 "The Formation of New States," in Ithiel de Sola Pool, ed., *Contemporary Political Science: Toward Empirical Theory* (New York: McGraw-Hill), 182–203.

Radzinowicz, Leon.

1957 *A History of English Criminal Law and its Administration from 1750* (New York: Macmillan; 4 vols.).

Rambaud, Placide.

1962 *Economie et sociologie de la montagne: Albiez-le-Vieux en Maurienne* (Paris: Colin).

Rashdall, Hastings.

1936 *The Universities of Europe in the Middle Ages, III. English Universities, Student Life* (Oxford: Clarendon Press), rev. edn., eds. F. M. Powicke and A. B. Emden.

Razzell, P. E.

1965 "Population Change in Eighteenth-Century England: A Reinterpretation," *Economic History Review*, 18: 312–332.

Redlich, Fritz.

1964– "The German Military Enterpriser and his Work Force," in *Viertel-*
1965 *jahresschrift für Sozial- und Wirtschaftsgeschichte*, Beiheft 47 and 48.

1964– *The German Military Enterpriser and his Work Force* (Wiesbaden:
1965a Steiner; 2 vols.).

Reid, Rachel Robertson.

1921 *The King's Council in the North* (London: Longmans, Green).

Reinhard, Marcel.

1956 "Elite et noblesse dans la deuxième moitié du XVIIIe siècle," *Revue d'histoire moderne et contemporaine*, 3.

Reinhard, Marcel, Armengaud, André, and Dupâquier, Jacques.

1968 *Histoire générale de la population mondiale* (Paris: Montchrestien).

Reith, Charles.

1948 *A Short History of the British Police* (London: Oxford University Press).

Richards, E. S.

1973 "Structural Change in a Regional Economy: Sutherland and the Industrial Revolution, 1780–1830, *Economic History Review* 2d series, 26: 63–76.

Richardson, Nicholas.

1966 *The French Prefectoral Corps, 1814–1830* (London: Cambridge University Press).

Richardson, Walter Cecil.

1952 *Tudor Chamber Administration, 1485–1547* (Baton Rouge: Louisiana State University Press).

1953 *Stephen Vaughan, Financial Agent of Henry VIII; A Study of Financial Relations with the Low Countries* (Baton Rouge: Louisiana State University Press; LSU Studies, Social Science Series, 3).

1961 *History of the Court of Augmentation, 1536–1554* (Baton Rouge: Louisiana State University Press).

Ridley, F., and Blondel, J.

1965 *Public Administration in France* (New York: Barnes and Noble).

Riedel, Adolph Friedrich.

1866 *Der Brandenburgisch-Preussische Staatshaushalt* (Berlin: Ernst & Korn).

Riggs, Fred W.

1970 "The Comparison of Whole Political Systems," in Robert T. Holt and John E. Turner, eds., *The Methodology of Comparative Research* (New York: Free Press).

Ringrose, David.

1968 "Transportation and Economic Stagnation in Eighteenth-Century Castile," *Journal of Economic History*, 28: 51–79.

1969 "Madrid y Castilla, 1560–1850. una capital nacional en una economía regional," *Moneda y Credito*, 111: 65–122.

Rokkan, Stein.

1969 "Models and Methods in the Comparative Study of Nation-Building," *Acta Sociologica*, 12: 53–73.

1970a *Citizens, Elections, Parties* (Oslo: Universitets Forlaget).

1970b "The Growth and Structuring of Mass Politics," *Scandinavian Political Studies*, 5: 65–83.

de Roover, Raymond.

1958 "The Concept of the Just Price: Theory and Economic Policy," *Journal of Economic History*, 18: 418–434.

Rose, R. B.

1959 "Eighteenth-Century Price-Riots, the French Revolution and the Jacobin Maximum," *International Review of Social History*, 4: 432–445.

Rosenau, James.

1970 *The Adaptation of National Societies: A Theory of Political System Behavior and Transformation* (New York: McCaleb-Seiler).

[675]

Rosenberg, Hans.

1943   "The Rise of the Junkers in Brandenburg-Prussia, 1410–1653," *American Historical Review*, 49: 1–22, 228–242.

1958   *Bureaucracy, Aristocracy and Autocracy: The Prussian Experience 1660–1815* (Cambridge: Harvard University Press).

1969   *Probleme der deutschen Sozialgeschichte* (Frankfurt a/M: Suhrkamp).

Rothman, Stanley.

1970   *European Society and Politics* (Indianapolis: Bobbs-Merrill).

Rowse, Alfred Leslie.

1950   *The England of Elizabeth: The Structure of Society* (London: Macmillan).

Royal Commission on the Police.

1962   *Final Report* (London: Her Majesty's Stationery Office).

Rudé, George.

1956   "La taxation populaire de mai 1775 à Paris et dans la region Parisienne," Annales historique de la Revolution Française, no. 143.

1961   "La taxation populaire de mai 1775 en Picardie, en Normandie et dans le Beauvisis," Annales historiques de la Revolution Française, no. 165.

1964   *The Crowd in History: A Study of Popular Disturbances in France and England, 1730–1848* (New York: Wiley).

1970   *Paris and London in the 18th Century* (London: Collins).

Rusche, George, and Kirchheimer, Otto.

1968   *Punishment and Social Structure* (New York: Russell and Russell).

Russell, J. C.

1958   "Late Ancient and Medieval Population," *Transactions of the American Philosophical Society* (Philadelphia: American Philosophical Society), new series, 48: part 3.

Russett, Bruce M.

1964   *World Handbook of Political and Social Indicators* (New Haven: Yale University Press).

Rustow, Dankwart.

1967   *A World of Nations: Problems of Political Modernization* (Washington: Brookings Institution).

Ruwet, Joseph.

1964   "Mesure de la production agricole sous l'Ancien Régime: le blé au pays mosan," *Annales; Economies, Sociétiés, Civilisations*, 19: 625–642.

Rybinski, Helga.

1964   "Der Grundsatz des Haushaltsgleichgewichts in historischer und dogmengeschichtlicher Sicht" (Berlin: dissertation, Wirtschafts- und Sozialwissenschaftliche Fakultät Freie Universität Berlin).

Saalfeld, Diedrich.

1968   "Produktion und Intensität der Landwirtschaft in Deutschland und angrenzenden Gebieten um 1800," *Third International Conference of Economic History, Munich 1965* (Paris: Mouton), II: 141–148.

Sánchez-Albornoz, Nicolas.

1963a "En Espagne, au XIXe siècle: géographie des prix," *Mélanges d'histoire économique et sociale en hommage au professeur Antony Babel* (Geneva: n.p.), II: 191–209.

1963b *Las crisis de subsistencias de España en el siglo XIX* (Rosario, Argentina: Instituto de Investigaciones Históricas, Universidad Nacional del Litoral).

1964 "Crisis de subsistencias y recesion demografía: España en 1868," *Anuario del Instituto de Investigaciones Históricas, Universidad Nacional del Litoral*, 6: 27–40.

1968 "El trasfondo económico de la Revolución," *Revista de Occidente*, 67: 39-63.

Sarrailh, Jean.

1954 *L'Espagne éclairée de la seconde moitié du XVIIIe siècle* (Paris: Imprimerie Nationale).

Seaville, John.

1969 "Primitive Accumulation and Early Industrialization in Britain," *Socialist Register*, 1969: 247–271.

Savine, Alexander.

1909 "English Monasteries on the Eve of Dissolution," in Paul Vinogradoff, ed. *Studies in Social and Legal History* (Oxford: Clarendon Press), I.

Schattschneider, E. E.

1960 *The Semi-Sovereign People* (New York: Holt, Rinehart & Winston).

Schiff, Otto.

1924 "Die Bauernaufstände von 1525 bis 1789," *Historische Zeitschrift*, 130: 189–209.

Schmoller, Gustav.

1877 "Die Epochen der preussischen Finanzpolitik," *Jahrbuch für Gesetzgebung, Verwaltung und Volkswirtschaft im Deutschen Reich* (Leipzig), I: 33–114.

1896 "Die Epochen der Getreidehandelsverfassung und -politik," *Jahrbuch für Gesetzgebung, Verwaltung und Volkswirtschaft im Deutschen Reich* [Schmollers Jahrbuch], 20: 695–744.

1909 "Historische Betrachtungen über Staatenbildung und Finanzentwicklung," *Jahrbuch für Gesetzgebung, Verwaltung und Volkswirtschaft im Deutschen Reich* (Leipzig), 33: no. 1, 1–64.

1921 *Preussische Verfassungs-, Verwaltungs- und Finanzgeschichte* (Berlin: Reimar Hobbing).

von Schröder, Wilhelm Freyherr.

1721 *Fürstliche Schatz- und Rent-Cammer* (Leipzig: T. Fritschen).

Schultze, Walther.

1888 "Geschichte der Preussischen Regieverwaltung von 1766 bis 1786. Ein historisch-kritischer Versuch," *Staats- und sozialwissenschaftliche Forschungen*, 7, Drittes Heft.

Schumpeter, Elizabeth Boody.

1938 "English Prices and Public Finance, 1660–1822," *The Review of Economic Statistics*, XX: 21–37.

Schumpeter, Joseph.

1918 "Die Krise des Steuerstaates," *Zeitfragen aus dem Gebiet der Soziologie*, 4: 1–71.

1954 "The Crisis of the Tax State," in Alan T. Peacock, Ralph Turvey, Wolfgang F. Stolper and Elizabeth Henderson, eds., *International Economic Papers: Translations Prepared for the International Economic Association* (New York: Macmillan), 4: 5–38.

Scott, James C.

1969 "The Analysis of Corruption in Developing Nations," *Comparative Studies in Society and History*, 11: 315–341.

1970 "Patron-Client Politics and Political Change" (unpublished paper presented to the annual meeting of the American Political Science Association, Los Angeles).

Sée, Henri.

1923 "Remarques sur le caractère de l'industrie rurale en France et les causes de son extension au XVIIIe siècle," *Revue historique*, 142: 47–53.

1948– *Histoire économique de la France* (Paris: A. Colin; 2 vols.).
1951

Seeley, Sir John Robert.

1968 *Life and Times of Stein, or, Germany and Prussia in the Napoleonic Age* (New York: Greenwood Press, first published 1879, vol. 1).

Seligman, Edwin R.

1914 Essais sur l'impôt (Paris: Suret).

Sentou, Jean.

1969 *Fortunes et groupes sociaux à Toulouse sous la Révolution* (Toulouse: Privat; Bibliothèque Méridionale, 2d series, 43).

Sereni, Emilio.

1948 *Il capitalismo nelle campagne* (1860-1900) (Turin: Einaudi).

Sharp, Walter R.

1935 "Public Personnel Management in France," in Leonard E. White et al., *Civil Service Abroad: Great Britain, Canada, France, Germany* (New York: McGraw-Hill), 83–157.

Siberling, Norman J.

1919 "British Financial Experience 1790-1830," *The Review of Economic Statistics*, preliminary vol. 1: 282–297; App.: 321–323.

da Silva, Jose Gentil.

1963 "Villages castillans et types de production au XVIe siècle," *Annales; Economies, Sociétés, Civilisations*, 18: 729–744.

1965 *En Espagne. Développement économique, subsistances, déclin* (Paris: Mouton).

Simon, Oskar.

1902 *Die Fachbildung des preussischen Gewerbe und Handelsstandes im 18. und 19. Jahrhundert nach den Bestimmungen des Gewerberechts und der Verfassung des gewerblichen Unterrichtswesens* (Berlin: J. J. Heine).

Skeel, Caroline Anne James.

1924 *The Council in the Marches of Wales: A Study in Local Government during the Sixteenth and Seventeenth Centuries* (London: first published by H. Rees, Ltd., London, 1904).

Slicher van Bath, B. H.

1960 "The Rise of Intensive Husbandry in the Low Countries," in J. S. Bromley and E. H. Kossman, eds., *Britain and the Netherlands* (London: Chatto and Windus).

1963 *The Agrarian History of Western Europe, A.D. 500–1850* (London: Arnold).

1968 "La productivité agricole. Les problémes fondamentaux de la société pre-industrielle en Europe occidentale," *Third International Conference of Economic History, Munich 1965* (Paris: Mouton), II: 23–30.

Smith, Denis Mack.

1968 *A History of Sicily: Modern Sicily* (London: Chatto and Windus).

1968 *The Making of Italy, 1796–1870* (New York: Walker).

Smith, Donald E.

in press *Religion and Political Development* (Boston: Little, Brown).

Smith, Munroe.

1928 *The Development of European Law* (New York: Columbia University Press).

Snow, Peter G.

1971 "A Scalogram Analysis of Political Development," in John A. Gillespie and Betty A. Nesvold, eds., *Macro-Quantitative Analysis* (Beverly Hills: Sage Publications).

Soetbeer, Adolph G.

1879 *Edelmetall-Produktion und Werth verhältniss Zwischen Gold und Silber, seit der Entdecking Amerika's bis zur Gegenwart* (Gotha: J. Perthes).

von Sonnenfels, Joseph.

1776 *Grundsätze der Polizei, Handlung und Finanzwissenschaft* (Wien: J. Kurzbock), I.

Spooner, F. C.

1968 "The Economy of Europe 1559–1609," in R. B. Wernham, ed. *The New Cambridge Modern History,* III. *The Counter-Reformation and Price Revolution, 1559–1610* (Cambridge: The University Press), 14–43.

Stalweit, August.

1931 *Die Getreidehandelspolitik und Kriegmagazinverwaltung Preussens 1756–1806* (Berlin: Parey; Acta Borussica, "Die Getreidehandelspolitik," IV).

Stavenhagen, Rodolfo.

1970 "Introduction," in Stavenhagen, ed., *Agrarian Problems and Peasant Movements in Latin America* (Garden City: Doubleday; Anchor).

Stead, Philip John.

1957 *The Police of Paris* (London: Staples Press).

Stenton, Frank Merry.

1943   *Anglo-Saxon England* (Oxford: Clarendon Press).

Stone, Lawrence.

1965   *The Crisis of the Aristocracy, 1558–1641* (Oxford: Clarendon Press).

1967   *The Crisis of the Aristocracy, 1558–1641* (London: Oxford University Press; abridge. edn.).

Stouff, L.

1969   "La viande à Carpentras," *Annales; Economies, Sociétés, Civilisations*, 24: 1431–1448.

Straube, Hans-Joachim.

1931   "Die Gewerbeforderung Preussens in der ersten Halfte des 19. Jahrhunderts mit besonderer Berucksichtigung der Regierungsmassnahmen zur Forderung der Industrie durch Erziehung und Fortbilding" (Berlin; thesis).

Strayer, Joseph.

1970   *On the Medieval Origins of the Modern State* (Princeton: Princeton University Press).

1971   *Medieval Statecraft and the Perspectives of History* (Princeton: Princeton University Press).

Sugar, Peter F.

1963   "The Nature of the Non-Germanic Societies under Habsburg Rule," *Slavic Review*, 22: 1–30.

Swart, Koenraad Wolter.

1949   *Sale of Offices in the Seventeenth Century* (The Hague: Nijhoff).

Tarschys, Daniel.

1971   *Beyond the State. The Future Polity in Classical and Soviet Marxism*, Swedish Studies in International Politics, 3 (Stockholm: Laromedels).

Taton, Rene.

1964   Ed., *Enseignement et diffusion des sciences en France au XVIIIe siècle* (Paris: Hermann; Histoire de la pensée, XI).

Tauscher, Anton.

1943   "Die Steuer als Gestaltungsmitted der Volkswirtschaft bei den deutschen Merkantilisten," *Finanzarchiv.*, 9; no. 2, 303–337.

Tawney, Richard Henry.

1958   *Business and Politics under James I: Lionel Cranfield as Merchant and Minister* (Cambridge: The University Press).

1967   *The Agrarian Problem in the Sixteenth Century*, ed. Lawrence Stone (New York: Harper Torchbooks; first published in 1912).

Taylor, Eva Germaine Rimington.

1930   *Tudor Geography 1485–1583* (London: Methuen).

1954   *The Mathematical Practitioners of Tudor and Stuart England* (Cambridge: published for the Institution of Navigation at the University Press).

1956   *The Haven-Finding Art: A History of Navigation from Odysseus to Captain Cook* (London: Hollis & Carter).

Thirsk, Joan.

1961   "Industries in the Countryside," in F. J. Fisher, ed., *Essays in the Economic and Social History of Tudor and Stuart England in Honor of R. H. Tawney* (Cambridge: The University Press).

1967   ed., *The Agrarian History of England and Wales, IV. 1500–1640* (Cambridge: The University Press).

Thompson, E. P.

1963   *The Making of the English Working Class* (London: Gollancz).

1971   "The Moral Economy of the English Crowd in the Eighteenth Century," *Past and Present*, 50: 76–136.

Thompson, Francis M. L.

1963   *English Landed Society in the Nineteenth Century* (Toronto: University of Toronto Press).

1966   "The Social Distribution of Landed Property in England since the Sixteenth Century," *Economic History Review*, 2d series, 19: 505–517.

1968   "The Second Agricultural Revolution, 1815–1880," *Economic History Review*, 2d series, 21: 62–77.

1969   "Landownership and Economic Growth in England in the Eighteenth Century," in E. L. Jones and S. J. Wolff, eds., *Agrarian Change and Economic Development: The Historical Problems* (London: Methuen), 41–60.

Thomson, Gladys Scott.

1923   *Lord Lieutenants in the Sixteenth Century: A Study of Tudor Local Administration* (London: Longmans, Green).

Thorner, Daniel.

1964   "L'Economie paysanne, Concept pour l'histoire économique," *Annales; Economies, Sociétés, Civilisations*, 19: 417–432.

Thyssen, Simon.

1954   *Die Berufsschule in Idee und Gestaltung* (Essen: W. Girardet).

Tilly, Charles.

1970   "Notes on West European Statemaking since 1500: (unpublished paper presented to the UNESCO Conference on State- and Nation-Building, Cérisy-la-Salle, France).

Tilly, Louise A.

1971   "The Food Riot as a Form of Political Conflict in France," *Journal of Interdisciplinary History*, 2: 23–57.

Tilly, Richard.

1966   *Financial Institutions and Industrialization in the Rhineland, 1815–1870* (Madison: University of Wisconsin Press).

1969   "The Political Economy of Public Finance and the Industrialization of Prussia, 1815–1866," *Journal of Economic History*, 26: 484–497.

————, and Tilly, Charles.

1971   "An Agenda for European Economic History in the 1970s," *Journal of Economic History*, 31: 184–198.

Tillyard, Eustace Mandeville Wetenhall.

1962 *Shakespeare's History Plays* (Harmondsworth: Penguin Books; Peregrine edn.).

de Tocqueville, Alexis.

1955 *The Old Regime and the French Revolution*. Trans. by Stuart Gilbert (Garden City, N.Y.: Doubleday; Anchor Books).

Tout, Thomas Frederick.

1916– "The English Civil Service in the Fourteenth Century," lecture de-
1917 livered in John Rylands Library, 15 Dec. 1915; printed in the
1932– *Bulletin of the Library*, 3 (1916–17); reprinted in *The Collected*
1934 *Papers of Thomas Frederick Tout*, III: 191–221 (Manchester: The University Press, 1932–1934).

1920– *Chapters in the Administrative History of Medieval England: The*
1933 *Wardrobe, the Chamber, and the Small Seals* (Manchester: The University Press; London: Longmans, Green; 6 vols.).

Toutain, Jean-Claude.

1963 *La population de la France de 1700 à 1959* (Paris: Institut de Science Economique Appliquée; Cahiers de l'ESEA, AF 3).

Treasure, G.R.R.

1966 *Seventeenth Century France* (London: Rivingtons).

Trevor-Roper, H. R.

1967 "The General Crisis of the Seventeenth Century," in *Religion, the Reformation and Social Change* (London: Macmillan), 46-89; first published in *Past and Present*, 1969.

Troizkii, S. J.

1968 "Die Evolution der direkten Steuern in Russland im XVII-XVIII Jahrhundert," *Third International Conference of Economic History*, Munich 1965 (Paris: Mouton), I: 741–742.

Turgot, Anne Robert Jacques.

1913– *Oeuvres de Turgot et documents le concernant*, Gustave Schelle, con-
1923 tributor (Paris: F. Alcan; 5 vols.), II.

Usher, A. P.

1913 *The History of the Grain Trade in France, 1400–1710* (Cambridge: Harvard University Press).

Válka, Josef.

1965 "La structure économique de la seigneurie tchèque au XVIe siècle," *Second International Conference of Economic History, Aix-en-Provence, 1962* (Paris: Mouton), II: 211–215.

Van Riper, Paul P.

1958 *History of the United States Civil Service* (White Plains: Row, Peterson).

Várkonyi, Ágnes.

1968 "Fiscalité et Société en Hongrie à la fin du XVIIe siècle," *Third International Congress of Economic History, Munich 1965* (Paris: Mouton), I: 737–739.

de Vauban, Sebastien le Prestre.

1888   *La dîme royale* (Paris: Guillaumin).

Vaucher, Paul.

1924   *La Crise du Ministère Walpole en 1733–1734* (Paris: Plon-Nourrit).

Vaughan, Michalina.

1969   "The Grandes Ecoles," in Rupert Wilkinson, ed., *Governing Elites: Studies in Training and Selection* (New York: Oxford University Press).

Verba, Sidney.

1971   "Sequences and Development," in Leonard Binder and others, *Crises and Sequences in Political Development* (Princeton: Princeton University Press).

Veverka, Jindrich.

1963   "The Growth of Government Expenditure in the United Kingdom since 1790," in *Scottish Journal of Political Economy*, x: 111–127.

Vignes, Joseph Bernard Maurice.

1961   *Histoire des doctrines sur l'impôt en France* (Paris: Librairie général de droit et de jurisprudence).

Vilar, Pierre.

1962   *La Catalogne dans l'Espagne moderne* (Paris: SEVPEN; 3 vols.).

Villari, Rosario.

1967   *La rivolta antispagnola a Napoli. Le origini (1585–1647)* (Bari: Laterza).

Vives, Jaime Vicens.

1969   *An Economic History of Spain* (Princeton: Princeton University Press).

Vocke, Wilhelm.

1866   *Geschichte der Steuern des britischen Reichs* (Leipzig: A. Felix).

1884   "Deutsche und englische Finanzverwaltung," in *Finanzarchiv*. i: no. 1, 159–204.

Wackernagel, Hans Georg.

1956   *Altes Volkstum der Schweiz* (Basel: Krebs; Schriften der Schweizerischen Gesellschaft für Volkskunde, Band 38).

Wagner, A., and Déité, H.

1909–   *Histoire de l'impôt depuis l'antiquité jusqu'à nos jours* Adolph Hein-
1913   rich Wagner, ed., *Traité de la science des finances* (Paris: V. Giard & E. Briere; vols. 4–5).

Wallerstein, Immanuel.

1974   *The Modern World-System* (New York: Academic Press).

Ward, Robert E., and Rustow, Dankwart A.

1964   Eds., *Political Modernization in Japan and Turkey* (Princeton: Princeton University Press).

Ward, William Reginald.

1953   *The English Land Tax in the Eighteenth Century* (London: Oxford University Press).

Waters, David Watkin.

1958   *The Art of Navigation in England in Elisabethan and Early Stuart Times* (London: Holis and Carter).

Webb, Sidney, and Webb, Beatrice.

1904   "The Assize of Bread," *The Economic Journal*, 14: 192–218.

1913   *English Local Government* (London: Longmans, Green).

Weber, Adna Ferrin.

1899   *Growth of Cities in the Nineteenth Century* (Ithaca: Cornell University Press).

Weber, Max.

1956   *Wirtschaft und Gesellschaft, Studienausgabe*, Johannes Winckelmann, ed. (Tübingen: Mohr).

1964   *Wirtschaft und Gesellschaft: Grundriss der verstehenden Soziologie: Studienausgabe*, Johannes Winckelmann, ed. (Tübingen: Mohr).

Wegmann, Dietrich.

1969   *Die leitenden Staatlichen Verwaltungsbeamten der Province Westfalen, 1815–1918* (Münster: Aschendorffsche Verlagsbuchhandlung).

Weiss, Eberhard.

1970   "Ergebnisse eines Vergleichs der grundherrschaftlichen Strukturen Deutschlands und Frankreichs vom 13. bis zum Ausgang des 18. Jahrhundert," *Vierteljahrschrift für Sozial- und Wirtschaftsgeschichte*, 1: 1–14.

Wernham, Richard Bruce.

1966   *Before the Armada: The Growth of English Foreign Policy, 1485–1588* (London: Cape).

van Werveke, Hans.

1955   "Les villes belges. Histoire des institutions économiques et sociales," in Société Jean Bodin, *La Ville* (Brussels: Librairie Encyclopédique), part II: 551–576.

Western, John R.

1965   *The English Militia in the Eighteenth Century* (London: Routledge & Kegan Paul).

White, Lynn, Jr.

1940   "Technology and Invention in the Middle Ages," *Speculum*, 15: 141–159.

White, Lynn Townsend.

1962   *Mediaeval Technology and Social Change* (Oxford: Clarendon Press).

Whittlesey, Derwent.

1944   *The Earth and the State* (New York: Holt; 2d edn.).

Wiese, H.

1968   "Die Fleischversorgung der nordwesteuropäischen Grossstädte unter besonder Berücksichtigung des interterritorialen Rinderhandels," *Third International Conference of Economic History, Munich 1965* (Paris: Mouton), 1: 125–130.

Wilke, Gustav.

1921 "Die Entwicklung der Theorie des staatlichen Steuersystems in der deutschen Finanzwissenschaft des 19. Jahrhunderts," *Finanzarchiv.*, Jg. 38, vol. 1: 1–108.

Wilkinson, Spencer.

1915 *The French Army before Napoleon* (Oxford: Clarendon Press).

Willcox, William Bradford.

1940 *Gloucestershire; A Study in Local Government, 1590–1640* (New Haven: Yale University Press).

Williams, Henry.

1958 *The Council in the Marches of Wales under Elisabeth I* (Cardiff: University of Wales Press).

Wilson, Charles Henry.

1965 *England's Apprenticeship, 1603–1763* (London: Longmans, Green).

Wöhner, Paul Gottlieb.

1804– *Steuerverfassung des platten Landes der Kurmark Brandenburg* (Berlin:
1805 Voss).

Wolf, Eric.

1955 "Types of Latin American Peasantry: A Preliminary Discussion," *American Anthropologist*, 57: 452–471.

1956 "Aspects of Group Relations in a Complex Society: Mexico," *American Anthropologist*, 58: 1065–1078.

1969 *Peasant Wars of the Twentieth Century* (New York: Harper and Row).

Wolfe, Martin.

1972 *The Fiscal System of Renaissance France* (New Haven: Yale University Press).

Wolters, Friedrich.

1915 *Geschichte der brandenburgischen Finanzen in der Zeit von 1640–1697; Darstellung und Akten, II. Die Zentralverwaltung des Heeres und der Steuern* (München; Urkunden und Aktenstücke zur Geschichte der inneren Politik des Kurfürsten Friedrich Wilhelm von Brandenburg, part 1).

Wright, Louis Booker.

1935 *Middle-Class Culture in Elisabethan England* (Chapel Hill: University of North Carolina Press).

Wrigley, E. A.

1966 "Family Limitation in Pre-Industrial England," *Economic History Review*, 2d series, 19: 82–109.

1967 "A Simple Model of London's Importance in Changing English Society and Economy, 1650–1750," *Past and Present*, 37: 44–70.

1969 *Population and History* (New York: McGraw-Hill).

Wunder, Gerd.

1971 "Die Sozialstruktur der Geheimratskollegien in den süddeutschen protestantischen Fürstentümern (1660–1720). Zum Verhältnis von sozialer Mobilitat und Briefadel im Absolutismus," *Vierteljahrschrift für Sozial- und Wirtschaftgeschichte*, 58: 145–220.

Yatkunsky, V. K.

1965 "Formation en Russie de la grande industrie textile sur la base de la production rurale," *Second International Conference of Economic History, Aix-en-Provence 1962* (Paris: Mouton), II: 365–376.

1968 "Principaux moments de l'histoire de la production agricole en Russie du XVIe siècle à 1917," *Third International Conference of Economic History, Munich 1965* (Paris: Mouton), II: 221–237.

Zanetti, Dante.

1963 "L'approvisionnement de Pavie au XVIe siècle," *Annales; Economies, Sociétés, Civilisations*, 18: 44–62.

Ziegler, Philip.

1969 *The Black Death* (New York: J. Day).

Zytkowicz, Leonid.

1968 "Production et productivité de l'économie agricole en Pologne aux XVIe-XVIIIe siècles," *Third International Conference of Economic History, Munich 1965* (Paris: Mouton), II: 149–170.

1972 "The Peasant's Farm and the Landlord's Farm in Poland from the 16th to the Middle of the 18th Century," *The Journal of European Economic History*, 1: 135–154.

CONTRIBUTORS

GABRIEL ARDANT, born in Bex, Switzerland, in 1906, is *inspecteur général des finances* and served as general commissioner on productivity from 1953 to 1954. Both an economist and sociologist he is especially interested in development problems. Working on the experiences he has been able to follow in developing countries, he has suggested general solutions in *Le Monde en friche* and in *Anti-Hunger Scheme*. Another of his preoccupations has been state reform. The outcome of his achievements and researches in this field include: *Technique de l'Etat*; *Histoire de l'impôt*; and, together with Pierre Mendes-France, *Science économique et lucidité politique*.

DAVID H. BAYLEY, born in New York, New York, in 1933, is professor of international relations at the Graduate School of International Studies, University of Denver. Trained in political science at Oxford and Princeton Universities, he has specialized in comparative politics. His major research interest has been the relationship between police institutions and practices and national political environments. He has done field work in India as a research fellow of the American Institute of American Studies, and in Japan on a grant from the National Science Foundation. He is author of *The Police and Political Development in India*, and co-author of *Minorities and the Police*, a study of American police-community relations.

RUDOLF BRAUN, born in Basel, Switzerland, in 1930, is professor of history at the University of Zürich, Switzerland. His main fields of interest are the relationships between industrialization and sociocultural changes. His publications include: *Industrialisierung und Volksleben* and *Sozialer und kultureller Wandel in einem ländlichen Industriegebiet im 19. und 20. Jahrhundert*.

SAMUEL E. FINER, born in London, England, in 1915, is professor of government and chairman of the department at the Victoria University of Manchester. He has been a visiting professor at Cornell, the Institute of Social Studies at The Hague, and at the Hebrew University of Jerusalem. He has just retired from the

Executive Committee of the International Political Science Association of which he was vice-president and is still a member of the Council. He is also a fellow of the Royal Historical Society, and his publications include: *The Life and Times of Edwin Chadwick*; *Anonymous Empire*; *A Study of the Lobby in Britain*; *Pareto: Sociological Writings*; *Man on Horseback*; *The Role of the Military in Politics*; and *Comparative Government*. He is currently working on a manuscript provisionally entitled "The Military in the Formation of the Modern European State."

WOLFRAM FISCHER, born in Weigelsdorf, Silesia, in 1928, is professor of economics and social history at the Free University of Berlin. He has specialized in the study of early industrialization and the relations between the economy and the government. Presently, he is involved in research on the problem of the world economy during the twentieth century. In addition to editing several readers on industrialization, his publications include: *Das Fürstentum Hohenlohe im Zeitalter der Aufklärung*; *Wirtschaft und Gesellschaft im Zeitalter der Industrialisierung*; and *Der Staat und die Anfänge der Industrialisierung in Baden*.

PETER LUNDGREEN, born in Berlin in 1936, is an assistant professor of economic history at the Free University of Berlin. He specializes in the history of education. Among his various articles and publications is *Bildung und Wirtschaftswachstum im Industrialisierungsprozess des 19. Jahrhunderts*.

STEIN ROKKAN, born in Lofoten, Northern Norway, in 1921, is professor of sociology at the University of Bergen and recurring visiting professor of political science at Yale. He has carried out extensive research on Norwegian politics and has also been active in the organization of cooperative studies within Europe. He has been vice-president of the International Sociological Association and president of the International Political Science Association, and is currently (1973-1975) president of the International Social Science Council set up by UNESCO. He is also chairman of the European Consortium for Political Research. His publications include: *Comparing Nations*; *Data Archives, Citizens, Elections, Parties*; *Comparative Survey Analysis*; *Building States and Nations*.

CHARLES TILLY, born in Lombard, Illinois in 1929, is professor of sociology, professor of history, and director of the Center for Research on Social Organization at the University of Michigan, Ann Arbor. He is a student of cities, urbanization, political change, and collective action in Europe and America. He is author or co-author of: *The Vendée*; *Race and Residence in Wilmington, Subsidizing the Poor*; *Strikes in France*; *An Urban World*; and of monographs on migration, population change and historical methods.

INDEX

absolutism, 268, 272, 276, 296, 304, 305, 316, 490, 492–494, 499, 507, 510, 511, 525, 545, 547, 549, 586, 588, 589

Académie d'Architecture, see Academy of Architecture

Academy: of Architecture, 552, 553; of Arts, 552; of Sciences, 546–548, 553

Achilles, Albrecht, 257

Acquitaine, 125

Act in Restraint of Appeals, 475

Act of Supremacy, 259, 261, 262

administradors: dels forments, 438; de les carns, 438

Admiralty, 461, 532–535, 539, 540

Aemterkommissarien, 274

affaire des fiches, 157, 160

Africa, 78, 238, 241, 562, 573, 578, 593–595, 634

Agincourt, 92, 104, 115, 174

agrarian demonstrations, 386

Agrarian Revolution, 302

agrarian socialism, 15

agrarian structure, 168, 169, 301, 302, 310, 318, 575, 606, 622

agriculture, 61, 62, 166, 174–176, 178, 180–183, 186, 193, 199, 208, 212, 220, 221, 226, 241, 303, 308, 319, 380–455, 502, 518, 596, 627, 632

aides, 494

Albert (duchy), 131

Alençon, 552

Alfred the Great, 468, 469

Algeria, 238

allodium (freehold), 276

Almond, Gabriel, 5, 79, 80, 601, 608, 609

Alps, 576

Alsace, 583, 619

America, 24, 41, 78, 134, 199, 217, 220, 223, 332, 369, 418, 616, 623, 628; Central America, 20, 419; Latin America, 200, 238, 241, 562, 573, 580, 581, 593–595, 599, 626; North America, 227, 233, 238, 595

Amicable Grant, 118

Amiens, 442

Amsterdam, 67, 252, 292, 416

Amstkammer, 139

Andalusia, 48

Andes, 20

Andorra, 619

Angevins, 116

Anglia, East, 118, 120, 383–385, 411

Anglo-Saxons, 113, 429, 466–469

Antarctica, 637

Antwerp, 416

Apter, David, 617

Apulia, 406

Arabs, 580, 594. *See also* Moslems

Aragon, 610; Aragon-Castile, 586; Aragon-Catalonia, 578

archers, 344

Ardant, Gabriel, 17, 47, 50, 52–55, 58, 73, 79, 80, 83, 349, 357

Argenson, Marquis d', 345

aristocracy, *see* nobility

Armada, Spanish, 528, 529, 544

army, armed forces, 6, 13, 16, 23, 24, 41, 42, 48, 50–52, 54, 57, 58, 62, 63, 65, 68, 71, 73–76, 81, 82, 84–163, 198, 205, 212, 213, 245, 254, 259, 268, 269, 271, 272, 275–277, 281, 283, 294, 300, 301, 304, 305, 310–313, 315, 319, 321, 323, 324, 328, 329, 339, 340, 344, 347, 348, 356, 358, 360, 361, 366, 367, 374, 381, 383, 385, 393, 411–413, 433, 440, 441, 445, 448, 452, 454, 456, 458, 462, 463, 479, 480, 488, 492, 499, 506, 507, 510, 520–524, 528, 538, 541–543, 550, 554, 565, 570, 609, 611, 620, 623, 632, 633; standing army, 94, 95, 113, 121, 123, 125, 134, 144, 154, 158, 239, 268, 276, 281, 282, 288, 348, 366, 396, 410, 448, 453, 511, 514; Revolutionary Armies (France), 441. *See also* artillery; cavalry; infantry; navy etc.

Arras, 161

arrière-ban, 94, 174

artillery, 103, 105–108, 149, 156, 159, 205, 522, 528, 529, 541, 550, 557

artisans, 167, 179, 186

Asia, 199, 217, 238, 241, 562, 573, 574, 595, 604; South Asia, 626

Assekuranztheorie (protection theory), 280

assemblies, provincial, 211

Assessorismus, 519

assignats, 150

Assisa Panis et Cervisiae, 429

Assize of Bread, 429

Athens, 3, 394

atimia, 630

Aubernon, comte d', 131

Auditeure, 520
Auerstädt, 305, 310
Aulic Council, 223
Auskultator, 518, 519
Ausreuter, 513, 520
Australia, 233
Austria, 92, 103, 143, 199–201, 208, 209, 233, 234, 359, 578, 580, 582, 583, 585, 586, 590, 591, 594, 637; Austria-Hungary, 75, 222–224, 412, 636
Austro-Spanish Commercial Treaty, 201
Aylmer, G. E., 483, 485–488

Bacon, Francis, 119, 464
Baden, 234
bailliages, 493–495
baillies, 126, 491
Baker, James, 531
Baker, Mathew, 531
Balkans, 380, 580
Baltic, 72, 415, 416, 422, 575, 576, 579, 588, 589
Balzac, Honoré de, 54
bandits, 434, 440
Bank: of Amsterdam, 290; of England, 122, 123, 291, 314; of Scotland, 291
banking, banks, 189, 190, 192, 199, 219, 252, 264, 267, 290–292
Baran, Paul, 627
Barbarossa, Frederick, 173
Barcelona, 450
Barker, Ernest, 85, 460
Barzini, Luigi, 339
Basques, 18, 580
Bastille, 388
Batavian Republic, 636
Bath, 391
Bauakademie, 552–557. *See also* Academy of Architecture
Baugh, Daniel A., 533, 534
Bauinspektoren, 514
Bavaria, 13, 234, 578, 586, 590, 619
Bayley, David, 46, 49, 50, 58–60, 70, 80, 83, 615
Beamtenstaat, 516
Beaumont-sur-Oise, 382
Beauvaisis, 405
Beckerath, Erwin von, 324
Becket, Thomas à, 457, 470, 473
Bede, 252, 253, 256
Bedford, Duke of, 534
Belgium, 4, 15, 75, 578, 582, 583, 594. *See also* Low Countries
Bellay, Joachim du, 439
Bellegarde, 131
Belmost, General, 134

Beloff, Max, 352, 390
Benavente, 431
Bendix, Reinhard, 80, 624, 626
Beresford, 423
Bergen, 576
Berlin, 140, 154, 346, 347, 351, 352, 360, 374, 413, 516, 521, 551, 552, 580; Berlin Academy of Sciences, 548; Berliners, 160
Berne, 352
Berthelot (family), 411
Beuth, 553, 555, 556
biens nationaux, 150
bienséance, droit de, 279, 306
Bill of Rights, 123, 289, 292
billets de monnaie, 192
Binney, J.E.D., 310
Biscay, 395
Bismarck, Otto von, 160, 232, 363
Black, Cyril, 605–607
Black Death, 250
Blackstone (English jurist), 123
Blenheim, 108
blockage (form of food riot), 386–388, 430, 442, 443, 448
Bluche, François, 498
Blücher, Gebhard von, 102
Blum, Jerome, 424
Board: of Ordnance, 542; of Trade, 317; of War, 356; of War and Domains, 358
Bobbies, 342, 343, 370
bocage (woodland), 405, 420
Bodin, Jean, 93, 243, 278, 623
Bohemia, 48, 226, 590, 591, 610
Boisguillebert, Pierre de, 183, 185
Boislisle, A.M. de, 176
Book of Rates, 267
Borchardt, Knut, 302
Bordeaux, 177
Borgia (family), 63
Borough, Stephen, 537
Borough, William, 537
borussische Geschichtsschreibung, 300
Bosher, John, 496
Bosworth Field, Battle of, 116
Boulainvilliers, Comte de, 176
Bourbonnais, 131, 210
Bourbons, 129, 130, 356, 458, 541
bourgeois, bourgeoisie, 11, 16, 20, 30, 206, 213, 223, 231, 232, 425, 489, 496–498, 522, 526, 560, 587, 628, 632; bourgeois militias, 441
Bourgeois, Léon, 169
Bourne, William, 537, 544
bouteillier, 492
Bowden, Peter, 415

Boyen (Prussian statesman), 158
Boynton, Lindsay, 118
Brabant, 408
Brandenburg, 16, 135, 137–140, 256, 270, 302, 412, 514; Mark of Brandenburg, 138; Brandenburg-Prussia, 13, 24, 40–41, 47, 55–58, 62, 67, 73, 78, 89, 96, 109–111, 134–144, 242–327, 409, 452–453, 606, 619, 636
Brandon, 384
Braudel, Fernand, 30–31, 72, 189, 407, 426, 439, 444, 595
Braun, Rudolf, 46, 59, 50, 55–58, 73, 83, 401
Brazil, 200, 238
Brecht, Arnold, 462
Bremervörde, 423
Bretons, 577
brigandage, 444. *See also* bandits
Briggs, Henry, 543
Brissotins, 149
Bristol, 391
Britain, Great Britain, 9, 42, 51, 57, 62, 64, 65, 83, 86, 95, 127, 145, 146, 152, 157, 158, 160, 177, 180, 182, 190, 193, 196, 201, 207, 220, 222, 226, 229, 231–234, 242–328, 330–336, 338, 341–343, 348, 350, 354, 357–366, 368–372, 374, 376–378, 389, 459–490, 528–545, 556, 558, 559, 586, 609, 611, 616, 628, 631, 632. *See also* England; Scotland; Wales
Britannica Book of the Year, 11
British Empire, 528
Brittany, 125, 344, 395, 578, 583, 619
Browne (family), 530
Bruges, 576
Brüning, Heinrich, 171, 238
Brunner, Otto, 584, 595, 596
Buddhists, 593
budgets, state, 9, 74, 128, 202, 203, 221. *See also* financial policy
bureau des parties casuelles, 496
bureaucracy, 3, 24, 29, 33, 38, 43, 44, 48, 56, 57, 60, 62, 65, 73, 78, 97, 125, 128, 129, 130, 136, 138, 140, 143, 144, 156, 163, 168, 199, 245, 252, 261, 263, 265, 269, 272, 273, 277, 278, 281, 282, 296, 298, 300, 301, 306, 309, 317, 319, 329, 334, 337, 341, 346, 358, 360, 364, 367, 369, 370, 372, 409, 412, 453, 454, 456–561, 597, 614, 616, 631
bureaux des finances, 500
Burghley, Lord, 544
Burgos, 430

Burgundy, 41, 103, 112, 125, 131, 610; Duke of Burgundy, 176
Burke, Edmund, 145
Burleigh (English statesman), 241
Bury St. Edmonds, 384
businessmen, 483, 484, 489. *See also* bourgeois, merchants
Bute, Lord, 203
Byzantine Empire, 30, 45

C.I.D., *see* Criminal Investigation Division
Cabot, Sebastian, 529, 536
cadaster, 183–185, 193, 208–210, 212, 241, 280, 318
cahiers de doléances, 217
Calais, 104
Calonne, Charles-Alexandre de, 173, 177, 182, 212, 213
Calvinists, 582
Cam, Helen Maud, 113
Cambrai, 93
Cambridge, 543
Cameralism, 97, 272, 278, 280, 281, 295, 316, 324, 326, 510, 514, 518, 519, 546
Canada, 594
Canterbury, Archbishop of, 470
canton system, 276
Capetians, 110, 125, 173
capitalism, 30–32, 45, 47, 62, 72, 73, 354, 387, 394, 403, 406, 420, 421, 424, 435, 519, 627, 629
capitation, 185, 501
Captain Swing, 389
Carabinieri, 339, 347, 348, 366, 374
Caribbean, 238
Carniola, 200
Carolingians, 155, 499
Carrera Pujal, Jaime, 451
cartographers, 536, 543
Casa da India, 536
Casa de la Contratación, 529, 536
Casanova, Giacomo, 317
Castile, 19, 450, 451, 453, 561, 590; Castile-Aragon, 580. *See also* Aragon, Spain
Castile Canal, 431
Castillon, 104
Catalonia, 37, 43, 167, 439, 450, 580, 584, 590
Cateau-Cambrésis, le, 129
Catherine II, 204, 207
Catholic Monarchs, 451
Cato, 147
Cavaignac, Louis-Eugène, 160
Cavalier Parliament, 289, 290

cavalry, 92, 102–106, 114, 115, 142, 159, 160, 479
Cavour, Camille Benso, count of, 142,
Celts, 18, 583
census, 323
Center for Advanced Study in the Behavioral Sciences, 5
Central Empire, 584
Central Europe, 580
Central Powers, 223
Chaka Zulu, 152
Chambers, 480, 526; Chamber Court, 273. See also chambres des comptes, Kammergericht
Chambers, J. D., 403
chambres des comptes, 494, 495
chambrier, 492
Chamillart (French financier), 173
Champagne, 129, 210
chancelier, 492; chancellor, 470
Chancellor, Richard, 537
chancery, 467, 469, 471, 472, 474, 488
Charing Cross, 342
Charlemagne, 135, 165, 173, 468
Charles I, 117, 119, 121, 122, 125, 204, 311, 463, 488
Charles II, 121, 170, 289, 358, 538, 539, 542
Charles III, 205
Charles V, 112, 164, 167, 189, 451
Charles VI, 201
Charles VII, 99, 112, 127
Charles the Bold, 105
Chartism. 169
Chastellet, Paul Hay du, 177
Châteauroux, 131
Chatillon, Walter, 475
Chaucer, Geoffrey, 474
Chaunu, Pierre, 409
China, 3, 5, 18, 20, 24, 45, 68, 76, 362, 509, 593, 594, 596, 631, 634, 637; Ch'ing China, 394
Chōnin, 595
church, churchmen, 18, 25–27, 33, 48, 63, 66, 81, 114, 170, 251, 252, 259, 261, 264, 311, 427, 435, 436, 457, 475, 476, 568, 572, 575, 583, 585, 596. See also clergy, ecclesiastics
Cinque Ports, 530
Cipolla, Carlo, 596
Cisalpine Republic, 637
cities, 20, 23, 30, 31, 61, 67, 72, 443, 444, 452, 513, 514, 568, 575, 576, 580, 591, 595, 596; cities and demand for food, 398, 437, 451
citizenship, 88, 97
Civil List, 293, 295; Civil Service, 81;

civil maintenance (Zivilversorgung), 521
Civil War: England, 56, 249, 282, 306, 356, 466; Spain, 452; U.S., 157, 159, 160, 220. See also revolution
Clark, George, 410
clavari del avituallement, 438
clergy, 214, 349, 471–476, 480, 530. See also church, ecclesiastics
Clerk of the Acts, 535
Clermont, 131
Cleve, 135, 137, 138, 140, 257
Cobban, Alfred, 500
Cobdenism, 447
Cocceji, 525
Coeur, Jacques, 172, 173
Cohen, E. W., 461
Colbert, Jean-Baptiste, 42, 60, 132, 167, 176, 180, 193, 195, 241, 297, 300, 344, 357, 448, 464, 492, 500, 501, 546, 547, 550, 551, 635
Cole, G.D.H., 390
collectivist states, 240–241
Colonial Department, 461
colonies, colonialism, 303, 446, 572, 618, 630, 637
Colquhoun, Patrick, 60, 352, 371
Columbus, Christopher, 418
Comité de Salut Public (Committee of Public Safety), 149
commander-in-chief, 461
commercialization, 11, 17, 62, 72, 262, 318, 400, 404, 414, 415, 417, 418, 428, 453, 454, 631
commissaires, 334, 337, 344, 491, 499–509, 511, 545. See also commissars, commissioners
commissarius loci, 271, 272, 513
commissars, 65, 270, 514; District Commissar, 271; District Commissariat, 272
commissioners, 336; commissioners for war, 507; Commissioners of Public Accounts, 292
Commissions of Array, 117; Commissions of Peace, 478
Committee on Comparative Politics, 5
Common Market, 584, 638
Common Pleas, 476
Commonwealth, 121, 356, 533
communal council; 334
Communists, 634
compagnie: souveraine, 495; d'ordonnance, 99, 348; Compagnies Républicaines de Sécurité, 337
comparative government, 4
comptables due trésor, 190

comptroller-general, *see* contrôleur-général des finances
Concordat: of 1515, 177; of 1516, 187
Condé (prince), 106, 127, 131, 134
Congo, Belgian, 636
connétable, 492. *See also* constable
Conquest, Norman, 112, 113, 466
conquistadores, 114
conscription, 9, 23, 71, 94, 134, 154, 158, 159, 167, 207, 219, 315, 322, 392, 521, 572, 625
conseil: de commerce, 503; *d'état*, 195, 492, 493, 503; *d'en haut*, 503, 505, 506; *des dépêches*, 503; *des finances*, 503; *des parties*, 503; *privé*, 494, 503
Conservatoire des arts et métiers, 549
constable, parish, 348, 356, 358, 370, 374; chief constables, 331, 333, 336
constabulary, civil, 341
Constantine, 238
Constantinople, 398
Constituent Assembly, 508
contribution mobilière, 216
Contribution (*Kontribution*), 136, 141, 269
contrôle générale des finances, 505; *contrôleur général des finances*, 172, 177, 180, 182, 185, 189, 195, 212, 216, 382, 492, 501, 503, 505, 547
Convention, 211, 229
Cooper, J. P., 56
Copenhagen, 67
Cordelle, Grégoire, 442
Corn Laws, 302, 303, 319, 320, 416
Cortes, 196, 231, 451
Cortes, Hernán, 22, 114
corvée, 167, 302, 392, 419, 421
cottage industry, *see* industry, rural
Council: in the Marshes of Wales, 463, 479; of Constance, 37; of the North, 463, 479
Counter-Reformation, 580, 581, 583, 593
Country commissioner, commissar, *see* Landrat
County and Borough Police Act of 1856, 343; County Council, 332; County Police Act of 1839, 343
cour: des monnaies, 494, 495, 498; des aides, 494, 495; souveraines, 493
Court: of Assizes, 477; of Augmentations, 463, 481; of Exchequer, 476; of First Fruits and Tenths, 481; of High Commission, 476; of Requests, 480; of Wards and Liveries, 463
courts, 111, 263–265, 289, 294, 299, 302, 308, 309, 338, 339, 465, 477, 478, 488, 517

Cranfield, Lionel, 56, 465
Crécy, 93, 104, 115, 174
credit, 217, 219, 252, 253, 290, 294, 295, 304, 308, 313, 314, 324, 327. *See also* banks
crime, 331, 352, 365, 378
Criminal Investigation Division (C.I.D.), 333, 362, 373
crises, developmental, 609, 611
Critchley, T. A., 352
Croatia, 591
Cromwell, Oliver, 121, 331, 356, 545
Cromwell, Thomas, 41, 463, 464, 480, 482, 490
cross-sectional analyses, 11, 12
Crusade, Third, 74, 102
Cuba, 238
cultural homogeneity, 6, 18, 31–33, 44, 49, 77. *See also* homogeneity
Cunningham (British historian), 297
Curia, 581; Curia Regis (royal council), 470
Curragh incident, 158
customs, 221, 222, 260, 261, 266, 267, 282, 284–286, 304, 319, 321, 426, 435, 458, 461, 462, 489, 586, 588
Custos Rotulorum, 479
Cutright, Phillips, 611–613
Czechoslovakia, 225, 226, 591, 594, 636

Dahrendorf, Ralf, 372
Danes, *see* Denmark
Dauphiny, 129
Davis, John, 537
Davis, Natalie, 388
Deal, 118
decentralization, political, 21, 27
Declaration of Indulgence, 122
Declaration of Rights (1791), 508
decolonization, 45, 171
Dee, Dr. John, 537, 544, 545
Denmark, 41, 110, 125, 415, 468, 577, 579, 581, 582, 585, 586, 588, 590, 591, 620
Dent, Julian, 380
dependence, economic, 628, 630
depressions, 239
Deptford, 531
dérogeance, 111
Desmarets, Nicolas, 128, 173
despotism, enlightened, 204–214. *See also* absolutism
development, political, *see* political development
developmental theories of political change, 602–621. *See also* political development

dextrarius, 102, 115
Diaz del Moral, Juan, 452
Dickens, Charles, 427
Dickson, P.G.M., 290, 292
dictatorship, military, 15
Diets, Provincial, 153
Dietz, Frederick C., 260
Digges (English mathematician), 544
Dijon, 131
dime, 182
Directory (France), 155
Dispositio Achillea, 256, 257
Disraeli, Benjamin, 312, 427
District Governments (*Regierungen*), 512
Divine Right, 289
domain, 276, 296, 297, 326, 356, 434, 435, 494, 506, 512
Domänenedikt, 274, 277
Domain-District Commissars, 274
Domains Chambers, 143, 512
Domesday Book, 468–470
dominium eminens, 255, 276, 279; *dominium excellenciae*, 255
Dore, Ronald, 599
Dorn, Walter L., 511
Doszá rising (1514), 421
Dover, 544
Dovring, Folke, 595
Downham Market, 384
Downing, Sir George, 490
Drake, Francis, 528, 537, 538
Dreiklassenwahlrecht, 323
Dreyfus, Alfred, and Dreyfus Case, 157, 158, 160
Dunstan, Archbishop, 468
Dupplin Moor, 104
Durand, G., 502
Durkheim, Emile, 603
Duverger, Maurice, 11

East Indies, 529
ecclesiastics, 245, 457, 468, 470, 479. *See also* church, clergy
échevins, 495
Ecole: Centrale des Arts et Manufactures, 555, 557; *d'Artillerie*, 554; des *Ponts et Chaussées*, 551, 552, 553; du *Génie*, 550, 554; *Polytechnique*, 158, 550, 553–555, 557
écoles: *d'arts et métiers*, 555, 556; *d'application*, 554, 557
Edgar (King), 113
Edinburgh, 352
Edward I, 117
Edward III, 471
Edward VI, 117, 120, 261, 311

Edward the Confessor, 469
efficiency, 155, 457, 458
Egypt, 68, 219, 598
Einjährig-Freiwilligen-Privileg, 522
Eisenstadt, S. N., 29
Elbe, 422
Elbeuf, Duke of, 442
élections, 494, 495
Elizabeth I, 118, 120, 260, 261, 267, 284, 287, 311, 363, 410, 420, 464, 479, 529–532, 544, 545
Elizabeth II, 475
Elton, G. R., 464
Ely, 384, 385
enclosures, 302, 319, 403–405, 414, 417, 420, 427
Engels, Friedrich, 89
Enghien, 131
engineers, 522, 528, 550–552, 557
England, 12, 15, 19, 20, 22–24, 35, 41, 45, 47, 48, 54–56, 59, 60, 62, 66, 74, 78, 80, 86, 89, 95, 99, 100, 101, 103, 108–125, 128, 129, 140, 142, 153, 154, 162, 163, 168–170, 177, 180, 187, 189, 190, 192, 197, 199, 202–205, 217, 219, 223, 224, 235, 297, 339, 349, 351, 353, 356, 391, 400, 402, 403, 405, 407–411, 414–417, 420, 421, 423, 424, 426–430, 432–437, 444–448, 453, 457, 458, 492, 510, 560, 577, 579, 581, 584, 585, 587, 588, 590, 594, 610, 614, 619, 625, 630, 636; Englishness, 88
Er.guerrard de Marigny (French financier), 172
Enlightenment, 183, 309
enregistrement, right of, 494
Erbpacht, 274
Erith, 531
Estates, 22, 37, 57, 77, 97, 111, 135–140, 251–253, 255, 256, 266, 268, 270–272, 277, 305, 321, 435, 491, 492, 510, 511, 513, 514, 517, 524, 588; Estates of the Empire, 249
Estates-General, 112, 127, 170, 182, 196, 213, 215, 217, 231
Etzioni, Amitai, 91, 620
European Organization for Cooperation and Development (OCDE), 237
Evelyn (family), 530
Everitt, Alan, 410, 411, 430, 432
exchange, economic, 186. *See also* commercialization; markets
exchange economy, 166, 192
Exchequer, 78, 259, 260, 288, 290, 291, 298, 318, 467, 469–472, 474, 477, 480, 481, 490, 532

excise, 136–139, 180, 181, 186, 223, 269, 270, 272, 278, 280, 281, 286, 300, 303, 304, 319, 321, 435, 458, 461, 513. *See also* taxation, indirect
Excise Bill of 1733, 287
Excise Office, 462
exempts, 344
exit, 567, 592

Fabrik-Inspektoren, 514
Facts on File, 11
Farmers General, 180, 496. *See also* taxes, farming of
Fascism, 34, 225
Fay, C. R., 447
Federal Criminal Police Bureau, 337
Fennomans, 582
Ferdinand (King), 177
Ferme Générale, see, Farmers General; taxes, farming of
fertility, 14
Festivals of Misrule, 388
Festy, Octave, 425
Feydeau, Georges, 130
Fideikommiss, 277
Fielding, Henry, 352, 371
Fielding, John, 371
Fifteenths, 252, 253, 261, 266
financial policy, 52–55, 83, 164–242. *See also* taxation
Financial Revolution, 311
Finanzräte, 512
Finer, Herman, 462, 464, 497, 510
Finer, Samuel, 17, 47, 49–51, 54, 70, 83, 315, 363
Finland, 573, 579, 581, 582, 584, 590, 591, 594
Firemaster, 542
First Somme, 161
fiscal policy, *see* taxation
Fischer, Wolfram, 17, 49, 62–65, 77, 79, 83, 458
Flanders, 20, 72, 104, 116, 148, 175, 189, 408, 438, 444, 575, 582
fleet, *see* navy
Fleury, 216
Flodden, 104
fonctionnaires, 545, 547, 548, 558
food: demand for, 397–414; supply, 6, 47, 60–62, 71, 83, 310, 318–320, 380–455, 414–424, 477, 513, 611. *See also* riots, food
format, 84, 85, 89, 90; military format, 91, 99
forment asegurat and *forment aventurer*, 438
Formigny, 104

Fouquet, Nicolas, 173
Fox, Henry, 203
France, 9, 13, 15, 22, 23, 35–37, 41–44, 48, 49, 51, 54, 59, 60, 62, 64–66, 69, 72, 75, 77, 78, 86, 89, 91–93, 95, 99–103, 105–107, 109–113, 115, 120, 124, 140, 142–155, 157–160, 162, 163, 169, 170, 172–174, 176, 177, 179–182, 184, 185, 187–192, 194, 195, 197–202, 204, 208–214, 220, 222–227, 231, 233, 234, 241, 249, 285, 291, 292, 300, 310, 311, 330, 334–345, 347–349, 351–355, 357–361, 363, 365, 366, 369–374, 377, 378, 386–388, 401, 405–407, 409, 410, 412, 415, 416, 420, 424, 426, 427, 431, 437, 441, 444, 445, 447–450, 453, 457, 458, 460, 461, 462, 464, 468, 478, 481, 482, 487, 489–509, 511, 512, 528, 529, 536, 540–543, 545–560, 577, 578, 582–588, 590, 591, 614, 619, 625, 628, 631, 636
franc-fief, 187
franchise, *see* suffrage
Francis I, 60, 112, 126, 128, 177, 188, 363
Francis II Rokoczi, 445
Frankfurt/Oder, 518
Franks, 102, 126
Frederick I, 274, 525
Frederick II (The Great), 69, 141, 170, 180, 204, 205, 207, 268, 275, 278, 281, 300, 346, 355, 358, 360, 511, 512, 525, 548, 552
Frederick III, 140
Frederick William (Great Elector), 97, 110, 111, 135–137, 139, 140, 142, 144, 180, 248, 268–270, 272–275, 313, 349, 355, 358, 364, 452, 453, 458, 470, 510, 516, 520, 525
Frederick William I, 141, 143, 268–272, 275–277, 518, 520, 525
Frederick William III, 549
free trade, 310, 382
French Empire, 159, 167, 177, 218, 229, 241
Fréville, Henri, 502
Frey, J. G., 346
Fried, Morton, 621
Fried, Robert, 344
Frobisher, Martin, 537
Fronde, 35, 129–131, 134, 194, 344, 357
Fronsac, 131
functional theories of political change, 602, 603, 621–624
Fürstenstaat, 85

Furtado, Celso, 627
fyrd, 94, 113

gabelle, 180, 215, 496
Garde: Bourgeoise, 349; *Mobile*, 334; *Nationale*, 170; *Républicaine*, 334
Gardiens de la Paix, 345
Garrison State, 358
Gascony, 125
Gdansk (Danzig)
Geertz, Clifford, 423, 627
Gemeiner Pfennig, 250
Gendarmerie, 334, 336, 338, 344, 346, 347, 356, 374, 443
Gendarmerie-Edict, 346
General: ·Aid, 283, 284; Book of Law, 278; Directory, 274, 275, 278, 317, 505, 511, 512, 514, 517, 520; Financial Directory, 274; -hufenschoss, 275; -ober-Finanz-Kriegs-und-Domänen-Direktorium, 274; -pacht, 274; -separation, 301; -Supreme-Finance-War-and-Domains-Directory, 143; War Commissariat, 139, 140, 143, 271, 273, 274; War Purse, 271
généralités, 344, 494, 495, 500, 505, 506, 547, 551, 552
généraux des finances, 494. *See also* *contrôle général des finances* génie, 557; *corps du génie*, 551; *corps du génie militaire*, 550. *See also* engineers
Genoa, 93, 189, 444
Gentil da Silva, José, 451
gentry, 302, 308, 465, 484, 485, 487, 489
George I, 41, 293, 358
George III, 293
Germany, 15, 22, 27, 37, 41, 45, 48, 51, 58, 59, 67–69, 75, 78, 86, 88, 105, 117, 118, 120, 122, 148, 154, 158, 159, 163, 164, 171, 180, 181, 189, 204, 223–226, 233, 238, 241, 243, 249, 300, 328, 330, 335, 336, 341, 342, 345–347, 350, 352, 354, 355, 358–360, 363, 366, 368, 370, 373, 374, 376–378, 398, 406–408, 412, 415, 416, 424, 468, 491, 509, 510, 529, 530, 575, 577, 581, 583–586, 591, 594, 606, 619, 631, 632, 636; German Empire, 222, 258, 346, 363, 556; German Reich, 579, 582, 619; East Germany, 337; West Germany, 331, 337, 338, 369, 370, 585. *See also* Brandenburg; Cleve; Prussia; etc.
Gerschenkron, Alexander, 301
Gewerbeinstitut, 556, 557
Ghana, 4

Gilbert, Sir Humphrey, 545
Gladstone, William, 318
gold, 191, 199
Goldscheid, Rudolf, 243, 311, 313, 315
Gonzalvo de Córdoba (Gran Capitan of Spain), 106
Goody, Jack, 595, 596
Gordon Riots, 357
Goubert, Pierre, 401, 405, 498, 585
Gournay, Vincent de, 206
gouvernements, 500; *gouverneurs*, 127, 155, 491–494, 500
grain, 23, 47, 55, 62, 381–388, 391–394, 402–404, 415–422, 429, 430, 433, 434, 437–442, 444–453. *See also* food
grand conseil, 494, 495
grand parti, 189
Grande Armée, 102, 146
grandes écoles, 509, 558, 560
Grandison, 92, 105
Granvelle, Nicolas Perrenot de, 167
Great Britain, *see* Britain
Great Elector, *see* Frederick William
Great Rebellion, 119
Greece, 31, 395, 565
Greek Orthodox Church, 593
Greenberg, Freddi, 380
Gresham College, 537, 543
Gross National Product, 11
growth, economic, 56, 62, 73. *See also* industrialization; infrastructure, economic
Gruder, Vivian, 503
Grundherrschaft, 585
Grundwirtschaft, 407
Guardia di Pubblica Sicurezza, 339, 347, 374
Guénée, Bernard, 37
Guernsey, 619
Guerre des Farines, 382
Guibert (French strategist), 108, 147–150
Guildford, 391
Guinegatte, Battle of, 105
Guise (family), 127, 129
Gunder Frank, André, 626–627
Gustavus Adolphus, 107, 108
Gutsherrschaft, 273, 585
Gutswirtschaft, 407, 419, 420
Gymnasium, 522, 553

Haandfaestning, 588
Habsburgs, *see* Hapsburgs
Hakluyt, Richard, 537, 545
Halidon, 104
Halle, 518

Hamburg, 233
Hamlet, 305
Hammond, J. L. and Barbara, 366, 391, 403
Hanoverians, 356
Hanse, Hanseatic League, 27, 72, 193, 576, 579, 586
Hapsburgs, 13, 18, 19, 27, 41, 54, 69, 104, 112, 128, 129, 208, 223, 578, 580, 595
Hardenberg, Karl Auguste von, 153, 357
Hariot (English explorer), 545
Harold II, 113
Hart, Jenifer, 353
Hartshorne, Richard, 583
Hartung, Fritz, 305
Hartwell, R. M., 417
Hastings, 101, 113, 162
Haushofer, Karl, 583
Hausstaat, 85
Hawkins, John, 531, 537
Head War Commissariat, 273
Heath, Edward, 331
Heckscher, Eli, 297, 300
Hegel, G.W.F., 297
Henry I, 114, 464, 470
Henry II, 78, 467, 470, 471, 475
Henry IV, 129, 134, 188, 492
Henry VI, 116
Henry VII, 100, 116, 117, 119, 120, 122, 258–261, 435
Henry VIII, 101, 118, 177, 259, 261, 262, 266, 311, 411, 435, 480, 529–531, 544
Heptarchy, 113
Hermandad, 100
Herrenhaus (First Assembly), 323
High Court, 468
Highlanders, 108
Hill, Christopher, 265, 292, 295, 298, 303, 306, 308
Hindenburg, Paul von Beneckendorff und, 160
Hintze, Otto, 243, 300, 584, 585, 626
Hirschman, Albert O., 567, 570, 584, 589, 599
historical analysis, role of, 3–4; historical theories of political change, 602, 603, 624–632
Historical Schools, 297
Hitler, Adolf, 225, 238, 337, 348, 359
Hobbes, Thomas, 287, 623
Hobsbawm, E. J., 389
Hoccleve, Thomas, 494
Hochdeutsch, 582
Hoffman, J. G., 322
Hofkammer, 139

Hohenzollerns, 57, 58, 89, 100, 110, 135, 256–258, 268, 269, 278, 345, 349, 356, 453, 458, 464, 509, 516
Holland, 45, 75, 110, 135, 152, 181, 190, 202, 292, 410, 426, 529, 614. *See also* Low Countries
Holy Alliance, 218
Holy Roman Empire, 18, 25, 26, 37, 151, 197, 202, 249, 258, 580, 582; Electors of the Empire, 22; Emperor, 201, 451
Home: Department, 461; Office, 364; Secretary, 332, 342, 368, 374
homogeneity, as a factor in statemaking, 27, 28, 40, 43, 67, 77–80. *See also* cultural homogeneity
Hooge, 161
Hounslow, 120
housecarles, 113
House of Commons, House of Lords, *see* Parliament
House Treaty of Gera, 257
Hubertusburg, Peace of, 278
Huguenots, 440, 492
Hungary, 200, 201, 419–421, 445, 529, 578, 586, 590, 591
Huntington, Samuel, 5, 598, 616
Hus, Jan, 37, 117
Huskisson (British statesman), 447
Husum, 428

I.R.A. (Irish Republican Army), 362
Iceland, 579, 582, 590, 591
Ile de France, 176
imperialism, 620, 628, 630. *See also* colonies
income, real, 422
indentured companies, 110, 113, 115, 117
India, 20, 68, 183, 201, 285, 362, 593, 594, 632, 634; Indian Civil Service, 483
Indigenatsrecht, 272, 273
Indochina, 578
Indonesia, 423, 622, 627
industrial production, 20, 72, 81, 186, 199, 221, 227, 238, 239, 407, 408, 414, 418, 421, 446, 447, 449, 450, 454, 476, 502, 622; industrialism, industrialization, 32, 33, 65, 155–163, 166, 196, 217, 234, 354, 378, 394, 409, 453, 520, 559, 605, 611, 615, 631
Industrial Reserve Army, 237
Industrial Revolution, 218–242, 297, 302–304, 310, 354, 372, 402, 625
industry, rural, 401, 405, 407–409, 453

infantry, 92, 102, 105–108, 142, 150, 159, 160
inflation, 190–192, 239
infrastructure, economic, 53, 55, 83, 164–242, 209, 219, 220, 223–225, 230, 233, 235, 236, 239, 241
Innes, H. A., 596, 597
Inns of Court, 476, 485
Inquisition, 60, 363
inspector of mills (*Mühlenbereuter*), 521
instrument makers, 537
insurrections, *see* rebellions, revolutions, riots
intendants, 127, 130–134, 155, 176, 185, 195, 199, 210–212, 344, 356–358, 365, 493, 499–503, 505–508, 547; intendancies, 167; *Intendant-General*, 347
Interior, Ministry of, 334, 335, 337, 339, 345, 347, 369
Interregnum, 282, 283, 286–288
Ireland, 24, 42, 118, 122, 311, 362, 391, 418, 461, 468, 573, 578, 584, 590, 594, 619
iron industry, 530
Israel, 4, 68, 94, 565, 598
Italy, 9, 13, 20, 27, 31, 46, 59, 67–69, 72, 75, 78, 80, 101, 104, 106, 118, 120 121, 128, 152, 163, 223, 225, 226, 234, 241, 252, 328, 330, 335, 336, 338–342, 347–350, 354, 355, 360, 366, 370, 373, 374, 377, 378, 391, 407, 408, 424, 434, 437, 444, 452, 529, 530, 575, 576, 577, 583, 586, 590, 636, 637

J. P., *see* Justices of the Peace
Jacobins, 147, 149, 150, 372
Jacquier (family), 411
Jamaica, 4
James I, 465, 530
James II, 121, 122
Janetz, 131
Japan, 20, 223, 224, 394, 574, 594–596, 599, 604, 631, 637
Jena, 47, 136, 141, 153, 305, 310
Jersey, 619
Jews, 38, 44, 252, 313, 317
John (King of England), 115
John II (of Portugal), 536
Johnson, Dale L., 628
Jones, E. L., 418
Jordan, 4
Joseph II, 198, 200, 202, 204, 205, 212, 214
Jourdain conscription law (1789), 150
judicial system, 6, 9, 245, 252, 268, 270,

273, 302, 374, 524, 525. *See also* courts; justice
July Monarchy, 169, 170
June Days, 160, 238
Junkers, 44, 55, 57, 58, 65, 78, 154, 269, 270, 273, 275–277, 301, 304, 312, 346, 453, 524, 586
Jura Mountains, 161
Jury, 469
justice, 37, 49, 228, 256
Justices of the Peace, 62, 117, 262, 264, 265, 289, 348, 409, 429, 432, 433, 446, 461, 477–479, 564, 632
justiciar, 470
Jutland, 581

Kadettenanstalten, 521; *Kadettenhaus*, 141, 158
Kaiserreich, 160
Kammergericht, 256, 273, 516
Kant, Immanuel, 297
Kapitulation, 100, 139, 141
Karlsbad, Decisions of, 320
Katzer, Nichols, 544
Keeper of the King's Ships, 530
Keir, D. L., 262, 298
Kellenbenz, Herrmann, 408
Kennecott Copper, 81
Kennedy, William, 267, 303, 306
Kent, 411
Key, V. O., 11
Keynes, J. M., 227, 230, 237, 239, 241
Killicrankie, 108
King, Gregory, 128, 402
King, James F., 500
King's Bench, 476; Chamber, 259; Council, 480
Klassensteuer (class tax), 321, 323
klassifizierte Einkommenssteuer (classified income tax), 323. *See also* taxation
Kloss, Heinrich, 593
Kluck, General von, 161
knights, 92, 93, 99, 102, 103, 114, 115
Knights of Malta, 444
Knights Templar, 172
Kommissarien, see commissars, commissioners
Kompaniewirtschaft, 301
Königsberg, 111, 135, 138, 346
Kontribution, see Contribution
Korea, 596
Kothari, Rajni, 5
Kreisdirektor, 137, 139–141
Kriegskommissar, 139, 271; *Kriegs- und Domänenkammern*, 512; *Kriegs- und Domänenräte*, 512; *Kriegsmagazinverwaltung*, 410

Krippendorff, Ekkehart, 623
Kubek, Baron de, 223
Kulischer, Joseph, 406

labor, landless, *see* proletariat
Labrousse, C. E., 216, 426
La Fère, 550
Laffemas, Barthélemy, 241
Lagos, Gustavo, 630
La Mare, Nicolas de, 441
Lancaster, Duke of, 116
landlords, landholding, 13, 19, 28, 34, 40, 44, 47, 57, 62, 64, 65, 72, 76, 77, 81, 120, 216, 217, 266, 302, 304, 307, 319, 346, 349, 362, 381, 393, 395, 400, 402, 403, 405, 406, 408, 419, 420, 422, 427, 436, 438, 452–454, 481, 484, 568, 576, 584, 606, 632, 633
Land- oder Kriegskommissarien, 271
Landrat (Country Commissioner), 57, 64, 141, 271, 273, 337, 338, 346, 355, 369, 502, 513–515, 524, 526, 560
Landry, Adolphe, 191
Landschaften (mortgage credit societies), 276
Landsknechten, 100, 105
Landsturm, 153
Landwehr, 153, 158
Lanfranc, 470
Lang, Karl Heinrich, 310
Langlois (inventor of quick-firing field gun), 156
Languedoc, 43, 129, 422, 583
Laos, 594
Laqueur, Walter, 74
La Reynie, Nicolas-Gabriel de, 60
La Rochefoucauld, Duc de, 555
Lasswell, Harold, 358
latifundia, 585
Latin language, 575, 581, 596, 597
Launey, Bernard-René, marquis de, 388
Lavisse, Ernest, 131
Law, John, 173, 177, 192
law faculties, 476
Law of Rome, 471. *See also* Roman Law
lawyers, 47, 480, 481, 483
Lefebvre de la Bellande, Jean Louis, 180
Lefebvre, Georges, 152
Legion of Honor, 170
Lehenspferdegeld, 276
Leibnitz, Gottfried Wilhelm, 548
Leicester, 544
Lemarchand, Guy, 449
Lemercier de la Rivière (French author), 206

Lenin, V. I., 628, 630
Lenoir, Jean-Charles-Pierre, 383
Lenski, Gerhard, 622
Le Roux, Jean, 442
Le Roy Ladurie, Emmanuel, 422
Le Tellier, Michel, 108, 132, 133, 448
levée en masse, 149. *See also* conscription
liberalism, 309, 425, 427, 449, 452, 453, 510, 519, 627
Liberals, 233
Lichtheim, George, 630
Liège, 428
Lieutenant-General, 351; Lieutenant-General of Police, 344–346, 360
Lieutenant of the Admiralty, 531
Limoges, 210
Limousin, 176, 210
Lincoln, Lincolnshire, 411
Lindsay, A. D., 85
linguistic divisions, 18, 19, 44, 49, 77, 78, 568, 582
Lionne, Hugues de, 132
Lisbon, 352, 416, 536
literacy, 634
Littleport, 384, 385
Lloyd George, David, 233
Local Government Act, 343
Locke, John, 287, 306, 308, 309
logistics, 108, 410
Lombards, 252
London, 9, 69, 117, 121, 175, 252, 264, 267, 292, 331–333, 336, 342, 350–353, 371–373, 398–400, 413, 429, 446, 447, 530, 576, 598; City of London, 342, 371; London Institute of Strategic Studies, 93–94; London Metropolitan Police, 332, 333, 342
Long Parliament, 249, 264, 265, 283–286, 288, 294, 298
Lord Admiral, 531
Lords Lieutenant, 479
Lorraine, 48, 129, 131, 583; Duke of Lorraine, 131
Lorwin, Val, 3, 380, 601
Lottery Office, 462
Louis IX, 112
Louis XI, 105, 128, 180
Louis XII, 164, 188
Louis XIII, 500
Louis XIV, 60, 100, 108, 109, 122, 126–128, 131–134, 155, 169, 174, 182, 185, 188, 190, 192, 195–198, 228, 229, 344, 357, 447, 448, 464, 500, 541, 550
Louis XV, 60, 143, 144, 204
Louis XVI, 170, 204, 214, 215
Louis XVIII, 344

Louis-Philippe, 231
Louvois, Michel Le Tellier, marquis de, 108, 132, 133, 448
Low Countries, 25, 49, 75, 106, 136, 189, 193, 201, 234, 311, 406, 408, 412, 415, 416, 422, 428, 446, 538, 542, 544, 576–578, 582, 584–586, 589–591, 620, 637. *See also* Belgium; Holland
loyalty, 94, 95, 118, 119, 123, 124, 126, 155, 300, 457, 458, 482, 496, 558, 567
Lübeck, 233
Lucy, Richard de, 470
Ludd, Ned, 389; Luddites, 357
Ludendorff, Erich von, 160
Lundgreen, Peter, 49, 62–65, 77, 79, 83, 458, 462
Lutherans, 581
Luxemburg, 256, 582
Lyon, 407

M.I.T. Study Group, 634
Macaulay, Thomas Babington, 538
Machault d'Arnouville, Jean-Baptiste, 173
Machiavelli, Nicolo, 93, 94
macinato, 434
MacPherson, C. B., 73, 289, 425
Madrid, 48, 413, 450
Magdeburg, 270
magistrature, 494, 495, 498, 507, 560
Magyars, 18
Mahl- und Schlachtsteuer (milling and slaughter tax), 321, 323
maires, see mayors
maîtres des requêtes, 503, 506, 507
Malowist, Marian, 421
Malthus, Thomas, 175, 403
Manchester, 352
Mandrou, Robert, 502
Mann, Fritz Karl, 243, 245, 246, 248
manufacturers, 288, 408. *See also* industrial production
Manufactures, Department of, 549
Manzoni, Alessandro, 380, 381
Map, Walter, 475
Marczewski, Jean, 220
Maréchaussée, 344
Marengo, 151, 155
Maria Theresa, 202, 204, 209, 212, 346, 360
Marion, Marcel, 188
markets, 19, 52, 61, 72, 73, 81, 166, 176, 182, 189, 190, 196, 206, 222, 242, 382, 386–389, 393, 397, 399–402, 404–407, 410, 411, 414, 417, 418, 420, 425–429, 432, 435, 437, 438, 440, 446–450, 452, 614, 620, 625, 638
Markovitch, Tikhomir, 220
Marlborough, John Churchill, Duke of, 108, 141
Marseille, 440, 444
Marshall, T. H., 80, 624
Martel, Charles, 103, 114
Marx, Fritz Morstein, 516, 524
Marx, Karl, 11, 89, 90, 168, 229, 237, 403, 421, 603, 630
Marxist-Leninist theories, 628
Mary (Queen), 118
Masaniello (Aniello), 434
Maskenrecht, 388
Master Attendant, 535; Master Gunner of England, 542; Master Shipwrights, 535
Mathias, Peter, 529
Matilda of Flanders (Queen of England), 114
Matrikularbeiträge, 250
Mauersberg, Hans, 428
Maupeou, René-Nicolas de, 174, 507
Maurice of Nassau, 106–108
Maximum, Jacobin, 449
Mayne (Commissioner of London Police), 373
mayors, 334, 336, 495
Mazarin, Cardinal, 63, 127, 130, 167, 195, 345, 357, 457; *mazarinades*, 173
McLuhan, Marshall, 597
Mecklenburg, 234
Mediterranean, 20, 30, 72
Mendès-France, Pierre, 238
mercantilism, 171, 196, 224, 278, 279, 284, 301, 316, 324, 490, 501, 514, 518, 549, 589
mercenaries, 113, 114, 129, 131, 135, 137, 144, 195, 219, 269, 313, 479, 511, 514
merchants, mercantile classes, 266, 267, 288, 290, 299, 308, 393, 394, 402, 437, 445, 453, 454, 460, 465, 483, 497, 530
Merle, Louis, 405
Mesopotamia, 394
Messina, 445
Mesta, 406, 423
Méthivier, Hubert, 502
Metternich-Winneburg, Klemens Lothar Wenzel, Prince of, 150
Meuvret, Jean, 411, 444
Mexico, 114, 617
Meyer, Jean, 392
Mézières, 550
Middle East, 626

Midlands, 73, 357
Milan, 164, 202, 209, 380–382, 438
Miliband, Ralph, 70, 628
militarism, 75. *See also* army
military, *see* army, cavalry, infantry, navy etc.
militia, 48, 99, 100, 109, 111, 113, 114, 117–119, 121–124, 129, 134, 276, 313, 315, 431, 443, 448, 479, 501
Ministerials, 468
Mirabeau, Victor Riqueti, marquis de, 180, 210
missi dominici, 499
mobilization, 32–35, 38, 589, 597
modernization, political, *see* political modernization
Mollien, François-Nicolas, 177, 190
Mols, Roger, 399
Momsen, Ingwer Ernst, 428
Monaco, 619
monarchy, absolute, *see* absolutism
Monck (English general), 122
monetization, 96, 135, 219, 248, 318, 421
Mongols, 18
Monmouth's Rebellion, 121, 122
monnaie de billion, 191
Montagu, Edward, 490
Montenegro, 395
Montesquieu, Charles de Secondat, baron de, 247
Monthly Assessment, 283
Montmorency, 121, 129–131
Montrond, 131
Moore, Barrington, Jr., 5, 44, 47, 77, 355, 406, 414, 584, 585, 586, 631–632
Moore, Charles, 542
Moors, 44. *See also* Arabs, Moslems
moral economy, 432
More, Thomas, 457, 544
Moreau de Beaumont, Jean Louis, 181
Morgarten, 105
Mosca, Gaetano, 87
Moscow, 69
Moslems, 18, 30, 183, 575, 578, 580, 593. *See also* Arabs
mouchard, 363
Mouchi, Antoine di, 363
Mousnier, Rold, 188, 411, 501, 507
Mughuls, 183
Mühlenbereuter (mill inspector), 520
Municipal Corporations Act, 343
municipal council, 335; municipal revolution, 448
Muret, 92, 105
Muscovy Company, 537

Muslims, *see* Moslems
Mussolini, Benito, 225
Musson, A. E., 543
Mutiny Acts, 123; Mutiny Bill, 144
Mykland, Knut, 588

Naples, 48, 145, 199, 201, 398, 400, 413, 434, 440–442; Kingdom of Naples, 202
Napoleon I, 67, 101, 102, 108, 144–155, 159, 160, 170, 211, 233, 324, 347, 356, 359, 447, 551, 577, 636
Napoleon III, 160, 356, 357, 359
nation-building, 6, 39, 55, 79, 86, 88–90, 97, 162–164, 218–242, 244, 363, 491, 562–600, 618–620
National Assembly, 218, 335; National Guard, 348, 441, 448
nationalism, 6, 43, 49, 55, 69, 88, 155–163, 229, 360
Naval Commissioner, 535
Navigation Acts, 285
navy, 122–124, 152, 205, 260, 283, 288, 410–412, 445, 446, 458, 479, 488, 530–535, 541, 632
Navy Board, 461, 464, 531–534; Navy Office, 462; Navy Reserve Officers, 539
Nazis, 224
Near East, 20, 27
Necker, Jacques, 190, 210, 211, 508
Nef, John U., 128
Nelson, Horatio, 528
Netherlands, *see* Low Countries
Nettl, J. P., 620
New East India Company, 291
New England, 418
New International Yearbook, 11
New Model Army, 74, 99, 282, 446
New Monarchy, 258
New Police, 350
New World, 189
New York Times, 11
New Zealand, 233
Nineteen Propositions, 264
Nisbet, Robert, 603
nobles, nobility, 19, 21, 57, 111, 116, 119–121, 125, 127, 129, 135–138, 140–142, 149, 153–155, 157, 168, 170, 174, 212–214, 251, 266, 272, 274, 276, 281, 286, 289, 305, 308, 323, 349, 362, 382, 405, 406, 419, 420, 423, 424, 445, 452, 464, 465, 475, 485, 487, 488, 493, 506, 521–527, 585, 587, 588, 630
noblesse: d'épée, 493; *d'Etat*, 507; *de fonction publique*, 558; *de robe*, 497, 498, 505, 507, 549, 558, 560

Nordic countries, *see* Scandinavia
Norfolk, Duke of, 118
Norman Kings, 113, 114, 473
Normandy, 113, 125, 176, 461
Normans, 101, 110, 116, 465–468, 473, 577. *See also* Conquest, Norman
Norsemen, 577
North Sea, 575, 576, 579
Northern Earls, 118
Norway, 573, 577, 579, 581, 582, 584–586, 590, 591, 594
Norwich, 384
notaries, 471, 472

Ober-Examinationskommission (State Examination Board), 517
Oberkriegskommissar, 139
Ocampo, José F., 628
Occitan, 577
Oder, 13
Office of Arms, 488
officers, officiers, 65, 491–499, 501–503, 505–509, 511, 525, 545, 548
offices, sale of, 48, 58, 64, 77, 82, 125, 128, 130, 170, 174, 188, 435, 444, 473, 486, 487, 495–498, 508, 523, 525, 587
officiers: comptables, 496; *des finances*, 500; *des monnaies*, 166, 191
Old English Treasury, 469
Oman, Sir Charles, 103, 464, 467
Order of Payment, 290
Ordinary Penny (*gemeiner Pfennig*), 250
Ordnance, 461; Ordnance Office, 462
Organski, A.F.K., 607
Orleans, 130
O'Shea, Ann, 380
Ostend Company, 201
Otto the Great, 173
Ottoman Empire, 75, 188, 219, 578, 580, 637
Ouvrard, Gabriel-Julien, 150
Overbury, Sir Thomas, 486
Oxford, 543

P.S., *see Guardia di Pubblica Sicurezza*
Pach, S. P., 419, 420
Pagès, G., 188
Pakistan, 68
Palencia, 431
Palermo, 67, 445
papacy, *see* pope
Papal States, 27, 37, 64
Paret, Peter, 380
Paris, 31, 60, 69, 113, 125, 161, 175–177, 184, 210, 334, 335, 344–346, 350–352, 363, 382, 383, 398, 400,

413, 415, 447, 493, 598; Paris Academy, 549
parish constable, *see* constable, parish
Parker, J. L., 353
Parkinson, C. Northcote, 64
parlements, 111, 130, 131, 188, 216, 349, 357, 382, 448, 453, 493, 494, 507; Parlement of Paris, 344
Parliament, 22, 56, 57, 109, 111, 112, 115, 117, 121–123, 140, 144, 146, 152, 170, 196, 203, 231, 233, 259, 261–267, 282, 285, 287–291, 293, 294, 296, 298, 299, 302, 308–311, 319, 326, 339, 342, 353, 357, 368, 371, 374, 435, 466, 475, 481. *See also* Long Parliament; Short Parliament
parliamentarism, Lancastrian, 37
parliamentary democracy, 15; parliamentary institutions, 16
Parsons, Talcott, 563, 565, 567, 570, 613–615
patentes, 216
Patiño, José, 241
patrimonium, 252, 254
patronage, 482–490, 496, 508, 523, 528, 540, 558, 560
Paulette, 128, 288, 496
Pavia, 437, 438, 470
Peacock, A. J., 383
Peasant Revolt, 448–449
peasants, 19–21, 27, 28, 31, 34, 44, 71, 72, 92, 111, 114, 135–137, 154, 165, 167, 192, 200, 212, 213, 221, 222, 226, 235, 237, 257, 266, 273, 277, 301, 304, 305, 324, 380, 389, 392–395, 401, 402, 404, 406, 412, 418, 420–422, 428, 431, 433, 435, 445, 452–455, 576, 582, 597, 627, 631
Peel, Sir Robert, 342, 372, 373, 447
Peking, 69, 598
Pepys, Samuel, 464, 490
Perronet, Jean-Rodolphe, 552
personnel, administrative and technical, 18, 62–65, 456–561; technical personnel, 6, 310, 317–318
Peter (Tsar), 360
Peterloo massacre, 357
Pett family (Joseph, Peter, Peter Jr., Phineas), 531, 533
Petty, Sir William, 177, 545
Phantom (aircraft), 103
Philip II, 164, 189, 196
Philippe-Auguste, 109, 126
Philippe le Bel, 109, 126
Philippines, 200
Philosophic Radicals, 307
Physiocrats, 175, 183, 185, 210, 221, 241

Picardy, 131
Piedmont, 201, 347, 348, 418. *See also*
Savoy
Pilgrimage of Grace, 22, 118, 119
Pilgrims, 118
Pilsudski, Joseph, 225
piracy, 426, 444, 445
Pirenne, Henri, 428, 429, 438
Pitt, William, The Elder, 203, 204, 311,
371; The Younger, 318
Pizzorno, Alessandro, 11
Plantagenets, 110, 204
Plumb, J. H., 23
Plymouth, 531
Po River, 175, 406
Poitiers, 104, 115, 174
Poland, 41, 44, 73, 135, 137, 138, 198,
225, 402, 415, 421, 445, 578, 586,
590, 591, 610, 620, 622
Polanyi, Karl, 73
police, 6, 9, 38, 49, 50, 58–60, 71, 83,
109, 141, 154, 160, 168, 245, 300,
304, 310, 316, 328–379, 383, 428,
440–443, 476, 501, 513, 514, 609,
611; definitions of, 328
Police: Act of 1964, 332, 343, 368, 376;
Administrative, 337; *des blés*, 441;
Générale, 335; *Judiciare*, 337; *Lieutenant de*, 60; Ministry of, 345; *Nationale*, 334–336; Prefect of, 335;
President, 346; police state, 58. *See
also Polizei; Polizeistaat*
political development, 3–5, 7, 10, 11, 16,
21, 38, 39, 82, 328–379, 563–570,
601, 602, 604, 607, 611–613, 615–
621, 623, 627, 632, 633, 635; developmental phase, 68. *See also* stages of
economic and political development
political modernization, 604, 616, 617
Polizei, 50; *Polizeistaat*, 272, 273, 299,
300, 510, 511, 514, 515, 518
Pombal, Sebastian, marquis of, 42
Pomerania, 135, 143, 270
Ponts et Chaussées, Corps des, 551
Poole, A. L., 467
Poor Laws, 303, 479
pope, 37, 74, 177, 188, 439, 440, 445,
470, 472, 581
population growth, 17, 18, 156, 175, 378,
397, 402, 403, 405, 423
Porchnev, Boris, 188
Porey, William, of Sutton, 411
Portsmouth, 530
Portugal, 41, 165, 199, 223, 529, 536,
538, 578, 580, 586, 690, 636
posse, 48

possessive individualism, 307, 308, 316,
426
Post Office, 461–463
Postan, M. M., 72
Postgate, Raymond, 390
Potato War, 160
Powell, Bingham, 79, 80
Pragmatic Sanction, 201
prefects, 151, 152, 155, 195, 334, 336,
338, 339, 344, 347, 356, 358, 508
Prerogative, 262–265, 289, 294, 298
présidiaux, 493–495
prests, 260
prévôt, 344, 348, 468; *prévôtée*, 493
Pride's Purge, 446
Prince's State, 85
Privy Council, 259, 289, 298, 479, 487,
488, 517, 544
Privy Seal, 471, 472, 474
probabilistic and deterministic analyses,
14–16, 48
proletarianization, 72, 403, 409, 423;
proletariat, 61, 72, 77, 400–409, 413,
414, 418, 422, 423, 430, 443, 449
prospective and retrospective analyses, 14,
15, 48
protection theory, 280
Protectorate, 121, 288
Protestant sects, 593; Protestant state
church, 593
Provence, 583
Provincial War and Domains Chamber,
514; Provincial War Commissariats,
140
provost, *see prévôt*
Prussia, 12, 22, 36, 44, 46, 48, 51, 54,
55, 57, 62, 64–67, 69, 73–75, 78, 83,
89, 95, 97, 99–101, 107, 110, 114,
140, 142–146, 148, 153, 154, 157–
160, 162, 170, 180, 181, 202, 205,
207, 223, 234, 247, 257, 331, 337,
345–347, 349, 355, 359, 360, 362–
365, 367, 369–372, 374, 378, 410,
412, 415, 433, 435, 437, 453, 458,
460–462, 464, 478, 481, 482, 489,
491–494, 497, 499, 502, 505, 508–
528, 545–560, 577, 579, 580, 582,
583, 585, 586, 590, 591, 595, 610,
622, 625; Duchy of Prussia, 110, 135,
137, 138; East Prussia, 275, 374;
Prussian Ministry of Finance, 462;
Prussian United Artillery and Engineering College. *See also* Brandenburg-
Prussia; Germany
public: assistance, 9; instruction, 44; order, 380–455
Pye, Lucian, 608, 609

Quarter Sessions, 109, 121
Quartermaster General, 462, 511, 514
Quesnay, François, 178, 205, 210
Questore, 339, 347

Radzinowicz, Leon, 352
railways, 157, 457
Raleigh, Sir Walter, 544, 545
Rasin (Czech statesman), 226
rationing, 224, 439
Ratzel, Friedrich, 583
Raynall, Carew, 285
Razzell, P. E., 403
Rebecca Riots, 389
rebellions, 50, 53, 79, 166, 167, 188, 194, 198, 237; against conscription, 61, 184; anticolonial, 24; peasant, 404; tax, 61, 71, 117, 134, 166, 167, 175, 200, 220, 282, 357, 445. *See also* revolutions, particular rebellions, e.g. Peasant Revolt, Pilgrimage of Grace
Recess of 1653, 47, 137, 139, 142, 273
receveurs, 494; *receveurs généraux*, 190
Rechenhaftigkeit, 38
Reconquista, 18, 580, 585
Recorde, Robert, 537
Recruitment Chest (*Rekrutenkasse*), 525
Red Belt, 339
Referendar, Referendariat, 518–520
Reform Period, 319
Reformation, 12, 33, 177, 187, 466, 479, 480, 597
regalia, 244
Régie, 512
Regierungen, 511, 517, 524, 526
régime censitaire, 587. *See also* suffrage
Regimentsquartiermeister, 520
regnum, 42, 43, 113
Reich, Second, 337, 345, 347, 369; Reichstag, 160; *Reichstände*, 249; *Reichswehr*, 160
Reinhard, Marcel, 509
Reith, Charles, 352
religion, 18, 77, 78. *See also* church; clergy; ecclesiastics
remonstrance, 494, 500
Renaissance, 57, 58, 93
Renseignements Généraux, 336
repression, governmental, 9, 10. *See also* army; public order; police
Resident Commissioner, 533
Restoration, 99, 121, 169, 284, 287, 288, 298, 299
retributive action (form of food riot), 386, 387, 442
revolts, *see* rebellions
revolutions, 17, 74, 159, 182, 284, 287,
344, 345, 409, 410, 441, 449; American Revolution, 145, 150, 172, 204, 216, 311, 316, 599; English Revolution (1640–), 13, 194, 356; Glorious Revolution (1688), 140, 283, 289, 292, 293, 298, 314, 587; French Revolution (1789–), 3, 13, 33, 59, 89, 95, 101, 108, 144–155, 170, 172, 187, 197, 200, 204, 214–218, 224, 229, 233, 324, 356, 425, 426, 443, 448, 508, 549, 553, 560, 587, 599; Mexican Revolution, 617; Revolutions of 1848, 160, 169, 212, 238, 322, 324, 357; Russian Revolution (1917), 13, 74, 387, 443; Spanish Revolution of 1868, 443. *See also* Civil War; rebellions
Rhine, 13; Rhineland, 72, 136, 143, 408, 409, 428, 586
Richard I, 115, 473
Richard II, 115, 116
Richardson, N., 508
Richelieu, Cardinal, 8, 126, 166, 167, 194, 195, 201, 228, 344, 457, 464, 493, 500, 501
Richemont, Arthur de Bretagne, comte de, 127
rights, political, 32, 35–38. *See also* political development; suffrage
Rioseco, 431
Riot Act, 391
riots, food, 61, 71, 175, 380–392, 430, 433, 442, 443, 448, 449, 452–454; price riots, 386–388, 430, 442, 443, 448. *See also* blockage; retributive action
Risorgimento, 347, 348, 350, 355, 356, 359
Rittergutsgesetz, 276, 277
Ritz Hotel View of Society, 306, 309
Robertson, Roland, 620
Robinson, Eric, 543
Rocroi, Battle of, 106
Roger of Hereford, 475
Rohan, Henri, duc de, 129
Rokkan, Stein, 17, 33, 34, 49, 65–69, 72, 79, 80, 83, 608
Roman Catholic Church, 466, 580, 581, 583, 593. *See also* church
Roman Empire, 18, 21, 24, 25, 29, 45, 66, 76, 77, 85, 197, 281, 394, 575, 576, 580, 596; Roman Law, 251, 457, 470, 475, 476, 558, 575, 583, 584, 596, 599
Romania, 591
Rome, 147–148, 177, 339, 347, 352, 359, 439, 440

Römermonate, 250
Rosenau, James, 622, 623
Rosenberg, Hans, 44, 250, 272, 300, 301, 453, 525
Rouen, 449
Rousseau, Jean-Jacques, 93
Rowan (London Commissioner of Police), 373
Royal Academy, 543; Royal Commission on the Police, 333, 352, 353; royal council (curia regis), 470; Royal Exchange, 543; royal power, 22; Royal Society, 537, 542, 543, 546
Rudé, George, 382
Rufus (William Rufus of Normandy), 114
Russett, Bruce, 11
Russia, 101, 145, 167, 197, 199, 207, 223, 224, 422, 537, 579, 591, 595, 596, 625, 631, 637. See also Soviet Union
Rustow, Dankwart, 593, 604

St. Cyr, 158
St. Petersburg, 360, 413
Saint-Pierre, Abbé de, 209
Saint-Simon, Louis de Rouvroy, duc de, 132
Salamanca, 536
Saldana, 431
Salisbury, 56
salt monopoly, 434; salt tax, 173, 215, 222, 303, 434. See also gabelle
Sanchez-Albornoz, Nicolas, 380
Sandhurst, 158
sanscoulottisme, 151
Sardinia, 201
Sartine, Gabriel de, 60, 346, 360
Savine, Alexander, 466
Savoy, 66, 68, 95, 201, 223, 356, 577, 580; Savoy-Piedmont, 67, 578. See also Piedmont
Saxons (in England), 99, 101, 110, 113, 114
Saxony, 181, 234
Scandinavia, 41, 234, 380, 412, 416, 570, 577
Scharnhorst, Gerhard von, 153
Schattschneider, E. E., 80
Schatullengüter, 274
Schellenburg, 108
Schleswig, 581
Schmoller, Gustav, 243, 258, 295–297, 398, 437, 513
Schumpeter, J. A., 11, 243, 245, 327
Scotland, 42, 48, 104, 112, 116–118,

120, 264, 311, 332, 395, 579, 581, 584, 590, 619
Scotland Yard, 333
Scott, James, 604
scutages, 114, 115
Seaford, 391
Secret Court Chamber, 274
secrétaires d'état, 492
Sée, Henri, 200
Seeley, J. R., 143
Séguier, Pierre, 167
Seine, 335
Self-Denying Ordinance, 282
Seligman, E. R., 184
Semblançay, 172
Sempach, 105
Senate, U.S., 635
seneschaux (sénéchaux), 126
Sentou, Jean, 427, 428
serfdom, 207, 208, 212, 257, 273, 402, 414, 419, 421, 424, 445
sergents de ville, 345
Seven Bishops, 122
Seville, 536
sheriffs, 117, 346, 468, 470
Ship Money, 264, 267
shipbuilding, 541
shire courts, 470
shire-reeves, see sheriffs
shock-cavalry, shock-infantry, 91
Short Parliament, 264
Shrewsbury, Earl of, 119
Sicily, 202, 204, 395, 406, 439, 445, 450, 585
Sidney, Philip, 544
Sieyès, Emmanuel-Joseph, abbé, 88
Silesia, 409
silver, 191, 199
Simiand, François, 178
Simnel, Lambert, 119
Sinn Fein, 362
Skinner, G. W., 5
Slicher van Bath, B. H., 415, 595
Slovaks, 591
smallpox, 403
Smith, Adam, 93, 206, 295–297, 299, 309, 432
Smith, Donald E., 592
smuggling, 203
Social Science Research Council, 5
socialists, 34
Sonnenfels, J., 279
Sound, The, 41, 588, 589
South Africa, 594
Southampton, 530
Soviet Union, 5, 68, 163, 165, 223, 225, 369, 594, 623

Spain, 12, 15, 16, 18, 22, 35, 41, 44–48, 56, 62, 72, 73, 99, 104, 106, 110, 112, 132, 145, 152, 177, 187, 191, 194, 199–201, 204, 214, 223, 363, 380–382, 406, 412, 415, 419, 420, 423, 424, 428, 430, 436–439, 441, 444, 445, 450–453, 461, 529, 536–538, 540, 541, 544, 578, 585, 586, 591, 594, 620, 622, 636
Spanish Match, 118
Special Branch, 333, 362
Spooner, F. C., 416
Staats- und Polizeiwissenschaft, 317
stages of economic and political development, 11, 563–565, 570–575, 604–611. *See also* political development
Stamp Office, 462
Standesherren, 247, 321
Ständestaat, 85, 251, 258, 271, 510
Standing Joint Committees, 331, 343
Ständisches Kreditwerk, 253
Star Chamber, 259, 264, 480
state, anthropological treatments of, 621; capitalist state, 628; definitions of state, 6, 26, 37, 66, 68, 70–71, 84–86; dynastic state, 85; modern state, 84, 85, 87; mosaic state, 42, 43; unitary state, 42, 43
state-building, state-making, 6–9, 13, 20, 85, 86, 88–90, 95, 109, 115, 129, 162–164, 172–218, 242–327, 361–363, 393, 396, 455, 456, 459, 466, 467, 480, 482, 491, 508, 510, 528, 562–600, 602, 610, 613, 622, 632; nature of evidence concerning state-making, 7–12; stateness, 32, 34, 35, 70; state-systems, 45, 52, 67, 69, 76, 81, 625–627, 637, 638
Stavenhagen, Rodolfo, 627
Stein, Heinrich von, 153, 296, 297, 346, 357
Stenai, 131
Stenton, F. M., 469
Stephen (king), 114
Steuerrat, 137, 139, 140, 143, 271, 346, 355, 502, 513–515, 520, 560
Stoke, 118, 119, 122
Stone, Lawrence, 120, 465
Stop of the Exchequer, 290
Strange, Lord, 119
stratification, international, 630; social stratification, 90, 91
Strayer, Joseph, 21, 25–27, 42, 43, 70, 74, 468
Stuarts, 22, 56, 112, 117, 121, 187, 231, 263–265, 267, 283, 284, 286, 287,

298, 432, 458, 465, 478, 483, 487, 532, 542
Stubbs, William, 37
Stuttgart, 352
styles of rule, 84, 87, 88, 109
Styria, 200
subdelegates (*subdélégués*), 132, 502
subsidy, 261, 262, 266
subsistence crises, 380–385, 390, 411, 412, 416, 426, 429, 430, 445. *See also* food supply; riots, food
suffrage, 35, 36, 55, 232, 247, 310, 326, 587, 588
Sully, Maximilien de Béthune, duc de, 492
Superintendent of Domains, 274
Surintendants, 172; *Surintendants des Finances*, 492
Surveillance du Territoire, 336
surveyor, 535; general surveyors and auditors, 260, 261
Sutherland, William, 534
Swabians, 104, 105
Swart, Martin, 118
Sweden, 41, 48, 110, 135, 137, 165, 445, 529, 573, 577, 579, 581–586, 588–591
Switzerland, 22, 25, 31, 94, 100, 103–105, 152, 233, 388, 576–578, 582, 585, 586, 589–591, 594

Tactics of Aelius, 106
taille, 127, 185, 209, 210, 494, 501
tanks, 92, 103
Tavannes, 131
Tawney, R. H., 414
Tax Commissar, 271, 272; Tax State, 311; Taxes Office, 462
taxation, taxes, 6, 9–11, 17, 23, 29, 30, 42, 50, 52–58, 60, 62, 63, 72, 83, 96, 97, 115, 122, 125–128, 130, 134, 135, 137, 138, 140, 141, 143, 151, 164–327, 365, 392, 414, 427, 433, 434, 445, 456, 458, 462, 489, 506, 511, 513, 514, 587, 609, 625, 630, 633; capital taxation, 183–185; direct taxes, 203, 207, 215, 216, 222, 223, 246, 252, 256, 258, 268–270, 283, 288, 291, 302, 303, 312, 319, 321, 323, 325, 435, 454; farming of taxes, 58, 496; hearth tax, 287, 299, 312; income tax, 169, 178, 186, 223, 232–236, 283, 284, 311, 312, 320, 321, 323; indirect taxes, 179–181, 200, 203, 215, 216, 222, 236, 256, 266, 268–270, 288, 312, 319, 320, 434, 496; land tax, 137, 154, 284, 302, 303, 319; milling

and slaughter tax, 321, 323; poll tax, 185, 284, 312; sales tax, 178; value-added tax, 178, 235. *See also* rebellions, tax; particular taxes, e.g. capitation, excise, gabelle
Technical Deputation, 549
Technische Hochschule, 553, 556
telegraph, 156, 457
Tenths, 252, 253, 261, 266
tercio, 106
Terray, Joseph-Marie, abbé, 173, 210, 216
Teutonic Knights, 114, 135
Thailand, 594
Theobald of Canterbury, Archbishop, 473
Thiers, Adolphe, 158, 232
Third Ypres, 161
Thirsk, Joan, 403, 404, 407
Thompson, E. P., 432
Thompson, Francis M. L., 402, 417
Thuringia, 423
Tilly, Charles, 5, 17, 60–62, 83, 175
Tilly, Louise, 175, 380
Tilsit, Peace of, 346
tithe, 182, 183, 193, 256, 387, 436
Tocqueville, Alexis de, 187, 188, 211, 372
tontines, 189
Torschreiber (city gates' comptroller), 521
Tory, 123, 290, 293
Toulouse, 428
Tournon, François, Cardinal de, 189
Tours, 103
Tout, T. F., 464, 467, 470, 472, 474
Toutain, J.-C., 220
town council, 332
trade, 199, 299, 413, 589, 597. *See also* commercialization; markets; merchants; monetization
Traditionspfand (traditional pledge), 252, 314
Trafalgar, 528
traitants, 190, 496
treasurers, 470, 533. *See also* trésoriers
treasury, 291–294, 299, 317, 318, 468; Treasury Office, 462
trésoriers, 494, 495; *trésoriers de France*, 500
Trevor-Roper, H. R., 57, 58
Trienio Bolchevista, 452
Trinity House, 537, 538, 540
Trivulce, 164
Trudaine (family), 551, 552
Tucker, Josiah, 303
Tudors, 22, 56, 112, 117, 120, 121, 231, 258–265, 267, 283, 298, 303, 306,

311, 316, 348, 410, 432, 435, 458, 463–466, 477–481, 483, 484, 487, 530, 533, 542, 543, 616
tumulto di San Martino, 380
Tunisia, 219
Tunstall, Cuthbert, 534
Turcaret (satire by Lesage), 173
Turenne, Henri de la Tour d'Auvergne, vicomte de, 134
Turgot, Anne-Robert-Jacques, 173, 176, 193, 210, 211, 382, 383
Turin, 201, 413
Turks, 18, 604
Tuscany, 439
Two Sicilies (Kingdom), 201, 204, 610

U.S.S.R., *see* Soviet Union
Ukraine, 148
Ulster, 591
unemployment, 237–239
Ungeld, 286
Unification (Italian), 354. *See also* Risorgimento
United East India Company, 291
United Provinces, 193
United States of America, 165, 222, 223, 229, 234, 335, 336, 350, 354, 355, 368, 372, 424, 516, 572, 626, 635
uprisings, *see* rebellions
urban growth, 398–400. *See also* cities
urbanization, 32, 61, 73, 378, 611
Utrecht, 201; Peace of Utrecht, 197, 291

Vachell, John, 384
Valencia, 438, 439
Valladolid, 430, 431
Valois, 104, 110, 129, 458
Vane Henry, 486
Vasa, Gustave, 177
Vauban, Sébastian le Prestre, seigneur de, 108, 177, 182, 185, 550
venality of offices, *see* offices, sale of
Vendée, 167
Vendôme, 130
Venice, 45, 193, 347, 440, 444
Verba, Sidney, 610
Vereinigte Artillerie und Ingenieurschule, 557
Vereinigte Landtag, 322, 323
Versailles, 48, 134, 176, 496; Treaty of Versailles, 46, 75, 226
Vertragspfand, 252, 314
Vespucci, Amerigo, 536
Vicens Vives, Jaime, 451
Victoria (Queen), 420
Victualling Office, 462
Vidal de la Blache, Paul, 444

Vienna, 201, 346, 360; Congress of Vienna, 46, 67, 75
Vietnam, 598, 634; Vietnam War, 96
Vigili Urbani, 339
Vilar, Pierre, 450
village council, 22
Villars, Claude, duc de, 108
vingtième, 209, 210, 501
violence, collective, 9, 11, 12. *See also* rebellion; revolution; riot
Visby, 576
voice, 567, 592

wages, 422. *See also* proletariat
Wagner, Richard, 90, 209
Wagram, 146
Wales, 112, 116, 332, 395, 468, 579, 594, 619
Wallerstein, Immanuel, 44, 45, 380, 627
Walpole, Robert, 203, 284, 287, 303, 533, 588
war, 29, 40, 42, 52, 54, 55, 58, 71, 73–76, 81, 89, 90, 108, 224, 246, 254, 285, 288, 305, 311–315, 393, 445, 453, 503, 633
War, American, *see* Revolution, American
War: and Domains Administration, 512; and Domains Chambers, 143, 153, 494, 502, 511, 512, 515, 517, 526, 560; and Domains Councillors, 515; Chambers, 273; Commissars, 271; Commissariat, 512; Ministry of, 334, 339, 347; State, 58. *See also* Kriegs-
Warbeck, Perkin, 118
Ward, Robert, 5, 604
wars: Austrian Succession, 203; Austro-Prussian, 108; Crimean, 156, 220, 359; of Devolution, 133; Dutch, 133, 290; First Silesian, 277; Franco-Prussian, 95, 159, 160, 220; Hundred Years, 100, 112, 126, 127, 492, 577; Italian, 99, 105; Napoleonic, 46, 52, 55, 75, 108, 162, 190, 270, 311, 365, 366, 384, 390, 523, 572, 574, 620; Nine Years, 133; in the North, 99; of Palatine Inheritance, 311; of Religion, 126, 129; of the Roses, 116, 120; Russo-Japanese, 160; Scottish, 116; Seven Years, 101, 203, 204; Spanish Succession, 101, 108, 122, 130, 133, 293, 311; Thirty Years, 45, 101, 130, 135, 139, 249, 251, 269, 270, 271, 416, 422, 452, 500, 589; World War I, 157, 160, 161, 220, 223–227, 238, 243, 297, 327, 626; World War II,

75, 169, 223, 225–227, 235, 236, 238, 338, 368, 372, 373. *See also* Civil War
Warsaw, 225
Warwick, Earl of, 118
Washington, 69, 598
Watch Committees, 331, 332, 343
Waterloo, 102, 127, 359
Webb, Sidney and Beatrice, 352
Weber, Max, 11, 85, 243, 247, 559, 560, 603
Weekly Assessment, 283
Weimar Republic, 160, 337, 338, 369, 374. *See also* Germany
Weiner, Myron, 5
Weiss, Eberhard, 585
welfare, 80, 82, 97
Wellesley, *see* Wellington
Wellington, Arthur Wellesley, Duke of, 357, 372
Wells, John, 543
Wernham, Bruce, 119
Wessex, 110
Western Rising, 120
Westphalia, Treaty of, 45, 46, 75, 249, 572
Whigs, 123, 290, 293, 294, 299
White, Lynn, 102
White Sea, 537
Whittlesey, Derwent, 583
William, George, 135
William I (The Conqueror), 113, 114, 468–470
William III, 78, 140, 292
William and Mary, 283, 289, 292
William of Newbury, 114
William of Orange, 170, 204, 510
William (Prince of Prussia), 522
Wilson, C. H., 306
Winter, William, 531
Wolf, Eric, 20, 394, 404, 419, 627
Wolsey, 118, 457, 482
wool, 19, 41, 55, 115, 116, 285, 402, 423, 588
Woolwich, 158, 530, 542
Worcester, Earl of, 530
workers, 34, 217, 225, 230, 236, 239, 597; working classes, 55, 221, 232, 320–322. *See also* proletariat
World Handbook of Political and Social Indicators, 11
Worms, Diet of, 250
Wrigley, E. A., 399
Württemberg, 234
Wyatt's Rebellion, 23, 118
Wycliff, John, 177

yeomanry, 349
Yorkists, 466
Yorkshire, 474
Yugloslavia, 636

Zabern incident, 158

Zacuto (Spanish astronomer), 536
Zaïre, 636, 637
Zivilversorgung (civil maintenance), 521
Zolberg, Aristide, 5
Zuckmayer (German author), 523
Zurich, 401

Library of Congress Cataloging in Publication Data
Main entry under title:

The Formation of National States in Western Europe.

   (Studies in political development; 8)
   Sponsored by the Committee on Comparative Politics, Social Science
Research Council.
   Bibliography: p.
   Includes index.
   1. Europe—Politics. I. Tilly, Charles, ed. II. Ardant, Gabriel. III. Social
Science Research Council. Committee on Comparative Politics. IV. Series.
JN94.A2F67 1975   320.9′4   74-20941
ISBN 0-691-05219-0
ISBN 0-691-00772-1 pbk.